The Gospel
According
to
St. Mark

The Gospel According to St. Mark

Alfred Plummer

BAKER BOOK HOUSE

Grand Rapids, Michigan 49506

Reprinted 1982 by
Baker Book House Company

First published in 1914 as part
of the Cambridge Greek Testament
for Schools and Colleges

ISBN: 0-8010-7072-4

PHOTOLITHOPRINTED BY CUSHING - MALLOY, INC.
ANN ARBOR, MICHIGAN, UNITED STATES OF AMERICA

PREFACE
BY THE GENERAL EDITOR.

THE General Editor does not hold himself responsible, except in the most general sense, for the statements, opinions, and interpretations contained in the several volumes of this Series. He believes that the value of the Introduction and the Commentary in each case is largely dependent on the Editor being free as to his treatment of the questions which arise, provided that that treatment is in harmony with the character and scope of the Series. He has therefore contented himself with offering criticisms, urging the consideration of alternative interpretations, and the like; and as a rule he has left the adoption of these suggestions to the discretion of the Editor.

The Greek Text adopted in this Series is that of Dr Westcott and Dr Hort with the omission of the marginal readings. For permission to use this Text the thanks of the Syndics of the Cambridge University Press and of the General Editor are due to Messrs Macmillan & Co.

TRINITY COLLEGE, CAMBRIDGE.
January, 1910.

19695

PREFACE

OUR estimate of the historical and critical value of the Second Gospel has risen enormously during the last thirty or forty years, and it is possible that further study will cause the estimate to rise even higher than it is at present. But the unique value of this Gospel is still very imperfectly realized by many of those who often read and to some extent study it; and it is one of the objects of this new edition of St Mark to make the knowledge of its unique character more widely diffused, and to enable more readers of the New Testament to see for themselves some of the particulars in which this hitherto underrated Gospel brings us closer than any other to our Lord, as He was known to those who watched His acts and listened to His teaching.

During the period in which the inestimable character of the Gospel according to St Mark has been more and more appreciated, a number of critical and controversial works have appeared in England and elsewhere which raise, or bring into greater prominence, questions respecting Christian doctrine that produce perplexity in many minds. With regard to not a few of these questions, the Second Gospel, fairly and intelligently used, will show the way, if not to a solution, at least to the direction in which a reasonable answer to doubts can be found. These Notes on the Gospel will do good service, if in any degree they render aid to such a quest.

The titles of some of the books which the writer of the Notes has found very helpful are given at the end of the Introduction, and the list might be greatly enlarged. Among English works he has found nothing equal to Dr Swete's Commentary, and among foreign ones nothing equal to that of Lagrange, who had the advantage of coming after Dr Swete. He has also to express his obligations to the General Editor for vigilant care in reading the proofs and for many valuable suggestions and criticisms.

The Greek Index is not a Concordance. It does not contain all, or even nearly all, the Greek words which occur in the Gospel; and in the case of many words only a selection of the references is given.

A. P.

BIDEFORD.
Easter, 1914.

TABLE OF CONTENTS

INTRODUCTION

CHAPTER I

St Mark the Evangelist

The name "Mark" occurs four times in Acts and four times in the Epistles. In Acts we are told three times of a Jew at Jerusalem named John who had Mark as an alternative or additional name (xii. 12, 25, xv. 37), and once he is called simply Mark, τὸν Μᾶρκον, "the Mark just mentioned" (xv. 39). The same person is twice called simply "John," without mention of an alternative name (xiii. 5, 13). In the Epistles the name "John" is dropped, and the person in question is called simply "Mark," Μᾶρκος without the article, as if those who are addressed would know who was meant (Col. iv. 10; Philem. 24; 2 Tim. iv. 11; 1 Pet. v. 13). The identification of the John in Acts with the Mark of the Epistles is probable on other grounds (see below), and it is confirmed by the fact that in Col. iv. 10 St Paul, after mentioning that Mark is the cousin (not "sister's son," as A.V.) of Barnabas, reminds the Colossians that they have been told that they need have no hesitation in receiving him, if he should visit them; which looks like an allusion to the defection of John Mark), as related in Acts xv. 37—39.

To speak of him as "John Mark," as if the combined names were analogous to "John Smith," is misleading. "Whose surname was Mark" (xii. 12, 25) encourages us to regard the cases as analogous, but in the modern combination the two names are intended to be used together and in some cases must be used together, whereas in the other case the two names were rarely, if ever, used together, but were alternatives; the second name was an *alias*. Although under the name of Simon, or Peter, or Kephas, the chief Apostle is mentioned more than 180 times in N.T., only

three times is he called Simon Peter (Mt. xvi. 16; Lk. v. 8;
2 Pet. i. 1) by any writer except John, who commonly gives both
names. "Saul, otherwise Paul" (Acts xiii. 9) is never called
"Saul Paul.". The Evangelist would be called "John" among
Jews and "Mark" among Gentiles. "Then it was the fashion
for every Syrian, or Cilician, or Cappadocian, who prided himself
on his Greek education, to bear a Greek name; but at the same
time he had his other name in the native language, by which he
was known among his countrymen. His two names were the
alternative, not the complement of each other; and the surroundings of the moment determined which name he was called by"
(Ramsay, *Paul the Traveller*, p. 81). Acts xiii. 5 is against
Deissmann's suggestion that in xiii. 13 Mark is called "John"
purposely, because he had forsaken the Apostle and had returned
to Jerusalem, whereas in xv. 39, when he goes with Barnabas to
Cyprus, he is called simply "Mark" (*Bib. St.*, p. 317). If the
change is not purely accidental, the reason would rather be that
at Antioch and Jerusalem he was in Jewish society and was known
as "John," whereas in travelling he would use the Gentile *alias*.
The employment of a Roman *praenomen* to serve as a single name
is found again in the case of Titus and of several persons who
bore the name of Gaius. In "Jesus, called Justus" (Col. iv. 11)
we have a combination of a Hebrew and a Latin name. Philo
had a nephew named Mark, son of Alexander the Alabarch (Joseph.
Ant. xviii. viii. 1, xix. v. 1), but the name was rare among Jews.
Μᾶρκος is the right accentuation; Μάαρκος occurs in inscriptions.

With regard to the identification, the connexion between the
mentions of Mark in three different Epistles is of importance.
In Col. iv. 10 St Paul commends him to a Church of proconsular
Asia; in 1 Pet. v. 13 Mark sends a salutation to Churches in
that region; in 2 Tim. iv. 11 he is found in that region. "The
Scriptural notices suggest that the same Mark is intended in all
the occurrences of the name, for they are connected together by
personal links (Peter, Paul, Barnabas); and the earliest forms of
tradition likewise identify them" (Lightfoot on Col. iv. 10).

Mark was the son of Mary (Mariam), who was a Jewish convert,
who seems to have been well-to-do, and to have been a Christian
of some importance. Her house at Jerusalem has a "porch"
(πυλών) and an upper room, and she has at least one female

slave. As soon as the chief of the Apostles is released from prison he goes to her house to report his freedom, for there members of the Church of Jerusalem were accustomed to meet. It is probable that her son John was already a believer, like herself. If he was not already known to Peter, this nocturnal visit of the released Apostle may have been the beginning of intimacy. St Peter may have converted both mother and son. As the father is not mentioned in Acts, we conclude that he was dead, a conclusion which is against the identification of the father of Mark with "the goodman of the house" (see on xiv. 14), but the conclusion may be wrong. Severus, a writer of the tenth century, gives the father the name of Aristobulus.

That Mark was one of the Seventy or Seventy-two disciples (Lk. x. 1) is a worthless tradition for which the credulous and uncritical Epiphanius gives no authority. The same statement is made about St Luke. There was a natural desire to show that all four Evangelists were personal disciples of the Lord. That Mark was a Levite is a reasonable conjecture from the fact that he was a "cousin" (ἀνεψιός) of the Levite Barnabas; but we are not sure that they were the sons of two brothers. There is more to be said for the theory that he was the young man mentioned in Mk xiv. 51, 52; see notes there.

Even if his parents were Jews of the Dispersion, it is probable that they had been settled in Jerusalem for some years, and the names Mary and John point to the family being Hebrews rather than Hellenists (Zahn, *Introd. to N.T.* ii. p. 487). Assuming that at any rate the married life of his mother had been spent in Jerusalem, Mark must have been familiar with the sensation which was caused there and in Judaea when, after centuries of silence, first one Prophet and then a second began to proclaim the coming of the reign of God. If Mark did not himself hear either of these new Prophets, he may often have talked to those who had listened to John the Baptist and Jesus of Nazareth. That he had often been with some who had known Jesus, and in particular with Peter, may be regarded as certain.

His cousin Barnabas came to Jerusalem with Saul to bring alms from the Christians in Antioch to the Christians in Judaea during the famine of A.D. 45, 46; and when the work of relieving the poor in Jerusalem was over, the two missionaries took Mark with them on their return to Syria. There can be little doubt whose doing this was. Of the two missionaries, Barnabas was as yet very decidedly the chief. He had introduced the notable convert, Saul of Tarsus, to the Church at Jerusalem and had been his sponsor and patron (Acts ix. 27, xi. 25). He and Saul needed helpers in their work, and when it came to selecting one, it would be Barnabas that would decide who should be chosen, and he chose his young cousin, who had probably been useful in distributing relief at Jerusalem: 2 Tim. iv. 11 indicates that Mark had powers of organization. Consequently, when Barnabas and Saul were again sent forth by the Church at Antioch, they had him as their "attendant," which probably means that he was the courier of the party and managed the details of the journey. That he baptized converts (Blass on Acts xiii. 5) is not improbable, but it is not likely that this was his only, or even his chief duty. He was not a missionary chosen by the Holy Spirit and solemnly sent forth by the Church at Antioch, but the two Apostles (as we may now call them) who were thus chosen "had *got* him as an attendant." This is a more probable meaning of εἶχον δὲ καὶ Ἰωάνην ὑπηρέτην than "And they had [with them] also John, the *synagogue minister*" (cf. Lk. iv. 20). D has ὑπηρετοῦντα αὐτοῖς, which gives the more probable meaning to ὑπηρέτην, which is of more importance than the exact force of εἶχον.

It is evident from what follows that Mark did not consider himself under any obligation either to Divine commands or to the Church at Antioch in this service. He was free to decide for himself how long he would continue to attend on his cousin and Saul. With them he sailed to Cyprus. They stay at Salamis, working among the Jews there, and then go through the island to its western extremity, and at Paphos come into conflict with Elymas the sorcerer, whose discomfiture leads to the conversion of the Proconsul, Sergius Paulus. After this success they cross to Pamphylia, and at Perga Mark refuses to go further and returns to Jerusalem. Possibly the risks and hardships of a journey into the interior frightened him; he felt that he could no longer do his work as dragoman satisfactorily under such conditions. Or he may have thought that home ties were more binding than those which attached him to Barnabas and Paul. Or he may have seen that it was becoming more and more difficult to work with *both* the Apostles, for Paul's teaching, especially with regard to the Gentiles, was now far in advance of that of his colleague, and was becoming more so. And the more advanced Apostle was now taking the lead. It is no longer "Barnabas and Saul" (Acts xiii. 2, 7) but "Paul and his company" or "Paul and Barnabas" (*vv.* 13, 43, 46). For any or all of these reasons Mark may have turned back. Whatever the reasons were, they were such as could be better appreciated, if not actually approved, by his cousin than by his cousin's energetic colleague, who condemned Mark severely (xv. 38). After an interval there is the so-called "Council" at Jerusalem (*c.* A.D. 49 or 50). Paul and Barnabas are again at Antioch, and Peter joins them there. Was Mark there also, and was he one of "the rest of the Jews" who "dissembled with Peter, insomuch that even Barnabas was carried away with their dissimulation"? Gal. ii. 13. That is not unreasonable conjecture; but it has against it the silence of both St Luke in Acts and St Paul in Galatians. When St Paul absolutely refused to give Mark another trial, and parted from Barnabas rather than do so, the only reason given is Mark's withdrawal from Pamphylia (xv. 38). The result was that he took Silas as a colleague and went on a mission through Syria and Cilicia, while Barnabas and his cousin sailed back to Cyprus, in which island both of them had connexions. This would be about A.D. 52. It is worth while noting in passing how these two incidents—Mark's separating from Barnabas and Paul, and Paul's separating from Barnabas—illustrate the saying that travel tests character. If you want to know a man, travel with him for a few months.

The frequently mentioned tradition that St Mark founded the Church of Alexandria may, with much reserve and uncertainty, be allowed to come in at this point. There is here a considerable gap of about ten years in what Scripture tells us about Mark, and it is credible that, during the period about which Scripture tells us nothing, he went from Cyprus to Alexandria and helped to make it a Christian centre. But it does not follow that, because the tradition helps to fill this gap, therefore the tradition is true. The Alexandrian Fathers, Clement and Origen, in all their various writings, nowhere allude to Mark's preaching at Alexandria. Another tradition makes Barnabas the founder of the Alexandrian

Church, and it is not impossible that both went from Cyprus to Alexandria and worked there. On the whole, however, it is more probable that the connexion of St Mark with Alexandria, if it be historical, did not begin until after the death of St Peter.

We are on sure ground once more when we find St Mark at Rome during the first Roman imprisonment of St Paul (Col. iv. 10; Philem. 24); but we cannot safely infer that it was the Apostle's imprisonment which brought Mark to Rome. What is certain is that he and the Apostle are now completely reconciled, and that the latter seems to have become anxious to show Mark that he now has complete confidence in him. He declares him to be one who joined in alleviating his sufferings as a prisoner. He claims him as a fellow-worker, and he inserts salutations from him in the letters to the Colossians and Philemon. Mark, Aristarchus, and Jesus who is called Justus are the only Jewish Christians who cleave to St Paul in his captivity, and the Apostle seems to have sent Mark back to Asia. A few years later, in the latest of the Pauline Epistles (2 Tim. iv. 11), Timothy, who was probably at Ephesus, is charged to "pick up Mark" and bring him with him to Rome.

And it is in Rome that we next hear of St Mark. It was probably after the deaths of the two Apostles with whom he had of old been associated that Mark attached himself to the old friend of the family, St Peter; and it is in 1 Pet. v. 13 that we have the last mention of him in the N.T.—"Mark, my son, saluteth you." "My son" may be a mere expression of affection; but it is not impossible that it means that Peter was instrumental in converting Mark to Christianity (cf. 1 Cor. iv. 14, 15). It is not fatal to this view that *St Paul* commonly uses τέκνον and not υἱός of the relationship between himself and his converts (1 Cor. iv. 14; Phil. ii. 22; 1 Tim. i. 2, 18; 2 Tim. i. 2, ii. 1; Tit. i. 4; Philem. 10; cf. 3 Jn 4), although it makes it a little less probable than the other view. But the sense in which ὁ υἱός μου is used does not affect the probability that Mark was instructed in the Gospel first by St Peter. One thing may be regarded as certain, that when 1 Peter was written, the Evangelist was with the Apostle in Rome. Beyond reasonable doubt "Babylon" is Rome (Hort, 1 *Peter*, p. 6; Lightfoot, *Clement*, ii. p. 492; Bigg, 1 *and 2 Peter*, pp. 22, 76).

That both St Peter and St Paul suffered martyrdom at Rome under Nero may be accepted as a sufficiently attested tradition. That they suffered at the same time is less probable; but, when we abandon this tradition, it is difficult to determine which Apostle suffered first. On the whole, it is safer to place the martyrdom of St Paul before that of St Peter, and to suppose that the death of the former was one reason for Mark's becoming closely connected with the latter; but the friendship of St Peter with Mark's family would account for this close connexion, even if St Paul were still alive.

The Author of the Second Gospel.

That Mark was the writer of the Second Gospel, and that in what he wrote he was largely dependent upon the teaching of St Peter, may also be accepted as sufficiently attested. That St Peter is the probable source of a great deal that we find in this Gospel can be shown in detail from the Gospel itself; but the evidence with regard to the exact relation between the Apostle and the Gospel of Mark is not harmonious. We begin with Papias, Bishop of Hierapolis. Irenaeus tells us that Papias was "a hearer of John and a companion of Polycarp." The first statement may be true, but it is perhaps only an inference from the second. After the destruction of Jerusalem some Christians migrated from Palestine to Hierapolis. Among these were Philip the Apostle and his daughters, two of whom lived to a great age, and from them Papias obtained various traditions about the Apostles and their contemporaries. He also obtained information from two disciples of the Lord, Aristion and John the Presbyter or the Elder. The former is interesting to us in connexion with the longer ending of this Gospel (xvi. 9—20), while the latter is connected with our present purpose. Papias collected traditions about Christ and His Apostles and used them to illustrate the Gospel narrative in a treatise called *An Exposition of the Oracles of the Lord,* some precious fragments of which have been preserved by Eusebius. He quotes the passage which concerns us *H. E.* iii. 39; and it will be seen from the opening words that in it Papias is quoting "the Presbyter" or "the Elder," which almost certainly means the Presbyter John. After the first sentence which is attributed to the Presbyter we cannot be quite sure whether we are reading his statements or those of Papias; but this is not of much moment, for Papias is certainly passing on information which he had received on what he believed to be good authority.

"This also the Presbyter used to say. Mark, having become Peter's interpreter, wrote accurately, though not in order (τάξει), all that he remembered of the things which were either said or done by Christ. For he was neither a hearer of the Lord nor a follower of Him, but afterwards, as I said, [followed] Peter, who used to adapt his instructions to the needs [of his hearers], but without making a connected report of the Lord's Sayings. So that Mark committed no error when he wrote down some things just as he remembered them; for of one thing he made a purpose from the first, not to omit any one of the things which he heard or state anything falsely among them."

This is evidence of the highest importance. Papias can hardly have got this information much later than A.D. 100, and he gets it from one who was contemporary with Apostles and the earliest Christian traditions. We shall have to return to the difficult statement that Mark, in contrast with other Evangelists, did *not* write "in order."

Irenaeus (III. i. 1) says that "after the death of Peter and Paul, Mark also, the disciple and interpreter of Peter, delivered to us in writing the things which had been preached by Peter."

Tertullian (*Adv. Marcion.* iv. 5) says much the same as Irenaeus; that Mark was Peter's interpreter, and reproduced his teaching.

Clement of Alexandria (*Hypotyposeis*), as quoted by Eusebius (*H. E.* ii. 15), states that Peter's hearers were so impressed by his teaching, that they "were not content with this unwritten teaching of the divine Gospel, but with all sorts of entreaties besought Mark, a follower of Peter, and the one whose Gospel is extant, that he would leave them a written monument of the doctrine which had been communicated to them orally. Nor did they cease till they had prevailed with the man, and had thus become the occasion of the written Gospel which bears the name of Mark. And they say that Peter, when he had learned through the Spirit that which had been done, was pleased with their zeal, and that the work won the sanction of his authority for the purpose of being used in the Churches." Elsewhere (*H. E.* vi. 25) Eusebius quotes Clement as having written that, when Peter learnt what Mark had done, "he neither directly forbade it nor encouraged it."

Origen, as quoted by Eusebius (*H. E.* vi. 25), states that Mark wrote as Peter dictated to him; and Jerome (Ep. 120, *Ad Hedibiam* 11) repeats this.

Where these writers disagree, the earlier witnesses are to be preferred. Papias was a contemporary of Mark; *i.e.* he was a boy about the time when Mark wrote his Gospel. His narrative states that Mark wrote down what he recollected of the teaching of Peter, which almost implies that he did not write until after Peter's death; and Irenaeus expressly states that this was the case. This is more probable than Clement's statement that Peter approved of the work, and much more probable than Origen's statement that Peter dictated it. Such enhancements of the value of the Gospel of Mark would be likely to be imagined in Alexandria, where Mark was believed to have laboured, and even to have founded the first Christian community.

What those who call Mark the "interpreter of Peter" mean by the expression is explained by none of them. The most natural, and not improbable, meaning of "Peter's interpreter" would be that Peter's knowledge of Greek was not equal to giving addresses to those whom he instructed in Rome, and that Mark translated into Greek what Peter said in Aramaic. It is true that Peter had probably been bilingual from childhood, speaking both Aramaic and Greek, as many Welsh peasants speak both Welsh and English. But such casual use of Greek would not necessarily enable him to preach in Greek any more than a Welsh peasant's casual use of English would enable him to preach in English. If this is the correct explanation of "interpreter," it is easy to see how Mark's services in this direction would impress Peter's teaching on his memory. According to any explanation, the term can hardly mean less than that in some way Mark acted as an instrument for conveying Peter's teaching to those who either did not hear it or could not understand it.

Hippolytus (*Philos.* vii. 30) says that Mark was called ὁ κολοβοδάκτυλος, "the stump-fingered," which implies that one of his fingers was defective through malformation or amputation. Various guesses have been made as to the origin of this nick-name, which is repeated in Latin Prefaces to the Gospel. Some take it literally: he *had* only a stump in place of a finger, either (1) because he was born so or had been accidentally maimed, or (2) because, being a Levite and not wishing to become a priest, he cut off one of his fingers. Others take it metaphorically: he was *called* stump-fingered, either (3) because, like a malingerer, he had deserted in Pamphylia, or (4) because his Gospel is maimed in its extremities, having lost its conclusion, and (as some think) its beginning. Of these four conjectures the first and fourth are most worthy of consideration.

We do not know either when, where, or how St Mark died. Jerome places his death in the eighth year of Nero at Alexandria; but we have no means of confirming or correcting this. The apocryphal *Acts of Mark* make him die a martyr's death; but these *Acts* are Alexandrian, and a desire to glorify the reputed founder of the Alexandrian Church may be the origin of the statement. No writer of the second, third, or fourth century says that Mark suffered martyrdom, and their silence may be regarded as decisive.

Shortly before his own martyrdom St Paul wrote of Mark that he was "useful for ministering" (2 Tim. iv. 11). This statement "assigns to Mark his precise place in the history of the Apostolic Age. Not endowed with gifts of leadership, neither prophet nor teacher, he knew how to be invaluable to those who filled the first rank in the service of the Church, and proved himself a true *servus servorum Dei*" (Swete).

CHAPTER II

THE SOURCES

One chief source has already been mentioned, the Apostle St Peter. The evidence for this goes back to the Presbyter John as quoted by Papias, who evidently gives his assent. It is confirmed by Irenaeus, Tertullian and many other writers; and it is by no means improbable that by the "Memoirs of

Peter" ('Απομνημονεύματα Πέτρου) Justin means the Gospel of
St Mark. These Memoirs contained the words ὄνομα Βοανεργές,
ὅ ἐστιν υἱοὶ βροντῆς, words which occur Mk iii. 17 and in no other
Gospel (Justin, *Try.* 106; comp. *Try.* 88 with Mk vi. 3). Nearly
everything which Mark records might have been told him by
St Peter, for St Peter was present when what is recorded was
done and spoken. But no one supposes that Peter was Mark's
only source. Even some things which Peter might have told
him may have been derived by Mark from others, for when he
wrote other eye-witnesses still survived and there was abundance
of oral tradition. On three occasions, however, only three disciples,
Peter, James, and John, were present as witnesses, and on two
of these—the Transfiguration and the Agony—they were the only
witnesses, for it cannot be regarded as probable that the "young
man" of Mk xiv. 51 was present at the Agony and saw and
listened while the Three were sleeping. From which of the
Three did Mark obtain information? James is excluded by his
early death, and we know of no special relations between Mark
and John. Peter is much more likely to have been Mark's in-
formant. It is true that some very interesting things about
Peter are omitted by Mark, e.g. Christ's high praise of his confession of faith, his walking on the sea, his paying the tribute
with the stater from the fish; but these are things about which
Peter might wish to be reticent, and which he himself omitted in
his public teaching. See Eusebius, *Demonstr. Evang.* iii. 5.
Although Mark is so much shorter than Matthew or Luke, yet
he mentions Peter nearly as often (Mk 25 times, Mt. 28, Lk. 27);
and Mark mentions Peter in four places where Matthew and Luke
do not mention him, and in all four passages we seem to have
personal recollections (i. 36, xi. 21, xiii. 3, xvi. 7). If we had no
information as to the authorship of the Second Gospel or the connexion of Mark with Peter, we should never have had any reason
for supposing that Mark might have written it; but the Gospel
itself would have suggested that Peter was connected with it.

The number of graphic details which are found in Mark, and
in Mark alone, has often been pointed out as a characteristic of
this Gospel. While Mark omits many sections which are found
in Matthew and Luke, yet in those sections which are common to
all three Mark almost always gives us something which is not in

either of the other two; and often these additional touches are of
great value. Many of them are pointed out in the notes, and the
whole of them can be seen very conveniently in the first column
of Abbott and Rushbrooke, *The Common Tradition of the Synoptic
Gospels*. It is of course possible that these details are in many
cases mere literary embellishments supplied by Mark himself,
who has a manifest liking for fullness of expression; but a good
many of them look like the recollections of an eye-witness. They
bear out what the Presbyter John, as quoted by Papias, said of
Mark, that in writing things down from memory he "made it his
purpose from the first, not to omit any of the things which he
heard or state anything falsely among them." This is praise
which could not so justly be given to Matthew, who rather often
either omits or alters what he does not like. When we see
how wanting in literary skill Mark often is, we are inclined to
think that the graphic descriptions which he gives us are due
less to exuberance of style than to conscientious or accidental
retention of what one who was there had told him. The ex-
pansions and descriptive touches in the apocryphal Gospels are
of a very different character. The student will be able to come
to some conclusion for himself on this point, if he compares the
Synoptic narratives of the three occasions when Christ took
Peter, James, and John apart, or of Peter's denials. The passages
peculiar to Mark, having no parallel in Matthew or Luke, are i. 1,
iii. 20, 21, iv. 26—29, vii. 2—4, 33—37, viii. 22—26, xiv. 51, 52.
Study of these will also help the attainment of some conclusion.

It is probable that, in addition to the teaching of St Peter and
much oral tradition of a general kind, Mark also used documentary
evidence; *e.g.* notes on the teaching and death of John the Baptist,
and on the last days of Christ's life on earth. But beyond this
vague probability it is not safe to go.

The question whether Mark used the lost document, commonly
designated "Q," which was abundantly used by Matthew and
Luke, and of which there are no sure traces in Mark, is one to
which no sure answer can be given. Mr Streeter thinks that he
has been able to "establish beyond reasonable doubt that Mark
was familiar with Q," and Dr Sanday thinks that his arguments
"seem to compel assent" (*Studies in the Synoptic Problem*, pp. xvi,
165—183). On the other side see Stanton, *The Gospels as*

Historical Documents, II. pp. 109—114; Moffatt, *Introd. to the
Literature of the N.T.,* pp. 204—206.   It may be doubted whether
there is any clear instance in which it is necessary to assume
that Mark derived his material from Q.   The items which are
supposed by some critics to come from Q are small in amount.
No doubt Mark knew of the existence of Q, and had a general
knowledge of its contents.   He may have seen it, and here and
there may have been influenced by what he had seen, but it is
difficult to believe that he worked with it at his side as Matthew
and Luke must have done.   Q is certainly earlier than any date
which can reasonably be given to Mark, and therefore the hypothesis that he had seen it is reasonable.   We are on sufficiently
safe ground when we assert that what Mark gives us comes from
Peter and cognate sources of information.   Peter's teaching may
have contained nearly all the Sayings of Christ which are reported
by Mark.

It is not necessary to examine what is called the "three-
stratum hypothesis" respecting the origin of this Gospel, either
in the form advocated by E. Wendling, or in the much more
moderate form put forward by Mr E. P. Williams (*Studies in
the Syn. Pr.,* pp. xxv, 388).   The theory of three editions of
Mark, whether issued by the Evangelist himself, or by him
with two subsequent editors, with considerable additions in
the second and third issues, needs to be supported by more
substantial arguments than those which are at present advanced
in its favour, before it becomes necessary for ordinary students
of the Gospel to pay attention to it.   The hypothesis of an *Ur-
Marcus,* a first edition considerably shorter than our Mark, is not
required.   Burkitt, *The Gospel History and its Transmission,* pp.
40 f.; Swete, *St Mark,* p. lxv; Jülicher, *Introd. to N.T.,* p. 326.

It is more to the point to remember that for some things in
the Gospel Mark's own experience may be the chief source.
The fullness of the narrative of the last week of our Lord's life
in all the Gospels has often been remarked in contrast to the
scantiness of the record respecting the previous thirty years.
It is quite possible that some of that fullness is the outcome of
what St Mark himself could remember.   Some events in the
Holy Week he may well have witnessed and never forgotten; at
some points he may have been present when Peter was not.

CHAPTER III

Plan and Contents

Critics are not agreed as to the analysis of this Gospel. Even their main divisions are not always the same. Yet certain broad features stand out clearly, although there is sometimes room for difference of opinion as to the exact point at which the dividing lines should be placed. There is a short Introduction. Then come two main divisions : the Ministry in Galilee and the neighbourhood, and the Ministry in Judaea. These are followed by the beginning of the Conclusion, and the Conclusion remains unfinished.

The Introduction may be made to contain the first eight verses (WH.), or the first thirteen (Salmond, Swete, Moffatt), or the first fifteen (Zahn). There is something to be said for each of these arrangements. The preparatory work of the Forerunner ends at *v.* 8 ; then he is eclipsed by the Messiah. On the other hand, the Messiah's own work does not begin till *v.* 14 ; but it does begin there in a real sense, although in the fullest sense it may be said to begin with the call of the first pair of disciples. The purely introductory portion ends with the Temptation, which prepared the Messiah for the work of the Ministry, just as the Baptist's preaching prepared the people for the reception of the Messiah's Ministry.

The line between the two main divisions may also be drawn at different places ; either just before or just after ch. x., or at x. 31. There is an interval of transition between the Galilean and the Judaean Ministries, and we can either attach the interval to the latter (Moffatt), or give it a place by itself (Swete), or divide it at the point where the Messiah begins His last journey to Jerusalem (WH., Salmond). Perhaps the last is the most satisfactory arrangement, but the question is not a matter of great moment.

It is obvious that thus far the order is chronological ; Introduction, Galilee, Judaea, Conclusion. But are the sections and sub-sections which make up the main divisions chronologically arranged ? That question cannot be answered with certainty.

Any narrator would endeavour to avoid confusing what took place in Galilee with what took place in Judaea and Jerusalem. Peter and others would remember fairly well where things of moment took place and where Sayings of still greater moment were spoken : and Mark, with the tenacious memory of an Oriental who had not ruined his powers of remembering by misuse, as we ruin ours, would recollect with general accuracy how things had been told to him. But we cannot assume that Peter would always care to insist upon the exact sequence of what took place either in Galilee or Judaea, or that Mark would regard exact sequence as a thing which he must be careful to preserve. A single perusal of the Gospels is enough to show that chronology is not a thing on which the writers lay a great deal of stress. Notes of time are few, and events are often grouped according to subject-matter rather than according to time. In the grouping of the contents of the main divisions of this Gospel it is not often possible to determine whether the sequence is chronological or not, but it is likely that Mark would follow a chronological order in the main, so far as he knew it. In the main, for it might sometimes seem to be instructive to group incidents together and Sayings together which in time were separated ; and Mark's knowledge of the time would sometimes be nil. Tradition often preserves a memory of what has been done or said without any definite setting of time or place ; and when unframed material of great value was known to the Evangelists they had to find a place for it by conjecture ; and they sometimes differ considerably as to the place in the Ministry to which they assign this or that event or Saying. This at times is very disconcerting to the student, but it detracts very little from the supreme usefulness of the Gospels. Their value would not be greatly increased if we could put exact dates to everything.

But, when all allowance has been made for this, the statement of the Presbyter in Papias, that Mark " wrote accurately, though *not in order*," is perplexing, because, with all its defects, his order is remarkably good. Its sufficiency was evidently recognized at once ; Matthew follows it, and so does Luke, and though each of them deviates from it somewhat, yet they never deviate from it together. Mark always has the support of either Matthew,

or Luke, or both.   We never have to balance the order of Matthew
and Luke against that of Mark.   Mark gives us what is really
an orderly and intelligent development.   Jesus is at first
enthusiastically welcomed as a great Teacher and Healer worthy
of being ranked with the greatest of the Prophets.   Gradually
His opposition to the formalism and perverse exegesis of the
Scribes provokes the hostility of the hierarchy and many of
the upper classes.   This hostility becomes so intense, and the
popular misconception of His aim becomes so embarrassing,
that at last He almost confines Himself to the training of the
Twelve in regions remote from the influence of His enemies and
from the disturbance caused by unspiritual crowds.   Finally the
time comes for open conflict with His implacable enemies in their
headquarters ; and in this conflict He is apparently vanquished
and destroyed.

We can explain the perplexing criticism of the Presbyter
when we consider the extract from Papias as a whole, and
recognize that the purpose of it is to defend the Gospel of St
Mark against objections which have been made to it.   Now that
there are three other Gospels, Mark is becoming discredited, as
being very inferior.   The Presbyter admits some inferiority, but
calls attention to conspicuous merits.   He is evidently contrasting Mark with some other Gospel which he regards as a
model, and there is little doubt that the model Gospel is the
Fourth.   It must be confessed that in the matter of arrangement Mark differs widely from John.   Therefore, if the Fourth
Gospel is written " in order," the Second Gospel is not so written.
In this way we get an intelligible meaning for the Presbyter's
criticism.

Dr Abbott suggests that by " not in order " is meant " without appropriate beginning and end."   In defence of this interpretation he quotes from Dionysius of Halicarnassus, *Judic. de
Thucyd.* § 10, what is said respecting criticisms on Thucydides ;
" Some find fault also with his *order*, since he has neither taken
for his history the beginning that he ought to have taken, nor
adjusted it to the end that is suitable."   Obviously, this fits the
statement that Mark did not write " in order " ; for his Gospel
begins very abruptly with the preaching of John, and we are
not told who " the Baptizer " is or whence he comes ; and

it ends still more abruptly with the words "for they were afraid."

But, however we may explain "not in order," which may after all be due to an unintelligent misunderstanding of the Presbyter by Papias, we are not driven to the extreme conclusion that the Gospel which is thus criticized is not the Mark which we possess.

St Mark does not aim at giving us either history or biography in the technical sense. And his work is so incomplete that we cannot suppose that he aimed at giving us a complete Gospel. We are tempted to think that he wrote to supplement what had already been written. Just as the desire to supplement, and in some particulars to correct, the Synoptics, was the reason which induced John to write his Gospel, and just as the desire to combine and supplement, and perhaps supersede, Mark and Q, was the chief reason which induced Matthew and Luke to write, so we might conjecture that one of Mark's reasons for writing was to supplement Q. Q, so far as we can ascertain its character and contents, seems to have supplemented what was well remembered in the infant Church. The contemporaries of Jesus Christ were not likely to forget the homely life at Nazareth, the Ministry consisting of much teaching and many miracles, the Crucifixion and the Resurrection. But the details of the homely life and the details of the Ministry, especially what was said by Jesus in His teaching, were likely to be forgotten, unless they were written down. Whether of the life at Nazareth before the Baptism many notes were taken, we do not know. But notes were taken of many of Christ's Sayings and of a few of His miracles, and these were the main contents, if not the only contents, of Q. How soon these notes were taken cannot be determined; but there is no great improbability in supposing, with Salmon and Ramsay, that some were written during the Ministry. Within ten years of the Ascension, especially after the Twelve had become dispersed and one or two of them had died, there would be a demand for something of the kind; and missionaries who had never seen or heard our Lord would need some such record badly. What we call Q was an early attempt to meet this demand.

When experience showed that Q was inadequate for mission

work, and that lapse of time was causing some precious facts to become blurred, Mark wrote his Gospel, not to supersede Q, and perhaps not directly and deliberately to supplement it, but to save from oblivion a great deal that was not yet written down and must not be allowed to perish. It has been stated already that Mark probably knew the contents of Q, and we may feel confident that there is at least this much of truth in the statement that he wrote his Gospel in order to supplement Q—he generally omitted what he knew to be in Q, because space was precious. That is the answer to those who argue against Mark's having any knowledge of Q by asking, If he knew it, why does he make so very little use of it? We may be sure that the writers of all four Gospels knew a great deal more than they record, and indeed Jn xxi. 25 tells us so. Books in those days had to be of very moderate length, and Luke and Acts reach extreme limits. When it was believed that Christ would return in a year or two at the latest, men's memories of what He had said and done sufficed. When a few years had passed, Q was produced, mainly to preserve precious Sayings. When thirty, forty, fifty, sixty years passed, and still the Lord did not return, more and more full records were required, ending in the Fourth Gospel. That Gospel, when added to its predecessors, has satisfied Christendom.

But Mark is too original to be a mere recorder of what Peter used to say or a mere supplier of what Q had omitted to say. His Gospel does not read like a series of notes strung together ; nor does it read like a supplement to another work. It is an early attempt to bring what we should call " the power of the press" to aid the living voice in making the good tidings known to the world. Mark had had years of experience with Saul of Tarsus, with Barnabas, and with Peter, in preaching the Gospel, and he knew well incidents and Sayings which again and again went home to the hearts of men. Of these he has put together enough to give, by means of a series of anecdotes, a movingly vivid picture of what the Messiah was to those who knew Him. He does not describe or interpret the Messiah; His greatness is sufficiently demonstrated by His own works and words. People who find in his Gospel controversial aims read into it what is not there. The Evangelist evidently takes delight in reproducing what he knows ; and, simple as his language is, it is that of a writer—one might almost say, of a talker—to whom narrating is a pleasure. Nothing of subtle suggestion or insinuation, in the interests of any school of thought, is to be detected in it. Those who profess to find such things do not discover but invent. "These touches in a host of cases are fresh, lifelike, inimitably historical. Nowhere in the Gospels do we stand so near to the eye-witness of Jesus' healings as in the two stylistically connected incidents, peculiar to this Gospel, vii. 31—37 and viii. 22—26. The sign language of Jesus to the deaf and dumb man interprets His thought as if He stood before us. The blind man's description of his returning sight is inimitable" (B. W. Bacon, *Introd. to N. T.*, p. 206).

CONTENTS OF THE GOSPEL

16—20. The Mockery by Pilate's Soldiers.
20—22. The Road to Calvary.
23—32. The Crucifixion and the first Three Hours.
33—41. The last Three Hours and the Death.
42—47. The Burial.
xvi. 1—8. The Visit of the Women to the Tomb.
[9—11. The Appearance to Mary Magdalen.
12—13. The Appearance to Two Disciples.
14—18. The Appearance to the Eleven.
19—20. The Ascension and After.]

The relation of the plan of Mark to Matthew and to Luke may be seen from the following table :

	Mark	Matthew	Luke
Introduction	i. 1—13	iii. 1—iv. 11	iii. 1—iv. 13
Galilee and Neighbourhood	i. 14—ix. 50	iv. 12—xviii. 35	iv. 14—ix. 17
Journey to Jerusalem	x. 1—52	xix. 1—xx. 34	
Last Work in Jerusalem	xi. 1—xv. 41	xxi. 1—xxvii. 56	xix. 28—xxiii. 49
Conclusion	xv. 42—xvi. 8	xxvii. 57—xxviii. 9	xxiii. 50—xxiv. 11

For some reason, probably deliberate, the matter contained in Mk vi. 45—viii. 26 is not much used by Luke, and Lk. ix. 51—xviii. 14 is for the most part independent of Mark. Possibly, or even probably, the great insertion is wholly independent of Mark, for even in the thirty-five verses which are more or less parallel to some of the contents of Mark it is quite possible that Luke got his material from some other source. See Sir John Hawkins in *Studies in the Synoptic Problem*, pp. 29—74.

CHAPTER IV

PLACE, TIME, AND LANGUAGE

Almost all early writers—Papias, Clement of Alexandria, Origen, Eusebius, Epiphanius, Jerome—either state or imply that St Mark wrote his Gospel in Rome. Chrysostom is alone in saying that Mark put together his Gospel in Egypt at the request of his disciples ; but it is incredible that on such a point he was better informed than Clement and Origen. If the Alexandrians could with any probability have claimed the Gospel as having been written in and for their Church, they would have done so. Other possibilities do not merit discussion. In the Gospel itself there are a few features which harmonize with the tradition that it was written in Rome, primarily for Roman readers, and there is nothing which militates against this. What are called the "Latinisms of Mark" are a slight confirmation of this ; but they are not numerous, and they are such as were being adopted in various parts of the Roman Empire by such as spoke and wrote Greek. The mention of Rufus (see on xv. 21) may be a more substantial confirmation. That the Evangelist began his Gospel in Rome, and probably wrote the whole of it there, is the most tenable theory. It is just possible that the abrupt conclusion at xvi. 8 is due to his being obliged to fly, leaving his MS. unfinished.

We may safely set aside the theory that St Mark wrote his Gospel about A.D. 43 at the dictation, or under the personal supervision, of St Peter. This theory is based upon the statement of Eusebius (*H. E.* ii. 14) and Jerome (*De Vir. ill.*) that Peter came to Rome early in the reign of Claudius ; whence comes the famous tradition that he was Bishop of Rome for twenty-five years. This statement, and with it the supposition that "interpreter of Peter" means "writer of a Gospel for Peter," may be treated as untenable. That either Peter or Mark was in Rome at this early date is incredible. St Paul, writing to the Romans A.D. 58, declares Rome to be virgin soil for Apostolic ministrations, and it was probably not till five years later that St Peter reached Rome and was there joined by Mark. As stated above, it is safest to abide by the express statement of Irenaeus that Mark wrote his Gospel after both St Peter and St Paul were dead. That means not earlier than A.D. 65, for Nero's persecution did not begin until the second half of 64, and perhaps both Apostles were not dead until 67. The Gospel itself, especially ch. xiii., indicates that it was written before A.D. 70, for there is no hint that Jerusalem had been destroyed in accordance with Christ's prediction, while there is a hint that an enemy is close to it (xiii. 14). A.D. 65—70 would seem to be the time of composition, and nearer to 70 than to 65. See on xiii. 14. Allen and Grensted (*Int. to N.T.* pp. 8, 13) favour the early date.

The question of language is simple. Assuming, as we have a right to assume from the evidence which exists, that the Second Gospel was written in Rome and primarily for Roman believers, we may be sure that it was written, as we possess it, in Greek, and that our Gospel is not a translation from an Aramaic original. St Paul wrote to Roman Christians in Greek; Clement writing in the name of Roman Christians wrote in Greek; and the early Roman liturgy was in Greek. That Mark wrote for Gentile Christians is evident; for (1) he only once quotes the O. T.; (2) explains Jewish usages (vii. 3), regulations (xiv. 12), and technical terms (ix. 43, xv. 42); and (3) translates the expressions which he sometimes gives in the original Aramaic (iii. 17, vii. 11, x. 46, xiv. 36, xv. 34). What use would an Aramaic Gospel be to Gentile Christians? Again, if Mark wrote in Aramaic, and our Gospel is a translation, why did the translator sometimes preserve the Aramaic in Greek letters and add a translation? This last argument is not a strong one, for the freaks of translators are endless, but other arguments are strong. The book nowhere reads like a translation. The writer has his own characteristic way of expressing things, and these characteristics appear again and again throughout. The intelligent use of tenses and prepositions, and the general freedom of narration, are decided marks of originality; and Wellhausen remarks that it is impossible, with any confidence, to re-translate Mark into Aramaic. We may translate, but we cannot feel sure that we are restoring the original language. Mark knew both Aramaic and Greek, and in writing his Gospel he used material which came to him in Aramaic; but what he writes comes from his pen in easy, and sometimes rather slipshod, conversational Greek. As Jülicher says, "the suggestion that there is an original Hebrew or Aramaic document at the bottom of our Gospel is conspicuously ill-judged. No translator could have created the originality of language shown by Mark" (*Introd. to N. T.* p. 322). And it is certain that the Mark which Matthew and Luke used was in Greek. That either or both of them had an Aramaic Mark and translated it, is incredible. Such frequent and striking coincidences in wording as exist could not have come into existence if either of them had been an independent translator.

It is true that in Mark's Greek there are more traces of Semitic idioms than even in Matthew or John ; *e.g.* δύο δύο (vi. 7), συμπόσια συμπόσια and πρασιαὶ πρασιαὶ (vii. 39, 40), the oath formula with εἰ (viii. 12), the pleonastic αὐτοῦ, αὐτῆς, &c. (i. 7, vii. 25), and the use of καί rather than ἀλλά in cases of contrast (vi. 19, xii. 12). See on i. 9. But these features are sufficiently accounted for by the fact that he spoke both Aramaic and Greek, and that in writing he often translated Aramaic oral tradition, and possibly Aramaic notes, into Greek. See on the one side Allen, *Expository Times*, 1902, xiii. pp. 328 f., and on the other, Lagrange, *S. Marc*, pp. lxxxii f.

For reasons already stated, the "Latinisms" in the Gospel are insufficient to show that St Mark knew Latin, or to give any support to the marginal note contained in two Syriac Versions that he preached in Rome in Latin. The theory that he wrote his Gospel in Latin need be no more than mentioned. The Latinisms are chiefly these: κεντυρίων (xv. 39, 44, 45), κῆνσος (xii. 14), ξέστης (vii. 4, 8), σπεκουλάτωρ (vi. 27), φραγελλόω (xv. 15). More remarkable are the two cases in which Mark explains Greek by Latin, λεπτὰ δύο, ὅ ἐστιν κυδράντης (xii. 42), and ἔσω τῆς αὐλῆς, ὅ ἐστιν πραιτώριον (xv. 16). Perhaps συμβούλιον διδόναι (iii. 6), ῥαπίσμασιν αὐτὸν ἔλαβον (xiv. 65), and ποιῆσαι τὸ ἱκανόν (xv. 16) may be added to the list.

CHAPTER V

Characteristics in Vocabulary and Style

Those who possess Sir John Hawkins' *Horae Synopticae* need very little information in addition to what is given there respecting the characteristic words and phrases in Mark. For the use of others some of the more important facts, taken largely from those collected by him and those collected by Dr Swete, are given here.

(1) Of course not all the 80 words which are found in Mark and nowhere else in N.T., nor all the 37 words which are found in Mark and nowhere else in either N. T. or LXX., are characteristic of Mark. Indeed, very few of them are such. Adopting the standard suggested by Hawkins, *we may count as characteristic expressions those which occur at least three times in Mark and are either not found at all in Matthew or Luke, or are found more often in Mark than in Matthew and Luke together.* Of such expressions 41 have been collected; but on five of these very little stress can be laid, while seven are remarkable as being in a high degree characteristic. These are :

ἐκθαμβέομαι, four times in Mark, and nowhere else.
περιβλέπομαι, six times in Mark, and nowhere else.
ἔρχεται, ἔρχονται (hist. pres.), 24 times in Mark, 19 elsewhere.
εὐθύς (εὐθέως), 41 times in Mark, 45 elsewhere.
ὅ ἐστιν, six times in Mark, once or twice elsewhere.
πολλά (adverbial), nine times in Mark, five elsewhere.
συνζητέω, six times in Mark, four elsewhere.

To these seven must be added the curious combination of the aor. ἀποκριθείς or -θέντες with the pres. λέγει or -ουσιν, which occurs eight times in Mark (iii. 33, viii. 29, ix. 5, 19, x. 24, xi. 22, 33, xv. 2; cf. vii. 28) and only twice elsewhere (Lk. xiii. 8, xvii. 37). Cf. Mt. xxv. 40 and Lk. xiii. 25, where we have aor. and fut. combined. Apparently ἀποκριθείς is timeless.

Other words for which Mark seems to show a preference are ἐκπορεύομαι, ἐπερωτάω, ἤρξατο or ἤρξαντο, πάλιν, πρωΐ, and ὑπάγω.

(2) There are also some *expressions, the avoidance of which is characteristic of Mark.* They are frequent in the other Gospels, but Mark seldom or never has them. He never uses καὶ ἰδού or (in narrative) ἰδού, or νόμος, or the form ἑστώς. While Matthew has πορεύομαι 28 times, Luke 50, Acts 37, John 13, Mark has it only once (ix. 30), and there it is a somewhat doubtful reading. Οὖν is freq. in Matthew and Luke, very freq. in John (194), but Mark has it only four times ; and καλέω, freq. in Matthew and Luke, is rare in both Mark (4) and John (2).

(3) Among the 80 words, not counting proper names, which

are peculiar to Mark in N. T., a considerable number are *non-classical*. Seven are found nowhere else in Greek literature ; ἐκπερισσῶς, ἔννυχα, ἐπιράπτω, ἐπισυντρέχω, κεφαλιόω, προμεριμνάω, ὑπερεκπερισσῶς. But none of these are out-of-the-way expressions coined for a special purpose. Most of them are quite common words with a preposition prefixed, and probably all of them were current in the language of the people, although only the word without the prefix is current in literature. Mark has a fairly extensive vocabulary and can find an unusual word when he wants it, yet in ordinary narrative he has no great command of language, either as regards variety of words or correct constructions. He is like a man who can talk freely and with tolerable correctness in a foreign language, but cannot make a speech or write an essay in it. The word which best describes his style is "conversational." He writes, as people often talk even in their own language, without much regard to niceties of style, or, in some cases, even of grammar. Mark uses the language of common life, rather than that which is employed in literature, whether secular or religious.

Among his colloquial expressions may be reckoned σχιζομένους of the opening of the heavens (i. 10), ἀμφιβάλλοντας without an acc. (i. 16), ἐπιράπτει (ii. 21), ἐσχάτως ἔχει (v. 23), μὴ προμεριμνᾶτε (xiii. 11), εἷς καθ᾽ εἷς (xiv. 19), ἀπέχει (xiv. 41), ἐπιβαλών (xiv. 72).

(4) *Many broken or imperfect constructions* are found ; see notes on i. 27, ii. 22, iii. 16—18, iv. 15, 26, 31, v. 23, vi. 8, 9 (a glaring instance), vii. 2—5, 11, 19, viii. 2, ix. 20, x. 30, xiii. 13, 34.

(5) *Combinations of participles* are very common, often in pairs, and sometimes in triplets : i. 15, 26, 31, 41, ii. 6, iii. 5, 31, iv. 8, v. 25—27 (seven participles in three verses), 30, 33, vi. 2, viii. 11, x. 17, 50, xii. 28, xiii. 34, xiv. 23, 67, xv. 21, 36, 43.

(6) *Repetition of the negative* is often found in Greek literature, but Mark is specially fond of it. We sometimes find that, where Mark repeats the negative, Matthew in the parallel passage does not. Repetition occurs with μή (i. 44, ii. 2, iii. 10, xi. 14), but far more often with οὐ (iii. 27, v. 3, 37, vi. 5, vii. 12, ix. 8, xi. 2, xii. 34, xiv. 25, 60, 61, xv. 45, xvi. 8).

(7) The *frequency of the historic present* in Mark is often noticed ; but it is nearly as common (allowing for the different length of the Gospels) in John. Hawkins gives Mark 151, Matthew 78, Luke 4 or 6, John 162. The vividness which the historic present gives in Mark and John is produced in Matthew and Luke to a large extent by the use of ἰδού, which neither Mark nor John employs in narratives. The most common instance of the historic present in Mark is λέγει or λέγουσιν. Matthew and Luke, in the parallel passages, generally either omit the verb or substitute an aorist. Thus, where Mark has λέγει (ii. 5, 8, 17, 25, iii. 4, 34, viii. 29, ix. 5, 19, x. 23, 27, 42, xiv. 13), Matthew and Luke have εἶπεν, or in a few cases ἔφη.

(8) In Mark's own narrative *asyndeton* is rare (ix. 38, x. 27, 28, 29, xii. 24, and a few other places), but it is very frequent in his terse and vigorous reports of sayings (i. 27, v. 39, viii. 15, x. 14, 24, 25, xii. 9, 10, 17, 20, 23, 27, 37, xiii. 6, 7, 8, 9, xiv. 6, xvi. 6). In nearly all these cases there is a connecting particle (καί, or γάρ, or δέ, or οὖν) in the parallel passages in Matthew and Luke ; and scribes have often inserted a connecting particle in inferior texts of Mark. In the true text of Mark οὖν is very rare.

(9) Mark greatly *prefers* καί *to* δέ, but in a number of cases scribes have changed καί to δέ (i. 14, 28, ii. 5, ix. 9, x. 42, xi. 48, xii. 3, 14, xiii. 11, 12, xv. 33). Of 88 sections in Mark, 80 begin with καί and only six have δέ in the second place. Hawkins estimates that δέ occurs 156 times in Mark, 496 in Matthew, 508 in Luke.

(10) A somewhat *superfluous fulness of expression* is a constant feature in Mark's colloquial style ; i. 16, 32, 42, ii. 20, 23, 25, iii. 26, 27, iv. 2, 39, v. 15, vi. 4, 25, vii. 13, 20, 21, 23, viii. 17, 28, ix. 2, 3, x. 22, 30, xi. 4, xii. 14, 44, xiii. 19, 20, 29, 34, xiv. 15, 43, 58, 61, 68, xv. 1, 26, xvi. 2. Some of these may be Semitic. Matthew and Luke evidently noticed this feature, for they often omit what is superfluous when they reproduce Mark's expression, and cases are pointed out in the notes in which each of them takes a different portion of Mark's complete statement.

With this trait may be connected such pleonastic expressions as ἀπὸ μακρόθεν, which is rare elsewhere, but freq. in Mark (v. 6, viii. 3, xi. 13, xiv. 54, xv. 40), and ἐκ παιδιόθεν, Mark only (ix. 21).

(11) The *imperf. tense* is much used by Mark, and "it conveys the impression of an eye-witness describing events which passed under his own eye; *e.g.* v. 18, vii. 17, x. 17, xii. 41, xiv. 55 " (Swete). Moreover, Mark regards conversation as a process, and therefore he often uses ἔλεγεν or ἔλεγον, where what is said is neither interrupted nor repeated, and where εἶπεν or εἶπαν (which Matthew often substitutes) would have been quite as exact. In other respects he handles his tenses with ease and accuracy, interchanging pres., imperf., perf., and aor. quite correctly according to the shade of meaning to be expressed; *e.g.* i. 30, 31, 35, ii. 2, 13, iii. 1, 2, 10, 11, 21, iv. 8, v. 24, vi. 41, 56, vii. 26, 35, 36, viii. 25, ix. 15, xii. 41, xv. 44.

(12) Mark is rather fond of *diminutives*, but there is only one that he alone uses among N. T. writers : θυγάτριον (v. 23, vii. 25). Other instances are—κοράσιον, Mark five times, Matthew three; κυνάριον, Mark two, Matthew two ; παιδίσκη, Mark two, Matthew one, Luke two, John one ; ἰχθύδιον, Mark one, Matthew one ; ψιχίον, Mark one, Matthew one ; ὠτάριον, Mark one, John one; βιβλίον, Mark one, Matthew one, Luke two, John two, &c.; παιδίον freq. in Mark, Matthew, Luke, rare in John. On the other hand, there are several diminutives which are used by one or more of the other Evangelists, but are not used by Mark : κλινίδιον, τεκνίον, ὀνάριον, παιδάριον, ὠτίον, and (in Acts) κλινάριον.

(13) We may attribute it to Mark's want of literary skill that he employs *the same framework for different narratives*. In the case of very similar events, such as the feeding of the 5000 (vi. 34—44) and the feeding of the 4000 (viii. 1—9), this might occur in any writer. But Mark exhibits a striking parallelism in recording the healings of the deaf stammerer (vii. 32—34) and of the blind man at Bethsaida (viii. 22—26), which are among the chief passages peculiar to Mark ; and even in recording miracles so different as the cure of a demoniac at Capernaum (i. 25, 27) and the calming of the storm on the Lake (iv. 39, 41). Compare also the narrative of Christ sending two disciples to

fetch the colt (xi. 1—6) with that of His sending two to prepare
the Paschal Supper (xiv. 13—16); also the narrative of His
preaching at Capernaum and its effects (i. 21, 22, 27) with that
of His preaching at Nazareth and its effects (vi. 1, 2). In such
cases we do not need the suggestion that the second narrative
has been inserted by a later writer who has imitated the work of
the original Evangelists. Such repetitions are common in the
simpler forms of literature, *e.g.* in Homer and in folklore. Compare Job i. 6—12 with Job ii. 1—6, and the reports of the
different messengers, Job i. 14—19.

Mark not only repeats the framework of his narratives, he
repeats also the grouping of his narratives; thus viii. 1—26
follows the grouping in vi. 30—vii. 37. In each section there is
a voyage on the Lake, a feeding of a multitude, and a healing by
means of spittle and touch.

Mark also *repeats the same word* when it suits his purpose.
He has a favourite word for multitude, crowd, populace, people;
and he does not even vary it, as Matthew and Luke do, with an
occasional plural. With one exception (x. 1), it is always ὄχλος
(37 times). In this he resembles John. Λαός, freq. in Matthew,
Luke, and Acts, occurs in Mark only once in a remark of the
hierarchy (xiv. 2) and once in a quotation (vii. 6); never in
Mark's own narrative (not xi. 32). Δῆμος is used in Acts, but
nowhere in the Gospels. Πλῆθος, so freq. in Luke and Acts,
occurs twice in Mark (iii. 7, 8).

(14) When we come to more general characteristics, we may
say, with Bruce, that the leading one is *realism*, by which is
meant the unreserved manner in which Mark gives us pictures
of Christ and His disciples. He is not reticent; what he has
been told he retells without scruple. He neither omits startling
facts, nor does he shrink from startling ways of telling them.
"The Spirit driveth Him forth" (i. 12); the cleansed leper disobeyed Him (i. 45); "I came not to call the righteous" (ii. 17);
"The Sabbath was made for man" (ii. 27); "He looked round
about on them with anger, being grieved" (iii. 5); "guilty of an
eternal sin" (iii. 29); "he that hath not, from him shall be
taken away even that which he hath" (iv. 25); "He could there
do no mighty work, save &c." (vi. 5); "He marvelled because of
their unbelief" (vi. 6); the Apostles' "heart was hardened"

(vi. 52); "whatsoever goeth into the man cannot defile him" (vii. 18); "He could not be hid" (vii. 24); the healed deaf-stammerer disobeyed Him (vii. 36); the Apostles "understood not the saying and were afraid to ask Him" (ix. 32); "Why callest thou Me good? none is good save one, even God" (x. 18). While the other Evangelists give us, to a large extent, what the Christians of the Apostolic age believed about Christ, Mark gives us what Peter and others remembered about Him. In Mark "we get nearest to the true human personality of Jesus in all its originality and power. And the character of Jesus loses nothing by the realistic presentation. Nothing is told that needed to be hid. The homeliest facts only increase our interest and admiration" (*Expository Greek Testament*, I. p. 33).

CHAPTER VI

LITERARY HISTORY

The early history of St Mark's Gospel is curious. That the Gospel which bears his name was written by him was never doubted from the time when it was first published, and we need have no doubt about the fact now. No rival claimant has ever existed. No good reason for assigning the Gospel to Mark can be suggested, except the fact that he wrote it. If a distinguished name was wanted for an anonymous writing of this character, Peter's name would be the obvious one to select. In the Apostolic age Mark is a person of quite secondary importance, and, if he had not written a Gospel, he would have remained as undistinguished as Silas. His two claims to distinction are his having written the earliest of the four Gospels which were accepted by the whole Church, and his having the honour of both assisting and being assisted by the chief of the Apostles. He helped St Peter in supplying an oral Gospel, and St Peter helped him in supplying a written one. Yet the abiding monument of their mutual service did not meet with much recognition in the Church. Neither its being first in the field, nor its known connexion with St Peter, secured its supremacy. Its authority was admitted wherever it was known; but, before it became widely known, it was superseded by Gospels which answered, much better than it could do, the cravings and needs of Christians. The unique merits of St Mark's work could not be appreciated until all four Gospels had been placed under the searchlight of modern criticism.

Among the Apostolic Fathers, Hermas is the only one who gives anything like clear evidence of being acquainted with Mark. The *Pastor* of Hermas may be dated *c.* A.D. 155, and by that time all four Gospels were recognized as being authoritative and having unique authority. Twenty-five years later we have Irenaeus treating the number four as not only appropriate but necessary; there must be four Gospels, neither more nor less. Evidently Irenaeus had never known a time when the Gospels of Matthew, Mark, Luke, and John were not generally accepted. That carries us back beyond the probable date of Hermas.

Within ten years of the publication of St Mark's Gospel, that which bears the name of St Matthew was given to the world; and within twenty years that which rightly bears the name of St Luke was published. The result was comparative neglect of Mark. The Gospel acc. to St Matthew quickly drove Mark almost into oblivion; and the neglect of Mark became still more complete after St Luke's Gospel appeared. Although Luke did not attain to the popularity which Matthew enjoyed, yet it at once became far more popular than Mark. That Matthew and Luke should be preferred to Mark was inevitable. They contained nearly everything that Mark contained, with a great deal more; and what they added to Mark was just what was most precious, viz. records of what the Lord had said. That Matthew should be preferred to either Mark or Luke was also inevitable, for it was believed to have been written by an Apostle, whereas it was known that St Mark and St Luke were not Apostles.

The depreciation of Mark seems to have arisen early. Papias (see p. xvi) is evidently answering objections. He quotes the high authority of the Presbyter John in answer to criticisms that had been passed on Mark, viz. that he was wanting in fullness and accuracy. The mistaken view that Mark is a mere abbreviation of Matthew seems to have arisen early; and when this error received the weighty sanction of Augustine, it was adopted without question. This of course helped to throw Mark into the background, for of what value was a greatly abbreviated copy of Matthew, when the complete Gospel was to be obtained as easily? Indeed, more easily; for copies of Matthew were more numerous than copies of Mark. Evidence of the preference for Matthew is abundant. One has only to look at the number of references to Matthew in any early writer and compare it with the references to Mark, and even with those to Luke, to see how much more frequently Matthew is quoted. Tertullian is a partial exception with regard to Luke. In his treatise against Marcion he goes through Luke almost verse by verse, and therefore in his writings the references to Luke slightly exceed the references to Matthew. But his references to Mark are only about a tenth of his references to either Matthew or Luke. It is hardly an exaggeration to say that at one time Mark was in danger of being lost as completely as that other document which was used by both Matthew and Luke side by side with Mark, the document which is now called Q. That was regarded as valueless after its contents had become embedded in Matthew and Luke, and no copy of it survives. Not even the fact, if it be a fact, that it was written by the Apostle Matthew saved it from perishing of neglect. And we may suppose that it was mainly because Mark was believed to be in substance the Gospel according to St Peter, that Mark did not suffer the same fate. It is not an unreasonable conjecture that St Mark's autograph was preserved with so little care that it lost its last portion, and hence the abrupt termination at xvi. 8.

In different MSS. and catalogues the order in which the four Gospels are placed varies considerably. The common order is probably meant to be chronological, for it was believed that Matthew was written first. Irenaeus states this erroneous opinion as a fact. Often in lists the two Gospels which were attributed to Apostles were placed first, either Matthew, John, or John, Matthew; and after them were placed those which were not written by Apostles, Mark, Luke, or Luke, Mark. But in no arrangement is Mark ever placed first in the quaternion.

Another fact seems to show that Mark appeared to the primitive Church to be not only a defective, but also a perplexing Gospel ; and a perplexing book is not likely to be popular. Christian students seem to have found a difficulty in deciding as to the distinctive character of St Mark's Gospel. Irenaeus and other writers make the four Cherubim in Ezek. i. 5—10, and the four Living Creatures in Rev. iv. 6—8, symbols of the four Gospels, but they do not always agree as to which Living Creature is the best representative of the respective Evangelists. The Man is generally assigned to Matthew, the Ox to Luke, and the Eagle to John, while the assignment of the Lion varies. But every one of the four symbols is by one writer or another assigned to Mark. Evidently there was something puzzling in the simplicity and objectivity of his Gospel, for no symbol seemed quite clearly to represent it to the exclusion of any other symbol. Its inestimable value as contemporary evidence, free from speculative or doctrinal colouring, was not understood. While the refusal to put it in its proper place as first among the four Gospels is intelligible, perhaps the giving to it each of the evangelical emblems in turn may be justified. It is in this primitive record that the elements of what each of these emblems represents can be found.

CHAPTER VII

The Integrity of the Gospel

This question is simply the question of the genuineness of the alternative endings. That from i. 1 to xvi. 8 we have the Gospel almost as the Evangelist wrote it, need not be doubted. Here and there a doubt may reasonably be raised as to the genuineness of a few words, and these cases are pointed out in the critical notes ; but, as has been stated in Ch. ii. of this Introduction, we have no sufficient grounds for supposing that considerable additions to the original Gospel have been made by subsequent editors. In discussing the integrity of our Gospel acc. to St Mark we may confine ourselves to the last twelve verses found in our Bibles (xvi. 9—20) and to the much shorter duplicate found in four uncial MSS., two of which are mere fragments.

That neither of these endings is part of the original Gospel is one of those sure results of modern criticism which ought no longer to need to be proved. Few who have even a moderate acquaintance with the subject would care to maintain the text about the Three Heavenly Witnesses, or the paragraph about the Woman taken in Adultery, or the words about the Angel troubling the water at the pool of Bethesda, as genuine portions of the writings in which they are found ; and the same ought to be true of the existing endings of Mark. It is true of the shorter ending, for no one defends that as even possibly genuine ; and we may hope that the time is near when it will be equally true of the longer and much more familiar ending.

The shorter ending may be dismissed with few words. It is found in Fragm. Sinaiticum (7th cent.), Fragm. Parisiense (8th cent.), Codex Regius, L (8th cent.), and Codex Athous Laurae, Ψ (8th or 9th cent.). In all four MSS. it is given not as a substitute for the familiar ending, but as an alternative to it, and in front of it, between xvi. 8 and xvi. 9. The archetype of the first three of these MSS. evidently ended at xvi. 8 with the words ἐφοβοῦντο γάρ, for in each MS. there is a break and a few words are inserted between *v.* 8 and *v.* 9. This shows that the scribes knew of the two endings and thought both of them worth preserving ; also that they thought the shorter ending preferable to the longer one, which is not surprising, for the shorter fits the rough edge of *v.* 8, whereas the longer one does not. In Ψ there is no break after *v.* 8, and it was probably copied from a MS. which had the shorter ending only. The Old Latin k (Bobiensis) is the only witness which has the shorter ending as the only ending to Mark. In all four of the Greek MSS. there is a note separating the shorter from the longer ending ; but in several MSS. of the Ethiopic Version the shorter is found between *v.* 8 and *v.* 9, without any separation. It is also found in the *margin* of one cursive (274), of Syr.-Hark., and of two MSS. of the Memphitic or Bohairic Version.

According to the best attested text the wording runs thus :

Πάντα δὲ τὰ παρηγγελμένα τοῖς περὶ τὸν Πέτρον συντόμως ἐξήγγειλαν. Μετὰ δὲ ταῦτα καὶ αὐτὸς ὁ Ἰησοῦς ἀπὸ ἀνατολῆς καὶ ἄχρι δύσεως ἐξαπέστειλεν δι᾽ αὐτῶν τὸ ἱερὸν καὶ ἄφθαρτον κήρυγμα τῆς αἰωνίου σωτηρίας.

"And they reported briefly to Peter and his friends all the things they were charged to tell. And after these things Jesus Himself sent forth through them from the East even to the West the holy and incorruptible message of eternal salvation."

This was evidently written *as* an ending, to finish the unfinished Gospel. Some scribe, feeling that ἐφοβοῦντο γάρ was intolerably abrupt as a last word, and that readers ought to be told that the women obeyed the Angel's command, added these few lines. It has little resemblance to anything in N.T., but the preface to Luke may be compared, *i.e.* the next four verses in the Bible. It is not certain that τοῖς περὶ τὸν Πέτρον means more than Peter. In late Greek οἱ περί τινα may mean simply the man himself.

For Fragm. Sinaiticum, see *Biblical Fragments* edited by J. R. Harris; for Fragm. Parisiense, Amélineau, *Notices et Extraits*; for Cod. L, see the facsimile in Burgon, *Last Twelve Verses*, p. 112; for Cod. Ψ see Gregory, *Prolegomena*, p. 445; for the Memphitic, Sanday, *Appendices ad N.T.*, p. 187. Swete gives the text of the four Greek MSS. in full.

The longer ending, as we have it in our Bibles, requires a longer discussion, because the strength of the case against the genuineness of the familiar words is still very imperfectly known, and because the other side has been fiercely defended by Burgon, and is still upheld as correct by Scrivener-Miller, Belser, and some others. It is perhaps worth while to state at the outset the judgment of some leading scholars. Tischendorf expunges the passage altogether. Alford, Tregelles, and Westcott and Hort emphatically reject it, separating it from the true text of the Gospel, with or without strong brackets as a mark of spuriousness. Lightfoot (*On Revision*, p. 28) discards it and thinks that placing it in brackets is the best way to treat it. Bruce, Credner, Ewald, Fritzsche, Keim, G. Milligan, Nestle, Schaff, B. Weiss, J. Weiss, A. Wright, and others, decide against it. Gould (p. 302), after summarizing the external evidence against the genuineness, says "But the internal evidence is much stronger than the external, proving conclusively that these verses could not have been written by Mark." Moffatt (*Introd. to the Lit. of N.T.* p. 240) considers that we have "overwhelming proof from textual criticism, stylistic considerations,

and internal contents, that this condensed and secondary fragment
was not the Marcan conclusion." Jülicher (*Introd. to N.T.* p. 328)
says that the "only passage in the existing text of Mark that we
must unconditionally reject is xvi. 9—20." So also Warfield
(*Textual Criticism*, p. 203): "The combined force of external
and internal evidence excludes this section from a place in
Mark's Gospel quite independently of the critic's ability to account
for the unfinished look of Mark's Gospel as it is left, or for the
origin of the section itself." Swete (p. cxiii): "When we add to
these defects in the external evidence the internal characteristics
which distinguish these verses from the rest of the Gospel, it is
impossible to resist the conclusion that they belong to another
work, whether that of Aristion or of some unknown writer of the
first century." Zahn (*Introd. to N.T.* II. 467) calls the decision
against the genuineness of the verses "one of the most certain of
critical conclusions." To these must be added those scholars
who have adopted the conjecture of F. C. Conybeare, based on a
statement in an Armenian MS. of A.D. 986, that these twelve
verses were written by Aristion, who is mentioned by Papias as
one of the disciples of the Lord. In this he has been followed by
Chapman, Eck, Harnack, Lisco, Mader, Rohrbach, and Sanday.

When we examine the external evidence, the question seems
at once to be decided in favour of the disputed twelve verses.
With the exception of the four MSS. already mentioned which
have the shorter ending between *v.* 8 and *v.* 9, and two other
uncial MSS. which end at ἐφοβοῦντο γάρ, the longer ending
follows *v.* 8, without a break, in every known Greek MS. It is
also found in seven representatives of the Old Latin (c ff g l n o q),
in Syr.-Cur., in the Memphitic and the Gothic. Finally, the
earliest Christian writings which exhibit clear evidence of the
influence of Mark exhibit evidence that these verses were accepted
as belonging to the Gospel. Irenaeus (III. x. 6) expressly quotes
v. 19 as being found at the end of Mark. "In fine autem evangelii
ait Marcus; Et quidem Dominus Jesus, postquam locutus est
eis, receptus est in caelos, et sedet ad dexteram Dei"; which
Irenaeus regards as a fulfilment of Ps. cx. 1. This external testimony to the genuineness of the twelve verses seems to be not
only conclusive, but superabundant. On the strength of this
evidence the passage has been defended by Bleek, Burgon, Cook,

De Wette, Eichhorn, Lange, E. Miller, McClellan, Morison, Olshausen, Salmon, Scrivener, Wordsworth, and others.

And yet even this strong documentary evidence is very seriously shaken when we notice that the two uncial MSS. which end at ἐφοβοῦντο γάρ are by far the best that we possess, the Vaticanus (B) and the Sinaiticus (א). When they agree, they are rarely wrong, and when they agree and are supported by other good witnesses, they are very rarely wrong. Here they are supported by Syr.-Sin., by the oldest MSS. of the Armenian and Ethiopic Versions, and by all the witnesses mentioned above which either place the shorter ending between ἐφοβοῦντο γάρ and the longer ending, or (as k) omit the longer ending altogether. Eusebius (*Ad Marinum*) says that the longer ending was not in the "accurate copies," which ended at ἐφοβοῦντο γάρ : "For at this point the end of the Gospel according to Mark is determined in nearly all the copies of the Gospel according to Mark ; whereas what follows, being but scantily current, in some but not in all (copies), will be redundant, and especially if it should contain a contradiction to the testimony of the other Evangelists." There is reason for suspecting that Eusebius is here reproducing some earlier writer, probably Origen, and in that case his evidence is greatly increased in weight. It is quite certain that this statement of Eusebius, whether borrowed or not, is reproduced almost word for word by Jerome in his letter to Hedibia (*Ep.* 120), written at Bethlehem A.D. 406 or 407. In it he says that "nearly all Greek MSS. have not got this passage"; and he would hardly have reproduced this statement of Eusebius without comment, if his own experience had shown him that nearly all Greek MSS. had the passage. It is also the fact that Victor of Antioch ends his commentary at xvi. 8. "On all the weighty matter contained in *vv.* 9—20 Victor is entirely silent; *vv.* 9—20 must have been absent from his copy of the Gospel" (WH. *App.* p. 34).

There is also the argument of silence, which needs to be carefully handled, for in some cases the silence may be accidental, owing to the loss of writings in which the passage was handled, or owing to the fact that the writer never had occasion to make use of the passage. Clement of Alexandria, Origen, Athanasius, Basil, both Gregorys, both Cyrils, and Theodoret, in no writing quote these verses, although some of them must have known of their existence. Cyril of Jerusalem (c. A.D. 350), when lecturing on the session at the right hand of the Father, quotes eleven passages from N.T., but does not quote xvi. 19. Among the early Latin Fathers, Tertullian and Cyprian exhibit no knowledge of these verses, and the same is true of Lucifer and Hilary.

But if the strong external evidence which favours the twelve verses is shaken by other documentary evidence, which tells heavily against them, it is completely shattered by the internal evidence, which by itself would be decisive.

The twelve verses not only do not belong to Mark, they quite clearly belong to some other document. While Mark has no proper ending, these verses have no proper beginning. . They imply that something has preceded, and that something is not found in Mk xvi. 1—8 or anywhere else in the Gospel; Ἀναστὰς ἐφάνη implies that "Jesus" has immediately preceded; but in v. 8 He is not mentioned. On the other hand, in the narrative immediately preceding the twelve verses, Mary Magdalen is mentioned three times (xv. 40, 47, xvi. 1) as a well-known person, yet in the first of these verses she is named as a new personage who needs to be described as one 'from whom He had cast out seven devils.'

Not only does v. 9 not fit on to v. 8, but the texture of what follows is quite different from the texture of what precedes. A piece torn from a bit of satin is appended to the torn end of a roll of homespun. Instead of short paragraphs linked quite simply by καί, we have a carefully arranged series of statements, each with its proper introductory expression, μετὰ δὲ ταῦτα, ὕστερον δέ —ὁ μὲν οὖν, ἐκεῖνοι δέ. Other expressions, utterly unlike Mark, are pointed out in the notes, and some are not found elsewhere in N.T. "Both sides of the juncture alike cry out against the possibility of an original continuity" (WH. *App.* p. 51).

These considerations and conclusions remain unshaken by the interesting numerical facts pointed out by Professor Albert C. Clark in his Essay on *The Primitive Text of the Gospels and Acts* (Oxford, 1914). They show that the twelve verses were appended as a conclusion to the unfinished Second Gospel, without the shorter ending between them and v. 8, at a very early date ; but they prove nothing as to the genuineness of either ending.

This result does not imply that the verses are devoid of authority.

They do not at all resemble the shorter conclusion in being evidently the composition of some scribe who desired to give a better conclusion to the Gospel. They were added to the Gospel so early as an appendix, that their composition as an independent document must have been very early indeed ; and they probably embody primitive traditions, some of which may be Apostolic. The name of the writer of them is given in an Armenian MS. of the Gospels, discovered by F. C. Conybeare in the Patriarchal Library at Edschmiatzin in November 1891. The MS. is dated A.D. 986, and these twelve verses are preceded by a note in the handwriting of the writer of the MS., "Of the presbyter Ariston." It is thought that the note may be correct, and that the presbyter in question is the same as Aristion, whom Papias mentions as a disciple of the Lord.

CHAPTER VIII

THE TEXT OF THE GOSPEL

The authorities for the text are various and abundant. They are classified under three main heads : (1) Greek MSS., (2) Ancient Versions, (3) Quotations from the Fathers and other writers. In each of these three classes, the earlier witnesses are, as a rule, more valuable than the later ones. But this rule is liable to considerable modification in particular cases. A MS. of the 8th or 9th century may be more important than one of the 6th or 7th, because it has been copied from a MS. with a better text. The value of a version depends less upon the date at which it was made than upon the type of text from which it was taken. Similarly, quotations from the writings of a Father who exercised discrimination as to the MSS. which he used, *e.g.* Origen, Eusebius, and Jerome, are more valuable than quotations from earlier writers who exhibit no such care. With regard to this third kind of evidence another consideration has to be weighed. Unless there is a critical edition of the Father whose quotation of Scripture is quoted, we cannot rely upon the wording of the quotation. Scribes in copying the writings of the Fathers freely altered the wording of quotations, whenever it differed from the wording with which they were familiar ; and they put into the copies which

they made the readings which were current instead of those
actually used by the Father whose works they were copying.   In
some cases the comment made by the Father shows the reading
which he knew, and perhaps had adopted in preference to some
other reading which he knew, but such cases are exceptional.   In
other cases a quotation of a Father which agrees with the ordinary
text is of much less weight than one which differs from it.
Again, the Fathers generally quoted from memory, the process
of consulting a MS. being difficult, and the same text is sometimes quoted by a writer in more than one form.   It is only
when a Father quotes a long passage, which must have been
copied from a MS., that we can put much confidence in the
wording.   Once more, in the Gospels the Fathers sometimes
used, not a MS. of any one Gospel, but a harmony of all four,
and then the wording of different Gospels becomes mixed, and
what the writer quotes as Matthew is really a blend of two or
three Gospels.   Nevertheless, in spite of these drawbacks,
quotations from the Fathers are of great value, especially in
determining the place in which a certain type of text prevailed ;
e.g. readings found chiefly in Tertullian and Cyprian tell us of
a text which prevailed in Africa ; readings found chiefly in
Clement, Origen, and Cyril tell us of a text which prevailed in
Alexandria, and that text is still a difficult problem.   There is
no pure Alexandrian text ; it is mixed with elements which are
called "Neutral," because they belong to no one locality more
than another, and therefore seem to be nearest to the readings of
the autographs.   Its chief representatives are ℵ and B, with the
Memphitic or Bohairic Version and many quotations in Origen.
L is perhaps the chief representative of the Alexandrian elements
which are not Neutral.   To L may be added C and many
quotations in Origen.   But the text which rivals the Neutral in
claiming to be nearest to the autographs is that which is called
"Western," because it came to prevail chiefly in Latin writers in
the West, but the name is unsatisfactory, for some of its early
representatives do not belong to the West.   These are D, Old
Syriac and Old Latin, and quotations in Irenaeus, Tertullian and
Cyprian.   It remains very doubtful whether the text which is
supported by these authorities is really nearer to the autographs
than that which is supported by ℵB, Memph. and Orig.

The Greek MSS.

These are divided into two classes, Uncials or Majuscules, and Cursives or Minuscules. Uncials are written in capital letters, and each letter is separate, but the words, as a rule, are not separate. Cursives are written in a running hand, the words separate, but the letters in each word connected as in modern writing. The common idea that, after some centuries of uncial writing, cursive writing gradually supplanted it, is only partly true. From very early times there was cursive writing, but it was not used for literary purposes, and hence was called "private." Books were written and copied in uncial letters ; but for correspondence, and business or household purposes, a cursive hand was used. This, as being so much more convenient, was at last used for literary purposes. Hence some prefer to call cursive MSS. of Scripture "minuscules," because "cursive" might mean the running private hand which is as old as the earliest MSS. of Scripture. There are two or three thousand cursive MSS. of different parts of Scripture. Only one of them is quoted in these notes, No. 33, which Eichhorn called "the queen of the cursives." It is of the 9th cent. and is at Paris. It has been copied from some excellent archetype.

Uncial MSS.

The word "uncial" comes from Jerome's preface to Job, in which he condemns the unnecessary size of the letters in some MSS. in his time. Books were written *uncialibus, ut vulgo aiunt, litteris,* "'in inch-long letters,' as people say." Of course "inch-long" is popular exaggeration, and hence the qualifying "as people say." The MS. called N has letters over half an inch, and capitals over an inch. The history of some of the uncial MSS. is of great interest, and in the case of the most important a few facts are here stated ; but for the most part it will suffice to give the date and the portions of Mark which the MS. contains.

ℵ. Codex Sinaiticus. 4th cent. Discovered by Tischendorf in 1859 at the Monastery of St Katharine on Mount Sinai. Now at St Petersburg. The whole Gospel, ending at xvi. 8. Photographic facsimile, 1911.

A. Codex Alexandrinus. 5th cent. Brought by Cyril Lucar, Patriarch of Constantinople, from Alexandria, and afterwards presented by him to King Charles I. in 1628. In the British Museum. The whole Gospel. Photographic facsimile, 1879.

B. Codex Vaticanus. 4th cent., but perhaps a little later than ℵ. In the Vatican Library almost since its foundation by Pope Nicolas V., and one of its greatest treasures. The whole Gospel, ending at xvi. 8. Photographic facsimile, 1889.

C. Codex Ephraemi. 5th cent. A palimpsest : the original writing has been partially rubbed out, and the works of Ephraem the Syrian have been written over it ; but a great deal of the original writing has been recovered ; of Mark we have i. 17—vi. 31, viii. 5—xii. 29, xiii. 19—xvi. 20. In the National Library at Paris.

D. Codex Bezae. 6th cent. Has a Latin translation (d) side by side with the Greek text, and the two do not quite always agree. Presented by Beza to the University Library of Cambridge in 1581. Remarkable for its frequent divergences from other texts. Contains Mark, except xvi. 15—20, which has been added by a later hand. Photographic facsimile, 1899.

E. Codex Basiliensis. 8th cent. At Basle.

F. Codex Boreelianus. Once in the possession of John Boreel. 9th cent. At Utrecht. Contains Mk i.—41, ii. 8—23, iii. 5—xi. 0, xi. 27—xiv. 54, xv. 6—39, xvi. 19—20.

G. Codex Seidelianus I. 9th or 10th cent. Contains Mk i. 13—xiv. 18, xiv. 25—xvi. 20.

H. Codex Seidelianus II. 9th or 10th cent. Contains Mk i. 1—31, ii. 4—xv. 43, xvi. 14—20.

K. Codex Cyprius. 9th cent. One of the seven uncials which have the Gospels complete, the others being ℵBMSUΩ. At Paris.

L. Codex Regius. 8th cent. An important witness. At Paris. Contains Mk i. 1—x. 15, x. 30—xv. 1, xv. 20—xvi. 20, but the shorter ending is inserted between xvi. 8 and xvi. 9, showing that the scribe preferred it to the longer one.

M. Codex Campianus. 9th cent. At Paris. Gospels complete.

N. Codex Purpureus. 6th cent. Full text in *Texts and Studies* v. No. 4, 1899. Contains Mk v. 20—vii. 4, vii. 20—viii.

32, ix. 1—x. 43, xi. 7—xii. 19, xiv. 25—xv. 23, xv. 33—42. See below on Ψ.

P. Codex Guelpherbytanus. 6th cent. Contains Mk i. 2—11, iii. 5—17, xiv. 13—24, 48—61, xv. 12—37.

S. Codex Vaticanus. 10th cent. Dated A.D. 949.

U. Codex Nanianus. 9th or 10th cent. Gospels complete.

V. Codex Mosquensis. 9th cent.

X. Codex Monacensis. 10th cent. Contains Mk vi. 47—xvi. 20. Many verses in xiv., xv., xvi. are defective.

Γ. Codex Oxoniensis. 9th cent. Contains Mark, except iii. 35—vi. 20.

Δ. Codex Sangallensis. 9th or 10th cent. Contains the Gospels nearly complete, with an interlinear Latin translation. The text of Mark is specially good, agreeing often with CL. At St Gall.

Π. Codex Petropolitanus. 9th cent. Gospels almost complete. Mk xvi. 18—20 is in a later hand.

Σ. Codex Rossanensis. 6th cent. Mk xvi. 14—20 is missing.

Φ. Codex Beratinus. 6th cent. Contains Mk i. 1—xiv. 62.

Ψ. Codex Athous Laurae. 8th cent. Like N and Σ, it is written in silver letters on purple vellum. Contains Mk ix. 5—xvi. 20, and, as in L, the shorter ending is inserted between xvi. 8 and xvi. 9. As in Δ, the text of Mark is specially good.

The fragments which contain the shorter ending inserted between *v.* 8 and *v.* 9 have already been mentioned (p. xliii).

Fragm. Sinaiticum. 6th cent. Contains Mk xiv. 29—45, xv. 27—xvi. 10.

Fragm. Parisiense. 8th cent. Contains Mk xvi. 6—18.

Ancient Versions.

The translations of the Greek N.T. which are of the highest value are the Latin, the Syriac, and the Egyptian. But in each of these three languages we have more than one version, and these versions in the same language sometimes differ from one another as much as our Revised Version differs from the Authorized.

In the *Latin Versions* it will suffice to distinguish the Old Latin from the Revised Version made by Jerome and commonly

called the Vulgate. The Old Latin is represented by about
twenty-seven MSS. in the Gospels, very few of which contain the
whole of Mark. Among these is d, the Latin translation in Codex
Bezae. Codex Palatinus (e) must be mentioned as of special importance. 5th cent. Now at Vienna. It contains Mk i. 20—iv.
8, iv. 19—vi. 9, xii. 37—40, xiii. 2—3, 24—27, 33—36. In character
it agrees with Codex Bobiensis (k), already mentioned as having
the shorter ending, without the longer one appended as an alternative. 4th or 5th cent. Now at Turin. Said to have belonged
to St Columban, the founder of the monastery of Bobbio, A.D.
613. Contains Mk viii. 8—11, 14—16, 19—xvi. 8. These two
MSS. differ considerably from other representatives of the Old
Latin, and show that early translations into Latin must have
been made in different places, or that considerable freedom was
taken in copying. While e and k represent the African translation, a, b and i represent the European, f and g the Italic.
Other MSS. exhibit a mixture of texts. Hence the necessity for
Jerome's revision and for the production of a uniform Latin
Version, such as the Vulgate. As will be seen from details given
in the notes, the revision in many places must have been rather
perfunctory. Capriciously varying translations of the same Greek
words abound.

In the *Syriac Versions* we seem to have three stages marked,
which we may call Old, Middle, and Late. The Old Syriac is
represented by the Sinaitic Syriac, the Curetonian, and Tatian ;
the Middle or Vulgate by the Peshitta ; the Late by the Philoxenian (A.D. 508) and the Harklean (A.D. 616). The latter, which
is a revision of the Philoxenian, as the Philoxenian of the Peshitta,
has marginal notes which are more valuable than the slavishly
literal text, for the notes represent an earlier and better Greek
text. Our knowledge of the Old Syriac was greatly increased in
Feb. 1892, when the twin-sisters, Mrs Lewis and Mrs Gibson,
discovered at the monastery of St Katharine on Mount Sinai a
palimpsest containing lives of female saints under which was the
Gospels. After a second visit with other scholars in 1893, and
a third by the two sisters in 1895, a revised and complete translation was published by Mrs Lewis in 1896 with the original
Syriac. It is certain that this version (Syr.-Sin.) is derived from
the same archetype as the Curetonian (Syr.-Cur.), and both may

have been made in the 5th cent. Scholars are not agreed as to which is the older of the two ; but the general view seems to be that Syr.-Sin. is nearer to the archetype, and may have been made in the 4th cent. This does not exclude the possibility that in some cases Syr.-Cur. retains the original reading, while Syr.-Sin. has been corrupted. Many of the remarkable readings of the latter are quoted in the notes.

In the *Egyptian Versions* we have to distinguish two dialects, the Sahidic or Thebaic, belonging to southern Egypt, and the Memphitic or Bohairic, belonging to northern Egypt. The latter is far the more valuable, the text which underlies it being Neutral or Alexandrian.

The Armenian, Aethiopic, and Gothic Versions are of less importance.

Even the very moderate amount of information which is given at the beginning of each chapter, respecting differences of reading, may easily give an exaggerated idea of the amount of uncertainty which exists respecting the text of the N.T. Can we be sure that we anywhere have got what the authors dictated or penned ? It is worth while to quote once more the deliberate estimate of Westcott and Hort, I. p. 561. "If comparative trivialities, such as changes of order, the insertion or omission of the article with proper names, and the like, are set aside, the words in our opinion still subject to doubt can hardly amount to more than a thousandth part of the N.T." For further information the reader is referred to that work, or at least to the handbooks of C. Hammond, F. G. Kenyon, E. Nestle, and Kirsopp Lake. The last (Rivington, 1900) gives a large amount of well sifted results, and costs one shilling.

In this volume the text of Westcott and Hort has generally, but not quite exclusively, been followed. The excellently printed text of A. Souter, with brief apparatus criticus, will be found useful, and for the Vulgate the handy little volume edited by H. J. White, Oxford, 1911.

CHAPTER IX

COMMENTARIES

The comparative neglect of the Gospel acc. to St Mark in the first few centuries has been already pointed out. This neglect had as a natural consequence an absence of commentaries upon it. Suidas says that Chrysostom wrote on St Mark, but we know nothing of any such work.

Victor, a presbyter of Antioch, who probably lived in the 6th cent., is the compiler of the earliest commentary on Mark that has come down to us. His work consists mainly of quotations from Chrysostom on St Matthew and from Origen, with occasional extracts from Basil, Apollinaris, Cyril of Alexandria, and a few others. Yet the work is not exactly a *catena*, though it is often quoted as such, for he adds something of his own, and he rarely gives the names of the writers whose words he adopts. It was first published in Rome in 1673 by Possinus in the *Catena Graecorum Patrum in ev. sec. Marcum*. It must have been very popular in the East, for it exists in more than fifty MSS. of the Gospels. It is often quoted in the commentaries of E. Klostermann, Lagrange, and Swete, all of which have been used in producing the present volume, the last two being the best that exist in French and in English respectively. Particulars will be found in Burgon, *Last Twelve Verses of St Mark*, pp. 60—65, 269—290.

Next comes the commentary of the Venerable Bede, who died on the Eve of the Ascension, A.D. 735. Migne, *P. L.* xcii. ; Giles, xi. ; ed. Colon. 1612, v. He thus describes his own work : " I have made it my business, for the use of me and mine, briefly to compile out of works of the venerable Fathers, and to interpret according to their meaning (adding somewhat of my own) these following pieces" and then follows a list of his writings (*H. E. sub fin.*). He says much the same in the Preface to St Mark. It is the added "something of his own" that is often the most attractive element. The reader will judge from the quotations in these notes.

Theophylact, Archbishop of Achridia (Ochrida) in Bulgaria (1071—1078). Migne, *P. G.* cxxiii. *If* Chrysostom wrote on Mark, we probably have a good deal of him in Theophylact, who makes much use of Chrysostom elsewhere ; but it is likely that, in this Gospel, we have a larger proportion of Theophylact's own excellent comments.

Euthymius Zigabenus, a monk of Constantinople, died later than A.D. 1118. Migne, *P.G.* cxxix. He also is largely dependent on Chrysostom. His commentary on Mark is meagre, for he usually contents himself with a reference to his notes on Matthew. But where Mark is alone or differs from Matthew, we get some valuable comments. His terseness is not unlike that of Bengel.

Joannes Maldonatus, a Spanish Jesuit, died 1583. Very good of its kind. He rarely shirks a difficulty, though his solutions are not always tenable.

Cornelius a Lapide (van Stein), a Jesuit, died 1637. Voluminous, including allegory and legend ; often edifying but sometimes puerile.

Bengel, died 1751. His *Gnomon N.T.* is a masterpiece of insight and terseness. Eng. tr. Clark, 1857.

Wetstein, died 1754. His *N.T. Graecum* is a monument of criticism and learning. His abundant illustrations have been largely used by subsequent commentators.

Among the best modern commentaries on Mark are—in *English*, Alford, 5th ed. 1863 ; Morison, 1873 ; G. A. Chadwick, in the Expositor's Bible, 1887 ; Gould, in the International Critical Commentary, 1896; Bruce, in the Expositor's Greek Testament, 1897 ; Menzies, 1901 ; Swete, 2nd ed. 1902. The last is indispensable to all who read Greek.

In *German*, De Wette, 1839 ; Schanz, 1881 ; B. and J. Weiss, in the 8th ed. of Meyer, 1892 ; Holtzmann, in the *Hand-commentar*, 1892 ; E. Klostermann, in the *Handbuch zum N.T.*, 1907 ; Wohlenberg, in Zahn's Comm., 1910.

In *French*, Lagrange, 1911, of great excellence, especially in his criticism of Loisy.

Other works of great usefulness are—Abbott and Rushbrooke, *The Common Tradition of the Synoptic Gospels*, 1884 ; Deissmann, *Bible Studies*, 1901 ; Dalman, *The Words of Jesus*, 1902 ; Arthur Wright, *A Synopsis of the Gospels in Greek*, 2nd ed. 1903; Stanton, *The Gospels as Historical Documents*, 1903, 1909; Burkitt, *The Gospel History and its Transmission*, 1906, *The Earliest Sources for the Life of Jesus*, 1910 ; Sir John Hawkins, *Horae Synopticae*, 2nd ed. 1909 ; J. M. Thompson, *The Synoptic Gospels in Parallel Columns*, 1910 ; Hastings, *Dictionary of Christ and the Gospels*, 1906, 1908.

ΕΥΑΓΓΕΛΙΟΝ ΚΑΤΑ ΜΑΡΚΟΝ

1 ¹Ἀρχὴ τοῦ εὐαγγελίου Ἰησοῦ Χριστοῦ[υἱοῦ Θεοῦ].
²καθὼς γέγραπται ἐν τῷ Ἡσαΐᾳ τῷ προφήτῃ, Ἰδοὺ
ἐγὼ ἀποστέλλω τὸν ἄγγελόν μου πρὸ προσώπου σου,
ὃς κατασκευάσει τὴν ὁδόν σου· ³φωνὴ βοῶντος ἐν τῇ
ἐρήμῳ, Ἑτοιμάσατε τὴν ὁδὸν κυρίου, εὐθείας ποιεῖτε
τὰς τρίβους αὐτοῦ, ⁴ἐγένετο Ἰωάννης ὁ βαπτίζων
ἐν τῇ ἐρήμῳ καὶ κηρύσσων βάπτισμα μετανοίας εἰς
ἄφεσιν ἁμαρτιῶν. ⁵καὶ ἐξεπορεύετο πρὸς αὐτὸν πᾶσα
ἡ Ἰουδαία χώρα καὶ οἱ Ἱεροσολυμεῖται πάντες, καὶ
ἐβαπτίζοντο ὑπ᾽ αὐτοῦ ἐν τῷ Ἰορδάνῃ ποταμῷ ἐξομολογούμενοι τὰς ἁμαρτίας αὐτῶν. ⁶καὶ ἦν ὁ Ἰωάννης ἐνδεδυμένος τρίχας καμήλου καὶ ζώνην δερματίνην περὶ τὴν
ὀσφὺν αὐτοῦ, καὶ ἔσθων ἀκρίδας καὶ μέλι ἄγριον. ⁷καὶ
ἐκήρυσσεν λέγων, Ἔρχεται ὁ ἰσχυρότερός μου ὀπίσω
μου, οὗ οὐκ εἰμὶ ἱκανὸς κύψας λῦσαι τὸν ἱμάντα τῶν
ὑποδημάτων αὐτοῦ. ⁸ἐγὼ ἐβάπτισα ὑμᾶς ὕδατι, αὐτὸς
δὲ βαπτίσει ὑμᾶς πνεύματι ἁγίῳ.

⁹Καὶ ἐγένετο ἐν ἐκείναις ταῖς ἡμέραις ἦλθεν Ἰησοῦς
ἀπὸ Ναζαρὲτ τῆς Γαλιλαίας καὶ ἐβαπτίσθη εἰς τὸν
Ἰορδάνην ὑπὸ Ἰωάννου. ¹⁰καὶ εὐθὺς ἀναβαίνων ἐκ τοῦ
ὕδατος εἶδεν σχιζομένους τοὺς οὐρανοὺς καὶ τὸ πνεῦμα
ὡς περιστερὰν καταβαῖνον εἰς αὐτόν. ¹¹καὶ φωνὴ ἐγένετο ἐκ
τῶν οὐρανῶν, Σὺ εἶ ὁ υἱός μου ὁ ἀγαπητός, ἐν σοὶ εὐδόκησα.

¹²Καὶ εὐθὺς τὸ πνεῦμα αὐτὸν ἐκβάλλει εἰς τὴν ἔρημον. ¹³καὶ ἦν ἐν τῇ ἐρήμῳ τεσσεράκοντα ἡμέρας πειραζόμενος ὑπὸ τοῦ σατανᾶ, καὶ ἦν μετὰ τῶν θηρίων, καὶ οἱ ἄγγελοι διηκόνουν αὐτῷ.

¹⁴Καὶ μετὰ τὸ παραδοθῆναι τὸν Ἰωάννην ἦλθεν ὁ Ἰησοῦς εἰς τὴν Γαλιλαίαν, κηρύσσων τὸ εὐαγγέλιον τοῦ θεοῦ ¹⁵καὶ λέγων ὅτι Πεπλήρωται ὁ καιρὸς καὶ ἤγγικεν ἡ βασιλεία τοῦ θεοῦ· μετανοεῖτε καὶ πιστεύετε ἐν τῷ εὐαγγελίῳ.

¹⁶Καὶ παράγων παρὰ τὴν θάλασσαν τῆς Γαλιλαίας εἶδεν Σίμωνα καὶ Ἀνδρέαν τὸν ἀδελφὸν Σίμωνος ἀμφι-βάλλοντας ἐν τῇ θαλάσσῃ· ἦσαν γὰρ ἁλεεῖς. ¹⁷καὶ εἶπεν αὐτοῖς ὁ Ἰησοῦς, Δεῦτε ὀπίσω μου, καὶ ποιήσω ὑμᾶς γενέσθαι ἁλεεῖς ἀνθρώπων. ¹⁸καὶ εὐθέως ἀφέντες τὰ δίκτυα ἠκολούθησαν αὐτῷ. ¹⁹καὶ προβὰς ὀλίγον εἶδεν Ἰάκωβον τὸν τοῦ Ζεβεδαίου καὶ Ἰωάννην τὸν ἀδελφὸν αὐτοῦ, καὶ αὐτοὺς ἐν τῷ πλοίῳ καταρτίζοντας τὰ δίκτυα. ²⁰καὶ εὐθὺς ἐκάλεσεν αὐτούς· καὶ ἀφέντες τὸν πατέρα αὐτῶν Ζεβεδαῖον ἐν τῷ πλοίῳ μετὰ τῶν μισθωτῶν ἀπῆλθον ὀπίσω αὐτοῦ.

²¹Καὶ εἰσπορεύονται εἰς Καφαρναούμ· καὶ εὐθὺς τοῖς σάββασιν [εἰσελθὼν] εἰς τὴν συναγωγὴν ἐδίδασκεν. ²²καὶ ἐξεπλήσσοντο ἐπὶ τῇ διδαχῇ αὐτοῦ· ἦν γὰρ διδάσ-κων αὐτοὺς ὡς ἐξουσίαν ἔχων, καὶ οὐχ ὡς οἱ γραμματεῖς. ²³καὶ εὐθὺς ἦν ἐν τῇ συναγωγῇ αὐτῶν ἄνθρωπος ἐν πνεύ-ματι ἀκαθάρτῳ, καὶ ἀνέκραξεν ²⁴λέγων, Τί ἡμῖν καὶ σοί, Ἰησοῦ Ναζαρηνέ; ἦλθες ἀπολέσαι ἡμᾶς; οἶδά σε τίς εἶ, ὁ ἅγιος τοῦ θεοῦ. ²⁵καὶ ἐπετίμησεν αὐτῷ ὁ Ἰησοῦς λέγων, Φιμώθητι καὶ ἔξελθε ἐξ αὐτοῦ. ²⁶καὶ σπαρά-ξαν αὐτὸν τὸ πνεῦμα τὸ ἀκάθαρτον καὶ φωνῆσαν φωνῇ μεγάλῃ ἐξῆλθεν ἐξ αὐτοῦ. ²⁷καὶ ἐθαμβήθησαν ἅπαντες,

ὥστε συνζητεῖν πρὸς ἑαυτοὺς λέγοντας, Τί ἐστιν τοῦτο; διδαχὴ καινή· κατ᾽ ἐξουσίαν καὶ τοῖς πνεύμασι τοῖς ἀκαθάρτοις ἐπιτάσσει, καὶ ὑπακούουσιν αὐτῷ· ²⁸καὶ ἐξῆλθεν ἡ ἀκοὴ αὐτοῦ εὐθὺς εἰς ὅλην τὴν περίχωρον τῆς Γαλιλαίας. ²⁹Καὶ εὐθὺς ἐκ τῆς συναγωγῆς ἐξελθὼν ἦλθεν εἰς τὴν οἰκίαν Σίμωνος καὶ Ἀνδρέου μετὰ Ἰακώβου καὶ Ἰωάννου. ³⁰ἡ δὲ πενθερὰ Σίμωνος κατέκειτο πυρέσσουσα, καὶ εὐθὺς λέγουσιν αὐτῷ περὶ αὐτῆς. ³¹καὶ προσελθὼν ἤγειρεν αὐτὴν κρατήσας τῆς χειρός· καὶ ἀφῆκεν αὐτὴν ὁ πυρετός, καὶ διηκόνει αὐτοῖς. ³²Ὀψίας δὲ γενομένης, ὅτε ἔδυσεν ὁ ἥλιος, ἔφερον πρὸς αὐτὸν πάντας τοὺς κακῶς ἔχοντας καὶ τοὺς δαιμονιζομένους· ³³καὶ ἦν ὅλη ἡ πόλις ἐπισυνηγμένη πρὸς τὴν θύραν. ³⁴καὶ ἐθεράπευσεν πολλοὺς κακῶς ἔχοντας ποικίλαις νόσοις, καὶ δαιμόνια πολλὰ ἐξέβαλεν, καὶ οὐκ ἤφιεν λαλεῖν τὰ δαιμόνια, ὅτι ᾔδεισαν αὐτόν [Χριστὸν εἶναι].

³⁵Καὶ πρωῒ ἔννυχα λίαν ἀναστὰς ἐξῆλθεν καὶ ἀπῆλθεν εἰς ἔρημον τόπον, κἀκεῖ προσηύχετο. ³⁶καὶ κατεδίωξεν αὐτὸν Σίμων καὶ οἱ μετ᾽ αὐτοῦ, ³⁷καὶ εὗρον αὐτόν, καὶ λέγουσιν αὐτῷ ὅτι Πάντες ζητοῦσίν σε. ³⁸καὶ λέγει αὐτοῖς, Ἄγωμεν ἀλλαχοῦ εἰς τὰς ἐχομένας κωμοπόλεις, ἵνα κἀκεῖ κηρύξω· εἰς τοῦτο γὰρ ἐξῆλθον. ³⁹καὶ ἦλθεν κηρύσσων εἰς τὰς συναγωγὰς αὐτῶν εἰς ὅλην τὴν Γαλιλαίαν καὶ τὰ δαιμόνια ἐκβάλλων.

⁴⁰Καὶ ἔρχεται πρὸς αὐτὸν λεπρός, παρακαλῶν αὐτὸν [καὶ γονυπετῶν] λέγων αὐτῷ ὅτι Ἐὰν θέλῃς δύνασαί με καθαρίσαι. ⁴¹καὶ σπλαγχνισθεὶς ἐκτείνας τὴν χεῖρα αὐτοῦ ἥψατο καὶ λέγει αὐτῷ, Θέλω, καθαρίσθητι. ⁴²καὶ εὐθὺς ἀπῆλθεν ἀπ᾽ αὐτοῦ ἡ λέπρα, καὶ ἐκαθερίσθη. ⁴³καὶ ἐμβριμησάμενος αὐτῷ εὐθὺς ἐξέβαλεν αὐτόν, ⁴⁴καὶ

λέγει αὐτῷ, Ὅρα μηδενὶ μηδὲν εἴπῃς, ἀλλὰ ὕπαγε σεαυτὸν δεῖξον τῷ ἱερεῖ καὶ προσένεγκε περὶ τοῦ καθαρισμοῦ σου ἃ προσέταξεν Μωϋσῆς εἰς μαρτύριον αὐτοῖς. ⁴⁵ ὁ δὲ ἐξελθὼν ἤρξατο κηρύσσειν πολλὰ καὶ διαφημίζειν τὸν λόγον, ὥστε μηκέτι αὐτὸν δύνασθαι φανερῶς εἰς πόλιν εἰσελθεῖν, ἀλλ' ἔξω ἐπ' ἐρήμοις τόποις ἦν, καὶ ἤρχοντο πρὸς αὐτὸν πάντοθεν.

2 ¹ Καὶ εἰσελθὼν πάλιν εἰς Καφαρναοὺμ δι' ἡμερῶν, ἠκούσθη ὅτι ἐν οἴκῳ ἐστίν. ² καὶ συνήχθησαν πολλοί, ὥστε μηκέτι χωρεῖν μηδὲ τὰ πρὸς τὴν θύραν, καὶ ἐλάλει αὐτοῖς τὸν λόγον. ³ καὶ ἔρχονται φέροντες πρὸς αὐτὸν παραλυτικὸν αἰρόμενον ὑπὸ τεσσάρων. ⁴ καὶ μὴ δυνάμενοι προσενέγκαι αὐτῷ διὰ τὸν ὄχλον, ἀπεστέγασαν τὴν στέγην ὅπου ἦν, καὶ ἐξορύξαντες χαλῶσι τὸν κράβαττον ὅπου ὁ παραλυτικὸς κατέκειτο. ⁵ καὶ ἰδὼν ὁ Ἰησοῦς τὴν πίστιν αὐτῶν λέγει τῷ παραλυτικῷ, Τέκνον, ἀφίενταί σου αἱ ἁμαρτίαι. ⁶ ἦσαν δέ τινες τῶν γραμματέων ἐκεῖ καθήμενοι καὶ διαλογιζόμενοι ἐν ταῖς καρδίαις αὐτῶν, ⁷ Τί οὗτος οὕτως λαλεῖ; βλασφημεῖ· τίς δύναται ἀφιέναι ἁμαρτίας, εἰ μὴ εἷς, ὁ θεός; ⁸ καὶ εὐθὺς ἐπιγνοὺς ὁ Ἰησοῦς τῷ πνεύματι αὐτοῦ ὅτι οὕτως διαλογίζονται ἐν ἑαυτοῖς, λέγει αὐτοῖς, Τί ταῦτα διαλογίζεσθε ἐν ταῖς καρδίαις ὑμῶν; ⁹ τί ἐστιν εὐκοπώτερον, εἰπεῖν τῷ παραλυτικῷ· ἀφίενταί σου αἱ ἁμαρτίαι, ἢ εἰπεῖν· ἔγειρε καὶ ἆρον τὸν κράβαττόν σου καὶ περιπάτει; ¹⁰ ἵνα δὲ εἰδῆτε ὅτι ἐξουσίαν ἔχει ὁ υἱὸς τοῦ ἀνθρώπου ἐπὶ τῆς γῆς ἀφιέναι ἁμαρτίας, λέγει τῷ παραλυτικῷ· ¹¹ Σοὶ λέγω, ἔγειρε ἆρον τὸν κράβαττόν σου καὶ ὕπαγε εἰς τὸν οἶκόν σου. ¹² καὶ ἠγέρθη, καὶ εὐθὺς ἄρας τὸν κράβαττον ἐξῆλθεν ἔμπροσθεν πάντων, ὥστε ἐξίστασθαι πάντας καὶ δοξάζειν τὸν θεὸν λέγοντας ὅτι Οὕτως οὐδέποτε εἴδαμεν.

¹³ Καὶ ἐξῆλθεν πάλιν παρὰ τὴν θάλασσαν· καὶ πᾶς ὁ ὄχλος ἤρχετο πρὸς αὐτόν, καὶ ἐδίδασκεν αὐτούς. ¹⁴ καὶ παράγων εἶδεν Λευεὶν τὸν τοῦ Ἀλφαίου καθήμενον ἐπὶ τὸ τελώνιον, καὶ λέγει αὐτῷ, Ἀκολούθει μοι. καὶ ἀναστὰς ἠκολούθησεν αὐτῷ. ¹⁵ καὶ γίνεται κατακεῖσθαι αὐτὸν ἐν τῇ οἰκίᾳ αὐτοῦ, καὶ πολλοὶ τελῶναι καὶ ἁμαρτωλοὶ συνανέκειντο τῷ Ἰησοῦ καὶ τοῖς μαθηταῖς αὐτοῦ· ἦσαν γὰρ πολλοί, καὶ ἠκολούθουν αὐτῷ ¹⁶ καὶ οἱ γραμματεῖς τῶν Φαρισαίων. καὶ ἰδόντες ὅτι ἐσθίει μετὰ τῶν ἁμαρτωλῶν καὶ τελωνῶν, ἔλεγον τοῖς μαθηταῖς αὐτοῦ, Ὅτι μετὰ τῶν τελωνῶν καὶ ἁμαρτωλῶν ἐσθίει καὶ πίνει; ¹⁷ καὶ ἀκούσας ὁ Ἰησοῦς λέγει αὐτοῖς, Οὐ χρείαν ἔχουσιν οἱ ἰσχύοντες ἰατροῦ ἀλλ᾽ οἱ κακῶς ἔχοντες· οὐκ ἦλθον καλέσαι δικαίους ἀλλὰ ἁμαρτωλούς. ¹⁸ καὶ ἦσαν οἱ μαθηταὶ Ἰωάννου καὶ οἱ Φαρισαῖοι νηστεύοντες. καὶ ἔρχονται καὶ λέγουσιν αὐτῷ, Διατί οἱ μαθηταὶ Ἰωάννου καὶ οἱ μαθηταὶ τῶν Φαρισαίων νηστεύουσιν, οἱ δὲ σοὶ μαθηταὶ οὐ νηστεύουσιν; ¹⁹ καὶ εἶπεν αὐτοῖς ὁ Ἰησοῦς, Μὴ δύνανται οἱ υἱοὶ τοῦ νυμφῶνος ἐν ᾧ ὁ νυμφίος μετ᾽ αὐτῶν ἐστιν νηστεύειν; ὅσον χρόνον ἔχουσιν τὸν νυμφίον μετ᾽ αὐτῶν, οὐ δύνανται νηστεύειν. ²⁰ ἐλεύσονται δὲ ἡμέραι ὅταν ἀπαρθῇ ἀπ᾽ αὐτῶν ὁ νυμφίος, καὶ τότε νηστεύσουσιν ἐν ἐκείνῃ τῇ ἡμέρᾳ. ²¹ οὐδεὶς ἐπίβλημα ῥάκους ἀγνάφου ἐπιράπτει ἐπὶ ἱμάτιον παλαιόν· εἰ δὲ μή, αἴρει τὸ πλήρωμα ἀπ᾽ αὐτοῦ, τὸ καινὸν τοῦ παλαιοῦ, καὶ χεῖρον σχίσμα γίνεται. ²² καὶ οὐδεὶς βάλλει οἶνον νέον εἰς ἀσκοὺς παλαιούς· εἰ δὲ μή, ῥήξει ὁ οἶνος τοὺς ἀσκούς, καὶ ὁ οἶνος ἀπόλλυται καὶ οἱ ἀσκοί. ἀλλὰ οἶνον νέον εἰς ἀσκοὺς καινούς. ²³ Καὶ ἐγένετο αὐτὸν ἐν τοῖς σάββασιν διαπορεύεσθαι διὰ τῶν σπορίμων, καὶ οἱ μαθηταὶ αὐτοῦ ἤρξαντο

ὁδὸν ποιεῖν τίλλοντες τοὺς στάχυας. ²⁴ καὶ οἱ Φαρισαῖοι
ἔλεγον αὐτῷ, Ἴδε τί ποιοῦσιν τοῖς σάββασιν ὃ οὐκ
ἔξεστιν; ²⁵ καὶ λέγει αὐτοῖς, Οὐδέποτε ἀνέγνωτε τί
ἐποίησεν Δαυείδ, ὅτε χρείαν ἔσχεν καὶ ἐπείνασεν αὐτὸς
καὶ οἱ μετ' αὐτοῦ; ²⁶ [πῶς] εἰσῆλθεν εἰς τὸν οἶκον τοῦ
θεοῦ ἐπὶ Ἀβιάθαρ ἀρχιερέως καὶ τοὺς ἄρτους τῆς προθέσεως ἔφαγεν, οὓς οὐκ ἔξεστιν φαγεῖν εἰ μὴ τοὺς ἱερεῖς,
καὶ ἔδωκεν καὶ τοῖς σὺν αὐτῷ οὖσιν; ²⁷ καὶ ἔλεγεν αὐτοῖς,
Τὸ σάββατον διὰ τὸν ἄνθρωπον ἐγένετο, καὶ οὐχ ὁ
ἄνθρωπος διὰ τὸ σάββατον· ²⁸ ὥστε κύριός ἐστιν ὁ υἱὸς
τοῦ ἀνθρώπου καὶ τοῦ σαββάτου.

3 ¹ Καὶ εἰσῆλθεν πάλιν εἰς συναγωγήν, καὶ ἦν ἐκεῖ
ἄνθρωπος ἐξηραμμένην ἔχων τὴν χεῖρα· ² καὶ παρετήρουν
αὐτὸν εἰ ἐν τοῖς σάββασιν θεραπεύσει αὐτόν, ἵνα κατη-
γορήσωσιν αὐτοῦ. ³ καὶ λέγει τῷ ἀνθρώπῳ τῷ τὴν
χεῖρα ἔχοντι ξηράν, Ἔγειρε εἰς τὸ μέσον. ⁴ καὶ λέγει
αὐτοῖς, Ἔξεστιν τοῖς σάββασιν ἀγαθοποιῆσαι ἢ κακο-
ποιῆσαι, ψυχὴν σῶσαι ἢ ἀποκτεῖναι; οἱ δὲ ἐσιώπων.
⁵ καὶ περιβλεψάμενος αὐτοὺς μετ' ὀργῆς, συνλυπούμενος
ἐπὶ τῇ πωρώσει τῆς καρδίας αὐτῶν, λέγει τῷ ἀνθρώπῳ,
Ἔκτεινον τὴν χεῖρά σου. καὶ ἐξέτεινεν, καὶ ἀπεκατεστάθη
ἡ χεὶρ αὐτοῦ. ⁶ καὶ ἐξελθόντες οἱ Φαρισαῖοι εὐθὺς μετὰ
τῶν Ἡρωδιανῶν συμβούλιον ἐδίδουν κατ' αὐτοῦ, ὅπως
αὐτὸν ἀπολέσωσιν.

⁷ Καὶ ὁ Ἰησοῦς μετὰ τῶν μαθητῶν αὐτοῦ ἀνεχώρησεν
πρὸς τὴν θάλασσαν, καὶ πολὺ πλῆθος ἀπὸ τῆς Γαλιλαίας
ἠκολούθησεν καὶ ἀπὸ τῆς Ἰουδαίας, ⁸ καὶ ἀπὸ Ἱεροσολύμων καὶ ἀπὸ τῆς Ἰδουμαίας καὶ πέραν τοῦ Ἰορδάνου
καὶ περὶ Τύρον καὶ Σιδῶνα, πλῆθος πολύ, ἀκούοντες
ὅσα ποιεῖ, ἦλθον πρὸς αὐτόν. ⁹ καὶ εἶπεν τοῖς μαθηταῖς
αὐτοῦ ἵνα πλοιάριον προσκαρτερῇ αὐτῷ διὰ τὸν ὄχλον,

ἵνα μὴ θλίβωσιν αὐτόν· ¹⁰πολλοὺς γὰρ ἐθεράπευσεν,
ὥστε ἐπιπίπτειν αὐτῷ, ἵνα αὐτοῦ ἅψωνται, ὅσοι εἶχον
μάστιγας. ¹¹καὶ τὰ πνεύματα τὰ ἀκάθαρτα, ὅταν αὐτὸν
ἐθεώρουν, προσέπιπτον αὐτῷ καὶ ἔκραζον λέγοντα ὅτι
Σὺ εἶ ὁ υἱὸς τοῦ θεοῦ. ¹²καὶ πολλὰ ἐπετίμα αὐτοῖς ἵνα
μὴ αὐτὸν φανερὸν ποιήσωσιν.

¹³Καὶ ἀναβαίνει εἰς τὸ ὄρος, καὶ προσκαλεῖται οὓς
ἤθελεν αὐτός, καὶ ἀπῆλθον πρὸς αὐτόν. ¹⁴καὶ ἐποίησεν
δώδεκα [οὓς καὶ ἀποστόλους ὠνόμασεν] ἵνα ὦσιν μετ᾽
αὐτοῦ, καὶ ἵνα ἀποστέλλῃ αὐτοὺς κηρύσσειν ¹⁵καὶ ἔχειν
ἐξουσίαν ἐκβάλλειν τὰ δαιμόνια· ¹⁶καὶ ἐποίησεν τοὺς
δώδεκα καὶ ἐπέθηκεν ὄνομα τῷ Σίμωνι Πέτρον· ¹⁷καὶ
Ἰάκωβον τὸν τοῦ Ζεβεδαίου καὶ Ἰωάννην τὸν ἀδελφὸν
τοῦ Ἰακώβου, καὶ ἐπέθηκεν αὐτοῖς ὀνόματα Βοανηργές,
ὅ ἐστιν υἱοὶ βροντῆς· ¹⁸καὶ Ἀνδρέαν καὶ Φίλιππον καὶ
Βαρθολομαῖον καὶ Μαθθαῖον καὶ Θωμᾶν καὶ Ἰάκωβον
τὸν τοῦ Ἀλφαίου καὶ Θαδδαῖον καὶ Σίμωνα τὸν Καναναῖον ¹⁹καὶ Ἰούδαν Ἰσκαριώθ, ὃς καὶ παρέδωκεν αὐτόν.

Καὶ ἔρχεται εἰς οἶκον· ²⁰καὶ συνέρχεται πάλιν ὁ
ὄχλος, ὥστε μὴ δύνασθαι αὐτοὺς μηδὲ ἄρτον φαγεῖν.
²¹καὶ ἀκούσαντες οἱ παρ᾽ αὐτοῦ ἐξῆλθον κρατῆσαι αὐτόν.
ἔλεγον γὰρ ὅτι Ἐξέστη. ²²καὶ οἱ γραμματεῖς οἱ ἀπὸ
Ἰερυσολύμων καταβάντες ἔλεγον ὅτι Βεελζεβοὺλ ἔχει,
καὶ ὅτι Ἐν τῷ ἄρχοντι τῶν δαιμονίων ἐκβάλλει τὰ
δαιμόνια. ²³καὶ προσκαλεσάμενος αὐτοὺς ἐν παραβολαῖς
ἔλεγεν αὐτοῖς, Πῶς δύναται Σατανᾶς Σατανᾶν ἐκβάλλειν; ²⁴καὶ ἐὰν βασιλεία ἐφ᾽ ἑαυτὴν μερισθῇ, οὐ δύναται
σταθῆναι ἡ βασιλεία ἐκείνη. ²⁵καὶ ἐὰν οἰκία ἐφ᾽ ἑαυτὴν
μερισθῇ, οὐ δυνήσεται ἡ οἰκία ἐκείνη σταθῆναι. ²⁶καὶ
εἰ ὁ Σατανᾶς ἀνέστη ἐφ᾽ ἑαυτόν, καὶ ἐμερίσθη, οὐ δύναται
στῆναι ἀλλὰ τέλος ἔχει. ²⁷ἀλλ᾽ οὐ δύναται οὐδεὶς εἰς

τὴν οἰκίαν τοῦ ἰσχυροῦ εἰσελθὼν τὰ σκεύη αὐτοῦ διαρπάσαι, ἐὰν μὴ πρῶτον τὸν ἰσχυρὸν δήσῃ, καὶ τότε τὴν οἰκίαν αὐτοῦ διαρπάσει. ²⁸ἀμὴν λέγω ὑμῖν ὅτι πάντα ἀφεθήσεται τοῖς υἱοῖς τῶν ἀνθρώπων τὰ ἁμαρτήματα καὶ αἱ βλασφημίαι, ὅσα ἐὰν βλασφημήσωσιν· ²⁹ὃς δ᾽ ἂν βλασφημήσῃ εἰς τὸ πνεῦμα τὸ ἅγιον, οὐκ ἔχει ἄφεσιν εἰς τὸν αἰῶνα, ἀλλὰ ἔνοχός ἐστιν αἰωνίου ἁμαρτήματος. ³⁰ὅτι ἔλεγον, Πνεῦμα ἀκάθαρτον ἔχει.

³¹ Καὶ ἔρχονται ἡ μήτηρ αὐτοῦ καὶ οἱ ἀδελφοὶ αὐτοῦ, καὶ ἔξω στήκοντες ἀπέστειλαν πρὸς αὐτὸν καλοῦντες αὐτόν. ³²καὶ ἐκάθητο περὶ αὐτὸν ὄχλος, καὶ λέγουσιν αὐτῷ, Ἰδοὺ ἡ μήτηρ σου καὶ οἱ ἀδελφοί σου ἔξω ζητοῦσίν σε. ³³καὶ ἀποκριθεὶς αὐτοῖς λέγει, Τίς ἐστιν ἡ μήτηρ μου καὶ οἱ ἀδελφοί μου; ³⁴καὶ περιβλεψάμενος τοὺς περὶ αὐτὸν κύκλῳ καθημένους λέγει, Ἴδε ἡ μήτηρ μου καὶ οἱ ἀδελφοί μου. ³⁵ὃς ἂν ποιήσῃ τὸ θέλημα τοῦ θεοῦ, οὗτος ἀδελφός μου καὶ ἀδελφὴ καὶ μήτηρ ἐστίν.

4 ¹ Καὶ πάλιν ἤρξατο διδάσκειν παρὰ τὴν θάλασσαν. καὶ συνάγεται πρὸς αὐτὸν ὄχλος πλεῖστος, ὥστε αὐτὸν εἰς πλοῖον ἐμβάντα καθῆσθαι ἐν τῇ θαλάσσῃ, καὶ πᾶς ὁ ὄχλος πρὸς τὴν θάλασσαν ἐπὶ τῆς γῆς ἦσαν. ²καὶ ἐδίδασκεν αὐτοὺς ἐν παραβολαῖς πολλά, καὶ ἔλεγεν αὐτοῖς ἐν τῇ διδαχῇ αὐτοῦ, ³Ἀκούετε. ἰδοὺ ἐξῆλθεν ὁ σπείρων σπεῖραι. ⁴καὶ ἐγένετο ἐν τῷ σπείρειν ὃ μὲν ἔπεσεν παρὰ τὴν ὁδόν, καὶ ἦλθεν τὰ πετεινὰ καὶ κατέφαγεν αὐτό. ⁵καὶ ἄλλο ἔπεσεν ἐπὶ τὸ πετρῶδες, ὅπου οὐκ εἶχεν γῆν πολλήν, καὶ εὐθὺς ἐξανέτειλεν διὰ τὸ μὴ ἔχειν βάθος γῆς· ⁶καὶ ὅτε ἀνέτειλεν ὁ ἥλιος, ἐκαυματίσθη, καὶ διὰ τὸ μὴ ἔχειν ῥίζαν ἐξηράνθη. ⁷καὶ ἄλλο ἔπεσεν εἰς τὰς ἀκάνθας, καὶ ἀνέβησαν αἱ ἄκανθαι καὶ

συνέπνιξαν αὐτό, καὶ καρπὸν οὐκ ἔδωκεν. ⁸καὶ ἄλλα
ἔπεσεν εἰς τὴν γῆν τὴν καλήν, καὶ ἐδίδου καρπὸν ἀναβαίνοντα καὶ αὐξανόμενα, καὶ ἔφερεν εἰς τριάκοντα καὶ
εἰς ἑξήκοντα καὶ εἰς ἑκατόν. ⁹καὶ ἔλεγεν· Ὃς ἔχει ὦτα
ἀκούειν, ἀκουέτω.
¹⁰Καὶ ὅτε ἐγένετο κατὰ μόνας, ἠρώτων αὐτὸν οἱ
περὶ αὐτὸν σὺν τοῖς δώδεκα τὰς παραβολάς. ¹¹καὶ
ἔλεγεν αὐτοῖς, Ὑμῖν τὸ μυστήριον δέδοται τῆς βασιλείας τοῦ θεοῦ· ἐκείνοις δὲ τοῖς ἔξω ἐν παραβολαῖς
τὰ πάντα γίνεται, ¹²ἵνα βλέποντες βλέπωσιν καὶ μὴ
ἴδωσιν, καὶ ἀκούοντες ἀκούωσιν καὶ μὴ συνίωσιν, μή
ποτε ἐπιστρέψωσιν καὶ ἀφεθῇ αὐτοῖς. ¹³καὶ λέγει
αὐτοῖς, Οὐκ οἴδατε τὴν παραβολὴν ταύτην, καὶ πῶς
πάσας τὰς παραβολὰς γνώσεσθε; ¹⁴ὁ σπείρων τὸν
λόγον σπείρει. ¹⁵οὗτοι δέ εἰσιν οἱ παρὰ τὴν ὁδὸν ὅπου
σπείρεται ὁ λόγος, καὶ ὅταν ἀκούσωσιν, εὐθὺς ἔρχεται ὁ
Σατανᾶς καὶ αἴρει τὸν λόγον τὸν ἐσπαρμένον ἐν αὐτοῖς.
¹⁶καὶ οὗτοι ὁμοίως εἰσὶν οἱ ἐπὶ τὰ πετρώδη σπειρόμενοι,
οἳ ὅταν ἀκούσωσιν τὸν λόγον εὐθὺς μετὰ χαρᾶς λαμβάνουσιν αὐτόν, ¹⁷καὶ οὐκ ἔχουσιν ῥίζαν ἐν ἑαυτοῖς ἀλλὰ
πρόσκαιροί εἰσιν, εἶτα γενομένης θλίψεως ἢ διωγμοῦ διὰ
τὸν λόγον εὐθὺς σκανδαλίζονται. ¹⁸καὶ ἄλλοι εἰσὶν οἱ
εἰς τὰς ἀκάνθας σπειρόμενοι· οὗτοί εἰσιν οἱ τὸν λόγον
ἀκούσαντες, ¹⁹καὶ αἱ μέριμναι τοῦ αἰῶνος καὶ ἡ ἀπάτη
τοῦ πλούτου καὶ αἱ περὶ τὰ λοιπὰ ἐπιθυμίαι εἰσπορευό-
μεναι συνπνίγουσιν τὸν λόγον, καὶ ἄκαρπος γίνεται.
²⁰καὶ ἐκεῖνοί εἰσιν οἱ ἐπὶ τὴν γῆν τὴν καλὴν σπαρέντες,
οἵτινες ἀκούουσιν τὸν λόγον καὶ παραδέχονται, καὶ
καρποφοροῦσιν ἐν τριάκοντα καὶ ἐν ἑξήκοντα καὶ ἐν
ἑκατόν. ²¹καὶ ἔλεγεν αὐτοῖς ὅτι Μήτι ἔρχεται ὁ λύχνος
ἵνα ὑπὸ τὸν μόδιον τεθῇ ἢ ὑπὸ τὴν κλίνην; οὐχ ἵνα ἐπὶ

τὴν λυχνίαν τεθῇ; ²²οὐ γὰρ ἔστιν κρυπτόν, ἐὰν μὴ ἵνα φανερωθῇ· οὐδὲ ἐγένετο ἀπόκρυφον, ἀλλ᾽ ἵνα ἔλθῃ εἰς φανερόν. ²³εἴ τις ἔχει ὦτα ἀκούειν, ἀκουέτω. ²⁴καὶ ἔλεγεν αὐτοῖς, Βλέπετε τί ἀκούετε. ἐν ᾧ μέτρῳ μετρεῖτε μετρηθήσεται ὑμῖν, καὶ προστεθήσεται ὑμῖν. ²⁵ὃς γὰρ ἔχει, δοθήσεται αὐτῷ· καὶ ὃς οὐκ ἔχει, καὶ ὃ ἔχει ἀρθήσεται ἀπ᾽ αὐτοῦ.

²⁶Καὶ ἔλεγεν, Οὕτως ἐστὶν ἡ βασιλεία τοῦ θεοῦ, ὡς ἄνθρωπος βάλῃ τὸν σπόρον ἐπὶ τῆς γῆς, ²⁷καὶ καθεύδῃ καὶ ἐγείρηται νύκτα καὶ ἡμέραν, καὶ ὁ σπόρος βλαστᾷ καὶ μηκύνεται, ὡς οὐκ οἶδεν αὐτός. ²⁸αὐτομάτη ἡ γῆ καρποφορεῖ, πρῶτον χόρτον, εἶτεν στάχυν, εἶτεν πλήρης σῖτον ἐν τῷ στάχυϊ. ²⁹ὅταν δὲ παραδοῖ ὁ καρπός, εὐθὺς ἀποστέλλει τὸ δρέπανον, ὅτι παρέστηκεν ὁ θερισμός.

³⁰Καὶ ἔλεγεν, Πῶς ὁμοιώσωμεν τὴν βασιλείαν τοῦ θεοῦ, ἢ ἐν τίνι αὐτὴν παραβολῇ θῶμεν; ³¹ὡς κόκκῳ σινάπεως, ὃς ὅταν σπαρῇ ἐπὶ τῆς γῆς, μικρότερον ὂν πάντων τῶν σπερμάτων τῶν ἐπὶ τῆς γῆς, ³²καὶ ὅταν σπαρῇ, ἀναβαίνει καὶ γίνεται μεῖζον πάντων τῶν λαχάνων, καὶ ποιεῖ κλάδους μεγάλους, ὥστε δύνασθαι ὑπὸ τὴν σκιὰν αὐτοῦ τὰ πετεινὰ τοῦ οὐρανοῦ κατασκηνοῦν. ³³καὶ τοιαύταις παραβολαῖς πολλαῖς ἐλάλει αὐτοῖς τὸν λόγον, καθὼς ἠδύναντο ἀκούειν· ³⁴χωρὶς δὲ παραβολῆς οὐκ ἐλάλει αὐτοῖς, κατ᾽ ἰδίαν δὲ τοῖς ἰδίοις μαθηταῖς ἐπέλυεν πάντα.

³⁵Καὶ λέγει αὐτοῖς ἐν ἐκείνῃ τῇ ἡμέρᾳ ὀψίας γενομένης, Διέλθωμεν εἰς τὸ πέραν. ³⁶καὶ ἀφέντες τὸν ὄχλον παραλαμβάνουσιν αὐτὸν ὡς ἦν ἐν τῷ πλοίῳ, καὶ ἄλλα δὲ πλοῖα ἦν μετ᾽ αὐτοῦ. ³⁷καὶ γίνεται λαῖλαψ μεγάλη ἀνέμου, καὶ τὰ κύματα ἐπέβαλλεν εἰς τὸ πλοῖον, ὥστε ἤδη γεμίζεσθαι τὸ πλοῖον. ³⁸καὶ ἦν αὐτὸς ἐν τῇ

πρύμνῃ ἐπὶ τὸ προσκεφαλαιον καθεύδων· καὶ ἐγείρουσιν αὐτὸν καὶ λέγουσιν αὐτῷ, Διδάσκαλε, οὐ μέλει σοι ὅτι ἀπολλύμεθα; ³⁹καὶ διεγερθεὶς ἐπετίμησεν τῷ ἀνέμῳ καὶ εἶπεν τῇ θαλάσσῃ, Σιώπα, πεφίμωσο. καὶ ἐκόπασεν ὁ ἄνεμος, καὶ ἐγένετο γαλήνη μεγάλη. ⁴⁰καὶ εἶπεν αὐτοῖς, Τί δειλοί ἐστε; οὔπω ἔχετε πίστιν; ⁴¹καὶ ἐφοβήθησαν φόβον μέγαν, καὶ ἔλεγον πρὸς ἀλλήλους· Τίς ἄρα οὗτός ἐστιν, ὅτι καὶ ὁ ἄνεμος καὶ ἡ θάλασσα ὑπακούει αὐτῷ;

5 ¹Καὶ ἦλθον εἰς τὸ πέραν τῆς θαλάσσης εἰς τὴν χώραν τῶν Γερασηνῶν. ²καὶ ἐξελθόντος αὐτοῦ ἐκ τοῦ πλοίου, εὐθὺς ὑπήντησεν αὐτῷ ἐκ τῶν μνημείων ἄνθρωπος ἐν πνεύματι ἀκαθάρτῳ, ³ὃς τὴν κατοίκησιν εἶχεν ἐν τοῖς μνήμασιν, καὶ οὐδὲ ἁλύσει οὐκέτι οὐδεὶς ἐδύνατο αὐτὸν δῆσαι, ⁴διὰ τὸ αὐτὸν πολλάκις πέδαις καὶ ἁλύσεσι δεδέσθαι καὶ διεσπάσθαι ὑπ᾽ αὐτοῦ τὰς ἁλύσεις καὶ τὰς πέδας συντετρίφθαι, καὶ οὐδεὶς ἴσχυεν αὐτὸν δαμάσαι, ⁵καὶ διὰ παντὸς νυκτὸς καὶ ἡμέρας ἐν τοῖς μνήμασιν καὶ ἐν τοῖς ὄρεσιν ἦν κράζων καὶ κατακόπτων ἑαυτὸν λίθοις. ⁶καὶ ἰδὼν τὸν Ἰησοῦν ἀπὸ μακρόθεν ἔδραμεν καὶ προσεκύνησεν αὐτῷ, ⁷καὶ κράξας φωνῇ μεγάλῃ λέγει, Τί ἐμοὶ καὶ σοί, Ἰησοῦ υἱὲ τοῦ θεοῦ τοῦ ὑψίστου; ὁρκίζω σε τὸν θεόν, μή με βασανίσῃς. ⁸ἔλεγεν γὰρ αὐτῷ, Ἔξελθε τὸ πνεῦμα τὸ ἀκάθαρτον ἐκ τοῦ ἀνθρώπου. ⁹καὶ ἐπηρώτα αὐτόν, Τί ὄνομά σοι; καὶ λέγει αὐτῷ, Λεγιὼν ὄνομά μοι, ὅτι πολλοί ἐσμεν. ¹⁰καὶ παρεκάλει αὐτὸν πολλὰ ἵνα μὴ αὐτὰ ἀποστείλῃ ἔξω τῆς χώρας. ¹¹ἦν δὲ ἐκεῖ πρὸς τῷ ὄρει ἀγέλη χοίρων μεγάλη βοσκομένη· ¹²καὶ παρεκάλεσαν αὐτὸν λέγοντες, Πέμψον ἡμᾶς εἰς τοὺς χοίρους, ἵνα εἰς αὐτοὺς εἰσέλθωμεν. ¹³καὶ ἐπέτρεψεν αὐτοῖς. καὶ ἐξελθόντα τὰ πνεύματα τὰ

ἀκάθαρτα εἰσῆλθον εἰς τοὺς χοίρους, καὶ ὥρμησεν ἡ
ἀγέλη κατὰ τοῦ κρημνοῦ εἰς τὴν θάλασσαν, ὡς δισχίλιοι, καὶ ἐπνίγοντο ἐν τῇ θαλάσσῃ. ¹⁴ καὶ οἱ βόσκοντες
αὐτοὺς ἔφυγον καὶ ἀπήγγειλαν εἰς τὴν πόλιν καὶ εἰς
τοὺς ἀγρούς· καὶ ἦλθον ἰδεῖν τί ἐστιν τὸ γεγονός. ¹⁵ καὶ
ἔρχονται πρὸς τὸν Ἰησοῦν, καὶ θεωροῦσιν τὸν δαιμονιζόμενον καθήμενον ἱματισμένον καὶ σωφρονοῦντα, τὸν
ἐσχηκότα τὸν λεγιῶνα, καὶ ἐφοβήθησαν. ¹⁶ καὶ διηγήσαντο αὐτοῖς οἱ ἰδόντες πῶς ἐγένετο τῷ δαιμονιζομένῳ
καὶ περὶ τῶν χοίρων. ¹⁷ καὶ ἤρξαντο παρακαλεῖν αὐτὸν
ἀπελθεῖν ἀπὸ τῶν ὁρίων αὐτῶν. ¹⁸ καὶ ἐμβαίνοντος
αὐτοῦ εἰς τὸ πλοῖον, παρεκάλει αὐτὸν ὁ δαιμονισθεὶς
ἵνα μετ' αὐτοῦ ᾖ. ¹⁹ καὶ οὐκ ἀφῆκεν αὐτόν, ἀλλὰ λέγει
αὐτῷ, Ὕπαγε εἰς τὸν οἶκόν σου πρὸς τοὺς σούς, καὶ
ἀπάγγειλον αὐτοῖς ὅσα ὁ κύριός σοι πεποίηκεν καὶ
ἠλέησέν σε. ²⁰ καὶ ἀπῆλθεν, καὶ ἤρξατο κηρύσσειν ἐν
τῇ Δεκαπόλει ὅσα ἐποίησεν αὐτῷ ὁ Ἰησοῦς, καὶ πάντες
ἐθαύμαζον.

²¹ Καὶ διαπεράσαντος τοῦ Ἰησοῦ ἐν τῷ πλοίῳ πάλιν
εἰς τὸ πέραν, συνήχθη ὄχλος πολὺς ἐπ' αὐτόν, καὶ ἦν
παρὰ τὴν θάλασσαν. ²² καὶ ἔρχεται εἷς τῶν ἀρχισυναγώγων, ὀνόματι Ἰάειρος, καὶ ἰδὼν αὐτὸν πίπτει πρὸς
τοὺς πόδας αὐτοῦ, ²³ καὶ παρακαλεῖ αὐτὸν πολλά, λέγων
ὅτι Τὸ θυγάτριόν μου ἐσχάτως ἔχει, ἵνα ἐλθὼν ἐπιθῇς
τὰς χεῖρας αὐτῇ, ἵνα σωθῇ καὶ ζήσῃ. ²⁴ καὶ ἀπῆλθεν
μετ' αὐτοῦ, καὶ ἠκολούθει αὐτῷ ὄχλος πολύς, καὶ συνέθλιβον αὐτόν.

²⁵ Καὶ γυνὴ οὖσα ἐν ῥύσει αἵματος δώδεκα ἔτη,
²⁶ καὶ πολλὰ παθοῦσα ὑπὸ πολλῶν ἰατρῶν καὶ δαπανήσασα τὰ παρ' αὐτῆς πάντα, καὶ μηδὲν ὠφεληθεῖσα
ἀλλὰ μᾶλλον εἰς τὸ χεῖρον ἐλθοῦσα, ²⁷ ἀκούσασα τὰ

περὶ τοῦ Ἰησοῦ, ἐλθοῦσα ἐν τῷ ὄχλῳ ὄπισθεν ἥψατο τοῦ ἱματίου αὐτοῦ· ²⁸ ἔλεγεν γὰρ ὅτι Ἐὰν ἅψωμαι κἂν τῶν ἱματίων αὐτοῦ, σωθήσομαι. ²⁹ καὶ εὐθὺς ἐξηράνθη ἡ πηγὴ τοῦ αἵματος αὐτῆς, καὶ ἔγνω τῷ σώματι ὅτι ἴαται ἀπὸ τῆς μάστιγος. ³⁰ καὶ εὐθὺς ὁ Ἰησοῦς ἐπι-γνοὺς ἐν ἑαυτῷ τὴν ἐξ αὐτοῦ δύναμιν ἐξελθοῦσαν, ἐπι-στραφεὶς ἐν τῷ ὄχλῳ ἔλεγεν, Τίς μου ἥψατο τῶν ἱμα-τίων; ³¹ καὶ ἔλεγον αὐτῷ οἱ μαθηταὶ αὐτοῦ, Βλέπεις τὸν ὄχλον συνθλίβοντά σε, καὶ λέγεις, Τίς μου ἥψατο; ³² καὶ περιεβλέπετο ἰδεῖν τὴν τοῦτο ποιήσασαν. ³³ ἡ δὲ γυνὴ φοβηθεῖσα καὶ τρέμουσα, εἰδυῖα ὃ γέγονεν αὐτῇ, ἦλθεν καὶ προσέπεσεν αὐτῷ καὶ εἶπεν αὐτῷ πᾶσαν τὴν ἀλήθειαν. ³⁴ ὁ δὲ εἶπεν αὐτῇ, Θύγατερ, ἡ πίστις σου σέσωκέν σε· ὕπαγε εἰς εἰρήνην, καὶ ἴσθι ὑγιὴς ἀπὸ τῆς μάστιγός σου.

³⁵ Ἔτι αὐτοῦ λαλοῦντος ἔρχονται ἀπὸ τοῦ ἀρχισυ-ναγώγου λέγοντες ὅτι Ἡ θυγάτηρ σου ἀπέθανεν, τί ἔτι σκύλλεις τὸν διδάσκαλον; ³⁶ ὁ δὲ Ἰησοῦς παρακούσας τὸν λόγον λαλούμενον λέγει τῷ ἀρχισυναγώγῳ, Μὴ φοβοῦ, μόνον πίστευε. ³⁷ καὶ οὐκ ἀφῆκεν οὐδένα μετ᾽ αὐτοῦ συνακολουθῆσαι εἰ μὴ τὸν Πέτρον καὶ Ἰάκωβον καὶ Ἰωάννην τὸν ἀδελφὸν Ἰακώβου. ³⁸ καὶ ἔρχονται εἰς τὸν οἶκον τοῦ ἀρχισυναγώγου, καὶ θεωρεῖ θόρυβον καὶ κλαίοντας καὶ ἀλαλάζοντας πολλά, ³⁹ καὶ εἰσελθὼν λέγει αὐτοῖς, Τί θορυβεῖσθε καὶ κλαίετε; τὸ παιδίον οὐκ ἀπέθανεν ἀλλὰ καθεύδει. ⁴⁰ καὶ κατεγέλων αὐτοῦ. αὐτὸς δὲ ἐκβαλὼν πάντας παραλαμβάνει τὸν πατέρα τοῦ παιδίου καὶ τὴν μητέρα καὶ τοὺς μετ᾽ αὐτοῦ, καὶ εἰσπορεύεται ὅπου ἦν τὸ παιδίον. ⁴¹ καὶ κρατήσας τῆς χειρὸς τοῦ παιδίου λέγει αὐτῇ, Ταλειθά, κούμ, ὅ ἐστιν μεθερμηνευόμενον, Τὸ κοράσιον, σοὶ λέγω, ἔγειρε. ⁴² καὶ

εὐθὺς ἀνέστη τὸ κοράσιον καὶ περιεπάτει· ἦν γὰρ ἐτῶν
δώδεκα· καὶ ἐξέστησαν εὐθὺς ἐκστάσει μεγάλῃ. ⁴³ καὶ
διεστείλατο αὐτοῖς πολλὰ ἵνα μηδεὶς γνοῖ τοῦτο, καὶ
εἶπεν δοθῆναι αὐτῇ φαγεῖν.

6 ¹ Καὶ ἐξῆλθεν ἐκεῖθεν, καὶ ἔρχεται εἰς τὴν πατρίδα αὐτοῦ, καὶ ἀκολουθοῦσιν αὐτῷ οἱ μαθηταὶ αὐτοῦ.
² καὶ γενομένου σαββάτου ἤρξατο διδάσκειν ἐν τῇ συνα-
γωγῇ· καὶ οἱ πολλοὶ ἀκούοντες ἐξεπλήσσοντο, λέγοντες,
Πόθεν τούτῳ ταῦτα, καὶ τίς ἡ σοφία ἡ δοθεῖσα τούτῳ;
καὶ δυνάμεις τοιαῦται διὰ τῶν χειρῶν αὐτοῦ γινόμεναι;
³ οὐχ οὗτός ἐστιν ὁ τέκτων, ὁ υἱὸς τῆς Μαρίας καὶ
ἀδελφὸς Ἰακώβου καὶ Ἰωσῆτος καὶ Ἰούδα καὶ Σίμωνος;
καὶ οὐκ εἰσὶν αἱ ἀδελφαὶ αὐτοῦ ὧδε πρὸς ἡμᾶς; καὶ
ἐσκανδαλίζοντο ἐν αὐτῷ. ⁴ καὶ ἔλεγεν αὐτοῖς ὁ Ἰησοῦς
ὅτι Οὐκ ἔστιν προφήτης ἄτιμος εἰ μὴ ἐν τῇ πατρίδι
αὐτοῦ καὶ ἐν τοῖς συγγενεῦσιν αὐτοῦ καὶ ἐν τῇ οἰκίᾳ
αὐτοῦ. ⁵ καὶ οὐκ ἐδύνατο ἐκεῖ ποιῆσαι οὐδεμίαν δύναμιν,
εἰ μὴ ὀλίγοις ἀρρώστοις ἐπιθεὶς τὰς χεῖρας ἐθεράπευσεν.
⁶ καὶ ἐθαύμασεν διὰ τὴν ἀπιστίαν αὐτῶν. καὶ περιῆγεν
τὰς κώμας κύκλῳ διδάσκων.

⁷ Καὶ προσκαλεῖται τοὺς δώδεκα, καὶ ἤρξατο αὐτοὺς
ἀποστέλλειν δύο δύο, καὶ ἐδίδου αὐτοῖς ἐξουσίαν τῶν
πνευμάτων τῶν ἀκαθάρτων, ⁸ καὶ παρήγγειλεν αὐτοῖς ἵνα
μηδὲν αἴρωσιν εἰς ὁδὸν εἰ μὴ ῥάβδον μόνον, μὴ ἄρτον, μὴ
πήραν, μὴ εἰς τὴν ζώνην χαλκόν, ⁹ ἀλλὰ ὑποδεδεμένους
σανδάλια, καί, Μὴ ἐνδύσασθε δύο χιτῶνας. ¹⁰ καὶ ἔλεγεν
αὐτοῖς, Ὅπου ἐὰν εἰσέλθητε εἰς οἰκίαν, ἐκεῖ μένετε ἕως
ἂν ἐξέλθητε ἐκεῖθεν. ¹¹ καὶ ὃς ἂν τόπος μὴ δέξηται ὑμᾶς
μηδὲ ἀκούσωσιν ὑμῶν, ἐκπορευόμενοι ἐκεῖθεν ἐκτινάξατε
τὸν χοῦν τὸν ὑποκάτω τῶν ποδῶν ὑμῶν εἰς μαρτύριον
αὐτοῖς. ¹² καὶ ἐξελθόντες ἐκήρυξαν ἵνα μετανοῶσιν. ¹³ καὶ

δαιμόνια πολλὰ ἐξέβαλλον, καὶ ἤλειφον ἐλαίῳ πολλοὺς
ἀρρώστους καὶ ἐθεράπευον.

¹⁴Καὶ ἤκουσεν ὁ βασιλεὺς Ἡρῴδης, φανερὸν γὰρ
ἐγένετο τὸ ὄνομα αὐτοῦ, καὶ ἔλεγον ὅτι Ἰωάννης ὁ βαπτίζων ἐγήγερται ἐκ νεκρῶν, καὶ διὰ τοῦτο ἐνεργοῦσιν αἱ
δυνάμεις ἐν αὐτῷ. ¹⁵ἄλλοι δὲ ἔλεγον ὅτι Ἡλείας ἐστίν·
ἄλλοι δὲ ἔλεγον ὅτι Προφήτης ὡς εἷς τῶν προφητῶν.
¹⁶ἀκούσας δὲ ὁ Ἡρῴδης ἔλεγεν, Ὃν ἐγὼ ἀπεκεφάλισα
Ἰωάννην, οὗτος ἠγέρθη. ¹⁷αὐτὸς γὰρ ὁ Ἡρῴδης ἀποστείλας ἐκράτησεν τὸν Ἰωάννην καὶ ἔδησεν αὐτὸν ἐν
φυλακῇ διὰ Ἡρῳδιάδα τὴν γυναῖκα Φιλίππου τοῦ
ἀδελφοῦ αὐτοῦ, ὅτι αὐτὴν ἐγάμησεν· ¹⁸ἔλεγεν γὰρ ὁ
Ἰωάννης τῷ Ἡρῴδῃ ὅτι Οὐκ ἔξεστίν σοι ἔχειν τὴν
γυναῖκα τοῦ ἀδελφοῦ σου. ¹⁹ἡ δὲ Ἡρῳδιὰς ἐνεῖχεν
αὐτῷ καὶ ἤθελεν αὐτὸν ἀποκτεῖναι, καὶ οὐκ ἐδύνατο·
²⁰ὁ γὰρ Ἡρῴδης ἐφοβεῖτο τὸν Ἰωάννην, εἰδὼς αὐτὸν
ἄνδρα δίκαιον καὶ ἅγιον, καὶ συνετήρει αὐτόν, καὶ
ἀκούσας αὐτοῦ πολλὰ ἠπόρει, καὶ ἡδέως αὐτοῦ ἤκουεν.
²¹καὶ γενομένης ἡμέρας εὐκαίρου, ὅτε Ἡρῴδης τοῖς
γενεσίοις αὐτοῦ δεῖπνον ἐποίησεν τοῖς μεγιστᾶσιν αὐτοῦ καὶ τοῖς χιλιάρχοις καὶ τοῖς πρώτοις τῆς Γαλιλαίας, ²²καὶ εἰσελθούσης τῆς θυγατρὸς αὐτῆς τῆς Ἡρῳδιάδος καὶ ὀρχησαμένης, ἤρεσεν τῷ Ἡρῴδῃ καὶ τοῖς
συνανακειμένοις. ὁ δὲ βασιλεὺς εἶπεν τῷ κορασίῳ, Αἴτησόν με ὃ ἐὰν θέλῃς, καὶ δώσω σοι· ²³καὶ ὤμοσεν αὐτῇ
ὅτι Ὃ ἐάν με αἰτήσῃς δώσω σοι ἕως ἡμίσους τῆς βασιλείας μου. ²⁴καὶ ἐξελθοῦσα εἶπεν τῇ μητρὶ αὐτῆς, Τί
αἰτήσωμαι; ἡ δὲ εἶπεν, Τὴν κεφαλὴν Ἰωάννου τοῦ βαπτίζοντος. ²⁵καὶ εἰσελθοῦσα εὐθὺς μετὰ σπουδῆς πρὸς τὸν
βασιλέα ᾐτήσατο λέγουσα, Θέλω ἵνα ἐξαυτῆς δῷς μοι ἐπὶ
πίνακι τὴν κεφαλὴν Ἰωάννου τοῦ βαπτιστοῦ. ²⁶καὶ περί-

λυπος γενόμενος ὁ βασιλεὺς διὰ τοὺς ὅρκους καὶ τοὺς ἀνακειμένους οὐκ ἠθέλησεν ἀθετῆσαι αὐτήν. ²⁷ καὶ εὐθὺς
ἀποστείλας ὁ βασιλεὺς σπεκουλάτορα ἐπέταξεν ἐνέγκαι
τὴν κεφαλὴν αὐτοῦ. ²⁸ καὶ ἀπελθὼν ἀπεκεφάλισεν αὐτὸν
ἐν τῇ φυλακῇ, καὶ ἤνεγκεν τὴν κεφαλὴν αὐτοῦ ἐπὶ
πίνακι καὶ ἔδωκεν αὐτὴν τῷ κορασίῳ, καὶ τὸ κοράσιον
ἔδωκεν αὐτὴν τῇ μητρὶ αὐτῆς. ²⁹ καὶ ἀκούσαντες οἱ
μαθηταὶ αὐτοῦ ἦλθαν καὶ ἦραν τὸ πτῶμα αὐτοῦ, καὶ
ἔθηκαν αὐτὸ ἐν μνημείῳ.

³⁰ Καὶ συνάγονται οἱ ἀπόστολοι πρὸς τὸν Ἰησοῦν, καὶ
ἀπήγγειλαν αὐτῷ πάντα ὅσα ἐποίησαν καὶ ὅσα ἐδίδαξαν.
³¹ καὶ λέγει αὐτοῖς, Δεῦτε ὑμεῖς αὐτοὶ κατ' ἰδίαν εἰς
ἔρημον τόπον καὶ ἀναπαύσασθε ὀλίγον. ἦσαν γὰρ οἱ
ἐρχόμενοι καὶ οἱ ὑπάγοντες πολλοί, καὶ οὐδὲ φαγεῖν
εὐκαίρουν. ³² καὶ ἀπῆλθον ἐν τῷ πλοίῳ εἰς ἔρημον τόπον
κατ' ἰδίαν. ³³ καὶ εἶδον αὐτοὺς ὑπάγοντας καὶ ἐπέγνω-
σαν πολλοί, καὶ πεζῇ ἀπὸ πασῶν τῶν πόλεων συνέδραμον ἐκεῖ καὶ προῆλθον αὐτούς. ³⁴ καὶ ἐξελθὼν
εἶδεν πολὺν ὄχλον, καὶ ἐσπλαγχνίσθη ἐπ' αὐτούς, ὅτι
ἦσαν ὡς πρόβατα μὴ ἔχοντα ποιμένα, καὶ ἤρξατο διδάσκειν αὐτοὺς πολλά. ³⁵ καὶ ἤδη ὥρας πολλῆς γινομένης
προσελθόντες αὐτῷ οἱ μαθηταὶ αὐτοῦ ἔλεγον ὅτι Ἔρημός
ἐστιν ὁ τόπος, καὶ ἤδη ὥρα πολλή· ³⁶ ἀπόλυσον αὐτούς,
ἵνα ἀπελθόντες εἰς τοὺς κύκλῳ ἀγροὺς καὶ κώμας ἀγο-
ράσωσιν ἑαυτοῖς τί φάγωσιν. ³⁷ ὁ δὲ ἀποκριθεὶς εἶπεν
αὐτοῖς, Δότε αὐτοῖς ὑμεῖς φαγεῖν. καὶ λέγουσιν αὐτῷ,
Ἀπελθόντες ἀγοράσωμεν δηναρίων διακοσίων ἄρτους,
καὶ δώσωμεν αὐτοῖς φαγεῖν; ³⁸ ὁ δὲ λέγει αὐτοῖς, Πόσους
ἔχετε ἄρτους; ὑπάγετε, ἴδετε. καὶ γνόντες λέγουσιν,
Πέντε, καὶ δύο ἰχθύας. ³⁹ καὶ ἐπέταξεν αὐτοῖς ἀνακλῖναι
πάντας συμπόσια συμπόσια ἐπὶ τῷ χλωρῷ χόρτῳ.

⁴⁰καὶ ἀνέπεσαν πρασιαὶ πρασιαί, κατὰ ἑκατὸν καὶ κατὰ πεντήκοντα. ⁴¹καὶ λαβὼν τοὺς πέντε ἄρτους καὶ τοὺς δύο ἰχθύας ἀναβλέψας εἰς τὸν οὐρανὸν εὐλόγησεν, καὶ κατέκλασεν τοὺς ἄρτους καὶ ἐδίδου τοῖς μαθηταῖς ἵνα παρατιθῶσιν αὐτοῖς, καὶ τους δύο ἰχθύας ἐμέρισεν πᾶσιν. ⁴²καὶ ἔφαγον πάντες καὶ ἐχορτάσθησαν· ⁴³καὶ ἦραν κλάσματα δώδεκα κοφίνων πληρώματα, καὶ ἀπὸ τῶν ἰχθύων. ⁴⁴καὶ ἦσαν οἱ φαγόντες τοὺς ἄρτους πεντακισχίλιοι ἄνδρες.

⁴⁵Καὶ εὐθὺς ἠνάγκασεν τοὺς μαθητὰς αὐτοῦ ἐμβῆναι εἰς τὸ πλοῖον καὶ προάγειν εἰς τὸ πέραν πρὸς Βηθσαϊδάν, ἕως αὐτὸς ἀπολύει τὸν ὄχλον. ⁴⁶καὶ ἀποταξάμενος αὐτοῖς ἀπῆλθεν εἰς τὸ ὄρος προσεύξασθαι. ⁴⁷καὶ ὀψίας γενομένης ἦν τὸ πλοῖον ἐν μέσῳ τῆς θαλάσσης, καὶ αὐτὸς μόνος ἐπὶ τῆς γῆς. ⁴⁸καὶ ἰδὼν αὐτοὺς βασανιζομένους ἐν τῷ ἐλαύνειν, ἦν γὰρ ὁ ἄνεμος ἐναντίος αὐτοῖς, περὶ τετάρτην φυλακὴν τῆς νυκτὸς ἔρχεται πρὸς αὐτοὺς περιπατῶν ἐπὶ τῆς θαλάσσης. καὶ ἤθελεν παρελθεῖν αὐτούς· ⁴⁹οἱ δὲ ἰδόντες αὐτὸν περιπατοῦντα ἐπὶ τῆς θαλάσσης ἔδοξαν φάντασμα εἶναι καὶ ἀνέκραξαν· ⁵⁰πάντες γὰρ αὐτὸν εἶδαν καὶ ἐταράχθησαν. ὁ δὲ εὐθὺς ἐλάλησεν μετ' αὐτῶν, καὶ λέγει αὐτοῖς, Θαρσεῖτε, ἐγώ εἰμι, μὴ φοβεῖσθε. ⁵¹καὶ ἀνέβη πρὸς αὐτοὺς εἰς τὸ πλοῖον, καὶ ἐκόπασεν ὁ ἄνεμος· καὶ λίαν ἐν ἑαυτοῖς ἐξίσταντο. ⁵²οὐ γὰρ συνῆκαν ἐπὶ τοῖς ἄρτοις, ἀλλ' ἦν αὐτῶν ἡ καρδία πεπωρωμένη.

⁵³Καὶ διαπεράσαντες ἦλθον ἐπὶ τὴν γῆν Γεννησαρὲτ καὶ προσωρμίσθησαν. ⁵⁴καὶ ἐξελθόντων αὐτῶν ἐκ τοῦ πλοίου εὐθὺς ἐπιγνόντες αὐτὸν ⁵⁵περιέδραμον ὅλην τὴν χωραν ἐκείνην καὶ ἤρξαντο ἐπὶ τοῖς κραβάττοις τοὺς κακῶς ἔχοντας περιφέρειν, ὅπου ἤκουον ὅτι ἐστίν.

⁵⁶ καὶ ὅπου ἂν εἰσεπορεύετο εἰς κώμας ἢ εἰς πόλεις ἢ εἰς ἀγρούς, ἐν ταῖς ἀγοραῖς ἐτίθεσαν τοὺς ἀσθενοῦντας, καὶ παρεκάλουν αὐτὸν ἵνα κἂν τοῦ κρασπέδου τοῦ ἱματίου αὐτοῦ ἅψωνται· καὶ ὅσοι ἂν ἥψαντο αὐτοῦ ἐσώζοντο.

7 ¹ Καὶ συνάγονται πρὸς αὐτὸν οἱ Φαρισαῖοι καί τινες τῶν γραμματέων ἐλθόντες ἀπὸ Ἱεροσολύμων. ² καὶ ἰδόντες τινὰς τῶν μαθητῶν αὐτοῦ ὅτι κοιναῖς χερσίν, τοῦτ᾽ ἔστιν ἀνίπτοις, ἐσθίουσιν τοὺς ἄρτους, —³ οἱ γὰρ Φαρισαῖοι καὶ πάντες οἱ Ἰουδαῖοι ἐὰν μὴ πυγμῇ νίψωνται τὰς χεῖρας οὐκ ἐσθίουσιν, κρατοῦντες τὴν παράδοσιν τῶν πρεσβυτέρων, ⁴ καὶ ἀπ᾽ ἀγορᾶς ἐὰν μὴ ῥαντίσωνται οὐκ ἐσθίουσιν, καὶ ἄλλα πολλά ἐστιν ἃ παρέλαβον κρατεῖν, βαπτισμοὺς ποτηρίων καὶ ξεστῶν καὶ χαλκίων—⁵ καὶ ἐπερωτῶσιν αὐτὸν οἱ Φαρισαῖοι καὶ οἱ γραμματεῖς, Διὰ τί οὐ περιπατοῦσιν οἱ μαθηταί σου κατὰ τὴν παράδοσιν τῶν πρεσβυτέρων, ἀλλὰ κοιναῖς χερσὶν ἐσθίουσιν τὸν ἄρτον; ⁶ ὁ δὲ εἶπεν αὐτοῖς· Καλῶς ἐπροφήτευσεν Ἡσαΐας περὶ ὑμῶν τῶν ὑποκριτῶν, ὡς γέγραπται ὅτι Οὗτος ὁ λαὸς τοῖς χείλεσίν με τιμᾷ, ἡ δὲ καρδία αὐτῶν πόρρω ἀπέχει ἀπ᾽ ἐμοῦ· ⁷ μάτην δὲ σέβονταί με διδάσκοντες διδασκαλίας ἐντάλματα ἀνθρώπων. ⁸ ἀφέντες τὴν ἐντολὴν τοῦ θεοῦ κρατεῖτε τὴν παράδοσιν τῶν ἀνθρώπων. ⁹ καὶ ἔλεγεν αὐτοῖς, Καλῶς ἀθετεῖτε τὴν ἐντολὴν τοῦ θεοῦ, ἵνα τὴν παράδοσιν ὑμῶν τηρήσητε. ¹⁰ Μωϋσῆς γὰρ εἶπεν, Τίμα τὸν πατέρα σου καὶ τὴν μητέρα σου, καί, Ὁ κακολογῶν πατέρα ἢ μητέρα θανάτῳ τελευτάτω. ¹¹ ὑμεῖς δὲ λέγετε, Ἐὰν εἴπῃ ἄνθρωπος τῷ πατρὶ ἢ τῇ μητρί, Κορβᾶν, ὅ ἐστιν δῶρον, ὃ ἐὰν ἐξ ἐμοῦ ὠφεληθῇς, ¹² οὐκέτι ἀφίετε αὐτὸν οὐδὲν ποιῆσαι τῷ πατρὶ ἢ τῇ μητρί, ¹³ ἀκυροῦντες τὸν λόγον τοῦ θεοῦ τῇ παραδόσει ὑμῶν ᾗ παρεδώκατε. καὶ παρόμοια τοιαῦτα πολλὰ ποιεῖτε. ¹⁴ καὶ προσκαλεσάμενος πάλιν τὸν ὄχλον ἔλεγεν αὐτοῖς, Ἀκούσατέ μου πάντες καὶ σύνετε. ¹⁵ οὐδέν ἐστιν ἔξωθεν τοῦ ἀνθρώπου εἰσπορευόμενον εἰς αὐτὸν ὃ δύναται αὐτὸν κοινῶσαι· ἀλλὰ τὰ ἐκ τοῦ ἀνθρώπου ἐκπορευόμενά ἐστιν τὰ κοινοῦντα τὸν ἄνθρωπον.* ¹⁷ Καὶ ὅτε εἰσῆλθεν εἰς οἶκον ἀπὸ τοῦ ὄχλου, ἐπηρώτων αὐτὸν οἱ μαθηταὶ αὐτοῦ τὴν παραβολήν. ¹⁸ καὶ λέγει αὐτοῖς, Οὕτως καὶ ὑμεῖς ἀσύνετοί ἐστε; οὐ νοεῖτε ὅτι πᾶν τὸ ἔξωθεν εἰσπορευόμενον εἰς τὸν ἄνθρωπον οὐ δύναται αὐτὸν κοινῶσαι, ¹⁹ ὅτι οὐκ εἰσπορεύεται αὐτοῦ εἰς τὴν καρδίαν ἀλλ᾽ εἰς τὴν κοιλίαν, καὶ εἰς τὸν ἀφεδρῶνα ἐκπορεύεται, καθαρίζων πάντα τὰ βρώματα; ²⁰ ἔλεγεν δὲ ὅτι Τὸ ἐκ τοῦ ἀνθρώπου ἐκπορευόμενον, ἐκεῖνο κοινοῖ τὸν ἄνθρωπον. ²¹ ἔσωθεν γὰρ ἐκ τῆς καρδίας τῶν ἀνθρώπων οἱ διαλογισμοὶ οἱ κακοὶ ἐκπορεύονται, πορνεῖαι, κλοπαί, φόνοι, ²² μοιχεῖαι, πλεονεξίαι, πονηρίαι, δόλος, ἀσέλγεια, ὀφθαλμὸς πονηρός, βλασφημία, ὑπερηφανία, ἀφροσύνη· ²³ πάντα ταῦτα τὰ πονηρὰ ἔσωθεν ἐκπορεύεται καὶ κοινοῖ τὸν ἄνθρωπον.

²⁴ Ἐκεῖθεν δὲ ἀναστὰς ἀπῆλθεν εἰς τὰ ὅρια Τύρου [καὶ Σιδῶνος]. καὶ εἰσελθὼν εἰς οἰκίαν οὐδένα ἤθελεν γνῶναι, καὶ οὐκ ἠδυνάσθη λαθεῖν· ²⁵ ἀλλ᾽ εὐθὺς ἀκούσασα γυνὴ περὶ αὐτοῦ, ἧς εἶχεν τὸ θυγάτριον αὐτῆς πνεῦμα ἀκάθαρτον, ἐλθοῦσα προσέπεσεν πρὸς τοὺς πόδας αὐτοῦ· ²⁶ ἡ δὲ γυνὴ ἦν Ἑλληνίς, Συροφοινίκισσα τῷ γένει· καὶ ἠρώτα αὐτὸν ἵνα τὸ δαιμόνιον ἐκβάλῃ ἐκ τῆς θυγατρὸς αὐτῆς. ²⁷ καὶ ἔλεγεν αὐτῇ, Ἄφες πρῶτον χορτασθῆναι τὰ τέκνα· οὐ γάρ ἐστιν καλὸν λαβεῖν τὸν ἄρτον τῶν τέκνων καὶ τοῖς κυναρίοις βαλεῖν. ²⁸ ἡ δὲ ἀπεκρίθη καὶ λέγει αὐτῷ, Ναί, κύριε· καὶ τὰ κυνάρια ὑποκάτω τῆς

* Verse 16 omitted on the best MSS. authority.

τραπέζης ἐσθίουσιν ἀπὸ τῶν ψιχίων τῶν παιδίων. ²⁹ καὶ
εἶπεν αὐτῇ, Διὰ τοῦτον τὸν λόγον ὕπαγε, ἐξελήλυθεν ἐκ
τῆς θυγατρός σου τὸ δαιμόνιον· ³⁰ καὶ ἀπελθοῦσα εἰς
τὸν οἶκον αὐτῆς εὗρεν τὸ παιδίον βεβλημένον ἐπὶ τὴν
κλίνην καὶ τὸ δαιμόνιον ἐξεληλυθός.

³¹ Καὶ πάλιν ἐξελθὼν ἐκ τῶν ὁρίων Τύρου ἦλθεν διὰ
Σιδῶνος εἰς τὴν θάλασσαν τῆς Γαλιλαίας ἀνὰ μέσον
τῶν ὁρίων Δεκαπόλεως. ³² καὶ φέρουσιν αὐτῷ κωφὸν
καὶ μογιλάλον, καὶ παρακαλοῦσιν αὐτὸν ἵνα ἐπιθῇ αὐτῷ
τὴν χεῖρα. ³³ καὶ ἀπολαβόμενος αὐτὸν ἀπὸ τοῦ ὄχλου
κατ᾽ ἰδίαν ἔβαλεν τοὺς δακτύλους αὐτοῦ εἰς τὰ ὦτα αὐτοῦ
καὶ πτύσας ἥψατο τῆς γλώσσης αὐτοῦ, ³⁴ καὶ ἀναβλέψας εἰς τὸν οὐρανὸν ἐστέναξεν, καὶ λέγει αὐτῷ, Ἐφφαθά,
ὅ ἐστιν διανοίχθητι. ³⁵ καὶ ἠνοίγησαν αὐτοῦ αἱ ἀκοαί,
καὶ ἐλύθη ὁ δεσμὸς τῆς γλώσσης αὐτοῦ, καὶ ἐλάλει
ὀρθῶς. ³⁶ καὶ διεστείλατο αὐτοῖς ἵνα μηδενὶ λέγωσιν·
ὅσον δὲ αὐτοῖς διεστέλλετο, αὐτοὶ μᾶλλον περισσότερον ἐκήρυσσον. ³⁷ καὶ ὑπερπερισσῶς ἐξεπλήσσοντό
λέγοντες, Καλῶς πάντα πεποίηκεν, καὶ τοὺς κωφοὺς
ποιεῖ ἀκούειν καὶ ἀλάλους λαλεῖν.

8 ¹ Ἐν ἐκείναις ταῖς ἡμέραις πάλιν πολλοῦ ὄχλου
ὄντος καὶ μὴ ἐχόντων τί φάγωσιν, προσκαλεσάμενος
τοὺς μαθητὰς λέγει αὐτοῖς, ² Σπλαγχνίζομαι ἐπὶ
τὸν ὄχλον, ὅτι ἤδη ἡμέραι τρεῖς προσμένουσίν μοι καὶ
οὐκ ἔχουσιν τί φάγωσιν. ³ καὶ ἐὰν ἀπολύσω αὐτοὺς
νήστεις εἰς οἶκον αὐτῶν, ἐκλυθήσονται ἐν τῇ ὁδῷ· καί
τινες αὐτῶν ἀπὸ μακρόθεν εἰσίν. ⁴ καὶ ἀπεκρίθησαν
αὐτῷ οἱ μαθηταὶ αὐτοῦ ὅτι Πόθεν τούτους δυνήσεταί
τις ὧδε χορτάσαι ἄρτων ἐπ᾽ ἐρημίας; ⁵ καὶ ἠρώτα
αὐτούς, Πόσους ἔχετε ἄρτους; οἱ δὲ εἶπαν, Ἑπτά.
⁶ καὶ παραγγέλλει τῷ ὄχλῳ ἀναπεσεῖν ἐπὶ τῆς γῆς· καὶ

λαβὼν τοὺς ἑπτὰ ἄρτους εὐχαριστήσας ἔκλασεν καὶ
ἐδίδου τοῖς μαθηταῖς αὐτοῦ ἵνα παρατιθῶσιν· καὶ παρέ-
θηκαν τῷ ὄχλῳ. ⁷ καὶ εἶχαν ἰχθύδια ὀλίγα· καὶ εὐλογήσας αὐτὰ εἶπεν παραθεῖναι καὶ αὐτά. ⁸ καὶ ἔφαγον
καὶ ἐχορτάσθησαν, καὶ ἦραν περισσεύματα κλασμάτων
ἑπτὰ σφυρίδας. ⁹ ἦσαν δὲ ὡς τετρακισχίλιοι· καὶ
ἀπέλυσεν αὐτούς.
¹⁰ Καὶ εὐθὺς ἐμβὰς εἰς τὸ πλοῖον μετὰ τῶν μαθητῶν
αὐτοῦ ἦλθεν εἰς τὰ μέρη Δαλμανουθά. ¹¹ καὶ ἐξῆλθον οἱ
Φαρισαῖοι καὶ ἤρξαντο συνζητεῖν αὐτῷ, ζητοῦντες παρ'
αὐτοῦ σημεῖον ἀπὸ τοῦ οὐρανοῦ, πειράζοντες αὐτόν.
¹² καὶ ἀναστενάξας τῷ πνεύματι αὐτοῦ λέγει, Τί ἡ γενεὰ
αὕτη ζητεῖ σημεῖον; ἀμὴν λέγω ὑμῖν εἰ δοθήσεται τῇ
γενεᾷ ταύτῃ σημεῖον. ¹³ καὶ ἀφεὶς αὐτοὺς πάλιν ἐμβὰς
ἀπῆλθεν εἰς τὸ πέραν. ¹⁴ καὶ ἐπελάθοντο λαβεῖν ἄρτους,
καὶ εἰ μὴ ἕνα ἄρτον οὐκ εἶχον μεθ' ἑαυτῶν ἐν τῷ πλοίῳ.
¹⁵ καὶ διεστέλλετο αὐτοῖς λέγων, Ὁρᾶτε, βλέπετε ἀπὸ τῆς
ζύμης τῶν Φαρισαίων καὶ τῆς ζύμης Ἡρώδου. ¹⁶ καὶ
διελογίζοντο πρὸς ἀλλήλους ὅτι Ἄρτους οὐκ ἔχομεν. ¹⁷ καὶ
γνοὺς ὁ Ἰησοῦς λέγει αὐτοῖς, Τί διαλογίζεσθε ὅτι ἄρτους
οὐκ ἔχετε; οὔπω νοεῖτε οὐδὲ συνίετε; πεπωρωμένην ἔχετε
τὴν καρδίαν ὑμῶν; ¹⁸ ὀφθαλμοὺς ἔχοντες οὐ βλέπετε, καὶ
ὦτα ἔχοντες οὐκ ἀκούετε, καὶ οὐ μνημονεύετε, ¹⁹ ὅτε τοὺς
πέντε ἄρτους ἔκλασα εἰς τοὺς πεντακισχιλίους, πόσους
κοφίνους κλασμάτων πλήρεις ἤρατε; λέγουσιν αὐτῷ,
Δώδεκα. ²⁰ ὅτε καὶ τοὺς ἑπτὰ εἰς τοὺς τετρακισχιλίους,
πόσων σφυρίδων πληρώματα κλασμάτων ἤρατε; καὶ
λέγουσιν, Ἑπτά. ²¹ καὶ ἔλεγεν αὐτοῖς, Οὔπω συνίετε;
²² Καὶ ἔρχονται εἰς Βηθσαϊδάν. καὶ φέρουσιν αὐτῷ
τυφλόν, καὶ παρακαλοῦσιν αὐτὸν ἵνα αὐτοῦ ἅψηται.
²³ καὶ ἐπιλαβόμενος τῆς χειρὸς τοῦ τυφλοῦ ἐξήνεγκεν

αὐτὸν ἔξω τῆς κώμης, καὶ πτύσας εἰς τὰ ὄμματα αὐτοῦ, ἐπιθεὶς τὰς χεῖρας αὐτῷ, ἐπηρώτα αὐτὸν Εἴ τι βλέπεις. ²⁴ καὶ ἀναβλέψας ἔλεγεν, Βλέπω τοὺς ἀνθρώπους, ὅτι ὡς δένδρα ὁρῶ περιπατοῦντας. ²⁵ εἶτα πάλιν ἐπέθηκεν τὰς χεῖρας ἐπὶ τοὺς ὀφθαλμοὺς αὐτοῦ, καὶ διέβλεψεν καὶ ἀπεκατέστη, καὶ ἐνέβλεπεν δηλαυγῶς ἅπαντα. ²⁶ καὶ ἀπέστειλεν αὐτὸν εἰς οἶκον αὐτοῦ λέγων, Μηδὲ εἰς τὴν κώμην εἰσέλθῃς.

²⁷ Καὶ ἐξῆλθεν ὁ Ἰησοῦς καὶ οἱ μαθηταὶ αὐτοῦ εἰς τὰς κώμας Καισαρείας τῆς Φιλίππου· καὶ ἐν τῇ ὁδῷ ἐπηρώτα τοὺς μαθητὰς αὐτοῦ λέγων αὐτοῖς, Τίνα με λέγουσιν οἱ ἄνθρωποι εἶναι; ²⁸ οἱ δὲ εἶπαν αὐτῷ λέγοντες ὅτι Ἰωάννην τὸν βαπτιστήν, καὶ ἄλλοι Ἡλείαν, ἄλλοι δὲ ὅτι Εἷς τῶν προφητῶν. ²⁹ καὶ αὐτὸς ἐπηρώτα αὐτούς, Ὑμεῖς δὲ τίνα με λέγετε εἶναι; ἀποκριθεὶς ὁ Πέτρος λέγει αὐτῷ, Σὺ εἶ ὁ Χριστός. ³⁰ καὶ ἐπετίμησεν αὐτοῖς ἵνα μηδενὶ λέγωσιν περὶ αὐτοῦ. ³¹ Καὶ ἤρξατο διδάσκειν αὐτοὺς ὅτι Δεῖ τὸν υἱὸν τοῦ ἀνθρώπου πολλὰ παθεῖν, καὶ ἀποδοκιμασθῆναι ὑπὸ τῶν πρεσβυτέρων καὶ τῶν ἀρχιερέων καὶ τῶν γραμματέων καὶ ἀποκτανθῆναι καὶ μετὰ τρεῖς ἡμέρας ἀναστῆναι. ³² καὶ παρρησίᾳ τὸν λόγον ἐλάλει. καὶ προσλαβόμενος ὁ Πέτρος αὐτὸν ἤρξατο ἐπιτιμᾶν αὐτῷ. ³³ ὁ δὲ ἐπιστραφεὶς καὶ ἰδὼν τοὺς μαθητὰς αὐτοῦ ἐπετίμησεν Πέτρῳ καὶ λέγει, Ὕπαγε ὀπίσω μου, Σατανᾶ, ὅτι οὐ φρονεῖς τὰ τοῦ θεοῦ ἀλλὰ τὰ τῶν ἀνθρώπων.

³⁴ Καὶ προσκαλεσάμενος τὸν ὄχλον σὺν τοῖς μαθηταῖς αὐτοῦ εἶπεν αὐτοῖς, Εἴ τις θέλει ὀπίσω μου ἀκολουθεῖν, ἀπαρνησάσθω ἑαυτὸν καὶ ἀράτω τὸν σταυρὸν αὐτοῦ, καὶ ἀκολουθείτω μοι. ³⁵ ὃς γὰρ ἐὰν θέλῃ τὴν ψυχὴν αὐτοῦ σῶσαι, ἀπολέσει αὐτήν· ὃς δ᾽ ἂν ἀπολέσει τὴν ἑαυτοῦ ψυχὴν ἕνεκεν ἐμοῦ καὶ τοῦ εὐαγγελίου, σώσει

αὐτήν. ³⁶τί γὰρ ὠφελεῖ ἄνθρωπον κερδῆσαι τὸν κόσμον
ὅλον καὶ ζημιωθῆναι τὴν ψυχὴν αὐτοῦ; ³⁷τί γὰρ δοῖ
ἄνθρωπος ἀντάλλαγμα τῆς ψυχῆς αὐτοῦ; ³⁸ὃς γὰρ ἐὰν
ἐπαισχυνθῇ με καὶ τοὺς ἐμοὺς λόγους ἐν τῇ γενεᾷ ταύτῃ
τῇ μοιχαλίδι καὶ ἁμαρτωλῷ, καὶ ὁ υἱὸς τοῦ ἀνθρώπου
ἐπαισχυνθήσεται αὐτόν, ὅταν ἔλθῃ ἐν τῇ δόξῃ τοῦ
πατρὸς αὐτοῦ μετὰ τῶν ἀγγέλων τῶν ἁγίων. 9 ¹καὶ
ἔλεγεν αὐτοῖς, Ἀμὴν λέγω ὑμῖν ὅτι εἰσίν τινες ὧδε τῶν
ἑστηκότων οἵτινες οὐ μὴ γεύσωνται θανάτου ἕως ἂν
ἴδωσιν τὴν βασιλείαν τοῦ θεοῦ ἐληλυθυῖαν ἐν δυνάμει.

²Καὶ μετὰ ἡμέρας ἓξ παραλαμβάνει ὁ Ἰησοῦς τὸν
Πέτρον καὶ τὸν Ἰάκωβον καὶ τὸν Ἰωάννην, καὶ ἀναφέρει
αὐτοὺς εἰς ὄρος ὑψηλὸν κατ᾽ ἰδίαν μόνους, καὶ μετεμορφώθη ἔμπροσθεν αὐτῶν, ³καὶ τὰ ἱμάτια αὐτοῦ ἐγένετο
στίλβοντα λευκὰ λίαν, οἷα γναφεὺς ἐπὶ τῆς γῆς οὐ
δύναται οὕτως λευκᾶναι. ⁴καὶ ὤφθη αὐτοῖς Ἡλείας
σὺν Μωϋσεῖ, καὶ ἦσαν συνλαλοῦντες τῷ Ἰησοῦ. ⁵καὶ
ἀποκριθεὶς ὁ Πέτρος λέγει τῷ Ἰησοῦ, Ῥαββεί, καλόν
ἐστιν ἡμᾶς ὧδε εἶναι, καὶ ποιήσωμεν τρεῖς σκηνάς,
σοὶ μίαν καὶ Μωϋσεῖ μίαν καὶ Ἡλείᾳ μίαν. ⁶οὐ γὰρ
ᾔδει τί ἀποκριθῇ· ἔκφοβοι γὰρ ἐγένοντο. ⁷καὶ ἐγένετο
νεφέλη ἐπισκιάζουσα αὐτοῖς, καὶ ἐγένετο φωνὴ ἐκ τῆς
νεφέλης, Οὗτός ἐστιν ὁ υἱός μου ὁ ἀγαπητός, ἀκούετε
αὐτοῦ. ⁸καὶ ἐξάπινα περιβλεψάμενοι οὐκέτι οὐδένα
εἶδον ἀλλὰ τὸν Ἰησοῦν μόνον μεθ᾽ ἑαυτῶν. ⁹Καὶ καταβαινόντων αὐτῶν ἐκ τοῦ ὄρους, διεστείλατο αὐτοῖς ἵνα
μηδενὶ ἃ εἶδον διηγήσωνται, εἰ μὴ ὅταν ὁ υἱὸς τοῦ ἀνθρώπου ἐκ νεκρῶν ἀναστῇ. ¹⁰καὶ τὸν λόγον ἐκράτησαν
πρὸς ἑαυτοὺς συνζητοῦντες τί ἐστιν τὸ ἐκ νεκρῶν ἀναστῆναι. ¹¹καὶ ἐπηρώτων αὐτὸν λέγοντες, Ὅτι λέγουσιν
οἱ Φαρισαῖοι καὶ οἱ γραμματεῖς ὅτι Ἡλείαν δεῖ ἐλθεῖν

πρῶτον ; ¹² ὁ δὲ ἔφη αὐτοῖς, Ἠλείας μὲν ἐλθὼν πρῶτον
ἀποκαθιστάνει πάντα. καὶ πῶς γέγραπται ἐπὶ τὸν
υἱὸν τοῦ ἀνθρώπου ; ἵνα πολλὰ πάθῃ καὶ ἐξουθε-
νωθῇ. ¹³ ἀλλὰ λέγω ὑμῖν ὅτι Καὶ Ἠλείας ἐλήλυθεν, καὶ
ἐποίησαν αὐτῷ ὅσα ἤθελον, καθὼς γέγραπται ἐπ᾽ αὐτόν.
¹⁴ Καὶ ἐλθόντες πρὸς τοὺς μαθητὰς εἶδον ὄχλον πολὺν
περὶ αὐτοὺς καὶ γραμματεῖς συνζητοῦντας πρὸς αὐτούς.
¹⁵ καὶ εὐθὺς πᾶς ὁ ὄχλος ἰδόντες αὐτὸν ἐξεθαμβήθησαν,
καὶ προστρέχοντες ἠσπάζοντο αὐτόν. ¹⁶ καὶ ἐπηρώτησεν
αὐτούς, Τί συνζητεῖτε πρὸς αὐτούς ; ¹⁷ καὶ ἀπεκρίθη
αὐτῷ εἷς ἐκ τοῦ ὄχλου, Διδάσκαλε, ἤνεγκα τὸν υἱόν μου
πρὸς σέ, ἔχοντα πνεῦμα ἄλαλον, ¹⁸ καὶ ὅπου ἐὰν αὐτὸν
καταλάβῃ ῥήσσει αὐτόν· καὶ ἀφρίζει καὶ τρίζει τοὺς ὀδόν-
τας καὶ ξηραίνεται· καὶ εἶπα τοῖς μαθηταῖς σου ἵνα αὐτὸ
ἐκβάλωσιν, καὶ οὐκ ἴσχυσαν. ¹⁹ ὁ δὲ ἀποκριθεὶς αὐτοῖς
λέγει, Ὦ γενεὰ ἄπιστος, ἕως πότε πρὸς ὑμᾶς ἔσομαι ;
ἕως πότε ἀνέξομαι ὑμῶν ; φέρετε αὐτὸν πρός με. ²⁰ καὶ
ἤνεγκαν αὐτὸν πρὸς αὐτόν. καὶ ἰδὼν αὐτόν, τὸ πνεῦμα
εὐθὺς συνεσπάραξεν αὐτόν, καὶ πεσὼν ἐπὶ τῆς γῆς
ἐκυλίετο ἀφρίζων. ²¹ καὶ ἐπηρώτησεν τὸν πατέρα αὐτοῦ, Πόσος χρόνος ἐστὶν ὡς τοῦτο γέγονεν αὐτῷ ; ὁ δὲ
εἶπεν, Ἐκ παιδιόθεν· ²² καὶ πολλάκις καὶ εἰς πῦρ αὐτὸν
ἔβαλεν καὶ εἰς ὕδατα, ἵνα ἀπολέσῃ αὐτόν· ἀλλὰ εἴ τι
δύνῃ, βοήθησον ἡμῖν σπλαγχνισθεὶς ἐφ᾽ ἡμᾶς. ²³ ὁ δὲ
Ἰησοῦς εἶπεν αὐτῷ Τὸ εἰ δύνῃ ; πάντα δυνατὰ τῷ πιστεύοντι. ²⁴ εὐθὺς κράξας ὁ πατὴρ τοῦ παιδίου ἔλεγεν,
Πιστεύω· βοήθει μου τῇ ἀπιστίᾳ. ²⁵ ἰδὼν δὲ ὁ Ἰησοῦς
ὅτι ἐπισυντρέχει ὄχλος, ἐπετίμησεν τῷ πνεύματι τῷ
ἀκαθάρτῳ λέγων αὐτῷ, Τὸ ἄλαλον καὶ κωφὸν πνεῦμα,
ἐγὼ ἐπιτάσσω σοι, ἔξελθε ἐξ αὐτοῦ καὶ μηκέτι εἰσέλθῃς
εἰς αὐτόν. ²⁶ καὶ κράξας καὶ πολλὰ σπαράξας ἐξῆλθεν·

καὶ ἐγένετο ὡσεὶ νεκρός, ὥστε τοὺς πολλοὺς λέγειν ὅτι
Ἀπέθανεν. ²⁷ὁ δὲ Ἰησοῦς κρατήσας τῆς χειρὸς αὐτοῦ ἤγειρεν αὐτόν, καὶ ἀνέστη. ²⁸ καὶ εἰσελθόντος αὐτοῦ εἰς οἶκον
οἱ μαθηταὶ αὐτοῦ κατ᾽ ἰδίαν ἐπηρώτων αὐτόν, Ὅτι ἡμεῖς
οὐκ ἠδυνήθημεν ἐκβαλεῖν αὐτό; ²⁹καὶ εἶπεν αὐτοῖς, Τοῦτο
τὸ γένος ἐν οὐδενὶ δύναται ἐξελθεῖν εἰ μὴ ἐν προσευχῇ.

³⁰ Κἀκεῖθεν ἐξελθόντες παρεπορεύοντο διὰ τῆς Γαλιλαίας, καὶ οὐκ ἤθελεν ἵνα τις γνοῖ· ³¹ ἐδίδασκεν γὰρ
τοὺς μαθητὰς αὐτοῦ, καὶ ἔλεγεν αὐτοῖς ὅτι Ὁ υἱὸς τοῦ
ἀνθρώπου παραδίδοται εἰς χεῖρας ἀνθρώπων, καὶ ἀποκτενοῦσιν αὐτόν, καὶ ἀποκτανθεὶς μετὰ τρεῖς ἡμέρας
ἀναστήσεται. ³² οἱ δὲ ἠγνόουν τὸ ῥῆμα, καὶ ἐφοβοῦντο
αὐτὸν ἐπερωτῆσαι.

³³ Καὶ ἦλθον εἰς Καφαρναούμ. καὶ ἐν τῇ οἰκίᾳ γενόμενος ἐπηρώτα αὐτούς, Τί ἐν τῇ ὁδῷ διελογίζεσθε; ³⁴ οἱ
δὲ ἐσιώπων· πρὸς ἀλλήλους γὰρ διελέχθησαν ἐν τῇ
ὁδῷ τίς μείζων. ³⁵ καὶ καθίσας ἐφώνησεν τοὺς δώδεκα,
καὶ λέγει αὐτοῖς, Εἴ τις θέλει πρῶτος εἶναι, ἔσται πάντων ἔσχατος καὶ πάντων διάκονος. ³⁶ καὶ λαβὼν παιδίον
ἔστησεν αὐτὸ ἐν μέσῳ αὐτῶν, καὶ ἐναγκαλισάμενος αὐτὸ
εἶπεν αὐτοῖς, ³⁷ Ὃς ἂν ἓν τῶν τοιούτων παιδίων δέξηται
ἐπὶ τῷ ὀνόματί μου, ἐμὲ δέχεται· καὶ ὃς ἂν ἐμὲ δέχηται,
οὐκ ἐμὲ δέχεται ἀλλὰ τὸν ἀποστείλαντά με.

³⁸ Ἔφη αὐτῷ ὁ Ἰωάννης, Διδάσκαλε, εἴδομέν τινα ἐν
τῷ ὀνόματί σου ἐκβάλλοντα δαιμόνια, καὶ ἐκωλύομεν
αὐτόν, ὅτι οὐκ ἠκολούθει ἡμῖν. ³⁹ὁ δὲ Ἰησοῦς εἶπεν,
Μὴ κωλύετε αὐτόν· οὐδεὶς γάρ ἐστιν ὃς ποιήσει
δύναμιν ἐπὶ τῷ ὀνόματί μου καὶ δυνήσεται ταχὺ κακο-
λογῆσαί με· ⁴⁰ ὃς γὰρ οὐκ ἔστιν καθ᾽ ἡμῶν, ὑπὲρ ἡμῶν
ἐστίν. ⁴¹ ὃς γὰρ ἂν ποτίσῃ ὑμᾶς ποτήριον ὕδατος ἐν
ὀνόματι ὅτι Χριστοῦ ἐστέ, ἀμὴν λέγω ὑμῖν ὅτι οὐ

μὴ ἀπολέσει τὸν μισθὸν αὐτοῦ. ⁴²Καὶ ὃς ἂν σκανδαλίσῃ ἕνα τῶν μικρῶν τούτων τῶν πιστευόντων εἰς ἐμέ,
καλόν ἐστιν αὐτῷ μᾶλλον εἰ περίκειται μύλος ὀνικὸς
περὶ τὸν τράχηλον αὐτοῦ καὶ βέβληται εἰς τὴν θάλασσαν. ⁴³ καὶ ἐὰν σκανδαλίσῃ σε ἡ χείρ σου, ἀπόκοψον
αὐτήν· καλόν ἐστίν σε κυλλὸν εἰσελθεῖν εἰς τὴν ζωήν,
ἢ τὰς δύο χεῖρας ἔχοντα ἀπελθεῖν εἰς τὴν γέενναν, εἰς
τὸ πῦρ τὸ ἄσβεστον.* ⁴⁵ καὶ ἐὰν ὁ πούς σου σκανδαλίζῃ
σε, ἀπόκοψον αὐτόν· καλόν ἐστίν σε εἰσελθεῖν εἰς τὴν
ζωὴν χωλόν, ἢ τοὺς δύο πόδας ἔχοντα βληθῆναι εἰς τὴν
γέενναν.* ⁴⁷ καὶ ἐὰν ὁ ὀφθαλμός σου σκανδαλίζῃ σε,
ἔκβαλε αὐτόν· καλόν σε ἐστὶν μονόφθαλμον εἰσελθεῖν
εἰς τὴν βασιλείαν τοῦ θεοῦ, ἢ δύο ὀφθαλμοὺς ἔχοντα
βληθῆναι εἰς τὴν γέενναν, ⁴⁸ ὅπου ὁ σκώληξ αὐτῶν οὐ
τελευτᾷ καὶ τὸ πῦρ οὐ σβέννυται. ⁴⁹ πᾶς γὰρ πυρὶ
ἁλισθήσεται. ⁵⁰ καλὸν τὸ ἅλας· ἐὰν δὲ τὸ ἅλα ἄναλον
γένηται, ἐν τίνι αὐτὸ ἀρτύσετε; ἔχετε ἐν ἑαυτοῖς ἅλα
καὶ εἰρηνεύετε ἐν ἀλλήλοις.

10 ¹ Καὶ ἐκεῖθεν ἀναστὰς ἔρχεται εἰς τὰ ὅρια τῆς
Ἰουδαίας καὶ πέραν τοῦ Ἰορδάνου, καὶ συνπορεύονται
πάλιν ὄχλοι πρὸς αὐτόν, καὶ ὡς εἰώθει πάλιν ἐδίδασκεν
αὐτούς. ² καὶ προσελθόντες Φαρισαῖοι ἐπηρώτων αὐτὸν εἰ ἔξεστιν ἀνδρὶ γυναῖκα ἀπολῦσαι, πειράζοντες
αὐτόν. ³ ὁ δὲ ἀποκριθεὶς εἶπεν αὐτοῖς, Τί ὑμῖν ἐνετείλατο Μωϋσῆς; ⁴ οἱ δὲ εἶπαν, Ἐπέτρεψεν Μωϋσῆς βιβλίον ἀποστασίου γράψαι καὶ ἀπολῦσαι. ⁵ ὁ δὲ Ἰησοῦς
εἶπεν αὐτοῖς, Πρὸς τὴν σκληροκαρδίαν ὑμῶν ἔγραψεν
ὑμῖν τὴν ἐντολὴν ταύτην. ⁶ ἀπὸ δὲ ἀρχῆς κτίσεως
ἄρσεν καὶ θῆλυ ἐποίησεν αὐτούς. ⁷ ἕνεκεν τούτου κατα-
λείψει ἄνθρωπος τὸν πατέρα αὐτοῦ καὶ τὴν μητέρα, ⁸ καὶ

* Verses 44 and 46 omitted on the best MSS. authority.

ἔσονται οἱ δύο εἰς σάρκα μίαν, ὥστε οὐκέτι εἰσὶν δύο ἀλλὰ μία σάρξ. ⁹ ὃ οὖν ὁ θεὸς συνέζευξεν, ἄνθρωπος μὴ χωριζέτω. ¹⁰ καὶ εἰς τὴν οἰκίαν πάλιν οἱ μαθηταὶ περὶ τούτου ἐπηρώτων αὐτόν. ¹¹ καὶ λέγει αὐτοῖς, Ὃς ἂν ἀπολύσῃ τὴν γυναῖκα αὐτοῦ καὶ γαμήσῃ ἄλλην, μοιχᾶται ἐπ᾽ αὐτήν· ¹² καὶ ἐὰν αὐτὴ ἀπολύσασα τὸν ἄνδρα αὐτῆς γαμήσῃ ἄλλον, μοιχᾶται.

¹³ Καὶ προσέφερον αὐτῷ παιδία ἵνα ἅψηται αὐτῶν· οἱ δὲ μαθηταὶ ἐπετίμησαν αὐτοῖς. ¹⁴ ἰδὼν δὲ ὁ Ἰησοῦς ἠγανάκτησεν καὶ εἶπεν αὐτοῖς, Ἄφετε τὰ παιδία ἔρχεσθαι πρός με, μὴ κωλύετε αὐτά· τῶν γὰρ τοιούτων ἐστὶν ἡ βασιλεία τοῦ θεοῦ. ¹⁵ ἀμὴν λέγω ὑμῖν, ὃς ἂν μὴ δέξηται τὴν βασιλείαν τοῦ θεοῦ ὡς παιδίον, οὐ μὴ εἰσέλθῃ εἰς αὐτήν. ¹⁶ καὶ ἐναγκαλισάμενος αὐτὰ κατευλόγει, τιθεὶς τὰς χεῖρας ἐπ᾽ αὐτά.

¹⁷ Καὶ ἐκπορευομένου αὐτοῦ εἰς ὁδόν, προσδραμὼν εἷς καὶ γονυπετήσας αὐτὸν ἐπηρώτα αὐτόν, Διδάσκαλε ἀγαθέ, τί ποιήσω ἵνα ζωὴν αἰώνιον κληρονομήσω; ¹⁸ ὁ δὲ Ἰησοῦς εἶπεν αὐτῷ, Τί με λέγεις ἀγαθόν; οὐδεὶς ἀγαθὸς εἰ μὴ εἷς ὁ θεός. ¹⁹ τὰς ἐντολὰς οἶδας, Μὴ μοιχεύσῃς, μὴ φονεύσῃς, μὴ κλέψῃς, μὴ ψευδομαρτυρήσῃς, μὴ ἀποστερήσῃς, τίμα τὸν πατέρα σου καὶ τὴν μητέρα. ²⁰ ὁ δὲ ἔφη αὐτῷ, Διδάσκαλε, ταῦτα πάντα ἐφυλαξάμην ἐκ νεότητός μου. ²¹ ὁ δὲ Ἰησοῦς ἐμβλέψας αὐτῷ ἠγάπησεν αὐτὸν καὶ εἶπεν αὐτῷ, Ἕν σε ὑστερεῖ· ὕπαγε, ὅσα ἔχεις πώλησον καὶ δὸς τοῖς πτωχοῖς, καὶ ἕξεις θησαυρὸν ἐν οὐρανῷ, καὶ δεῦρο ἀκολούθει μοι. ²² ὁ δὲ στυγνάσας ἐπὶ τῷ λόγῳ ἀπῆλθεν λυπούμενος· ἦν γὰρ ἔχων κτήματα πολλά. ²³ καὶ περιβλεψάμενος ὁ Ἰησοῦς λέγει τοῖς μαθηταῖς αὐτοῦ, Πῶς δυσκόλως οἱ τὰ χρήματα ἔχοντες εἰς τὴν βασιλείαν τοῦ θεοῦ εἰσελεύσονται.

²⁴οἱ δὲ μαθηταὶ ἐθαμβοῦντο ἐπὶ τοῖς λόγοις αὐτοῦ. ὁ δὲ Ἰησοῦς πάλιν ἀποκριθεὶς λέγει αὐτοῖς, Τέκνα, πῶς δύσκολόν ἐστιν εἰς τὴν βασιλείαν τοῦ θεοῦ εἰσελθεῖν· ²⁵εὐκοπώτερόν ἐστιν κάμηλον διὰ τῆς τρυμαλιᾶς τῆς ῥαφίδος διελθεῖν ἢ πλούσιον εἰς τὴν βασιλείαν τοῦ θεοῦ εἰσελθεῖν. ²⁶οἱ δὲ περισσῶς ἐξεπλήσσοντο λέγοντες πρὸς αὐτόν, Καὶ τίς δύναται σωθῆναι; ²⁷ἐμβλέψας αὐτοῖς ὁ Ἰησοῦς λέγει, Παρὰ ἀνθρώποις ἀδύνατον, ἀλλ' οὐ παρὰ θεῷ· πάντα γὰρ δυνατὰ παρὰ τῷ θεῷ. ²⁸ἤρξατο λέγειν ὁ Πέτρος αὐτῷ, Ἰδοὺ ἡμεῖς ἀφήκαμεν πάντα καὶ ἠκολουθήκαμέν σοι. ²⁹ἔφη ὁ Ἰησοῦς, Ἀμὴν λέγω ὑμῖν, οὐδείς ἐστιν ὃς ἀφῆκεν οἰκίαν ἢ ἀδελφοὺς ἢ ἀδελφὰς ἢ μητέρα ἢ πατέρα ἢ τέκνα ἢ ἀγροὺς ἕνεκεν ἐμοῦ καὶ ἕνεκεν τοῦ εὐαγγελίου, ³⁰ἐὰν μὴ λάβῃ ἑκατονταπλασίονα νῦν ἐν τῷ καιρῷ τούτῳ οἰκίας καὶ ἀδελφοὺς καὶ ἀδελφὰς καὶ μητέρας καὶ τέκνα καὶ ἀγροὺς μετὰ διωγμῶν, καὶ ἐν τῷ αἰῶνι τῷ ἐρχομένῳ ζωὴν αἰώνιον. ³¹πολλοὶ δὲ ἔσονται πρῶτοι ἔσχατοι καὶ οἱ ἔσχατοι πρῶτοι.

³²Ἦσαν δὲ ἐν τῇ ὁδῷ ἀναβαίνοντες εἰς Ἱεροσόλυμα, καὶ ἦν προάγων αὐτοὺς ὁ Ἰησοῦς, καὶ ἐθαμβοῦντο, οἱ δὲ ἀκολουθοῦντες ἐφοβοῦντο. καὶ παραλαβὼν πάλιν τοὺς δώδεκα ἤρξατο αὐτοῖς λέγειν τὰ μέλλοντα αὐτῷ συμβαίνειν ³³ὅτι Ἰδοὺ ἀναβαίνομεν εἰς Ἱεροσόλυμα, καὶ ὁ υἱὸς τοῦ ἀνθρώπου παραδοθήσεται τοῖς ἀρχιερεῦσιν καὶ τοῖς γραμματεῦσιν, καὶ κατακρινοῦσιν αὐτὸν θανάτῳ καὶ παραδώσουσιν αὐτὸν τοῖς ἔθνεσιν, ³⁴καὶ ἐμπαίξουσιν αὐτῷ καὶ ἐμπτύσουσιν αὐτῷ καὶ μαστιγώσουσιν αὐτὸν καὶ ἀποκτενοῦσιν, καὶ μετὰ τρεῖς ἡμέρας ἀναστήσεται.

³⁵Καὶ προσπορεύονται αὐτῷ Ἰάκωβος καὶ Ἰωάννης

οἱ υἱοὶ Ζεβεδαίου, λέγοντες αὐτῷ, Διδάσκαλε, θέλομεν ἵνα ὃ ἐὰν αἰτήσωμέν σε ποιήσῃς ἡμῖν. ³⁶ ὁ δὲ εἶπεν αὐτοῖς, Τί θέλετε ποιήσω ὑμῖν ; ³⁷ οἱ δὲ εἶπαν αὐτῷ, Δὸς ἡμῖν ἵνα εἷς σου ἐκ δεξιῶν καὶ εἷς ἐξ ἀριστερῶν σου καθίσωμεν ἐν τῇ δόξῃ σου. ³⁸ ὁ δὲ Ἰησοῦς εἶπεν αὐτοῖς, Οὐκ οἴδατε τί αἰτεῖσθε. δύνασθε πιεῖν τὸ ποτήριον ὃ ἐγὼ πίνω, ἢ τὸ βάπτισμα ὃ ἐγὼ βαπτίζομαι βαπτισθῆναι ; ³⁹ οἱ δὲ εἶπαν αὐτῷ, Δυνάμεθα. ὁ δὲ Ἰησοῦς εἶπεν αὐτοῖς, Τὸ ποτήριον ὃ ἐγὼ πίνω πίεσθε, καὶ τὸ βάπτισμα ὃ ἐγὼ βαπτίζομαι βαπτισθήσεσθε· ⁴⁰ τὸ δὲ καθίσαι ἐκ δεξιῶν μου ἢ ἐξ εὐωνύμων οὐκ ἔστιν ἐμὸν δοῦναι, ἀλλ᾽ οἷς ἡτοίμασται. ⁴¹ καὶ ἀκούσαντες οἱ δέκα ἤρξαντο ἀγανακτεῖν περὶ Ἰακώβου καὶ Ἰωάννου. ⁴² καὶ προσκαλεσάμενος αὐτοὺς ὁ Ἰησοῦς λέγει αὐτοῖς, Οἴδατε ὅτι οἱ δοκοῦντες ἄρχειν τῶν ἐθνῶν κατακυριεύουσιν αὐτῶν καὶ οἱ μεγάλοι αὐτῶν κατεξουσιάζουσιν αὐτῶν. ⁴³ οὐχ οὕτως δέ ἐστιν ἐν ὑμῖν· ἀλλ᾽ ὃς ἂν θέλῃ μέγας γενέσθαι ἐν ὑμῖν, ἔσται ὑμῶν διάκονος, ⁴⁴ καὶ ὃς ἂν θέλῃ ὑμῶν γενέσθαι πρῶτος, ἔσται πάντων δοῦλος. ⁴⁵ καὶ γὰρ ὁ υἱὸς τοῦ ἀνθρώπου οὐκ ἦλθεν διακονηθῆναι, ἀλλὰ διακονῆσαι καὶ δοῦναι τὴν ψυχὴν αὐτοῦ λύτρον ἀντὶ πολλῶν.

⁴⁶ Καὶ ἔρχονται εἰς Ἱερειχώ. καὶ ἐκπορευομένου αὐτοῦ ἀπὸ Ἱερειχὼ καὶ τῶν μαθητῶν αὐτοῦ καὶ ὄχλου ἱκανοῦ ὁ υἱὸς Τιμαίου Βαρτιμαῖος, τυφλὸς προσαίτης, ἐκάθητο παρὰ τὴν ὁδόν. ⁴⁷ καὶ ἀκούσας ὅτι Ἰησοῦς ὁ Ναζαρηνός ἐστιν, ἤρξατο κράζειν καὶ λέγειν, Υἱὲ Δαυεὶδ Ἰησοῦ, ἐλέησόν με. ⁴⁸ καὶ ἐπετίμων αὐτῷ πολλοὶ ἵνα σιωπήσῃ· ὁ δὲ πολλῷ μᾶλλον ἔκραζεν, Υἱὲ Δαυείδ, ἐλέησόν με. ⁴⁹ καὶ στὰς ὁ Ἰησοῦς εἶπεν, Φωνήσατε αὐτόν. καὶ φωνοῦσιν τὸν τυφλὸν λέγοντες αὐτῷ, Θάρσει, ἔγειρε, φωνεῖ

σε. ⁵⁰ὁ δὲ ἀποβαλὼν τὸ ἱμάτιον αὐτοῦ ἀναπηδήσας ἦλθεν πρὸς τὸν Ἰησοῦν. ⁵¹καὶ ἀποκριθεὶς αὐτῷ ὁ Ἰησοῦς εἶπεν, Τί σοι θέλεις ποιήσω; ὁ δὲ τυφλὸς εἶπεν αὐτῷ, Ῥαββουνεί, ἵνα ἀναβλέψω. ⁵²ὁ δὲ Ἰησοῦς εἶπεν αὐτῷ, Ὕπαγε, ἡ πίστις σου σέσωκέν σε. καὶ εὐθὺς ἀνέβλεψεν, καὶ ἠκολούθει αὐτῷ ἐν τῇ ὁδῷ.

11 ¹Καὶ ὅτε ἐγγίζουσιν εἰς Ἱεροσόλυμα εἰς Βηθφαγὴ καὶ Βηθανίαν πρὸς τὸ ὄρος τὸ Ἐλαιών, ἀποστέλλει δύο τῶν μαθητῶν αὐτοῦ ²καὶ λέγει αὐτοῖς, Ὑπάγετε εἰς τὴν κώμην τὴν κατέναντι ὑμῶν, καὶ εὐθὺς εἰσπορευόμενοι εἰς αὐτὴν εὑρήσετε πῶλον δεδεμένον, ἐφ᾽ ὃν οὐδεὶς οὔπω ἀνθρώπων κεκάθικεν· λύσατε αὐτὸν καὶ φέρετε. ³καὶ ἐάν τις ὑμῖν εἴπῃ, Τί ποιεῖτε τοῦτο; εἴπατε, Ὁ κύριος αὐτοῦ χρείαν ἔχει, καὶ εὐθὺς αὐτὸν ἀποστέλλει πάλιν ὧδε. ⁴καὶ ἀπῆλθον καὶ εὗρον τὸν πῶλον δεδεμένον πρὸς τὴν θύραν ἔξω ἐπὶ τοῦ ἀμφόδου, καὶ λύουσιν αὐτόν. ⁵καὶ τινες τῶν ἐκεῖ ἑστηκότων ἔλεγον αὐτοῖς, Τί ποιεῖτε λύοντες τὸν πῶλον; ⁶οἱ δὲ εἶπαν αὐτοῖς καθὼς εἶπεν ὁ Ἰησοῦς· καὶ ἀφῆκαν αὐτούς. ⁷καὶ φέρουσιν τὸν πῶλον πρὸς τὸν Ἰησοῦν, καὶ ἐπιβάλλουσιν αὐτῷ τὰ ἱμάτια αὐτῶν, καὶ ἐκάθισεν ἐπ᾽ αὐτόν. ⁸καὶ πολλοὶ τὰ ἱμάτια αὐτῶν ἔστρωσαν εἰς τὴν ὁδόν, ἄλλοι δὲ στιβάδας, κόψαντες ἐκ τῶν ἀγρῶν. ⁹καὶ οἱ προάγοντες καὶ οἱ ἀκολουθοῦντες ἔκραζον, Ὡσαννά, εὐλογημένος ὁ ἐρχόμενος ἐν ὀνόματι κυρίου· ¹⁰εὐλογημένη ἡ ἐρχομένη βασιλεία τοῦ πατρὸς ἡμῶν Δαυείδ, ὡσαννὰ ἐν τοῖς ὑψίστοις. ¹⁵καὶ εἰσῆλθεν εἰς Ἱεροσόλυμα εἰς τὸ ἱερόν· καὶ περιβλεψάμενος πάντα, ὀψίας ἤδη οὔσης τῆς ὥρας, ἐξῆλθεν εἰς Βηθανίαν μετὰ τῶν δώδεκα.

¹²Καὶ τῇ ἐπαύριον ἐξελθόντων αὐτῶν ἀπὸ Βηθανίας ἐπείνασεν. ¹³καὶ ἰδὼν συκῆν ἀπὸ μακρόθεν ἔχουσαν

φύλλα, ἦλθεν εἰ ἄρα τι εὑρήσει ἐν αὐτῇ, καὶ ἐλθὼν ἐπ᾽
αὐτὴν οὐδὲν εὗρεν εἰ μὴ φύλλα· ὁ γὰρ καιρὸς οὐκ ἦν
σύκων. ¹⁴ καὶ ἀποκριθεὶς εἶπεν αὐτῇ, Μηκέτι εἰς τὸν
αἰῶνα ἐκ σοῦ μηδεὶς καρπὸν φάγοι. καὶ ἤκουον οἱ μαθηταὶ αὐτοῦ. ¹⁵ καὶ ἔρχονται εἰς Ἱεροσόλυμα. καὶ
εἰσελθὼν εἰς τὸ ἱερὸν ἤρξατο ἐκβάλλειν τοὺς πωλοῦν-
τας καὶ τοὺς ἀγοράζοντας ἐν τῷ ἱερῷ, καὶ τὰς τραπέζας τῶν κολλυβιστῶν καὶ τὰς καθέδρας τῶν πω-
λούντων τὰς περιστερὰς κατέστρεψεν, ¹⁶ καὶ οὐκ ἤφιεν
ἵνα τις διενέγκῃ σκεῦος διὰ τοῦ ἱεροῦ, ¹⁷ καὶ ἐδίδασκεν
καὶ ἔλεγεν αὐτοῖς, Οὐ γέγραπται ὅτι ὁ οἶκός μου
οἶκος προσευχῆς κληθήσεται πᾶσιν τοῖς ἔθνεσιν; ὑμεῖς
δὲ πεποιήκατε αὐτὸν σπήλαιον λῃστῶν. ¹⁸ καὶ ἤκου-
σαν οἱ ἀρχιερεῖς καὶ οἱ γραμματεῖς, καὶ ἐζήτουν
πῶς αὐτὸν ἀπολέσωσιν· ἐφοβοῦντο γὰρ αὐτόν, πᾶς
γὰρ ὁ ὄχλος ἐξεπλήσσετο ἐπὶ τῇ διδαχῇ αὐτοῦ.
¹⁹ καὶ ὅταν ὀψὲ ἐγένετο, ἐξεπορεύοντο ἔξω τῆς πόλεως.

²⁰ Καὶ παραπορευόμενοι πρωῒ εἶδον τὴν συκῆν ἐξηραμμένην ἐκ ῥιζῶν. ²¹ καὶ ἀναμνησθεὶς ὁ Πέτρος λέγει
αὐτῷ, Ῥαββεί, ἴδε ἡ συκῆ ἣν κατηράσω ἐξήρανται. ²² καὶ
ἀποκριθεὶς ὁ Ἰησοῦς λέγει αὐτοῖς, Ἔχετε πίστιν θεοῦ.
²³ ἀμὴν λέγω ὑμῖν ὅτι ὃς ἂν εἴπῃ τῷ ὄρει τούτῳ, Ἄρθητι,
καὶ βλήθητι εἰς τὴν θάλασσαν, καὶ μὴ διακριθῇ ἐν
τῇ καρδίᾳ αὐτοῦ, ἀλλὰ πιστεύῃ ὅτι ὃ λαλεῖ γίνεται,
ἔσται αὐτῷ. ²⁴ διὰ τοῦτο λέγω ὑμῖν, πάντα ὅσα
προσεύχεσθε καὶ αἰτεῖσθε, πιστεύετε ὅτι ἐλάβετε,
καὶ ἔσται ὑμῖν. ²⁵ καὶ ὅταν στήκετε προσευχόμενοι,
ἀφίετε εἴ τι ἔχετε κατά τινος, ἵνα καὶ ὁ πατὴρ ὑμῶν ὁ
ἐν τοῖς οὐρανοῖς ἀφῇ ὑμῖν τὰ παραπτώματα ὑμῶν.*

* Verse 26 omitted on the best MSS. authority.

²⁷ Καὶ ἔρχονται πάλιν εἰς Ἱεροσόλυμα. καὶ ἐν τῷ ἱερῷ περιπατοῦντος αὐτοῦ ἔρχονται πρὸς αὐτὸν οἱ ἀρχιερεῖς καὶ οἱ γραμματεῖς καὶ οἱ πρεσβύτεροι, ²⁸ καὶ ἔλεγον αὐτῷ, Ἐν ποίᾳ ἐξουσίᾳ ταῦτα ποιεῖς; ἢ τίς σοι τὴν ἐξουσίαν ταύτην ἔδωκεν ἵνα ταῦτα ποιῇς; ²⁹ ὁ δὲ Ἰησοῦς εἶπεν αὐτοῖς, Ἐπερωτήσω ὑμᾶς ἕνα λόγον, καὶ ἀποκρίθητέ μοι, καὶ ἐρῶ ὑμῖν ἐν ποίᾳ ἐξουσίᾳ ταῦτα ποιῶ. ³⁰ τὸ βάπτισμα τὸ Ἰωάννου ἐξ οὐρανοῦ ἦν ἢ ἐξ ἀνθρώπων; ἀποκρίθητέ μοι. ³¹ καὶ διελογίζοντο πρὸς ἑαυτοὺς λέγοντες Ἐὰν εἴπωμεν, Ἐξ οὐρανοῦ, ἐρεῖ. Διατί οὖν οὐκ ἐπιστεύσατε αὐτῷ; ³² ἀλλὰ εἴπωμεν, Ἐξ ἀνθρώπων; ἐφοβοῦντο τὸν ὄχλον· ἅπαντες γὰρ εἶχον τὸν Ἰωάννην ὄντως ὅτι προφήτης ἦν. ³³ καὶ ἀποκριθέντες τῷ Ἰησοῦ λέγουσιν, Οὐκ οἴδαμεν. καὶ ὁ Ἰησοῦς λέγει αὐτοῖς, Οὐδὲ ἐγὼ λέγω ὑμῖν ἐν ποίᾳ ἐξουσίᾳ ταῦτα ποιῶ.

12 ¹ Καὶ ἤρξατο αὐτοῖς ἐν παραβολαῖς λαλεῖν. Ἀμπελῶνα ἄνθρωπος ἐφύτευσεν, καὶ περιέθηκεν φραγμὸν καὶ ὤρυξεν ὑπολήνιον καὶ ᾠκοδόμησεν πύργον, καὶ ἐξέδετο αὐτὸν γεωργοῖς, καὶ ἀπεδήμησεν. ² καὶ ἀπέστειλεν πρὸς τοὺς γεωργοὺς τῷ καιρῷ δοῦλον, ἵνα παρὰ τῶν γεωργῶν λάβῃ ἀπὸ τῶν καρπῶν τοῦ ἀμπελῶνος· ³ καὶ λαβόντες αὐτὸν ἔδειραν καὶ ἀπέστειλαν κενόν. ⁴ καὶ πάλιν ἀπέστειλεν πρὸς αὐτοὺς ἄλλον δοῦλον· κἀκεῖνον ἐκεφαλίωσαν καὶ ἠτίμασαν. ⁵ καὶ ἄλλον ἀπέστειλεν· κἀκεῖνον ἀπέκτειναν, καὶ πολλοὺς ἄλλους, οὓς μὲν δέροντες, οὓς δὲ ἀποκτέννοντες. ⁶ ἔτι ἕνα εἶχεν υἱόν, ἀγαπητόν· ἀπέστειλεν αὐτὸν ἔσχατον πρὸς αὐτοὺς λέγων ὅτι Ἐντραπήσονται τὸν υἱόν μου. ⁷ ἐκεῖνοι δὲ οἱ γεωργοὶ πρὸς ἑαυτοὺς εἶπαν ὅτι Οὗτός ἐστιν ὁ κληρονόμος· δεῦτε ἀποκτείνωμεν αὐτόν, καὶ ἡμῶν ἔσται ἡ κληρονομία. ⁸ καὶ λαβόντες ἀπέκτειναν αὐτόν, καὶ ἐξέβαλον αὐτὸν ἔξω τοῦ ἀμπελῶνος. ⁹ τί ποιήσει ὁ κύριος τοῦ ἀμπελῶνος; ἐλεύσεται καὶ ἀπολέσει τοὺς γεωργούς, καὶ δώσει τὸν ἀμπελῶνα ἄλλοις. ¹⁰ οὐδὲ τὴν γραφὴν ταύτην ἀνέγνωτε, Λίθον ὃν ἀπεδοκίμασαν οἱ οἰκοδομοῦντες, οὗτος ἐγενήθη εἰς κεφαλὴν γωνίας· ¹¹ παρὰ κυρίου ἐγένετο αὕτη καὶ ἔστιν θαυμαστὴ ἐν ὀφθαλμοῖς ἡμῶν; ¹² καὶ ἐζήτουν αὐτὸν κρατῆσαι, καὶ ἐφοβήθησαν τὸν ὄχλον· ἔγνωσαν γὰρ ὅτι πρὸς αὐτοὺς τὴν παραβολὴν εἶπεν. καὶ ἀφέντες αὐτὸν ἀπῆλθον.

¹³ Καὶ ἀποστέλλουσιν πρὸς αὐτὸν τινὰς τῶν Φαρισαίων καὶ τῶν Ἡρωδιανῶν, ἵνα αὐτὸν ἀγρεύσωσιν λόγῳ. ¹⁴ καὶ ἐλθόντες λέγουσιν αὐτῷ, Διδάσκαλε, οἴδαμεν ὅτι ἀληθὴς εἶ καὶ οὐ μέλει σοι περὶ οὐδενός· οὐ γὰρ βλέπεις εἰς πρόσωπον ἀνθρώπων, ἀλλ᾽ ἐπ᾽ ἀληθείας τὴν ὁδὸν τοῦ θεοῦ διδάσκεις· ἔξεστιν κῆνσον Καίσαρι δοῦναι ἢ οὔ ; δῶμεν ἢ μὴ δῶμεν ; ¹⁵ ὁ δὲ εἰδὼς αὐτῶν τὴν ὑπόκρισιν εἶπεν αὐτοῖς, Τί με πειράζετε ; φέρετέ μοι δηνάριον ἵνα ἴδω. ¹⁶ οἱ δὲ ἤνεγκαν. καὶ λέγει αὐτοῖς, Τίνος ἡ εἰκὼν αὕτη καὶ ἡ ἐπιγραφή ; οἱ δὲ εἶπαν αὐτῷ, Καίσαρος. ¹⁷ ὁ δὲ Ἰησοῦς εἶπεν αὐτοῖς, Τὰ Καίσαρος ἀπόδοτε Καίσαρι καὶ τὰ τοῦ θεοῦ τῷ θεῷ. καὶ ἐξεθαύμαζον ἐπ᾽ αὐτῷ.

¹⁸ Καὶ ἔρχονται Σαδδουκαῖοι πρὸς αὐτόν, οἵτινες λέγουσιν ἀνάστασιν μὴ εἶναι, καὶ ἐπηρώτων αὐτὸν λέγοντες, ¹⁹ Διδάσκαλε, Μωϋσῆς ἔγραψεν ἡμῖν ὅτι Ἐάν τινος ἀδελφὸς ἀποθάνῃ καὶ καταλίπῃ γυναῖκα καὶ μὴ ἀφῇ τέκνον, ἵνα λάβῃ ὁ ἀδελφὸς αὐτοῦ τὴν γυναῖκα καὶ ἐξαναστήσῃ σπέρμα τῷ ἀδελφῷ αὐτοῦ. ²⁰ ἑπτὰ ἀδελφοὶ ἦσαν· καὶ ὁ πρῶτος ἔλαβεν γυναῖκα, καὶ ἀποθνήσκων οὐκ ἀφῆκεν σπέρμα. ²¹ καὶ ὁ δεύτερος ἔλαβεν αὐτήν,

καὶ ἀπέθανεν μὴ καταλιπὼν σπέρμα· καὶ ὁ τρίτος ὡσαύτως· ²²καὶ οἱ ἑπτὰ οὐκ ἀφῆκαν σπέρμα. ἔσχατον πάντων καὶ ἡ γυνὴ ἀπέθανεν. ²³ἐν τῇ ἀναστάσει τίνος αὐτῶν ἔσται γυνή; οἱ γὰρ ἑπτὰ ἔσχον αὐτὴν γυναῖκα. ²⁴ἔφη αὐτοῖς ὁ Ἰησοῦς, Οὐ διὰ τοῦτο πλανᾶσθε μὴ εἰδότες τὰς γραφὰς μηδὲ τὴν δύναμιν τοῦ θεοῦ; ²⁵ὅταν γὰρ ἐκ νεκρῶν ἀναστῶσιν, οὔτε γαμοῦσιν οὔτε γαμίζονται, ἀλλ᾽ εἰσὶν ὡς ἄγγελοι ἐν τοῖς οὐρανοῖς. ²⁶περὶ δὲ τῶν νεκρῶν, ὅτι ἐγείρονται, οὐκ ἀνέγνωτε ἐν τῇ βίβλῳ Μωϋσέως ἐπὶ τοῦ βάτου πῶς εἶπεν αὐτῷ ὁ θεὸς λέγων, Ἐγὼ ὁ θεὸς Ἀβραὰμ καὶ ὁ θεὸς Ἰσαὰκ καὶ ὁ θεὸς Ἰακώβ; ²⁷οὐκ ἔστιν ὁ θεὸς νεκρῶν ἀλλὰ ζώντων. πολὺ πλανᾶσθε.

²⁸Καὶ προσελθὼν εἷς τῶν γραμματέων, ἀκούσας αὐτῶν συνζητούντων, εἰδὼς ὅτι καλῶς ἀπεκρίθη αὐτοῖς, ἐπηρώτησεν αὐτόν, Ποία ἐστὶν ἐντολὴ πρώτη πάντων; ²⁹ἀπεκρίθη ὁ Ἰησοῦς ὅτι Πρώτη ἐστίν, Ἄκουε Ἰσραήλ, κύριος ὁ θεὸς ἡμῶν κύριος εἷς ἐστίν, ³⁰καὶ ἀγαπήσεις κύριον τὸν θεόν σου ἐξ ὅλης τῆς καρδίας σου καὶ ἐξ ὅλης τῆς ψυχῆς σου καὶ ἐξ ὅλης τῆς διανοίας σου καὶ ἐξ ὅλης τῆς ἰσχύος σου. ³¹δευτέρα αὕτη, Ἀγαπήσεις τὸν πλησίον σου ὡς σεαυτόν. μείζων τούτων ἄλλη ἐντολὴ οὐκ ἔστιν. ³²καὶ εἶπεν αὐτῷ ὁ γραμματεύς, Καλῶς, διδάσκαλε, ἐπ᾽ ἀληθείας εἶπες ὅτι Εἷς ἐστὶν καὶ οὐκ ἔστιν ἄλλος πλὴν αὐτοῦ. ³³καὶ τὸ ἀγαπᾶν αὐτὸν ἐξ ὅλης τῆς καρδίας καὶ ἐξ ὅλης τῆς συνέσεως καὶ ἐξ ὅλης τῆς ἰσχύος, καὶ τὸ ἀγαπᾶν τὸν πλησίον ὡς ἑαυτὸν περισσότερόν ἐστιν πάντων τῶν ὁλοκαυτωμάτων καὶ τῶν θυσιῶν. ³⁴καὶ ὁ Ἰησοῦς, ἰδὼν αὐτὸν ὅτι νουνεχῶς ἀπεκρίθη, εἶπεν αὐτῷ, Οὐ μακρὰν εἶ ἀπὸ τῆς βασιλείας τοῦ θεοῦ. καὶ οὐδεὶς οὐκέτι ἐτόλμα αὐτὸν ἐπερωτῆσαι.

³⁵ Καὶ ἀποκριθεὶς ὁ Ἰησοῦς ἔλεγεν διδάσκων ἐν τῷ
ἱερῷ, Πῶς λέγουσιν οἱ γραμματεῖς ὅτι ὁ Χριστὸς υἱὸς
Δαυείδ ἐστιν; ³⁶ αὐτὸς Δαυεὶδ εἶπεν ἐν τῷ πνεύματι τῷ
ἁγίῳ, Εἶπεν ὁ κύριος τῷ κυρίῳ μου· κάθου ἐκ δεξιῶν
μου ἕως ἂν θῶ τοὺς ἐχθρούς σου ὑποκάτω τῶν ποδῶν
σου. ³⁷ αὐτὸς Δαυεὶδ λέγει αὐτὸν κύριον, καὶ πόθεν
αὐτοῦ ἐστιν υἱός; καὶ ὁ πολὺς ὄχλος ἤκουεν αὐτοῦ ἡδέως.
³⁸ καὶ ἐν τῇ διδαχῇ αὐτοῦ ἔλεγεν, Βλέπετε ἀπὸ τῶν
γραμματέων τῶν θελόντων ἐν στολαῖς περιπατεῖν καὶ
ἀσπασμοὺς ἐν ταῖς ἀγοραῖς ³⁹ καὶ πρωτοκαθεδρίας ἐν
ταῖς συναγωγαῖς καὶ πρωτοκλισίας ἐν τοῖς δείπνοις· ⁴⁰ οἱ
κατεσθίοντες τὰς οἰκίας τῶν χηρῶν καὶ προφάσει μακρὰ
προσευχόμενοι, οὗτοι λήμψονται περισσότερον κρίμα.
⁴¹ Καὶ καθίσας κατέναντι τοῦ γαζοφυλακίου ἐθεώρει
πῶς ὁ ὄχλος βάλλει χαλκὸν εἰς τὸ γαζοφυλάκιον· καὶ
πολλοὶ πλούσιοι ἔβαλλον πολλά, ⁴² καὶ ἐλθοῦσα μία
χήρα πτωχὴ ἔβαλεν λεπτὰ δύο, ὅ ἐστιν κοδράντης.
⁴³ καὶ προσκαλεσάμενος τοὺς μαθητὰς αὐτοῦ εἶπεν αὐ-
τοῖς, Ἀμὴν λέγω ὑμῖν ὅτι ἡ χήρα αὕτη ἡ πτωχὴ πλεῖον
πάντων ἔβαλεν τῶν βαλλόντων εἰς τὸ γαζοφυλάκιον·
⁴⁴ πάντες γὰρ ἐκ τοῦ περισσεύοντος αὐτοῖς ἔβαλον, αὕτη
δὲ ἐκ τῆς ὑστερήσεως αὐτῆς πάντα ὅσα εἶχεν ἔβαλεν,
ὅλον τὸν βίον αὐτῆς.

13 ¹ Καὶ ἐκπορευομένου αὐτοῦ ἐκ τοῦ ἱεροῦ, λέγει
αὐτῷ εἷς τῶν μαθητῶν αὐτοῦ, Διδάσκαλε, ἴδε ποταποὶ
λίθοι καὶ ποταπαὶ οἰκοδομαί. ² καὶ ὁ Ἰησοῦς εἶπεν
αὐτῷ, Βλέπεις ταύτας τὰς μεγάλας οἰκοδομάς; οὐ μὴ
ἀφεθῇ ὧδε λίθος ἐπὶ λίθον, ὃς οὐ μὴ καταλυθῇ. ³ καὶ
καθημένου αὐτοῦ εἰς τὸ ὄρος τῶν ἐλαιῶν κατέναντι τοῦ
ἱεροῦ, ἐπηρώτα αὐτὸν κατ᾽ ἰδίαν Πέτρος καὶ Ἰάκωβος καὶ
Ἰωάννης καὶ Ἀνδρέας, ⁴ Εἰπὸν ἡμῖν, πότε ταῦτα ἔσται;

καὶ τί τὸ σημεῖον ὅταν μέλλῃ ταῦτα συντελεῖσθαι
πάντα; ⁵ὁ δὲ Ἰησοῦς ἤρξατο λέγειν αὐτοῖς, Βλέπετε
μή τις ὑμᾶς πλανήσῃ. ⁶πολλοὶ ἐλεύσονται ἐπὶ τῷ
ὀνόματί μου, λέγοντες ὅτι Ἐγώ εἰμι, καὶ πολλοὺς πλανή-
σουσιν. ⁷ὅταν δὲ ἀκούσητε πολέμους καὶ ἀκοὰς πολέ-
μων, μὴ θροεῖσθε· δεῖ γενέσθαι, ἀλλ᾽ οὔπω τὸ τέλος.
⁸ἐγερθήσεται γὰρ ἔθνος ἐπὶ ἔθνος καὶ βασιλεία ἐπὶ
βασιλείαν, ἔσονται σεισμοὶ κατὰ τόπους, ἔσονται λιμοί.
ἀρχὴ ὠδίνων ταῦτα. ⁹βλέπετε δὲ ὑμεῖς ἑαυτούς· παραδώσουσιν [γὰρ] ὑμᾶς εἰς συνέδρια καὶ εἰς συναγωγάς,
δαρήσεσθε, καὶ ἐπὶ ἡγεμόνων καὶ βασιλέων σταθήσεσθε
ἕνεκεν ἐμοῦ, εἰς μαρτύριον αὐτοῖς. ¹⁰καὶ εἰς πάντα τὰ
ἔθνη πρῶτον δεῖ κηρυχθῆναι τὸ εὐαγγέλιον. ¹¹καὶ ὅταν
ἄγωσιν ὑμᾶς παραδιδόντες, μὴ προμεριμνᾶτε τί λαλή-
σητε, ἀλλ᾽ ὃ ἐὰν δοθῇ ὑμῖν ἐν ἐκείνῃ τῇ ὥρᾳ, τοῦτο
λαλεῖτε· οὐ γάρ ἐστε ὑμεῖς οἱ λαλοῦντες, ἀλλὰ τὸ
πνεῦμα τὸ ἅγιον. ¹²καὶ παραδώσει ἀδελφὸς ἀδελφὸν
εἰς θάνατον καὶ πατὴρ τέκνον, καὶ ἐπαναστήσονται
τέκνα ἐπὶ γονεῖς καὶ θανατώσουσιν αὐτούς. ¹³καὶ
ἔσεσθε μισούμενοι ὑπὸ πάντων διὰ τὸ ὄνομά μου· ὁ δὲ
ὑπομείνας εἰς τέλος, οὗτος σωθήσεται.

¹⁴Ὅταν δὲ ἴδητε τὸ βδέλυγμα τῆς ἐρημώσεως
ἑστηκότα ὅπου οὐ δεῖ, ὁ ἀναγινώσκων νοείτω, τότε
οἱ ἐν τῇ Ἰουδαίᾳ φευγέτωσαν εἰς τὰ ὄρη, ¹⁵ὁ δὲ ἐπὶ
τοῦ δώματος μὴ καταβάτω, μηδὲ εἰσελθάτω ἆραί τι
ἐκ τῆς οἰκίας αὐτοῦ, ¹⁶καὶ ὁ εἰς τὸν ἀγρὸν μὴ ἐπι-
στρεψάτω εἰς τὰ ὀπίσω ἆραι τὸ ἱμάτιον αὐτοῦ. ¹⁷οὐαὶ
δὲ ταῖς ἐν γαστρὶ ἐχούσαις καὶ ταῖς θηλαζούσαις
ἐν ἐκείναις ταῖς ἡμέραις. ¹⁸προσεύχεσθε δὲ ἵνα μὴ
γένηται χειμῶνος. ¹⁹ἔσονται γὰρ αἱ ἡμέραι ἐκεῖναι
θλίψις, οἵα οὐ γέγονεν τοιαύτη ἀπ᾽ ἀρχῆς κτίσεως, ἣν

ἔκτισεν ὁ θεός, ἕως τοῦ νῦν καὶ οὐ μὴ γένηται. ²⁰ καὶ εἰ
μὴ ἐκολόβωσεν κύριος τὰς ἡμέρας, οὐκ ἂν ἐσώθη πᾶσα
σάρξ· ἀλλὰ διὰ τοὺς ἐκλεκτοὺς οὓς ἐξελέξατο ἐκολόβωσεν τὰς ἡμέρας. ²¹ καὶ τότε ἐάν τις ὑμῖν εἴπῃ, Ἴδε ὧδε
ὁ Χριστός, ἢ ἴδε ἐκεῖ, μὴ πιστεύετε. ²² ἐγερθήσονται γὰρ
ψευδόχριστοι καὶ ψευδοπροφῆται καὶ δώσουσιν σημεῖα
καὶ τέρατα πρὸς τὸ ἀποπλανᾶν, εἰ δυνατόν, τοὺς ἐκλεκτούς. ²³ ὑμεῖς δὲ βλέπετε· προείρηκα ὑμῖν πάντα.
²⁴ Ἀλλὰ ἐν ἐκείναις ταῖς ἡμέραις μετὰ τὴν θλίψιν
ἐκείνην ὁ ἥλιος σκοτισθήσεται, καὶ ἡ σελήνη οὐ δώσει
τὸ φέγγος αὐτῆς, ²⁵ καὶ οἱ ἀστέρες ἔσονται ἐκ τοῦ
οὐρανοῦ πίπτοντες, καὶ αἱ δυνάμεις αἱ ἐν τοῖς οὐρανοῖς σαλευθήσονται. ²⁶ καὶ τότε ὄψονται τὸν υἱὸν
τοῦ ἀνθρώπου ἐρχόμενον ἐν νεφέλαις μετὰ δυνάμεως
πολλῆς καὶ δόξης. ²⁷ καὶ τότε ἀποστελεῖ τοὺς ἀγγέλους
καὶ ἐπισυνάξει τοὺς ἐκλεκτοὺς ἐκ τῶν τεσσάρων ἀνέμων
ἀπ᾽ ἄκρου γῆς ἕως ἄκρου οὐρανοῦ. ²⁸ Ἀπὸ δὲ τῆς συκῆς
μάθετε τὴν παραβολήν. ὅταν αὐτῆς ἤδη ὁ κλάδος
ἁπαλὸς γένηται καὶ ἐκφύῃ τὰ φύλλα, γινώσκετε ὅτι ἐγγὺς
τὸ θέρος ἐστίν· ²⁹ οὕτως καὶ ὑμεῖς ὅταν ἴδητε ταῦτα γι-
νόμενα, γινώσκετε ὅτι ἐγγύς ἐστιν ἐπὶ θύραις. ³⁰ ἀμὴν
λέγω ὑμῖν ὅτι οὐ μὴ παρέλθῃ ἡ γενεὰ αὕτη μέχρις οὗ
ταῦτα πάντα γένηται. ³¹ ὁ οὐρανὸς καὶ ἡ γῆ παρελεύσονται, οἱ δὲ λόγοι μου οὐ μὴ παρελεύσονται.
³² Περὶ δὲ τῆς ἡμέρας ἐκείνης ἢ τῆς ὥρας οὐδεὶς οἶδεν,
οὐδὲ οἱ ἄγγελοι ἐν οὐρανῷ οὐδὲ ὁ υἱός, εἰ μὴ ὁ πατήρ.
³³ βλέπετε, ἀγρυπνεῖτε [καὶ προσεύχεσθε]· οὐκ οἴδατε γὰρ
πότε ὁ καιρός ἐστιν. ³⁴ ὡς ἄνθρωπος ἀπόδημος ἀφεὶς
τὴν οἰκίαν αὐτοῦ καὶ δοὺς τοῖς δούλοις αὐτοῦ τὴν ἐξουσίαν, ἑκάστῳ τὸ ἔργον αὐτοῦ, καὶ τῷ θυρωρῷ ἐνετείλατο
ἵνα γρηγορῇ. ³⁵ γρηγορεῖτε οὖν· οὐκ οἴδατε γὰρ πότε

ὁ κύριος τῆς οἰκίας ἔρχεται, ἢ ὀψὲ ἢ μεσονύκτιον ἢ ἀλεκτοροφωνίας ἢ πρωΐ· ³⁶ μὴ ἐλθὼν ἐξαίφνης εὕρῃ ὑμᾶς καθεύδοντας. ³⁷ ὃ δὲ ὑμῖν λέγω, πᾶσιν λέγω, γρηγορεῖτε.

14 ¹ Ἦν δὲ τὸ πάσχα καὶ τὰ ἄζυμα μετὰ δύο ἡμέρας, καὶ ἐζήτουν οἱ ἀρχιερεῖς καὶ οἱ γραμματεῖς πῶς αὐτὸν ἐν δόλῳ κρατήσαντες ἀποκτείνωσιν· ² ἔλεγον γάρ, Μὴ ἐν τῇ ἑορτῇ, μήποτε ἔσται θόρυβος τοῦ λαοῦ.

³ Καὶ ὄντος αὐτοῦ ἐν Βηθανίᾳ ἐν τῇ οἰκίᾳ Σίμωνος τοῦ λεπροῦ, κατακειμένου αὐτοῦ ἦλθεν γυνὴ ἔχουσα ἀλάβαστρον μύρου νάρδου πιστικῆς πολυτελοῦς· συντρίψασα τὸν ἀλάβαστρον κατέχεεν αὐτοῦ τῆς κεφαλῆς. ⁴ ἦσαν δέ τινες ἀγανακτοῦντες πρὸς ἑαυτούς, Εἰς τί ἡ ἀπώλεια αὕτη τοῦ μύρου γέγονεν; ⁵ ἠδύνατο γὰρ τοῦτο τὸ μύρον πραθῆναι ἐπάνω δηναρίων τριακοσίων καὶ δοθῆναι τοῖς πτωχοῖς· καὶ ἐνεβριμῶντο αὐτῇ. ⁶ ὁ δὲ Ἰησοῦς εἶπεν, Ἄφετε αὐτήν· τί αὐτῇ κόπους παρέχετε; καλὸν ἔργον ἠργάσατο ἐν ἐμοί. ⁷ πάντοτε γὰρ τοὺς πτωχοὺς ἔχετε μεθ᾽ ἑαυτῶν καὶ ὅταν θέλητε δύνασθε αὐτοῖς εὖ ποιῆσαι, ἐμὲ δὲ οὐ πάντοτε ἔχετε. ⁸ ὃ ἔσχεν ἐποίησεν· προέλαβεν μυρίσαι μου τὸ σῶμα εἰς τὸν ἐνταφιασμόν. ⁹ ἀμὴν δὲ λέγω ὑμῖν, ὅπου ἐὰν κηρυχθῇ τὸ εὐαγγέλιον εἰς ὅλον τὸν κόσμον, καὶ ὃ ἐποίησεν αὕτη λαληθήσεται εἰς μνημόσυνον αὐτῆς.

¹⁰ Καὶ Ἰούδας Ἰσκαριώθ, ὁ εἷς τῶν δώδεκα, ἀπῆλθεν πρὸς τοὺς ἀρχιερεῖς ἵνα αὐτὸν παραδοῖ αὐτοῖς. ¹¹ οἱ δὲ ἀκούσαντες ἐχάρησαν καὶ ἐπηγγείλαντο αὐτῷ ἀργύριον δοῦναι· καὶ ἐζήτει πῶς αὐτὸν εὐκαίρως παραδοῖ.

¹² Καὶ τῇ πρώτῃ ἡμέρᾳ τῶν ἀζύμων, ὅτε τὸ πάσχα ἔθυον, λέγουσιν αὐτῷ οἱ μαθηταὶ αὐτοῦ, Ποῦ θέλεις ἀπελθόντες ἑτοιμάσωμεν ἵνα φάγῃς τὸ πάσχα; ¹³ καὶ

ἀποστέλλει δύο τῶν μαθητῶν αὐτοῦ καὶ λέγει αὐτοῖς,
Ὑπάγετε εἰς τὴν πόλιν, καὶ ἀπαντήσει ὑμῖν ἄνθρωπος
κεράμιον ὕδατος βαστάζων· ἀκολουθήσατε αὐτῷ, [14] καὶ
ὅπου ἐὰν εἰσέλθῃ εἴπατε τῷ οἰκοδεσπότῃ ὅτι Ὁ διδάσκαλος λέγει· ποῦ ἐστιν τὸ κατάλυμά μου, ὅπου τὸ
πάσχα μετὰ τῶν μαθητῶν μου φάγω; [15] καὶ αὐτὸς ὑμῖν
δείξει ἀνάγαιον μέγα ἐστρωμένον ἕτοιμον, καὶ ἐκεῖ ἑτοιμάσατε ἡμῖν. [16] καὶ ἐξῆλθον οἱ μαθηταὶ καὶ ἦλθον εἰς
τὴν πόλιν καὶ εὗρον καθὼς εἶπεν αὐτοῖς, καὶ ἡτοίμασαν
τὸ πάσχα.

[17] Καὶ ὀψίας γενομένης ἔρχεται μετὰ τῶν δώδεκα.
[18] καὶ ἀνακειμένων αὐτῶν καὶ ἐσθιόντων ὁ Ἰησοῦς εἶπεν,
Ἀμὴν λέγω ὑμῖν ὅτι εἷς ἐξ ὑμῶν παραδώσει με, ὁ
ἐσθίων μετ᾽ ἐμοῦ. [19] ἤρξαντο λυπεῖσθαι καὶ λέγειν αὐτῷ
εἷς κατὰ εἷς, Μήτι ἐγώ; [20] ὁ δὲ εἶπεν αὐτοῖς, Εἷς τῶν
δώδεκα, ὁ ἐμβαπτόμενος μετ᾽ ἐμοῦ εἰς τὸ [ἓν] τρύβλιον.
[21] ὅτι ὁ μὲν υἱὸς τοῦ ἀνθρώπου ὑπάγει, καθὼς γέγραπται
περὶ αὐτοῦ· οὐαὶ δὲ τῷ ἀνθρώπῳ ἐκείνῳ δι᾽ οὗ ὁ
υἱὸς τοῦ ἀνθρώπου παραδίδοται· καλὸν [ἦν] αὐτῷ εἰ
οὐκ ἐγεννήθη ὁ ἄνθρωπος ἐκεῖνος. [22] Καὶ ἐσθιόντων
αὐτῶν λαβὼν ἄρτον εὐλογήσας ἔκλασεν καὶ ἔδωκεν
αὐτοῖς καὶ εἶπεν, Λάβετε· τοῦτό ἐστιν τὸ σῶμά μου.
[23] καὶ λαβὼν ποτήριον εὐχαριστήσας ἔδωκεν αὐτοῖς,
καὶ ἔπιον ἐξ αὐτοῦ πάντες. [24] καὶ εἶπεν αὐτοῖς, Τοῦτό
ἐστιν τὸ αἷμά μου τὸ τῆς διαθήκης τὸ ἐκχυννόμενον
ὑπὲρ πολλῶν. [25] ἀμὴν λέγω ὑμῖν ὅτι οὐκέτι οὐ μὴ πίω
ἐκ τοῦ γενήματος τῆς ἀμπέλου ἕως τῆς ἡμέρας ἐκείνης
ὅταν αὐτὸ πίνω καινὸν ἐν τῇ βασιλείᾳ τοῦ θεοῦ.

[26] Καὶ ὑμνήσαντες ἐξῆλθον εἰς τὸ ὄρος τῶν ἐλαιῶν.
[27] καὶ λέγει αὐτοῖς ὁ Ἰησοῦς ὅτι Πάντες σκανδαλισθή-
σεσθε, ὅτι γέγραπται, Πατάξω τὸν ποιμένα, καὶ τὰ

πρόβατα διασκορπισθήσονται. ²⁸ ἀλλὰ μετὰ τὸ ἐγερθῆναί με προάξω ὑμᾶς εἰς τὴν Γαλιλαίαν. ²⁹ ὁ δὲ Πέτρος ἔφη αὐτῷ, Εἰ καὶ πάντες σκανδαλισθήσονται, ἀλλ᾽ οὐκ ἐγώ. ³⁰ καὶ λέγει αὐτῷ ὁ Ἰησοῦς, Ἀμὴν λέγω σοι ὅτι σὺ σήμερον ταύτῃ τῇ νυκτὶ πρὶν ἢ δὶς ἀλέκτορα φωνῆσαι τρίς με ἀπαρνήσῃ. ³¹ ὁ δὲ ἐκπερισσῶς ἐλάλει, Ἐάν με δέῃ συναποθανεῖν σοι, οὐ μή σε ἀπαρνήσομαι. ὡσαύτως δὲ καὶ πάντες ἔλεγον.

³² Καὶ ἔρχονται εἰς χωρίον οὗ τὸ ὄνομα Γεθσημανεί, καὶ λέγει τοῖς μαθηταῖς αὐτοῦ, Καθίσατε ὧδε ἕως προσεύξωμαι. ³³ καὶ παραλαμβάνει τὸν Πέτρον καὶ Ἰάκωβον καὶ Ἰωάννην μετ᾽ αὐτοῦ, καὶ ἤρξατο ἐκθαμβεῖσθαι καὶ ἀδημονεῖν, ³⁴ καὶ λέγει αὐτοῖς, Περίλυπός ἐστιν ἡ ψυχή μου ἕως θανάτου· μείνατε ὧδε καὶ γρηγορεῖτε. ³⁵ καὶ προελθὼν μικρὸν ἔπιπτεν ἐπὶ τῆς γῆς, καὶ προσηύχετο ἵνα εἰ δυνατόν ἐστιν παρέλθῃ ἀπ᾽ αὐτοῦ ἡ ὥρα, ³⁶ καὶ ἔλεγεν, Ἀββᾶ ὁ πατήρ, πάντα δυνατά σοι· παρένεγκε τὸ ποτήριον τοῦτο ἀπ᾽ ἐμοῦ, ἀλλ᾽ οὐ τί ἐγὼ θέλω ἀλλὰ τί σύ. ³⁷ καὶ ἔρχεται καὶ εὑρίσκει αὐτοὺς καθεύδοντας, καὶ λέγει τῷ Πέτρῳ, Σίμων, καθεύδεις; οὐκ ἴσχυσας μίαν ὥραν γρηγορῆσαι; ³⁸ γρηγορεῖτε καὶ προσεύχεσθε, ἵνα μὴ εἰσέλθητε εἰς πειρασμόν. τὸ μὲν πνεῦμα πρόθυμον, ἡ δὲ σὰρξ ἀσθενής. ³⁹ καὶ πάλιν ἀπελθὼν προσηύξατο τὸν αὐτὸν λόγον εἰπών. ⁴⁰ καὶ ὑποστρέψας εὗρεν αὐτοὺς πάλιν καθεύδοντας· ἦσαν γὰρ οἱ ὀφθαλμοὶ αὐτῶν καταβαρυνόμενοι, καὶ οὐκ ᾔδεισαν τί ἀποκριθῶσιν αὐτῷ. ⁴¹ καὶ ἔρχεται τὸ τρίτον καὶ λέγει αὐτοῖς, Καθεύδετε τὸ λοιπὸν καὶ ἀναπαύεσθε· ἀπέχει· ἦλθεν ἡ ὥρα, ἰδοὺ παραδίδοται ὁ υἱὸς τοῦ ἀνθρώπου εἰς τὰς χεῖρας τῶν ἁμαρτωλῶν. ⁴² ἐγείρεσθε, ἄγωμεν· ἰδοὺ ὁ παραδιδούς με ἤγγικεν.

⁴³ Καὶ εὐθὺς ἔτι αὐτοῦ λαλοῦντος παραγίνεται Ἰούδας εἷς τῶν δώδεκα, καὶ μετ' αὐτοῦ ὄχλος μετὰ μαχαιρῶν καὶ ξύλων παρὰ τῶν ἀρχιερέων καὶ τῶν γραμματέων καὶ τῶν πρεσβυτέρων. ⁴⁴ δεδώκει δὲ ὁ παραδιδοὺς αὐτὸν σύσσημον αὐτοῖς λέγων, Ὃν ἂν φιλήσω, αὐτός ἐστιν· κρατήσατε αὐτὸν καὶ ἀπάγετε ἀσφαλῶς. ⁴⁵ καὶ ἐλθὼν εὐθὺς προσελθὼν αὐτῷ λέγει, Ῥαββεί, καὶ κατεφίλησεν αὐτόν· ⁴⁶ οἱ δὲ ἐπέβαλαν τὰς χεῖρας αὐτῷ καὶ ἐκράτησαν αὐτόν. ⁴⁷ εἷς δέ τις τῶν παρεστηκότων σπασάμενος τὴν μάχαιραν ἔπαισεν τὸν δοῦλον τοῦ ἀρχιερέως καὶ ἀφεῖλεν αὐτοῦ τὸ ὠτάριον. ⁴⁸ καὶ ἀποκριθεὶς ὁ Ἰησοῦς εἶπεν αὐτοῖς, Ὡς ἐπὶ λῃστὴν ἐξήλθατε μετὰ μαχαιρῶν καὶ ξύλων συλλαβεῖν με· ⁴⁹ καθ' ἡμέραν ἤμην πρὸς ὑμᾶς ἐν τῷ ἱερῷ διδάσκων, καὶ οὐκ ἐκρατήσατέ με· ἀλλ' ἵνα πληρωθῶσιν αἱ γραφαί. ⁵⁰ καὶ ἀφέντες αὐτὸν ἔφυγον πάντες. ⁵¹ καὶ νεανίσκος τις συνηκολούθει αὐτῷ περιβεβλημένος σινδόνα ἐπὶ γυμνοῦ, καὶ κρατοῦσιν αὐτόν· ⁵² ὁ δὲ καταλιπὼν τὴν σινδόνα γυμνὸς ἔφυγεν.

⁵³ Καὶ ἀπήγαγον τὸν Ἰησοῦν πρὸς τὸν ἀρχιερέα, καὶ συνέρχονται πάντες οἱ ἀρχιερεῖς καὶ οἱ πρεσβύτεροι καὶ οἱ γραμματεῖς. ⁵⁴ καὶ ὁ Πέτρος ἀπὸ μακρόθεν ἠκολούθησεν αὐτῷ ἕως ἔσω εἰς τὴν αὐλὴν τοῦ ἀρχιερέως, καὶ ἦν συνκαθήμενος μετὰ τῶν ὑπηρετῶν καὶ θερμαινόμενος πρὸς τὸ φῶς. ⁵⁵ οἱ δὲ ἀρχιερεῖς καὶ ὅλον τὸ συνέδριον ἐζήτουν κατὰ τοῦ Ἰησοῦ μαρτυρίαν εἰς τὸ θανατῶσαι αὐτόν, καὶ οὐχ εὕρισκον· ⁵⁶ πολλοὶ γὰρ ἐψευδομαρτύρουν κατ' αὐτοῦ, καὶ ἴσαι αἱ μαρτυρίαι οὐκ ἦσαν. ⁵⁷ καί τινες ἀναστάντες ἐψευδομαρτύρουν κατ' αὐτοῦ λέγοντες ⁵⁸ ὅτι Ἡμεῖς ἠκούσαμεν αὐτοῦ λέγοντος ὅτι ἐγὼ καταλύσω τὸν

ναὸν τοῦτον τὸν χειροποίητον καὶ διὰ τριῶν ἡμερῶν
ἄλλον ἀχειροποίητον οἰκοδομήσω. ⁵⁹ καὶ οὐδὲ οὕτως
ἴση ἦν ἡ μαρτυρία αὐτῶν. ⁶⁰ καὶ ἀναστὰς ὁ ἀρχιερεὺς
εἰς μέσον ἐπηρώτησεν τὸν Ἰησοῦν λέγων, Οὐκ ἀποκρίνῃ
οὐδέν; τί οὗτοί σου καταμαρτυροῦσιν; ⁶¹ ὁ δὲ ἐσιώπα
καὶ οὐκ ἀπεκρίνατο οὐδέν. πάλιν ὁ ἀρχιερεὺς ἐπηρώτα
αὐτὸν καὶ λέγει αὐτῷ, Σὺ εἶ ὁ Χριστὸς ὁ υἱὸς τοῦ
εὐλογητοῦ; ⁶² ὁ δὲ Ἰησοῦς εἶπεν, Ἐγώ εἰμι, καὶ
ὄψεσθε τὸν υἱὸν τοῦ ἀνθρώπου ἐκ δεξιῶν καθήμενον
τῆς δυνάμεως καὶ ἐρχόμενον μετὰ τῶν νεφελῶν τοῦ
οὐρανοῦ. ⁶³ ὁ δὲ ἀρχιερεὺς διαρήξας τοὺς χιτῶνας
αὐτοῦ λέγει, Τί ἔτι χρείαν ἔχομεν μαρτύρων; ⁶⁴ ἠκούσατε τῆς βλασφημίας· τί ὑμῖν φαίνεται; οἱ δὲ
πάντες κατέκριναν αὐτὸν ἔνοχον εἶναι θανάτου. ⁶⁵ καὶ
ἤρξαντό τινες ἐμπτύειν αὐτῷ καὶ περικαλύπτειν αὐτοῦ τὸ πρόσωπον καὶ κολαφίζειν αὐτὸν καὶ λέγειν
αὐτῷ, Προφήτευσον, καὶ οἱ ὑπηρέται ῥαπίσμασιν αὐτὸν
ἔλαβον.

⁶⁶ Καὶ ὄντος τοῦ Πέτρου κάτω ἐν τῇ αὐλῇ ἔρχεται
μία τῶν παιδισκῶν τοῦ ἀρχιερέως, ⁶⁷ καὶ ἰδοῦσα τὸν
Πέτρον θερμαινόμενον ἐμβλέψασα αὐτῷ λέγει, Καὶ σὺ
μετὰ τοῦ Ναζαρηνοῦ ἦσθα τοῦ Ἰησοῦ. ⁶⁸ ὁ δὲ ἠρνήσατο
λέγων, Οὔτε οἶδα οὔτε ἐπίσταμαι σὺ τί λέγεις. καὶ
ἐξῆλθεν ἔξω εἰς τὸ προαύλιον. ⁶⁹ καὶ ἡ παιδίσκη
ἰδοῦσα αὐτὸν ἤρξατο πάλιν λέγειν τοῖς παρεστῶσιν
ὅτι Οὗτος ἐξ αὐτῶν ἐστίν. ⁷⁰ ὁ δὲ παλιν ἠρνεῖτο. καὶ
μετὰ μικρὸν πάλιν οἱ παρεστῶτες ἔλεγον τῷ Πέτρῳ,
Ἀληθῶς ἐξ αὐτῶν εἶ· καὶ γὰρ Γαλιλαῖος εἶ. ⁷¹ ὁ δὲ
ἤρξατο ἀναθεματίζειν καὶ ὀμνύναι ὅτι Οὐκ οἶδα τὸν
ἄνθρωπον τοῦτον ὃν λέγετε. ⁷² καὶ εὐθὺς ἐκ δευτέρου
ἀλέκτωρ ἐφώνησεν. καὶ ἀνεμνήσθη ὁ Πέτρος τὸ ῥῆμα

ὡς εἶπεν αὐτῷ ὁ Ἰησοῦς ὅτι Πρὶν ἀλέκτορα φωνῆσαι δὶς
τρίς με ἀπαρνήσῃ. καὶ ἐπιβαλὼν ἔκλαιεν.

15 ¹ Καὶ εὐθὺς πρωῒ συμβούλιον ποιήσαντες οἱ
ἀρχιερεῖς μετὰ τῶν πρεσβυτέρων καὶ γραμματέων καὶ
ὅλον τὸ συνέδριον, δήσαντες τὸν Ἰησοῦν ἀπήνεγκαν
καὶ παρέδωκαν Πειλάτῳ. ² καὶ ἐπηρώτησεν αὐτὸν ὁ
Πειλᾶτος, Σὺ εἶ ὁ βασιλεὺς τῶν Ἰουδαίων; ὁ δὲ ἀποκριθεὶς αὐτῷ λέγει, Σὺ λέγεις. ³ καὶ κατηγόρουν αὐτοῦ
οἱ ἀρχιερεῖς πολλά. ⁴ ὁ δὲ Πειλᾶτος πάλιν ἐπηρώτα αὐτόν, λέγων, Οὐκ ἀποκρίνῃ οὐδέν; ἴδε πόσα σου κατηγοροῦσιν. ⁵ ὁ δὲ Ἰησοῦς οὐκέτι οὐδὲν ἀπεκρίθη, ὥστε θαυμάζειν
τὸν Πειλᾶτον. ⁶ κατὰ δὲ ἑορτὴν ἀπέλυεν αὐτοῖς ἕνα δέσ-
μιον ὃν παρῃτοῦντο. ⁷ ἦν δὲ ὁ λεγόμενος Βαραββᾶς μετὰ
τῶν στασιαστῶν δεδεμένος, οἵτινες ἐν τῇ στάσει φόνον
πεποιήκεισαν. ⁸ καὶ ἀναβὰς ὁ ὄχλος ἤρξατο αἰτεῖσθαι
καθὼς ἀεὶ ἐποίει αὐτοῖς. ⁹ ὁ δὲ Πειλᾶτος ἀπεκρίθη αὐτοῖς
λέγων, Θέλετε ἀπολύσω ὑμῖν τὸν βασιλέα τῶν Ἰουδαίων;
¹⁰ ἐγίνωσκεν γὰρ ὅτι διὰ φθόνον παραδεδώκεισαν αὐτὸν
οἱ ἀρχιερεῖς. ¹¹ οἱ δὲ ἀρχιερεῖς ἀνέσεισαν τὸν ὄχλον
ἵνα μᾶλλον τὸν Βαραββᾶν ἀπολύσῃ αὐτοῖς. ¹² ὁ δὲ
Πειλᾶτος πάλιν ἀποκριθεὶς ἔλεγεν αὐτοῖς, Τί οὖν
ποιήσω ὃν λέγετε τὸν βασιλέα· τῶν Ἰουδαίων; ¹³ οἱ δὲ
πάλιν ἔκραξαν, Σταύρωσον αὐτόν. ¹⁴ ὁ δὲ Πειλᾶτος
ἔλεγεν αὐτοῖς, Τί γὰρ ἐποίησεν κακόν; οἱ δὲ περισσῶς
ἔκραξαν, Σταύρωσον αὐτόν. ¹⁵ ὁ δὲ Πειλᾶτος βουλό-
μενος τῷ ὄχλῳ τὸ ἱκανὸν ποιῆσαι ἀπέλυσεν αὐτοῖς τὸν
Βαραββᾶν, καὶ παρέδωκεν τὸν Ἰησοῦν φραγελλώσας
ἵνα σταυρωθῇ.

¹⁶ Οἱ δὲ στρατιῶται ἀπήγαγον αὐτὸν ἔσω τῆς αὐλῆς,
ὅ ἐστιν πραιτώριον, καὶ συνκαλοῦσιν ὅλην τὴν σπεῖραν·
¹⁷ καὶ ἐνδιδύσκουσιν αὐτὸν πορφύραν καὶ περιτιθέασιν

αὐτῷ πλέξαντες ἀκάνθινον στέφανον· [18] καὶ ἤρξαντο
ἀσπάζεσθαι αὐτόν, Χαῖρε βασιλεῦ τῶν Ἰουδαίων·
[19] καὶ ἔτυπτον αὐτοῦ τὴν κεφαλὴν καλάμῳ καὶ ἐνέ-
πτυον αὐτῷ, καὶ τιθέντες τὰ γόνατα προσεκύνουν αὐτῷ.
[20] καὶ ὅτε ἐνέπαιξαν αὐτῷ, ἐξέδυσαν αὐτὸν τὴν πορφύραν καὶ ἐνέδυσαν αὐτὸν τὰ ἱμάτια αὐτοῦ. καὶ ἐξάγουσιν αὐτὸν ἵνα σταυρώσωσιν αὐτόν. [21] καὶ ἀγγαρεύουσιν παράγοντά τινα Σίμωνα Κυρηναῖον, ἐρχόμενον
ἀπ᾽ ἀγροῦ, τὸν πατέρα Ἀλεξάνδρου καὶ Ῥούφου, ἵνα
ἄρῃ τὸν σταυρὸν αὐτοῦ. [22] καὶ φέρουσιν αὐτὸν ἐπὶ τὸν
Γολγοθᾶν τόπον, ὅ ἐστιν μεθερμηνευόμενον, Κρανίου
τόπος. [23] καὶ ἐδίδουν αὐτῷ ἐσμυρνισμένον οἶνον· ὃς δὲ
οὐκ ἔλαβεν. [24] καὶ σταυροῦσιν αὐτόν, καὶ διαμερίζονται
τὰ ἱμάτια αὐτοῦ, βάλλοντες κλῆρον ἐπ᾽ αὐτὰ τίς τί ἄρῃ.
[25] Ἦν δὲ ὥρα τρίτη καὶ ἐσταύρωσαν αὐτόν. [26] καὶ
ἦν ἡ ἐπιγραφὴ τῆς αἰτίας αὐτοῦ ἐπιγεγραμμένη, Ὁ
βασιλεὺς τῶν Ἰουδαίων.
[27] Καὶ σὺν αὐτῷ σταυροῦσιν δύο λῃστάς, ἕνα ἐκ δεξιῶν
καὶ ἕνα ἐξ εὐωνύμων αὐτοῦ.* [29] καὶ οἱ παραπορευόμενοι
ἐβλασφήμουν αὐτὸν κινοῦντες τὰς κεφαλὰς αὐτῶν καὶ
λέγοντες, Οὐὰ ὁ καταλύων τὸν ναὸν καὶ οἰκοδομῶν τρισὶν
ἡμέραις, [30] σῶσον σεαυτὸν καταβὰς ἀπὸ τοῦ σταυροῦ.
[31] ὁμοίως καὶ οἱ ἀρχιερεῖς ἐμπαίζοντες πρὸς ἀλλήλους
μετὰ τῶν γραμματέων ἔλεγον, Ἄλλους ἔσωσεν, ἑαυτὸν
οὐ δύναται σῶσαι· [32] ὁ Χριστὸς ὁ βασιλεὺς Ἰσραήλ,
καταβάτω νῦν ἀπὸ τοῦ σταυροῦ, ἵνα ἴδωμεν καὶ πιστεύ-
σωμεν. καὶ οἱ συνεσταυρωμένοι αὐτῷ ὠνείδιζον αὐτόν. [33] καὶ γενομένης ὥρας ἕκτης σκότος ἐγένετο ἐφ᾽ ὅλην
τὴν γῆν ἕως ὥρας ἐνάτης. [34] καὶ τῇ ἐνάτῃ ὥρᾳ ἐβόησεν
ὁ Ἰησοῦς φωνῇ μεγάλῃ, Ἐλωί ἐλωί λαμὰ σαβαχθανεί, ὅ

* Verse 28 omitted on the best MSS. authority.

ἐστιν μεθερμηνευόμενον, Ὁ θεός μου ὁ θεός μου, εἰς τί ἐγκατέλιπές με ; ³⁵ καί τινες τῶν παρεστηκότων ἀκούσαντες ἔλεγον, Ἴδε Ἠλείαν φωνεῖ. ³⁶ δραμὼν δέ τις καὶ γεμίσας σπόγγον ὄξους περιθεὶς καλάμῳ ἐπότιζεν αὐτόν, λέγων, Ἄφετε ἴδωμεν εἰ ἔρχεται Ἠλείας καθελεῖν αὐτόν. ³⁷ ὁ δὲ Ἰησοῦς ἀφεὶς φωνὴν μεγάλην ἐξέπνευσεν. ³⁸ καὶ τὸ καταπέτασμα τοῦ ναοῦ ἐσχίσθη εἰς δύο ἀπ' ἄνωθεν ἕως κάτω.

³⁹ Ἰδὼν δὲ ὁ κεντυρίων ὁ παρεστηκὼς ἐξ ἐναντίας αὐτοῦ ὅτι οὕτως ἐξέπνευσεν, εἶπεν, Ἀληθῶς οὗτος ὁ ἄνθρωπος υἱὸς ἦν θεοῦ. ⁴⁰ ἦσαν δὲ καὶ γυναῖκες ἀπὸ μακρόθεν θεωροῦσαι, ἐν αἷς καὶ Μαρία ἡ Μαγδαληνὴ καὶ Μαρία ἡ Ἰακώβου τοῦ μικροῦ καὶ Ἰωσῆτος μήτηρ καὶ Σαλώμη, ⁴¹ αἳ ὅτε ἦν ἐν τῇ Γαλιλαίᾳ ἠκολούθουν αὐτῷ καὶ διηκόνουν αὐτῷ, καὶ ἄλλαι πολλαὶ αἱ συναναβᾶσαι αὐτῷ εἰς Ἱεροσόλυμα.

⁴² Καὶ ἤδη ὀψίας γενομένης, ἐπεὶ ἦν παρασκευή, ὅ ἐστιν προσάββατον, ⁴³ ἐλθὼν Ἰωσὴφ ὁ ἀπὸ Ἀριμαθαίας, εὐσχήμων βουλευτής, ὃς καὶ αὐτὸς ἦν προσδεχόμενος τὴν βασιλείαν τοῦ θεοῦ, τολμήσας εἰσῆλθεν πρὸς τὸν Πειλᾶτον καὶ ᾐτήσατο τὸ σῶμα τοῦ Ἰησοῦ. ⁴⁴ ὁ δὲ Πειλᾶτος ἐθαύμασεν εἰ ἤδη τέθνηκεν, καὶ προσκαλεσάμενος τὸν κεντυρίωνα ἐπηρώτησεν αὐτὸν εἰ ἤδη ἀπέθανεν· ⁴⁵ καὶ γνοὺς ἀπὸ τοῦ κεντυρίωνος ἐδωρήσατο τὸ πτῶμα τῷ Ἰωσήφ. ⁴⁶ καὶ ἀγοράσας σινδόνα, καθελὼν αὐτὸν ἐνείλησεν τῇ σινδόνι καὶ ἔθηκεν αὐτὸν ἐν μνημείῳ ὃ ἦν λελατομημένον ἐκ πέτρας, καὶ προσεκύλισεν λίθον ἐπὶ τὴν θύραν τοῦ μνημείου. ⁴⁷ ἡ δὲ Μαρία ἡ Μαγδαληνὴ καὶ Μαρία ἡ Ἰωσῆτος ἐθεώρουν ποῦ τέθειται.

16 ¹ Καὶ διαγενομένου τοῦ σαββάτου Μαρία ἡ Μαγδαληνὴ καὶ Μαρία ἡ Ἰακώβου καὶ Σαλώμη ἠγό-

ρασαν ἀρώματα, ἵνα ἐλθοῦσαι ἀλείψωσιν αὐτόν. ² καὶ
λίαν πρωῒ τῇ μιᾷ τῶν σαββάτων ἔρχονται ἐπὶ τὸ
μνημεῖον, ἀνατείλαντος τοῦ ἡλίου. ³ καὶ ἔλεγον πρὸς
ἑαυτάς, Τίς ἀποκυλίσει ἡμῖν τὸν λίθον ἐκ τῆς θύρας
τοῦ μνημείου ; ⁴ καὶ ἀναβλέψασαι θεωροῦσιν ὅτι ἀνακεκύλισται ὁ λίθος· ἦν γὰρ μέγας σφόδρα. ⁵ καὶ εἰσελ-
θοῦσαι εἰς τὸ μνημεῖον εἶδον νεανίσκον καθήμενον ἐν
τοῖς δεξιοῖς περιβεβλημένον στολὴν λευκήν, καὶ ἐξεθαμβήθησαν. ⁶ ὁ δὲ λέγει αὐταῖς, Μὴ ἐκθαμβεῖσθε.
Ἰησοῦν ζητεῖτε τὸν Ναζαρηνὸν τὸν ἐσταυρωμένον·
ἠγέρθη, οὐκ ἔστιν ὧδε· ἴδε ὁ τόπος ὅπου ἔθηκαν αὐτόν.
⁷ ἀλλὰ ὑπάγετε εἴπατε τοῖς μαθηταῖς αὐτοῦ καὶ τῷ
Πέτρῳ ὅτι Προάγει ὑμᾶς εἰς τὴν Γαλιλαίαν· ἐκεῖ αὐτὸν
ὄψεσθε, καθὼς εἶπεν ὑμῖν. ⁸ καὶ ἐξελθοῦσαι ἔφυγον ἀπὸ
τοῦ μνημείου· εἶχεν γὰρ αὐτὰς τρόμος καὶ ἔκστασις,
καὶ οὐδενὶ οὐδὲν εἶπον· ἐφοβοῦντο γάρ.   ⁘   *

⁹[Ἀναστὰς δὲ πρωῒ πρώτῃ σαββάτου ἐφάνη πρῶτον
Μαρίᾳ τῇ Μαγδαληνῇ, παρ᾽ ἧς ἐκβεβλήκει ἑπτὰ δαιμόνια. ¹⁰ ἐκείνη πορευθεῖσα ἀπήγγειλεν τοῖς μετ᾽ αὐτοῦ
γενομένοις, πενθοῦσιν καὶ κλαίουσιν. ¹¹ κἀκεῖνοι ἀκούσαντες ὅτι ζῇ καὶ ἐθεάθη ὑπ᾽ αὐτῆς ἠπίστησαν.
¹² Μετὰ δὲ ταῦτα δυσὶν ἐξ αὐτῶν περιπατοῦσιν ἐφανερώθη ἐν ἑτέρᾳ μορφῇ, πορευομένοις εἰς ἀγρόν. ¹³ κἀκεῖνοι
ἀπελθόντες ἀπήγγειλαν τοῖς λοιποῖς· οὐδὲ ἐκείνοις
ἐπίστευσαν.
¹⁴Ὕστερον ἀνακειμένοις αὐτοῖς τοῖς ἔνδεκα ἐφανερώθη, καὶ ὠνείδισεν τὴν ἀπιστίαν αὐτῶν καὶ σκληροκαρδίαν, ὅτι τοῖς θεασαμένοις αὐτὸν ἐγηγερμένον
οὐκ ἐπίστευσαν. ¹⁵ καὶ εἶπεν αὐτοῖς, Πορευθέντες εἰς
τὸν κόσμον ἅπαντα κηρύξατε τὸ εὐαγγέλιον πάσῃ τῇ

κτίσει. ¹⁶ ὁ πιστεύσας καὶ βαπτισθεὶς σωθήσεται, ὁ δὲ ἀπιστήσας κατακριθήσεται. ¹⁷ σημεῖα δὲ τοῖς πιστεύσασιν ταῦτα παρακολουθήσει· ἐν τῷ ὀνόματί μου δαιμόνια ἐκβαλοῦσιν, γλώσσαις λαλήσουσιν [καιναῖς], ¹⁸ ὄφεις ἀροῦσιν, κἂν θανάσιμόν τι πίωσιν οὐ μὴ αὐτοὺς βλάψῃ, ἐπὶ ἀρρώστους χεῖρας ἐπιθήσουσιν καὶ καλῶς ἕξουσιν.

¹⁹ Ὁ μὲν οὖν κύριος Ἰησοῦς μετὰ τὸ λαλῆσαι αὐτοῖς ἀνελήμφθη εἰς τὸν οὐρανὸν καὶ ἐκάθισεν ἐκ δεξιῶν τοῦ θεοῦ· ²⁰ ἐκεῖνοι δὲ ἐξελθόντες ἐκήρυξαν πανταχοῦ, τοῦ κυρίου συνεργοῦντος καὶ τὸν λόγον βεβαιοῦντος διὰ τῶν ἐπακολουθούντων σημείων.]

NOTES

In the remarks on the results of textual revision prefixed to the Notes on each chapter, special attention has been paid to those cases in which differences between the A.V. and the R.V. depend upon differences of reading.

CHAPTER I.

The title of the Gospel exists in various forms, none of which can be part of the original autograph. No Evangelist would write such a heading ; least of all would the earliest Evangelist do so. These titles point to a time when the Gospels had already been collected into one volume, with the general title Εὐαγγέλιον. The earliest form of the title is the simplest; κατὰ Μᾶρκον (ℵBF), *secundum Marcum*, or, in some Latin MSS., *cata Marc.* (so *Codex Bobiensis*, one of the most important Old Latin MSS.). Other forms are εὐαγγέλιον κατὰ Μᾶρκον (ADEH), τὸ κατὰ M. ἅγιον εὐαγγ. (some cursives) and ἐκ τοῦ κατὰ M. ἁγίου εὐαγγ. (69).

The κατά implies conformity to a type, without necessarily asserting authorship ; but the Christians of the first four centuries who affixed these titles believed that each Gospel was written by the Evangelist whose name they affixed. Had they intended the κατά to mean no more than "according to the teaching of," this Gospel would have been called κατὰ Πέτρον, for it was commonly held that Mark wrote according to the teaching of Peter.

1. υἱοῦ θεοῦ (ℵᵃBDL), υἱοῦ τοῦ θεοῦ (AEFHKM etc.), Latt. Syrr. Memph. Arm. Goth. Aeth., Iren-lat. ⅔ Amb. Aug. Omit ℵ* 28 (omits Χριστοῦ also) 255, Iren-lat. ⅓, Orig. Bas. "The evidence for omission is weighty but meagre" (Swete). "Neither reading can be safely rejected" (W.H.). Mk uses the expressions υἱὸς θεοῦ and ὁ υἱὸς τ. θ. (iii. 11, v. 7, xv. 39 ; cf. i. 11, ix. 7, xiv. 61). But it is difficult to believe that any scribe or editor would omit the words ; and viii. 29, compared with Mt. xvi. 16 and Lk. ix. 20, supports the shorter reading. On the other hand xv. 39 may look back to this.

2. ἐν τῷ 'Ησαΐᾳ τῷ προφήτῃ (אBDLΔ 33, Latt. Syrr. Memph. Goth.) rather than ἐν τοῖς προφήταις (AEFHKM etc., Aeth.), which is an obvious correction. For a similar reason Bas. Epiph. Victorin. omit 'Ιδού...τὴν ὁδόν σου, as not being in Isaiah.

4. B 33 omit καί before κηρύσσων.

6. The form ἔσθων (אBL* 33) is freq. in the B text of LXX.

8. Many texts (ADP etc.) insert ἐν before ὕδατι and before πνεύματι ἁγίῳ. The evidence for the latter insertion is stronger than that for the former, but in neither should it be made. R.V. retains ἐν in both places.

10. εὐθύς (אBLΔ 33), not εὐθέως (APΛΠ), is the form used in Mk. So in vv. 18, 21, 29, etc. Elsewhere in N.T. εὐθέως is more freq. ἐκ τοῦ ὕδατος (אBDL 33) rather than ἀπὸ τ. ὕδ. (APΓΔΠ). εἰς αὐτόν (BD) rather than ἐπ' αὐτόν (אALP etc.). אΔ insert καὶ μένον after καταβαῖνον (from Jn i. 33).

11. ἐν σοί (אBDLP 33) rather than ἐν ᾧ (AΓH) ; cf. Mt. iii. 17.

14. καὶ μετά (BD) rather than μετὰ δέ (אAL). Mk throughout prefers καί to δέ. So v. 28, ii. 5, ix. 9, x. 42, xi. 4, 8, xii. 3, 14, xiii. 11, 12, xv. 33. Contrast vii. 24, x. 32. אBL 33 omit τῆς βασιλείας.

16. καὶ παράγων (אBDL 33) rather than περιπατῶν δέ (AΓΔΠ) ; cf. Mt. iv. 18. ἀμφιβάλλοντας (אABDE) rather than βάλλοντας ἀμφίβληστρον (AΓΔΠ); cf. Mt. iv. 18.

21. Καφαρναούμ (אBDΔ 33) rather than the softer Καπερναούμ (ACLΓΠ). אCLΔ, Syr-Sin. Syr-Pesh. Memph., Orig. omit εἰσελθών. Syr-Sin. omits καὶ εἰσπορεύονται εἰς Καφ.

23. εὐθύς (אBL 33, Memph., Orig.) may be retained, although ACD, Syr-Sin., and many other authorities omit.

24. Ἔα (א³ACLΓΔΠ) is an interpolation from Lk. iv. 34; א*BD, Latt. Syr-Sin. Syr-Pesh. Memph. omit.

27. Τί ἐστιν τοῦτο; διδαχὴ καινή (אBL 33). These abrupt sentences have been smoothed in different ways in A and C and other texts.

29. For ἐξελθὼν ἦλθεν (BD good cursives, f g Arm. Aeth.) many witnesses have ἐξελθόντες ἦλθον.

34. Χριστὸν εἶναι (BLΣ 33, Syr-Hark. Arm. Memph. Aeth.) is powerfully supported (τὸν Χν εἶναι, א°GM), but א*ADEF etc., Latt. Syr-Sin. Syr-Pesh. Goth. omit. It may come from Lk. iv. 41.

39. ἦλθεν (אBL) rather than ἦν (ACDΓΔ) ; cf. Lk. iv. 44.

1—8. Preparatory Ministry of the Baptizer.

Mt. iii. 1—12.   Lk. iii. 1—6.   Cf. Jn i. 6—31.

1. Ἀρχή τ. εὐαγγελίου Ἰησοῦ Χριστοῦ.   This superscription
is probably original; *The beginning of the good tidings about Jesus
Christ* (Acts v. 42; Gal. i. 16; cf. Mt. iv. 23); or possibly, *brought
by Jesus Christ.* Indeed, both may be meant; see on *v.* 14. But
the dominant meaning is that He is the subject of the glad tidings;
all that is known about Christ is the good news for every human
being. See how St Paul sums up the Gospel which he preached,
1 Cor. xv. 3, 4. Χριστοῦ is here a proper name and has no art. Cf.
Enoch xlviii. 10, lii. 4.

If ἀρχή = ἄρχεται, *Here begins the Gospel*, we must suppose that
the superscription has been added by a later editor; for (1) this
formula is not found in the oldest MSS.; (2) it implies that some
other document precedes the one which now begins, *e.g.* another
Gospel; (3) it implies that εὐαγγέλιον means the *record* of the good
news.   Zahn, *Intr. to N.T.* ii. pp. 456 f.

Εὐαγγέλιον (8 times in Mk, 4 in Mt., not in Lk. or Jn, but very
freq. in Paul) is neither "a reward for good tidings" (in which sense
the plur. is usual both in class. Grk and in LXX.), nor "a written
narrative" (a meaning nowhere found in N.T.), but the "message
of salvation" (Acts xx. 24; Gal. ii. 2, 5; Eph. vi. 15; etc.).

A full stop at the end of the verse is right. Attempts to connect
it in construction with any of the three verses which follow may be
safely rejected.   The Greek of Mark is not literary and he rarely
deals in periodic sentences. It is not likely that he would begin with
a complicated construction.

υἱοῦ θεοῦ.   The words may be accepted as possibly genuine (see
critical note); but they are just such as an early scribe would be
likely to add to the superscription of a Gospel. They proclaim the
Messiahship of Jesus Christ, not His metaphysical relationship to
the Father. Mk is anxious to make clear the Messiahship. The
confession of the centurion is recorded as Gentile testimony to the
truth of the theme of this Gospel, "Truly this man was the Son of
God." There, as here, neither word has the article (xv. 39). Mt.,
writing for Jews, is concerned with showing that Jesus is the Son
of David and the Son of Abraham (i. 1). The close of the Fourth
Gospel (Jn xx. 31) is similar in import to what we have here.

This verse forms a heading for the whole book, not for i. 2—13
only. No other headings follow. The life of the Messiah from the
Preaching of the Baptist to the Resurrection was the *beginning* of

the glad tidings, which spread rapidly and widely during the years between the Resurrection and the time of writing. While Mt. begins his record with the pedigree and nativity of the Messiah, Lk. with the parentage and nativity of the Forerunner, and Jn with the pre-existence of the Messiah, Mk begins with the public work of the Forerunner. This at once is evidence that he gives us a very early tradition, to which these prefaces had not yet been added.

Spitta, however, contends that Mk is defective, not only at the end but at the beginning. He regards *v.* 1 as a heading supplied by a later hand after the original beginning of the Gospel had been lost; and he thinks that before *v.* 2 there once stood a page or two containing the Nativity and childhood (*Lücken im Markusevangelium*, pp. 115—122).

2. **καθὼς γέγραπται.** *Even as it stands written.* The difference between καθώς and ὡς (which many texts have here) is worth noting, and γέγραπται has the full force of the Greek perf., abiding result of past action. This formula of quotation (ix. 13, xiv. 21) is freq. in LXX. and N.T., esp. in the Pauline Epp. In the Hellenistic world, γέγραπται was "the formula with which people referred to the terms of an unalterable agreement" (Deissmann, *St Paul*, p. 103, *Bible Studies*, pp. 112, 249). The καθώς has *v.* 4 as its real apodosis, and the meaning is that John's preaching was an exact fulfilment of prophecy, and therefore a confirmation of the Messiahship of Jesus.

ἐν τῷ Ἡσαΐᾳ τῷ προφήτῃ. See critical note. As Origen points out, the words which follow are a conflation of two prophecies, Mal. iii. 1 and Is. xl. 3. Here Mt. and Lk. agree against Mk in quoting Isaiah only, the Malachi prophecy being given in a different connexion (Mt. xi. 10; Lk. vii. 97). All three Evangelists illustrate the facility with which N.T. writers transfer words, which in the O.T. refer to Jehovah, to Christ. In Malachi, Jehovah speaks of Himself, here of His Son. It was one of Porphyry's criticisms that the attributing of both prophecies to Isaiah was a blunder. It may be due to lapse of memory. But collections of Messianic texts seem to have been common, and Mk may be quoting from one in which a series of texts from Isaiah was preceded by this one from Malachi, and he may not have noticed the change of author. The existence of such collections is indicated by the fact that the same combinations of texts are found in different writers. Hatch, *Essays in Bibl. Grk*, p. 204. Nowhere else does Mk himself quote Scripture (xv. 28 is not genuine), for the O.T. would not greatly interest Gentile readers. Where the O.T. is quoted by others, there is generally fairly close agreement with LXX., but with the text of *cod.* A rather than with that of our oldest uncial B. Here there are several divergences, LXX. having ἰδοὺ ἐξαποστέλλω τ. ἄγγ. μου, καὶ ἐπιβλέψεται ὁδὸν πρὸ προσώπου μου. In all three Synoptists the first half of the quotation seems to be influenced by Exod. xxiii. 20, καὶ ἰδοὺ ἐγὼ ἀποστέλλω τ. ἄγγ. μου πρὸ προσώπου σου, ἵνα φυλάξῃ σε ἐν τῇ ὁδῷ.

3. Here the only variation from LXX. is αὐτοῦ instead of τοῦ θεοῦ ἡμῶν, a change which allows Κυρίου to be understood of the Messiah. We may take ἐν τῇ ἐρήμῳ with ἑτοιμάσατε, but the usual connexion with βοῶντος is probably correct. The imagery is taken from the practice of eastern conquerors, who sent heralds to tell the nations through which they were about to pass to prepare a "king's highway" by levelling ground and straightening roads. John prepared the way by inviting all men to prepare it. Mt. and Lk. again agree against Mk in placing the quotation from Is. xl. 3 *after* the appearance of the Baptist, not before, as here. See Hawkins, *Horae Synopticae*[2], pp. 210 f. ; Burkitt, *The Gospel History*, pp. 40—58. The application of the prophecy to the Baptist was made by himself (Jn i. 23). Place only a comma at the end of *v.* 3 (W.H.).

4. ἐγένετο Ἰωάννης ὁ βαπτίζων ἐν τῇ ἐρήμῳ. *There came John the Baptizer in the wilderness.* This is the apodosis of καθὼς γέγραπται: in exact accordance with written prediction, John *arose* in the wilderness, *i.e.* the uninhabited part of the valley of the Jordan. The preaching of the Baptist is just the point at which a Gospel influenced by Peter might be expected to begin. Peter would remember it well. Mk alone uses ὁ βαπτίζων (vi. 14, 24) as well as ὁ βαπτιστής (vi. 25, viii. 28), and the difference, though slight, is worth marking in translation ; cf. ὁ καταλύων τὸν ναόν, "the Temple-destroyer" (Mt. xxvii. 40), and ὁ διώκων ἡμᾶς ποτέ, "our former persecutor" (Gal. i. 23). Josephus (*Vita*, 2) tells us that as a lad he imitated one Banus, who lived in the wilderness and got his food and clothing from what grew on trees.

καὶ κηρύσσων. If with all uncials, except B, and all ancient versions we read καί before κηρύσσων, the ὁ belongs to both participles ; "There arose in the wilderness John the Baptizer and the Preacher, etc." All four Gospels give the historical relation between Jesus and John as the starting-point of the Gospel narrative. On Ἰωάνης or Ἰωάννης see W.H. *App.* p. 159.

βάπτισμα μετανοίας. Cf. Lk. iii. 3 ; Acts xiii. 24, xix. 4. The gen. is equivalent to an adjective, "repentance-baptism," baptism which implied and symbolized a "change of mind" as regards both past and future ; and if real repentance was there, forgiveness

followed. This is in favour of taking εἰς ἄφεσιν ἁμαρτιῶν with
βάπτισμα rather than with μετανοίας (Acts ii. 38, xxii. 16). To
preach repentance-baptism means to proclaim the value of baptism
as a seal of repentance, a pledge of a new life; and the purpose (εἰς)
was to assure those who accepted such baptism that by repentance
they could be delivered from the penalty and the bondage of sin.
Some Jews believed that it was the sins of the nation that delayed
the coming of the Messiah. Nowhere else does Mk use μετάνοια, and
he has μετανοέω only twice (i. 15, vi. 12). In Lk. and Acts both noun
and verb are freq., but neither is found in Jn. In LXX., as in
class. Grk, μετάνοια is rare (Prov. xiv. 15; Wisd. xi. 23, xii. 10, 19;
Ecclus. xliv. 16). Neither βάπτισμα nor -μός is found in LXX., nor
is ἄφεσις with the meaning of "forgiveness." The language here
may be influenced by Christian phraseology. On ἄφεσις see Trench,
N.T. Syn. § xxxiii.; Cremer, *Lex.* p. 297.

The description of the Baptist by Josephus (*Ant.* xviii. v. 2)
should be compared with this. Evidently each is independent of the
other.

5. ἐξεπορεύετο...ἐβαπτίζοντο. Both actions went on continually.
The latter verb is passive (i. 9, viii. 3), not middle (Acts xxii. 16;
1 Cor. x. 2).

πᾶσα...πάντες. Popular hyperbole, which misleads no one, cf.
v. 37. But it is difficult for us to estimate the enthusiasm caused by
the hope that, after centuries of silence, Jehovah was again speaking
to His people through a Prophet. Most of the people regarded John
as a Prophet, most of the hierarchy did not; but the hierarchy did
not dare to avow their denial openly (xi. 27—33). Mark at the time
of John's preaching was quite old enough to remember the excitement, and he was living in Jerusalem. He may here be giving his
own recollections.

ἡ Ἰουδαία χώρα. Elsewhere Mk says simply ἡ Ἰουδαία (iii. 7,
x. 1, xiii. 14). Judaea proper is meant, not the whole of Palestine.

Ἰεροσολυμεῖται. Smooth breathing; the aspirate has come from
a mistaken connexion with ἱερός. So also in Ἰεροσόλυμα. See on
x. 32.

ἐβαπτίζοντο. *Were one after another baptized.*

ἐξομολογούμενοι. *Confessing right out, in full and openly.* Not
classical, and rare in late Grk, except in LXX. and N.T. See on
Jn i. 9. The meaning may be "*thereby* confessing their sins";
their asking for baptism was *ipso facto* a confession of sin. More
probably it means that they there and then made an acknowledgment
in words. Cf. Acts xix. 18; Jas. v. 16. In LXX. it commonly means

"giving praise"; cf. Lk. x. 21; Rom. xiv. 11, xv. 9. The two meanings are connected, Josh. vii. 19, Δὸς δόξαν τῷ κυρίῳ καὶ δὸς τὴν ἐξομολόγησιν, when Joshua urges Achan to confess his guilt. See also LXX. of Dan. ix. 20. Here, as in *vv.* 13, 39, ii. 23, iii. 1, we have an important fact expressed by a participle attached to the finite verb.

6. ἦν ἐνδεδυμένος. The periphrastic tense, freq. in Lk., is not rare in Mk (*v.* 33, ii. 6, v. 5, ix. 4, x. 32, xiii. 13, 23, xv. 43). Cloth was made of camel's hair, and either this or a camel's skin may be meant. It is probable that actual locusts (Lev. xi. 22) and honey made by wild bees (Deut. xxxii. 13) are meant. The wilderness food was in harmony with the rough dress. This picture of the Baptist is the more remarkable because there is no corresponding picture of the Christ. But it is an exaggeration to say that we have a clear picture of John, but not of Jesus. There is uncertainty about the unusual dress and unusual food of John. Jesus wore the usual dress and ate the usual food. We know the details of neither. John perhaps deliberately imitated Elijah, in order to teach the people that he was a Prophet (2 Kings i. 8; cf. Zech. xiii. 4); but the suddenness with which he appears in Mk, Mt. and Jn, like Elijah in 1 Kings xvii. 1, cannot be his doing. It is neither said nor implied that it was his asceticism which attracted such crowds; the belief that he was a Prophet did that.

7. ἐκήρυσσεν. Mk alone has this imperf. of continued action, which fits on well to ἦν ἐνδεδ. κ. ἔσθων. Mt., Lk. and Jn have aorists of other verbs. By some John was believed to be the Messiah, and this compelled him to be more explicit about his relation to the Messiah.

ἱκανός. It is clear from Mt. viii. 8 and Lk. vii. 6 that this = ἄξιος (Jn i. 27); *the thong* (Acts xxii. 25) *of whose sandals I am not fit to*, etc. Note the characteristically graphic fulness of κύψας λῦσαι, where the aor. may mean that he was unworthy to render even once the humble service which a slave rendered often to his master. Mt. speaks of the sandals being carried, a custom common in Palestine, but unknown to Mk's Roman readers. With the superfluous αὐτοῦ comp. vii. 25 and οὗ ἀρᾶς τὸ στόμα αὐτοῦ γέμει (Ps. ix. 28), μακάριος ἀνὴρ οὗ ἐστὶν ἡ ἀντίλημψις αὐτοῦ παρὰ σοῦ, Κύριε (Ps. lxxxiii. 6). The pleonasm is a Hebraism. Blass, § 50. 4 ; J. H. Moulton, *Gr. of N.T. Grk*, p. 95.

8. ἐγὼ ἐβάπτισα. He is addressing his baptized converts. Mt. and Lk. have βαπτίζω. They have μέν after ἐγώ, and some texts insert it here. The classical μέν...δέ... is comparatively rare in N.T.;

only three or four times in Mk, and in some books (2 Thess., 1 Tim., Tit., 2 Pet., 1, 2, 3 Jn, Rev.) not at all. Jn has ἐν before ὕδατι, Mt. and Lk. before πνεύματι, Mk in neither place; see crit. note. Here we have dat. of the instrument; *with water, with (the) Holy Spirit*. There is no art. and the Spirit is hardly personal; John would not think of a Person. In Mk the Baptist utters no warning about a judgment that is near at hand; there is no axe or fan or fire, and the mission of the Forerunner is almost immediately lost in that of the Messiah. But the effect of his teaching is seen long after his death; even at Ephesus, where St Paul found men ready to accept the Gospel, having previously known only the baptism of John (Acts xix. 2), and in the zeal of Apollos (Acts xviii. 22—28).

9—11. The Messiah is baptized by John.

Mt. iii. 13—17. Lk. iii. 21, 22. Cf. Jn i. 32—34.

9. Καὶ ἐγένετο...ἦλθεν. A Hebraism, introducing a fact that is of importance. Burton, *Moods and Tenses*, § 357.

ἐν ἐκείναις ταῖς ἡμέραις. *Sc. ἐν αἷς ἐκήρυσσε τὸ βάπτισμα τῆς μετανοίας ὁ 'Ιωαν.* (Euthym. Zig.). Another Hebraism (viii. 1, xiii. 17, 24). The date is very vague.

ἦλθεν 'Ιησοῦς. The ἰσχυρότερος at once comes on the scene, and John decreases in significance.

Ναζαρέτ. This form occurs also in Mt., Lk. and Jn, but not in LXX. or Josephus. Mk does not use Ναζαρέθ (Mt., Acts) or Ναζαρά (Mt., Lk.). The addition of τῆς Γαλιλαίας indicates that the situation of Nazareth was not likely to be known to Mk's readers; the insignificant town is not mentioned in O.T. But it was well known that the new Teacher came from Nazareth (i. 24, xiv. 67, xvi. 6).

The surprise that the Messiah should submit to baptism is evident in Mt. (iii. 13—15); and Jerome (*Adv. Pelag.* iii. 2) tells us that it was met in the Gospel acc. to the Hebrews in a way which is an instructive contrast to the narrative in Mt. But it does not appear in Mk, and this is in harmony with the primitive simplicity of his narrative. That the first Christians felt this difficulty, and explained it in different ways, is evidence that the baptism of John is historical fact.

εἰς τὸν 'Ιορδάνην. The εἰς, like the ἐκ in *v.* 10, may point to actual immersion; but in this late Greek, as papyri show, the difference between εἰς and ἐν is becoming blurred.

10. εὐθὺς...εἶδεν. As usual, εὐθύς belongs to the finite verb rather than to the participle. This is the first occurrence of Mk's favourite

adv., which he uses 41 times (Mt. 18 times, Lk. 7, Jn 6, Acts 10);
cf. Job v. 3. Mt.'s favourite adv. is τότε, which is rare in Mk, while
Lk.'s is παραχρῆμα, which Mk does not use at all.

εἶδεν σχιζομένους τοὺς οὐρανούς. Jesus *saw the heavens being rent
asunder.* We must mark the pres. part. and also the difference between Mk's bold expression and ἀνοίγω, which is the verb almost
invariably used of the heavens being opened. So elsewhere in N.T.,
as in LXX. (Is. lxiv. 1; Ezek. i. 1) and Testaments of the XII.
Patriarchs (*Levi* xviii. 6; *Judah* xxiv. 2, which are Messianic parallels to the Gospel narrative). In the Apocalypse of Baruch (xxi. 1)
we have the heavens opened and a voice coming from on high. Mk
may be thinking of Is. lxiv. 1, *Utinam dirumperes coelos et descenderes*;
but there we have ἀνοίξῃς in LXX.

The nom. to εἶδεν is certainly 'Ιησοῦς (*v.* 9). We know from
Jn i. 32 that the Baptist saw also, but the grammatical construction
and ἐν σοὶ εὐδόκησα show that the vision, like the voice, was sent to
the Christ. It is unnecessary to ask whether, if others were there,
which is doubtful (Lk. iii. 21), they also saw and heard, or whether
Jesus and John saw and heard with eye and ear. *Aperiuntur coeli,
non reseratione elementorum, sed spiritualibus oculorum* (Bede). What
is clear is that there was no hallucination, but a real reception of
the Spirit of God and of the word of God. Euthymius says that
these signs were given ἵνα μάθωμεν ὅτι ἐπὶ παντὸς ἀνθρώπου βαπτιζομένου
ἀνοίγονται οἱ οὐρανοί, καλοῦντες αὐτὸν εἰς τὴν ἄνω κατοικίαν. Theophylact adds that the Spirit descended, not because the Christ was in
need of it, "but that thou mayest know that, when thou art baptized,
the Spirit will come to thee." In Hebrew poetry and in Philo the
Dove is a symbol of heavenly attributes; ἐκ φύσεως μιμήματα ἔχει τ.
ἁγ. πνεύματος (Euthym.). See Lagrange, *S. Marc*, p. 12.

εἰς αὐτόν. See crit. note. The prep. indicates that ὡς περιστεράν
is not to be taken literally; *non veritas sed similitudo monstratur*
(Jerome). Mt. and Lk. have ἐπ' αὐτόν, possibly because εἰς αὐτόν
might suggest that until then Jesus had been devoid of the Spirit.

11. φωνὴ ἐγένετο. The first of the three Voices from Heaven;
the second being at the Transfiguration (ix. 7), and the third being
before the Passion (Jn xii. 28). Then and at the conversion of
St Paul sight and sound depended upon the condition of those
present, whether they had eyes to see and ears to hear. The same
was true at the Baptism.

ὁ ἀγαπητός. In LXX. the same Heb. word is translated sometimes ἀγαπητός and sometimes μονογενής. In N.T., ἀγαπητός is freq.
and "it is exclusively a title of Christ, or applied to Christians as

such.   As a Messianic title (cf. Mk ix. 7, xii. 6), it indicates a
unique relation to God " (Swete).   Here Vulg. has *dilectus*, but
ix. 7 and xii. 6 *carissimus*.   Here it is possibly a separate title,
Thou art my Son, the Beloved, but the usual translation (A.V., R.V.)
cannot safely be set aside.   J. A. Robinson, *Ephesians*, p. 229;
Hastings' *D.C.G.* art. " Voice " ; Dalman, *Words of Jesus*, pp. 204,
276 ; Tisserant, *Ascension d'Isaie*, p. 8.

ἐν σοὶ εὐδόκησα.   The timeless aorist ; *In Thee I am well pleased*
gives the force of verb and tense sufficiently well.   It is rash to give
any definite limit to the past tense ; *e.g.* pre-existence, or life on
earth up to this point, or the reception of Baptism.   Burton, § 55;
J. H. Moulton, *Gr.* p. 134.   Theophylact renders ἐν ᾧ ἀναπαύομαι,
and Jerome (on Is. xi. 2) quotes from the Nazarene Gospel, *descendit
fons omnis Spiritus Sancti et requievit super eum et dixit illi, Fili mi,
in omnibus prophetis expectabam te, ut venires et requiescerem in te.
Tu es enim requies mea.   Tu es filius meus primogenitus qui regnas in
aeternum.*

By accepting baptism from John our Lord not only "fulfilled all
righteousness," *i.e.* complied with the Levitical Law, in the eyes of
which He was unclean through connexion with an unclean people,
but He also thereby consecrated Himself for His work of inaugurating
the Kingdom of God.   John's baptism was a preparation for the
Kingdom.   For everyone else it was repentance-baptism.   Jesus
needed no repentance, but He could make use of preparation.

12, 13.   THE MESSIAH IS TEMPTED BY SATAN.
Mt. iv. 1—11.   Lk. iv. 1—13.

12.   Καὶ εὐθύς.   All three Synoptists intimate that the Temptation
followed immediately after the Baptism, and that it took place under
the guidance of the Spirit.   Mt. has his favourite τότε, and Mk his
favourite εὐθύς.   Jesus knows that He is the Messiah, and He must
meditate on His work, and the means, and the method.   Cf. Lk.
xiv. 25 f. ; Gal. i. 15—18.   The information must have come from
Christ Himself.   The hypothesis of fiction is inadmissible, for no
one at the time when the first Gospels were written had sufficient
insight to invent such temptations.   Indeed, but for His own statement, the first Christians would not have supposed that He ever
was tempted.   We know of later temptations (Mt. xvi. 23 ; Lk. xxii.
28, 42—44), and we may believe in earlier ones.   But here Satan
attempts to vanquish the Messiah just as He is about to begin the
work of rescuing mankind from his power.

ἐκβάλλει. Neither Mt. (ἀνήχθη) nor Lk. (ἤγετο) adopts this verb, perhaps because it might seem to imply that the Lord was unwilling to go. *Expellit* (Vulg.) and "driveth forth" (R.V.) suggest the same idea. *Cod. Brixianus* (f), the best representative of the Old Latin, has *eduxit* ; others have *duxit* (a) or *tulit* (ff₂), and perhaps *urgeth* or *sendeth forth* would suffice. Βάλλω in late Greek is often reduced in meaning; see on Jn v. 7. Here we have the first of the historic presents which are such a strong characteristic of Mk (151) and Jn (162), as compared with Mt. (78) and Lk. (4 to 6). Mt. 69 times alters or omits the historic presents of Mk, as here. In this chapter we have seven other instances, mostly λέγει or λέγουσιν (*vv*. 21, 30, 37, 38, 40, 41, 44). In LXX., 337 instances have been counted, nearly all of them in historical passages. Hawkins, *Hor. Syn.*² pp. 143 f., 213. This pres. is followed by three imperfects of what continued for some time.

εἰς τὴν ἔρημον. Apparently not the wilderness of *v.* 4, for Christ leaves the Jordan to go to it. Hastings' *D.C.G.* art. "Wilderness" and "Temptation."

13. τεσσεράκοντα ἡμέρας. Vulg. adds *et quadraginta noctibus* from Mt. iv. 2. Mt. mentions the nights to show that the fasting was continuous ; but Mk does not mention fasting. Mk and Lk. indicate that temptations continued throughout the forty days; cf. Exod. xxxiv. 28 of Moses, and 1 Kings xix. 8 of Elijah. Mt. might lead us to suppose that they did not begin till acute hunger was felt.

πειραζόμενος. In N.T. the verb is often used of the attacks of the evil one, a use not found in LXX., in which God's trying man, or man's trying God, is the usual meaning. Often in N.T. "try" or "test" would be a better rendering than "tempt." Here, as in *vv.* 5 and 39, we have a leading idea expressed by a participle.

ὑπὸ τοῦ σατανᾶ. Mt. and Lk. say ὑπὸ τοῦ διαβόλου, a word more widely used in N.T. than Σατανᾶς, but not found in Mk. "Satan" (="Adversary") is found in all four Gospels, Acts, Pauline Epp. and Revelation. Cf. Job i. 6, ii. 1; 1 Chron. xxi. 1; Zech. iii. 1. Here the Adversary of God and man begins his conflict with ὁ ἰσχυρότερος αὐτοῦ (Lk. xi. 22) about the method of overcoming the world. Mk thinks it unnecessary to state which was victor.

ἦν μετὰ τῶν θηρίων. Short as Mk's narrative is, he here gives a particular which is not in Mt. or Lk. The wild beasts indicate the solitariness of the place, διὰ τὴν ἄγαν ἐρημίαν τοῦ τόπου (Euthym.), rather than a special terror. One who knew Himself to be the Messiah would not be afraid of being killed by wild animals. That the beasts are meant to suggest a Paradise for the Second Adam is an idea alien from the context. They intimate the absence of human beings (Is. xiii. 21), and hence the need of Angels. Still less need we suppose that here there is confusion between two similar Hebrew words, one of which means "wild beasts" and the other "fast," so that "wild beasts" here becomes "hungered" in Mt. and Lk. Least of all that there is here any borrowing from Buddha's fasting or the temptation of Zarathustra. "Such ideas can only occur to those who will not try first of all to find in the story its own explanation" (Clemen). See p. 92.

διηκόνουν. Cf. i. 31, xv. 41. The imperf. seems to imply that the Angelic ministrations, like the Satanic assaults, continued throughout. Mt. places both at the end. Bede's antithesis is hardly right : *inter bestias commoratur ut homo, sed ministerio utitur angelico ut Deus.* It was as man that He needed the support of Angels (Lk. xxii. 43). There is a striking parallel in the Testaments (*Naph.* viii. 4) : "And the devil shall fly from you, [And the wild beasts shall fear you,] And the Lord shall love you, [And the Angels shall cleave to you]." But the words in brackets are not found in all texts. Christian interpolations are freq. in the Testaments.

14, 15.　The Messiah begins His Ministry.

Mt. iv. 12—17.　Lk. iv. 14, 15.

14. Καὶ μετὰ τὸ παραδοθῆναι. See crit. note. *And after that John was delivered up,* into the hands of Herod Antipas; cf. vi. 17. We are not told by whom John was delivered up, and some understand "by God," who in a similar sense "delivered up" Jesus (ix. 31, x. 33). The instruments were the Pharisees, and perhaps there is a hint that, as in the case of the Messiah (iii. 19, xiv. 10), there was treachery. The view that Mk gives is that, when the Forerunner's work ended (μετά), that of the Messiah began, but there is no hint given as to the amount of interval, which did not seem to Mk to be of importance. The Law passed, and the Gospel came ; *desinente lege consequenter oritur evangelium* (Jerome). Mk says nothing, and perhaps knew nothing, of an earlier ministry in which the Baptist and Jesus were preaching simultaneously (Jn iv. 1).

εἰς τὴν Γαλιλαίαν. Galilee was the most populous of the provinces into which Palestine was divided. Experience proved that it was a far more hopeful field than Jerusalem and Judaea (Jn ii. 13—iv. 3).

τὸ εὐαγγέλιον τ. θεοῦ. See crit. note. Either the gracious message which God sends or that which tells of Him ; cf. *v.* 1. Both meanings may be included. St Paul was perhaps the first to use the phrase (1 Thess. ii. 8, 9; Rom. i. 1, xv. 16; 2 Cor. xi. 7). Because the expression seemed strange, τῆς βασιλείας was inserted at an early date (AD, Latt. Syr-Pesh.). Τὸ εὐαγγ. is freq. in Mk, rare in Mt. and Acts, and is not found at all in Lk. or Jn. Only in ch. i. does Mk use κηρύσσω of Christ; elsewhere He is said διδάσκειν.

15. καὶ λέγων. Mk often accumulates participles; vv. 31, 41, ii. 6, iii. 5, 31, iv. 8, v. 25—27, 30, 33, vi. 2, viii. 11, x. 17, xii. 28, xiii. 34, xiv. 23, 67, xv. 21, 36, 43.

ὅτι. When ὅτι introduces, in the *oratio recta*, the words spoken, it is omitted in translation, being equivalent to inverted commas; vv. 37, 40, ii. 12, iii. 11, 21, 22, etc. But we need not suppose that Christ used these very words. He was not constructing set phrases to be impressed on the memory by repetition; but in these sentences the Evangelist sums up the substance of the Messiah's preaching.

Πεπλήρωται ὁ καιρός. "The time has been completed and *is complete*"; a Jewish idea, freq. in O.T. As usual ὁ καιρός means "the appointed time, right season, opportune moment," not necessarily a short time; ὁ καιρὸς ὁ ἀφορισθεὶς παρὰ θεοῦ τῇ πολιτείᾳ τῆς Παλαιᾶς Διαθήκης (Euthym.).

ἤγγικεν. "Has come near" and therefore *is at hand* (A.V., R.V.). Cf. xiv 42. Christ appears as a Revivalist of religion.

ἡ βασιλεία τοῦ θεοῦ. Mk has this expression 14 times, Lk. 32 times. Mt. nearly always omits or paraphrases Mk's expression, or substitutes ἡ βασ. τῶν οὐρανῶν, which he has 32 times. This Kingdom or Reign is *the rule of God* in men's hearts and in society. It exists already, but many have not even begun to try to attain to it, and no one gains it in its fulness. God's rule will be complete in eternity (1 Cor. xv. 24—28). See the full discussion of the phrase, esp. in its eschatological sense, in Dalman, *The Words of Jesus*, pp. 91—143; *D.C.G.* art. "Kingdom of God."

πιστεύετε ἐν τῷ εὐαγγελίῳ. Πιστ. εἰς is freq. in N.T., and πιστ. ἐπί occurs several times in Acts and Romans and elsewhere; but neither is found in LXX. Πιστ. ἐν occurs Eph. i. 13, and perhaps nowhere else in N.T., for Jn iii. 15 is doubtful, and it is rare in LXX. All three expressions are stronger than πιστ. with the simple dat. (xi. 31)—the difference between reposing trust in and merely believing what is stated. J. H. Moulton, *Gr.* p. 67. Mk elsewhere attributes the use of the word εὐαγγέλιον to Christ (viii. 35, x. 29, xiii. 10, xiv. 9); but he nowhere represents Him as speaking of "My Gospel." It would be natural to give Christ's meaning in the language which was current when Mk wrote. Dalman, *Words of Jesus*, pp. 102, 106. Syr-Sin. has "believe *His* Gospel."

16—20. The Messiah calls His first Disciples.

Mt. iv. 18—22.   Cf. Lk. v. 1—11.

Here, in the fullest sense, the main portion of the Gospel begins, and the authority for it goes back to eye-witnesses, of whom St Peter may be regarded as the chief.   We do not know how long an interval there is between this section and the preceding one ; but the connexion in thought is close.   If τὸ εὐαγγέλιον was to be proclaimed to all the world, many preachers would be required, and the Messiah at once seeks such helpers.

16. Καὶ παράγων. See crit. note. The intrans. use of παράγω is found in Mk (ii. 14, xv. 21), Mt., Jn, and the Pauline Epps. ; also once or twice in the Psalms. In Mk and Mt. παρά c. acc. is always local. Blass, § 43. 4.

τὴν θάλασσαν τῆς Γαλιλαίας. This is its usual designation in N.T. (vii. 31 ; Mt. iv. 18, xv. 29 ; Jn vi. 1, where " of Tiberias " is added). Lk. more accurately calls it a lake (λίμνη). But more frequently it is simply "the Sea." Mk has θάλασσα 19 times, 17 times of the lake, and twice (ix. 42, xi. 23) of the sea. The familiar " of Gennesaret " (Lk. v. 1) appears first 1 Macc. xi. 67. In LXX., we have θάλασσα Χενέρεθ (Josh. xii. 3, xiii. 27) or Χενέρα (Num. xxiv. 11). The lake is still remarkable for abundance of fish, esp. near the hot springs.

Σίμωνα. The name may be a Greek contraction of Symeon or an independent Greek name. It is very common in N.T. In the Gospels we have seven Simons ; in Josephus there are twenty-five. Simon Maccabaeus may have made the name popular. As was natural, the name given to the Apostle by our Lord almost drove his original name out of use. After it was given (iii. 16), Mk uses " Peter " 18 times and " Simon " only in Christ's address to him (xiv. 37). A similar use is found in Mt., Lk. and Acts. In Jn, both " Peter " and " Simon Peter " are freq. In Gal. ii. 7, 8, St Paul has " Peter," but elsewhere always " Kephas." Hort, 1 *Peter*, p. 151. The usage with regard to " Saul " and " Paul " is similar.

Ἀνδρέαν. A purely Greek name, but not rare among the Jews. Andrew had been a disciple of the Baptist (Jn i. 35, 40). The repetition of Simon's name illustrates Mk's fulness of expression. The father, Jonas or John, is not mentioned.

ἀμφιβάλλοντας. See crit. note. The verb occurs nowhere else in N.T. : in LXX. only Hab. i. 17, ἀμφιβαλεῖ τὸ ἀμφίβληστρον αὐτοῦ. See Trench, *Syn.* § lxiv.

17. Δεῦτε ὀπίσω μου. Cf. 2 Kings vi. 19. A magisterial invitation, almost a command. No reason is given, except the promise which follows, and we assume that He is already known to the two brothers. As in xi. 24, 29, the imperative takes the place of a protasis with εἰ or ἐάν. Δεῦτε = δεῦρο ἴτε.

γενέσθαι ἁλεεῖς ἀνθρώπων. Mt. omits γενέσθαι, which points to the preparatory training: ἀνθρώπους ἔσῃ ζωγρῶν (Lk. v. 10) is more explicit; *men* instead of fish, and for *life* instead of for death; *vivos capies homines* (Beza). This implies an invitation to permanent service; they are to cease to catch fish and to become fishers of men. This is the earliest instance of Christ's parabolic teaching; cf. ii. 19, 21, 22. In the result Christ Himself appears as a successful fisher, ἵνα ἁλιεύσῃ τοὺς ἁλιεῖς (Euthym.). Cf. the hymn, sometimes attributed to Clem. Alex.: ἁλιεὺς μερόπων τῶν σωζομένων κ.τ.λ.

18. καὶ εὐθέως ἀφέντες τ. δ. There is no hesitation. Like Bartimaeus with his ἱμάτιον (x. 50), they leave their valuable possessions; and apparently there is neither father nor servant present to take care of the nets. As Theophylact says, τὸν Ἰάκωβον σαγηνεύει καὶ τὸν Ἰωάννην. Mt. often omits the εὐθύς of Mk (comp. i. 12, 29, 43, ii. 8, 12 with Mt. iv. 1, viii. 4, 14, ix, 4, 7), but not here.

19. τοῦ Ζεβεδαίου. We may infer from xv. 40 that the mother's name was Salome. As James is mentioned first and John is described as "his brother," we conclude that John was the younger, or that, at the time when this Gospel was written, James was the better known. In Acts xii. 2, "James the brother of John" indicates that at that time John was better known than Zebedee. See on iii. 16.

καὶ αὐτοὺς ἐν τῷ πλοίῳ. *They also in their boat.* We were not told that Simon and Andrew were in their boat, but it might be inferred from ἀμφιβάλλοντας, for an ἀμφίβληστρον could not be used to much purpose from the shore.

καταρτίζοντας. James and John were not fishing but getting their nets in proper order for the next expedition. Theophylact strangely makes this a sign of poverty; they repaired their nets because they could not afford to get new ones! Hired servants imply that Zebedee was well off. Καταρτίζω in profane writers often means setting a joint or bone. St Paul has it in all of the four great Epistles.

20. καὶ εὐθὺς ἐκάλεσεν. As soon as He saw them, being certain of success, He called them. Mt. again preserves the εὐθύς, but employs it, as before, to mark the immediate response to Christ's invitation. James and John apparently had more to leave than Peter and Andrew had, but in each case all was left (x. 28). Mk does not

repeat the words of invitation and he varies the description of the
response. To follow Christ is a call superior even to parental claims
(Mt. viii. 22, x. 37; Lk. xiv. 26). " With the hired servants " is one
of the unessential details in Mk which Mt. omits; cf. *v.* 29, iv. 38, v.
13, vi. 37, xiv. 5, etc.

The Messiah has chosen four simple fishermen with whom to
begin the work of converting the world. *Piscatores et illitterati
mittuntur ad praedicandum, ne fides credentium, non in virtute Dei,
sed eloquentia atque doctrina putaretur* (Bede). But Christ did not
prefer ignorance to education. There was much in the patient endurance necessary for a fisherman's calling that was good training
for the work of converting the world.

21—28. CURE OF A DEMONIAC AT CAPERNAUM.

Lk. iv. 31—37. Omitted by Mt.

21. Καφαρναούμ. See crit. note. Christ came thither from
Nazareth (Mt., Lk.), and for a time it became His headquarters.
"Caphar" means "hamlet" or "village"; Capharsalama (1 Macc. vii.
31) and Capharsaba (Joseph. *Ant.* xvi. v. 2). The site of Capernaum
is still much debated; either *Tell Hum,* or *Khan Minyeh,* which
is about 2½ miles S.W. of *Tell Hum,* may be right. Mk speaks
thrice of Christ's coming to Capernaum (i. 21, ii. 1, ix. 33) and thrice
of His entering Jerusalem (xi. 11, 15, 27). We cannot safely infer
from this that were was an intention " to convey that both cities
received a three-fold warning from the Messiah."

εὐθὺς τοῖς σάββασιν. *On the very first sabbath* after the call of
the first disciples; cf. εὐθὺς πρωί (xv. 1). Like Peter (Acts x. 38), Mk
lays stress on Christ's healing demoniacs, and he places an act of this
kind first among the miracles. Both in LXX. and in N.T., both
σάββατον and σάββατα are used for "a Sabbath." In N.T., σάββατον
is more common (ii. 27, 28, vi. 2, xvi. 1; etc.), and σάββατα is
" Sabbaths " in Acts xvii. 2, where a numeral (ἐπὶ σαβ. τρία) requires
the plur. Elsewhere σάββατα is plur. in sound, perhaps in imitation
of the Hebrew or because Greek festivals are neut. plur. (vi. 21;
Jn x. 22), but is sing. in meaning. In N.T., σάββασιν is the usual
form of the dat., with σαββάτοις as *v. l.* in some authorities (Mt. xii.
1, 12 in B); in LXX., σαββάτοις prevails. Josephus has both. Mk
uses neither σάββατον nor σάββατα in the sense of " a week "; xvi. 9
is not by Mk.

εἰσελθών...ἐδίδασκεν. See crit. note. "He entered their synagogue
and was teaching there, and thereupon they were in a state of amaze-

ment." If εἰσελθών be omitted, cf. *v.* 39, x. 10, xiii. 9, xiv. 9. The
art. is probably possessive, or it may imply that there was only
one; but that built by the good centurion is not likely to have been
the only one in so large a place as Capernaum; see on Lk. vii. 5.
At *Tell Hum* there are ruins of two, but perhaps neither is as old
as the first century. In LXX., both συναγωγή and ἐκκλησία are used
of a *congregation* of the Israelites, especially in an organized form,
but sometimes of other gatherings (Prov. v. 14; cf. συναγωγὰς ὁσίων,
Ps. Sol. xvii. 18). In N.T., Josephus, and Philo, συναγωγή is used,
as here, of the *building* in which the congregation met. There were
many such in Jerusalem, and we read of them at Nazareth (vi. 2;
Mt. xiii. 54; Lk. iv. 16) as well as at Capernaum. In Asia Minor and
in Greece, St Paul could find a synagogue in most cities, and could
count on being allowed by the officials to address the congregation.
The origin of synagogues is unknown. The service in them consisted
largely of instruction. Philo calls them " houses of instruction"
and regards them primarily as schools. They were also courts of
justice (Lk. xii. 11, xxi. 12), and punishment was inflicted in them
(xiii. 9).

22. ἐξεπλήσσοντο. *They began to be amazed*, or *they continued
to be amazed*. Amazement was a common result of Christ's teaching
and acts (v. 20, vi. 2, 6, vii. 37, x. 26, xi. 18). What amazed people
in His teaching was its authoritative tone. Jewish teachers quoted
Scripture, or tradition, or the sayings of some famous Rabbi, as the
authority for what they taught; " It is written," or "It has been
said." Jesus taught as One who needed no such justification, and
He sometimes corrected, not only traditions, but even the accepted
expositions of the Law; *But I say unto you* (Mt. v. 22, 28, 32, 34,
39, 44). Hort, *Judaistic Christianity*, p. 33.

ἦν γὰρ διδάσκων. See on *v.* 6. The periphrastic tense covers
more than the previous imperf.; ἐδίδασκεν refers to His teaching on
this occasion, ἦν διδ. to the general tone of His teaching; *His way
was to teach*. Cf. ii. 6, 18.

ὡς ἐξουσίαν ἔχων. Adverbial, stating the manner of the action,
viz. " authoritatively." We may treat the participle as used sub-
stantively and expand, " He taught as one who has authority teaches";
but the words are intelligible without such expansion, as in ὡς οὐκ
ἀέρα δέρων (1 Cor. ix. 26; cf. 1 Cor. vii. 25; 1 Pet. ii. 16). Burton,
§ 446. 'Εξουσία is legitimate power derived from a source which is
competent to confer it. The source of Christ's ἐξουσία was His
Father (Mt. xxviii. 18; Lk. xxii. 29; Jn iii. 35, xiii. 3, xvii. 2), and
from the outset stress is laid on it.

οἱ γραμματεῖς. Those who were learned in τὰ γράμματα, the professional exponents of Scripture. For the history of the term see Deissmann, *Bible Studies*, p. 110 ; cf. 1 Esdr. viii. 3 ; 2 Macc. vi. 18. The scribes in 1 Macc. v. 42, and perhaps in vii. 12, are a different class of officials. In N.T., "the Scribes," *Sopherim*, are the professors of exegesis, and most of them were Pharisees or held similar views. They are the Clerical party.

23. εὐθὺς...αὐτῶν. See crit. note. Lk. omits both words as unnecessary, but they are part of Mk's fulness ; "On that very occasion, just as He was thus teaching in the local synagogue, etc."

ἐν πνεύματι ἀκαθάρτῳ. "In the control of, in the power of, an unclean spirit" (v. 2) ; we have the same use of ἐν when the spiritual influence is a good one (xii. 36 ; Mt. xii. 28, 43 ; Lk. ii. 27, iv. 1). In iii. 30, vii. 25, ix. 17 the afflicted person "has" the evil spirit. Mk and Lk., who wrote for Gentiles, to whom spirits or demons were indifferent, add a distinctive epithet much more often than Mt., who wrote for Jews, for Jews distinguished evil spirits from good. Mk has ἀκάθαρτον eleven times, Lk. six times and πονηρόν twice, while Mt. has ἀκάθαρτον only twice. Mk and Lk. add this epithet the first time they mention these beings (here and Lk. iv. 33), whereas Mt. mentions them several times before he adds it (x. 1). Nowhere in the Epistles is it used of spirits.

On the difficult subject of demoniacal possession see Hastings' *D.C.G.* art. "Demon" ; W. M. Alexander, *Demonic Possession in the N.T.* pp. 12, 200—212, 249 ; Plummer, *S. Matthew*, pp. 134 f. The other instances in Mk should be compared ; *v.* 34, iii. 11, 12, v. 6, 7, ix. 20.

ἀνέκραξεν. "Lifted up his voice," "cried loudly" ; in N.T., the verb is peculiar to Mk and Lk. The crying out of demons is mentioned iii. 11, v. 5, 7, ix. 26.

24. Τί ἡμῖν καὶ σοί ; Lit. "What is there that belongs to us and to Thee?" *i.e.* "What hast Thou to do with us?" Only one unclean spirit is mentioned, but it recognizes in Christ a power hostile to the whole class of demons. The man with the Legion (v. 7) begins with the same cry. Like Peter's Ἔξελθε ἀπ' ἐμοῦ (Lk. v. 8), it expresses consciousness of the incompatibility of perfect purity with sin. The form of expression is found in LXX. (Josh. xxii. 24 ; Judg. xi. 12 ; 2 Sam. xvi. 10) and in class. Grk (Demosth., Aristoph., and often in Arrian, *Epict.*). Cf. 2 Cor. vi. 14, and the proverb τί κοινὸν λύρᾳ καὶ ὄνῳ (Lucian, *De merc. cond.* 25).

Ναζαρηνέ. This is Mk's form ; Mt. and Jn have Ναζωραῖος. Lk. has both forms in his Gospel, in Acts always Ναζωραῖος (seven times).

ἦλθες ἀπολέσαι ἡμᾶς ; *Didst Thou come to destroy us ?* Τί ἐμοὶ καὶ σοί ; in 1 Kings xvii. 18, is followed by a similar question, εἰσῆλθες πρὸς μέ...θανατῶσαι τὸν υἱόν μου ; and here the sentence is probably interrogative (A.V., R.V.). But this and Lk. iv. 34 should be treated alike. Ναζαρηνέ might suggest that ἦλθες means " Didst Thou come from Nazareth? " But the plur. ἡμᾶς points the other way, "Didst Thou come into the world ? " This is confirmed by what follows ; but the thought that the Saviour ought not to destroy would be clearer if ὁ σωτὴρ τοῦ κόσμου (Jn iv. 42) stood in place of ὁ ἅγιος τ. θ. Cf. Jn vi. 69 ; Acts ii. 27, iv. 27. " Let us alone " (A.V.) is an interpolation ; see crit. note. Cf. Jas. ii. 19, τὰ δαιμόνια πιστεύουσιν καὶ φρίσσουσιν. *Praesentia Salvatoris tormenta sunt daemonum* (Bede). Lucian points out that in these cases the afflicted person is silent and the demon speaks (*Philops*. 16), and that the afflicted person is specially irate with a doctor who tries to heal him (*Abdicat*. 6).

οἶδά σε. The distinction between οἶδα and γινώσκω is not rigidly observed, the latter being sometimes used of God's knowing (Jn x. 15) and οἶδα of knowledge gained by experience (x. 42) ; but here οἶδα is quite in place ; the demon knew instinctively the absolute holiness of Jesus.

ὁ ἅγιος τ. θ. As in Peter's confession (Jn vi. 69 ; cf. Jn x. 36 ; 1 Jn ii. 20). Here was One who fulfilled the ideal of complete consecration to God. Aaron is ὁ ἅγιος Κυρίου (Ps. cv. 16) as being consecrated and set apart for the service of Jehovah. The confession of the unclean spirits in iii. 11 is more definite ; they know Him to be the Son of God.

25. ἐπετίμησεν. In class. Grk the verb has three meanings, the second and third growing out of the first ; (1) " lay a value on, *rate* " ; (2) " lay an estimated penalty on, sentence " ; (3) " chide, rebuke, *rate*." In Greek there is a real connexion between the first and third meanings ; but in English we have a mere accident of language, for " rate " = " value " is a word of different origin from " rate " = " scold." Excepting 2 Tim. iv. 2 and Jude 9, the verb occurs only in the Synoptists in N.T., always in the sense of " rebuke," or " give a strict order," and often of rebuking violence ; so also in LXX., where it is rare, except in the Psalms.

Φιμώθητι καὶ ἔξελθε. The two commands show why the demon was rebuked ; he had no authority to proclaim who Jesus was, and he had no right to have possession of the man. Euthymius (κολακεύων) follows Tertullian (*male adulantem*) in attributing the demon's utterance to flattery, which is not probable. It is rather a confession of the power of perfect goodness. Excepting 1 Cor. ix. 9 (?) and 1 Tim.

v. 18, where Deut. xxv. 4 is quoted, φιμόω is always used of silencing, not of muzzling. Cf. Josephus (*B.J.* i. xxii. 3), ἀλλ' ὁ μὲν πεφίμωτο τοῖς ἱμέροις. It is probably colloquial rather than literary, and it is said to have been used in exorcisms. Papyri may throw light on it. In iv. 39 we have perf. imperat. πεφίμωσο, which is stronger than aor. imperat. Whatever may be the truth about demoniacal possession, all the evidence that we have shows that Christ, in dealing with those who were believed to be possessed, went through the form of commanding evil spirits to *go out* (v. 8, vii. 29, ix. 25 ; cf. i. 34, 39, iii. 15 ; Mt. xii. 28, 43 ; etc.). And His miracles were not wrought by uttering spells, but by speaking a word of command. He bade the demons to depart, the lepers to be cleansed (*v.* 41), the lame to walk (ii. 11), the deaf to hear (vii. 34), the blind to see (x. 52), the dead to arise (v. 41), the storm to be still (iv. 39). With this simple ἔξελθε ἐξ αὐτοῦ contrast the elaborate form of exorcism quoted by Deissmann, *Light from the Ancient East*, pp. 251 f. Of the seven miracles wrought on the Sabbath, Mk gives three (i. 25, 31, iii. 5), Lk. two (xiii. 13, xiv. 4), and Jn two (v. 9, ix. 14).

The command to demons not to make His Messiahship known among Jews (here and iii. 12), a prohibition which was not made in the case of Gentiles (v. 19), is in harmony with the well-attested fact, that even the Twelve were slow in recognizing Him as the Messiah, and that the nation refused to accept Him as such. So far from proclaiming Himself as the Messiah, He was anxious that this fact should not be disclosed until men's minds were prepared to receive it on other grounds than the fact that He worked miracles. Miracles did not prove that He was the Messiah ; Prophets had healed lepers and raised the dead. And it is not irreverent to conjecture that He knew that a premature recognition of Him as the Messiah might produce a renewal of the temptations in the wilderness, temptations to gain the glory of victory without the necessary suffering (Mt. iv. 8—10, xvi. 21—23).

26. σπαράξαν...φωνῆσαν. Accumulation of participles ; see on *v.* 15. *Convulsing him and crying with a loud voice, came out.* "Tearing him" suggests that there was permanent injury, and Lk. tells us that there was none ; cf. ix. 20, where D has ἐτάραξεν for συνεσπάραξεν. Here, for σπαράξαν (*discerpens*, Vulg.), Lk. has ῥῖψαν εἰς τὸ μέσον (*cum projecisset in medium*), and Syr-Sin. has "threw him down" in Mk. Dan. viii. 7, where LXX. has ἐσπάραξεν, Theod. has ἔριψεν. The adverbial φωνῇ μεγάλῃ is much more freq. in Lk. (iv. 33, viii. 28, xix. 37, xxiii. 46) than in Mk (v. 7, xv. 34).

27. ἐθαμβήθησαν ἅπαντες. Lk. has ἐγένετο θάμβος ἐπὶ πάντας. In

N.T. Mk alone uses θαμβέομαι, and Lk. alone uses θάμβος. But Lk., far more often than all other N.T. writers put together, uses the strong form ἅπας. Just as Christ's rebuke to the demon reveals the two things which provoked the rebuke (see on *v.* 25), so the people's utterance reveals the two things which excited their astonishment, His authoritative teaching and His casting out the unclean spirit with a word. Cf. Mt. vii. 28.

συνζητεῖν. Freq. in Mk, elsewhere twice in Lk. and twice in Acts. It is usually followed by πρός.

Τί ἐστιν τοῦτο; See crit. note. The text of אBL 33 and other cursives gives the utterances of the congregation in abrupt short sentences and is probably original. But the punctuation is doubtful: διδαχὴ καινή may be interrogative, and κατ' ἐξουσίαν may be taken either with what precedes or with what follows. Διδαχὴ καινή is probably the answer to τί ἐστιν τοῦτο; and Lk. is in favour of taking κατ' ἐξ. with what follows. It is barely possible to take κατ' ἐξ. (with ἐστιν understood) as a separate sentence. The recently discovered MS. acquired by Mr C. L. Freer has "What is this new, this authoritative teaching, and that He commandeth even the unclean spirits and they obey Him?" See Appendix.

καινή. "New" in reference to quality, "fresh," not worn out or obsolete; whereas νέος is "new" in reference to time, "young," not aged. But, excepting in ii. 22 and parallels, καινός cannot be translated "fresh": "fresh covenant," "fresh heaven," "fresh Jerusalem" are intolerable.

καὶ τοῖς πνεύμασι τ. ἀκ. *Even the spirits, the unclean ones.* The repetition of the art. makes the adj. a separate idea. They had often heard of exorcisms; they had not so often heard that the demons at once obeyed. Cf. the Testaments (*Benj.* v. 2), καὶ τὰ ἀκάθαρτα πνεύματα φεύξονται ἀφ' ὑμῶν. Cf. καὶ ὁ ἄνεμος (iv. 41), καὶ τὰ δαιμόνια (Lk. x. 17). Christ's miracles, like His teaching, were not an art which He had acquired, but ἐξουσία with which He was endowed.

28. ἀκοή. Here again (see on *v.* 25) we have a word with three meanings, of which the second and third spring directly from the first: (1) "hearing," as "by hearing ye shall hear," Is. vi. 9; then, seeing that "hearing" may mean either the sense of hearing or hearsay, we have (2) "the ear," vii. 35, and (3) "rumour" or "report," as here. Cf. Jer. vi. 24.

εὐθὺς [πανταχοῦ]. *From that moment in all directions.* Some important witnesses (א* 33, Lat-Vet.) omit εὐθύς, and still more (א*ADΓΔΠ, Latt. Syrr.) omit πανταχοῦ, but perhaps both may be retained (R.V.). Syr-Sin. omits both and adds "and many followed Him."

ὅλην τὴν περίχωρον τῆς Γαλιλαίας. Either A.V. or R.V. may be
right; *all the region round about Galilee, i.e.* the whole of Syria
(Mt. iv. 24), or *all the region of Galilee round about, i.e.* the whole of
Galilee (Lk. iv. 37). In the latter case, τῆς Γαλ. merely explains
τ. περίχωρον.

This curing of a demoniac is the first miracle recorded by Mk,
who may have regarded it as symbolical of the Messiah's work—His
victory over the forces of evil.

29—31. HEALING OF SIMON'S WIFE'S MOTHER.

Mt. viii. 14, 15. Lk. iv. 38, 39.

29. εὐθὺς...ἐξελθών. See on *v.* 10. The coincidence with ἐξῆλθεν...
εὐθύς (*v.* 28) is accidental. No parallel is intended between the report
going forth at once and His at once going forth. As soon as the synagogue service was over, Christ went to the home of the first pair of
disciples accompanied by the second pair; and this house now becomes His headquarters (ii. 1, iii. 20, vii. 24, ix. 33, x. 10). Those
who adopt the reading ἐξελθόντες ἦλθον (אAC, etc.) think that here we
can trace the words of Peter, ἐξελθόντες ἤλθομεν. The change to the
plur. was probably made in order to include the disciples who accompanied Him to Peter's house. Mt. omits "with James and John."
Syr-Sin. has "And He came out of the synagogue, and they came to
the house of Simon Cepha and of Andrew; and James and John
were with Him."

30. πενθερά. It is certain that πενθερά means "mother-in-law"
(Lk. xii. 53; Ruth i. 14, ii. 11, 18, 19, 23; Mic. vii. 6); "step-mother"
is μητρυιά; and it is clear from 1 Cor. ix. 5 that Peter was married.
Clem. Alex. (*Strom.* iii. 6) says that Peter had children and that his
wife helped the Apostle in ministering to women; and here her mother
ministers to Christ and His disciples. See also *Strom.* vii. 11, quoted
by Eusebius, *H.E.* iii. 30. Jonas or John (Jn xxi. 15), the father of
Simon and Andrew, was probably dead.

Note the accurate changes of tense in *vv.* 30, 31, imperf. of what
continued, hist. pres. or aor. of what was done once for all; also the
two participles, as in *vv.* 14, 15.

κατέκειτο. *Was in bed;* Jn v. 3, 6; Acts ix. 33, xxviii. 8; cf.
Wisd. xvii. 7. She *was keeping her bed, being in a fever.*

εὐθὺς λέγουσιν. As soon as He enters the house Peter and Andrew
tell Him of their sick relation, for after what they had seen in the
synagogue they were confident that He could and would heal her.
To suppose that they were merely explaining her non-appearance is
inadequate. Mt. omits this. Euthymius notes how often ὁ Χριστὸς

τῇ ἑτέρων πίστει χαρίζεται τὴν ἑτέρων ἴασιν, and continues ὑποδεξώμεθα καὶ ἡμεῖς τὸν Χριστόν, ἵνα τῶν ἐν ἡμῖν παθῶν τὴν πύρωσιν ἀποσβέσῃ.

31. κρατήσας τῆς χειρός. We have the same action in the cases of Jairus's daughter (v. 41), the blind man at Bethsaida (viii. 23), and the demoniac boy (ix. 27) ; cf. ix. 36. Lk. substitutes that " He stood over her and rebuked the fever." Κρατέω *c. acc.* implies complete control (iii. 21, vi. 17, xii. 12, etc.), *c. gen.*, grasping only a part (v. 41, ix. 27). On the aor. part. see Blass, § 58. 4. On the combination of participles see on *v.* 15.

διηκόνει. All three have this imperf., and the beloved physician, who states that the fever was a "great" one, emphasizes διηκόνει with his favourite παραχρῆμα. A person just recovered from a fever is usually too weak to minister to others ; *verum sanitas quae Domini confertur imperio simul tota redit* (Bede). It is at the Sabbath meal after the synagogue service that she waits on Christ and His disciples. In this she showed her gratitude and her joy in regained strength. Ἐὰν κατεχόμενον νοσήματι ἰάσηταί σε ὁ θεός, τῇ ὑγιείᾳ κέχρησο πρὸς τὴν τῶν ἁγίων διακονίαν (Theoph.).

32—34. HEALINGS AFTER SUNSET.

Mt. viii. 16. Lk. iv. 40, 41.

32. Ὀψίας δὲ γενομένης, ὅτε ἔδυσεν ὁ ἥλιος. The Sabbath ended at sunset, and then the work of moving the sick could begin. The double statement illustrates Mk's love of fulness of expression ; cf. *v.* 42, ii. 23, 25, iii. 27, vi. 25, vii. 13, 20, ix. 3, x. 30, xi. 4, xii. 14, 44, xiii. 20, 34, xiv. 43, 58, 61, 68, xv. 1, xvi. 2. It is also one of several instances in which Mk has the whole expression, of which Mt. and Lk. each take a different half. Here Mt. has ὀψίας δὲ γενομένης, Lk. δύνοντος δὲ τοῦ ἡλίου, and Syr-Sin. here agrees with Lk. See on *v.* 13, and comp. xiv. 30 with Mt. xxvi. 34 and Lk. xxii. 34, also xv. 26 with Mt. xxvii. 37 and Lk. xxiii. 38. From ii. 25, Mt. and Lk. take the same half, omitting "hath need " ; also from xii. 14, omitting "Shall we give, or shall we not give?" So also from xiv. 68, omitting "nor understand." There are also other instances in which Mk has superfluous words, which either Mt. retains but not Lk., or Lk. retains but not Mt. Hawkins, *Hor. Syn.*[2] pp. 139 f.

ἔδυσεν...ἔφερον. The change from imperf. to aor., and from aor. to imperf., is again quite accurate.

τοὺς δαιμονιζομένους. Syr-Sin. omits. As usual, these are distinguished from ordinary sick folk. The verb does not occur in LXX.

and in N.T. is found only in the Gospels, freq. in Mt. and Mk, and
once each in Lk. and Jn.

33. ὅλη ἡ πόλις. Popular hyperbole, like πᾶσα and πάντες in *v.*
5, and πάντες in *v.* 37.

ἐπισυνηγμένη πρὸς τὴν θύραν. "Flocked towards the door and
formed a dense crowd there." Note the periphrastic tense (*vv.* 6, 22),
and the double compound ; one concourse came on the top of another.
Cf. ἐπισυνάγαγε ἡμᾶς ἐκ τῶν ἐθνῶν (Ps. cvi. 47). Mt., as often, omits
the dense crowds which impeded Christ.

34. πολλούς. They brought πάντας and He healed πολλούς, which
does not mean that some went away without treatment. To avoid
this misinterpretation, Mt. transposes πολλούς and πάντας : they
brought many and He healed all. The physician tells us the method
of healing : "He laid His hands on each one." He also has the more
accurate ἐθεράπευεν, for such individual treatment was a long process,
and persistent energy was evident through it all. All three distinguish
casting out demons from healing the sick, and it is because of
the preceding δαιμονιζομένους that Mk has δαιμόνια instead of πνεύματα
ἀκάθαρτα. Syr-Sin. omits κακῶς...νόσοις.

ἤφιεν. We have the same form xi. 16 ; cf. xi. 4 ; Rev. xi. 9 ;
συνίω is a similar form. W.H. *App.* p. 167 ; Blass, § 23. 7. The use
of λαλεῖν (not λέγειν) shows that ὅτι means "because," not "that."
The two verbs are not confused in N.T.

ᾔδεισαν. See on οἶδα, *v.* 24. It was the demons, not the demoniacs, who recognized Him. If the demoniacs were only insane or
epileptic persons, how did they know who Jesus was ? See crit. note.
If Χριστὸν εἶναι is a gloss, it is a correct gloss; "knew Him" means
"knew Him to be the Messiah." But Mk writes with reserve as
to what they knew, and perhaps we ought to write and speak with
reserve also. We do not know enough about it to speak with confidence ; but perhaps it is more correct to say that as yet Jesus
was the Messiah-designate rather than the Messiah, because He had
not yet been revealed to mankind as having this office. The time
for that revelation had not yet come. In God's sight He was the
Messiah, a fact declared to Him and to John at the Baptism. And we
are told here that this was known also to the demons. But it had not
yet been revealed to men ; and it was for God to make this revelation
at the fitting time, not for demons, nor even for Apostles. Hence the
silence about the fact which is strictly enjoined upon Peter and
the rest (viii. 30). At first sight that requirement of silence from
those who had to proclaim the coming of the reign of God seems inconsistent ; but the nearer we get to the view given us by St Mark, the

more intelligible it will become. We need not be surprised at finding
that there are "things concerning Jesus of Nazareth" which we
cannot fully explain; but we can understand that it was not God's
will that His Son should be prematurely proclaimed as the promised
Messiah, or be proclaimed as such by demons.

35—39. Departure from Capernaum.
Circuit in Galilee.

Lk. iv. 42—44.

35. πρωῒ ἔννυχα. Either word would suffice, and Syr-Sin. omits
ἔννυχα : and either ἐξῆλθεν or ἀπῆλθεν would suffice : καὶ ἀπῆλθεν
may come from vi. 32, 46 ; it is omitted by B and other witnesses.
Nowhere else does ἔννυχα occur; cf. πάννυχα (Soph. *Ajax*, 929). *A
great while before day* (A.V., R.V.) is a good equivalent for ἔννυχα
λίαν, lit. "well in the night," *He rose up and went out.*

κἀκεῖ προσηύχετο. *And there He continued in prayer.* Accurate
change from aor. to imperf. The Evangelist who is most often alone
in recording that Christ prayed is Lk. (iii. 21, v. 16, vi. 12, ix. 18, 28,
xi. 1, xxiii. [34,] 46) ; but here Mk is alone. Both Mk (vi. 46) and
Mt. (xiv. 23) mention His retiring to pray after feeding the 5000,
and all three record the praying in Gethsemane. He was liable to
physical exhaustion, and He might pray for help to overcome that.
He was not omniscient, and He might pray for illumination. He
was liable to temptation, and He might pray for strength to overcome
that (Heb. ii. 18, iv. 15, v. 7, 8). It is rash to say that all Christ's
prayers were intercessions for others ; it was not so in Gethsemane.
Here, as usual, the best MSS. have κἀκεῖ : in *v.* 38 and xiv. 15, καὶ
ἐκεῖ may be right.

36. κατεδίωξαν. "Pursued Him *closely*," "followed Him *down*."
Freq. in LXX., but here only in N.T. The verb generally implies
interference with the person pursued, and sometimes implies persecution. But cf. Ps. xxiii. 6. Considering the simple character of
Mk's Greek, he uses compound words more often than we should
expect. It is instructive to take a page here and there and count.
In N.T., διώκω is freq. Peter at once begins to lead.

οἱ μετ' αὐτοῦ. Andrew, James, and John. In Lk. this is blurred
into οἱ ὄχλοι. The earliest tradition says that the disciples pleaded
the desires of the multitudes : Lk. says the people came and urged
their own wishes.

37. Πάντες ζητοῦσίν σε. *All men are seeking Thee.* He had no house of His own at which they could be sure of finding Him. Cf. *vv.* 5, 33.

38. "Αγωμεν. Intrans. as in xiv. 42 and always in N.T. Cf. ἔγειρε, ii. 11.

ἀλλαχοῦ. *Elsewhere*; nowhere else in N.T., and omitted in many texts here. But it is certainly to be retained with אBC*L 33, Arm. Memph. Aeth.

κωμοπόλεις. A rare word, which D and Vulg. divide into its component parts, κωμὰς καὶ πόλεις, *vicos et civitates*. It occurs only here in N.T., and in LXX. not at all, but is used once or twice by Strabo, and it means a town which, as regards its constitution, has only the rank of a village. Perhaps the chief distinction was the absence of walls; προσπίπτοντες πόλεσιν ἀτειχίστοις καὶ κατὰ κώμας οἰκουμέναις (Thuc. i. 5). In LXX. we often read of towns which are "daughters" of other towns (Num. xxi. 22, 32, xxxii. 42, etc.). Here only in N.T. is ἐχόμενος used of *local* proximity; of nearness in *time*, Lk. xiii. 33; Acts xx. 15, xxi. 26. Cf. τὰς ἐχομένας πόλεις (Joseph. *Ant.* xi. viii. 6).

ἵνα καὶ ἐκεῖ κηρύξω. This shows the point of the rebuke. They must not try to monopolize Him; He has been sent to bring the good tidings to as many as possible. The emphasis is on καὶ ἐκεῖ (see on *v.* 35). There is no hint that He is rebuking them for interrupting His preaching by asking for more healings. His healings were an important element in His teaching, for He was sent as the Healer of maladies of body and soul. Divine compassion was conspicuous in both spheres.

ἐξῆλθον. Lk. gives the right meaning: ἐπὶ τοῦτο ἀπεστάλην. His Father did not send Him to a favoured few, but to all; ἦλθον καλέσαι ἁμαρτωλούς (ii. 17; cf. x. 45). *Primi sermones Jesu habent aenigmatis aliquid, sed paulatim apertius de se loquitur. Postea dicturus erat, Exii a Patre* (Beng.).

39. εἰς τὰς συναγωγάς. The εἰς may give the direction of the preaching or may be influenced by ἦλθεν (iv. 15, xiv. 9; Jn viii. 26). Cf. ἐς τὸν δῆμον ταῦτα λέγωσιν (Thuc. v. 45). But in late Greek εἰς and ἐν have become less distinct. The verse illustrates Mk's lack of literary skill. While εἰς τὰς συν. belongs to κηρύσσων, εἰς ὅλην τ. Γ. must belong to ἦλθεν. Mt. puts the construction straight. Note the combination of participles (*v.* 15).

τὰ δαιμόνια ἐκβάλλων. With Mk this is the representative miracle; iii. 15, vi. 7.

40—45. The Cleansing of a Leper.

Mt. viii. 2—4.   Lk. v. 12—16.

The three Evangelists give this miracle in different connexions. Mt. places it first in his three triplets of specimens of the Messiah's mighty works, just after Christ had come down from delivering the Sermon on the Mount. Lk. places it just after the call of the first disciples. On the impossibility of eliminating miracles from the career of Jesus Christ see Sanday, *Outlines of the Life of Christ*, p. 113; Illingworth, *Divine Immanence*, p. 90; R. J. Ryle, M.D., *Hibbert Journal*, Apr. 1907, pp. 572—586. The healing of a leper cannot be explained as a case of "suggestion" or ordinary "faith-healing." We have twelve cases of leprosy in N.T., this one, Simon the Leper (xiv. 3), and the ten in Lk. xvii. 12. The literature on the subject is enormous; see artt. in *D.B.*, *D.C.G.*, *Enc. Brit.*, etc. Lepers were probably numerous in Palestine then as now, and the malady probably differed greatly in malignity, some skin-diseases being reckoned as "leprosy." The disciples were commissioned to heal lepers (Mt. x. 8).

40. λεπρός. The physician (Lk. v. 12) says that he was "full of leprosy," which perhaps shows that he was not ceremonially unclean (Lev. xiii. 12, 13), and therefore was able to approach Christ. But his misery might make him desperate, and those near Christ would draw away when the leper approached.

[καὶ γονυπετῶν]. Cf. x. 17. The humble prostration is in all three, but differently expressed: Mt. προσεκύνει (his favourite word), Lk. πεσὼν ἐπὶ πρόσωπον. If καὶ γονυπετῶν had been an interpolation (BDGΓ omit), we should probably have had a word taken from Mt. or Lk. The combination of participles is in Mk's style.

Ἐὰν θέλῃς. He fears that Jesus may judge him to be unworthy of so enormous a boon. *De voluntate Domini non quasi pietatis incredulus dubitavit, sed quasi colluvionis suae conscius non praesumpsit* (Bede). Contrast the father's εἴ τι δύνῃ (ix. 22).

δύνασαί με καθαρίσαι. Leprosy was believed to be incurable, except by Him who had inflicted this "stroke." The man's faith, therefore, is great, esp. if this was the first instance of Christ's healing a leper. The form δύνασαι (Mt. v. 36, viii. 2; Lk. v. 12, vi. 42; Jn xiii. 36) is well attested here, though B has δύνῃ, which is right in ix. 22, 23; Lk. xvi. 2.

καθαρίσαι. After δύναμαι the aor. infin. is normal; v. 45, ii. 4, iii. 20, 24—27, v. 3, vi. 5, 19, vii. 15. In Lev. xiii. 6, 7, 13, etc., καθαρίζειν is used of the priest pronouncing the leper to be clean; here, as elsewhere in N.T., it is used of the actual cleansing.

41. σπλαγχνισθείς. See Lightfoot on Phil. i. 8. The verb in N.T. is found in the Synoptists only, and (except in parables) it is used of no one but Christ. It is the moving cause of His mighty works (ix. 22; Mt. ix. 36, xiv. 14, xv. 32, xx. 34; Lk. vii. 13). The outstretched hand (a Hebraistic fulness of writing which is in all three) expresses this compassion and confirms the faith which secured the cleansing. It was owing to His compassion for mankind that He had a hand with which to lay hold. Euthymius points out that Christ healed sometimes with a touch, sometimes with a word, sometimes, as here, with both. Cf. i. 31, 41, v. 41, vi. 5, vii. 34, viii. 23. Theophylact says that He touched the leper to show that He was Δεσπότης τοῦ νόμου, and that τῷ καθαρῷ οὐδὲν ἀκάθαρτον. The latter is nearer the truth. It indicates that the greatest pollution will not make Christ shrink from one who desires to be freed from his pollution, and comes to Him believing that He can free him. That Christ was asserting His sacerdotal character (priests were allowed to handle lepers) is less probable. Priests pronounced lepers, when healed, to be clean, and this Christ pointedly abstained from doing. On the combination of participles see *v.* 15.

D, a ff₂ r have the strange reading ὀργισθείς for σπλαγχνισθείς. Ephraem had both words in his text, and he thinks that Christ was angry because the leper doubted His willingness to heal. Seeing that the σπλάγχνα were regarded as the seat of anger as well as of pity, it is possible that ὀργισθείς was a marginal gloss, to produce harmony with *v.* 43, and that it was afterwards substituted for σπλαγχνισθείς. But see Nestle, *Textual Criticism of N.T.* p. 262; he suggests a different meaning for ὀργισθείς or a difference of translation. Nowhere in N.T. has ὀργισθείς any other meaning than "being angry," and the Latin texts which support this reading have *iratus*.

42. Here again (see on *v.* 32) Mk expresses one fact in two ways, of which Mt. and Lk. each have one. Lk. has ἡ λέπρα ἀπῆλθεν ἀπ' αὐτοῦ, while Mt. has ἐκαθαρίσθη αὐτοῦ ἡ λέπρα. Both have εὐθύς. Syr-Sin. has "And in that hour he was cleansed." In Naaman's case (2 Kings v. 14) ἐκαθαρίσθη is used. Naaman expected to be touched, but he was not a Jew.

43. ἐμβριμησάμενος...ἐξέβαλεν. The two verbs, esp. when rendered *comminatus...ejecit* (Vulg.), give the impression that our Lord was angry with the man; but the impression is probably wrong. Ἐμβριμάομαι occurs in four other places in N.T. (xiv. 5; Mt. ix. 30;

Jn xi. 33, 38), and nearly always of Christ. From meaning
(1) "snort" or "growl," it comes to mean (2) "exhibit indignation,"
or (3) "show sternness." The last seems to be the meaning here.
Christ saw that the man would be likely to disobey His injunctions,
and He was stringent in giving them. Allowing him no time to
raise objections or to talk to others, *He straightway sent him forth.*
Syr-Sin. omits these words. See on iii. 5; also *D.C.G.* artt. "Anger,"
"Fierceness"; *Ecce Homo*, ch. xxi. It illustrates the variations of
Vulg. that it has *expellit v.* 12 and *ejecit* here. R.V. has "driveth
him forth," *v.* 12 and "sent him out" here. We need not suppose
from ἐξέβαλεν that Christ was in a house or a synagogue (*v.* 39). The
leper would not have intruded into a building.

44. Ὅρα μηθενὶ μηδὲν εἴπῃς. Winer, p. 625. The ὅρα and the
double negative indicate the urgency of the command. Mk is fond
of double negatives; ii. 2, iii. 27, v. 3, 37, vii. 12, ix. 8, xi. 2, 14,
xii. 34, xiv. 25, xv. 4, 5, xvi. 8. Neither here nor at iii. 27, ix. 8,
xiv. 25 is there a double neg. in Mt. Elsewhere Mt. omits the
sentence. The change from pres. imperat. to aor. is correct : *Continually take care that thou do not begin to say to anyone at all*; so
also the change from ὕπαγε to δεῖξον. Compare the commandments
with aorists (x. 19), and contrast the presents (v. 36, vi. 50, ix. 39).
On these charges to keep silence see Sanday, *J.T.S.* Apr. 1904. In
this case silence would prevent the man from mixing with others till
he was pronounced clean by proper authority, and from producing
unhealthy excitement in himself and his hearers ; and there may
have been other reasons affecting Christ Himself.

ὕπαγε. Cf. ii. 11, v. 19; not in LXX., but found in Eur. and
Aristoph. See on vi. 38.

σεαυτὸν δεῖξον. The emphasis on the pronoun makes the command
more urgent. Christ does not assume the right to pronounce the
man clean; for that He sends him to the proper official; cf. Lk.
xii. 14.

ἃ προσέταξεν Μωϋσῆς. Christ is making no statement as to the
authorship of the Pentateuch or of Lev. xiv. In accordance with
current thought and language He speaks of the Pentateuch as
"Moses" (vii. 10, x. 3, 4, xii. 26, etc.) and of the Psalms as
"David" (xii. 36, 37). Questions of authorship had not been
raised, and He did not raise them or give any decision about them.
See Plummer, *S. Matthew*, p. 311, and the literature there quoted.
The important thing here is that He was no revolutionary teacher;
He did not encourage men to ignore the Law. Hort, *Jud. Chris.*
p. 29.

εἰς μαρτύριον αὐτοῖς. The words are in all three. The gift which the man offers is the "testimony," and "to them" means "to the priests.'' The offering would show them that there was among them One who could heal leprosy and yet did not take upon Himself to absolve men from their obligation to observe the Law. It would be *testimonium de Messia praesente, legi non derogante* (Beng.).

45. ἐξελθών. "From the place" or "from the crowd." The man, of necessity, yields to the ἐξέβαλεν, but he forthwith disregards the μηδενὶ μηδὲν εἴπῃς. Cf. vii. 36; Mt. ix. 30, 31.

ἤρξατο. Very freq. in Mk and Lk., but only once in Jn. Cf. v. 17, vi. 7. Such fulness of expression is Hebraistic. Blass, § 69. 4.

κηρύσσειν πολλά. *To publish much, i.e.* "at great length" or "often" (iii. 12, v. 10, 23, 38, 43, ix. 26); *it* (R.V.) should be in italics, or omitted. Probably τὸν λόγον goes with both infinitives, πολλά being adverbial. D, Latt. omit πολλά. Cf. vii. 36; Mt. ix. 30, 31.

διαφημίζειν τὸν λόγον. Vulg. has *diffamare sermonem*, whereas διεφημίσθη ὁ λόγος (Mt. xxviii. 15) is rendered *divulgatum est verbum*. *Spread abroad the matter* (R.V.) is right; ὁ λόγος does not mean Christ's healing word, or His teaching, but the whole story of his marvellous cure. Luther has *die Geschichte*. Bede thinks that our Lord submitted to be disobeyed that many might profit by what the cleansed leper had to tell, and *unius perfecta salvatio multas ad Dominum cogit turbas*. This explanation ignores the disastrous result which Christ tried to prevent. Mt. again omits the impeding crowd; he does not like to say that Christ was unable to do what He wished. See on *v.* 33, vi. 48, vii. 24.

ὥστε μηκέτι αὐτὸν δύνασθαι. His *public* work in towns (φανερῶς is emphatic), and therefore His teaching in synagogues, had to be suspended. Instead of seeking the lost in their own homes, He had to go into the wilderness and wait for them to seek Him. This was a serious drawback, although His Ministry still went on.

ἐρήμοις τόποις. Places in which there were no houses or culti-vated lands.

ἤρχοντο. Graphic imperf. There was a continual stream of visitors; cf. ii. 13; Jn iv. 30.

πάντοθεν. Cf. Lk. xix. 43. The hyperbole is similar to that in *vv.* 5, 28, 32. In Heb. ix. 4, πάντοθεν may mean "inside and out." The classical πανταχόθεν is not found in N.T., though a few inferior MSS. have it here (EGUV etc.); in popular language the shorter form would prevail.

CHAPTER II.

2. אBL 33 and versions omit εὐθύς.

4. προσενέγκαι (אBL 33) rather than προσεγγίσαι (ACDΓΔ).

5. καὶ ἰδών (אBL) rather than ἰδὼν δέ: cf. i. 14, 28. ἀφίενται (B 33, Latt. Syrr. Goth., Orig.) rather than ἀφέωνται (אACDL etc.), which may come from Lk. v. 20. Mt. ix. 2, 5 has ἀφίενται. So also here v. 9, where א joins B. σου αἱ ἁμαρτίαι (אBDLΔ 33) rather than σοι αἱ ἁμ. σου (AC³EH etc.).

7. λαλεῖ; βλασφημεῖ (אBDL) rather than λαλεῖ βλασφημίας (ACG etc.).

9. ἐγείρου (BL) may be original, but it looks like a correction of the intrans. ἔγειρε. Mt. and Lk. have ἔγειρε here, and all three have ἔγειρε at v. 11.

11. אBCDL 33 omit καί before ἆρον.

14. For Λευείν (אᶜBLM), Λευίν (CFGHSUV), Λευί (AKΓΔΠ 33), Λευεί (א*), D, some cursives and Lat-Vet. have Ἰάκωβον. The Gospel of Peter sub fin. has Λευείς. Vulg. has Leuin.

15. γίνεται (אBL 33) rather than ἐγένετο (ACDΓΔΠ).

16. γραμματεῖς τῶν Φαρισαίων καὶ ἰδόντες (אBDLΔ 33) rather than γρ. καὶ οἱ Φαρισαῖοι ἰδόντες (ACΓΠ). ὅτι ἐσθίει (B 33) is probably to be preferred to ὅτι ἤσθιεν (אDL) or αὐτὸν ἐσθίοντα (ACΓΔΠ). ἁμαρτωλῶν κ. τελωνῶν (BDL 33) rather than τελ. κ. ἁμαρτ. (אACΓΔΠ) by assimilation to next line.

17. אABDKLΔΠ and versions omit εἰς μετάνοιαν, which comes from Lk. v. 32.

20. ἐκείνῃ τῇ ἡμέρᾳ (אABCDKLΔ) rather than ἐκείναις ταῖς ἡμέραις (Γ, Latt.).

22. The text is much confused, but the reading which is best attested, and best explains variations, is ῥήξει ὁ οἶνος τοὺς ἀσκοὺς καὶ ὁ οἶνος ἀπόλλυται καὶ οἱ ἀσκοί. This text is supported throughout by BL, joined in different details by other witnesses. After καινούς many witnesses add βλητέον (from Lk.); אB omit. A few add καὶ ἀμφότεροι συντηροῦνται (from Mt.).

23. ὁδὸν ποιεῖν τίλλοντες (אACLΓΔΠ), supported by ὁδοποιεῖν τίλλοντες (BGH) rather than τίλλειν (D, Lat-Vet.).

25. λέγει (אCL 33) rather than ἔλεγεν (ΑΒΓΔΠ), which looks like assimilation to the preceding ἔλεγον.

26. πῶς before εἰσῆλθεν should probably be omitted with BD, t. D, Lat-Vet. Syr-Sin. omit ἐπὶ 'Αβιάθαρ ἀρχιέρεως.

<h3 style="text-align:center">1—12. HEALING OF A PARALYTIC AT CAPERNAUM.
THE FORGIVENESS OF SINS.</h3>

Mt. ix. 1—8. Lk. v. 17—26.

This incident gives the dominant thought to a group of narratives which record the hostile criticisms of the Scribes and Pharisees (ii. 1—iii. 6). It comes after—we do not know how long after— the healing of the leper; so also in Lk. The other narratives seem to be selected because of their resemblance to this one, and are perhaps arranged so as to form a climax. Here the hostile party do not openly express their criticisms. In *vv.* 15—17 they utter them to the disciples. In 18—22 and 23—28 they utter them to Christ Himself. In iii. 1—6 they seek plans for His destruction.

1. Καὶ εἰσελθὼν πάλιν. Unless ἠκούσθη is personal, to which Blass, § 72. 4, with hesitation inclines, εἰσελθών is a *nom. pend.* AC, Latt. Syrr. Goth. smooth the constr. by reading εἰσῆλθεν...καὶ ἠκούσθη. If ἠκούσθη is personal, the constr. is not broken : *And having entered again into C., He was heard of as being*, etc. The πάλιν looks back to i. 21. Mk often notes the recurrence of scenes and incidents (*v.* 13, iii. 1, 20, iv. 1, etc.). One missionary circuit is ended ; but there is no hint that it was the disobedience of the leper (i. 45) which brought it to a conclusion ; his disobedience changed the character of it from town to country. Here He returns to His headquarters. Mt. calls Capernaum "His own city."

δι' ἡμερῶν. *After some days, interjectis diebus*, seems to be the meaning. Cf. δι' ἐτῶν δὲ πλειόνων (Acts xxiv. 17), διὰ δεκατεσσάρων ἐτῶν (Gal. ii. 1). This use of διά is classical. Winer, p. 475. Cf. xiv. 58.

ἠκούσθη. Probably impersonal, as in Jn ix. 32 ; and, as in 2 Esdr. xvi. 6 (Neh. vi. 6), ὅτι may be recitative and be omitted in translation; *People were heard to say, He is at home.* For this use of ἐν οἴκῳ cf. 1 Cor. xi. 34, xiv. 35, where it is in emphatic contrast to ἐν ἐκκλησίᾳ. Ἐν τῷ οἴκῳ would mean "in the house already mentioned" (i. 29), viz. Simon's, and this may have been the house in which He was "at home"; εἰς οἶκον (ΑΓΔ) suggests "He has gone indoors and is there."

2. ὥστε μηκέτι χωρεῖν. *So that there was no longer room, no,*

not even about the door. A.V. ignores μηκέτι (cf. i. 45) and renders
ἐλάλει "He preached," which would be ἐκήρυσσε. The imperf.
indicates the continuation of Christ's discourse indoors while the
crowd in the street blocked the entrance. The multitude would
not lose the opportunity of witnessing miracles; Christ would not
lose the opportunity of instructing them. Mt., as usual, omits the
impeding crowd; see on i. 33, 44. For συνήχθησαν cf. Mt. xxiv. 28;
Rev. xix. 17: for χωρεῖν cf. Jn ii. 6, xxi. 25. This graphic verse has
no parallel in Mt. or Lk., who are here very independent of Mk. Of
the narrative as a whole even Loisy admits : *La scène est prise sur le
vif, et on croirait la recueillir de la bouche d'un témoin.*

τὸν λόγον. We have ἐλάλει τὸν λόγον again iv. 33, which shows
that the first Christians used ὁ λόγος as a technical term for "the
good tidings"; cf. iv. 14; Acts xiv. 25, viii. 4. *He was speaking
the word.*

3. παραλυτικόν. Lk., as usual (Acts viii. 7, ix. 33), has the
more classical παραλελυμένος.

αἰρόμενον ὑπὸ τεσσάρων. Mk alone has this detail. There is
perhaps design in using the same verb of his being carried and of his
carrying his bed (*vv.* 9, 11, 12), a point which Lk. makes clearer by
saying ἄρας ἐφ' ὃ κατέκειτο. If so, the point is lost in A.V. and R V.,
"*borne* of four" and "*took up* the bed"; also in Vulg., with *porto*
and *tollo*. Cf. ἐπὶ χειρῶν ἀροῦσίν σε (Ps. xci. 12).

4. μὴ δυνάμενοι. The μή does not necessarily give their view;
"*because they saw that* they could not": in N.T., μή with participles
is normal; v. 26, vi. 34, viii. 1, xii. 21, 24. Blass, § 75. 5; J. H.
Moulton, p. 231.

προσενέγκαι. See crit. note. An outside staircase leading to the
flat roof is not uncommon in Palestinian houses, the roof being used
for various purposes. If there was no staircase, ladders could be
obtained, and the roof would be no great distance from the ground.
Men who were so much in earnest would not think getting on to the
roof and removing a small portion of it an insuperable difficulty.
There has been needless discussion of a simple matter; and to treat
the whole narrative as fiction, because we have no certain explanation of this interesting detail, is not sane criticism. It is not even
necessary to surmise that Mk and Lk. are thinking of two different
kinds of houses.

διὰ τὸν ὄχλον. Mk commonly has ὄχλος (*v.* 13, iii. 9, 20, 32, iv. 1,
36, etc., etc.), the others, ὄχλοι.

ἀπεστέγασαν τὴν στέγην. *They unroofed the roof.* A rare verb,
not found elsewhere in N.T., or in LXX. Lk.'s διὰ κεράμων shows

that only part of the roof was removed, just the part above the place
where Christ was teaching.   This verb and ἐξορύξαντες illustrate Mk's
correct use of compound verbs; cf. *v.* 15, iii. 5, iv. 5, 7.   The men
would "dig *out*" whatever clay or mortar had to be removed, so as to
cause as little inconvenience as possible to those in the room below;
in Gal. iv. 15 and in LXX., ἐξορύσσω is used of gouging out eyes.
Burglars who break into houses are said to "dig *through*" (διορύσσω)
the mud walls (Mt. vi. 20).   These difficulties in bringing the patient
to the Healer tested the faith of all five, and thereby strengthened
it.

χαλῶσι τὸν κράβαττον.   *They let down the pallet on which the
paralytic was lying.* Cf. Acts ix. 25 and 2 Cor. xi. 33 of St Paul
being let down in a basket.   The κράβαττος (vi. 55 ; cf. Jn v. 8—11 ;
Acts v. 15, ix. 33) would be the rug or mattress on which they carried
him to the house.   Mt. and Lk. adopt a more literary word ; but
κλίνη, like "bed," suggests something larger than a κράβαττος, and
therefore less likely to be used.   When Lk. comes to the letting down
through the roof, he changes κλίνη, "bed" to κλινίδιον, "couch"
(A.V., R.V.), but no distinction is made in A.V. or R.V. between
κράβαττος and κλίνη.   The spelling of κράβαττος varies greatly in
MSS. of N.T. and in papyri.   The Latin *grabatus* or *grabatum* commonly means a poor kind of bed, a pallet; *grabatis tegetibusque
concepti* (Mart. vi. 39).   Coelius Aurelianus, the famous physician,
says, *eos quiescere jubemus lecto mutato, ad grabata aegros trans-
ferendo.*   Κραβάρειος = *cubicularius* is found in inscriptions.

κατέκειτο.   *Was lying.* Christ does not rebuke him or his bearers
for interrupting His teaching.

5.   ἰδὼν τὴν πίστιν αὐτῶν.   All three preserve the words.   Belief
in the power and good will of Christ is meant.   The αὐτῶν includes
the paralysed man.   Theophylact and Euthymius remark that he
would not have consented to be brought, if he had not believed that
he could be cured.   Here, as in the case of the father of the demoniac
boy (ix. 24), and of Jairus (v. 36), the faith of representatives is
taken into account.   Cf. vii. 32.   This would hold good in the case
of most demoniacs.

Τέκνον.   *My child.* This affectionate address is preserved by Mk
and Mt.   It was doubtless intended to encourage the man and
strengthen his hopes.   We must insert "My," for "Child" would
sound like the beginning of a rebuke.   Lk. has ἄνθρωπε, which is
much less sympathetic.   Τέκνα is addressed to the Twelve (x. 24);
also τεκνία (Jn xiii. 36).   Cf. 1 Cor. iv. 14, 17, and Θύγατερ, Mk v. 34.
We must not infer from τέκνον that the sick person was a lad;

teachers often addressed their disciples in this way (Prov. i. 8, 10, ii. 1, etc.).

ἀφίενταί σου αἱ ἁμαρτίαι. See crit. note. *Thy sins are* forgiven thee (R.V.), rather than "*be* forgiven thee" (A.V.), which might be understood as a wish. This "aoristic present" (Burton § 13; Blass § 56. 4) means "are forgiven now and here"; it = "I forgive thee." Possibly, as in the case of the man at the pool of Bethesda, this man's palsy was the result of sin (Jn v. 14), and the thought of this lessened the man's hope of recovery. Therefore Christ healed the man's conscience before healing his body, and thereby greatly strengthened his faith. See Clem. Alex. *Paed.* i. 2. The belief that suffering is a judgment on the sufferer's sin is wide-spread, and it was strong in Jews (Acts xxviii. 4; Lk xiii. 1—5; Jn ix. 2). "Rabbi Ami said, No death without sin, and no pains without some transgression." And "Rabbi Alexander said, The sick ariseth not from his sickness until his sins are forgiven" (Talmud). Cf. Job iv. 7, xxii. 4, 5. The silence of the paralytic and his friends is impressive.

6. τινες τῶν γραμματέων. See on i. 22. The first appearance of the Scribes in Mk, but Mt. (ii. 4) has them in connexion with the Magi.

καθήμενοι. Lk. preserves this graphic detail and adds that they had come "out of every village of Galilee and Judaea and from Jerusalem." That is popular hyperbole, but it shows that Christ's teaching had already excited the misgivings of the hierarchy (Jn iv. 1), as the Baptist's teaching had done (Jn i. 19, 24). Their sitting may have been accidental (iii. 34), but it may have been a mark of distinction such as they loved (xii. 39). In so crowded a room most would have to stand. On the combination of participles see on i. 15.

ἐν ταῖς καρδίαις. It is remarkable that this Hebraistic expression is in Mk, while Mt., as also in xvi. 7, 8, xxi. 25, has ἐν ἑαυτοῖς. In *v.* 8 all three have ἐν τ. καρδίαις: in xi. 23 Mk alone has it. The heart is regarded as the seat of thought (vii. 21) as well as of emotion. The Scribes had not yet got so far as to express their hostile criticisms openly in Christ's hearing.

7. Τί οὗτος οὕτως λαλεῖ; B has ὅτι for τί, and if it is adopted, ὅτι is interrogative, as in ix. 11, 28. Both οὗτος and οὕτως express disapproval; *Quid iste ita loquitur?* As in i. 27, we have what was thought given in rough, disjointed expressions, which some texts have made smooth. See crit. note.

βλασφημεῖ. Used in this absolute way it means blasphemy

against God, punishable with death (Lev. xxiv. 16; 1 Kings xxi.
10, 13). Jesus had claimed the Divine attribute of being able to
forgive sins; He was " blaspheming." Cf. Mt. xxvi. 66; Jn x. 33.

εἰ μὴ εἶς, ὁ θεός. We have the same words in x. 18, where all
three have εἶς. Here Lk. has μόνος, and Mt. omits the words. In
Enoch, the Son of Man judges, but does not forgive sins.

8. καὶ εὐθὺς ἐπιγνοὺς κ.τ.λ. Mk alone states that Christ knew
instantaneously, and that it was in His spirit that He did so. It
was in the higher part of His human nature (viii. 12), in which He
had communion with the Father, that Jesus possessed this supernatural knowledge (Jn ii. 25). In Jn xi. 33, xiii. 21, it is Christ's
πνεῦμα which is affected by the presence of moral evil. In Mk xiv. 34;
Mt. xxvi. 38; Jn xii. 27, it is His ψυχή that is troubled at the thought
of impending suffering. Bengel draws a questionable distinction
when he says that *prophetae cognoscebant res in Dei spiritu, non in
suo, Christus in spiritu suo divino.* Was it not *in Dei spiritu* in both
cases? The difference may have been that this exceptional knowledge was always open to Christ, but not always to the Prophets.
Lk. also has ἐπιγνούς here. That the compound sometimes, and
perhaps often, implies more complete knowledge than the simple
verb, is clear from 1 Cor. xiii. 12. Here, as in v. 30, the compound
has fuller meaning. All three use ἐπιγινώσκω much less often than
γινώσκω : the case is not parallel to ἀποθνήσκω, which takes the
place of θνήσκω without difference of meaning and almost drives
θνήσκω out of use. In all three Synoptists, as well as in Jn, Christ
shows Himself as ὁ καρδιογνώστης (Acts i. 24, xv. 8).

Τί ταῦτα διαλογίζεσθε ; This reply to the Scribes' unuttered
criticism is almost verbally the same in all three, with the parenthesis in the same place in each—clear evidence that the narratives
are not independent. The Scribes themselves hardly knew how far
their adverse judgment was provoked by jealousy of a rival teacher
rather than by jealousy for God's honour. By reading their thoughts
Christ gave them evidence of His authority, for only He who knows
the hearts of men can pardon men's sins.

9. τί ἐστιν εὐκοπώτερον ; See on x. 25. Here Christ gives them a
test by which they can see whether their adverse judgment is just. It
was easy to *say* " Thy sins are forgiven," because no one could prove
that the claim to work this invisible miracle was baseless. But the
claim to have power to heal with a word could be tested at once ; and
if it proved to be true, it was a guarantee that the other claim was
true also. His healing the body was evidence that He could heal the
soul. But Christ healed the man in answer, not to the unbelief of the

Scribes, but to the belief of the man and his bearers. He would have
healed him, if the Scribes had not been there. As they were there,
He made the healing serve a double purpose.

10. ἐξουσίαν ἔχει. *Hath authority.* God has the power, and has
given authority to the Son of Man to exercise it (Jn v. 27, 30).

ὁ υἱὸς τοῦ ἀνθρώπου. This remarkable expression is used 14
times by Mk. All of these are preserved in Mt., who adds 19, most
of which have come from Q. The total for the four Gospels is 81, 12
of which are in Jn. Lk. has it 8 times in common with Mk and Mt.,
8 times in common with Mt., and 8 times without either. All
four Evangelists represent Christ as using this title of Himself. They
never call Him "the Son of Man," and they nowhere record that anyone gave Him this title. The theory that He never used this title of
Himself is untenable. Even if it were certain, which it is not, that the
difference between υἱὸς ἀνθρώπου, "son of man" or "human being,"
and ὁ υἱὸς τοῦ ἀνθρώπου, "the Son of Man," could not be expressed
in Aramaic, it is incredible that all four Evangelists have gone wrong
on this point. Christ sometimes spoke Greek, and He may have used
the expression ὁ υἱὸς τοῦ ἀνθρώπου. Even if He did not, the Evangelists, whoever they were, represent the memories of numerous
persons who knew whether or no Christ had applied this unusual
title to Himself. Allen, *S. Matthew*, pp. lxxi. f.; Driver, Hastings
D.B. iv. pp. 579 f.; Dalman, *Words*, pp. 249, 253, 259. If the first
Christians had invented a designation for the now risen and glorified
Lord, they would not have chosen an expression so indeterminate as
"the Son of Man."

Here, as in *v.* 28, it is possible to conjecture that the Aramaic original
meant mankind in general. The meaning then would be, not that all
men possess this power, but that it is possible for a man to have it.
Such an interpretation makes good sense, and Mt. ix. 8 favours it.
But this is not often the case: in viii. 13, 38, ix. 9, 12, 31, x. 33, 45,
xiv. 21, 41, such an interpretation is scarcely possible, and in xiii. 26,
xiv. 62 is quite impossible.

ἐπὶ τῆς γῆς. In Mt. and Lk. these words immediately precede
ἀφιέναι ἁμαρτίας, and it is possible that they did so in the original
text of Mk. So ℵCDHLMWᶜΔΣ, Latt. Syr-Pesh. Memph. Arm. Goth.
But B here has ἀφ. ἁμ. ἐπὶ τ. γῆς, and is supported by Φ and two cursives. A third reading, ἀφ. ἐπὶ τ. γ. ἁμ. (AEFGKSUVΓΠ, Syr-Hark.)
adds weight to B, as indicating that ἐπὶ τ. γ. belongs to ἀφ. ἁμαρτ.
rather than to ὁ υἱὸς τ. ἀν. The absolution which the Son of Man
declares takes effect on earth, for it is in accordance with Divine rule.

11. Σοὶ λέγω. The emphatic pronoun marks the change of

address from the Scribes to the sufferer. This change is quite
different from the changes which want of power to keep the *oratio
obliqua* through a long sentence sometimes produces, as in vi. 8, 9.
This speech, with its explanatory parenthesis, is as clear as literary
skill can make it; and it is in the parenthesis, which is no part of
Christ's utterance, that the Evangelists have differences of wording,
Mt. inserting his favourite τότε, and Lk. using his παραλελυμένῳ. Cf.
xi. 32 ; Exod. iv. 4, 5.

ἔγειρε. See crit. note. Here comes the test of the man's faith,
which Christ knew to be sufficient, for He read his thoughts as easily
as the thoughts of the Scribes. The man could give no proof of his
belief that he had received forgiveness of his sins, but he could show
his belief that he had received power to get up and walk. Like ἄγωμεν
(i. 38), ἔγειρε is intrans. Cf. iii. 3, x. 49. Note the asyndeton ; in
the true text there is no καί before ἆρον. For ὕπαγε Lk. has πορεύου, a
verb which is exceptionally freq. in his writings. It is quite in the
narrative style of the O.T. that Mk. has the same fulness of expression
here as in *v.* 9 ; cf. 1 Kings xii. 4, 9, 10, 14 ; Dan. iii. 5, 7, 10, 15.
There is close similarity between *vv.* 11, 12 and Jn v. 8, 9.

εἰς τὸν οἶκόν σου. Doubtless at Capernaum. There is no command to silence. Such a command would have had little meaning
respecting a miracle wrought before such a multitude.

12. ἠγέρθη, καὶ εὐθὺς ἄρας...ἐξῆλθεν ἔμπροσθεν πάντων. Lk.
substitutes three words, each of which is characteristic of his
style, παραχρῆμα ἀναστὰς ἐνώπιον, of which ἀναστάς is an improvement, showing that the man raised himself and was not raised by
others, which ἠγέρθη might mean. See on v. 29, x. 52. Both Mt.
and Lk. emphasize the suddenness of the cure (cf. i. 42) ; and, like
Simon's wife's mother (i. 31), the person healed gives proof of the
completeness of the cure. He not only can use his limbs, but he has
strength to carry his pallet. The crowd would gladly make way for
the exit of so interesting a person, and some would come with him.

ἐξίστασθαι πάντας. Does this include the Scribes? Mt. says
οἱ ὄχλοι. It was natural that amazement should be the first feeling
(v. 43, vi. 51) ; Mt. calls it fear ; Lk. gives us both, and tells us that
the healed man led the way in glorifying God. Lk. is fond of mentioning this effect of Christ's miracles.

δοξάζειν. Note the tense ; *continued glorifying.*

εἴδαμεν. Both Mk and Lk. represent them as impressed by what
they had *seen*, viz., the healing. Mt. thinks of the authority to
forgive sins. On the mixture of first and second aor. forms in εἴδαμεν,
ἐπέβαλαν, ἦλθαν, κ.τ.λ., see Winer, p. 86 ; W.H. *App.* p. 164 ; Blass

§ xxi. 1; Deissmann, *Bib. St.* p.190. As in Mt. ix. 33, οὕτως = τοιαῦτα: it may be a Hebraism.

13, 14.   THE CALL OF LEVI.

Mt. ix. 9. Lk. v. 27, 28.

13. ἐξῆλθεν. From the house and the city; that He did so in order to escape from the concourse is conjecture.

πάλιν παρὰ τ. θάλασσαν. The πάλιν may be a mere mark of transition; or it may refer to a previous scene by the Lake, perhaps i. 16, where παρὰ τ. θ. means "along the shore." Here it would seem to mean "to the shore"; cf. Acts xvi. 13.

ἤρχετο...ἐδίδασκεν. The change to imperfects is accurate; cf. i. 31, 32. In wording, Mt. and Lk. differ considerably from Mk and from one another.

14. παράγων εἶδεν. As in i. 16; the repetition confirms the view that πάλιν refers to i. 16. Once more, on the shore of the Lake, He becomes a fisher of men.

Λευείν. See crit. note. The fact that James the Less was son of an Alphaeus (iii. 18) may have led to the reading Ἰάκωβον. That Levi and James were brothers, sons of the same Alphaeus, is improbable. They are associated in no list of the Apostles. With Λευείν Lk. has his favourite ὀνόματι, and with Μαθθαῖον Mt. has his λεγόμενον. Mk has λεγόμενος once (xv. 7) and ὀνόματι not at all.

καθήμενον ἐπὶ τὸ τελώνιον. *Sitting at or near the place where toll was collected.* The *douane* of the Lake; the word occurs only in this connexion; cf. δεκατώνιον, the office of a collector of tenths. In N.T., ἐπί c. acc. often answers the question Where? Blass § 43. 1. Capernaum was on some of the main trade routes, and here tolls were collected for the tetrarch; hence the πολλοὶ τελῶναι (*v.* 15), some of whom would be sitting with Levi. There is no serious ground for doubting the identity of Levi the toll-gatherer with Matthew the toll-gatherer. The two names do not cause great difficulty, although they are not quite parallel to the other instances among the Apostles. In those of Simon Peter and Thomas Didymus, one name is Semitic, the other Greek. Bartholomew (who is probably Nathaniel) has a patronymic for one name. But both Levi and Matthew are Semitic, and neither is a patronymic.

Ἀκολούθει μοι. A call to be a disciple (viii. 34), and perhaps to be an Apostle (i. 17): cf. Mt. viii. 22; Lk. ix. 59. It certainly meant leaving his lucrative post at the τελώνιον, and therefore it was a severer test than the call to the four fishermen: Lk. inserts καταλιπὼν πάντα. They could, and did, return to their fishing, when the work to which Jesus had called them seemed to be at an end. Once more Jesus appears as the reader of hearts. If He had not known Levi's character, He would not have called one of his very unpromising profession to be an Apostle : his ministrations would be unacceptable to every Jew who had known him as a toll-collector. There may have been a religious stir among the toll-collectors. Many of them had come to listen to John (Lk. iii. 12).

ἀναστὰς ἠκολούθησεν αὐτῷ. The Hebraistic pleonasm ἀναστάς is in all three. We may suppose that Levi heard Christ teach, or that he knew something of His teaching, and had thought about it. But there is nothing incredible in the thought that there was something in Christ's look and manner and sudden invitation which answered to a craving in the toll-gatherer's heart, and that he felt at once, like Francis of Assisi at the Portiuncula, that this was a call which came home to him. Such feeling may show want of mental ballast, as Porphyry thought. The outcome is the only practical test of its value ; " By their fruits ye shall know them."

15—17. The Feast in Levi's House.

Mt. ix. 10—13. Lk. v. 29—32.

15. γίνεται κατακεῖσθαι. See crit. note. *Reclining* at meals was usual. Of the six words used in the Gospels to denote this posture (ἀνακεῖσθαι, ἀνακλίνειν, ἀναπίπτειν, κατακεῖσθαι, κατακλίνειν, συνανακεῖσθαι), Mk uses all but κατακλίνειν, Mt. all but κατακεῖσθαι and κατακλίνειν, Lk. all six, while Jn uses only ἀνακεῖσθαι and ἀναπίπτειν. This is in accordance with the fulness of Lk.'s vocabulary and the sparseness of John's. For these six words, Vulg. has only three, *accumbere*, *discumbere*, and *recumbere*, and it uses them almost promiscuously. All three are employed to translate both ἀνακεῖσθαι and ἀνακλίνειν.

ἐν τῇ οἰκίᾳ αὐτοῦ. In Levi's house, as Lk. expressly states; Peter's house would not hold a large reception. In Mt., αὐτοῦ is omitted. If Levi = Matthew, and Matthew is the authority for this part of the First Gospel, αὐτοῦ would be unnecessary.

πολλοὶ τελῶναι καὶ ἁμαρτωλοί. The combination is here in all three ; cf. Mt. xi. 19, xxi. 31 ; Lk. vii. 34, xv. 1, xviii. 11. It is paralleled in Lucian (*Necyom.* 11) ; μοιχοὶ καὶ πορνοβόσκοι καὶ τελῶναι καὶ κόλακες καὶ συκοφάνται, καὶ τοιοῦτος ὅμιλος τῶν πάντα κυκώντων ἐν τῷ βίῳ. Cf. Aristoph. *Equit.* 248 ; Theoph. *Charac.* 6. Theocritus in answer to the question, which are the worst of wild beasts, says, " On the mountains bears and lions, in cities publicans and pettifoggers." The word is derived from τέλη (Mt. xvii. 25 ; Rom. xiii. 7) and ὠνέομαι, and therefore in etymology τελῶναι = *publicani*, the wealthy persons, commonly *equites*, who *bought* or farmed the taxes or Government *revenues*. But in usage τελῶναι = *portitores*, who collected the taxes. This usage is invariable in N.T. and freq. elsewhere. Taxes were usually collected for the Emperor, and for a Jew to undertake such work for a heathen conqueror was the deepest disgrace ; all such were excommunicated. But this was not Levi's case ; he would be disliked for being a tax-collector, but at Capernaum tolls were collected, not for Rome, but for the tetrarch. Rome allowed the Herods some powers of taxation.

τῷ Ἰησοῦ. So always in N.T. In LXX., Ἰησοῖ is sometimes found. Levi had invited his colleagues and acquaintances to meet the Master ; it was his first missionary act. After the call of Simon and Andrew Christ is entertained at their humble house (i. 29—31) ; and after the call of the well-to-do toll-collector He is entertained at his spacious house.

ἦσαν γὰρ πολλοί. Sc. οἱ μαθηταί. Like other teachers of repute, Jesus had hearers who followed Him in His movements. His "mighty works" attracted numbers, many of whom were retained by the "authority" of His teaching. It was the number of His adherents that roused the jealousy of the hierarchy, and the character of His teaching made them bitterly hostile. It is making the πολλοί tautological to refer it to τελῶναι κ. ἁμαρτωλοί.

καὶ ἠκολούθουν αὐτῷ. If the καί before ἰδόντες is genuine (see crit. note) these words are best taken with what follows. W.H., A.V., R.V. omit καί and connect κ. ἠκολ. αὐτῷ with ἦσαν γὰρ πολλοί. There is, however, more point in saying that Christ had hostile followers as well as friendly ones, than in saying that friendly people followed Him.

16. **οἱ γραμματεῖς τῶν Φαρισαίων.** *Those of the Scribes who belonged to the Pharisees.* There were Scribes before there were Pharisees, but most of them seem to have been Pharisees (cf. Acts xxiii. 9). The phrase is unusual, and hence the reading of ΑΓΠ, etc. D also has γρ. κ. οἱ Φ. These unfriendly followers of course would not enter the house in which τελῶναι and ἁμαρτωλοί were being entertained. The strongest characteristic of the Pharisees was their holding that the unwritten tradition was as binding as the written Law ; indeed some held that to transgress the tradition of the elders was worse than transgressing the Law.

ἔλεγον τοῖς μαθηταῖς. The question was perhaps asked several

times ; but they do not as yet assail Jesus Himself. It is probably
as another collision between Christ and the Scribes that this narrative
is placed here.

῞Οτι μετὰ τῶν τελωνῶν. We have ὅτι for τί again ix. 11, 28,
where Mt. has τί or διὰ τί : here both Mt. and Lk. have διὰ τί. In
class. Grk ὅστις sometimes introduces an indirect question, but in
these passages the question is direct. Here, however, the ὅτι may
be merely recitative ; *He eateth and drinketh*, etc. (R.V.). The
changes of order in *vv.* 15, 16 are curious (τελ. κ. ἁμαρ., ἁμαρ. κ.
τελ., τελ. κ. ἁμαρ.), and it is not the Scribes who differ from the
Evangelist, but the Evangelist from himself. In *v.* 16 the two classes
are twice coupled under one art. as a single class, and A.V. ignores
the art. in both places. See on iv. 3. As the disciples were eating
with them, the criticism touched them as well as the Master, and
Lk. has ἐσθίετε for ἐσθίει. The same criticism was made by Celsus
in the second century. He taunts Christians with His having as His
disciples infamous persons, τελώνας καὶ ναύτας τοὺς πονηροτάτους (Orig.
Cels. i. 62).

17. καὶ ἀκούσας. Probably He overheard. In all three accounts
He takes the whole responsibility. It is His doing, not the disciples',
that they eat with sinners, with excommunicated toll-collectors and
their associates. He asserts His mission as the Physician of souls ;
physicians do not visit healthy persons, and they are not afraid of
being infected by the diseases of the sick. Moreover, they cannot
heal the sick without visiting them. It is possible that this aphorism
was current in Palestine before Christ used it, and that it came to
Palestine from the Cynics, but the idea is " such an obvious one
that different men may quite well have stumbled on it independently"
(Jülicher). As Euthymius remarks, ὁ μὲν νόμος ἐξέβαλλε τὸν κακόν,
ὁ δὲ Χριστὸς μετέβαλλεν.

οἱ ἰσχύοντες. *They that are strong.* Cf. Soph. *Trach.* 234.

οὐκ ἦλθον καλέσαι δικαίους. An *argumentum ad hominem.* They
believed themselves to be δίκαιοι : He came to call those who knew
themselves to be sinners, and He had no remedy for those who
were convinced that they needed no remedy. The interpolation of
εἰς μετάνοιαν weakens the incisiveness of the parallel ; see crit. note.
With ἦλθον cf. i. 38, x. 45. Those who attributed these expressions
to Christ believed in His pre-existence ; and whence came that
belief? Salmon, *Human Element,* p. 170. Christ seems to have
often used the form " not...but "; it is freq. in the Gospels, and
specially freq. in Mk (iii. 26, 29, iv. 17, 22, v. 39, vi. 9, vii. 19,
ix. 37, x. 8, etc.).

18—22. The Question of Fasting.

Mt. ix. 14—17. Lk. v. 33—39.

Mt. is not wholly in agreement with Mk, but the discrepancy need not trouble us. It does not matter who put the question, or whether it arose out of the feast in Levi's house, which may have lasted till the evening on which one of the two weekly fasts which some Pharisees observed (Lk. xviii. 12) had begun.

18. οἱ μαθηταὶ ᾽Ιωάννου. They imitated the strictness of the Baptist's life (cf. Lk. xi. 1) and *were fasting* (R.V.), not "used to fast" (A.V.). It is the periphrastic tense again, as in i. 6, 33, ii. 6. John was in prison, so they could not ask him as to the difference of practice, and it would seem strange to them that their master should be in prison while Jesus was free and at a feast.

λέγουσιν αὐτῷ. This time the critics (*vv.* 6, 16) address Him, but in their criticism they do not mention Him. Here both Mk and Mt. have διὰ τί, while Lk. has a mere statement of fact; Christ's disciples do not keep the weekly fasts. *The disciples of the Pharisees* is an unusual expression.

οἱ δὲ σοί. The possessive pronouns are rare in Mk; σός here and v. 19; ἐμός, viii. 38, x. 40; ἡμέτερος and ὑμέτερος nowhere either in Mk or Mt.

19. Μὴ δύνανται; Like *num*, μή expects a negative reply. Blass § 75. 2; Winer, p. 641; cf. iv. 21; Mt. xxvi. 25; Lk. vi. 39. In Jn iv. 29, xviii. 17, 25, A.V. goes wrong on this point. The analogy of a wedding might come home to those whose master had declared his own relation to Jesus to be that of Bridegroom's friend to Bridegroom (Jn iii. 29). It is morally impossible to combine ascetic fasting with a festival of exceptional joyousness. Lk. has "Can ye *make* them fast?" Mt. has "Can they *mourn*?"

οἱ υἱοὶ τοῦ νυμφῶνος. *Filii nuptiarum* (Vulg.). The common Hebraism for "those closely connected with" whatever the gen. denotes; iii. 17; Lk. x. 6, xvi. 8, xx. 36; etc. In LXX. such phrases are somewhat rare; Gen. xi. 10; 2 Sam. xii. 5; 1 Kings i. 52; 1 Macc. iv. 2. Deissmann (*Bib. St.* p. 161) prefers to call them "Hebraisms of translation," and he thinks that some of them are not Hebraisms at all. With this phrase compare the "comrades" of Samson (Judg. xiv. 11, 20), and the νυμφευταί, παράνυμφοι, or πάροχοι among the Greeks. They are analogous to our bridesmaids. Hort (*Jud. Christ.* p. 23) says that by custom those who were in attendance on a bridegroom were dispensed from certain religious observances. Here again (see on i. 12) there is no reason to suspect that the saying is borrowed from heathen sources, such as myths about the marriage of the gods (Clemen, *Primitive Christianity*, p. 320). Νυμφών (Tobit vi. 14, 17) is analogous to ἀνδρῶν, γυναικῶν, παρθενών, κ.τ.λ.

ὁ νυμφίος. In Hos. ii., the relation of Jehovah to Israel is repeatedly spoken of as betrothal. Jesus transfers the figure to the relation between Himself and His disciples, and it is often used in N.T. both by Himself (Jn iii. 29 ; Mt. xxv. 1—11) and the Apostles (2 Cor. xi. 2 ; Eph. v. 27 ; Rev. xix. 7, xxi. 9). "As long as they have the Bridegroom with them" has much more point than "as long as the wedding-feast lasts." The sentence gives a solemn fulness to Christ's reply to the questioners. The preceding question would have sufficed. The metaphor is not an obvious one to use of disciples, and the adoption of it by Christ in a saying which is certainly His is all the more remarkable.

20. ἐλεύσονται δὲ ἡμέραι. *But days will come.* There is no art. ; yet even R.V. inserts it here in all three Gospels, and also Lk. xvii. 22, xix. 43, xxi. 6, xxiii. 29.

ὅταν ἀπαρθῇ. The verb is in all three, and nowhere else in N.T. He does not say simply ἀπέλθῃ or πορευθῇ (Jn xvi. 7), but implies, for the first time, that His death will be a violent one ; ὅτι αἴρεται ἀπὸ τῆς γῆς ἡ ζωὴ αὐτοῦ (Is. lxiii. 8). Dalman, *Words*, p. 263. Cf. xiv. 7.

τότε νηστεύσουσιν. *Then they will fast*, of their own accord, *ex arbitrio, non ex imperio* (Tert.). Not, "they *can* fast," or "they *shall* fast"; the fut. here is not imperative. We have instances of the ful-filment of this prediction, Acts ii. 13, xiii. 2, 3, xiv. 23. The fast before Easter was observed from very early times, but for several centuries great diversity existed as to its duration; see Irenaeus in Eus. *H.E.* v. 24; Socrates *H.E.* v. 22 ; Sozomen *H.E.* vii. 19.

ἐν ἐκείνῃ τῇ ἡμέρᾳ. See crit. note. "In that sad day," *atra dies* ; cf. the superfluous, but impressive, ὁ ἄνθρωπος ἐκεῖνος, xiv. 21. Mt. omits these words as implied in τότε, while Lk. has his characteristic ἐν ἐκείναις ταῖς ἡμέραις, in agreement with the preceding ἡμέραι, which Mk seems to have forgotten. If a change is made it should rather have been the other way ; "*A* day will come when He will be taken away, and then will they fast in those *days*." Is Mk influenced by the usage in his own day, which may have been that of fasting on the Friday?

21. οὐδεὶς ἐπίβλημα. This parable and its companion are a further reply to the criticism in *v.* 18. All three have the pair in this connexion. Both parables set forth the truth that a new spirit

requires a new form, and the second expresses it more strongly than
the first. Possibly the allusion to a wedding-feast in *v.* 19 suggested
lessons from garments and wine.

ἐπίβλ. ῥάκους ἀγνάφου. *A patch of undressed rag,* a patch torn
from new cloth. Lk. augments the folly by representing the patch
as torn from a new *garment.* Nowhere else in Bibl. Grk does ἐπιράπτω
occur. Vulg. here has *adsumentum* for ἐπίβλημα, in Mt. and Lk.
commissura ; other Latin renderings are *insumentum* (a) and *immis-
sura* (d). Similarly, for αἴρει τὸ πλήρωμα and χεῖρον σχίσμα, Vulg.
here has *auferet supplementum* and *major scissura,* in Mt. *tollit
plenitudinem* (as if τὸ πλ. were acc.) and *pejor scissura.*

εἰ δὲ μή. "But if a man acts not so," *i.e.* if he does commit this
folly. Cf. Jn xiv. 2 ; Rev. ii. 5. Syr-Sin. has "else the new filling
up draws away the weakness of the worn-out one."

αἴρει τὸ πλήρωμα ἀπ' αὐτοῦ. *The filling takes away from it.* The
new material shrinks and tears the old garment on which it is sewn.

τὸ καινὸν τοῦ παλαιοῦ. Explanatory of τὸ πλ. ἀπ' αὐτοῦ, *the new
from the old* (R.V.) ; or possibly, the ἀπό not being repeated, "the new
complement of the old " (Swete, Gould). The contrast between παλαιός
and καινός is found Eph. iv. 23 ; Heb. viii. 13. See Westcott on
Heb. viii. 8.

22. καὶ οὐδεὶς βάλλει. This second parable (1) puts the lesson
that a new system needs a new form more strongly, and (2) carries
it further. (1) The ἐπίβλημα is only a piece of the new system, the
οἶνος νέος is the whole of it. The new piece is wasted and the old
garment is made worse, but the new wine and the old skins perish
utterly. (2) In Mt. and Lk. certainly, and probably in Mk, although
D, a b ff i omit, the right method is pointed out. Here again, Mt. and
Lk. agree against Mk. They both say that the wine is *spilled,* while
Mk merely says that it *perishes* as well as the skins ; instead of abbre-
viating Mk (i. 32) they both expand him. Hawkins, *Hor. Syn.*[2]
p. 210 ; Burkitt, *Gosp. Hist.* p. 42. Βάλλει illustrates the tendency of
words to become weaker in meaning ; not "throws," but simply
"puts," as in vii. 33. Jn xiii. 5 is parallel ; cf. Mt. ix. 2 ; Jn xx.
25, 27 ; Jas. iii. 3.

οἶνον νέον. Wine recently made, in which fermentation might
still continue. *Quemadmodum musto dolia ipsa rumpuntur, et omne
quod in imo jacet in summam partem vis caloris ejectat* (Seneca, *Ep.*
lxxxiii. 14).

ἀσκοὺς παλαιούς. Old skins, already stretched to the utmost and
perhaps patched ; cf. Ps. cxix. 83 ; Job xiii. 28 ; and esp. Josh. ix.
4, 5, 13.

ἀλλὰ οἶνον νέον κ.τ.λ. See crit. note. Another instance of Mk's rough brevity; see on i. 27. Only in this passage is it worth while to mark in translation the difference between νέος and καινός : *But new wine into fresh wine-skins.* Vulg. ignores it in all three Gospels ; *vinum novum in utres novos.* Papyri do not observe it.

We have now had four instances of Christ's parabolic teaching; Fishers of men, the Bridegroom, the Garment and the Patch, the Wine and the Wine-skins (i. 17, ii. 19, 21, 22), all very brief. The last two form a pair, like the Mustard-seed |and the Leaven, the Lost Sheep and the Lost Coin, the Unwise Builder and the Unwise King; cf. Mt. xiii. 44—46. See Hort, *Judaistic Christianity*, pp. 22 f.

23—28. PLUCKING CORN ON THE SABBATH.

Mt. xii. 1—8. Lk. v. 1—5.

23. Καὶ ἐγένετο...διαπορεύεσθαι. Contrast the constr. in i. 9, iv. 4. Mt. places this incident much later, but Lk. agrees with Mk. For ἐν τοῖς σάββασιν see on i. 21.

διὰ τῶν σπορίμων. *Through the sown-lands*, which the context shows to have been corn-fields ; *per sata* (Vulg.). The word is rare, but is found in papyri.

ὁδὸν ποιεῖν. See crit. note. Not " to make a road," although this is the usual meaning of the phrase, but " to make their way " (R.V. marg.), " to go onwards," *progredi*, although the usual Greek for this is ὁδὸν ποιεῖσθαι (Judg. xvii. 8). Ὁδοποία has been found in a papyrus of the third cent. B.C. Plucking ears would not make a path where there was none, and Jesus was walking in front of the disciples. Vulg. has *praegredi* for ὁδὸν ποιεῖν, which makes the disciples go in front. It is possible that what Mk means is "began, as they went along, to pluck." In any case it is an instance of his superfluous fulness (cf. i. 32, 42) ; ὁδὸν π. is not needed after διαπορεύεσθαι, and it has no equivalent in Mt. or Lk. The Pharisees do not accuse the disciples of damaging property, or of making a path on the Sabbath ; it is the plucking (to which Lk. adds " rubbing in their hands ") that is questioned. This was regarded as harvesting, which might not be done on the Sabbath. Plucking as one went along was allowed (Deut. xxiii. 25, 26) ; but not on the Sabbath. Philo (*Vit. Mo.* ii. 4, M. 137) says that not a sprig or leaf might be cut, nor any kind of fruit gathered. As in i. 5, 13, 39, we have a leading fact expressed by a participle, τίλλοντες.

24. ἔλεγον. With Mk, conversation is a *process*, and he often

introduces what was said by an imperf., without meaning that the
remark was repeated.

Ἴδε. "Behold," "See." Mt. has ἰδού, Lk. neither. They are
attacking the Master through the disciples ; He must be aware of
what they are doing. In Lk. the reproach is addressed to the disciples ;
τί ποιεῖτε ; Evidently Christ Himself was not plucking.

25. Οὐδέποτε ἀνέγνωτε ; *Did ye never read ?* They had appealed
to the traditional interpretation of Scripture ; He appeals to Scripture
itself. Cf. xii. 10, 26 ; Mt. xix. 4, xxi. 16, 42, xxii. 31. The aor. is
used in all places ; and ἀναγινώσκω, which occurs more than 30 times
in N.T., seems always to mean "read," and never "recognize," or
"admit." See on 2 Cor. i. 13, iii. 2. The emphatic "never" is a
pointed rebuke. He might have shown that their interpretation was
wrong, and that the disciples had not broken the Sabbath. But He
takes higher ground ; charity comes before ritual propriety. The
Pharisees' error is a common one ; when we appeal to Scripture, we
often mean our inferences from Scripture.

Δαυείδ. 1 Sam. xxi. 1—6.

χρείαν ἔσχεν. Mk alone has this ; like ὁδὸν ποιεῖν, it is superfluous, for ἐπείνασεν suffices. Mt. alone *tells* us that the disciples
were hungry ; but their conduct indicates it ; thus "David and his
men find their counterpart in the Son of David and His disciples"
(Swete) Mk perhaps inserts χρείαν ἔσχεν to show that the disciples,
like David, could plead necessity ; cf. Acts ii. 45, iv. 35 ; Eph. iv. 28 ;
1 Jn iii. 17.

26. τὸν οἶκον τ. θεοῦ. Judg. xviii. 31 ; cf. 1 Sam. i. 7, 24, iii.
15. In 1 Sam. xxi. 1—6 it is not stated that David entered the House
of God, but it is just possible that the expression includes the τέμενος
or sacred enclosure in which the Tabernacle stood. The Tabernacle
was then at Nob, which was probably a little N. of Jerusalem.

ἐπὶ Ἀβιάθαρ ἀρχιερέως. *When Abiathar was high-priest* (R.V.).
Cf. Lk. iii. 2, iv. 27 ; Acts xi. 28. AC 33 insert τοῦ before ἀρχ.,
which would mean "in the time of Ab., who was high-priest," without
limiting the date to the duration of the high-priesthood. Mt. and Lk.
omit the date, which is erroneous, for Ahimelech was the high-priest
who gave David the shewbread. Syr-Sin. omits the date here. The
error may be compared with that of Mt. xxiii. 35, and in both cases
we probably have a slip of the Evangelist (or of a *very* early copyist),
who inserted a note of his own into our Lord's words and made a mistake in doing so. No date is required here. Conjectures that both high-
priests had both names, or that ἐπὶ Ἀβ. may mean "in the passage
about A." (cf. xii. 6), are unsatisfactory. Here, as in the coupling of

a prophecy from Malachi with one from Isaiah, as if both were from
Isaiah (i. 2), Mt. and Lk. omit what is erroneous in Mk.

τοὺς ἄρτους τῆς προθέσεως. *The bread* or *The loaves of the setting
forth, panes propositionis* (Vulg.). This expression occurs Exod. xl.
23; 1 Chron. ix. 32, xxiii. 29. Other names in LXX. are ἀρ. τοῦ
προσώπου, "of the Presence of God" (1 Sam. xxi. 6), τῆς προσφορᾶς,
(1 Kings vii. 28), ἄρ. ἐνώπιοι (Exod. xxv. 30), or οἱ διὰ παντός, "the
perpetual loaves" (Num. iv. 7) ; cf. 2 Chron. xiii. 11, xxix. 18. In
Heb. ix. 2 we have ἡ πρόθεσις τῶν ἄρτων. See Deissmann, *Bib. St.*
p. 157. "Shewbread" appears first in Coverdale (A.D. 1535), probably
from Luther's *Schaubrote*. Hebrew has few adjectives expressing
such attributes, and hence the freq. use of the gen. Twelve loaves
were placed on "the pure table" and renewed every Sabbath. Similar
offerings of twelve or thirty-six loaves were made by other Semitic
nations in the sacrifices to their gods as food for the gods to eat. To
the Jew they signified the Presence of God and His perpetual ac-
ceptance of worship.

οὐκ ἔξεστιν. Lev. xxiv. 9 says that this bread is for Aaron and his
sons, who are to eat it in a holy place. This οὐκ ἔξεστιν was therefore
stronger than the οὐκ ἔξεστιν in *v.* 24, and yet Ahimelech allowed an
exception to be made. Only here and Lk. vi. 4, xx. 22, does ἔξεστιν
c. acc. et infin. occur in N.T. Contrast vi. 18, x. 2 ; Mt. here has the
dat., and ACD, against אBL, have the dat. in Mk. Bede thinks that
allowing David and his followers to eat the priests' bread may point to
the fact that *omnes filii Ecclesiae sacerdotes sunt.*

ἔδωκεν καὶ τοῖς σὺν αὐτῷ. This also is not stated in 1 Sam. xxi.,
but it may be inferred from David's asking for five loaves, and from
his assuring Ahimelech that the wallets of his followers were Levitically clean. Thus David allowed his followers, as the Son of David
allowed His followers, to do what usage forbade.

27. καὶ ἔλεγεν αὐτοῖς. This introductory formula may indicate
that the cornfield incident is over, and that Mk is appending to it, as
a sort of moral, a principle on which Christ used to insist. The
formula is superfluous, if *vv.* 26, 27 were spoken as a continuous
utterance.

Τὸ σάββατον διὰ τὸν ἄνθρωπον ἐγένετο. Neither Mt. nor Lk. has
any parallel to this. Mt. may have omitted it as "a hard saying"
for Jewish Christians (Hawkins, *Hor. Syn.*² p. 122). Mt. substitutes
the argument that the priests in the Temple were allowed to violate
the Sabbath, on which day their work was not lessened, but increased;
an argument which does not lead on to what follows in *v.* 28 as *v.* 27
does. And he again quotes Hos. vi. 6. We owe the preservation of

this wide-embracing principle, "The Sabbath for man, not man for
the Sabbath," to Mk, who may have seen its value for Gentile readers.
The rigid observance of the Sabbath by Jewish Christians might
sometimes hinder the conversion of heathen hearers. Cf. Ezek.
xx. 12, "I *gave* them *My* Sabbaths." The Sabbath is a boon, not a
burden, as the Rabbis sometimes saw; "The Sabbath is handed over
to you; not, ye are handed over to the Sabbath" (Edersheim, *Life
and Times*, II. p. 58). Charity comes before ritual. Cf. οὐκ ἐκτίσθη
ἀνὴρ διὰ τὴν γυναῖκα, ἀλλὰ γυνὴ διὰ τὸν ἄνδρα (1 Cor. xi. 9): and Οὐ διὰ
τὸν τόπον τὸ ἔθνος, ἀλλὰ διὰ τὸ ἔθνος τὸν τόπον ὁ κύριος ἐξελέξατο (2 Macc.
v. 19). A few cursives, with Syr-Sin. and Syr-Pesh., read ἐκτίσθη
here for ἐγένετο.

διὰ τὸν ἄνθρωπον. Not merely for the Jew. A periodic day of
rest is a boon for the whole human race. When the observance of
Sunday was abolished during the French Revolution, it was found
necessary to make every tenth day a holiday. Syr-Sin. omits καὶ
οὐχ...σάββατον.

28. ὥστε. Here, as in x. 8, c. *indic.* If *v.* 27 is omitted, the
argument is incomplete. Mt. has γάρ, making the saying a premise
rather than a conclusion. Lk. has neither. In all three, κύριος
comes first with emphasis. The Sabbath has been given to mankind
for their benefit; therefore the Representative of mankind may decide
how the gift can best be used for their benefit, and it must not be
used in such a way as to turn a blessing into a curse. Thus Christ
not only takes the responsibility for His disciples' action but claims
it. St Paul argues in a similar way about our liberty in things indifferent; we must not use it in such a way as to *lose* it, by becoming
slaves to a habit (1 Cor. vi. 12). See Hort, *Jud. Chris.* p. 33. Some
Fathers seem to have thought that, because the Jews made the Sabbath a burden, it was given them as a burden, to punish them for
their carnal way of life.

καὶ τοῦ σαββάτου. Either "also" (A.V.) or "even" (R.V.) may
be right. If "also," it means "in addition to other things of which
He has control." Cf. vii. 18.

CHAPTER III.

5. אABCD etc. omit ὑγιὴς ὡς ἡ ἄλλη, which comes from Mt. xii. 13 and has little support here.

6. ἐδίδουν (BL) rather than ἐποίησαν (אCΔ), or ἐποίουν (ΑΡΓΠ), or ποιοῦντες (D). The variants are substitutions of a more usual verb. Cf. xv. 1.

8. ἀκούοντες (אBΔ and versions) rather than ἀκούσαντες (ACDL etc.). ποιεῖ (BL, Syrr.) rather than ἐποίει (אACD, Latt.). Syr-Sin. omits πλῆθος πολύ.

11. ἐθεώρουν (אBCDGL 33), προσέπιπτον (אACDFGKLMP), and ἔκραζον (אABCD) rather than ἐθεώρει (AP), προσέπιπτεν (EHSUV), and ἔκραζεν (EHSUV), which are grammatical corrections. Syr-Sin. omits ὅταν αὐτὸν ἐθ.

12. ποιήσωσιν (אAB*CΓΔ) rather than ποιῶσιν (B²DKL).

14. οὓς καὶ ἀποστόλους ὠνόμασεν (אBC*Δ, Memph.) is omitted by AC²DLP, Latt. Syrr. Goth. Arm., and may come from Lk. vi. 13.

15. אBC*LΔ omit θεραπεύειν τὰς νόσους καί.

16. καὶ ἐποίησεν τοὺς δώδεκα (אBC*ΔΦ) is to be retained ; AC²DL etc. omit as superfluous.

17. ὄνομα (BD, Syr-Pesh.) may be right; but ὀνόματα (אACLΓΔΠΦ, Latt. Syr-Hark. Arm. Memph. Goth. Aeth.) would be corrected to ὄνομα, as only one name follows.

18. Καναναῖον (אBCDLΔ 33) rather than Κανανίτην (ΑΓΠΦ).

19. Ἰσκαριώθ (אBCLΔ 33) rather than Ἰσκαριώτην (ΑΓΠΦ). ἔρχεται (א*BΓ) rather than ἔρχονται (א³CLΔΠΦ).

25. δυνήσεται (אBCLΔ) rather than δύναται (ΑDΓΠ).

29. ἁμαρτήματος (אBLΔ, Latt. Memph. Arm. Goth. [ἁμαρτίας, C*D]) rather than κρίσεως (AC²ΓΠ, Syrr.).

35. γάρ, though strongly attested (אACDL etc., Latt. Syrr. Arm. Goth.) is the kind of connexion which scribes often insert; B, b c Memph. omit. B has τὰ θελήματα, which is freq. in LXX.

1—6. A WITHERED HAND HEALED ON THE SABBATH.

Mt. xii. 9—14. Lk. vi. 6—11.

1. Καὶ εἰσῆλθεν πάλιν εἰς συναγωγήν. *And He entered again into a synagogue.* Mt. and Lk. have τὴν συν., "*the* synagogue in that place." It would perhaps be more exact if we sacrificed the compound verb and rendered, "He went again to synagogue." Cf. ἐν συναγωγῇ, "in synagogue" (Jn vi. 59, xviii. 20), and our "went to church," "was in church," ἐν ἐκκλησίᾳ (1 Cor. xiv. 19). The πάλιν looks back to i. 21; cf. ii. 1, 13. Mt. says that it was the same Sabbath; He went from the cornfields to the synagogue. Lk. says that it was a different Sabbath, and Mk seems to agree with Lk.; and he is probably right. It would be after the synagogue service that they would have gone to the cornfield. But the matter is of small importance.

ἐξηραμμένην ἔχων τὴν χεῖρα. *Who had his hand withered.* The passive participle implies that his hand had been paralysed by an accident or illness. Mt. and Lk. say simply ξηρά, and Lk. adds ἡ δεξιά. The ἔχων is another case of a main fact being expressed by a participle (i. 5, 13, 39, ii. 23). In the Canonical Gospels the man does not speak; in one which was used by the Nazarenes and Ebionites he asks to be restored to health.

2. παρετήρουν. *They kept watching Him closely.* That they did so with a sinister purpose (Lk. xx. 20; Dan. vi. 11) comes from the context. The middle is more common, and some texts (ACDΔ) have it here; it is used of observing ordinances scrupulously (Gal. iv. 10). From *v.* 6 we learn that it was the Pharisees who watched Christ.

εἰ τοῖς σάββασιν θ. αὐτόν. *To see if He will heal him on the Sabbath*; cf. τί οἶδας εἰ τὸν ἄνδρα σώσεις; (1 Cor. vii. 16). In the *Acta Pilati* i. (ed. Tisch. 215), the Jews say that they have a law not to heal on the Sabbath, and yet Jesus healed all kinds of people on the Sabbath. When this accusation is made before Pilate, he asks "Is it for a good deed that they wish to put Him to death?" They say to Him, "Yea." To formalists a breach of external propriety is more shocking than a breach of principle. As in ii. 8, Jesus reads their thoughts and replies to them both by word and action.

3. Ἔγειρε εἰς τὸ μέσον. *Arise and come into the midst*; condensed constr., as in x. 10; Lk. xi. 7; Acts viii. 40. Whatever is done shall be manifest to all. He has no need of secret methods, and there is no need to spy upon Him. Victor of Antioch is hardly right in sug-

gesting that Christ called the man into the midst in order to kindle
sympathy in the hostile critics. See on *v.* 12.

4. It might have been sufficient to say that it was no violation
even of their rules respecting the Sabbath for the man to stretch out
his hand. But Christ appeals to a broader principle (cf. ii. 17, 27).
To refuse to do good is to do evil (Jas. iv. 17), and, Sabbath or no
Sabbath, it is wrong to do evil and right to do good. His enemies
cared nothing about the man's hand. Κακοποιεῖν is class. Grk,
but not ἀγαθοποιεῖν, which in LXX. takes the place of the class. εὖ
ποιεῖν.

ψυχὴν σῶσαι ἢ ἀποκτεῖναι. This second way of putting the
alternative has two points. (1) The Rabbis themselves allowed attending to suffering when life was in danger, and life being in danger
was interpreted liberally. (2) They were plotting to kill Jesus. Which
did more honour to the Sabbath, His healing or their plotting? "To
save" means more than "to preserve from death"; it includes
restoring to health. Mt. here inserts the argument about the animal
fallen into a pit, which Lk. (xiv. 1—6) has in the healing of the man
with the dropsy.

ἐσιώπων. *They remained silent.* They cannot refute His arguments, but they will not yield. Mk alone mentions the silence of the
Pharisees, which, like the watching, continued for some time. See
on x. 48. Here and in *v.* 5 we seem to have the vivid recollections of
an eye-witness, such as Peter.

5. περιβλεψάμενος. Mk five times mentions the fact of Christ's
"looking round" on those who were near Him (here, iii. 34, v. 32,
x. 23, xi. 11), and only once (ix. 8) does he record this of anyone else.
Excepting Lk. in this passage, no other N.T. writer uses the verb.
There was someone who remembered this frequent looking round.
Cf. x. 21, 27. Here He may have looked round to see if anyone would
answer His question; and hence His anger when He found that no
one had the moral courage to do so. On the combination of participles see i. 15.

μετ' ὀργῆς, συνλυπούμενος. Peculiar to Mk. Nowhere else is
anger attributed to Jesus; but see x. 14 and cf. Rev. vi. 16, 17. He
was "not easily provoked." The anger accompanied the look (μετά
as in Heb. xii. 17), and the momentary (aor.) glance of anger is contrasted with their continued silence and His continued grief. Anger
may be a duty (Eph. iv. 26), and Christ's anger is never personal.
His love is sometimes personal (x. 21; Jn xi. 5), but not His wrath.
Mk's fondness for detail is here conspicuous; also his readiness to
record the human emotions of the Messiah: σπλαγχνισθείς (i. 41),

ἐμβριμησάμενος (i. 43), ἐστέναξεν (vii. 34), ἀναστενάξας (viii. 12), ἠγανάκτησεν (x. 14), ἐμβλέψας αὐτῷ ἠγάπησεν αὐτόν (x. 21). The pres. part.
συνλυπούμενος expresses lasting distress; but the συν- can hardly
point to sympathy with those who had the πώρωσις, for they felt no
λύπη. It points rather to the inwardness and intensity of the
distress; see on iv. 7 and cf. σύνοιδα, συνείδησις, συντηρέω, συνκύπτω,
συνκαλύπτω. The compound is found here only in N.T.

ἐπὶ τῇ πωρώσει. Vulg., A.V., and R.V. fluctuate as to the rendering of this noun and the cognate πωρόω. Vulg. nearly everywhere
prefers the idea of blindness; *caecitas, caecatum, excaecati, obcaeca-
tum,* and once (2 Cor. iii. 14) *obtunsi.* Here A.V. has "hardness,"
with "blindness" in the margin; R.V. has "hardening." Eph.
iv. 18, A.V. has "blindness," with "hardness" in the margin; R.V.
has "hardening." Rom. xi. 7, 25, A.V. has "blinded" and "blindness," with "hardened" and "hardness" in the margin; R.V. has
"hardened" and "hardening." Mk vi. 52, viii. 17, both have
"hardened." In all these places both renderings are possible, but
in some "blindness" or "blinded" seems to be preferable; see on
2 Cor. iii. 14. Here and elsewhere πήρωσις or πηρόω is found as a
variant, but everywhere the evidence for πώρωσις or πωρόω is decisive.
See Sanday and Headlam on Rom. xi. 7; J. A. Robinson on Eph.
iv. 18. Mt. omits the look, the anger, and the grief, probably as
suggesting a low conception of Christ; cf. vi. 56, viii. 12, x. 14, 21.
Loisy admits that these very human details, *qui n'ont aucune signification pour la Christologie,* give the impression of coming from an
eye-witness.

ἐξέτεινεν. The man's obedience proved his faith, and the wish
and endeavour to obey won the power to obey.

ἀπεκατεστάθη. The cure was immediate and complete. Cf. viii.
25 and note the double augment, which this verb always has in N.T.
Here אABLΓΔ against D. In the Testaments (*Symeon* ii. 13) a
withered hand is restored, and the same verb is used as here.

6. ἐξελθόντες. The service would be over before the healing;
Christ would not have interrupted it. They had expected that Christ
would heal, and that in healing He would do something which they
could denounce as a violation of the Sabbath; but He had not even
touched the man.

εὐθὺς μετὰ τῶν Ἡρωδιανῶν. To be taken with what follows;
"they at once took counsel with the Herodians." The Herodians
are mentioned only here and at the close of the Ministry (xii. 13=Mt.
xxii. 16). They seem to have been a political rather than a religious
party, and they would be opposed to one whose teaching was revolu-

tionary. Perhaps we might call them the Royalist party or the
Government party. That " in the country of the tetrarch Antipas there
could not be a party called the Herodians " is both erroneous and
irrelevant. In Galilee, as well as in Judaea, there might be those
who wished Antipas to become what Herod the Great had been; and
we are not told that this plot against Christ was laid in Galilee.
With the termination comp. that of Χριστιανός.

συμβούλιον ἐδίδουν. See crit. note. Apparently, συμβούλιον is an
official attempt to find an equivalent for *consilium*. Deissmann, *Bib.
St.* p. 238. As with us, the usual phrase is " to *take* counsel," λαμβάνειν συμβ. (So always in Mt.) Mk may mean that it was the
Pharisees who originated and gave forth the idea, and that this was the
beginning of a series of plots (imperf.). In fact, it was the beginning
of the end. " The final rupture of Jesus with the religious authorities in Galilee arose out of the healing of the man with the withered
hand in the Synagogue on the Sabbath " (Burkitt). We have reached
" the parting of the ways." Cf. xv. 1.

ὅπως. The only question was, How? Here only does Mk use
ὅπως, which is freq. in Mt. and Lk. Only once in Jn (xi. 57).

7—12. Withdrawal to the Sea of Galilee.

Mt. xii. 15—21. Lk. vi. 17—19.

The three accounts are here very independent and there is not
much similarity of wording. It is clear from the context that Mt.
xii. 15—21, and not iv. 24, 25, is the true parallel to this section.
Mt. states, what we might infer from Mk, that Jesus retired to the
Lake because He knew of the plots to destroy Him. Some friendly
Herodian may have told the disciples.

7, 8. ἀνεχώρησεν πρὸς τὴν θάλασσαν. The verb does not imply
retreat from danger (Jn vi. 15; Acts xxiii. 19, xxvi. 31), but it is often
used in this sense (Mt. ii. 14, iv. 12, xiv. 13). Arrest or assassination
would be more easy in a town; by the Lake there were boats in which
He could escape. Euthymius remarks that it was right to take these
precautions, for He had still much teaching and healing to do.

καὶ πολὺ πλῆθος. "And a *great* multitude"; contrast πλῆθος
πολύ in *v.* 8. This is the nom. to ἠκολούθησεν, and this constr. may
be continued down to Σιδῶνα, by which time both nom. and verb are
almost forgotten, and therefore πλῆθος is repeated and a new verb
(ἦλθον) is supplied (A.V.). But it is better to put a colon at ἠκολούθησεν and take all the items that follow with ἦλθον (R.V.). Only the
Galileans *followed* Him to the Lake, and there were a *great* many of

them, for they had *seen* His mighty works. The others could hardly be said to follow Him, but they *came* to Him afterwards, for they had *heard* of the many things which He did. Almost the whole of Palestine is represented; but there is no contingent from Samaria. Here, as in x. 1 and Mt. iv. 25, the art. is omitted before πέραν τοῦ Ἰορδάνου. For Ἰεροσόλυμα see on x. 32.

As the persecution which followed the martyrdom of Stephen caused a great extension of the Gospel, so also this conspiracy against Christ; it drove Him to become a roving Teacher and Healer.

ἀκούοντες ὅσα ποιεῖ. One expects ἀκούσαντες ὅσα ἐποίει, which many texts have (see crit. note); but the pres. part. and verb are more vivid. The whole is a process which continues. "As they hear (almost, 'as *fast* as they hear') how many things He is doing, they came to Him." The ἦλθον, rather than ἤρχοντο, is determined by ἠκολούθησεν: the Galileans followed, the rest came. Both A.V. and R.V. have "what *great* things He did"; but ὅσα refers to number rather than to importance (v. 10, vi. 30, 56, x. 21, xi. 24, xii. 44, etc.). These multitudes are not disciples; it is not His teaching which attracts them, but His cures. They want to be healed, or to see Him heal. The disciples are the four fishermen (i. 16—20), and possibly Levi.

9. εἶπεν τοῖς μαθηταῖς. *He told His disciples.* He gave orders to that effect.

ἵνα πλοιάριον προσκαρτερῇ. This defines the purport rather than the purpose of the request or command; cf. v. 10, vi. 8, ix. 9; Mt. iv. 3; 1 Cor. i. 10. The telic force of ἵνα is so completely in the background as to be lost. The boat would be a small one, to keep close along the shore, so as to be ready at any moment to take Him in. The verb suggests persevering observance, and Vulg. renders it in seven different ways; *deservire* (here), *servire, perseverare, perdurare, instare, adhaerere, parere.* He did not want the boat as a pulpit, but as a refuge, in case the pressure of the immense multitude should become dangerous. Syr-Sin. has "that they should bring a ship to Him." *Admirabilis patientia et benignitas Domini* (Beng.). Mt. again omits the impeding crowd; see on ii. 2.

10. Very graphic. *He healed many* by word or touch, *so that* those near Him were *falling upon Him*, and those at a distance were frantic to get near Him. Those on the outskirts would press forward all who were between them and Him. Like the woman with the issue (v. 28), they believed that their laying hold of Him would be as efficacious as His laying His hands on them. Mt. and Lk. say that *all* were healed, Mt. repeating Mk's ἐθεράπευσεν, while the physician has his characteristic ἰᾶτο. See on i. 34. Field quotes Thuc. vii. 84. 3 in illustration.

μάστιγας. Distressing bodily diseases are meant (v. 29; Lk. vii. 21), and the word implies Divine chastisement; ἀλλὰ Διὸς μάστιγι κακῇ ἐδάμημεν Ἀχαιοί (Hom. *Il.* xiii. 812; cf. Aesch. *Prom.* 682). In LXX. it is not used specially of disease.

11. See crit. note. As often, the unclean spirits and those whom they obsess are spoken of interchangeably. It was the demoniacs who *fell down before Him, whensoever they beheld Him* (R.V.); it was the demons who recognized Him as the Son of God. Indefinite repetition in the past is expressed by ὅταν c. *imperf. indic.*; so also ὅπου ἄν (vi. 56): also with the less intelligible aor.; ὅσοι ἄν (vi. 56) and ὅταν (xi. 19). Blass, § 63. 7; Burton, § 290, 315. Syr-Sin. condenses; "and they who had plagues of unclean spirits upon them fell down before them." The contrast between ἐπιπίπτειν and προσέπιπτον is perhaps accidental. Cf. the Philippian jailor (Acts xvi. 29) and Cornelius (Acts x. 25; also Ps. xcv. 6).

ἔκραζον. The separate instances are thought of throughout, and hence the plurals: cf. Lk. xxiv. 11; Jn xix. 31: and the separate instances are thought of because of the nature of the cry. "The earliest confession of the Sonship seems to have come from evil spirits, who knew Jesus better than He was known by His own disciples" (Swete).

12. πολλὰ ἐπετίμα. The adverbial πολλά may mean either "much" or "often"; *vehementer comminabatur* (Vulg.). There were so many cases, and the spirits were so rebellious, that both "much" and "often" would be true. But "often" is questionable. This use of πολλά is freq. in Mk, rare in Mt., and not found in Lk., Acts, or Jn. It is variously rendered in Vulg.; *multum*, v. 10, 23, 38, ix. 26; *vehementer*, v. 43; *in multis*, xv. 3; *frequenter*, Mt. ix. 14. In i. 45, D, Vulg. omit πολλά. Victor again thinks that this was done for the sake of the Scribes and Pharisees, lest the homage of the unclean spirits should madden them. See on *v. 3*.

13—19. THE APPOINTMENT OF THE TWELVE.

Mt. x. 1—4. Lk. vi. 12—16.

13. Καὶ ἀναβαίνει. As between ii. 28 and iii. 1, Mk indicates no interval of time; and, as in i. 35, the place is not very definite.

εἰς τὸ ὄρος. The hill-country round the Lake is meant (vi. 56; cf. v. 5). As in ii. 16, iv. 3, etc., A.V. ignores the art. Lk. tells us that He went up to pray and continued all night in prayer. The

momentous crisis of choosing His Apostles is at hand, and this vigil
is the preparation for it,—"the first Ember night" (Swete). It is
the first act in organizing the Church which is to convert the world.

προσκαλεῖται. The verb is freq. in Mk, Mt., Lk., Acts; elsewhere
only James v. 14. It was not until this vigil was over that He gave
this summons.

οὓς ἤθελεν αὐτός. The αὐτός is emphatic. The crowd of listeners
are sifted according to His pleasure, not theirs; He does not invite
any who *like* to follow Him, to do so. This is clear both in Mk
and Lk.

ἀπῆλθον πρὸς αὐτόν. *They came away unto Him*, implying that
they left something in order to come. These are not casual listeners
or spectators, but attached disciples, and out of their number He
selects the Twelve.

14. ἐποίησεν δώδεκα. *He appointed* (Acts ii. 36; Heb. iii. 2;
Rev. v. 10) *twelve*. That "the Twelve" quickly became an official
designation, is clear from all the Gospels. Mk mentions "the
Twelve" nine times, Mt. and Jn each four times, Lk. six times. Mt.
alone speaks of "the twelve *disciples*" (x. 1, xi. 1, xx. 17, xxvi. 20).
Still earlier, St Paul uses "the Twelve" of the Apostolic body even
when not all the Twelve were present (1 Cor. xv. 5). Their correspondence with the Twelve Tribes is also soon recognized (Mt. xix.
28; Lk. xxii. 30; Rev. xxi. 14; Ep. of Barnabas viii. 3); they are
the Twelve Patriarchs of the new Israel. The modern attempt to
connect them with the twelve signs of the Zodiac is a curiosity of
criticism; and it is hardly worth mentioning, even as a coincidence,
that on one occasion Buddha is said to have had just twelve
disciples.

οὓς καὶ ἀποστόλους ὠνόμασεν. See crit. note. It is difficult to
decide whether these strongly attested words are an early interpolation
from Lk. vi. 13. We cannot say that vi. 30 implies a previous mention of this title, for in Jn vi. 67, 70, "the Twelve" are spoken of
without previous mention of appointment or number. We need not
suppose that Christ named them "Apostles" at the time when He
appointed them; but it was He who sent them out to do His work
who gave them a title which implies a special mission. *DCG.* art.
"Apostles"; Lightfoot, *Galatians*, pp. 92—101.

ἵνα...καὶ ἵνα. Two separate purposes of the appointment, one
relating to the present and one to the future, are clearly marked;
(1) they are to remain with Him to be trained, and (2) He is to send
them out to proclaim the good tidings and to have authority to cast
out the demons. This is exactly His own work as defined i. 39.

Everything is kept in His own hands. He selects the larger circle of disciples; out of these He selects the Twelve; He trains them; He sends them to do work chosen by Himself, and their power over evil spirits is conferred by Him. They originate nothing, and they have nothing but what He bestows.

ἀποστέλλῃ. The verb which corresponds with ἀπόστολος is deliberately used; it implies, what πέμπω does not, a definite mission. As in i. 39, κηρύσσειν is used absolutely. Bede remarks that He who had forbidden unclean spirits to proclaim Him, now sends men of pure minds to proclaim the Gospel.

15. ἔχειν ἐξουσίαν. The nearest parallel to this in O.T. is 2 Kings ii. 11, 15. But here supernatural powers are given to many. Exorcism is again the representative miracle; cf. i. 39, vi. 7. "To send them to have authority" is one of Mk's clumsy expressions; He sent them to cast out demons.

16. καὶ ἐποίησεν τοὺς δώδεκα. See crit. note. This repetition is some slight confirmation of the genuineness of οὓς καὶ ἀπ. ὧν. It implies that so much has intervened as to make repetition advisable; but, without οὓς καὶ ἀπ. ὧν., the interruption is slight. Καὶ is almost our "Well." "Well, as I said, He appointed the Twelve"; "*the* Twelve" because they have been mentioned before and because the expression was so familiar. Similarly, we have first "seventy-two" and then "*the* seventy-two" (Lk. x. 1, 17).

καὶ ἐπέθηκεν ὄνομα. This need not mean that the name was given there and then, any more than v. 14 need mean that the title Apostle was given there and then. Mk's want of literary skill is conspicuous here; the meaning is clear, but the construction is confused, owing to the list of the Apostles being broken by the mention of the special names given to Simon and the sons of Zebedee. Cf. iv. 15, 26, 31, vi. 8, 9, vii. 2—5, 11, 12, xiii. 34.

Πέτρον. The Aramaic equivalent Κηφᾶς occurs Jn i. 43 and four times each in 1 Cor. and Gal. It means "a rock," or more often "a stone," and is used of precious stones, hailstones, etc. It is uncertain whether the name points to the character which Simon already possessed (which is hardly in harmony with facts), or to the character which he was to acquire, or to the office which was conferred on him, or to the fact that he was the first stone in laying the foundation of the Church (Mt. xvi. 18). Outside the four lists, Peter is mentioned, by one name or another, 182 times in N.T.

It is often observed that in all four lists (Mk, Mt., Lk., and Acts) the Twelve are arranged in three quaternions, with Peter head of the first quaternion, Philip of the second, and James of Alphaeus of the third. The other three names in each quaternion vary in order, but in Mk, Mt., and Lk. the traitor is always last, and in Acts his place is vacant. Here the sons of Zebedee are between the other two brothers, either because they, like Simon, received a special name from Christ, or because, with him, they form the ἐκλεκτῶν ἐκλεκτότεροι on various occasions (v. 37, ix. 2, xiv. 33). If James and John were first cousins of our Lord, their mother Salome being sister of His Mother (Jn xix. 25), this might be another reason for placing them next to the πρῶτος. Here and v. 37, and nowhere else in N.T., John is designated " the brother óf James," while in Acts xii. 2 we have "James the brother of John." Here it is necessary to distinguish John the Apostle from John the Baptist; in Acts it is necessary to distinguish James the Apostle from James the brother of the Lord. Is it possible that Mk is also distinguishing "John the brother of James" from "John whose surname was Mark"? Those who did not know, might fancy that the Evangelist was an Apostle.

17. Βοανηργές. Such is the spelling in אABCKLM 33; D has Βοανεργής, while EFGHUVΓ have Βοανεργές. The name and its interpretation are well-known difficulties. (1) How are the two vowels *o a* to be got from the Hebrew? (2) What Hebrew or Aramaic root resembling ργש means "thunder"? (3) If ὀνόματα is the right reading (see crit. note), why is only one name given? Syr-Sin. has "He called them Beni-Ragshi," and gives no explanation of the name. It is possible that in the oral tradition sounds became confused, and perhaps two names were fused into one; but no satisfactory solution has been found. Whence did Luther get *Bnehargem*, which is as strange as his *asabthani* in xv. 34? Justin quotes the words Βοανεργές, ὅ ἐστιν υἱοὶ βροντῆς as occurring in the "Memoirs of Peter," which is good reason for believing that by the Ἀπομνημονεύματα Πέτρου he means Mk (*Try.* 106). He also speaks of Christ as being regarded as a carpenter (*Try.* 88), and in Mk alone (vi. 3) is He so called. The fiery temper of the brothers appears ix. 38 and Lk. ix. 54, and this may have caused James to have been soon put to death (Acts xii. 2). Like Stephen, he may have infuriated those in authority by strong language. If in the first instance it was only John who was called "a son of thunder," the Fathers who point to the heavenly resonance of the Johannine writings may be near the truth. Jerome and Pseudo-Jerome apply the name to Peter as well as to James and John, and the latter interprets it of their hearing the voice from heaven at the Transfiguration. It is remarkable how often Mk's translations of Aramaic cause difficulty. In v. 41 σοὶ λέγω is superfluous, and in xv. 34 there is more than one puzzle. Outside the four lists, John is mentioned 50 times in N.T. and James 21 times. Some think Boanerges may = 'the twins.'

18. Ἀνδρέαν. Cf. i. 16, 29; he is mentioned again xiii. 3. Almost all that we know of him comes from Jn (i. 41, 44, vi. 8, xii. 22).

Φίλιππον. All that we know of him comes from Jn (i. 44—49, vi. 5—7, xii. 21, 22, xiv. 8, 9). Both Andrew and Philip are purely Greek names, and there seems to have been some connexion between the two Apostles. Both came from Bethsaida. In Acts i. 13 their names are placed together, as here. Philip is mentioned 12 times, and Andrew 9 times, outside the four lists.

Βαρθολομαῖον. "Son of Talmai," or (as some think) "of Ptolemäus." This patronymic is in all the lists, and the Synoptists place him next to Philip. If he is the same as Nathanael, Philip brought him to Christ (Jn i. 46). All the companions who are named in Jn xxi. 2 are Apostles. Jn never mentions Bartholomew, and Mk., Mt., and Lk. never mention Nathanael. Nevertheless, this ancient identification cannot be assumed as certain.

Μαθθαῖον καὶ Θωμᾶν. In all three Gospels these two names come together, but Mt. puts Thomas before Matthew and adds ὁ τελώνης to the latter, an addition found in no other list. This points to the influence of Matthew on the First Gospel, and to his wish to make it clear that Matthew the Apostle and Levi the toll-collector are the same person. See on ii. 14. All that we know of Thomas is told us by Jn (xi. 16, xiv. 5, xx. 24—29, xxi. 2). Δίδυμος is a translation, and Θωμᾶς is a transliteration, of the Hebrew for "twin." Tradition says that his original name was Judas, and in that case it would be almost necessary to give him another name, as there were two other Apostles named Judas.

Ἰάκωβον τὸν τοῦ Ἀλφαίου. The father's name is added to distinguish him from the son of Zebedee. This Alphaeus is not the father of Levi (ii. 14), nor is this James the brother of the Lord (vi. 3; Mt. xiii. 55; Gal. i. 19), who was the first overseer of the Church of Jerusalem (Acts xii. 17, xv. 13; Gal. ii. 9, 12). The brethren of the Lord at this time did not believe on Him (Jn vii. 5). But James of Alphaeus may be identical with James the Little (xv. 40; Mt. xxvii. 56; Jn xix. 25), for Alphaeus may *perhaps* = Clopas.

Θαδδαῖον. This is the only name about which there is material difference in the lists. Mk and Mt. have "Thaddaeus," with "Lebbaeus" as an alternative reading, while Lk. and Acts have "Judas the son of James." Here and in Mt. the reading Θαδδαιον may safely be adopted, Λεββαῖον (D, Lat-Vet.) being perhaps due to a wish to identify him with Levi.

Κανανᾶιον. See crit. note. "Canaanite" would be Χαναναῖος, and "man of Cana" would be Καναῖος. Καναναῖος is the Greek form of the Aramaic *Kanan*, which = ζηλωτής, as Lk. renders it. Lightfoot, *On Revision²,* pp. 154 f. We need not suppose that this Simon ever belonged to the fanatical extremists from whom sprang the *Sicarii*. Like St Paul, he may have been περισσοτέρως ζηλωτὴς τῶν πατρικῶν παραδόσεων (Gal. i. 14), and may have been equally zealous respecting Christ's teaching, after his call. Onias, who was head of the orthodox party, is said to be "zealous of the laws" (2 Macc. iv. 2).

19. Ἰσκαριώθ. See crit. note. Mt. and Jn write Ἰσκαριώτης: Lk. has both forms. The epithet probably means "man of Kerioth," but the site of Kerioth is uncertain. Both he and his father Simon have this epithet (Jn vi. 71, xiii. 26), which is in favour of its having a local meaning. He seems to have been the only Apostle who was not a Galilean, and this may have caused estrangement from the first. It is not necessary to do more than mention the suggestion that "Iscariot" comes from "Ashharti " = "Ashhurite " = N. Arabian; or that it is a thinly disguised form of *sikkarti* (Is. xix. 4) and means "surrender," so that Judas is a personification of the Jewish people.

ὃς καὶ παρέδωκεν αὐτόν. The force of the καὶ is "who was *identical with* the one who betrayed Him." Each Evangelist gives the appalling fact in a different way; Mt. ὁ καὶ παραδοὺς αὐτόν, Lk. ὃς ἐγένετο προδότης, i.e. "who *became* a traitor," or "who *turned* traitor," not "which *was the* traitor" (R.V.). Nowhere in Scripture is Judas called "*the* traitor." After Peter, John, and James, Judas Iscariot is mentioned in Scripture more often than any of the remaining eight Apostles. Of most of them we know nothing, except as members of the Twelve, and of none of them do we know much. Traditions as to their subsequent labours are for the most part unworthy of trust. With the first Christians it was the Gospel rather than those who preached it that was of supreme importance. And it was so with the Apostles themselves; "whether it were I or they" did not matter, if only their hearers believed.

Mk places a considerable interval between the appointment of the Twelve and the sending them out as missionaries (vi. 7). Mt. with much less probability has no interval. The theory that at this point there is a gap in Mk, owing to the loss of a portion of the original document, is not one that repays investigation. To insert here a long discourse, mediating between the Sermon in Mt. and the Sermon in Lk., is pure conjecture. Along with this, other things which are in Mt. or Lk. but not in our Mk may be added. There is no end to such guesswork. Spitta, *Lücken im Markusevangelium*, pp. 126—138.

19ᵇ—30. By whose Power are Demons cast out?

Mt. xii. 22—32.   Lk. xi. 14—23, xii. 10.

Καὶ ἔρχεται εἰς οἶκον. *And He cometh into a house.* This is to
remind us that the shore (*v.* 7) and the mountain (*v.* 13) are left,
and to prepare us for the incident with His Mother and brethren
(*vv.* 31—35), which took place when He was in a house. The
division of the verses is unfortunate. These words belong to *v.* 20.
A.V. puts only a colon after "betrayed Him," and continues "and
they went into a house." See crit. note. Between the descent from
τὸ ὄρος (*v.* 13) and this incident, Lk. (vi. 17 f.) inserts the Sermon
"on a level place," which Mk seems not to have known. If he was
acquainted with Q, the acquaintance must have been slight.

20. συνέρχεται πάλιν ὁ ὄχλος. The πάλιν looks back to iii. 7, 8.
The crowd, with the freedom of Orientals (Trench, *Parables*, p. 302 n. ;
Tristram, *Eastern Customs in Bible Lands*, p. 36), came in and filled
the house. These verses (20, 21) are preparatory to 31—35, which
show who come next to the chosen Twelve ; it is a circle which anyone can enter.

ὥστε μὴ...μηδέ. The authority for μηδέ is ample (ABKLUΔΠ*),
and μηδέ is required by the obvious meaning. With μήτε the sentence
would mean "so that they were not able nor ate bread," which
is hardly sense ; but in modern Greek the difference between μηδέ and
μήτε seems to have vanished. Winer, p. 614. This was no solitary
instance of the difficulty ; ii. 2 and vi. 31 show that the pressure of
the multitudes was a grave inconvenience. It hindered the training
of the Twelve. As usual, it is omitted by Mt.

ἄρτον φαγεῖν. See on vii. 2 ; also Dalman, *Words*, p. 112.

21. οἱ παρ᾽ αὐτοῦ. An expression as vague as our "His people."
It might include relations, acquaintances, domestics, and all who had
a special interest in Him. "*Her household* are clothed in scarlet"
(Prov. xxxi. 21) is οἱ παρ᾽ αὐτῆς ἐνδιδύσκονται (LXX., xxix. 39). Cf.
Josephus (*Ant.* i. x. 5) Ἄβραμος περιτέμνεται καὶ πάντες οἱ παρ᾽ αὐτοῦ.
In papyri, οἱ παρ᾽ αὐτοῦ often means "his agents" or "his representatives," but also "his family." J. H. Moulton, p. 106. Vulg.
has *sui*, which is as vague as the Greek ; Coverdale, "they that were
aboute him." Syr-Sin. is more definite, "His brethren," perhaps
from a feeling that the strong measure intended and the strong word
used were against His Mother being included. Cf. Susann. 33 ;
1 Macc. xiii. 52.

ἐξῆλθον. Not from the house in which He was, but from their own
house, which may have been at a distance.

κρατῆσαι αὐτόν. *To get possession of His person* ; see on i. 31. It is arbitrary to supply a fresh nom. for ἔλεγον, "for *people* were saying." His brethren did not believe on Him (Jn vii. 5). Ἐξέστη. "He has gone out of His mind," *He is beside Himself* (A.V., R.V.). This use of the aor. comes close to that of the perf., expressing present result of past action; but the aor. may imply that the past action was recent; ἀπέθανεν (v. 35), ἠγέρθη (xvi. 6 ; Lk. vii. 16), ἠγόρασα (Lk. xiv. 18, 19). Burton, § 47 ; J. H. Moulton, p. 134. Euthymius says that οἱ παρ' αὐτοῦ were envious, τὴν φιλανθρωπίαν νομίζοντες μανίαν, καὶ ὄντως αὐτοὶ μαινόμενοι. This is unlikely; more probably they regarded His open defiance of Scribes and Pharisees from Jerusalem as fanatical folly. They may have known that there were projects for His destruction. But it is possible that *He is beside Himself* is more than ἐξέστη means; excepting 2 Cor. v. 13, the verb nowhere has this meaning in N.T. Cf. ii. 12, v. 42, vi. 51 ; Lk. ii. 47, viii. 56, xxiv. 22 ; Mt. xii. 23 ; and often in Acts. Nevertheless, this meaning fits the context; but *in furorem versus est* (Vulg.) is too strong.

22. οἱ ἀπὸ Ἱεροσολύμων. The hostile criticism seems to have emanated from Jerusalem, and Scribes who were Pharisees (ii. 6, 16, 18, 24, iii. 6) dogged His footsteps to collect evidence against Him. Emissaries from Jerusalem appear as His deadliest foes (vii. 1), a presentiment, as Bede remarks, of the fact that it was the inhabitants of Jerusalem who were to put Him to death. Mk does not tell us what gave His critics an opening on this occasion. Mt. and Lk. say that it was the healing of a demoniac who was dumb and blind. Some suggested that the Healer must be the Messiah ; and then His foes gave this explanation.

Βεελζεβοὺλ ἔχει. Like Βοανηργές (v. 17), Βεελζεβούλ is an unsolved problem as regards orthography and derivation. Other forms are Βεεζεβούλ and Βεελζεβούβ. The last is found in no Greek MS., but has prevailed through the influence of Vulg.; but even there some MSS. have *beelzebul*. "Lord of the habitation" and "Lord of dung" are the more approved conjectures as to the meaning ; but all that is certain is that it is a term of reproach and abomination. Syr-Sin. has "B. is in Him," and again in v. 30, "an unclean spirit is in Him."

Ἐν τῷ ἄρχοντι τῶν δαιμονίων. *In the power of the prince of the demons.* It is not known whether the Jews regarded Beelzebub as the same as Satan or as an inferior evil power. There is the same use of ἐν in Mt. and Lk., and a similar use of ὁ ἄρχων in Jn xii. 31, xiv. 30, xvi. 11 ; Eph. ii. 2.

This charge is recorded in all three Gospels here, in Mt. also in
x. 24. Jn has it vii. 20, viii. 45, 52; cf. Mt. xi. 18. No doubt it was
made on various occasions. It has an important bearing on Christ's
"mighty works." There must have been some very marvellous
works, and they must have been notorious at the time, or the
Pharisees would not have propounded so desperate an explanation.
A little later it was said that Jesus had learned magic in Egypt.

23. προσκαλεσάμενος αὐτούς. The hostile Scribes were so far
off that He had to summon them in order to address them. This
shows that they had made this monstrous charge behind His back,
when He was too far off to hear. Therefore, as in ii. 8 and iii. 4, it
was because "He knew their thoughts" that He surprised them with
this unanswerable question. As in ii. 8, 17, 19, 25, iii. 4, He meets
their indirect and underhand methods directly and openly.

ἐν παραβολαῖς. The original meaning of "comparison" occurs
iv. 30 and is not wholly absent here; Euthymius has ἐν παραδείγμασιν.
His questions are *parallels* to their accusation. To say that by evil
spiritual power He casts out evil spirits is to say that Satan casts out
himself, which is like saying that a kingdom or a house is divided
against itself. But here the O.T. meaning of παραβολή may be
uppermost, a "trite and terse saying" or a "symbolical saying."

Πῶς δύναται; This question elsewhere implies that the thing is
morally impossible (Mt. xii. 34), or physically impossible (Mt. xii. 29;
Jn vi. 52), or that no one would have the face to do it (Lk. vi. 42).
Here it means that such conduct would be not only morally impossible
but unthinkable; it involves a contradiction. The Satanic corporation
does not violate the conditions of its existence. Note the pres. infin.;
cannot go on casting out. We have here one of the many occasions of
which it is recorded that Christ spoke of the great power of evil as a
personal agent; iv. 15; Lk. x. 18, xiii. 16, xxii. 31; Mt. xxv. 41;
Jn viii. 44. See on i. 13. It is difficult to believe that Christ was
ignorant on this momentous point, or that, if He knew it to be a
superstition, He yet encouraged men to hold it.

24. ἐφ᾽ ἑαυτήν. "In relation to itself," and so *in itself.*
Neither A.V. nor R.V. makes any distinction between καθ᾽ ἑαυτῆς
(Mt. xii. 25 *bis*) and ἐφ᾽ ἑαυτήν (Mk, Lk.). In Mt., Vulg. distinguishes
καθ᾽ ἑαυτῆς, *contra se*, from ἐφ᾽ ἑαυτόν, *adversus se*; but here it is
very capricious, *si regnum in se dividatur...si domus super semet ipsam
dispertiatur...si Satanas consurrexit in semet ipsum.* Possibly no
distinction is intended between σταθῆναι and στῆναι, and the readings
are confused; σταθῆναι (without variant) is right in *v.* 24, and στῆναι
(אBCL) is right in *v.* 26. In *v.* 25, στῆναι (BKLΠ) is preferable

to σταθῆναι (אAF etc.). Cf. "They shall not be able to stand" (Ps. xvii. 39, xxxvi. 12), οὐ μὴ δυνῶνται στῆναι. Unity is strength; it is not only good and joyful (Ps. cxxxiii. 1), it is indispensable to success (Rev. xvii. 17).

25. οἰκία. Household or *family* rather than "house." Lk. has οἶκος and means a building. Cf. Cic. *Laelius* vii. 23.

οὐ δυνήσεται. See crit. note. Mt. has οὐ σταθήσεται, Lk. has πίπτει. These striking illustrations would cause these Sayings to be easily remembered.

26. εἰ ἀνέστη...καὶ ἐμερίσθη. All three make the change to εἰ c. *indic.*, which represents the monstrous supposition of the Scribes as a fact; "And if, as you say, Satan has really risen against himself and is divided, it is now impossible for him to stand, but he is at an end"; τέλος ἔχει is classical, and here is peculiar to Mk. In Lk. xxii. 37, τέλος ἔχει has not quite the same meaning.

27. οὐ δύναται οὐδείς. See on i. 44; neither here nor there is there a double neg. in Mt. This is a fourth παραβολή, but it is not parallel to the other three. It shows that, so far from being Satan's agent, He is an enemy who is conquering him by driving out his agents. The picture comes from Is. xlix. 25, where Jehovah says "Even the captives of the strong one shall be taken away," because the stronger than he has come, a saying which may have been proverbial.

τὴν οἰκίαν τοῦ ἰσχυροῦ. The world is Satan's home, and he and his demons are the household. See on τῷ ἄρχοντι, v. 22, and cf. Eph. vi. 12.

εἰσελθών. This Christ did at the Incarnation.

τὰ σκεύη. Like *vasa* (Vulg.), a very comprehensive term. We need not interpret the σκεύη: Victor makes them mean mankind.

δήσῃ. It may be doubted whether this refers to anything so definite as the Temptation. Lk. has νικήσῃ, but he varies the picture considerably.

καὶ τότε. Again we have a somewhat superfluous statement; cf. i. 32, 42, ii. 23, 25, etc. The ἰσχυρότερος deprives ὁ ἰσχυρός of his ill-gotten possessions. This seems to refer to the driving out of the demons; they are Satan's representatives, and they are expelled from their usurped habitations. On the other hand, not even Satan can snatch (δύναται ἁρπάζειν) His sheep out of the hand of the Good Shepherd (Jn x. 27).

28. ἀμὴν λέγω ὑμῖν. This solemn formula, which introduces a statement of special import, occurs 13 times in Mk, 30 in Mt., 6 in Lk. Christ does not quote Moses; nor does He say "Thus saith the

Lord " ; He speaks out of His own ἐξουσία, "Verily I say to you."
Cf. the O.T. formula, "As I live, saith the Lord." In O.T., as in
our prayers, "Amen" confirms what precedes (1 Kings i. 36;
Jer. xi. 5, xxviii. 6); but in the Gospels it affirms what is coming.
Jerome regards it as equivalent to an oath; *debemus Christo juranti
credere.* But this use of 'Αμήν is unfamiliar to the whole range of
Jewish literature. Jesus seems to have given the word a new
meaning as a form of asseveration in place of the oath which He
forbade. Dalman, *Words*, p. 226.

πάντα. This can hardly be taken directly with the too distant
τὰ ἁμαρτήματα, "all their sins shall be forgiven" (R.V.); τὰ ἁμαρτήματα κ.τ.λ. is epexegetic of πάντα: *all things shall be forgiven to the
sons of men, yea all their sins and their blasphemies.* In the Gospels,
ἁμάρτημα, "an act of sin," is found only in these verses; elsewhere, only Rom. iii. 25 and 1 Cor. vi. 18. The word is interpolated
in some texts of Mk iv. 12.

τοῖς υἱοῖς τῶν ἀνθρώπων. This plur. is found only here and
Eph. iii. 5; in LXX. it is freq. Syr-Sin. has "all sins which they
shall blaspheme shall be forgiven unto men."

ὅσα ἐὰν βλασφ. *Constr. ad sensum*; ACFKL, etc., substitute
ὅσας. Cf. φυλάσσεσθε τὰς ἐντολὰς...ὅσα ἐγὼ ἐντέλλομαι (Deut. iv. 2).
We have ἐάν for ἄν in hypothetical relative clauses Mt. vii. 12;
Lk ix. 57; Acts ii. 21. J. H. Moulton, pp. 42 f. The clause is omitted
in Lat-Vet.

29. βλασφημήσῃ εἰς. Cf. Acts vi. 11; Dan. iii. 29 (LXX. 96).
The constr. is classical (Dem., Aesch.).

τὸ πνεῦμα τὸ ἅγιον. *The Spirit, the Holy Spirit.* The second
art. puts a strong emphasis on ἅγιον, perhaps in opposition to the
πνεῦμα ἀκάθαρτον (*v.* 30). Cf. xiii. 11; 1 Thess. iv. 8; Eph. iv. 30.
The repeated art. in various expressions is freq. in Jn. See on
Jn iv. 9 and viii. 31.

οὐκ ἔχει ἄφεσιν εἰς τὸν αἰῶνα. Mt. expands this into οὐκ ἀφεθήσεται
αὐτῷ οὔτε ἐν τούτῳ τῷ αἰῶνι οὔτε ἐν τῷ μέλλοντι, and the context here
seems to show that the expansion is correct. The ἐξουσία of the Son
of Man to forgive sins (ii. 10) in this case cannot be exercised; there
is no repentance, and therefore no forgiveness. Jesus had repeatedly
freed men from the obsession of spirits whom the Scribes themselves
recognized as the agents of Satan. Such acts *could* not be evil;
they were acts of the Spirit, the Holy Spirit of God. Yet, in order to
destroy the influence of One whose teaching often condemned their
traditions, the Scribes had declared that these acts of the Holy
Spirit were the acts of the prince of the demons. Such monstrous

perversity was evidence of a spiritual condition which was becoming hopeless—a condition of constant and deliberate preference of darkness to light. The blasphemy against the Holy Spirit did not consist in *saying* " He has Beelzebub," or " He casts out demons by the help of Satan " ; no single utterance could be said to be unpardonable. It was the state of heart which produced these utterances that was so perilous ; and that state was known to Him who pronounced this stern warning. We have not got our Lord's exact words (Dalman, *Words*, p. 147). The report of them which has come down to us in three different forms does not require us to believe that these Scribes were already guilty of unpardonable wickedness ; but their being capable of these utterances shows that they were perilously near to this. Repentance is not said to be impossible for them ; but so long as they maintained that manifestations of Divine beneficence were Satanic, their recovery was impossible.

No hint is given as to whether repentance and forgiveness are possible in the next world. The only safe course is to repent here and now. From Mt. xii. 32 Bede draws as inference *quasdam culpas in hoc saeculo, quasdam vero in futuro laxari* ; but the inference is precarious.

ἀλλὰ ἔνοχός ἐστιν.   " But lies under the consequences of an act of sin which belongs to the sphere of the world to come " (Swete). Cf. 2 Macc. xiii. 6. In N.T. ὁ αἰών without οὗτος is sometimes used of this present life (iv. 19, xi. 14) ; in O.T., but not in N.T., this is also true of αἰώνιος. There is no need to say here to whom such an offender has to answer for such a sin (Mt. v. 21, 22). It is the character of the sin itself that is emphasized. Note that αἰωνίου precedes its substantive, not follows, as in ζωὴ αἰώνιος, the only other connexion in which Mk uses the word (x. 17, 30). Elsewhere the gen. after ἔνοχος indicates either the penalty (xiv. 64 ; Mt. xxvi. 66 ; Heb. ii. 15), or that which is injured by the sin (1 Cor. xi. 27 ; cf. Jas ii. 10). On εἰς τὸν αἰῶνα and αἰώνιος see App. E in the volume on S. John. On the difficult subject of the unpardonable sin see on 1 Jn v. 16 ; Westcott on Heb. vi. 1—8 and *Historic Faith*, pp. 150 f. ; Agar Beet, *The Last Things*, pp. 246 f. ; *D.C.G.* art. "Blasphemy."

30. ὅτι ἔλεγον. It was because they gave such a wicked interpretation of His beneficent acts that He uttered His solemn warning. They had blasphemed the Son of Man, and were in danger of becoming blasphemers of the Holy Spirit, for their theory made any proof of Christ's Divine Sonship and mission impossible. To accept it was to become incurable. This verse is the Evangelist's own explanation of Christ's stern utterance ; it is no part of His utterance.

Cf. vii. 19, καθαρίζων πάντα τὰ βρώματα. Mk says πνεῦμα ἀκάθαρτον
instead of Βεελζεβούλ in antithesis to τὸ πνεῦμα τὸ ἅγιον. The explanation is not in Mt. or Lk.

31—35. Who are Christ's true Relations?

Mt. xii. 46—50. Lk. viii. 19—21.

31. Καὶ ἔρχονται. Mk has his historic pres.; Mt. and Lk. have
past tenses. It is possible that ἔρχονται, arrival at destination, is
meant to correspond with ἐξῆλθον, departure from home, in v. 21.
Neither Mk nor Lk. gives any connexion; Mt. says that this visit of
Christ's Mother and brethren took place while He was still speaking.
Both she and they are mentioned by name, vi. 3, where sisters also
are mentioned. But Mk tells us no more about her, and he nowhere
speaks of Joseph, who was probably dead before this Gospel opens.
We cannot be sure that these are οἱ παρ' αὐτοῦ (v. 21), who have
arrived to take Him away, as being too excited to take care of Himself.
It may be that His Mother and His brethren came to warn Him of
what οἱ παρ' αὐτοῦ are meditating. In any case He remains un-
molested. They are unable to reach Him, because He is in a house
blocked with people; and, as they cannot proclaim their intentions,
whatever these may have been, they are obliged to stand outside and
send a message to ask Him to come to them. Cf. ii. 4.

στήκοντες...καλοῦντες. Again (see on i. 15) we see a fondness for
participles. The readings στήκοντες (BC*Δ) and καλοῦντες (אBCL)
are firmly established. As στήκω is a rare form, perhaps not earlier
than N.T., it would be likely to be altered to στάντες (א), ἑστῶτες (AD),
or ἑστηκότες (GL). It is found xi. 25; Jn i. 26, viii. 44 (?); several
times in Paul. Nestle (*Text. Crit.* p. 263) prefers φωνοῦντες (DΓΠ) to
καλοῦντες, because the latter is more usual.

32. ἐκάθητο. They would sit on the ground, the most intimate
disciples being nearest; and the message sent by His family from the
outside was passed on by them to Him. *A multitude*, not "the
multitude" (A.V.). This error in A.V. is not so common as that of
ignoring the art. when it is present. See on iv. **3.**

καὶ οἱ ἀδελφοί σου. The addition of καὶ αἱ ἀδελφαί σου (AD) is
doubtless an interpolation from vi. 3 to harmonize with ἀδελφή in
v. 35; אBCL omit. To say that these witnesses omit the clause
because it is not in Mt. or Lk. is perverse criticism; it is not in Mt. or
Lk. because it was not in the copies of Mk which they used.

33. ἀποκριθεὶς αὐτοῖς λέγει. "To them" means to those who
had passed on the message to Him. The Hebraistic pleonasm

ἀποκριθεὶs λέγει or ἀποκ. εἶπεν is very freq. in N.T. and LXX., but
the curious combination of aor. with pres. is in N.T. almost peculiar
to Mk. See on viii. 29 *sub fin.* Nowhere in Jn does ἀποκριθεὶs occur.
Syr-Sin. omits it here. Occasionally the converse is found, ἀπεκρίθη
λέγων (xv. 9), but never ἀπεκρίθη εἰπών. In vii. 28 we have ἀπεκρίθη
καὶ λέγει, and in LXX. the more logical ἀπεκρίθη καὶ εἶπεν (Exod. iv. 1;
Num. xxii. 18; Josh. vii. 20; etc.). Blass, § 74, 3; Winer, p. 327.

T ίs ἐστιν ἡ μήτηρ μου; There is no need to surmise that here
Christ raised His voice so that His family might hear; *v.* 34 shows
whom He is addressing. He is not repudiating His Mother, still less
rebuking her before the whole crowd. Although Jn ii. 12 probably
does not mean "What does that matter to either of us?," but
amounts to a rebuke (see note *ad loc.*), yet it was spoken to her
privately. Here *non maternae refutat obsequia pietatis* (Bede). But
He never neglected an opportunity of doing good, and this interruption
gave Him an opening for teaching an important lesson. It is not
blood-relationship to the Son of Man which counts, but loyal
obedience to the will of God. Those who have that are bound to Him
by closer ties than the ties of family; for the former are spiritual,
while the latter are carnal. He is not slighting the latter, but inti-
mating that they do not come first and that they do not last for
ever: indeed in this life they may have to be severed (Mt. x. 37;
Lk. xiv. 26). That much is clear; He is teaching His audience that
they can be as strongly united to Him as His nearest relations are.
It is not so clear that He is teaching them that healing men's bodies
and saving their souls are more important than care of one's relations (Euthym.), or that His Mother is to be honoured, not merely
because she gave birth to Him, but because of her great virtues
(Theoph.).

34. περιβλεψάμενος. See on *v.* 5 and cf. Hom. *Od.* viii. 278;
Hdt. iv. 182; Plato *Phaedo* 72 B. Mt. says that He stretched forth
His hand over His disciples. In what follows we need not see any
discouragement of undue devotion to His Mother. The policy of
His family here ran counter to His work. He had left them in
order to fulfil the mission of His Father; they wanted Him to
abandon the mission and come back to them. Evidently they themselves were in need of His teaching (Jn vii. 5). Syr-Sin. omits
the superfluous κύκλῳ.

"Ἴδε ἡ μήτηρ. Like ἰδού (*v.* 32), ἴδε is an interjection. Both call
attention to something worth noting, and the mid. form does this
more strongly. Winer, pp. 229, 319. Cf. Hom. *Il.* vi. 429. The
Synoptists prefer ἰδού. Jn prefers ἴδε. In LXX., ἰδού is far more

common, and ἴδε, or ἴδετε, is generally a verb, often followed by ὅτι. They may be distinguished in translation by *en* and "Lo" for ἴδε, *ecce* and "Behold" for ἰδού. But Vulg. has *ecce* for both, A.V. and R.V. have "Behold" and "Lo" for both. A.V. here makes ἴδε a verb. Vulg. does the same xiii. 1, *aspice quales lapides*, and xv. 4, *vide in quantis*.

35. ὃς ἂν ποιήσῃ. See crit. note ; the "For" (A.V., R.V.) is probably an interpolation.

τὸ θέλημα τοῦ θεοῦ. Here only in Mk. When used of the Divine Will, τὸ θέλημα in N.T. almost always has a distinguishing gen. See esp. Mt. vii. 21. Rom. ii. 18 is hardly an exception, for θεῷ has preceded ; and in 1 Cor. xvi. 12 the context shows that the Divine Will is not the meaning. He Himself was doing the Divine Will in ministering to those whom "He is not ashamed to call brethren" (Heb. ii. 11; Mt. xxv. 40, xxviii. 10 ; Jn xx. 17).

καὶ ἀδελφή. This is added, because women were present, not because His sisters were outside. He does not say καὶ πατήρ : in spiritual relationship that position could not be approached by human beings ; cf. Mt. xii. 50. Almost certainly Joseph was dead before the Ministry began.

On the insoluble question of "the Brethren of the Lord" two theories are worthy of consideration; (1) that they were the sons of Joseph and Mary, born after the virgin-birth of Christ ; (2) that they were the children of Joseph by a former wife, of whom there is no mention in Scripture or in tradition. Any theory which makes Apostles to be brethren of the Lord is excluded by Jn vii. 5. Nothing in Scripture forbids us to adopt (1), which is confirmed by Mt. i. 25 and by the fact that the brethren here accompany Mary. See J. B. Mayor, *Ep. of S. James*, pp. v—xxxvi, and his thorough reinvestigation of the subject, *Expositor*, July and August, 1908 ; Lightfoot, *Galatians*, pp. 253—291 ; *D.C.G.* artt. "Brethren of the Lord" and "Mary the Virgin."

CHAPTER IV.

1. συνάγεται (אBCLΔ) rather than συνήχθη (DΠ) or συνήχθησαν (A). πλεῖστος (אBCLΔ) rather than πολύς (ADΠ). אBCL 33 omit τό before πλοῖον.

4. After τὰ πετεινά, אABCL etc. omit τοῦ οὐρανοῦ (from Lk.).

5. καὶ ἄλλο (אBCLΔ) rather than ἄλλο δέ (ΔΠ) ;ʹD has καὶ ἄλλα. Mk throughout prefers καί to δέ. See on i. 14.

8. ἄλλα (אBCL 33) rather than ἄλλο (ADΔΠ).

9. אABCDLΔ omit αὐτοῖς.

10. καὶ ὅτε rather than ὅτε δέ. See on v. 5. ἠρώτων (אABCLΔ) rather than ἠρώτησαν (Π). τὰς παραβολάς (אBCLΔ) rather than τὴν παραβολήν (AΠ).

11. אABC*KL omit γνῶναι (from Mt. and Lk.).

12. W.H. write συνίωσιν from the unused συνίω : συνιῶσιν is from συνίημι or the unused συνιέω. אBCL omit τὰ ἁμαρτήματα.

15. εἰς αὐτούς (B and some cursives) or ἐν αὐτοῖς (אCLΔ) rather than ἐν ταῖς καρδίαις αὐτῶν (DΠ) or ἀπὸ τῆς καρδίας αὐτῶν (A). Syr Sin. omits ὅπου σπ. ὁ λόγος and εὐθύς.

18. ἄλλοι (אBC*DLΔ) rather than οὗτοι (AC²Π).

19. אBCDLΔ omit τούτου.

20. ἐκεῖνοι (אBCLΔ) rather than οὗτοι (ADΠ).

21. As in viii. 4, the ὅτι is omitted in the large majority of witnesses, but is probably genuine (BL); ὅτι recitative is very freq. in Mk. For ἐπὶ τὴν λυχνίαν, אB*Σ 33 have the impossible ὑπό τ. λ., an interesting example of a very early corruption.

22. ἐὰν μὴ ἵνα (אBΔ) rather than ἐὰν μή (ACLΠ) or ἀλλ' ἵνα (D).

24. אBCDLΔ omit τοῖς ἀκούουσιν.

26. ὡς (אBDLΔ 33) rather than ὡς ἐάν (ACΠ), an obvious correction ; but ἐάν might get lost before ἄνθρ.

27. βλαστᾷ (BC*DLΔ) rather than βλαστάνῃ (אAC²) or βλαστάνει (EFH 33). μηκύνεται (BDHΣ) rather than μηκύνηται (אAC² etc.).

28. אABCL omit γάρ. Cf. iii. 35. It is impossible to determine the original Greek for "the full corn" ; perhaps πλήρη σῖτον (אAC²LΔΠ) is right ; but it may be a correction of πλήρης σῖτον (C*).

30. πῶς (אBCLΔ) rather than τίνι (ADΠ). θῶμεν (אBC*LΔ) rather than παραβάλωμεν (AC²DΠ).

34. τοῖς ἰδίοις μαθηταῖς (אBCLΔ) rather than τ. μαθ. αὐτοῦ (ADΠ).

37. ὥστε ἤδη γεμίζεσθαι τὸ πλοῖον (BCDLΔ) rather than ὥστε αὐτὸ ἤδη γεμ. (AΠ).

40. אBDLΔ omit οὕτως. οὔπω (אBDLΔ) rather than πῶς (ACΠ).

1—12. TEACHING BY PARABLES ; THE SOWER.

Mt. xiii. 1—9. Lk. viii. 4—8.

1. **πάλιν.** There is no hint as to the interval between iii. 35 and iv. 1. The Evangelists do not care much about exact chronology, which had seldom been preserved by tradition. The lessons are the same, in whatever order the incidents are placed. Here πάλιν is not simply transitional (ii. 13); it looks back to iii. 7.

ἤρξατο. This favourite amplification is here omitted by both Mt. and Lk.; cf. v. 17, 20, vi. 7, and see on x. 47.

παρὰ τὴν θάλασσαν. See on x. 46.

συνάγεται. See crit. note. Here again (cf. iii. 31) Mt. turns Mk's historic pres. into a past tense, which has got into some texts of Mk.

ὄχλος πλεῖστος. *A very great multitude.* Here also some texts of Mk have been influenced by Mt. and Lk. While Mk tells us that the crowd was still larger than before, Mt. and Lk. simply say that it was great.

εἰς πλοῖον. He may have again directed that a boat should be at hand (iii. 9). AB²DΔ insert τό and thus suggest that it was the same boat as that which was used before. Lk. says that the parable of the Sower was delivered as Christ was going about among the towns and villages in Galilee.

πρὸς τὴν θάλασσαν. *Facing the sea,* a feature worth preserving; cf. i. 33, ii. 2. He sat in the boat, throwing His net to catch all within hearing. See on xiii. 3.

2. **ἐδίδασκεν.** The imperf. is again accurate; cf. i. 21, 32, 35, 45, ii. 2, 13, iii. 2, 11, 23. Both A.V. and R.V. make πολλά a cogn. acc., but it is probably adverbial as usual, meaning "often," *i.e.* "in many parables," *in paravolis multis* (d). See on iii. 2. Parables appear to have become more freq. as Christ's audiences became larger and more mixed in character. Of these Mk gives us only four, of which only one, the Seed growing secretly (*vv.* 26—29), is peculiar to his Gospel. Parables instructed the real disciples, without harming

the careless, and without giving openings to hostile listeners. See Hastings' *D.B.* art. "Parable."

ἐν τῇ διδαχῇ. *In the course of His teaching.* Here and xii. 38 only; 2 Jn 9 is different. In the Gospels, διδασκαλία occurs only in vii. 7 = Mt. xv. 9. Burkitt calls attention to the fact that the Sower, the Seed growing secretly, and the Mustard-seed "are extraordinarily appropriate in the setting given them by S. Mark. The seed had been sown, the first harvest of disciples had just been reaped, although much of what had been said had fallen on deaf or forgetful ears."

3. Ἀκούετε. *Hear ye.* This translation preserves the resemblance to Deut. vi. 4 (quoted Mk xii. 29), and also shows the connexion between the opening note and the concluding one, "let him hear" (*v.* 9). This preparatory "Hear ye" is preserved by Mk alone. The people on the beach were talking to one another, and it was necessary more than once (ἔλεγεν) to call their attention: ἰδού serves the same purpose. Cf. Prov. iv. 1, v. 1, xxii. 17; Ecclus. iii. 1, etc.

ὁ σπείρων. *The sower,* the representative of his class. Winer, p. 132. The art. is in all three, and in all three places is ignored in A.V.; cf. ii. 16, iii. 13, iv. 13, v. 13, xi. 4, xiii. 28, xiv. 66. Moreover, A.V. varies the order of the opening words, although the Greek order is the same in all three Gospels.

σπείραι. The infin. of purpose is often preceded by τοῦ. Lk. is specially fond of τοῦ in this connexion, and both Mt. and Lk. have it here. Winer, p. 408.

4. ἐν τῷ σπείρειν. "During the sowing" or *as he sowed*; cf. ἐν τῷ ἐλαύνειν (vi. 48). D has ἐν τῷ σπεῖραι, which would mean "after he had sowed." Both constructions are freq. in Lk. Contrast the aor. Lk. ii. 27, ix. 36, xi. 37, xiv. 1 with the pres. v. 1, 12, viii. 42, ix. 18, 29, 33, 51. For the constr. ἐγένετο...ἔπεσεν cf. i. 9. Mt. and Lk. omit the superfluous ἐγένετο.

ὁ μέν. *Sc.* σπέρμα. As in 1 Thess. ii. 18; 1 Cor. v. 3; Rom. vii. 12, x. 1, no δέ follows. Winer, p. 719; Blass, § 77, 12.

παρὰ τὴν ὁδόν. Cf. ii. 13, iv. 1. Not "along the way," but "by the side of the way"; so close to the path that it was trampled on (Lk.). The change of prepositions is graphic; παρά (*v.* 4), ἐπί (*v.* 5), εἰς (*v.* 7). Mk has the sing. of the three failures, ὁ μέν, ἄλλο, ἄλλο, and the plur. of the one success, ἄλλα. What fell on the good ground was more abundant than what did not do so. This important distinction is lost in Mt. and Lk. Mt. has the plur. throughout and Lk. has the sing. throughout.

5. ἐπὶ τὸ πετρῶδες. Not "on stony ground" (A.V.), *i.e.* ground full of stones, but *on the rocky ground* (R.V.), *i.e.* with rock close to the surface, ἐπὶ τὴν πέτραν (Lk.). Thin soil would cause rapid germination and rapid withering, and such soil is common in Galilee (Stanley, *Sin. and Pal.* pp. 425, 432). Cf. Jonah's gourd.

ἐξανέτειλεν. In both N.T. and LXX., ἀνατέλλω is both transitive (Mt. v. 45; Gen. iii. 18) and intransitive (xvi. 2; Jas i. 11, which resembles this passage; Gen. xix. 25). In LXX., ἐξανατέλλω is trans. (Gen. ii. 9).

7. ἀνέβησαν αἱ ἄκανθαι. The thorns were as yet hardly above the surface; but they were more vigorous.

συνέπνιξαν. Vulg. *suffocaverunt*; Wic. "strangliden." The συν- expresses intensity; see on iii. 5. Mt. and Lk. have ἀπέπνιξαν, "choked *off.*"

καὶ καρπὸν οὐκ ἔδωκεν. Hardly necessary after συνέπνιξαν, and omitted by Mt. and Lk. See on καὶ τότε, iii. 27.

8. τὴν γῆν τὴν καλήν. All three have the double art., which emphasizes the adj. (iii. 29); Lk. has ἀγαθήν, which is stronger than καλήν. Only twice, and then of persons, does Mk use ἀγαθός, x. 17, 18; in iii. 4 we should read ἀγαθοποιῆσαι. Mt. and Lk. have ἀγαθός often; it means what is good in its results, while καλός is what is good as an object of contemplation.

ἐδίδου...ἔφερεν. The change from aorists to imperfects is accurate. The mistake of taking ἀναβαίνοντα with καρπόν (fruit does not spring up) produced the false reading αὐξανόμενον, which is followed in A.V. On the participles see i. 15.

εἰς τριάκοντα. The texts are so tangled that it is impossible to determine what word should precede the numeral in each case; but we must have the same word in each case. An estimate of the evidence which gives a change of word (εἰς...ἐν...ἐν) is intolerable. When we have decided for εις...εις...εις, or for εν...εν...εν, we have then to choose between εἰς and εἶς, or between ἐν and ἕν. If εις is preferred, εἰς "up to" is better than εἶς. If εν is preferred, ἕν is better than ἐν. In any case, after three groups of failures in the neut. sing., we have three groups of successes, the gender of which depends on the reading adopted. A hundredfold is not an imaginary increase; cf. Gen. xxvi. 12. Herodotus (i. 193) speaks of even threehundredfold.

9. ἔλεγεν. Perhaps this concluding appeal, corresponding to the opening Ἀκούετε, was uttered more than once. Cf. *v.* 23; Lk. xiv. 35; Mt. xi. 15, xiii. 43. Deut. xxix. 4 may be the basis. In Rev. we have the sing., ὁ ἔχων οὖς (ii. 7, 11, 17, 29, iii. 6, 13, 22), and there, as in the Gospels, the appeal is made by Christ. Rev. xiii. 9 is an exception.

10. **κατά μόνας.** The expression is freq. in LXX., but in N.T. only here and Lk. ix. 18; perhaps χώρας was originally understood. Cf. Thuc. i. 32, 37. *When they came to be by themselves,* after other parables had been spoken, is the meaning. That there had been other parables is shown by what follows.

ἠρώτων τὰς παραβολάς. See crit. note. Mk always uses the imperf. of ἐρωτάω, never the aor. (vii. 26, viii. 5). He regards conversation as a *process*; see on v. 9. Mt., as often, substitutes an aor., εἶπαν. Usually ἐρωτάω = "I question" is followed by περί or ὑπέρ. The reading, τὴν παραβολήν, was substituted because only one parable has been recorded.

11. **ἔλεγεν.** Conversational imperf.; or possibly it introduces His customary explanation of the use of parables. Christ's reply, as often, goes deeper than the question put to Him. They want explanations of the parables just spoken; He explains the purpose of parabolic teaching.

τὸ μυστήριον δέδοται. Emphasis on τὸ μυσ. Mt. and Lk. have δέδοται γνῶναι τὰ μυστήρια, which is not the same thing. Some texts here have γνῶναι, and some have τὰ μυστήρια. Christ Himself, the revelation of the Father, had been given to the disciples. He, as the embodiment of the Gospel, was τὸ μυστήριον, of the import of which they as yet knew very little. He was the embodiment of the Good Tidings that the Kingdom of Heaven had been sown here and would produce a glorious harvest hereafter. Nowhere else in the Gospels does μυστήριον occur, but it is very freq. in Paul. Dalman, *Words,* p. 233.

τοῖς ἔξω. "The multitude of followers who were outside the circle of disciples." The meaning of such an expression, like our "outsiders," must depend on the context. To Jews it means non-Jews; to Christians, non-Christians; to the initiated, the uninitiated. It is not found elsewhere in the Gospels; cf. 1 Cor. v. 12, 13; Col. iv. 5; 1 Thess. iv. 12; 1 Tim. iii. 7.

τὰ πάντα γίνεται. In Mk only. Not "all these things" (A.V.), nor "all things" (R.V.), but *the whole,* the whole contents of the mystery of the Gospel. Not "are done" (A.V., R.V.), but *proves to be* to them, because of the πώρωσις of their hearts. It was given as illumination and instruction, but in their case it becomes a riddle; cf. Lk. x. 36, xi. 26.

12. **ἵνα βλέποντες κ.τ.λ.** An adaptation of the LXX. of Is. vi. 9, 10, but in LXX. there is no ἵνα. It intimates that parables may serve as a judgment on those who have rejected Christ's teaching. They have shut their eyes so persistently to the truth that now they are

unable to see it, and this is in accordance with God's purpose. "He that hath not, from him shall be taken away even that which he hath." But this judgment is a merciful one. The parable which the cold-hearted multitudes hear without understanding they remember, because of its penetrating and impressive form ; and when their hearts become able to receive its meaning, the meaning will become clear to them. Meanwhile they are saved from the guilt of rejecting plain truth. See below on *v.* 22. Failure to see this point has caused some to say that it is incredible that Jesus can have given this explanation of the *purpose* of parabolic teaching, and the difficulty is perhaps the cause of Mt. substituting ὅτι for ἵνα. Hastings' *D.B.* and *D.C.G.* art. "Parable." Vulg. here ignores the difference between βλέπωσι and ἰδῶσιν, *ut videntes videant et non videant,* but in Acts xxviii. 27, *et videntes videbitis et non perspicietis.* Syr-Sin. has "that seeing they may not see." See on viii. 24.

μή ποτε ἐπιστρέψωσιν. It is possible that here tradition has carried the quotation from Is. vi. 10 further than Christ did, or has confused His use of it. In LXX. it is *the people* who hardened their hearts μή ποτε ἐπιστρέψωσιν, not Jehovah who did so; they refused to understand and be healed. Lk. (viii. 10) does not carry the quotation beyond συνίωσιν, and Mt. preserves καὶ ἰάσομαι αὐτούς, as in LXX., for which Mk has καὶ ἀφεθῇ αὐτοῖς. Their not being converted and forgiven was the just consequence of their own obstinacy; in that sense, and in that only, was it part of the Divine purpose. See on Mt. xiii. 13. βλέποντες· τοῦτο τοῦ θεοῦ. μὴ βλέπωσι· τοῦτο τῆς κακίας αὐτῶν (Theoph.).

13—20.　Interpretation of the Parable of the Sower.

Mt. xiii. 18—23.　Lk. viii. 11—15.

13. καὶ λέγει αὐτοῖς. This introductory formula marks the beginning of a new section and breaks the connexion with *vv.* 10—12. It does not introduce a customary utterance (ἔλεγεν), but the explanation given on one occasion of a particular parable. This verse is peculiar to Mk.

Οὐκ οἴδατε. All English versions follow Beza in making two questions; but Luther, and apparently Vulg., make οὐκ οἴδατε categorical, *Ye know not,* which is probably right. In Lk. xx. 44 and Jn xii. 34, καὶ πῶς is preceded by a statement. In either case we have an expression of surprise and disappointment; see on vi. 6. The view that parables were a common method of instruction among the Jews does not seem to be well founded. In O.T. there are few, and to Christ's hearers they were a novelty.

καὶ πῶς; The καί accepts what has just been said and leads on to a question which καί emphasizes, *How then?* Cf. καὶ τίς; x. 26; Lk. x. 29, xviii. 26; Jn ix. 36; 2 Cor. ii. 2. Winer, p. 545. The question implies that the Sower is a leading and testing parable, *prima et fundamentalis* (Beng.). It is one of the three which all three record, the others being the Mustard-seed and The Wicked Husbandmen. It is probably accidental that all three, together with the parable which is peculiar to Mk, have to do with vegetation. The question implies a rebuke to the disciples as well as surprise on the part of Christ. Mt. does not like either and substitutes "Hear then ye the parable of the Sower." See Mt.'s treatment of Mk ix. 10, 32, 34, xiv. 40. Lk. is like Mt. in sparing the Twelve, and he omits the rebuke. Both A.V. and R.V. ignore the change from οἴδατε to γνώσεσθε, and A.V. ignores the τάς : *How then shall ye come to know all My parables?* Cf. xiii. 28 ; Lk. vii. 5 and see on *v.* 3.

14. ὁ σπείρων. The sower in the parable. He is not explained, and the interpretation must vary ; Christ, or one of His ministers, or the Church. The emphasis is on τὸν λόγον, giving the key to the parable ; *What the sower sows is the word.* See on ii. 2. The comparison between sowing and teaching is common in literature, in Plato, Plutarch, Philo. See the remarkable parallel 2 Esdr. viii. 41. The suggestion that this parable is borrowed from any external source is unnecessary. Bede notes that ἐξῆλθεν is not explained, and he interprets *quia Dominus de sinu Patris egrediens venit in mundum,* which is probably too definite.

15. οὗτοι δέ εἰσιν κ.τ.λ. Another instance of Mk's lack of literary skill; the sense is clear, but the constr. is not. *These are they by the wayside where the word is sown* is an incomplete sentence, without any relative to correspond to "these." "By the wayside" does not mean "casually" as distinct from listening to instruction.

ὅταν ἀκούσωσιν, εὐθὺς ἔρχεται. *Whensoever they hear* (xiii. 7, 14, 28), *Satan,* like the birds, *at once is there.*

ὁ Σατανᾶς. Mt. has ὁ πονηρός, Lk. ὁ διάβολος. See on i. 13 and iii. 23. This is strong evidence that Christ taught the existence of a personal evil spirit. In iii. 23 f. He might be said to be answering the Scribes according to the folly of their own hypothesis. But here there is nothing that requires such accommodation. He might have explained τὰ πετεινά as impersonal temptations, and the plur. invites such interpretation.

αἴρει. By doubt, ridicule, counter-attractions.

16. ὁμοίως. Peculiar to Mk. It means that this interpretation is parallel to the preceding one ; cf. xv. 31.

οἱ σπειρόμενοι. There is no confusion between the seed and the soil. We talk of seed being sown and of soil being sown, *i.e.* receiving seed. The latter is the meaning here. Imperf. part., *who were being sown*, in the parable. Syr-Sin. omits σπειρόμενοι and εὐθύς.

εὐθὺς...λαμβάνουσιν. In the former case Satan allowed no time, in this case the hearers take none. There is no counting of the cost (Lk. xiv. 28—33), but an immediate enthusiasm. Lk. drops εὐθύς, but compensates by substituting his favourite δέχονται = " welcome " for λαμβάνουσιν.

17. ῥίζαν. Another of the commonplaces of literature ; cf. Eph. iii. 17 ; Col. ii. 7 ; 2 Kings xix. 30: ἐν ἑαυτοῖς, because they are the soil.

ἀλλὰ πρόσκαιροί εἰσιν. *On the contrary, they are short-lived.* Cf. 2 Cor. iv. 18 ; Heb. xi. 25. "Husbandmen, when there is warm weather too early, are afraid lest the seeds should be too luxuriant, and then a single frost should lay hold of them " (Epict. *Dis.* iv. 8 *sub fin.*). See on *v.* 29.

θλίψεως. Frequent in N.T. and LXX. It implies being either *pressed down* or *in great straits*. Vulg. varies between *tribulatio* (here), *pressura* (Jn xvi. 21, 33), and *passio* (Col. i. 24). R.V. has " affliction " 2 Cor. iv. 8, but changes "affliction " (A.V.) to "tribulation " here and xiii. 19. In 2 Thess. i. 4, θλίψις is joined with διωγμός.

διὰ τὸν λόγον. Cf. xiii. 13 ; Mt. v. 11. This could not be expressed in the parable. The thin soil was not dried up because it contained good seed.

εὐθύς. This answers to the εὐθύς in *v.* 16. They receive hastily, and they abjure hastily, in each case without considering the consequences.

σκανδαλίζονται. The verb is freq. in Mk and Mt., but is rare elsewhere in N.T. It combines the ideas of "trip up " and "entrap," and in N.T. is always figurative of " causing to sin." Cf. Ecclus. ix. 5, xxiii. 8, and see on Mt. v. 29. Awkward questions caused Peter to deny his Master (xiv. 27, 29).

18. ἄλλοι εἰσίν. See crit. note. *Others are they* (R.V.). In the following οὗτοί εἰσιν we have an anacoluthon ; but, as in *v.* 15, the meaning is clear. A.V. again ignores the art.

19. καὶ αἱ μέριμναι τ. αἰῶνος. See crit. note. A different constr. begins here. *The cares of the age, aerumnae saeculi* (Vulg.), are such as divide and distract the mind. Cf. 1 Pet. v. 7, where human anxiety (μέριμνα) is set against Divine care (μέλει).

ἡ ἀπάτη τοῦ πλούτου. *The deceitful power of riches* (x. 23, 24; 1 Tim. vi. 10); cf. ἀπάτη ἀδικίας (2 Thess. ii. 10), ἀπ. τῆς ἁμαρτίας (Heb. iii. 13). Here, as in 2 Pet. ii. 13, ἀπάτη and ἀγάπη have been confused in MSS.

αἱ περὶ τὰ λοιπὰ ἐπιθυμίαι. Mk alone has this. Mt., who is fond of making triplets, by dropping these words destroys a triplet. τὰ λοιπά, "the rest" (Lk. xii. 26; 1 Cor. xi. 34), "*all the* other things besides riches." "The lusts of other things" (A.V., R.V.) is not quite adequate. The germs of these desires are in human nature before the word enters it. Philo (*Leg. Alleg.* iii. § 89, M. p. 136) explains the thorns in Gen. iii. 18 of the passions which spring up in the fool's soul.

20. καὶ ἐκεῖνοι. *And those* (R.V.). The change from οὗτοι... οὗτοι...ἄλλοι...οὗτοι (*vv.* 15, 16, 18) to ἐκεῖνοι marks the difference between the first three classes and the last, and the change should be kept in translation. A.V. has "these" in all five places. Here and Mt. xx. 4, καὶ ἐκεῖνοι is found in the best MSS.; elsewhere (xii. 4, 5, [xvi. 11, 13]) κἀκεῖνος prevails.

σπαρέντες. The change from imperf. (σπειρόμενοι) to aor. may have point. In the other cases the sowing never reached fruitful completion; the good soil was sown once for all successfully.

οἵτινες. "Who are of such a character as to"; cf. ix. 1, xii. 18.

παραδέχονται. Mk alone has this, and the compound occurs nowhere else in the Gospels; cf. Acts xv. 4; Heb. xii. 6.

ἐν τριάκοντα. See on *v.* 8. Here there is no question between εἰς and ἐν: we have to decide between ἕν, "one group," or possibly "one seed," and ἐν, "at the rate of." The question is unimportant. Lk. omits the differentiation; with him it suffices to distinguish between fruitful and unfruitful. Christ could see in the hearts of His hearers counterparts of the different kinds of soils. Characteristically, Jerome gives 100 to the celibates, 60 to the widows, and 30 to the married; Augustine prefers martyrs, celibates, and married; and there are other guesses on similar lines. It is enough to recognize that there are differences among the fruitful. There is a Buddhist parable which is similar; "The best sort of land is like my monks and nuns...the medium sort like the lay associates...The bad sort is like the adherents of other religious societies. Even to them I preach my doctrine" (Clemen, *Primitive Christianity*, p. 322).

The interpretations of the parables of the Sower and of the Tares show us that, although each of Christ's parables has only one main lesson, yet it is lawful to seek for meaning in some of the details. But it requires sober judgment to do this correctly; and it does not

follow, because some details lend themselves to allegorical explanation, that therefore these meanings were intended by our Lord.
Sanday, *Outlines*, pp. 68 f.

21—25. THE RESPONSIBILITY OF HEARING THE WORD.

Lk. viii. 16—18; cf. Lk. xi. 33.

21. καὶ ἔλεγεν αὐτοῖς. As in *v.* 13, we have a new section
marked. It consists of isolated Sayings, the setting of which has not
been preserved by tradition. Cf. ἔλεγεν in *v.* 11. Mt., as often,
omits the imperf. The Sayings are scattered in Mt., and to some
extent in Lk. also.

Μήτι ἔρχεται; *Does it come into the room? Is it brought in?*
Like the interrogative μή (ii. 19), μήτι expects a negative reply (xiv. 19;
Mt. vii. 16, xii. 23; etc.). We talk of letters and presents "coming."
Just as the seed has to be sown everywhere, so the light must shine
everywhere.

ὁ λύχνος. Not "a candle" (A.V.), but *the lamp* (R.V.). See
on *v.* 3. See Trench, *Syn.* § xlvi.; *D.B.* art. "Lamp." In each case
the article denotes that which is commonly found in houses, "the
bushel," "the bed," "the lampstand"; and in each case A.V.
ignores the art. The λύχνος is the inner meaning of parables, the
light of the Gospel without parabolic covering. The disciples who
hear and understand are the λυχνίαι (Rev. i. 20); it is their business
to make others understand; *debet esse non modius sed candelabrum*
(Beng.).

τὸν μόδιον. *The bushel*; Lk. has the vague word σκεῦος. "Hiding
one's light under a bushel" has become an English proverb, and we
must not alter the translation; but the Roman *modius* was about a
quarter of a bushel. The Greek μέδιμνος, which is often rendered
"bushel," was about a bushel and a half. Μόδιος occurs in papyri.

ὑπὸ τὴν κλίνην. Probably the bed for sleeping on (vii. 30;
Lk. xvii. 34) rather than the couch for reclining at table.

22. οὐ γάρ ἐστιν κρυπτόν. *For nothing is hidden, except for the
purpose of being brought to light, nor yet anything become secret* to
remain so, *but rather for the purpose of coming to light.*

For this elliptical use of ἀλλ' ἵνα = ἀλλὰ τοῦτο γέγονεν ἵνα cf. xiv. 49,
where Mt. (xxvi. 56) supplies the ellipse. The ellipse is freq. in the
Johannine writings; Jn i. 8, ix. 3, xiii. 18, xv. 25; 1 Jn ii. 19. Neither
here nor x. 40 does ἀλλά mean "except"; but see J. H. Moulton,
pp. 191, 241. The difference between φανερωθῇ and ἔλθῃ εἰς φανερόν
is worth keeping in translation; and we have a good instance of κρυπτά

becoming φανερά 1 Cor. xiv. 25. The saying may have been proverbial; our Lord uses it in different connexions. In Lk. xii.
2 the fact that nothing remains secret is applied to condemn hypocrisy;
hypocrisy is not only wicked but futile, for one day there will be a
merciless exposure. In Mt. x. 26 the meaning seems to be that the
Apostles proclaim publicly what Christ teaches them in private.
Here and Lk. viii. 17 the saying indicates that parables are not given
in order that unsympathetic hearers should *never* see or understand
(*v.* 12), but that in the end they should become sympathetic and be
able to see and understand. This good result the disciples must effect
by making known the light of Christ's teaching. Things which are
precious are hidden to prevent them from being misappropriated or
misused; they are not hidden to prevent them from being ever
seen or used. Things which are never to be seen again are not
"hidden," but "lost"; and what is put underground to remain
there is not "sown," but "buried."

23. **εἴ τις ἔχει.** In *v.* 9 this appeal was made to the whole
audience. Here the disciples are told that it applies to them as well
as to outsiders.

24. **καὶ ἔλεγεν.** The imperf. may be conversational, or it may
introduce another caution which He used to give them. Mt. omits.

Βλέπετε. Not quite in the same sense as in *v.* 12, nor yet as in
xiii. 5, 9, 23, 33, where it means "take heed," "be on your guard."
Here it is rather *Heed*, "look at it carefully and see that you understand it." A. V. and R. V. have "take heed," which is misleading.
Cf. vii. 14. Sight, the nobler sense, directs hearing—*oculus, non
auris, se movet* (Beng.)—is not quite the point.

ἐν ᾧ μέτρῳ. "The spiritual profit which you receive from what
you hear will depend upon your attention to it and apprehension of it:
you will get proportionate return (μετρηθήσεται ὑμῖν), and you will
receive a generous addition to it" (προστεθήσεται ὑμῖν). The disciple
who heeds what he hears is bounteously repaid. This saying, like
the one in *v.* 22, seems to have been proverbial, and it is applied in
quite other ways elsewhere (Mt. vii. 2; Lk. vi. 38). "Let the wise
man hear and increase in learning" (Prov. i. 5); his insight will
increase by being used. Bede says that he who loves the word will
receive the power to understand what he loves; Euthymius, that the
measure of one's προσοχή is the measure of one's γνῶσις. On the
use of the passive to avoid using the Name of God see Dalman,
Words, p. 224.

25. **ὃς γὰρ ἔχει.** Another proverb-like utterance which is used
with different applications (Mt. xiii. 12, xxv. 29; Lk. xix. 26). We

have a parallel saying, which holds good of spiritual progress, as well
as of worldly advancement, "Nothing succeeds like success." The
γάρ introduces a reason for the previous statement about measure for
measure.

ὃς οὐκ ἔχει. Christ often utters startling sayings which arrest
attention and make people think ; *e.g.* that self-seeking is self-
destruction, that the dead must be left to bury their own dead, that
those who mourn are blessed, etc. The Beatitudes are paradoxes ;
they tell us that blessedness begins where man deems that misery
begins. And how can a man be deprived of that which he does
not possess? The answer is that something is taken from him, which
he never used, and therefore never really possessed: or that something is taken, *because* he does not possess something else. To some
extent he can grasp and appreciate the truth ; but he has no desire to
increase this power, and he has no desire to learn more of the truth.
At last he loses the power of grasping and appreciating it. Darwin's
losing the power of appreciating music and poetry illustrates the
principle. Cf. Juv. iii. 208,

> *Nil habuit Codrus, quis enim negat? et tamen illud*
> *Perdidit infelix totum nihil.*

Lk. lessens the paradox by substituting δοκεῖ ἔχειν for ἔχει.

26—29. The Seed growing secretly and automatically.

Omitted by Mt. and Lk.

26. Καὶ ἔλεγεν. In *vv.* 10—25 we have had specimens of Christ's
private instructions to the disciples, given probably on different
occasions, and in some cases more than once. We now (26—34) have
a little more of His public teaching. The omission of αὐτοῖς may
intimate that the audience is changed. Certainly we have another
specimen of the parables which He addressed to mixed audiences
(*v.* 33). This parable is the only one which is recorded by Mk alone.
Tatian places it immediately before the Tares, with which it has,
almost of necessity, a few words in common, χόρτος, σῖτος, θερισμός :
but the words for "seed" differ, σπόρος and σπέρμα, and also for
"sow," βάλλω and σπείρω. The one remarkable resemblance is the
sleeping (καθεύδω) of the sower. The more simple parable might
easily lead on to the more elaborate one.

Οὕτως...ὡς ἄνθρωπος βάλῃ. Another imperfect constr. We require ὡς ἐὰν ἄνθρ. βάλῃ (1 Thess. ii. 7). See crit. note and J. H.
Moulton, p. 185. Οὕτως in the Gospels hardly ever looks forwards, as

here; it nearly always refers to something already said. The chief actor in a parable is elsewhere simply ἄνθρωπος (xii. 1, xiii. 34). No carelessness on the man's part is implied in βάλῃ (ii. 22, vii. 33; Mt. iv. 18, viii. 6, xxv. 27; Lk. xiii. 19; etc.). We have aor. of what is done once for all, and pres. of the habitual actions which follow the sowing. Why does R.V. change "ground" to "earth" here and not in *v.* 20?

τὸν σπόρον. "The seed which he has to sow," *his seed* (cf. *v.* 36). In *v.* 31 we have the more usual σπέρμα. In class. Grk σπόρος is "sowing" more often than "seed," and sometimes means "crop" (Hdt. iv. 53, viii. 109). In the Sower, Lk. has σπόρος for seed.

27. νύκτα καὶ ἡμέραν. Acc. of duration of time, as in Lk. ii. 37; Acts xx. 31, xxvi. 7. We say both "night and day" and "day and night." So also in Greek; "night and day" is more common in N.T., "day and night" in O.T. The order seems to make no difference of meaning, but here νύκτα καὶ ἡμέραν follows the order of καθεύδῃ καὶ ἐγείρηται, *should go on sleeping and rising night and day.* The husbandman, having sown his seed, goes on with other occupations, and the seed works on without him.

καὶ ὁ σπόρος βλαστᾷ καὶ μηκύνεται. See crit. note. This is an independent constr., showing that the development of the seed is now independent of the sower. Βλαστᾷ may be either indic. or subj., and some texts, followed by A.V. and R.V., have μηκύνηται, to make the original constr. run on; but the evidence for μηκύνεται is decisive. *And the seed goes on springing and growing up.* Μηκύνω occurs thrice in LXX. and here only in N.T.

ὡς οὐκ οἶδεν αὐτός. *In a way not known to him*, with emphasis on "him." This does not mean that he takes no care of it; but he cannot do what soil and moisture do, and he does not understand the mysteries of growth. Some make ὡς temporal, *dum nescit ille* (Vulg.); then we might render, "without *his* knowing"; but the other is better, *quomodo ipse nescit* (Beza). Erasmus takes αὐτός of the seed, Bengel of God!

28. αὐτομάτη. First with emphasis; *It is of herself that the earth beareth fruit.* Similarly, αὐτομάτη ἠνοίχθη αὐτοῖς (Acts xii. 10), the only other occurrence in N.T. Cf. τὰ αὐτόματα ἀναβαίνοντα τοῦ ἀγροῦ σου (Lev. xxv. 5), of that which grows without cultivation in the sabbatical year. Theophylact interprets this of the freewill of man; αὐτεξούσιοι γάρ ἐσμεν, καὶ ἐν τῇ ἡμετέρᾳ προαιρέσει κεῖται τὸ τὸν σπόρον ἢ αὐξάνεσθαι ἢ μή. But Euthymius is probably right in saying that here only the righteous are signified, the good seed on good ground.

καρποφορεῖ. The crowning result of the soil's action is stated first, and then the chief stages are noted.

πρῶτον χόρτον κ.τ.λ. *First blade, then ear, then full corn in the ear.* A.V. and R.V. thrice insert the art., without putting "the " in italics. Cf. iii. 32.

εἶτεν...εἶτεν. This very rare form of εἶτα is well attested here, although in v. 17 we have εἶτα without variant. It occurs in a Messenian inscription of A.D. 91. It is said to be Ionic ; Blass § 6. 2.

πλήρης σῖτον. With this reading πλήρης is indeclinable. See crit. note. If πλήρης σῖτος is the original reading, the nom. gives a sort of triumphant ring to the conclusion ; " then there is the full corn in the ear." Cf. the change to the indic. in v. 27.

29. παραδοῖ. Aor. subj. = παραδῷ (WH. *App.* p. 168). Cf. γνοῖ v. 43, δοῖ viii. 37, παραδοῖ xiv. 10. The meaning is uncertain ; either *alloweth* (R.V. marg.), or " bringeth itself forth " ; cf. 1 Pet. ii. 23, where παρεδίδου may mean " committed himself."

ἀποστέλλει. *He sendeth forth* (iii. 14, vi. 7, xiii. 27). Perhaps an echo of Joel iii. 13, ἐξαποστείλατε δρέπανα, ὅτι παρέστηκεν τρυγητός. Cf. Rev. xiv. 15, πέμψον τὸ δρέπανόν σου...ὅτι ἐξηράνθη ὁ θερισμός. It is the husbandman who does this. The earth has done her mysterious work, and now he is wanted again. In class. Grk δρεπάνη is more common.

παρέστηκεν. *Is ready*, ready for the sickle, as in Joel iii. 13, where Vulg. has *maturavit*, not *adest*, as here.

We have Christ's interpretation of the Sower and of the Tares, but not of this kindred parable. As in the Sower, the seed is the Gospel and the soil is the hearts of those who receive it. The Sower and Reaper is Christ. Between His first and second coming we have the mysteriously combined action of soil and seed in the whole history of the Church. There is a remarkable parallel in Epictetus (*Dis.* iv. 8 *sub fin.*) ; " Fruit grows thus. The seed must be buried for some time, be hid, grow slowly, that it may come to perfection... Let the root grow, then acquire the first joint, then the second, then the third. Then in this way the fruit will naturally force its way out, even if I do not wish it." See on v. 17.

30—32. The Mustard Seed.

Mt. xiii. 31, 32. Lk. xiii. 18, 19.

30. Καὶ ἔλεγεν. Mt., as often, substitutes an aor.

ὁμοιώσωμεν. Delib. subj., as in xii. 14 ; 1 Cor. xi. 22. A double question, as in Lk. vii. 31, but there we have ὁμοιώσω. Nowhere else

does Mk use ὁμοιόω, which occurs seven times in Mt. and thrice in Lk.
Its use here might be quoted as evidence of Mk's acquaintance with
Q. Mk nowhere has ὅμοιος, which is freq. in Mt. and Lk. This
passage stands alone in coupling Christ with His hearers. Nowhere
does He use the plur. of Himself, as St Paul often does. Teaching by
asking questions and answering them oneself is universal. Mt. omits
the questions, perhaps as suggesting that Christ was in doubt or
difficulty. The wording in Lk. is very different.

ἐν τίνι. The ἐν is literal; *in what parable must we place it?*
The parable is a case or wrapper to contain the truth. The expression
is unique.

31. ὡς κόκκῳ σινάπεως. The verse is a medley of confused
constructions, but with its meaning sufficiently plain. The three
words seem to mix the forms of reply to the two questions, ὡς
answering to πῶς and κόκκῳ to τίνι. Hence the reading κόκκον (ACL).
After the second ἐπὶ τῆς γῆς, the constr. is lost in the superfluous καὶ
ὅταν ὑπαρῇ. The corrections in MSS. are various, and it is difficult
to determine how much of the defective grammar is due to the
Evangelist. Lk. connects the parable with the healing of a woman
in a synagogue on the Sabbath. Neither Mk nor Mt. gives any hint
of time or place.

μικρότερον ὄν πάντων τ. σπ. This is the main feature; the
smallness of the seed compared with the greatness of the development.
This use of the comparative is freq. in N.T. Cf. ix. 34; Lk. vii. 28,
ix. 48. The seed now is, not the Gospel, but the Kingdom. Again
Christ seems to be using a current proverbial saying; cf. vv. 22, 24.
"Small as a mustard-seed" was a Jewish proverb. Lk. says that the
man sows the seed "in his own garden."

32. πάντων τῶν λαχάνων. More accurate than Lk., who says
that it becomes a δένδρον. Lk. (xi. 42) gives λάχανα as the class to
which ἡδύοσμον and πήγανον belong; St Paul (Rom. xiv. 2), as the
food which the weak vegetarian eats. Its derivation (λαχαίνω=dig)
points to its meaning cultivated herbs, "vegetables." Stanley (*Sin.
and Pal.* p. 427) thinks that σίναπι in this parable probably means
Salvadora Persica; but *Sinapis nigra* is the more usual identification (Tristram, *Nat. Hist. of the Bible*, p. 472). What follows seems
to be an echo of Dan. iv. 11, 12, 21 or Ezek. xvii. 23, xxxi. 6; the
description may have been a commonplace.

κατασκηνοῦν. B* here, and B*D in Mt. xiii. 32, have κατασκηνοῖν.
Cf. ἀποδεκατοῖν, BD* in Heb. vii. 5; φιμοῖν, א* in 1 Pet. ii. 15.
Similar forms are found in inscriptions, but not in papyri or in LXX.
Blass § 22. 3; WH. II. § 410.

In this chapter we have three parables, which all point in the same direction, while each in addition has its own lesson. Seed is sown on good ground, and produces 30, 60, 100 fold. Seed is sown, and the sower has a sure return. A very small seed is sown, and the result is a very large plant. In each case the necessary thing is that the seed should be *sown*. In like manner the reign of God has been, and must continue to be, preached, and that reign, with immense development, will surely at last be absolute and complete. Even if this parable stood alone, which it does not, it would be conclusive against the view that Jesus believed that the end of the world was very near.

33, 34. The Principle of Christ's Parabolic Teaching.

Mt. xiii. 34.

33. ἐλάλει…ἠδύναντο. The imperfects are again accurate (cf. *vv.* 2, 10), yet Mt. has ἐλάλησεν. Αὐτοῖς refers to hearers who have not been mentioned ; τὸν λόγον as in ii. 2.

καθώς. *Just as* (i. 2, xi. 6, xiv. 16) ; the correspondence between His teaching and their capacity was exact. Here, xiv. 16, and xv. 7, R.V. has "as" for καθώς, as if ὡς were used. This seems to imply that Christ's parables were not elaborated beforehand. On each occasion He fitted them to His audience, whose hearts He read. Cf. iv. 11, 12 ; Jn xvi. 12. In *v.* 36 R.V. treats ὡς as καθώς.

34. χωρὶς…οὐκ. Cf. Philem. 14 ; Heb. ix. 22, xii. 14. *Nullus facile sermo ejus invenitur, in quo non aliquid parabolarum sit intermistum* (Bede).

κατ᾽ ἰδίαν δὲ τοῖς ἰδίοις μαθ. *But privately to His private disciples.* The repetition of ἴδιος is doubtless intentional. With κατ᾽ ἰδίαν (freq. in Mk and Mt.) comp. κατὰ μόνας (*v.* 10) : Gal. ii. 2 is parallel. With τοῖς ἰδίοις, "His own" (stronger than αὐτοῦ) comp. εἰς τὴν ἰδίαν πόλιν, εἰς τὸν ἴδιον ἀγρόν (Mt. ix. i, xxii. 5).

ἐπέλυεν. *He expounded, explicabat.* The verb is used of interpreting dark sayings and questions. Solomon ῥᾳδίως ἐπελύετο τὰ προβαλλόμενα σοφίσματα of the Queen of Sheba (Joseph. *Ant.* VIII. vi. 5). Cf. ἐπίλυσις (2 Pet. i. 20) of the interpretation of Scripture.

35—41. The Stilling of the Wind and the Waves.

Mt. viii. 23—27. Lk. viii. 22—25.

35. ἐν ἐκείνῃ τῇ ἡμέρᾳ. This takes us back to iii. 20. Mt. gives the incident quite a different setting.

Διέλθωμεν. The verb is more often used of traversing land than of crossing water. It is freq. in Lk. and Acts, and in Acts it is almost a technical word for a missionary journey on land (xiv. 24, xv. 3, 41, xviii. 23, xix. 1, 21, xx. 2). For crossing water we have διαπεράω (v. 21, vi. 53 ; Mt. ix. 1, xiv. 34 ; Acts xxi. 2 ; also in LXX.). Where διέρχομαι is used of traversing water, it means going on foot (1 Cor. x. 1).

36. ἀφέντες τὸν ὄχλον. Mt. says that it was when He saw such a multitude that He gave the order to cross. He had been teaching from the boat (v. 1). Apparently He was already lying down, too weary to help in dispersing the multitude.

παραλαμβάνουσιν αὐτὸν ὡς ἦν. *They take Him with them* (Acts xv. 39), *as He was, in their boat* (cf. v. 26). It is because it was their boat that they take Him rather than He them (ix. 2, x. 32).

ἄλλα πλοῖα. Their occupants had probably come round the boat in which Christ was, to listen to Him. We hear no more of them ; they would disperse when the teaching ceased. As they contribute nothing to the narrative, they are omitted by Mt. and Lk., but the mention of them here is a considerable guarantee for the truth of the tradition. Their presence was remembered.

37. λαῖλαψ. The word is in all three. It perhaps expresses the swishing slap with which the wind struck ; λα- is sometimes an intensive prefix ; λαδρέω, λακατάρατος.

ἐπέβαλλεν. *The waves continued to beat into the boat.* The imperf. (ABC etc.) is better than the aor. (ΝDE etc.). The intrans. use of ἐπιβάλλω is found in the later books of LXX. and in Polybius. Vulg. makes it trans., with λαῖλαψ as nom., *procella...fluctus mittebat in navem.*

ἤδη γεμίζεσθαι. *Was now filling* (R.V.). The needless repetition of τὸ πλοῖον is characteristic. Cf. τὸν ἄνθρωπον in vii. 15.

38. καὶ αὐτός. *And He Himself*, as distinct from the anxious crew. Cf. vi. 47, viii. 29 ; καὶ αὐτὸς is very freq. in Lk.

ἐν τῇ πρύμνῃ ἐπὶ τὸ προσκεφάλαιον. This graphic detail is peculiar to Mk. In the stern He was less in the way of the crew, and "*the* head-rest" indicates the usual furniture (v. 21), or the only one in the boat. A.V. again ignores the article. He was wearied with much teaching, and all three mention that He fell asleep ; καθεύδων comes with effect at the end of the sentence—*fast asleep.* Nowhere else is His sleeping mentioned ; but He needed sleep, as He needed food. His humanity was in all respects real.

ἐγείρουσιν αὐτόν. *They awake Him* (Acts xii. 7).

Διδάσκαλε. Mt. has Κύριε, Lk. his favourite Ἐπιστάτα. Only

once in Mk (vii. 28) is Christ addressed as Κύριε. It is freq. in the other Gospels.

οὐ μέλει σοι. Cf. Wisd. xii. 13; 1 Pet. v. 7. This reproachful question is omitted by Mt., who substitutes σῶσον, and by Lk., who substitutes a second Ἐπιστάτα. Both Mt. and Lk. are disposed to omit what seems to tell against the Twelve; see on v. 13. Cf. *Nate dea, potes hoc sub casu ducere somnos?* Virg. *Aen.* iv. 560. Bede compares the helpless dismay of the disciples at the death of Christ. In neither case did their belief that He was the Messiah convince them that disaster was impossible. All three have ἀπολλύμεθα, *we are perishing.*

39. διεγερθείς. Pointing back to ἐγείρουσιν (v. 38); *He awoke* (R.V.); not "He arose" (A.V.).

Σιώπα, πεφίμωσο. Mk alone preserves these words. Cf. i. 25 and the rebuke to the braggart fig-tree (xi. 14). The asyndeton is peremptory. The rare perf. imperat. indicates that what is commanded is to continue in its effects; *be still* and remain so. Cf. ἔρρωσθε, Acts xv. 29. For σιωπάω see on x. 48.

ἐγένετο γαλήνη. In all three. This was more marvellous than the "sinking to rest" of the wind. Wind sometimes has dropped suddenly, and yet "the sea wrought and was tempestuous" long after the wind ceased. In Jonah i. 11, κοπάζω is used of the sea sinking to rest. There are several points of similarity between the two narratives; but there are more and far stronger points of contrast.

40. Τί δειλοί ἐστε; οὔπω ἔχετε πίστιν; Mt. slightly, and Lk. still more, tones down the rebuke, which is more severe than A.V. and R.V. represent. Neither here nor Rev. xxi. 8 does "fearful" adequately render δειλός, which means "cowardly" or "craven." In Rev. xxi. 8 the δειλοί and ἄπιστοι are put in the front rank of those who are to receive the greater condemnation. Cf. Deut. xx. 8; Judg. vii. 3; and esp. Ecclus ii. 12, 13. The two questions are closely connected. It is their want of trust in Him that has made them cowards. If they had had firm faith, they would not have feared that the Messiah could perish in a storm, or allow them to perish for obeying His command; οὔπω, after all that they had heard Him say and seen Him do; see crit. note and cf. vii. 18. Caesar's encouragement to the terrified pilot, "Thou bearest Caesar and his fortunes," may be compared. For the asyndeton cf. vi. 38.

41. ἐφοβήθησαν φόβον μέγαν. Cf. v. 42; Is. viii. 12; Jonah i. 10; 1 Macc. x. 8. Mk says that they feared, Mt. that they marvelled, Lk. gives both. We have the same cogn. acc. Lk. ii. 9. This

fear is different from their terror during the storm, and it is not
rebuked. To be suddenly conscious of the presence of the supernatural commonly engenders fear ; vi. 50 ; Lk. i. 12, 30, v. 10, 26,
viii. 37, ix. 32; etc. The disciples had seen His power over demons
and over disease; but this power over wind and wave was a new
thing.

ἔλεγον πρὸς ἀλλήλους. See on x. 26. It is remarkable that in
none of the accounts do they say anything to Him; and this also
is natural (ix. 32, x. 32). Even Peter is silent; contrast Lk. v. 8;
Jn xxi. 7. This was a miracle which, as fishermen, they could
appreciate. In a legend they would have taken the miracle as a
matter of course.

ὑπακούει. Sing. verb with a plurality of nominatives, the so-
called σχῆμα Πινδαρικόν, which is more common when the verb
precedes (xiii. 3 ; Mt. v. 18; Rev. ix. 12) ; but the other order is not
rare (Mt. vi. 19 ; 1 Cor. xv. 50). Here "wind and sea" are regarded
as one entity. ADΠ have ὑπακούουσιν.

A comparison of the three narratives shows substantial agreement,
with some difference in details, esp. as to the words spoken. Augustine
(*De Cons. Evan.* ii. 24) says, supposing Christ used words which no
Evangelist records, but which mean much the same as what is
recorded, "what does it matter?" See on x. 46.

It is instructive also to compare the three narratives with the
description of a storm at sea in the Testaments (*Naphtali* vi. 1 9).
It seems to be based on all three Gospels, esp. Mk and Lk., with
a remarkable conclusion taken from Jn vi. 21. Note especially γίνεται
λαῖλαψ ἀνέμου μεγάλη καὶ ἐπληρώθη τὸ πλοῖον ὑδάτων, ὥστε καὶ συντρί-
βεσθαι αὐτό. ὡς δὲ ἐπαύσατο ὁ χειμών, ἔφθασε τὸ σκάφος ἐπὶ τῆς γῆς ἐν
εἰρήνῃ. It is difficult to believe that this narrative was written first
and influenced two, three, and possibly all four of the Gospels. The
above quotation is condensed, but without change of a word, in order
to show the chief points of resemblance.

CHAPTER V.

1. Γερασηνῶν (א*BD) rather than Γαδαρηνῶν (ACΠ) or Γεργεσηνῶν (אᶜLΔ 33).

3. ἁλύσει (BC*L 33) rather than ἁλύσεσιν (אAC²DΔΠ).

5. ἐν τοῖς μνήμασιν καὶ ἐν τοῖς ὄρεσιν (אABCKL etc.) rather than ἐν τ. ὄρεσιν κ. ἐν τ. μν. (D).

9. λέγει αὐτῷ (אABCKLΔΠ) rather than ἀπεκρίθη λέγων (EFGetc.). Scribes often insert ἀπεκρίθη or ἀποκριθείς, cf. vii. 6, ix. 12, x. 5, 20, xi. 29, 30, xii. 17.

12. אBCLΔ omit πάντες οἱ δαίμονες (from Mt. viii. 31).
παρεκάλεσαν (אBCLΔ) rather than παρεκάλουν (ADKM).

13. אBCLΔ omit εὐθέως ὁ Ἰησοῦς. Cf. vi. 34, viii. 1, x. 52, xii. 41. The insertion of names for the sake of clearness is freq., esp. at the beginning of lections. See also in the Gospels in our Prayer Book. On St John's Day both "Jesus" and "Peter" are inserted in Jn xxi. 19. אBC*DLΔ omit ἦσαν δέ. Syr-Sin. omits κατὰ τοῦ κρημνοῦ.

14. καὶ οἱ βόσκοντες (אABCDLMΔ) rather than οἱ δὲ βόσκοντες. See on i. 14. αὐτούς (אBCDLΔ) rather than τοὺς χοίρους (AΠ). ἦλθον (אᶜABKLM 33) rather than ἐξῆλθον (א*CD etc.).

18. ἐμβαίνοντος (אABCD) rather than ἐμβάντος (EFG).

19. καί (אABCLΔ 33) rather than ὁ δὲ Ἰησοῦς (D etc.). See on vv. 13, 14.

22. אBDLΔ omit ἰδού.

23. ἵνα σωθῇ καὶ ζήσῃ (אBCDLΔ) rather than ὅπως σωθῇ καὶ ζήσεται (ANΠ). Syr-Sin. omits ἵνα σωθῇ.

25. אABCLΔ omit τις after γυνή.

36. παρακούσας (א*BLΔ) rather than ἀκούσας (אᶜACD). אBDLΔ omit εὐθέως. See on v. 13.

37. μετ᾽ αὐτοῦ συνακολουθῆσαι (אBCLΔ) is the text from which several other readings have sprung.

38. ἔρχονται (אABCDFΔ) rather than ἔρχεται (LNΠ).

40. אBDLΔ 33 omit ἀνακείμενον.

41. κούμ (אBCLMN) rather than κοῦμι (DΔΠ).

43. γνοῖ (ABDL) rather than γνῷ (אCNΔΠ).

1—20. CURE OF THE GERASENE DEMONIAC.

Mt. viii. 28—34. Lk. viii. 26—39.

1. ἦλθον. This is all that we learn of the disciples in this
section. Throughout the incident Jesus alone acts and directs. Even
when the company returns to the other side (*v.* 21), it is Jesus only
who is mentioned. **τῶν Γερασηνῶν.** See crit. note. All three readings are found
in all three places. The evidence shows that "Gadarenes" is right
in Mt. and "Gerasenes" in Mk and Lk., while "Gergesenes" has
little claim to be considered original anywhere. Origen supports
"Gergesenes," but on topographical grounds, not on textual evidence.
The ruins now known as *Gersa*, *Kersa*, or *Kursi* may represent the
place which Mk and Lk. call Gerasa, but which was known to Origen
as Gergesa. But we cannot be sure that the modern names are
corruptions of Gerasa or Gergesa : they may have had independent
origin. "The country of the Gerasenes" may mean a large district,
but the country round the Gerasa which was situated more than
30 miles S.E. of the Lake cannot be meant. Only at one place on the
E. shore of the Lake is there a κρημνός. *D.C.G.* art. "Gerasenes."

2. ἐξελθόντος αὐτοῦ. The more idiomatic ἐξελθόντι αὐτῷ (ΑΠ)
is an obvious correction, and ἐξελθόντων αὐτῶν (D) is influenced by
ἦλθον, keeping the disciples in view a moment longer. Cf. v. 18 and
xiii. 1, and see Blass § 74, 5.

εὐθὺς ὑπήντησεν αὐτῷ. The characteristic εὐθύς, though omitted
in B, Lat.-Vet. Syrr. Arm., may be accepted as probably original.
No sooner had Christ come on shore than the demoniac appeared and
moved towards Him. Its seeming inconsistence with *v.* 6 may have
caused εὐθύς to be omitted. That ὑπαντάω means "meet accidentally," while ἀπαντάω means "go to meet," does not always hold ;
see xiv. 13, where ἀπαντήσει is undisputed, and Lk. xvii. 12, where
ἀπήντησαν is probably right.

ἐκ τῶν μνημείων. No rock-hewn tombs have been found near
Kersa, but a tomb built on the ground would be more likely to be
chosen as a dwelling. Cf. οἰκοδομεῖτε τὰ μνημεῖα τῶν προφητῶν
(Lk. xi. 47).

ἄνθρωπος. Lk. says ἀνήρ τις, Mt. δύο. Mt. xx. 30 has two blind
men, where Mk and Lk. mention only one. Probably in both cases
Mt. represents a tradition in which the greatness of the miraculous
benefit has been enhanced by increasing the number of the recipients ;
the narrative in Mk is distinct and consistent throughout. The plur.,
τῶν μνημείων and τοῖς μνήμασιν (*vv.* 3, 5), may, however, be said to

give some support to the tradition of two demoniacs. Lichtenstein compares 2 Kings xviii. 17, where three ambassadors are named, while Is. xxxvi. 2 names Rabshakeh only. See S. J. Andrews, *Life of our Lord*, pp. 300 f., for other suggestions.

ἐν πνεύματι ἀκαθάρτῳ. See on i. 23.

3. ὃς τὴν κατ. εἶχεν. The change from aor. to imperf. is accurate. Κατοίκησις, not rare in LXX., occurs nowhere else in N.T., and Mk nowhere has κατοικέω, which is freq. in N.T., esp. Acts and Rev.

ἐν τοῖς μνήμασιν. *In the tombs* (R.V.) rather than "amongst" them (A.V.). He took shelter sometimes in one and sometimes in another. Cf. Ps. lxviii. 7, ἐξάγων...τοὺς κατοικοῦντας ἐν τάφοις, and Is. lxv. 4, ἐν τοῖς μνήμασιν...κοιμῶνται. In N.T. μνημεῖον is freq., while μνῆμα is rare. In class. Greek both words mean a "memorial" or "monument"; the meaning "tomb" is Biblical and perhaps colloquial. The fondness of those who suffer from mania or melancholia for tombs is well known; many instances in Wetstein. Calvin says of some of the questions which have been raised about this narrative, *frivola est, imo stulta eorum divinatio.*

οὐδὲ ἁλύσει οὐκέτι οὐδείς. See crit. note. The accumulation of negatives is here peculiar to Mk. See on i. 44 and note the expressive οὐδέ and οὐκέτι. "Not even a chain was any longer of any use," implying that at one time it had sufficed. The statement explains how such a man came to be àt large and to have his abode in the tombs. Contrast Lk. viii. 29. After δύναμαι the aor. infin. (δῆσαι) is normal; see on i. 41.

4. διὰ τὸ...δεδέσθαι. The διά is not quite logical. His having been often bound ineffectually was not the cause of its being impossible to bind him effectually; it was the cause of their ceasing to try, and of his being free, in spite of his being a peril to the inhabitants. Syr-Sin. has "because he had broken many fetters and chains and *had escaped.*" Cf. Acts xix. 16.

πέδαις καὶ ἁλύσεσι. It is more certain that πέδαι means "fetters" than that ἁλύσεις means "manacles" or "hand-cuffs." Vulg. has *compedibus et catenis*, not *pedicis et manicis*. The ἁλύσεις might fasten him to a wall, as St Paul was fastened to a soldier (Eph. vi. 20; 2 Tim. i. 16). But διεσπάσθαι would express the tearing asunder of manacles, and συντετρίφθαι the crushing of the fetters or smashing them with a stone; cf. xiv. 3; Mt. xii. 20; Jn xix. 36.

οὐδεὶς ἴσχυεν. Coordinate with οὐδεὶς ἐδύνατο in *v.* 3. The difference between the verbs should be marked; *no man could any more bind him...and no man had strength to tame him* (R.V.).

St James does not use ἰσχύω of taming the tongue (iii. 7, 8); but it may be used of the physical effort to keep awake (xiv. 37). Cf. Jn xxi. 6, where even R.V. has "not able."

5. διὰ παντός. Neither here nor Lk. xxiv. 53 does διὰ π. mean that there were no intervals; διὰ π. expresses what is usual, and rather implies that there *are* breaks in what is generally continuous (Acts ii. 25; Heb. ix. 6, xiii. 15).

νυκτὸς καὶ ἡμέρας. See on iv. 27; here the gen. indicates intervals.

ἦν κράζων. The periphrastic imperf. emphasizes the continuance of the action.

κατακόπτων ἑαυτόν. *Pounding himself*, or perhaps *gashing himself*; lit. "cutting himself to pieces"; *concidens se* (Vulg.). Cf. *concisus pugnis* (Juv. iii. 300), and for the compound, κατέκλασεν (vi. 41). For the combination of participles see on i. 15.

6. καὶ ἰδὼν τὸν Ἰησοῦν. He had not come out of his dismal shelter because he saw Jesus land, so that his meeting Him (*v.* 2) was accidental on his part.

ἀπὸ μακρόθεν. A pleonasm of which Mk is fond; viii. 3, xi. 13, xiv. 54, xv. 40. Cf. ἐκ παιδιόθεν (ix. 21). In Mt. xxvi. 58 the ἀπό is omitted in אCDF, and in Mt. xxvii. 55 ἀπ' is omitted in אL. In class. Greek we should have πρόσωθεν or πόρρωθεν rather than μακρόθεν. Blass § 29. 3.

7. Τί ἐμοὶ καὶ σοί. See on i. 24.

τοῦ ὑψίστου. The girl with a Python uses the same expression (Acts xvi. 17); elsewhere in N.T. "it occurs only in passages with an O.T. ring, Lk. i. 32, 35, 76, vi. 35, viii. 28; Heb. vii. 1" (Swete). In LXX. it is freq. But the title is not exclusively Jewish, and may have been used by heathen before it was adopted by the Jews. It savours of polytheism in the sense of highest among many, and the demoniac may have been a heathen. In Jewish writings it is specially freq. in those of the second cent. B.C. See Charles, *Book of Jubilees*, p. 213; Clemen, *Primitive Christianity*, p. 81. Theophylact points out that Christ's enemies, the demons, exhibited better knowledge of Him than His friends had shown (iv. 41), or showed even later (vi. 50).

ὁρκίζω σε τὸν θεόν. The common phrase; cf. Acts xix. 13 and ἐνορκίζω ὑμᾶς τὸν κύριον (1 Thess. v. 27). The double acc. is found in inscriptions. Deissmann, *Bib. St.* p. 281. In LXX. we find both κατὰ τοῦ θεοῦ and ἐν τῷ θεῷ. In order to influence Jesus, the demon uses the very phrase that was commonly employed in exorcisms.

μή με βασανίσῃς. While the man runs to Jesus and prostrates himself, the evil power by which he is obsessed shrinks in terror from Him. Immediate punishment is expected from One who has the power to inflict it. Mt. inserts the significant πρὸ καιροῦ. Cf. Rev. xiv. 10, xx. 10; also βάσανος in Lk. xvi. 23, 28. The history of the noun indicates the delusion which has produced, and still produces, hideous suffering, that torture is a touch-stone or test of truth. Bede and Theophylact suggest that it was torture to the malignant spirits to be made to cease from tormenting a human being; but this is not what the cry means.

8. ἔλεγεν γάρ. Here the force of the imperf., as referring to action which preceded something already mentioned, is best represented in English by the pluperf.; *For He had been saying*, or *had said*; cf. *v.* 28, vi. 18; Mt. xiv. 4; also Acts ix. 39, ὅσα ἐποίει, "which Dorcas *had been making* while she was with them." Burton, § 29.

τὸ πνεῦμα τὸ ἀκάθαρτον. Nom. with art. for voc., as often in N.T. (v. 41, ix. 25; Lk. viii. 54, x. 21, xviii. 11, 13; Col. iii. 18; Eph. vi. 1; etc.). It is specially common with imperatives and may be due in some cases to Heb. influence (2 Kings ix. 31; Jer. xlvii. 6).

9. ἐπηρώτα. Mk, who regards conversation as a process, nearly always puts ἐπερωτάω in the imperf. (vii. 5, 17, viii. 23, 27, 29, ix. 11, 28, 33, x. 2, 10, 17, etc.); so that we cannot infer that the question had to be repeated, although it may have been. Asking for the name excited suspicion; it might be used for βασανισμός. It was a common belief that, in order to exorcize a demon, you must address it by name. Deissmann, *Light from the Ancient East*, pp. 252, 257. But the purpose of the question was rather to get the man to distinguish his own personality. This it fails to do; the obsession is still too strong. Mt., as usual, omits a question which seems to imply that Christ was ignorant and needed information. On the reply see crit. note.

Λεγιών. This introduction of a Latin word is a mark of authenticity; it is in place, but it would not be likely to be invented. In conquered Palestine, "legion" would suggest numbers, strength, and relentless oppression. Cf. Lk. viii. 2, xi. 26. *Legio non pro finito numero, sed tantum pro magna turba accipitur* (Calvin). The man felt as if he were possessed by a legion of demons. Syr-Sin. has "*Our* name is Legion." Cf. the "seven demons" in Mary Magdalen (Lk. viii. 2).

10. παρεκάλει. In spite of the masc. πολλοί ἐσμεν, the sing. is retained, because the demons use the man as their organ. Lk. has παρεκάλουν (as ΑΔ here), marking the plurality of the hostile forces, although neut. plur. (δαιμόνια πολλά) has preceded.

πολλά. Adverbial, as usual, *deprecabatur illum multum* (Vulg.). See on i. 45, and for ἵνα on iii. 9.

ἔξω τῆς χώρας. If this expresses the wish of the man, it means that he fears to be sent away from his familiar haunts and his home (*v.* 19). If, as Lk. takes it, it expresses the wish of the demons, it means that they fear to be sent εἰς τὴν ἄβυσσον, which probably means the penal part of Hades.

11.   πρὸς τῷ ὄρει. "*At* the mountain," or *on the mountain side* (R.V.); cf. Lk. xix. 37; Jn xviii. 16, xx. 11, 12.

12.   παρεκάλεσαν. All three have the plur. here, showing that the request is that of the demons; already they are dissociating themselves from the man. See crit. note.

Πέμψον. Here only does Mk use πέμπω, which is more suitable than Mt.'s ἀπόστειλον, for that would imply that Christ was to give the demons a mission as well as permission. Lk. has neither verb. See on iii. 14.

13.   ἐπέτρεψεν αὐτοῖς. See crit. note. *He gave them leave.* The distinction between permitting and commanding is not of much value for the purpose of freeing our Lord from responsibility for the entrance of the demons into the swine. The suggestion that He who was capable of surprise (iv. 13, 40, vi. 6; Mt. viii. 10, xv. 28, xvi. 8), and of ignorance (xiii. 32; Mt. xxiv. 36) did not foresee the consequences of giving permission, does free Him from responsibility for the destruction of the swine. But some striking proof that the unclean spirits had left the man may have been necessary in order to assure him and the inhabitants that he had been, not merely quieted, but permanently cured. On the enormous superiority of man to brutes, Bede remarks, *ob unius hominis salutem duo millia porcorum suffocantur.* On the fate of the demons, Euthymius says, μελετήσαντες βλάψαι, πλεῖον ἐβλάβησαν. See Salmon, *Human Element*, pp. 277 f. ; Plummer, *S. Matthew*, pp. 132 f., *S. Luke*, pp. 228 f.

εἰσῆλθον εἰς τοὺς χοίρους. Science raises no difficulty here. Of the marvellous power of mind over matter our knowledge is increasing rapidly, and it would be rash to deny that brutes can be influenced by spirits. The plur. verb keeps the plurality of the spirits in sight.

τοῦ κρημνοῦ. "The well-known steep." Travellers think that it can be identified. Cf. 2 Chron. xxv. 12.

ὡς δισχίλιοι. Mk alone gives this estimate. Mt. omits it, as also the "200 pennyworth" (vi. 37) and the "300 pence" (xiv. 5). This estimate may have come from the owners, who might exaggerate their loss. An inventor would have said 4000 or 5000, to correspond with the legion. It is not very probable that the owners were Jews, who had no right to keep these unclean animals; and the plea that they were justly punished for their disobedience cannot be pressed. The population on the E. side of the Lake was largely heathen.

14. τοὺς ἀγρούς. "Farms" or "hamlets" (vi. 36, 56); so only in the plur. Excepting Acts iv. 37, the word occurs only in Mk, Mt. and Lk.

τὸ γεγονός. "What had really happened"; they hardly knew what to believe, and they came to see for themselves.

15. θεωροῦσιν. Much stronger than the previous ἰδεῖν. Cf. iii. 11, xii. 41, xv. 40.

τὸν δαιμονιζόμενον. This is their view of him; to them he is still "the demoniac," unless the participle be imperf. Contrast ὁ δαιμονισθείς (v. 18) and see on i. 32. The three participles which follow form a climax. He was sitting quietly, instead of roaming and raving; that was not much, for he had his quiet moments. He was clothed; that was still more, for he had for a long time worn no clothes (Lk.). Above all, he was no longer controlled by diabolical influences, but could control himself. Lk. adds that they found him "at the feet of Jesus." In contrast to all this, τὸν ἐσχηκότα τὸν λεγιῶνα is added. Syr-Sin. omits it as superfluous, but it has point. They had come out at the report of a great disaster, and they find the proof of a marvellous cure.

ἐφοβήθησαν. See on iv. 41. Evidence of the presence of supernatural power again inspires fear.

16. διηγήσαντο. Cf. Lk. ix. 10; Acts ix. 27, xii. 17. The compound indicates the fulness with which the spectators narrated what had taken place. The spectators would be chiefly the Twelve and the swineherds.

17. ἤρξαντο. We return to the inhabitants mentioned in *v.* 15. Jesus had just freed them from a great terror, by delivering one who had relations and friends among them from an obsession of extraordinary violence; *and they began to beseech Him*—one expects some such conclusion as "to abide with them," or "to heal their sick"; but there comes, with tragic irony, the conclusion—*to depart from their borders.* As in Lk. xiv. 18, there is no ἀλλά or δέ to prepare one for this surprising conclusion, a conclusion which a writer of fiction would not be likely to invent. But ἐφοβήθησαν and περὶ τῶν χοίρων give the explanation. They were afraid of this mighty Wonder-worker, and they did not want any more losses. *Hoc foedi stuporis signum est, quod eos magis terret porcorum jactura quam animae salus* *exhilarat* (Calvin). The widow of Zarephath (1 Kings xvii. 18) is a somewhat similar case. Christ at once granted their request. They were not worthy, and He could do more effective work elsewhere.

18. ἐμβαίνοντος αὐτοῦ...αὐτόν. See crit. note. For the constr. see on *v.* 2. Mt. omits this incident.

ὁ δαιμονισθείς. No longer ὁ δαιμονιζόμενος.

ἵνα μετ᾽ αὐτοῦ ᾖ. The man fears the populace who had treated him with such rigour, and who were so hostile to his Deliverer. He naturally clings to the latter. For ἵνα see on iii. 9.

19. ῞Υπαγε...καὶ ἀπάγγειλον. It is startling to find that, while the Twelve are kept to be trained at His side (iii. 14), this healed demoniac, who wishes to be kept with Him, is at once sent to be an evangelist and prepare the way for Christ's teaching (vii. 31); also that, whereas He usually told those who were cured to say nothing about these benefits (i. 44, v. 43, vii. 36; Mt. ix. 30), He charges this man to let his family and his acquaintances know all the mercy that had been shown to him. The explanation seems to be that there was no one else to send; Christ would be there again before any one could be trained for evangelistic work, and the man could do more good at home than by remaining with Christ. Secondly, in Peraea there was no risk of political capital being made out of His fame as a Worker of miracles. See on i. 44. Here ὅσα refers to importance rather than number; see on iii. 8. Great things had been done for the man, but not very many.

ὁ κύριος. In Lk., both Κύριος and ὁ Κύριος are used of Jehovah, while ὁ Κύριος (but never Κύριος) is sometimes used of Christ. In Mk, Κύριος is always Jehovah, while ὁ Κύριος occurs only twice, here and xi. 3. Here it doubtless means Jehovah, as Lk. interprets it, placing ὁ θεός at the end with emphasis. In xi. 3 it means Christ, but probably in the sense of "Master" rather than "Lord."

πεποίηκεν καὶ ἠλέησεν. The change from perf. to aor. is remarkable. Actual confusion of tenses is not uncommon in illiterate writings, and perfects are used without much difference of meaning from aorists; but in most examples in N.T. of mixture of tenses, as here, each tense may have its proper force; "what things the Lord hath done for thee, the results of which still remain, and how in expelling the demons He had mercy on thee." The perf. gives the permanent cure, the aor. the moment of deliverance. Such changes are rather freq. in Rev. (iii. 3, viii. 5, xi. 17). Cf. 1 Jn i. 1. Conversely (Acts xxi. 28; Rev. v. 7). It is more difficult to give a distinctive force to each tense in ἑώρακεν καὶ ἤκουσεν (Jn iii. 32); and still more difficult in πέπρακεν καὶ ἠγόρασεν (Mt. xiii. 46). Winer,

p. 340; Burton § 80, 88; Blass § 50. 3, 4; J. H. Moulton, p. 142.
The irregularity here is not in the change of tense, but in carrying on
ὅσα to ἠλέησεν instead of supplying ὡς.

20. ἤρξατο κηρύσσειν. Cf. i. 45, where the cleansed leper does
the same, and vii. 36, where the healed deaf-mute and his friends do
the same.

ὅσα ἐποίησεν αὐτῷ ὁ Ἰησοῦς. He had been told to report all that
God had done for him, but it was natural that he should name the
visible Benefactor. Lk. marks the contrast strongly, with ὁ θεός at
the end of one sentence and ὁ Ἰησοῦς at the end of the other. Mk
intimates that in other respects the man did more than execute his
commission; κηρύσσειν (i. 4, 7, 39, 45, iii. 14, vi. 12, etc.) is stronger
than ἀπάγγειλον (vi. 30; Lk. vii. 18, 22, etc.); and ἐν τῇ Δεκαπόλει is
much wider than πρὸς τοὺς σούς. "The 'Decapolis' was used loosely,
without strict reference to the federated cities, the lists of which
varied (vii. 31; Mt. iv. 25)."

καὶ πάντες ἐθαύμαζον. Mk only. It was an unfruitful kind of
wonder at present; cf. ii. 12, v. 42.

21—34. The Petition of Jairus and the Healing of the Woman with the Issue.

Mt. ix. 18—22. Lk. viii. 40—48.

21. διαπεράσαντος. The usual word for crossing water; see on
iv. 35. He crosses from the E. to the W. shore of the Lake, from
those who had begged Him to leave them, to those who at once
gather together and throng Him. Lk. using his special verb says
that they *welcomed* Him, ἀπεδέξατο αὐτὸν ὁ ὄχλος, Mk that *a great
multitude were crowded together upon Him.*

ἐπ᾽ αὐτόν. This kind of constr. is freq. in Mk after a gen. abs.
Cf. *v.* 2, ix. 28, x. 17, xi. 27, xiii. 1, 3. Winer, p. 259.

ἦν παρὰ τὴν θάλασσαν. *He was by the sea*; probably no motion
to the sea is suggested; παρά c. acc. in late Greek is freq. after verbs
of rest; iv. 1; Acts x. 6; see on x. 46. Winer, 503. The remark
here is quite in place. Finding a large audience awaiting the arrival
of the boat, Jesus remained on the shore and addressed them. In
Mt. ix. 18, Jesus is in a house when Jairus comes.

22. εἷς τῶν ἀρχισυναγώγων. There was usually only one to each
synagogue. These officials regulated the services and perhaps had
charge of the buildings.

Ἰάειρος. Usually those on whom or for whom Jesus does His
mighty works are nameless. Jair (Num. xxxii. 41; Judg. x. 3)

means "he will give light" rather than "he will awaken"; but
even if the latter derivation were correct, it would not prove that the
name was invented to match the story, nor would the invention of
the name prove that the whole story was invention. As in the case
of Lazarus and his sisters, the name of the leading person in this
incident would be likely to be remembered. The daughter may have
been a well known person, like Alexander and Rufus (xv. 21), when
Mk wrote. Bartimaeus, Mary Magdalen, and Malchus are similar
instances.

πρὸς τοὺς πόδας αὐτοῦ. In the Synoptics αὐτοῦ generally follows
its substantive (*vv.* 27, vi. 1, 4, etc.); in Jn it often precedes (xi. 32,
i. 27, etc.), about 16 times in all.

23. παρεκάλει πολλά. Vulg. again has *multum* (*v.* 10), which is
evidently right. See on iii. 12.

Τὸ θυγάτριόν μου. Peculiar to Mk, and he alone in N.T. uses this
diminutive; cf. vii. 25. He also uses κοράσιον, κυνάριον, ἰχθύδιον,
πλοιάριον, ψιχίον, ὠτάριον, παιδίσκη. This little maid was an *only*
child, like the widow's son at Nain and the lunatic boy. In all three
cases we owe this detail to Lk. She was about twelve.

ἐσχάτως ἔχει. *In extremis est* (Vulg.). Josephus (*Ant.* ix. viii. 6)
has ἐν ἐσχάτοις ὄντα Mt. says that Jairus reported that she was
already dead; and he begs to have her restored to life.

ἵνα ἐλθὼν ἐπιθῇς. It is easy to understand some such verb as
παρακαλῶ or θέλω. Cf. 2 Cor. viii. 7; Eph. v. 33. In x. 51 the
preceding θέλεις supplies the ellipse. Blass § 64. 4. Vulg. makes
two imperatives, *veni impone manus*; so also Syr-Sin. D is similar,
ἐλθὲ ἅψαι αὐτῆς ἐκ τῶν χειρῶν σου. Here, as in i. 27, strong feeling
breaks the utterance. Jairus believes that Christ can heal, but that
He must come and touch in order to do so. As a symbol of blessing
the imposition of hands aided the sufferer's faith, and Christ often
used it (i. 41, vi. 5, vii. 32, viii. 23, 25).

24. ἀπῆλθεν. "He went away with him at once, and the crowd
kept on following and pressing on Him," so that He moves with
difficulty. The change from aor. to imperf. is accurate, and the
change from sing. (ἠκολούθει) to plur. (συνέθλιβον) is natural.

25. οὖσα ἐν ῥύσει αἵματος. "Being in a condition of hemor-
rhage." Cf. ἐν ἐκστάσει, ἐν φθορᾷ, ἐν ἔχθρᾳ: ῥύσις is from the unused
ῥύω, whence the late forms ἔρρυσα and ἔρρυκα. The accumulation of
participles is here very remarkable: we have seven in three verses.
See on i. 15.

26. πολλὰ παθοῦσα ὑπὸ πολλῶν. Elegant classical Greek.
Multa perpessa a compluribus (Vulg.) does not reproduce the effective

repetition. Here probably πολλά is cogn. acc. rather than adverbial; *many things of many physicians* (A.V., R.V.). The remedies employed by Jewish doctors, some severe, and others silly and disgusting, are given by John Lightfoot. This verse is peculiar to Mk. The beloved physician, in consideration to the profession, tones it down to οὐκ ἴσχυσεν ὑπ' οὐδενὸς θεραπευθῆναι, for ἰατροῖς προσαναλώσασα ὅλον τὸν βίον αὐτῆς are omitted in BD, Syr-Sin. and are of doubtful authority. Even if they are admitted, there is no mention of her sufferings at the hands of the doctors, or of her having been made worse by them, and the cause of failure is her want of strength to profit by treatment rather than their want of skill. In the ℵ text of Tobit ii. 10, it is said that he went (every morning, Chal.) to the physicians to be treated for his eyesight, and that the more they anointed him with their drugs, the worse the white films became, until he was totally blind. Wetstein quotes Menander, πολλῶν ἰατρῶν εἴσοδός μ' ἀπώλεσε. Plin. *Hist. Nat.* xxix. 5, *Hinc illa infelicis monumenti inscriptio, turba se medicorum periisse.* Petronius 42, *Plures medici illum perdiderunt.*

δαπανήσασα. This verb of simple meaning occurs five times in N.T., and Vulg. uses four different words in translating it, *erogo* here, *dissipo* Lk. xv. 14, *inpendo* Acts xxi. 24 and 2 Cor. xii. 15, *insumo* Jas. iv. 3. Note the combination of participles.

τὰ παρ' αὐτῆς. Cf. τὰ παρ' αὐτῶν Lk. x. 7, τὰ παρ' ὑμῶν Phil. iv. 18. In each case παρά indicates the *passage* of something from one to another: τό or τά before prepositions is freq. in Lk. and Acts, rare in Mk and Mt., and nowhere in Jn.

μηδὲν ὠφεληθεῖσα. The μηδέν (not οὐδέν) does not prove that this is given as her conviction rather than as an actual fact; in N.T., μή with participles is usual, even when facts are stated. See on ii. 4.

27. τὰ περὶ τοῦ Ἰησοῦ. His fame as a Healer. Cf. Lk. xxiv. 19, 27; Acts xviii. 25, xxviii. 31. The τά is genuine (ℵ*BC*Δ).

ὄπισθεν. So that He might not see her. Mt. and Lk. say that she touched His κράσπεδον, the "tassel" or "corner," two of which would hang behind. See Driver on Deut. xxii. 12. Nowhere else in Mk have we so long a sentence (25—27).

28. ἔλεγεν γάρ. *For she had been saying*; see on *v.* 8. Mt. adds ἐν ἑαυτῇ, which DKNΠ 33 insert in Mk, and no doubt it is true in fact. She would not speak aloud of her malady or of her intention.

Ἐὰν ἅψωμαι κἂν τῶν ἱματίων. *If I should lay hold of if even His garments.* Cf. vi. 56; Winer, p. 730. The plur. denotes the clothes as a whole, not two ἱμάτια (xv. 20). There is a superficial resemblance to the action of Valeria, sister of Hortensius, who came

behind Sulla in the theatre and took a little of the nap off his robe.
Replying to his amazement she said, "I only wish to have a little
share in your prosperity" (Plut. *Sulla, sub fin.*).	Theophylact con-
trasts the woman's faith in the power of Christ's robe with the half-
faith of Jairus, who thought that Christ could heal with a touch, but
not with a word spoken at a distance.	He adds that he who believes
in the Incarnation has touched Christ's robe.

29.	ἴαται.	The suddenness (εὐθύς, Lk. παραχρῆμα) of the cure
convinced her of its permanence; hence the perf.	The verb occurs
here only in Mk, but in "the physician" it is freq.	See on x. 52.

30.	καὶ εὐθύς...ἐπιγνούς.	His perception of what had taken place
was simultaneous with the sudden cure.

ἐπιγνοὺς ἐν ἑαυτῷ...ἐξελθοῦσαν.	Cf. ii. 8.	The compound seems
to indicate the superiority of His knowledge to hers (ἔγνω).	Neither
A.V. nor R.V. is correct as to ἐξελθοῦσαν.	It does not mean that the
power went forth without Christ's knowledge, and that He did not
know of its operation until after it had gone forth and worked the
cure.	The ἐπιγνούς and the ἐξελθοῦσαν were simultaneous, and to
express this in English, as in Latin, the participle must become an
infinitive; *perceiving in Himself His miraculous power go forth.*
R.V. has a similar error Lk. x. 18, where ἐθεώρουν and πεσόντα are
simultaneous; therefore *I beheld Satan fall* (A.V.) is right, and
"fallen" (R.V.) cannot stand.	Christ did not mean that He saw
Satan prostrate.	Here the meaning is that as soon as the hand of
faith touched Christ's robe there was a response on His part, a
response of which He was conscious.	We may think of Him as
ceaselessly willing to respond to such calls, however imperfectly they
might be made.

ἐπιστραφείς.	Another combination of participles; see on i. 15.
As in viii. 33, this passive form is middle in sense.	He turned
because the touch had come from behind.

Τίς μου ἥψατο τῶν ἱματίων; *Who laid hold of My garments?*
"Touched" is hardly adequate; cf. i. 41, iii. 10.	It was good for
the woman that she should come forward and confess her faith and
its result, and Christ may have asked the question for her sake.	For
educational purposes He sometimes asked questions of which He
knew the answer (ix. 33).	But He seems to have abstained from
using supernatural power in cases in which the knowledge could
be obtained without it.	"How many loaves have ye? go and see"
(vi. 38; cf. viii. 5), "How long time is it since this hath come to
him?" (ix. 21), "Where have ye laid him?" (Jn xi. 34), are
questions in which He asked for information.	Mt. omits these and

other questions which seem to imply ignorance on the part of Christ;
see on viii. 12, 23, ix. 16, xiv. 14.

31. οἱ μαθηταί. Lk. says that it was Peter, and the impulsive
remark is characteristic of him; cf. i. 36, viii. 32. The difference
between unsympathetic pressing and sympathetic grasping in spiritual
contact with Christ has been often pointed out. *Caro premit, fides
tangit* (Aug.).

32. περιεβλέπετο ἰδεῖν. Lk. records a reply to Peter; but it
seems to be constructed out of our *v.* 30. Here Christ makes no
reply, but follows up His own question with a searching look all
round (iii. 5, 34, x. 23, xi. 11); and this is more impressive. The
fem. τὴν τ. ποιήσασαν *may* mean that He already knew who she was.
But it probably merely anticipates the discovery, for the imperf.
implies that He continued looking around before the ἰδεῖν (iv. 12) took
place.

33. φοβηθεῖσα καὶ τρέμουσα, εἰδυῖα. The change of tense
intimates that she had been frightened and was still trembling. But
see on *v.* 36. The three participles (i. 15) indicate that even if she
had denied it (Lk.'s favourite πάντων need not include her), her
manner would have betrayed her. She may have feared that she
had been too bold and that her malady might return; she was not
afraid that she had made Him Levitically unclean by touching His
clothes. Chrysostom suggests that she was made to declare her
malady and the manner of its cure in order to sustain the failing faith
of Jairus.

πᾶσαν τὴν ἀλήθειαν. A classical expression; *the whole truth.*
Socrates (Plato *Apol.* 17), after saying that his accusers have uttered
scarcely a word that is true, promises the Athenians that they shall
hear from him πᾶσαν τὴν ἀλήθειαν.

34. ἡ πίστις σου σ. σ. Cf. x. 52. Calvin points out that these
words do not encourage a belief in the efficacy of relics. With the
address comp. τέκνον (ii. 5).

ὕπαγε εἰς εἰρήνην. Cf. Lk. vii. 50, viii. 48, 1 Sam. i. 17, xx. 42.
Stronger than ἐν εἰρήνῃ (Acts xvi. 36; Jas ii. 16), which attaches the
peace to the moment of departure rather than to the subsequent life.
Vade in pace (Vulg.) is inadequate.

ἴσθι ὑγιὴς ἀπό. *Be safe from*; there is no fear of a return of the
infliction. See on iii. 10.

Bernice or Veronica as the name of this woman first appears in
the Acts of Pilate, Gospel of Nicodemus i. 7. Eusebius (*H.E.* vii. 18)
saw statues at Caesarea which were erroneously believed to represent
Christ and this woman. Sozomen (v. 21) and Philostorgius (vii. 3)

say that Julian removed the statue of Christ and set up one of himself, which was destroyed by lightning. Ps.-Ambrosius (*serm.* 46) has the strange idea that this woman was Martha, the sister of Lazarus. Macarius Magnes (i. 6) makes her a princess of Edessa.

35—43. RAISING OF THE DAUGHTER OF JAIRUS.
Mt. ix. 23—26. Lk. viii. 49—56.

35. Ἔτι αὐτοῦ λαλοῦντος. As in xiv. 43. Cf. Acts x. 44; Job i. 16, 17, 18. *While He was yet speaking.*

ἔρχονται. This may be impersonal; "some one comes." Cf. δώσουσιν (Lk. vi. 38), αἰτοῦσιν and αἰτήσουσιν (Lk. xii. 20, 48). See on Lk. xii. 20.

ἀπὸ τοῦ ἀρχισυναγώγου. From his *house*, probably sent by his wife (*v.* 40); the ruler himself is with Christ, and the message is addressed to him. His anxiety during the delay caused by the woman with the issue must have been intense. Evidently, the family had no hope of a resurrection, if the child died. Mt. omits this message and makes the ruler report the death of the child and ask for restoration to life, which is much less probable. A man who believed that Christ must be present in order to heal would not expect a resurrection.

ἀπέθανεν. Cf. ix. 26; Jn xi. 14. As in the case of ἐξέστη (iii. 21), these aorists are almost perfects, expressing present effect of recent past action; therefore not "she died," but *she is dead*. In Jn viii. 52, 53, the aor. has its proper force, the point being that *they died* then rather than that they "are dead" (A.V., R.V.) now. In that case the past action was not recent.

σκύλλεις. Like βάλλω (ii. 22, iv. 26), σκύλλω illustrates the tendency of words to become weaker in meaning; it signifies (1) "flay," (2) "mangle," (3) "vex," "annoy" (Mt. ix. 36; Lk. vii. 6). Comp. the French *gêner* and *gêne*, which is a doublet of *gehenne*.

36. παρακούσας. *Not heeding* (R.V.) rather than "overhearing" (R.V. marg.). So Mt. xviii. 17 *bis* and always (7 times) in LXX. The aor. part. of antecedent action is often rightly translated by pres. part. Cf. ἐπιγνούς in *v.* 30, and perhaps φοβηθεῖσα, *v.* 33. Burton, § 138.

Μὴ φοβοῦ, μόνον πίστευε. The pres. imperat. in each case has its full force; *Cease to fear; only continue to believe.* Fear that his petition to Christ would now be useless had begun to shake the father's faith. See on vi. 38.

37. οὐκ ἀφῆκεν οὐδένα. Double negative; see on i. **44.** Perhaps most of the crowd dispersed at the news of the girl's death, and Christ dismissed the rest. He wished to disturb the mourning household as little as possible ; but a few independent witnesses might be needed. Peter, James and John is the order in Mk (iii. 16, ix. 2, xiii. 3, xiv. 33). Lk. usually puts John before James (viii. 51, ix. 28 ; Acts i. 13). When Lk. wrote, John was the better known of the two. It was to these three, and to these three alone, that Christ Himself gave names, Peter and Boanerges. See crit. note.

38. θεωρεῖ θόρυβον. *Beholdeth a tumult.* The house is full of an excited throng who are screaming lamentations (Jer. iv. 8) to express sympathy with the bereaved parents, and Christ gazes (*v.* 15) at the unseemly tumult (xiv. 2; Mt. xxvii. 24; Acts xxi. 34). He must have been some distance from the house when Jairus found Him. Since the father left home the child has died and the professional mourners (Amos v. 16) have arrived.

39. Τί θορυβεῖσθε; He stills this tumult, like that of the storm on the Lake, and that made by the demoniac (i. 25, iv. 39) ; but here, as He has rational beings to deal with, He reasons with them first.

οὐκ ἀπέθανεν. Aor. as in *v.* 35. The probable meaning is that Christ knew that He was about to recall her to life, and therefore He says *καθεύδει* of her, as He says *κεκοίμηται* of Lazarus (Jn xi. 11). The Evangelists regard her as dead, Lk. expressly so. *Hominibus mortua, Deo dormiebat* (Bede). But it is possible that He knew that she was only in a trance.

40. κατεγέλων αὐτοῦ. They laughed derisively at Him; *laughed Him to scorn.* Cf. *καταγινώσκω, κατακρίνω, καταψηφίζομαι.* The gen. is normal. Sadler may be right in suggesting that their ridicule was interested, for their pay as mourners depended upon her being dead, not asleep.

ἐκβαλὼν πάντας. These mourners, whether hired or friends of the family, would be unwilling to go ; cf. xi. 15, and for *αὐτὸς δέ*, " But He on His part," i. 8, and often in Lk.

παραλαμβάνει. This is the common use of *παραλαμβάνω* in the Gospels, of Christ taking others with Him (ix. 2, x. 32, xiv. 33); iv. 36 is exceptional. Euthymius suggests that the father and mother were witnesses in the family's interests, the chosen Three in Christ's interest. All five were sympathetic and believing witnesses, like the bearers of the paralytic (ii. 3). See crit. note.

41. κρατήσας τῆς χειρός. See on i. 31.

Ταλειθά, κούμ. See crit. note. The extraordinary shapes which these Aramaic words are made to assume in some texts may be ignored. English Versions have not escaped; Wiclif has *Tabita*, Tyndale has *Tabitha*, and Coverdale *Thabitha*. Cf. vii. 34, xi. 9, xiv. 36, xv. 34. On the Aramaic expressions preserved in the Gospels, esp. in Mk and Jn, see Zahn, *Intr. to N.T.*, i. pp. 2 f. Both Christ and His disciples habitually spoke Aramaic, although He, and perhaps most of them, sometimes spoke Greek. G. Milligan, *N.T. Documents*, p. 36.

Τὸ κοράσιον. See on *v.* 8; Lk. ἡ παῖς. The diminutive occurs only in Mk and Mt., and only of this maiden and the dancing girl (vi. 22). The Aramaic hardly justifies the insertion of σοὶ λέγω. As in iii. 17 and xv. 34, the rendering of Aramaic given by Mk raises questions.

42. εὐθὺς ἀνέστη...περιεπάτει. Lk. again has παραχρῆμα where Mk has εὐθύς (*v.* 29). The change of tense is accurate; the rising was instantaneous, the walking continued. The latter, mentioned by Mk only, like διηκόνει αὐτοῖς (i. 31), showed the completeness of the restoration. Bede remarks that spiritual resurrection must be followed by virtuous activity.

ἦν γὰρ ἐτῶν δώδεκα. "For she was old enough to walk." Bengel notes that her life began when the woman's affliction began (*v.* 25).

ἐξέστησαν εὐθὺς ἐκστάσει μεγάλη. See crit. note and cf. iv. 41; Gen. xxvii. 33. We have ἔκστασις = "amazement" xvi. 8; Lk. v. 26; Acts iii. 10; elsewhere "a trance," Acts x. 10, xxii. 17.

43. διεστείλατο. One of Mk's words; he has it five times; elsewhere in N.T. thrice.

ἵνα μηδεὶς γνοῖ τοῦτο. See crit. note. The charge is perplexing, for it would be impossible to keep such a miracle secret, and perhaps for this reason Mt. omits it; but his narrative throughout is greatly abbreviated. The object would be to let no one know till He had time to leave the place and avoid the unspiritual admiration of the crowd. Christ seems to have wished to minimize the miracle (*v.* 39), certainly not to astound them with it. When the child arose and walked, they would say, "He was right after all; she was only asleep" (Lagrange). And it was best for the recipients of this great benefit that they should not talk, but be thankful. Cf. vii. 36, ix. 9, where διαστέλλομαι is again used. For γνοῖ see on παραδοῖ, iv. 29.

δοθῆναι αὐτῇ φαγεῖν. In the joy of recovering their child the parents might have forgotten this. "Life restored by miracle must be supported by ordinary means; miracle has no place where human care will suffice" (Swete). Christ does not employ supernatural means of knowing where information can be gained by asking (see on *v.* 30). The stone that closed the tomb of Lazarus was removed by human labour (Jn xi. 39, 41). The gate which Rhoda could unfasten did not open of its own accord (Acts xii. 10, 16). Some Fathers regard this command as given to prove the reality of the restoration to life, because Christ ate in order to prove the reality of His Resurrection (Lk. xxiv. 43); but the idea is out of place here. For εἶπεν, *told* = *bade*, cf. viii. 7.

CHAPTER VI.

1. ἔρχεται (אBCLΔ) rather than ἦλθεν (ANII).
2. δοθεῖσα τούτῳ (אBCLΔ) rather than δοθ. αὐτῷ (ADII). After these words omit ὅτι, which has little authority. γινόμεναι (אBLΔ 33) rather than γίνονται (AC²E etc.).
3. ὁ τέκτων ὁ υἱός (אABCDLΔII) rather than ὁ τοῦ τέκτονος υἱός (33, Lat-Vet. Aeth.). καὶ ἀδελφός (אBCDLΔ) rather than ἀδελφὸς δέ (see on i. 14).
4. καὶ ἔλεγεν (אBCDLΔ) rather than ἔλεγεν δέ.
9. It is difficult to decide between ἐνδύσασθε (B*33), ἐνδύσασθαι (B²SII), and ἐνδύσησθε (אACDΔ). Perhaps the first would most easily have produced the other readings.
11. ὃς ἂν τόπος μὴ δέξηται (אBLΔ) rather than ὅσοι ἐὰν μὴ δέξωνται (AC²DII). אBCDLΔ omit ἀμὴν λέγω ὑμῖν κ.τ.λ. (from Mt. x. 15).
12. ἐκήρυξαν (אBCDLΔ) rather than ἐκήρυσσον (ANII), assimilation to ἐξέβαλλον. μετανοῶσιν (BDL) rather than μετανοήσωσιν (אACΔII).
14. ἔλεγον (B, a b ff, Aug.) seems preferable to ἔλεγεν (אACLΔII); ελεγοσαν (D) supports the plur. The context confirms B; we have three popular views, then Herod's agreement with the first. Cf. Lk. ix. 7–8. ἐγήγερται (אBDLΔ 33) rather than ἠγέρθη (CN) or ἀνέστη (A).
16. The text is much confused; but that which is supported throughout by אBDL, and in details by other witnesses, is probably original; ὁ Ἡρῴδης ἔλεγεν Ὃν ἐγὼ ἀπεκεφάλισα Ἰ. οὗτος ἠγέρθη.
20. ἠπόρει (אBL, Memph.) rather than ἐποίει (ACDΔII, Latt. Syrr.).
22. αὐτῆς τῆς Ἡρῳδιάδος (ACNΓII etc., Latt. Syrr. Memph. Arm. Goth. Aeth.) rather than αὐτοῦ Ἡρῳδιάδος (אBDLΔ). External evidence for the latter reading is strong, but on other grounds it is intolerable. ἤρεσεν (אBC*L 33) rather than καὶ ἀρεσάσης (AC³DNΓII).
24. αἰτήσωμαι (אABCD etc. 33) rather than αἰτήσομαι (EFHK etc.). βαπτίζοντος (אBLΔ) rather than βαπτιστοῦ (ACDNΓII).
26. ἀνακειμένους (BC*LΔ) rather than συνανακειμένους (אAC²DNΓ).

27. ἐνέγκαι (ℵBCΔ) rather than ἐνεχθῆναι (ADLNΓΠ).

31. λέγει (ℵBCLΔ 33) rather than εἶπεν (ADΓΠ).

33. οἱ ὄχλοι has very little authority. Mk writes ὁ ὄχλος elsewhere (ii. 4, 13, iii. 9, etc.): but here no nom. is expressed. ℵB, Vulg. Memph. Arm. omit καὶ συνῆλθον πρὸς αὐτόν. WH. *Introd.* pp. 95 f. show that the reading of AEF etc., followed by AV., is a conflation of καὶ προῆλθον αὐτούς (ℵB) with καὶ συνῆλθον αὐτοῦ (D).

34. ℵBL, Memph. Arm. omit ὁ ᾽Ιησοῦς. Seen on v. 13.

36. After ἑαυτοῖς read simply τί φάγωσιν (BDLΔ).

41. ℵBLΔ omit αὐτοῦ after μαθηταῖς.

43. κλάσματα δ. κοφίνων πληρώματα (BLΔ) rather than κλασμάτων δ. κοφίνους πλήρεις (ADΓΠ) from Mt.

44. ὡσεί has very little authority.

45. ἀπολύει (ℵBDL) rather than ἀπολύσῃ (AFG etc.) from Mt.

51. ℵBLΔ omit ἐκ περισσοῦ (ἐκπερισσῶς, περισσῶς), and καὶ ἐθαύμαζον.

52. ἀλλ᾽ ἦν (ℵBLΔ) rather than ἦν γάρ (AD).

1—6. CHRIST IS DESPISED AT NAZARETH.

Mt. xiii. 54—58. Cf. Lk. iv. 16—30.

1. ἐκεῖθεν. From Capernaum.

ἔρχεται εἰς τὴν πατρίδα αὐτοῦ. See critical note. "His country" means "His home," Nazareth (i. 9, 24), where His family was well known (*v.* 3). Cf. Joseph. *Ant.* x. vii. 3.

οἱ μαθηταὶ αὐτοῦ. Mk alone mentions them here. Jesus had left Nazareth as a private individual, and He comes back as a famous Teacher with a band of pupils; see on ii. 15.

2. ἤρξατο διδάσκειν. Apparently this was the first time that He taught publicly at Nazareth, and He was not encouraged to continue doing so.

οἱ πολλοὶ ἀκ. ἐξεπλήσσοντο. Most of them (ix. 26) were astounded at His preaching, as i. 22 and xi. 18, where the same verb is used. But they could not bear that one whom they had known as an equal should exhibit such superiority, and they make little of it. ℵACDΔΠ omit οἱ. In ix. 26, CDNXΓΠΦ omit τούς.

Πόθεν τούτῳ ταῦτα. "What right has this man to all this?" No other person had ever left the village as a carpenter and come back a Rabbi working miracles. As often, τούτῳ is contemptuous; "this man whom we have known for years." They cannot deny His powers; but they know all about Him and His family, and therefore He cannot have any mission from Heaven. Cf. Jn vii. 15.

τίς ἡ σοφία; "What sort of wisdom is it? whence comes it?" Cf. iv. 41. Nowhere else does Mk mention σοφία.

δυνάμεις. Cf. *vv.* 5, 14, ix. 39. A.V. varies between "mighty works," "wonderful works" and "miracles." In xiii. 22 Mk uses σημεῖα καὶ τέρατα of the wonders wrought by false Christs, but nowhere of the signs wrought by Christ and the disciples. The people of Nazareth do not question His mighty works, but they are jealous of His power to do them.

3. ὁ τέκτων. See critical note. Mt. will not call Him "the carpenter," but says "the carpenter's son," and states the relationship to Mary separately. Justin (*Try.* 88) preserves the tradition that He made ploughs and yokes. Cf. Orig. *Cels.* vi. 4.

ὁ υἱὸς τῆς Μαρίας. It is remarkable that Mk does not say "the son of Joseph and Mary." Joseph was probably dead, and hence Jesus is called "the carpenter." This is perhaps the reason why Joseph is not mentioned here; but Mk may have purposely avoided saying that Jesus was Joseph's son in the same sense that He was Mary's son. Contrast Lk. iv. 22; Jn vi. 42.

ἀδελφός. See on iii. 35. The names of His brothers are those of O.T. patriarchs.

Ἰακώβου. The most famous of the brethren, president of the church of Jerusalem (Acts xii. 17, xv. 13, xxi. 18; Gal. ii. 9, 12). Hort thinks that after James the brother of John was slain (Acts xii. 2), James the brother of the Lord was counted as one of the Twelve (*Chris. Eccl.* pp. 76 f.). He had the influence of an Apostle, and is the author of the Epistle of James. Josephus (*Ant.* xx. ix. 1) mentions him, and Eusebius (*H.E.* ii. 23) gives an extract from Hegesippus describing his martyrdom.

Ἰωσῆτος. Not the Joses of xv. 40. The name is another form of Joseph.

Ἰούδα. The author of the Epistle of Jude. The brethren were married (1 Cor. ix. 5), and Jude's humble grandsons were treated with contemptuous clemency by Domitian (Eus. *H.E.* iii. 20).

Σίμωνος. Nothing is known of him.

ἀδελφαί. Their existence is suggested in iii. 35. Mt. here adds πᾶσαι, which shows that there were several sisters, but they are mentioned nowhere else. The brothers, at first unbelievers (Jn vii. 5), became missionaries after the Resurrection (1 Cor. ix. 5). The sisters perhaps neither left Nazareth nor became in any way notable. The way in which the Nazarenes speak of them indicates that these brothers and sisters had not much sympathy with the Teacher who is here criticized.

πρὸς ἡμᾶς. "In constant intercourse with us"; ix. 19, xiv. 49. This does not imply that the brothers are *not πρὸς ἡμᾶς*.

ἐσκανδαλίζοντο. Astonishment led on, not to reverence, but to repulsion. They could not tolerate a fellow-villager's fame and success. Jealousy is never reasonable; the Nazarenes were offended at the very thing which brought them great honour. How soon Christ became aware that He must suffer and die is not revealed. The process was perhaps gradual. The conduct of His own people towards Him would be some intimation of what must follow. The contrast between the feeling at Nazareth and the feeling at Capernaum is extraordinary, seeing that the places were only about 20 miles apart. But there is mountainous country between, and there would be little intercourse.

4. καὶ ἔλεγεν. Their dissatisfaction was frequently expressed, and He used to reply with this aphorism. Mt., as often, substitutes an aor., εἶπεν.

Οὐκ ἔστιν προφήτης. Jesus made no public claim to be the Messiah, but His miracles and teaching caused Him to be generally accepted as a Prophet (*v.* 15, viii. 28; Mt. xxi. 11; Lk. vii. 16, xxiv. 19). The saying was doubtless proverbial before Christ uttered it, and it is given in different forms in Jn iv. 44 and Lk. iv. 24; also in Oxyrhyn. log. 6, which agrees with Lk. in inserting δεκτός. Plutarch (*De exil.* 13, p. 604 D) says that few very wise men receive attention ἐν ταῖς ἑαυτῶν πατρίσι. Pliny (*H. N.* xxxv. 36), *sordebat suis, ut plerumque domestica*. Christ had been rejected by the Gerasenes. As often, He states a general truth and leaves His hearers to find the limitations by thought and experience.

ἄτιμος. Cf. Is. iii. 5, liii. 3; Job xxx. 8.

συγγενεῦσιν. With this form for συγγένεσιν comp. γονεῦσιν (Rom. i. 30; 2 Cor. xii. 14). This may point back to iii. 21. Mt. omits it, as does Lk. (iv. 24).

5. οὐκ ἐδύνατο...δύναμιν. The verbal play is perhaps intentional; "He had no power to do any work of power" (McLaren). Mt. does not like οὐκ ἐδύνατο of Christ and says οὐκ ἐποίησεν. Origen points out that Mk does not say οὐκ ἤθελεν: the defect was on their side not His. Faith was necessary on both sides, where faith was possible. Christ always believed that He had the ἐξουσία to heal, but faith on the part of the afflicted (or those who were responsible for them) might be wanting; then, οὐκ ἐδύνατο · ἐνεπόδιζε γὰρ αὐτῷ ἡ ἀπιστία. οὐκ ἔδει βιαίως εὐεργετεῖν αὐτούς (Euthym.). He was not ἀσθενής, but they were ἄπιστοι (Theoph.). Jerome needlessly remarks that He could do much good even to those who did not believe; but the good in question was healing of body, not of soul: and Bede introduces an idea foreign to the passage when he suggests that it was in mercy that Christ did few mighty works, for, had He done many, the guilt of their unbelief would have been increased. Dr Abbott thinks that Jn (v. 19, 30) may be covering Mk's statement, which was disliked by some, when he quotes Christ as saying "The Son can do nothing of Himself" (*The Fourfold Gospel, Introd.* p. 23).

ποιῆσαι. Aor. infin. after δύναμαι. See on i. 40.

οὐκ...εἰ μὴ. Cf. viii. 14; and for ἐπιθεὶς τ. χεῖρας, v. 23.

6. ἐθαύμασεν. This also is omitted by Mt., although he admits surprise in Christ at the great faith of the centurion (viii. 10). Jn iv. 13 and ix. 19 we have expressions which imply surprise. Surprise is also implied in His treatment of the braggart fig-tree, on which He expected to find fruit because of its show of leaves (xi. 13). Just as οὐκ ἐδύνατο involves limitation of power, so ἐθαύμασεν involves limitation of knowledge: marvelling is incompatible with omniscience. The διά is intelligible, *on account of their unbelief,* but the usual constr. is ἐπὶ c. dat. (Lk. iv. 22, xx. 26; Acts iii. 12). Unless διὰ τοῦτο in Jn vii. 22 belongs to what precedes, which is improbable, θαυμάζω διά τι occurs nowhere else in N.T.

περιῆγεν...διδάσκων. *Beneficium tamen praestitit Jesus patriae suae* (Beng.). This is another missionary circuit in Galilee.

7—13. THE MISSION OF THE TWELVE.

Mt. x. 1, 5—15. Lk. ix. 1—6.

7. τοὺς δώδεκα. The number is regarded as final, but we cannot be sure that they were already known as "the Twelve." The expression is especially freq. in Mk (iv. 10, ix. 35, x. 32, xi. 11, xiv. 10, 17, 20, 43).

ἤρξατο αὐτοὺς ἀποστέλλειν. They were appointed (1) to be with Him to be trained, (2) that He might send them forth to preach (iii. 14). The first of these purposes has been to some extent accomplished, and now the second is to begin. Note the ἤρξατο: the pairs were not sent out all at one moment.

δύο δύο. The more classical expression would be either κατὰ δύο (1 Cor. xiv. 27), or ἀνὰ δύο, which D has here, and Lk. has x. 1 of the sending out of the Seventy-two. Cf. ix. 14. The double numeral (Gen. vi. 19, 20, vii. 2, 3, 9, etc.) is not purely Hebraistic. We have μυρία μυρία, "by tens of thousands" (Aesch. *Pers.* 981), and μίαν μίαν = κατὰ μίαν is quoted from the *Eris,* a lost play of Sophocles: δήσῃ τρία τρία occurs in a papyrus of the 3rd cent. A.D. Deissmann,

Light, p. 124. In the Gospel of Peter ix., and in the Acts of Philip xxxvi., we have the two constructions mixed, ἀνὰ δύο δύο. The duplication occurs in modern Greek.

The advantages of pairs are obvious (Eccles. iv. 9—12). The Baptist had adopted this method (Lk. vii. 19; Jn i. 37), and we find it repeatedly in the Apostolic Church; Barnabas and Saul, Judas and Silas, Barnabas and Mark, Paul and Silas, Timothy and Silas, Timothy and Erastus. Our Lord and the six pairs now made seven centres of preaching and healing. Cf. xi. 1, xiv. 13.

ἐδίδου. Here and in *v.* 41, Mt. has ἔδωκεν, as usual preferring aor. to imperf. But as each pair was dismissed, He continued the bestowal of this ἐξουσία. It represents miraculous power of healing generally (i. 39, iii. 15). It is strange to think of Judas having ἐξουσία to cast out demons. In the Testaments (*Benj.* v. 2), "If ye do well, even the unclean spirits will flee from you"; cf. *Issachar* vii. 7.

8. παρήγγειλεν. This charge seems to have been given once for all (aor.), before any were sent out. For ἵνα see on iii. 9.

εἰς ὁδόν. *For a journey*, for travel; cf. x. 17; also ἐξ ὁδοῦ (Lk. xi. 6).

εἰ μὴ ῥάβδον. Mt. and Lk. say, on the contrary, that they were forbidden to take a staff; and Mt. says that they were forbidden to wear ὑποδήματα, which seems to contradict the command to wear σανδάλια. These discrepancies are of no moment. In all three Gospels the charge means, "Make no elaborate preparations, as if you were going a long journey on your own business; you are going a short journey on Mine." *Contrariis verbis eandem sententiam uterque expressit; Christum Apostolis praecepisse, ne quid haberent, praeter ea quae essent in praesentem usum necessaria* (Maldonatus). The directions recall those for eating the Passover (Exod. xii. 11; cf. Gen. xxxii. 10).

μὴ ἄρτον κ.τ.λ. A climax; no food, no wallet for carrying food that might be given, no money for buying food. This is the order in אBCLΔ 33. There is no mention of gold or silver; they were not likely to have any or be offered any. They might accept a meal, but they were to have no other provision. The πήρα is a bag for provisions, not for money, as the context shows. Cf. Judith x. 5. Mt. enlarges "copper for your purse" into "get no gold, nor yet silver, nor yet copper for your purses," thus making one of his favourite triplets.

9. ἀλλὰ ὑποδεδεμένους σανδάλια. A violent anacoluthon, illustrating Mk's want of literary skill, and showing how completely ἵνα after verbs of exhorting has become equivalent to the *acc. c. infin.* Mk goes on here as if he had used the *acc. c. infin.*, for εἶναι or πορεύεσθαι is understood here. The identity of σανδάλια (Acts xii. 8)

and ὑποδήματα (i. 7; Mt. x. 10; etc.) is clear, for both are used to
translate the same Hebrew, *naal* (Josh. ix. 5; Is. xx. 2 and Exod. iii.
5, xii. 11). Here and in Acts, σανδάλια may have been preferred in
order to avoid the unpleasing repetition, ὑποδέομαι ὑποδήματα.

Μὴ ἐνδύσασθε. If this is the right reading, we have a change from
or. obliqua to *or. recta*, as in Lk. v. 14; Acts xxiii. 22. Mk xi. 32 is
different. There is a similar change if we read ἐνδύσησθε (R.V.). We
may take ἐνδύσασθαι as coordinate with the infin. understood with
ὑποδεδεμένους, or as an infin. imperat. It is strange criticism to see
in these broken constructions signs of clumsy copying from a document. They are signs of Mk writing just as he would talk. In Mt.
the Twelve are forbidden to *get* two chitons, in Lk. to *have* two, in
Mk to *put on* two. The χιτών was the less necessary garment, worn
under the almost indispensable ἱμάτιον (Mt. v. 40; Jn xix. 23); therefore a "shirt" rather than a "coat." The Baptist told those who had
two chitons to "give a share," *i.e.* one of the two, to some one who
had none (Lk. iii. 11). The high-priest rends "his chitons" (xiv. 63),
and two were sometimes worn in travelling (Joseph. *Ant.* xvii. v. 7).
We learn from Lk. xxii. 35 that the Twelve found this very small
outfit sufficient. Origen thinks that these regulations were not intended to be taken literally, and Bede interprets the prohibition of
two chitons as an admonition *non dupliciter sed simpliciter ambulare.*

10. ἔλεγεν αὐτοῖς. Mt. omits this imperf., which may be conversational, or may mean that this direction was repeated. Mk perhaps
regards this as the earliest Christian missionary experiment, and
hence records these directions as being of importance.

Ὅπου ἐάν. All three Evangelists record that the household first
selected was not to be changed for one that seemed to be more eligible.
"Go not from house to house" was said to the Seventy-two (Lk. x. 7);
and that is the meaning here. Calvin points out that forbidding
change of domicile would prevent lingering in any one place. The
Apostles would not like to become burdensome to their entertainers.
Didache xi. 5 limits the stay to two days; see also xii. 2. The right to
hospitality is recognized 1 Cor. ix. 14; and this use of a hospitable
house as a missionary centre is the germ of ἡ κατ᾽ οἶκον αὐτῶν ἐκκλησία (Rom. xvi. 5; 1 Cor. xvi. 19; Col. iv. 15; Philem. 2).

11. ὃς ἄν τόπος. This principle would apply to the town and to
any house in the town, and Mt. applies it both ways.

μηδὲ ἀκούσωσιν ὑμῶν. *Nor even listen to you.* Paul and Barnabas
shake off the dust at Antioch in Pisidia, and Paul shakes out his
raiment against the unbelieving Jews at Corinth (Acts xiii. 51, xviii.
6). This dramatic action did not express personal resentment; it was

a solemn declaration to those who rejected offers of grace that the person thus acting would make no more offers. He declined all further communication or responsibility. Pharisees are said to have performed this act on returning from pagan lands to Palestine; even the dust of heathendom was a pollution. Neh. v. 13 is different. Note the aor. imperat.; it is to be done at once.

εἰς μαρτύριον αὐτοῖς. *For a testimony unto them* (R.V.), not "against them" (A.V.). Cf. i. 44, xiii. 9. See crit. note. St Theresa is said to have done this at Salamanca.

12. ἐκήρυξαν...ἐξέβαλλον. Their main duty is mentioned first and it is regarded as a whole (aor.): the healings were numerous, but occasional (imperf.).

ἵνα μετανοῶσιν. Cf. *v.* 8 and see on iii. 9; but here something of the idea of purpose remains; "they preached in order to produce a *condition* of repentance." See crit. note. The pres. subj. is better attested and gives a fuller meaning than the aor.

13. ἐλαίῳ. Oil was believed to have healing properties (Lk. x. 34; Jas. v. 14), and this would aid faith on both sides. See on Jn ix. 6 and Knowling on Jas. v. 14. This anointing for healing purposes is very different from that which is administered when healing is believed to be impossible and death imminent. It is mentioned nowhere else in the Gospels and seems not to have been employed by Christ. Mk says nothing about cleansing lepers or raising the dead (Mt. x. 8). Mt. may possibly have had some other source.

14—29. The Murder of the Baptizer.

Mt. xiv. 1—12. Lk. ix. 7—9, iii. 19, 20.

14. ἤκουσεν ὁ βασιλεύς. The proclamation of the Kingdom of God in seven different places in Galilee would make some stir, and this reached the ears of Antipas. Mt. and Lk. give him his correct title of "tetrarch," a word which Mk never uses. Mk gives him the courtesy title of "king," as Appian gives Deiotarus, tetrarch of Galatia, the title of king; so also Cicero, who defended him. Under Caligula, Antipas tried to get the formal title of "king," and thereby brought about his own ruin. He is alluded to again viii. 15.

φανερὸν γὰρ ἐγένετο τὸ ὄνομα αὐτοῦ, καὶ ἔλεγον. *For His name had become known* (R.V.), *and they had been saying.* See crit. note, and on v. 8. This does not mean that Antipas had never heard even the name of Jesus until now. In his conversations with the Baptist (*v.* 20) Jesus had probably been mentioned; but now everyone was talking about Him. It was these rumours which excited Herod, and his remark comes in *v*. 16. For ὁ βαπτίζων see on i. 4.

ἐγήγερται. "Has been raised and remains alive"; the true perf. Cf. 1 Cor. xv. 12, 13, 16, 20. In this phrase νεκρῶν commonly has no art. (ix. 9, 10, xii. 25, etc.). Origen suggests that there was a personal resemblance between Jesus and John.

διὰ τοῦτο. This argument would apply to anyone who has risen from the dead. During his lifetime John did no "sign" (Jn x. 41); but a person who had returned from the grave might be expected to do wonderful things.

ἐνεργοῦσιν. *Work in him* (R.V.). This intrans. use occurs in the Gospels here and Mt. xiv. 2 only; cf. Gal. ii. 8; Eph. ii. 2. The verb seems to have acquired a special use to express supernatural activity. J. A. Robinson, *Ephesians*, pp. 241 f.

αἱ δυνάμεις. *The powers* which Jesus was said to exhibit; cf. 1 Cor. xii. 10, 28, 29. A.V. again ignores the art. (see on iv. 3) and translates "mighty works," which is right *vv*. 2, 5, ix. 39, but not here. See Lightfoot on Gal. iii. 5.

15. ἄλλοι δέ. In both places we must read δέ after ἄλλοι (ℵABCDΔΠ), and omit the rather senseless ἤ before ὡς (ℵABCLΠ). *But others* had a different explanation of the miraculous powers; they *said that it is Elijah* who has returned to earth; *while others said a prophet, as one of the Prophets,* equal in dignity with Isaiah and Jeremiah. The chief contrast is between those who said that it was John and those who said it was someone else; therefore the first δέ must be "but": the second may be "while" or "and." See on Jn i. 21 for Jewish beliefs about Prophets returning to life.

16. ἀκούσας. After Antipas had heard all these theories, he decided for the one which touched him most nearly: the pronouns are emphatic. "John whom *I* beheaded, *he* is risen"; or perhaps, "John whom *I* beheaded, is *he* risen?" Cf. the question in Lk. in. 0: ὁ φονεύσας φοβεῖται τὸν φονευμένον· τοιοῦτος γὰρ ὁ κακός (Euthym.). The late verb ἀποκεφαλίζω is used by all three of the beheading of John; elsewhere in Bibl. Grk only Ps. cli. 7 of David and Goliath. Vulg. has *decollo*, which is mostly post-class. With Antipas the main thought is that decapitation proved ineffectual (aor.); with the people (*v*. 14) it was that John is more active than ever (perf.).

17. αὐτὸς γὰρ Ἡρῴδης. This confirms the emphatic ἐγώ of Antipas; *For it was Herod himself who sent and laid hold on John*; cf. iii. 21.

ἐν φυλακῇ. Josephus (*Ant.* xviii. v. 4) tells us that this was Machaerus, near the N.E. corner of the Dead Sea, a fortress, palace,

and prison all in one, like that of the Popes at Avignon. It was close
to the wilderness of Judaea. Tristram, *Discoveries East of the Dead
Sea*, ch. xiv.

Φιλίππου, Not the son of Herod the Great by Cleopatra (Lk. iii.
1), but his son by Mariamne the daughter of Simon. It is possible
that Mk is in error in calling him Philip (Joseph. *Ant.* xviii. v. 4);
but, if so, it is of no moment. Antipas divorced the daughter of
Aretas IV., king of Arabia Petraea, in order to marry Herodias, for
which insult Aretas afterwards attacked and defeated Antipas; see on
2 Cor. xi. 32. Herodias was a granddaughter of Herod the Great, and
therefore niece of both Antipas and Philip.

18. ἔλεγεν γάρ. *For John had said* (A.V.) or "had been saying"
(see on v. 8), is here more accurate than "for John said" (R.V.).
In *v.* 17, R.V. agrees with A.V. in "for he *had* married her."
The English pluperf. is right in both cases.

Οὐκ ἔξεστιν. Lev. xviii. 16 admitted of one exception—where
the brother was dead and had left no son. Philip was still alive. It
is not said that the divorce of the daughter of Aretas was a bar to the
marriage with Herodias. Josephus says that Antipas imprisoned
John because of his great influence; he might cause a revolution.
That was the reason publicly given for putting John in prison, and
Antipas perhaps really feared disturbance; he could not avow his
private reason. John seems to have been leniently treated; he was
allowed to receive visits (Mt. xi. 2 f.; Lk. vii. 18 f.), and Antipas
himself conversed with him (*v.* 20). There is nothing to suggest that
John had publicly denounced Antipas; rather that he had privately
remonstrated with him. Aenon (Jn iii. 23) was close to Tiberias,
and John could easily visit Antipas. For ἔχειν = "marry" cf. xii. 23;
1 Cor. v. 1.

19. ἡ δὲ Ἡρῳδιὰς ἐνεῖχεν αὐτῷ. Antipas would have been content with imprisoning John, *but Herodias nursed enmity against
him.* Neither "therefore" (A.V.) nor "and" (R.V.) gives the force of
δέ, which marks a contrast between what Herod himself did (*v.* 17)
and what Herodias did. The only parallel in Bibl. Grk to 'this
intrans. use of ἐνέχω is the accidental iambus ἐνεῖχον αὐτῷ κύριοι
τοξευμάτων (Gen. xlix. 23), where Vulg. has *inviderunt illi*, although
elsewhere Jerome has *irascebantur adversus eum.* Here Vulg. has
insidiabatur, whence the "laid wait" of earlier versions. Beza has
imminebat. It may be doubted whether ἔχθραν, or χόλον (which Hdt.
expresses i. 118, vi. 119, viii. 27) is to be understood. But ἐπέχων,
sc. τὸν νοῦν (Lk. xiv. 7; &c.), suggests that here there is some forgotten ellipse. The provincialism, "to have it in for a man" or

"with a man," *i.e.* to be on bad terms with him, is parallel. "Had an inward grudge" (A.V. marg.) is near the mark. The imperfects (*vv.* 18—20) are quite in place; the rebukes of John, the resentment and malignity of Herodias, and the fears of Antipas were continual, just as in the case of Elijah, Jezebel, and Ahab. καὶ οὐκ ἐδύνατο. We might have expected ἀλλ' οὐκ ἐδύνατο. This adversative use of καί is perhaps Hebraistic. Cf. xii. 12.

20. Ἡρῴδης ἐφοβεῖτο τ. Ἰωάννην. *Argumentum verae religionis timor malorum* (Beng.). Cf. Felix and Paul (Acts xxiv. 25). Herod instinctively felt (εἰδώς) the sanctity of John. Δίκαιος, freq. in Mt. and Lk., is used elsewhere by Mk only ii. 17, and he nowhere else uses ἅγιος of a man. Acts iii. 14 we have τ. ἅγιον καὶ δίκαιον. συνετήρει αὐτόν. *Kept him safe* (R.V.), *custodiebat eum* (Vulg.), rather than "observed him" (A.V.), which is tautological with what follows; it explains οὐκ ἐδύνατο. Herodias could never compass John's death, because Antipas had him safely guarded (Tobit iii. 15; 2 Macc. xii. 42). This is against the theory that the oath of Antipas was "pre-arranged." The imperfects in this verse seem to form a climax.

πολλὰ ἠπόρει. See crit. note. The familiar "he did many things," *multa faciebat* (Vulg.), is vague. Lagrange says that, taken with what follows, ἐποίει is *absolument banal*. If it means that he did many things at John's bidding, the brevity is surprising. Hence Syr-Sin. has "and many things he heard from him he did." The objection that "was much perplexed" would require πολλὰ ἠπορεῖτο does not hold in Bibl. Grk. Lk. ix. 7 we have διηπόρει, Wisd. xi. 5 and 17 we have ἀποροῦντες εὐεργετήθησαν and οὐ γὰρ ἠπόρει ἡ παντοδύναμός σου χείρ. The objection would not hold even in class. Grk. τὸ δ' ἀπορεῖν ἀνδρὸς κακοῦ (Eur. *Herc. Fur.* 106); ἀποροῦντες οὖν ταῦτα οἱ Ἀργεῖοι (Thuc. v. 40); cf. Hdt. iii. 4, iv. 179, vi. 34. What is true is that ἀπορεῖσθαι is more freq. than ἀπορεῖν. *Was much perplexed* between his respect for John and his passion for Herodias, between conscience and inclination, makes excellent sense. But Nestle (*Text. Crit. of Grk T.*, p. 274) is a little inclined to follow Field and Burkitt in preferring ἐποίει.

ἡδέως αὐτοῦ ἤκουεν. Antipas could appreciate the loftiness and vigour of John's mind, so different from those with whom he daily lived; *he used to hear him gladly.*

21. γενομένης ἡμέρας εὐκαίρου. Mk has the deadly enmity of Herodias in mind. She was always on the watch, and at last found an opportune day. Cf. Heb. iv. 16.

τοῖς γενεσίοις αὐτοῦ. *On his birthday.* This meaning is firmly established, although in Attic Grk we should have τὰ γενέθλια or ἡ γενέθλιος ἡμέρα (2 Macc. vi. 7). Hdt. iv. 26 shows that τὰ γενέσια meant a festival in commemoration of a *dead* person. But in late Grk the distinction was not strictly observed. Joseph. *Ant.* xii. iv. 7 we have ἑορτάζοντες τὴν γενέσιον ἡμέραν τοῦ παιδίου, at the birth of a son to Ptolemy Epiphanes. On the other hand, Plutarch uses γενέθλια of commemoration of the dead. In papyri, γενέσια seems always to mean "birth-day fête." Christianity tended to obliterate the distinction between the two words by regarding the death of the faithful as their birthday into eternal life (*Mart. Pol.* 18; Tert. *De Coron.* 3, *Scorp.* 15). Seneca (*Ep.* cii. 24) has the same thought; *Dies iste, quem tanquam extremum reformidas, aeterni natalis est.* On the proposal to make τὰ γενέσια the anniversary of Herod's accession see Schürer, *Jewish People* i. ii. p. 26 note. Origen and Jerome condemn the keeping of birthdays; no good man in Scripture keeps them, but only Pharaoh and Herod.

δεῖπνον ἐποίησεν. At Machaerus; there is no ground for thinking that Mk places the banquet at Tiberias; see Schürer, *loc. cit.*

τοῖς μεγιστᾶσιν κ.τ.λ. The three classes are civil magistrates, military officers, and leading men. The chiliarchs are his own officers, not Roman tribunes. Elsewhere we have πρῶτοι τοῦ λαοῦ (Lk. xix. 47), τῆς πόλεως, τῶν 'Ιουδαίων, τῆς νήσου (Acts xiii. 50, xxv. 2, xxviii. 7, 17). In the later books of O.T. μεγιστᾶνες is freq., and Vulg. varies greatly in translation; *principes*, *magnates*, *fortes*, *optimates*, *magnifici*, etc.

22. τῆς θυγατρὸς αὐτῆς τῆς ʿΗρ. See crit. note. Her name was Salome (Joseph. *Ant.* xviii. v. 4), daughter of Herodias by Philip. That Herodias should degrade her daughter, to satisfy her own hatred of John, is credible. That Antipas should suffer *his* daughter to be thus degraded, to please his guests, is not credible. Moreover, a child of Antipas and Herodias could be only about two years old. If αὐτοῦ ʿΗρῳδιάδος be accepted as original, Mk has made a mistake.

ἤρεσεν. We have a similar constr. after a gen. abs. Mt. i. 18.

τῷ κορασίῳ. Not a term of disparagement; v. 41; Ruth ii. 8, 22.

Αἴτησόν με ὅ. The double acc. is freq.; Mt. vii. 9; Jn xvi. 23; etc.

23. ἕως ἡμίσους τ. βασ. μ. Cf. Ahasuerus and Esther (Esth. v. 2, 3), a story which may have influenced this narrative. But, in his cups, Antipas would not stop to consider whether he *could* give away his dominions. Cf. 1 Kings xiii. 8. The contracted gen. is late Greek.

24. ἐξελθοῦσα. Syr-Sin. inserts "she took counsel with." In Mt. she replies at once without going out.

Τί αἰτήσωμαι; *What am I to ask for myself?* Delib. subj. midd.
The change from αἴτησον, αἰτήσῃς to αἰτήσωμαι, ᾐτήσατο (v. 25) marks
a slight change of meaning. Salome's personal gain in the transaction is indicated by the midd. (xv. 8, 43). Cf. x. 35, 38; Jn xvi. 26;
1 Jn. v. 15; Jas. iv. 23.

25. μετὰ σπουδῆς. Almost superfluous after εὐθύς, but it emphasizes her intense eagerness. She is as keen as her mother for
vengeance, and Antipas might change his mind. Superfluous additions are frequent in Mk. See on i. 32. We have μετὰ σπουδῆς Lk.
i. 39; but neither ἐν σπουδῇ (in this sense), nor ἐπὶ σπουδῆς, nor κατὰ
σπουδήν is found in N.T. Syr-Sin. omits μετὰ σπουδῆς here.

Θέλω ἵνα. Cf. x. 35, and (without ἵνα) x. 36, 51, etc.

ἐξαυτῆς. Sc. τῆς ὥρας. This again emphasizes the passion with
which she presses home her ghastly request,—*matre vili filia vilior.*
A.V. has "by and by," which is now misleading. Formerly, it meant
"instantly," and that is what Salome demands; now it means "*not*
instantly." Except in Acts, ἐξαυτῆς is rare in N.T., and it does not
occur in LXX.

ἐπὶ πίνακι. She makes clear that the head is to be off. Vulg.
here has *discus*, a rare word in the sense of "dish," but in Lk. xi. 39
it has *catinus*. Other words for dish are παροψίς (Mt. xxiii. 25, 26)
and τρύβλιον (Mt. xxvi. 23), where Vulg. has *parapsis* for both, but
catinus for τρύβλιον (Mk xiv. 20). The distinction between dishes and
plates was probably not yet made. Hom. *Od.* i. 141.

τοῦ βαπτιστοῦ. Only here and viii. 28 does Mk use this term;
elsewhere ὁ βαπτίζων. See on i. 4.

26. περίλυπος. *Contristatus* (Vulg. here and Lk. xviii. 24) but,
when it is used of the Agony (xiv. 34; Mt. xxvi. 28), simply *tristis*.
The compound implies extreme grief, "wrapped in distress," "grieved
all round": cf. περιδεής, περικαλλής, περικλυτός. Mt. shows his de-
pendence on Mk by saying that the king was grieved, which is
inconsistent with his statement that Herod *wished* to kill John.
Strangely enough, Vulg. has *contristrare* here for ἀθετῆσαι as well as
for περίλυπος. The participle is concessive; *although the king was
deeply distressed.*

διὰ τοὺς ὅρκους. The oath was repeated (2 Macc. iv. 34, vii. 24:
Hdt. i. 146, vi. 62). Ὁ ἀνόητος καὶ ἐρωτόληπτος Ἡρῴδης δέδοικε τοὺς
ὅρκους· ἔδει δὲ ἐπιορκῆσαι (Theoph.). *Scelus excusat juramento, ut sub
occasione pietatis impius fieret* (Bede).

> "A sin it were to swear unto a sin,
> But greater sin to keep a sinful oath."

Comp. the ἀτελέστατος ὅρκος of Ptolemy Philopator (3 Macc. v. 42).

ἀθετῆσαι. Lit. " to displace what has been placed," and therefore
more applicable to his oath than the girl; hence it is far more often
used of things (vii. 9; 1 Cor. i. 19; Gal. ii. 21, iii. 15; 1 Tim. v. 12;
etc.) than of persons (Lk. x. 16; Jn xii. 48). Field suggests "disap-
point," quoting Ps. xv. 5, where LXX. has ἀθετῶν. In LXX. it
translates seventeen Hebrew words. Syr-Sin. has "he could not
change."

27. εὐθὺς ἀποστείλας. He allows himself no time for consideration. Mk has his usual verb, while Mt. has πέμψας. See on v. 12,
where the converse is found.

σπεκουλάτορα. Antipas followed the Roman custom of having
speculatores as in having tribunes (*v.* 21). Each legion had several.
The name shows that they were originally scouts, and the form
spiculator, as if from *spiculum*, is misleading. The *speculatores*
carried despatches (Livy xxxi. 24 ; Tac. *Hist.* ii. 73); and they sometimes formed a body-guard (Suet. *Claud.* 35) and acted as executioners
(Seneca *De ira* i. 16, *De benef.* iii. 25). Cf. Suet. *Calig.* 32, where
miles decollandi artifex quibuscunque e custodia capita amputabat.
At Athens the *public* executioner was ὁ δήμιος sc. δοῦλος, at Rome,
carnifex. Wetstein on Mt. xiv. 11 gives numerous instances of executions at a banquet. Here the contrast between the ascetic Prophet
and the profligate ruler who puts him to death is tragic.

ἐπέταξεν ἐνέγκαι. *Commanded to bring* (R. V.). See crit.
note.

28. ἔδωκεν αὐτὴν τῇ μητρὶ αὐτῆς. We may compare Fulvia with
the head of Cicero. Stories about the discovery of the Baptist's head
and its removal to Constantinople (Sozomen *H.E.* vii. 21) and its
subsequent removal to Amiens, may be disregarded (*Dict. of Chr. Ant.*
i. p. 883). The history of the head ends here; but it was necessary
to record the burial of the body in order to complete the explanation
of the fear of Antipas, οὗτος ἠγέρθη (*v.* 16).

29. οἱ μαθηταὶ αὐτοῦ. Antipas would try to lessen his remorse
by allowing John's disciples to come and remove the corpse.

τὸ πτῶμα. Used also of the Body of Jesus (xv. 45), and it is
possible that a parallel between the death and burial of the Forerunner
and the death and burial of the Messiah is intended. Cf. Mt. xxiv. 28
and esp. Rev. xi. 8, 9. John's disciples would probably take his body
far away from Machaerus and from the dominions of Antipas. The
bones which were dug up at Samaria and burnt in the time of Julian
(Thdrt *H.E.* iii. 3) may have been his. Legends about the body, as
about the head, would multiply as the craze for relics increased. In
class. Grk πτῶμα commonly has a gen., πτῶμα Ἑλένης, πτώματα

νεκρῶν. Polybius uses the word of the ruins of buildings. The commemoration of the martyrdom, 29 Aug., is early.

The 2nd aor. with 1st aor. termination, ἦλθαν, is here well attested: also ἀνέπεσαν (*v.* 40), εἶδαν (*v.* 50). See on εἴδαμεν, ii. 12.

30—44. RETURN OF THE TWELVE. FEEDING OF FIVE THOUSAND.

Mt. xiv. 13—21. Lk. ix. 10—17. Jn vi. 1—14.

30. οἱ ἀπόστολοι. Mk used the title iii. 14 by anticipation; here it is in place after their return from their first missionary journey, but Mk does not use it again. Οἱ ἀπόστολοι is freq. in Lk. and Acts; in all four Gospels οἱ δώδεκα is freq. It is probable that a date had been fixed for the return of the Apostles, and they arrived about the time when John's disciples reported his death. Mt. makes this report the cause of Christ's withdrawal.

ὅσα ἐποίησαν. Not unnaturally, they put their deeds, including miracles, before their teaching. Cf. Lk. x. 17. Christ's estimate made the miracles secondary. Syr-Sin. has "what *he* (John) had done and taught." Cf. Acts i. 1.

31. ὑμεῖς αὐτοί. *You yourselves*, or *you by yourselves*. The former rendering implies that others are resting, and now the missionaries themselves must rest. But who are these others? Syr-Sin. omits the words.

ὀλίγον. Only a short breathing time is possible. The compound and the aor. ἀναπαύσασθε imply that relaxation and not cessation is meant, refreshment and not final rest. Lightfoot on Philem. 7. אDL etc. have ἀναπαύεσθε.

ἦσαν γὰρ...πολλοί. *For those who were coming and those who were going were many*, and between the two there was no leisure even for meals. Mt., as usual, is silent about the pressure of the crowds; see on iii. 9, 20.

εὐκαίρουν. Here Vulg. has *spatium habebant*, Acts xvii. 21 *vacabant*, 1 Cor. xvi. 12 *ei vacuum fuerit*. Not found in LXX.

32. ἀπῆλθον ἐν τῷ πλοίῳ. *They went away in their boat* (art. as in iv. 36) to an uninhabited spot (Mk, Mt.), to a town called Bethsaida (Lk.). The difference is insignificant, and there need be no error. They may have left their boat near the town and have gone into the country. Lk. (ix. 12) does not suppose that the miracle took place in a town. The Bethsaida of Lk. is Bethsaida Julias, E. of the Jordan, near the place where it flows into the Lake. The existence of another Bethsaida on the lake W. of the Jordan is doubtful; see on *v.* 45. The repetition of Christ's κατ' ἰδίαν and εἰς ἔρημον τόπον marks the exact compliance with His request. Nothing is said about fear of Antipas.

33. καὶ εἶδον πολλοί. See on *v.* 29. The direction in which they sailed would be seen, and perhaps the whole course of the boat was visible from the shore. Christ's presence in the boat might be distinguishable at times.

πεζῇ. *By land* (R.V. marg.) as distinct from "by boat," but nearly all of them would go *on foot* (R.V.). Except in this narrative, πεζῇ is not found in N.T. Cf. πεζεύω (Acts xx. 13).

συνέδραμον ἐκεῖ. *They ran there together* (R.V.), fresh groups joining them as they hurried along the shore.

προῆλθον αὐτούς. See crit. note. Although the distance by land was more than double, they might arrive before a boat, if the wind was contrary. Cf. Lk. xxii. 47; ἔφθασαν αὐτούς would be better Greek; 1 Thess. iv. 15; Wisd. vi. 13, xvi. 28. Mk alone has συνέδραμον κ. προῆλθον, and it does not agree with Jn vi. 3, 5, which says that Christ and the disciples sat on the heights and watched the multitude coming. Christ then foresaw that much food would be required. Syr-Sin. omits the words.

34. ἐξελθὼν εἶδεν. This does not mean that He saw no multitude till He left the boat; He would see them from the boat. But now the sight excites compassion and leads to action. Mk, as usual, has ὄχλον, not ὄχλους. See on ii. 4. It is instructive to note how each Evangelist uses his favourite expressions.

ἐσπλαγχνίσθη ἐπ' αὐτούς. See on i. 41 and cf. viii. 2, ix. 22. They had frustrated His purpose (*v.* 31), yet His compassion at once went out to them; or (as Lk.'s favourite ἀποδεξάμενος puts it) He *welcomed* them; and the physician adds, that "He healed (ἰᾶτο) those who had need of treatment." All this is evidence of the reality of Christ's human nature. He might have prevented the frustration of His purpose.

ὡς πρόβατα μὴ ἔχοντα ποιμένα. A proverbial expression (Num. xxvii. 17; 1 Kings xxii. 17; 2 Chron. xviii. 16; Judith xi. 19). Cf. Ezek. xxxiv. 5, 8, which is parallel to this; in both cases it is a faithful and capable spiritual shepherd which God's people need, a true successor of Moses (Num. xxvii. 17 f.). The people ran after Christ in order to see others healed (Jn vi. 2). As usual (see on ii. 4), we have μή, not οὐ, with a participle; but we might have μή in class. Grk.

ἤρξατο διδάσκειν. This was their primary need. Some had never heard Him before, and all had the first elements of true religion to learn; so "He *began* to teach them many things." Here, as in v. 26, πολλά is cogn. acc. rather than adverbial, *multa* not *multum*. For this Mt. (xiv. 15) substitutes "He healed their sick," a change which he makes in xix. 2 = Mk x. 1 and in xxi. 14, 15 = Mk xi. 17, 18. Here Lk. has both the teaching and the healing.

35. ἤδη ὥρας πολλῆς γενομένης. *When it was already a late hour*, but not yet ὀψία (v. 47). The expression is found in Pol. v. 8, "Philip arrived at a late hour (πολλῆς ὥρας) at Thermus"; and in Dion. Hal. *Ant.* ii. 54, "They fought till a late hour (ἄχρι πολλῆς ὥρας) contending vigorously, until night overtook them and separated them." In Latin we have *multus dies*, for *multa hora* would be ambiguous; *multo denique die Caesar cognovit* (Caes. *B. G.* i. 22); *multus sermo ad multum diem* (Cic. *Att.* xiii. 9).

οἱ μαθηταί. The Synoptists represent the disciples as taking the initiative; in Jn, Christ does so by addressing a testing question to Philip. He thinks of their physical, as well as of their spiritual needs. Mt., as often, omits the imperf. ἔλεγον.

36. ἀπόλυσον. *Send away*, as v. 45, and viii. 3, 9 of the 4000. The verb is used of individuals (x. 2, xv. 6), and does not imply dispersion.

τοὺς κύκλῳ ἀγροὺς κ. κώμας. *The farms* (v. 14) *and villages round about*; κύκλῳ belongs to both nouns; cf. 1 Thess. ii. 12, iii. 7. These would be nearer than Bethsaida. D, Latt. read ἔγγιστα for κύκλῳ, *proximas villas et vicos*. In strict grammar the art. ought to be repeated (τοὺς ἀγροὺς τῆς πόλεως καὶ τὰς κώμας αὐτῆς, Josh. xxi. 12); but where the nouns are similar in meaning although different in gender, the art. of the first suffices (Lk. i. 6, xiv. 23; Col. ii. 22; Rev. v. 12).

τί φάγωσιν. See crit. note and cf. viii. 2; Lk. xvii. 8.

37. Δότε αὐτοῖς ὑμεῖς. The very emphatic ὑμεῖς is in all three; "They are not to be sent away; *you* must feed them."

Ἀπελθόντες ἀγοράσωμεν; *Are we to go and buy?* Cf. iv. 30, vi. 24, xii. 14. Jn here differs considerably and is more precise than the Synoptists, whose narrative seems to be partly a condensation of what Jn reports as having taken place between our Lord and Philip and Andrew.

δηναρίων διακοσίων. Mt. omits this, as he omits "about 2000" (v. 13) and "300 denarii" (xiv. 5). The retention in R.V. of "penny" for δηνάριον is as deplorable as that of "publican" for τελώνης. In amount of silver a *denarius* was nearly a shilling, in purchasing power it was more than a florin (Mt. xx. 2 f.). To speak of 200 pennyworths to feed 5000 people is so incongruous as to be almost grotesque. The "two pence" of the Good Samaritan and the "penny a day" of the owner of the vineyard make them seem niggardly instead of generous. In Rev. vi. 6, maximum prices are turned into incredibly low prices by the translation "penny." The meaning here is "A sum far greater than Judas carries for us would be quite insufficient." Lk. inserts an emphatic ἡμεῖς answering to Christ's ὑμεῖς. The question suggests that what Christ has ordered is impossible; οἱ δὲ καταμέμφονται αὐτὸν ὡς μὴ γνόντα (Theoph.).

38. Πόσους ἔχετε ἄρτους; ὑπάγετε, ἴδετε. The question and abrupt commands are a rebuke. "Never mind what is impossible; see what is possible. How *much* food have we got?" In Jn the suggestion of buying comes from Christ. Mk alone records the question and commands. Mt. again omits what seems to imply a limitation of Christ's knowledge and power. See on *v.* 5. The rendering "loaves" must not be disturbed; but the ἄρτοι resembled biscuits or oatcake rather than our own loaves.

ὑπάγετε, ἴδετε. The asyndeton is characteristic; i. 41, iv. 40, v. 36, viii. 17, 18, ix. 19, x. 14.

γνόντες. *Having ascertained.* Jn is far more definite. Andrew had found a lad who had five barley loaves and two fishes, which seems to imply that the disciples had no food with them. Philip and Andrew, as coming from Bethsaida, would know people in the crowd and would have some idea of the resources of the neighbourhood. The Fathers often find mystical meanings in numbers and do so here with "five" and "two"; *e.g.* the five Books of the Law with the Psalms and the Prophets, or with the Gospel and the Apostle.

δύο ἰχθύας. Dried or salted fish were often eaten as a relish (ὀψώνιον, προσφάγιον) with bread, so much so that these words may mean "fish"; see on Jn vi. 9, xxi. 5. Cf. πᾶν τὸ ὄψος (? ὄψον) τῆς θαλάσσης (Num. xi. 22).

39. ἀνακλῖναι πάντας. *That all should recline.* If the people had stood, they would have crowded round the distributors, and equal distribution would have been impossible. Arranging them in "messes" (τραπέζας διαφόρους, Theoph.) still further contributed to orderly and equal feeding.

συμπόσια. Lit. "drinking-parties," and then any gatherings for taking refreshment. Hence the addition of οἴνου (Ecclus. xxxi. 31, xxxii. 5, xlix. 1) when drinking is specially meant. Cicero has *compotatio*, but the usual words are *commissatio* and *convivium*. Vulg. has *secundum contubernia* here and *in partes* for πρασιαὶ πρασιαί. The reduplication (see on δύο δύο, *v.* 7) should be similarly rendered in both verses; but A.V. and R.V. have "*by* companies" and "*in* ranks."

Company by company and *rank by rank* preserves the reduplication and the similarity of construction.

ἐπὶ τῷ χλωρῷ χόρτῳ. The desert was not sand, but prairie, and the green grass confirms Jn's mention of a Passover here. Contrast *Clem. Recog.* ii. 70, iii. 30.

40. πρασιαί. Lit. "garden-beds" (Ecclus. xxiv. 31) or "plots." The word indicates the shape of the "messes," and perhaps implies that they were rectangular (Euthym.). See Wetstein for illustrations and cf. Exod. viii. 14.

κατὰ ἑκατὸν κ. κ. π. All four give the total as 5000 males, which would easily be estimated by counting the συμπόσια.

41. λαβὼν τ. πέντε ἄρτους κ.τ.λ. Cf. λαβὼν ἄρτον εὐλογήσας ἔκλασεν κ. ἔδωκεν αὐτοῖς (xiv. 22). He is now the host (Lk. xxiv. 30), with His staff of servants, and with what in His hands was a sufficient supply of food, and as such He utters the usual blessing and directs everything. The gifts are His, bestowed, however, not directly, but through the Twelve, εὐσχημόνως καὶ κατὰ τάξιν, and herein we have the germ of Church organization.

ἀναβλέψας. In all three; cf. vii. 34; Jn xi. 41.

εὐλόγησεν, In all three; Jn has the equivalent εὐχαριστήσας. Both verbs are used of the Eucharist (xiv. 22, 23). The "grace" at meals was virtually a thanksgiving; "Blessed art Thou, O Lord our God, who bringest forth bread out of the earth."

κατέκλασεν. *He broke in pieces; zerbrach.* Mt. has simply κλάσας, and all three, with Paul, have ἔκλασεν of the Eucharist. The compound occurs nowhere else in N.T. The breaking was part of the ceremony of saying grace and was done once (aor.). The breaking *in pieces* indicated the completeness of the munificence; διάθρυπτε πεινῶντι τὸν ἄρτον σου (Is. lviii. 7).

ἐδίδου. The giving continued (imperf.), either to each Apostle in turn, or to all of them as they returned for fresh supplies, if they did return. The manner of the multiplication is not revealed, and conjectures are futile. We are told that it "must have taken place in the hands of the Apostles." "Must" is out of place in such matters. "*His* disciples" (A.V.) is as correct as "*the* disciples" (R.V.): cf. iv. 26, 36, vi. 32. Note the πᾶσιν and the πάντες following. The disciples' share in the work would impress the events on their memory (Euthym.), but they did not see its significance.

42. ἐχορτάσθησαν. In all three; Jn has ἐνεπλήσθησαν. Originally used of supplying animals with fodder (χόρτος), χορτάζω implied brutish feeding when used of men (Plato *Rep.* ix. p. 586). In N.T. it is nowhere used of cattle (of birds, Rev. xix. 21), and has no degrading meaning when used of men (vii. 27, viii. 4, 8; etc.). In LXX. χορτάζω and πίμπλημι translate the same Hebrew word, even in the same verse (Ps. cvii. 9).

43. ἦραν κλάσματα. See crit. note. Jn tells us that it was by the Entertainer's order that this security against waste was taken; a remarkable order to come from One who had just fed 5000 with the food for five, and an order not likely to be invented by a writer of fiction. The amount saved far exceeded the amount supplied by the lad, but Christ did not allow it to be wasted. And the fragments are of the loaves and fishes; nothing new has been created.

κοφίνων. The word always used of this miracle, σφυρίδες being always used of feeding the 4000. The κόφινος was the wallet in which travelling Jews carried provisions, to avoid eating Gentile food; *Judaeis quorum cophinus foenumque supellex* (Juv. iii. 14), *Cophino foenoque relicto Arcanam Judaea tremens mendicat in aurem* (*Ib.* vi. 542). A σφυρίς would hold a man (Acts ix. 25). Wiclif has "coffyns" here and viii. 19.

44. ἄνδρες. In all four; *men*; ἄνθρωποι would be "people," including women and children, whom Mt. mentions separately. Mt., Lk., and Jn have ὡσεί or ὡς before πεντακισχίλιοι.

The attempts to explain away the miracle as a myth, or a parable, or a gross exaggeration, are very unsatisfying. The first Temptation, as recorded by Mt. and Lk. (a narrative which must have had its origin in Christ Himself), points strongly to His having powers such as are indicated here. He would not have put His temptation into a form that implied that He had power which He knew that He did not possess. At the time when He told the disciples about His temptations experience would have taught Him whether there was the supposed limit to His supernatural power. We are not in a position to draw a hard and fast line between what is only unknown and what is certainly impossible. This consideration applies also to the narrative which immediately follows.

45—52. The Walking on the Water.

Mt. xiv. 22—33. Jn vi. 16—21.

45. εὐθὺς ἠνάγκασεν τ. μαθητάς. Jn again differs considerably from the Synoptists. They say that He sent away the disciples and then dismissed the multitude. He says that Christ escaped from the people without dismissing them. But Jn shows why Christ insisted upon the disciples going away at once. There was a tradition that the Messiah would feed Israel with bread from heaven as Moses had

done. Even without that belief, the miracle that had saved them
from exhaustion in the wilderness might lead to the conclusion that
Jesus was the Messiah, and their idea of the Messiah was that of an
earthly conqueror and king. Jesus must be made to declare Himself
as such. The disciples might be inclined to join such a movement
(Lk. xix. 39); and to save them from such disastrous enthusiasm,
Christ compelled them to leave Him. Compulsion was necessary, for
they had only recently returned to Him, and this time they were
being sent away without any mission. Mk's interest is centred in
what Christ did; Jn's narrative is concerned with what the disciples
did.

ἐμβῆναι καὶ προάγειν. The combination of tenses is unusual; cf.
γαμῆσαι ἢ πυροῦσθαι (1 Cor. vii. 9).

εἰς τὸ πέραν πρὸς Βηθσαϊδάν. Mt. omits πρὸς B., possibly because
it seemed to contradict the tradition that the Feeding took place near
Bethsaida. Jn says ἤρχοντο πέραν τῆς θαλάσσης πρὸς Καφαρναούμ, and
both Mk (v. 53) and Mt. (xiv. 34) say that they came to land εἰς
Γεννησαρέτ. This has led some to suppose that there was another
Bethsaida, on the W. shore of the Lake, near Capernaum. The
existence of this Bethsaida is doubtful (Hastings' D.B., Enc. Bibl. art.
"Bethsaida"), but it may be admitted as a possibility (D.C.G.). The
improbability of two places called "Fishinghouse" near to one
another is not great. There are three Torringtons and two Little-
hams in Devon. But if we reject the W. Bethsaida, then εἰς τὸ
πέραν does not mean across the Lake, but across the bay which
separates the scene of the Feeding from Bethsaida Julias. The storm
prevented them from reaching Bethsaida, and they went homewards
to Capernaum. To render πρὸς B. "looking towards B.," i.e. opposite
B., or take πρὸς B. with ἀπολύει, is not admissible.

ἕως αὐτὸς ἀπολύει. See crit. note and cf. Jn xxi. 22; 1 Tim. iv.
13. While He Himself sendeth the multitude away (R.V.). Then He
is to rejoin them, as προάγειν implies, and this is against Bethsaida
being on the W. shore. The distance round the N. end of the Lake
would be very considerable, while that round the little bay would be
only a moderate walk. For τὸν ὄχλον Mt. has τοὺς ὄχλους. See on ii. 4.

46. ἀποταξάμενος αὐτοῖς. After He had taken leave of them (R.V.),
parting from them in a friendly way (Lk. ix. 61; Acts xviii. 21). Mt.
loses this point, and Beza gives just the wrong shade of meaning,
quum amandasset eos, which implies dismissing with contempt. Vulg.
points to a text with ἀπολύσας αὐτούς, dum dimitteret populum. Cum
dimisisset eos. Elsewhere Vulg. renders ἀποτάσσομαι vale facio or
renuncio.

εἰς τὸ ὄρος προσεύξασθαι. The human nature of our Lord is again conspicuous, not merely in His praying, but in His seeking solitude at sunset on the mountain side as a help to prayer, σχολῆς γὰρ καὶ ἀταραξίας δεῖται ἡ προσευχή (Theoph.). Jn mentions these accessories, but not the prayer. On two other occasions Mk records that Christ prayed, the first day's work at Capernaum (i. 35) and the last night's Agony (xiv. 35).

47. ὀψίας γενομένης. It was late in the day (v. 35) when arrangements for the Feeding began, and now the brief twilight was ending in darkness.

ἐν μέσῳ τῆς θαλάσσης. See on Jn vi. 17.

48. ἰδὼν αὐτοὺς βασανιζομένους. There is no need to suppose supernatural power of sight. The Paschal moon would give light enough. See on v. 7. Syr-Sin. has "tormented with the fear of the waves."

ἐν τῷ ἐλαύνειν. See on iv. 4. It was too stormy for sailing, and for hours they had been rowing against the wind making very little progress. Syr-Sin. omits.

τετάρτην φυλακήν. Mk (xiii. 35) and Mt. (xiv. 25) follow the Roman division into four watches. Lk. (xii. 38) probably follows the Jewish division into three (Judg. vii. 19); but see Acts xii. 4. Syr-Sin. omits the mention of the hour.

ἐπὶ τῆς θαλάσσης. Cf. ἐπὶ τῆς γῆς (v. 47), and περιπατῶν ὡς ἐπ᾽ ἐδάφους ἐπὶ θαλάσσης (Job ix. 8). Christ was walking not *by* the sea, but on it, over the surface of its stormy waters. His walking by the sea would not have terrified them, nor could He and they have conversed. We may refuse to believe the miracle, but the narrative has not arisen through misinterpretation of language. Nor is it an imitation of O.T. miracles; Christ does not divide the Jordan and walk over on dry land (Josh. iii. 14—17; 2 Kings ii. 8, 14). "These attempts are usually unconvincing, and provoke the remark how much ingenuity can be combined with a lack of common sense" (Salmon, *Human Element*, p. 323). It is rash to be positive as to what would be possible or impossible for a unique Personality such as that of Jesus Christ.

ἤθελεν παρελθεῖν. Cf. vii. 27; Lk. xxiv. 28; and for the conative imperf. Mt. iii. 14; Lk. i. 59. We have here the impression of an eye-witness; the figure looked as if it meant to pass by them. Mt. omits this; see on i. 45 and vii. 24.

49. φάντασμα. *An apparition* (R.V.). A word is required which answers to the derivation (φαίνομαι) and which occurs only in this connexion in N.T. The Syriac points to a reading δαιμόνιον. In Lk. xxiv. 37, D has φάντασμα for πνεῦμα.

ἀνέκραξαν. See on i. 23. τὸν ἀπὸ τοῦ κλύδωνος φόβον ἕτερος δια-δέχεται (Euthym.).

50. πάντες γὰρ εἶδαν. See on *v.* 29. It was no subjective delusion; there was something objective which all of them perceived. The aorists indicate what was of short duration; He addressed them at once, and their trouble was at an end. Syr-Sin. has "*when* they all saw Him, they cried out." The difference between λαλέω, "speak," and λέγω, "say," is manifest here. Trench, *Syn.* § 76.

Θαρσεῖτε. Cf. x. 49; Mt. ix. 2, 22; Jn xvi. 33. This form pre-vails in Gospels and Acts, θαρρέω in 2 Cor. and Heb. In LXX. θαρσέω is common, θαρρέω rare and late.

μὴ φοβεῖσθε. *Cease to fear:* v. 36, x. 14. Contrast the aorists in x. 19. For the asyndeton see on *v.* 38.

51. ἀνέβη. The verb is freq. in class. Grk of going on board a ship. Mk and Jn omit Peter's walking on the water. Lk. omits the whole narrative.

ἐκόπασεν. See on iv. 39. *In quocunque corde Deus per gratiam sui adest amoris, mox universa bella compressa quiescunt* (Bede).

λίαν ἐν ἑαυτοῖς. See crit. note. This time they keep their thoughts to themselves; contrast iv. 41. Mt. attributes to them the confession afterwards made by Peter (viii. 29; Mt. xvi. 16), which is out of harmony with what follows in the next verse.

52. οὐ γὰρ συνῆκαν ἐπὶ τοῖς ἄρτοις. "For the miracle of the loaves afforded them no *basis* for comprehending." See crit. note. Neither A.V. nor R.V. seems to be right here. As often, Mt. and Lk. omit what is discreditable to the Twelve, and Mt. substitutes what does honour both to them and to Christ. It was natural that His walking on the waves and the sudden cessation of the gale should amaze them more than the feeding of the multitudes (viii. 17 f.); as fishermen they could appreciate the former, but they were still very defective in insight. See on iii. 5. This miracle is part of their education.

53—56. MINISTRY IN THE PLAIN OF GENNESARET.
Mt. xiv. 34—36.

53. διαπεράσαντες ἐπὶ τ. γῆν. *When they had crossed over to the land* (R.V. marg.); cf. διασωθῆναι ἐπὶ τ. γῆν (Acts xxvii. 44). The δια- points to their getting through their perils and toils. Jn says that they did so εὐθέως, on their welcoming Christ into the boat.

Γεννησαρέτ. Mt. says the same; elsewhere only Lk. v. 1. It was a little S. of Capernaum, and was then a fertile and populous district (Joseph. *B. J.* iii. x. 8).

προσωρμίσθησαν. Here only in Bibl. Grk. Wetstein gives classical examples. Syr-Sin. omits καὶ πρ.

54. εὐθὺς ἐπιγνόντες αὐτόν. It was still early (v. 48), but there were people who recognized Him and, as before, were eager to get their sick folk healed. Cf. Lk. xxiv. 31; Acts iii. 10, xxvii. 39; Mt. is much less graphic.

55. περιέδραμον. Not elsewhere in N.T. The aorists indicate the rapidity with which all was done, while the news of His arrival kept spreading (ὅπου ἤκουον).

περιφέρειν. They were sometimes too late; and they then carried the sick from place to place, till they overtook Him.

ἐστίν. The very word of the report; "He *is* in such a place."

56. ὅπου ἂν εἰσεπορεύετο. Cf. the constr. in iii. 11; Acts ii. 45, iv. 35.

ἐν ταῖς ἀγοραῖς. *In the open places.* "In the streets" (A.V.) is from ἐν ταῖς πλατείαις (D, Vulg.), which looks like a correction, because no κῶμαι, and not all πόλεις, would have market-places. But ἀγορά has its original meaning, "a place where people assemble." Cf. Acts v. 15 and the curious Babylonian custom commended in Hdt. i. 197.

ἐτίθεσαν. So אBLΔ. For ἵνα cf. v. 18, 23, vii. 32. The way in which the woman with the issue had been cured had doubtless become widely known, and the faith of these applicants was as efficacious as hers. Mt. again has aor. where Mk has imperf.

CHAPTER VII.

2. ὅτι...ἐσθίουσιν (ℵBLΔ 33) rather than ἐσθίοντας (ADNX etc.). ℵABLΔ 33 omit ἐμέμψαντο, which was added to complete the construction; D adds κατέγνωσαν.

3. πυγμῇ (ABLNXΓΠ) rather than πυκνά (ℵ, Vulg.). D has πυκμη. Syr-Sin. omits.

4. ῥαντίσωνται (ℵB and 8 cursives) should probably be preferred to βαπτίσωνται (ADΓΠ) and other variants. ℵBLΔ omit καὶ κλινῶν.

5. καὶ ἐπερωτῶσιν (ℵBDL, Latt.) rather than ἔπειτα (ΑΧΓΠ), which is another attempt to mend the construction broken by vv. 3, 4. κοιναῖς (ℵ*BD 33) rather than ἀνίπτοις (ℵ°ALX etc.).

6. ℵBLΔ 33 omit ἀποκριθείς. See on x. 5.

8. ℵBLΔ omit γάρ and βαπτισμοὺς...ποιεῖτε (from v. 4).

12. ℵBDΔ omit καί.

14. πάλιν (ℵBDLΔ) rather than πάντα (ΑΧΓΠ).

16. ℵBLΔ*, Memph. omit the verse; an early interpolation from iv. 9, for Syr-Sin. has it.

17. τὴν παραβολήν (ℵBDLΔ) rather than περὶ τῆς π. (ΑΧΓΠ).

19. καθαρίζων (ℵABEFGHLSXΔ and many cursives) rather than καθαρίζον (KMUVΓΠ), or καθαρίζει (D).

21. πορνεῖαι, κλοπαί, φόνοι, μοιχεῖαι (ℵBLΔ) rather than μ., π., φ., κλ. (ΑΝΧΓΠ).

24. ἐκεῖθεν δέ (ℵBLΔ) rather than καὶ ἐκεῖθεν (ΑΝΧΓΠ). See on i. 14. ὅρια (ℵBDLΔ) rather than μεθόρια (ΑΝΧΓΠ). καὶ Σιδῶνος may come from Mt. xv. 21; BLΔ omit.

25. ἀλλ' εὐθὺς ἀκούσασα (ℵBLΔ 33) rather than ἀκούσασα γάρ (ΑΝΧΓΠ). Syr-Sin. omits εὐθύς, περὶ αὐτοῦ, τ. πόδας.

30. τὸ δαιμόνιον ἐξεληλυθός after τὸ παιδίον κ.τ.λ. (ℵBDLΔ).

31. ἦλθεν διὰ Σιδῶνος (ℵBDLΔ) rather than καὶ Σιδῶνος ἦλθεν (ΑΝΧΓΠ).

35. ℵBDLΔ omit εὐθέως. ἠνοίγησαν (ℵBDΔ) rather than διηνοίχθησαν (ΑΝΧΓΠ). See WH. App. p. 170; Deissmann, Bib. St. p. 189; Veitch, Greek Verbs, p. 66.

1—13. QUESTIONS OF CEREMONIAL CLEANSING.

Mt. xv. 1—20.

1. συνάγονται. Hitherto it has been a not unfriendly company that has gathered together where the great Teacher and Healer was to be found (i. 33, ii. 2, iii. 10, 32, iv. 1, v. 21, vi. 31, 55). Hostile elements have sometimes intruded (ii. 6, 16, 18, iii. 6, 22), but they have been exceptional. Here the gathering consists of hostile critics.

οἱ Φαρισαῖοι. See on ii. 16; they were last mentioned as plotting His death (iii. 6).

ἐλθόντες ἀπὸ Ἱεροσολύμων. See on x. 32. This may mean that a new party of Scribes (iii. 22) had arrived. *Non ad verbum audiendum, non ad quaerendam medelam, sed ad movendas solum quaestionum pugnas, ad Dominum concurrunt* (Bede). Put a full stop at the end of the verse (A.V.); ἰδόντες is not to be coupled with ἐλθόντες.

2. καὶ ἰδόντες. The beginning of a new sentence, which is broken by a long parenthesis (*vv.* 3, 4) and left unfinished.

ὅτι κοιναῖς χερσίν. See crit. note. We have ὅτι instead of infin. xi. 32, xii. 34. Κοινός was a technical term for what was "common" to the Gentiles but ceremonially unclean to the Jews; κοινὸν καὶ ἀκάθαρτον (Acts x. 14, 28, xi. 8; cf. Rom. xiv. 14; 1 Macc. i. 47, 62). Cf. εἰ δέ τις αἰτίαν ἔσχε κοινοφαγίας ἤ τινος ἄλλου τοιούτου ἁμαρτήματος (Joseph. *Ant.* xi. viii. 7; cf. xiii. i. 1). In N.T. κοινός is opposed to καθαρός and ἅγιος (Heb. x. 29). Syr-Sin. has "when they had not washed their hands."

τοῦτ' ἔστιν ἀνίπτοις. Added for Gentile readers.

ἐσθίουσιν τοὺς ἄρτους. "Eat *their* bread"; cf. iv. 26, 36, vi. 32. In this phrase the art. and the plur. are unusual both in N.T. (iii. 20; Mt. xv. 2; Lk. xiv. 1, 2) and in LXX. (Gen. xxxvii. 25; Exod. ii. 20; 2 Sam. ix. 7). See crit. note.

3. οἱ γὰρ Φαρισαῖοι. Another explanation inserted for Gentile readers. Mt. has nothing corresponding to *vv.* 3, 4.

πάντες οἱ Ἰουδαῖοι. "All strict Jews," those who wished to be δίκαιοι according to the regulations of the Scribes (Lk. i. 6, ii. 25, xviii. 9). The regulations of the Law (Lev. xi.—xv.; Num. v. 1—4, xix.) had been enormously increased by the Scribes, with the result that the right sense of proportion had been lost. People confounded what was ceremonially trivial with what was ceremonially important, and also what was purely ceremonial with what was moral, the former being often preferred to the latter. The longest of the six books of the Mishna (*Tohărôth*) treats of purification, and thirty chapters are given to the cleansing of vessels. Schürer, ii. ii. pp. 106 f. *D.C.G.* art. "Purification."

πυγμῇ. The word remains a puzzle in this connexion. "Up to the elbow" and "up to the fist" are impossible translations. "With the fist" is the best rendering; and this may be explained either literally, of rubbing a closed hand in the palm of the other hand, or metaphorically, of vigorous washing, = "diligently" (A.V. marg.).

νίψωνται. The verb is used of washing part of the body (Mt. vi. 17, xv. 2; 1 Tim. v. 10; Gen. xviii. 4; etc.), λούομαι being used of bathing the whole body (Acts ix. 37; Heb. x. 22; etc.), and πλύνω of washing clothes, nets, etc. (Rev. vii. 14, xxii. 14; Lk. v. 2). In Lev. xv. 11 we have all three verbs thus distinguished. See on Jn xiii. 10.

τὴν παράδοσιν τῶν πρεσβυτέρων. Traditions handed down for generations and sanctioned by great teachers were regarded by the Pharisees and their followers as of equal obligation with Scripture. The traditions were seldom wrong in themselves, but they were treated as of such importance that moral duties were neglected. This inevitably follows when right conduct is regarded as keeping certain rules. The acc. is used because the whole of the tradition (iii. 21, vi. 17), and not a part (i. 31, v. 41), is held. Only in this and the parallel passage (Mt. xv. 2—6) is παράδοσις used in the Gospels. In 2 Thess. ii. 15, κρατεῖτε τὰς παραδόσεις is said of holding Christian traditions; cf. 1 Cor. xi. 2.

4. ἀπ' ἀγορᾶς. *On coming from market*, where they might come in contact with persons or things that were ceremonially unclean. We have ἀπὸ δείπνου (Hdt. i. 126, ii. 78, v. 18) similarly used; ἀπὸ νεκροῦ (Ecclus. xxxi. [xxxiv.] 25).

ἐὰν μὴ ῥαντίσωνται. See crit. note. Sprinkling did not seem to be in harmony with πυγμῇ νίψωνται, and hence the change to βαπτίσωνται. If βαπτ. be adopted, it would mean bathing the hands rather than the whole person. Either verb might be used of holding the hands over a basin and having water poured over them. Cf. Justin, *Try.* 46. Tatian seems to have understood the sentence as meaning that the Jews do not eat what they bring from market without purifying it, which is not the meaning.

παρέλαβον. The right verb to use of those who received παραδόσεις.

ξεστῶν. The jugs in which the water for drinking or purifying was kept. A μετρητής (Jn ii. 6) held about 50 ξέσται. Here, however, the word is not used of a definite measure, *sextarius*, but of a house-

hold vessel without reference to size. Vulg. has *urceus*, a jug with
one handle. The addition, καὶ κλινῶν (see crit.
note), would not mean
"and tables," but "and couches," for reclining at table, or possibly
"and beds," for sleeping on at night. Syr-Sin. omits καὶ χαλκίων.

5. Διὰ τί; As in ii. 16, the question is a form of hostile criticism.
"Eat *their* bread," as in *v*. 2.

6. Καλῶς ἐπροφήτευσεν. "With beautiful appropriateness Isaiah
prophesied." Cf. xii. 28, 32; Lk. xx. 39; and esp. Acts xxviii. 25.
Everywhere in N.T., including Jude 14, and almost everywhere in
LXX., ἐπροφ. is to be preferred to προεφ. There is no simple verb
φητεύω. But in other verbs late writers sometimes put the augment
before the preposition. Blass, § 15, 17.

ὑποκριτῶν. This word, so freq. in Mt., occurs here only in Mk,
and here it is omitted in Syr-Sin. In Job xxxiv. 30, xxxvi. 13 it
means the godless man and = παράνομος (xvii. 8, xx. 5). It is not
found in Jn.

ὡς γέγραπται. See on i. 2. Mt. agrees with Mk in this quotation
from Is. xxix. 13, and both abbreviate the LXX., omitting ἐγγίζει and
ἐν τῷ στόματι αὐτοῦ.

7. μάτην. Freq. in LXX., but not found in N.T., except in this
quotation. St Paul has εἰς κενόν. See on 2 Cor. vi. 1.

διδάσκοντες διδασκαλίας ἐντ. ἀνθ. Here again Mk and Mt. differ
from LXX., which has διδάσκοντες ἐντάλματα ἀνθρώπων καὶ διδασκαλίας. One is inclined to translate "teaching for *teachings*," reserving
"doctrine" for διδαχή. But this would be no improvement, for διδαχή
is teaching as a whole, while διδασκαλία (freq. in Past. Epp.) is a particular part of teaching, a doctrine. But the distinction is not always
sharply made.

ἐντάλματα ἀνθρώπων. In apposition with διδασκαλίας, *teaching
doctrines (which are) commands of men.* This was the source of the
evil; their doctrines were of their own devising. They burdened the
conscience with external details which had no spiritual value. We
must distinguish in translation between ἔνταλμα, "command," or
"precept," and ἐντολή, "commandment." Vulg. *praeceptum* and
mandatum. Ἔνταλμα is used of the Divine commands Job xxiii. 11,
12; the word is not found in profane writers. Lightfoot thinks that
St Paul had this discourse in his mind when he wrote Col. ii. 21—23.

8. τὴν ἐντολήν. Commonly used of a single commandment (x. 5,
19, xii. 28), but here of the Divine Law as a whole; see on 1 Tim. vi. 14.
The verse looks like another version of *v*. 9. There is no such repetition in Mt., and his wording is closer to *v*. 9. Syr-Sin. omits the
verse.

9. καὶ ἔλεγεν αὐτοῖς. The insertion of this introductory formula confirms the impression that *v.* 8 and *v.* 9 come from two different sources. Syr-Sin. omits the words.

Καλῶς. See on Jn iv. 17 and 2 Cor. xi. 4. The irony is stronger here. This was the beautiful result of their putting a fence about the Law; their fence had shut off the Law so completely that the sight of it was lost.

ἀθετεῖτε. See on vi. 26; as applied to such words as ἐντολή, νόμος, διαθήκη, it means not merely violating, but treating as null and void (Heb. x. 28; Gal. iii. 15). The oral tradition had supplanted the written Law—everywhere by engrossing men's attention, and in some cases by contravening its spirit. *D.C.G.* art. "Tradition."

10. Μωϋσῆς γὰρ εἶπεν. Mt. makes the connexion more clear and the contrast more pointed by writing ὁ γὰρ Θεὸς εἶπεν. The Pentateuch was quoted as "Moses" (i. 44, x. 3, xii. 19). But the Law was given διὰ (not ὑπὸ) Μωυσέως (see on Jn i. 17). Moses was not the giver of it any more than of the manna (Jn vi. 32). See on xii. 26.

Ὁ κακολογῶν. *He that speaketh evil of* (R.V.) rather than "he that curseth" (A.V.); in ix. 39, and Acts xix. 9, A.V. has "speak evil of," and in the Corban case there is no cursing, but the parents are dishonoured. These quotations from Exod. xx. 12 and xxi. 17 illustrate the fact that citations which are found in more than one Synoptist, "with few exceptions, adhere closely to the LXX., the differences being only textual or in the way of omission" (Swete, *Introd. to O.T. in Greek,* p. 393).

11. ὑμεῖς δὲ λέγετε. "But *ye* say." As in *vv.* 2—5 and iv. 26 and 31, we have a confused constr. Mk forgets that he began with ὑμεῖς δὲ λέγετε and leaves the ἐὰν εἴπῃ sentence unfinished. Omit λέγετε and the constr. will stand; with λέγετε *v.* 12 should run οὐκέτι οὐδὲν ποιήσει. Cf. iii. 22.

Κορβᾶν, ὅ ἐστιν Δῶρον. As in v. 41, vii. 34, xiv. 36, we have Aramaic with a translation. Κορβάν is not found in LXX., but Josephus (*Ant.* IV. iv. 4) gives it with this translation. It means a *dedicated* or *vowed* gift, a gift not to be revoked by the giver (*Ibid. c. Apion.* i. 22). The Scribes taught that a vow, however unrighteous, must stand. Even if the man who made it desired to remedy the wrong, and even if the wrong was to his own parents, he could not be allowed to remedy it. Such ruling cuts right across the Fifth Commandment. See Wright, *Synopsis,* p. 69; Driver on Deut. xxiii. 24. The sentence means, "Whatsoever support thou mightest have from me is Korban, irrevocably given elsewhere." Luther, putting a comma after *me* in Vulg.—*Corban quodcunque ex me, tibi profuerit*

—took it to mean, "If I dedicate it, it is far more valuable to thee."

12. οὐκέτι ἀφίετε. *Ye no longer suffer;* "so far from telling him that his duty to his parents is paramount, you do not allow him to perform it." See crit. nc†e.

οὐδὲν ποιῆσαι τῷ πατρί. Cf. v. 19, 20, x. 36; the expression is found in Attic. Blass, § 34. 4. Syr-Sin. has "honour." For the double negative see on i. 44.

13. ἀκυροῦντες. Not merely *treating* as null and void (ἀθετεῖτε, v. 9), but *making void* (R.V.). Both verbs occur Gal. iii. 15—17. Excepting 4 Macc., ἀκυρόω is very rare in Bibl. Grk. In papyri it is used of annulling contracts. Passages in the Talmud definitely put tradition and comment above Scripture. "The words of the Scribes are lovely above the words of the Law; for the words of the Law are weighty and light, but the words of the Scribes are all weighty."

τῇ παραδόσει ᾗ παρεδώκατε. The connexion between noun and verb cannot be reproduced in English. The aor. seems to be out of place; παραδίδοτε would be better; or (if aor.) παρελάβετε. The relative is dative by attraction.

παρόμοια τοιαῦτα πολλά. Superfluous fulness; *many such similar things.* Cf. vi. 25. Παρόμοιος, freq. in class. Grk, occurs nowhere else in N.T. or LXX.

14—23. THE SOURCE OF REAL DEFILEMENT.

Mt. xv. 10—20.

14. προσκαλεσάμενος πάλιν. We need not limit the πάλιν to the crowd at Gennesaret. He often invited people to come to Him, and here He does so again. Having answered the cavils of the Scribes, He now resumes the more profitable work of freeing the multitude from the unspiritual traditions of Pharisaism. οὐκ ἔτι τοῖς Φαρισαίοις διαλέγεται, ὡς ἀθεραπεύτοις (Theoph.). Mk (about 27 times) even more than Mt. (about 17) is fond of πάλιν. Lk. (3) seems to avoid it, often omitting it where Mk has it. For ἔλεγεν Mt. again has εἶπεν. Cf. v. 27.

15. οὐδὲν ἔστιν ἔξωθεν κ.τ.λ. This illuminating principle is given by Mk in the most comprehensive terms; *There is nothing external to a man which by entering into him can defile him.* Mt. narrows it by limiting it to meat and drink. Externals cannot pollute a man, because they do not touch the man's self, but only his body. Epictetus enlarges on this difference; *e.g. Dis.* i. 19. Plato points out that what enters into the mouth is perishable, but what comes

out of it, viz. speech, may be imperishable (*Tim.* 75 D). Cf. Deut.
xxiii. 23. Like other parabolic utterances of Christ, this Saying was
not understood even by the Twelve at the time, nor indeed even
after Pentecost (Acts x. 14). But when this Gospel was written the
practical result of this principle was recognized;—Levitical prohibitions of certain foods as unclean had been abolished (*v.* 19 *b*). The
art., τοῦ or τὸν ἄνθρ., is generic, as in ii. 27, iv. 21. For the aor.
infin. see on i. 41. Syr-Sin. omits ἔξωθεν as superfluous.

ἀλλά. "On the contrary, the things which defile the man, are
the thoughts, words, and deeds which come out of him." As both τὰ
ἐκπορευόμενα and τὰ κοινοῦντα have the art., either may be the subject.
The repetition of τὸν ἄνθρ. instead of using a pronoun is characteristic;
cf. iv. 37.

16. See crit. note.

17. εἰς οἶκον. *When He came indoors.* The particular house is of
no moment; "indoors" means away from the multitude. It appears
repeatedly when private instruction is given (ix. 28, 33, x. 10). It
is possible that in all these cases we have personal recollection of a
detail. To the multitude He often spoke in parables, and now the
disciples once more ask for an interpretation of τὸν σκοτεινὸν λόγον
(iv. 2, 10, 11). See crit. note.

18. Οὕτως καὶ ὑμεῖς. As before (iv. 13), He expresses surprise at
their want of discernment. The position of οὕτως is against its being
taken with ἀσύνετοι, "so wanting in discernment," *tam insipientes.*
Better, "Is it so," *siccine?* Vulg. has *Sic et vos imprudentes estis?*
Either "Even you" (i. 27; Mt. v. 46) or "you also" (Mt. xx. 4, 7;
Jn vi. 68, where the context is decisive) may be right; see on ii. 28.
"Even you, whom I have instructed," or "you also, as well as the
multitude." We have similar surprise again in viii. 17, οὔπω νοεῖτε
οὐδὲ συνίετε; Syr-Sin. has "Are ye *yet* so stubborn? Do ye not yet
understand *anything*? that not everything which entereth into a man
defileth him?"

οὐ δύναται κοινῶσαι. Cannot pollute him in any religious sense;
he is not morally the worse. The Scribes taught otherwise. This
repetition from *v.* 15 is omitted in Mt.

19. οὐκ εἰσπορεύεται κ.τ.λ. This important explanation is also
omitted in Mt. Aristophanes has ἄφοδος (*Eccl.* 1059), ἀπόπατος
(*Ach.* 81) and κοπρών (*Thesm.* 485) for ἀφεδρών (ἕδρα), which occurs
nowhere else in Bibl. Grk. Vulg. has *in secessum*, Beza *in latrinam.*
D reads ὀχετός here, but ἀφεδρών in Mt.

καθαρίζων πάντα τὰ βρώματα. See crit. note. The happy restoration of the true reading makes excellent and important sense of a

passage which was reduced almost to nonsense by the false reading.
No intelligible meaning can be given to καθαρίζον, "purging all
meats" (A.V.). "*This He said*, making all meats clean" (R.V.)
is the comment of the Evangelist, who saw that Christ's words
abolished the distinction between clean and unclean food, even when
made by the Law. We have similar remarks iii. 30, v. 8. Origen
and Chrysostom have this reading and meaning, while Gregory
Thaumaturgus calls our Lord ὁ σωτὴρ ὁ πάντα καθαρίζων τὰ βρώματα.
Miller's Scrivener, ii. pp. 336 f. So also Field.

20. **ἔλεγεν δέ.** The Lord's words are resumed after the interjected
remark of the Evangelist.

21. **ἔσωθεν γάρ.** Nothing that comes from without brings moral
pollution, but a great deal that comes from within may do so, pro-
ceeding not ἐκ τῆς κοιλίας, but ἐκ τῆς καρδίας. Deut. xxiii. 23 has
a germ of this; τὰ ἐκπορευόμενα διὰ τῶν χειλέων φυλάξῃ. Cf. Mt. xii.
35 = Lk. vi. 45, and Mt. xxiii. 25 = Lk. xi. 39; and see on ὁ ἔξω and
ὁ ἔσω ἄνθρωπος, 2 Cor. iv. 16. Syr-Sin., like Mt., omits the superfluous
ἔσωθεν. Cf. i. 32, 42, ii. 23, vi. 25, where Syr-Sin. omits what is
superfluous.

οἱ διαλογισμοὶ οἱ κακοί. *The thoughts that are evil* is the genus
of which twelve species are enumerated, six in the plur. and six in the
sing. In N.T. διαλογισμός is almost always bad thought and generally
plur., but in LXX. it is sometimes used of the thoughts of God (Ps.
xl. 5, xcii. 5). Of the twelve evil things in Mk, Mt. omits seven, and
he adds ψευδομαρτυρίαι. In Gal. v. 19—21 we have sixteen or seventeen
sins, of which only two or three are in Mk; in Wisd. xiv. 25, 26, fifteen
or sixteen, of which five are in Mk; in Didache v. 9, twenty-two, of
which six are in Mk. These catalogues strikingly illustrate the multi-
plicity of evil. There is no classification of the vices, such as we
should have in a treatise on ethics. Both Mk and Mt. begin, where
all sin begins, in the region of thought. Then Mt. follows the order
of the Commandments, sixth to ninth.

22. **πλεονεξίαι.** Efforts to get more than one's due, forms of
selfishness; see on 2 Cor. ix. 5 and cf. Lk. xii. 15; Col. iii. 5. In
Rom. i. 29 we have πλεον· coupled with πονηρία.

δόλος. Conspicuous in Christ's enemies (iii. 6, 22, xiv. 1); the
true Israelite has none of it (Jn i. 48).

ἀσέλγεια. Unblushing licentiousness defying public opinion, such
as was seen at the court of Antipas (vi. 22 f.). Like ὕβρις, it cares
nothing for the feelings of others. Vulg. has *impudicitia* here.

ὀφθαλμὸς πονηρός. A belief in the "evil eye," which brings ill to
the person or thing on which it rests, seems to be almost universal in

savage and half-civilized nations. But belief in a person whose look
blighted without his willing it, the Italian *jettatore*, is not found in
Scripture. There the ἀνὴρ βάσκανος (Prov. xxiii. 6, xxviii. 22) is
envious, jealous, and grudging, and his "evil eye" is φθόνος and
πλεονεξία combined; ὀφθαλμὸς πονηρὸς φθονερὸς ἐπ' ἄρτῳ, "an evil eye
is envious over bread" (Ecclus. xiv. 8, 10; cf. xxxi. 12—14; Tobit
iv. 7; Deut. xv. 9, xxviii. 54, 56). See on 2 Cor. ix. 6, 7, and on the
whole subject F. T. Elworthy, *Evil Eye* (1895); Lightfoot on Gal.
iii. 1.

βλασφημία. Not "blasphemy" (A.V.), but *railing* (R.V.), or
"backbiting," καταλαλία. See on 2 Cor. xii. 20. In 1 Pet. ii. 1 we
have φθόνους καὶ πάσας καταλαλίας, which is much the same as ὀφθ.,
πον. and βλασφημία.

ὑπερηφανία. Here only in N.T., but freq. in LXX. See esp.
Ecclus. x. 7, 12, 18. It is the sin of the "superior" person, who
loves to make himself conspicuous and "sets all others at nought"
(Lk. xviii. 9). The ὑπερήφανοι are condemned Lk. i. 51; Rom. i. 30;
2 Tim. iii. 2; 1 Pet. v. 5; Jas. iv. 6, the last two being quotations
from Prov. iii. 32. In the Psalms of Solomon, ὑπερηφανία is often
used of the insolent pride of the heathen as opponents of Jehovah.

ἀφροσύνη. The fool in Scripture (ἄφρων, μωρός, ἀνόητος, ἄνοφος)
is one who does not know the moral value of things; he thinks that
sin is a joke, and mocks at those who treat it seriously. Hence the
severity with which he is condemned. In the Shephord of Hermas
there is much about ἀφροσύνη, *Man.* v. ii. 4, *Sim.* vi. v. 2, 3, ix. xv. 3,
xxii. 2, 3. It renders other vices incurable.

24—30.　THE SYROPHOENICIAN WOMAN.

Mt. xv. 21—28.

24. 'Εκεῖθεν δέ. See crit. note. Here the unusual δέ marks the
transition to different scenes and different work. Out of 88 sections
in Mk, only 6 have δέ at the outset, while 80 begin with καί.

ἀναστὰς ἀπῆλθεν. Cf. x. 1. Mt. has ἀνεχώρησεν. Christ is
retiring once more from the hostility which His teaching provoked
(iii. 7) and from the pressure of inconsiderate followers (vi. 31). His
hour is not far off, but it is not yet come, and He must have opportunity for giving further instruction to the Twelve. 'Αναστάς refers to
the change of place rather than the change of posture, viz. sitting
to teach; ἐκεῖθεν means "from Capernaum," not "from a seat."
Sitting has not been mentioned.

εἰς τὰ ὅρια Τύρου. Cf. v. 17; Mt. ii. 16. Tyre had been independent since B.C. 126, and Pompey had confirmed the independence, but Augustus had curtailed it B.C. 20. *The borders of Tyre* [*and Sidon*] are called Φοινίκη in LXX. and Acts, but nowhere in the Gospels. Some of the inhabitants had been attracted to the Lake to see Jesus (iii. 8), and, like the Gerasenes, they were probably pagan (Joseph. *c. Apion.* i. 13). Christ now visits their country, which was 40 or 50 miles from Capernaum, to escape publicity. Christ had forbidden the disciples to go to the Gentiles; they were to devote themselves to the house of Israel (Mt. x. 5). He here takes them to the Gentiles, yet not to teach the Gentiles, but to find quiet for being taught by Him themselves. It is only by setting aside the plain statements of Mk that it can be maintained that Christ came to this place for one purpose only,—" an extraordinary example of persevering faith." Cf. ix. 30.

οὐδένα ἤθελεν γνῶναι. "He wished to know no one " is not a probable rendering; *would have no one know it* is doubtless right. He did so, not because He feared being denounced by the Scribes for mixing with heathen (Theoph.), but because He wished to avoid interruption.

οὐκ ἠδυνάσθη λαθεῖν. Mt. characteristically omits the statement that Christ was unable to do what He wished. He could not be hid, because some who had seen Him in Galilee recognized Him. The double augment is Epic and Ionic. Blass, § 24. The aor. infin. is normal; see on i. 40.

25. ἀλλ' εὐθὺς ἀκούσασα. See crit. note. "On the contrary, a woman who had heard about Him came at once." For the superfluous αὐτῆς see on i. 7; the pleonasm is specially common after relatives (Rev. iii. 8, vii. 2, xiii. 8). It is found in modern Greek.

26. Ἑλληνίς, Συροφοινίκισσα τῷ γένει. *A Greek-speaking woman, a Phoenician of Syria by race.* In this context, Ἑλληνίς can hardly mean anything else (Acts xvii. 12). She spoke Greek, but she was not a Greek. The conversation, like that with Pilate, would be in Greek. Syr-Sin. has "a *widow*, from the borders of Tyre of Phoenicia." These Phoenicians came from the Canaanites, and Mt. calls her Χαναναία. The *Clem. Hom.* (ii. 19, iii. 73, iv. 6) calls her Justa, and her daughter Bernice. Syr-Sin. omits Ἑλληνίς and τῷ γένει.

ἠρώτα αὐτὸν ἵνα. See on iii. 9. The change from aor. (προσέπεσεν) to imperf. is accurate. Mt. gives her words, in which she addresses Him as "Son of David," an address which Mk does not record until the healing of Bartimaeus, near the time of the Passion (x. 47, 48). In Mt. the woman makes three appeals, of which Mk

omits one and also the appeal of the disciples that He would grant
her request and send her away.

27. ἔλεγεν. Mt. again substitutes εἶπεν, as in *v.* 14.
Ἄφες πρῶτον χορτασθῆναι τὰ τέκνα. See on vi. 42 and cf. x. 14.
In xv. 36 we have the subj. after ἄφετε. "The children" are the Jews,
but πρῶτον implies that the others will have their turn (Jn x. 16, xii.
32, xvii. 20; Acts i. 8, xiii. 47). This important πρῶτον is omitted in
Mt. It mitigates the harsh refusal.

ἐστιν καλόν. The expression is freq. in Mk. Cf. ix. 5, 42, 43, 45,
47, xiv. 21. Christ's reply illustrates the principle that, where faith
is strong, He seems to hold aloof, to bring the faith to perfection;
whereas weak faith is encouraged (v. 36, ix. 23).

τοῖς κυναρίοις. The diminutive is another mitigation. The Gentiles are not called "dogs" but "doggies," not outside scavengers
(Ps. lix. 7, 15), but household companions (τὰ κυνίδια τῆς οἰκίας, Orig.).
In late Greek, diminutives sometimes lose their force, *e.g.* ὠτάριον
(xiv. 47), ὠτίον (Mt. xxvi. 51); but the dimin. has point here. Contrast κύνες (Mt. vii. 6; Phil. iii. 2; Rev. xxii. 15). Vulg. spoils this
by having *canibus* in Christ's Saying and *catelli* in her reply.

28. ἡ δὲ ἀπεκρίθη καὶ λέγει. The ἀπεκρίθη is not mere amplification; it was an answer and a witty answer. She seizes on Christ's
repelling words and turns them into an argument in her favour:
δραξαμένη τῶν τοῦ Χριστοῦ ῥημάτων, ἀπ' αὐτῶν πλέκει συνηγορίαν
ἑαυτῆς (Euthym.). The historic pres. is recognized so completely
as historic that it can be combined with an aor. See on viii. 29
sub fin.

Ναί, κύριε· καὶ τὰ κυνάρια. *Yea, Lord, and the doggies*; not "*yet*
the dogs" (A.V.), nor "*even* the dogs" (R.V.). She fully assents to
the Lord's utterance and carries it on to her own conclusion; "Quite
so, Lord; and in that case I may have a crumb." Mt. has καὶ γάρ,
giving an additional reason for her request. Ναί—ἀμήν, but without
the religious tone of the Hebrew word (2 Cor. i. 20; Rev. i. 7, xxii. 20).
Syr-Sin. has "the crumbs which are over from the children's table."
The words may mean the crumbs thrown by the children to their pets.
In N.T., ἐσθ. ἐκ (Jn vi. 26, 50, 51; 1 Cor. ix. 7, xi. 28; etc.) is more
common than ἐσθ. ἀπό (Gen. ii. 16, iii. 1, 2, 5).

29. Διὰ τοῦτον τὸν λόγον. The Lord commends the ready reply,
and admits that in the argument she has won: διὰ τὸν λόγον, ᾧτινι
πρὸς συνηγορίαν ἐχρήσω συνετῶς ἄγαν (Euthym.). Like the centurion
(Mt. viii. 5—13), she believes that Christ can heal at a distance, and,
like him, she wins Christ's admiring approval (Mt. xv. 28). This is
the only case in Mk in which Christ heals at a distance.

30. ἀπελθοῦσα. His assurance is enough, as in the case of the royal official; see on Jn iv. 50, 52.

βεβλημένον ἐπὶ τὴν κλίνην. Like the demoniac boy (ix. 26), she was suffering from exhaustion after the final convulsion. The perf. part. is accurate.

This crumb, won from our Lord by the heathen woman's "shamelessness" (Lk. xi. 8), pertinacity (Lk. xviii. 2—5), and faith (Lk. vii. 9), remains isolated. He at once returns to the principle of feeding the children first.

31—37. RETURN TO DECAPOLIS.

HEALING OF A DEAF STAMMERER.

Cf. Mt. xv. 29—31.

31. ἐκ τῶν ὁρίων Τύρου ἦλθεν διὰ Σιδῶνος εἰς τ. θαλ. This means a very long circuit; about 20 or 30 miles northward to Sidon, then eastward and southward, till He reached the E. shore of the Lake. He would cross the Leontes twice, first between Tyre and Sidon, and again between Libanus and Anti-Libanus, but there is no hint as to where the second crossing took place. The object of the long circuit was to gain the retirement necessary for the training of the Twelve. He had twice failed in securing this (vi. 31—34, vii. 24).

διὰ Σιδῶνος. See crit. note. The other reading avoids the statement that He entered a city that was wholly heathen.

Δεκαπόλεως. He is once more in or near the country of the Gerasenes, where the healed demoniac has been acting as a pioneer (v. 20).

32. κωφὸν καὶ μογιλάλον. Deaf people, being unable to hear the sounds which they make, often speak very imperfectly, and sometimes cease to attempt to speak at all. Mt. is here very different; instead of a single healing he gives us an indefinite number of various kinds. Μογιλάλος occurs here only in N.T., and Is. xxxv. 6 only in LXX. In Exod. iv. 11, LXX. has δύσκωφος, the Heb. in both places being the same. Many MSS. have μογγιλάλον, as if from μογγός, "with harsh voice," a rare word; μόγις λαλῶν is the true derivation.

παρακαλοῦσιν. The man could not speak for himself and his friends act for him, as in the case of the paralytic (ii. 3—5). See on viii. 22.

ἐπιθῇ αὐτῷ τ. χεῖρα. Cf. v. 23, vi. 5. Christ does more than this, apparently in order to secure faith on the man's part.

33. ἀπολαβόμενος. It was necessary to free the man from all distraction; this taking him apart and the using of appropriate means increased his confidence in Christ's goodwill and power. Spittle was believed to be remedial; see on Jn ix. 6. Syr-Sin. has "He led him from the multitude, and put His finger, and spat in his ears, and touched his tongue." Cf. viii. 23; not v. 37.

34. ἀναβλέψας. Praying for help; Jn xi. 41.

ἐστέναξεν. Contrast the strong compound (ἀναστενάξας) used of the unbelief of the Pharisees (viii. 12). Signs of Christ's perfect humanity are again evident; see on iii. 5 and Jn xi. 38.

'Εφφαθά. Aramaic with a translation; see on v. 41. Deaf people understand what is spoken by watching the lips of the speaker, and a word like Ephphatha could easily be read from the lips. "Both the word and the use of saliva passed at an early time into the Baptismal rite as practised at Milan and Rome" (Swete).

διανοίχθητι. Lucian (*Contemplantes* 21) uses this compound of opening the ears; ὡς μηδ' ἂν τρυπάνῳ ἔτι διανοιχθῆναι αὐτοῖς τὰ ὦτα. Vulg. has *adaperire*, which Curtius (ix. vii. 24) uses of the ears; *adaperire aures ad criminationem*.

35. ἠνοίγησαν. Cf. Mt. xx. 33; Acts xii. 10; Rev. xi. 19, xv. 5.

ἀκοαί. See on i. 28.

ὁ δεσμὸς τῆς γλώσσης. We need not think of an actual ligament; he was released from the impediment in speech caused by his deafness. Deissmann (*Light*, pp. 306 f.) gives instances of spells to bind the tongue. But here there is no hint that the man was obsessed. The release took place once for all (aor.); his speaking articulately continued (imperf.).

36. διεστείλατο. See on v. 19 and 43. He gave the charge once; and then, the more He repeated it (διεστέλλετο), the more they continued to disregard it (ἐκήρυσσον). The comparative is sometimes strengthened by μᾶλλον (2 Cor. vii. 13; Phil. i. 23), sometimes by ἔτι (Heb. vii. 15), and περισσεύω may have both (Phil. i. 9). But here μᾶλλον might mean *potius*, "instead of being silent they published it more exceedingly." These commands to be silent were usually disregarded, but that does not prove that they ought not to have been given. The Decalogue is not abrogated because of man's disobedience. Wrede (*Messiasgeheimnis*, p. 133) sees a contradiction between this and *v.* 33. But *v.* 33 does not say that Christ took the man away from everybody. No doubt some of the crowd followed, and they were people who previously had seen little or nothing of His work as a Healer. They would naturally be very demonstrative.

37. ὑπερπερισσῶς. Here only in Bibl. Grk, and perhaps nowhere else. See on 2 Cor. vii. 4.

ἐξεπλήσσοντο. See on i. 22. This is simple history; Mk is not suggesting in an allegory the conversion of the Gentiles. He has not told us that the crowd was composed of Gentiles.

ποιεῖ. Mt. seems to have understood this as implying a number of miracles, and they appear to be required by this verse and to explain the great multitude in viii. 1.

ἀλάλους λαλεῖν. The combination of words is doubtless delibe-rate; *the speechless to speak.* Cf. ix. 24; Is. xxxv. 5. Syr-Sin. has "He maketh the deaf-mutes to hear and to speak."

CHAPTER VIII.

1. πάλιν πολλοῦ (אBDGLMNΔ 33) rather than παμπόλλου (AEF etc.), a word not found elsewhere in Bibl. Grk. אABDLΔΠ omit ὁ Ἰησοῦς. See on v. 13.

2. ἡμέραι τρεῖς (אALNΓΠ) rather than ἡμέραις τρισίν (B) or ἡμέρας τρεῖς (Δ), which look like grammatical corrections.

3. καί τινες (אBLΔ) rather than τινὲς γάρ (ANXΓΠ). ἀπὸ μακρόθεν (אBDLΔ) rather than μακρόθεν (ANXΓΠ). εἰσίν (BLΔ) rather than ἥκασιν (אADN) or ἥκουσιν (EFG etc.).

4. As in iv. 21, ὅτι is omitted in most authorities, but is probably original (BLΔ).

6. παραγγέλλει (אBDLΔ) rather than παρήγγειλεν (ACNXΓΠ). παρατιθῶσιν (אBCLMΔ) rather than παραθῶσιν (ΔDNΓΠ).

8. καὶ ἔφαγον (אBCLΔ) rather than ἔφαγον δέ (ANXΓΠ). See on i. 14.

9. אBLΔ omit οἱ φαγόντες.

13. אBCDLΔ omit εἰς τὸ πλοῖον after πάλιν ἐμβάς. Hence the italics in R.V.

16. אBDL omit λέγοντες after ἀλλήλους.

17. אBCDLΔ omit ἔτι.

21. οὔπω (אCKLΔΠ) rather than πῶς οὔπω (ADMX) or πῶς οὐ (BΓ,d). Note the difference between D and d.

22. ἔρχονται (אᶜBCDLᴬΛ 33) rather than ἔρχεται (א*ANXΓΠ).

23. βλέπεις (BCD*Δ) rather than βλέπει (אAD²LNΓΠ).

24. ὅτι ὡς δένδρα ὁρῶ περιπατοῦντας (אABC*LΓΔΠ) rather than ὡς δεν. περιπ. (C²D, Versions).

25. ἐνέβλεπεν (אᶜBLΔ) rather than ἐνέβλεψεν (ACΓΠ). ἅπαντα (אB*LΔ) rather than ἅπαντας (AC²ΓΠ).

26. The confusion in this verse is great; see WH., *Introd.* § 140. אBL omit μηδὲ εἴπῃς κ.τ.λ.

28. εἶπαν αὐτῷ λέγοντες (אBCLΔ) rather than ἀπεκρίθησαν (ANXΓΠ). ὅτι εἷς (אBC*L) rather than ἕνα (AC³ΓΔΠ).

29. ἐπηρώτα αὐτούς (אBC*DLΔ) rather than λέγει αὐτοῖς (AC²NXΓΠ).

31. ὑπό (אBCDLΠ) rather than ἀπό (AC²NXΓΠ). μετὰ τρεῖς ἡμέρας (אABCD etc.) rather than τῇ τρίτῃ ἡμέρᾳ (dg Arm. Aeth.). Cf. ix. 31, x. 34.

33. καὶ λέγει (אBCLΔ) rather than λέγων (ADΓΠ).

34. εἴ τις (אBC*DLΔ) rather than ὅστις (AC²ΓΠ).

36. ὠφελεῖ (אBL) rather than ὠφελήσει (ACDΓΔΠ). κερδῆσαι... ζημιωθῆναι (אBL) rather than ἐὰν κερδήσῃ...ζημιωθῇ (ACDΓΔΠ).

37. τί γάρ (אBLΔ) rather than ἢ τί (ACΓΠ). δοῖ (אB) rather than δώσει (ACDΓΠ).

1—9. THE FEEDING OF THE FOUR THOUSAND.

Mt. xv. 32—39.

1. Ἐν ἐκείναις τ. ἡμ. During the concluding part of the journey mentioned in vii. 31. The asyndeton is rare in Mk; cf. x. 28. Here D, Syr-Sin. and Lat-Vet. insert δέ, while in x. 28 D, Latt. Syrr. insert καί.

πάλιν πολλοῦ ὄχλου. See crit. note. The people of Decapolis had heard of His fame (v. 19; Mt. iv. 25) and both Jews and Gentiles would flock to Him when they heard that He was healing in the neighbourhood.

μὴ ἐχόντων. For μή cf. ii. 4, vi. 34, xii. 21, 24.

προσκαλεσάμενος. Here, as in Jn's account of the 5000, our Lord takes the initiative.

2. Σπλαγχνίζομαι. Nowhere else does Christ say that He feels compassion, although this is often said of Him; i. 41, vi. 34, ix. 22. He is continuing His training of the Twelve. He tells them His own feelings and points out the need of help. What do they suggest?

ἡμέραι τρεῖς. See crit. note. We can make ἡμέραι τρεῖς grammatical by taking προσμένουσιν and ἔχουσιν as datives with εἰσίν understood. More probably ἡμέραι τρεῖς is a parenthetic nominative, as in Lk. ix. 28; cf. Acts v. 7; also ἤδη αἱ ἡμέραι ἐρχόμεναι τὰ πάντα ἐπελήσθη (Eccles. ii. 16). In such cases the insertion of "and" smooths the construction; "There are now three days *and* they are attending Me and have nothing to eat." In Josh. i. 11 the καί is inserted; ἔτι τρεῖς ἡμέραι καὶ ὑμεῖς διαβαίνετε τὸν Ἰορδάνην τοῦτον. J. H. Moulton, p. 70. Mt., who sometimes improves the awkward constructions in Mk, leaves this unchanged, as if it had no need of correction. D has ἡμέραι τρεῖς εἰσιν ἀπὸ πότε ὧδέ εἰσιν, *triduum est ex quo hic sunt*; so also a b i.

προσμένουσίν μοι. Cf. προσμένειν τῇ χάριτι τοῦ θεοῦ (Acts xiii. 43); οἱ πιστοὶ ἐν ἀγάπῃ προσμενοῦσιν αὐτῷ (Wisd. iii. 9). BD omit μοι:

cf. Acts xviii. 18. "Three days" would mean that "they have been with Me since the day before yesterday," a much longer time than in the case of the 5000, which was hardly a whole day.

τί φάγωσιν. Cf. vi. 35 and Lk. xvii. 8.

3. ἐὰν ἀπολύσω αὐτούς. This looks like a reference to the suggestion made by the disciples in the former case (vi. 36). Have they anything better to suggest now?

νήστεις. In class. Grk νήστιδες (Aesch. *Ag.* 194, 1622) or νήστιες (Hom. *Od.* xvii. 370): cf. ἔρεις (? Tit. iii. 9) for ἔριδες: νῆστις (אΔ) is simply bad spelling. Blass, § 8. 3.

εἰς οἶκον αὐτῶν. Cf. *v.* 26; the omission of the art. is Hebraistic. Blass, § 46. 9.

ἐκλυθήσονται. *Deficient* (Vulg.). In Gal. vi. 9 and Heb. xii. 3, 5 (from Prov. iii. 11) the verb is used of faintness of spirit; in LXX. of bodily faintness (1 Sam. xiv. 28; 2 Sam. xvi. 2, xvii. 2; etc.). See crit. notes.

4. ὅτι Πόθεν. The ὅτι is recitative; see crit. note. Syr-Sin. has "Whence art Thou able?" The disciples' question is urged as an argument for regarding this miracle as a doublet of vi. 34—44. Could the disciples, who had seen how the 5000 were fed, have made such a reply? They would have said, "*Thou canst feed them.*" Their question diffidently suggests this; they confess their own powerlessness and leave the solution to Him. Note the emphatic ἡμῖν in Mt. "How can *we* have enough food?" Moreover, Christ does not rebuke them. They were still dull of apprehension (*v.* 16), and were sometimes afraid to ask questions (ix. 32).

χορτάσαι ἄρτων. Cf. τοὺς πτωχοὺς αὐτῆς χορτάσω ἄρτων (Ps. cxxxii. 15). The gen. after verbs of filling is freq. (xv. 36). Blass, § 36. 4.

ἐρημίας. Cf. 2 Cor. xi. 26; Heb. xi. 38. The more usual term is ἡ ἔρημος or ἔρημος τόπος.

5. ἠρώτα. The imperf. is probably conversational; Mt. has λέγει. See notes on vi. 38 f. The first aor. εἶπα is freq. in class. Grk.

6. παραγγέλλει. See crit. note. Mk twice keeps the fishes distinct from the bread where Mt. combines them; moreover, Mk has εὐχαριστήσας of the bread and εὐλογήσας of the fishes, perhaps without difference of meaning, but marking the blessing and distribution of the bread as the main thing.

7. εἶχαν. So אBDΔ. Cf. Rev. ix. 8 and 2 Jn 5; also παρεῖχαν, Acts xxviii. 2.

ἰχθύδια. Like κυνάρια (vii. 27, 28), this diminutive has its proper force; *small fishes.*

8. περισσεύματα. As in the former miracle, there was enough and to spare, and what was over was carefully gathered up.

ἑπτὰ σφυρίδας. The twelve κόφινοι corresponded with the twelve disciples, each having one. It is mere coincidence that the σφυρίδες are the same in number as the ἄρτοι. Σφυρίς (v. 20; Mt. xv. 37, xvi. 10; Acts ix. 25) is well attested as the N.T. form of σπυρίς, and the aspirate is vernacular. Both forms, with σφυρίδιον and σπυρίδιον, are found in papyri. Deissmann, *Bib. St.* pp. 158, 185. A σπυρίς (σπεῖρα) was probably woven of twigs or rushes, and might hold a man (Acts ix. 25). The marked difference of the words for "baskets" in the narratives of the two miracles, and also in the allusions to them afterwards (vv. 19, 20; Mt. xvi. 9, 10), is one of the strongest arguments against the identification of the two. And here there is no excitement after the miracle; Jesus does not force the disciples to go away without Him, but they leave quietly together. Yet the possibility that we are dealing with doublets must be admitted. All that is certain is that Mk believed in two miraculous feedings. The silence of Lk. proves nothing; he makes no use of this portion of Mk. See the Westminster Comm. on Mt. Mt., as often, emphasizes the magnitude of the miracle; but he does not report that the multitude (in which many were heathen) saw in Jesus the Messianic King.

10—13. Another Attack of the Pharisees.

Mt. xv. 39 b—xvi. 5 a.

10. εἰς τὸ πλοῖον. *Into the boat* which He often used (iii. 9, iv. 36, vi. 32). Syr-Sin. has "He went up and *sat in* the ship"; and again in v. 13, "He left them again and *sat in* the ship."

εἰς τὰ μέρη Δαλμανουθά. Mt. says εἰς τὰ ὅρια Μαγαδάν. Neither Dalmanutha nor Magadan is known, and in both Gospels there are differences of reading. In Mt. we have "Magedan," "Magdala," and "Magdalan"; here we have "Malegada" and "Magaida." Dalman (*Words*, p. 66) conjectures "Magalutha" as the original name, which was corrupted and corrected in a variety of ways. Syr-Sin. has "the *hill* of Magdan." If there were two places, they must have been near to one another, but we do not know on which side of the Lake either of them was. Hastings, *D.B.*, art. "Magdan"; *Enc. Bibl.* 985, 1635, 2894.

11. ἐξῆλθον. As if from an ambush.

οἱ Φαρισαῖοι. Mt. adds the Sadducees, and he does so six times. Mk and Lk. mention the Sadducees only once, Jn not at all. *They* *began* once more *to question with Him*; for some time He had escaped them. See on i. 27.

σημεῖον ἀπὸ τοῦ οὐρανοῦ. A voice, a return of the manna or of the Shechinah, the sun and the moon to stand still. They believed that with the help of Beelzebub He could work "signs" on earth, but Satanic agency would be powerless in heaven (Theoph.). This demand was made more than once (Mt. xii. 38, xvi. 1). Lk xi. 15, 16 gives one occasion and Mk here gives the other. Such a challenge would be likely to be repeated; but the popular taste for miracles is not encouraged by Christ (see on Jn iv. 48, xx. 29) and is disparaged by St Paul (1 Cor. i. 22). Deissmann, *Light from the Ancient East*, p. 393.

πειράζοντες αὐτόν. They did not want to be convinced that He *was* the Messiah; they wanted material for proving that He was not. Unconsciously, they were renewing the temptation in the wilderness. Note the combination of participles. See on i. 15.

12. ἀναστενάξας. "Sighed from the bottom of His heart"; stronger than στενάζω (vii. 34; Rom. viii. 23; etc.), and here only in N.T. In Lam. i. 4 of the sighing of Zion's priests; Ecclus. xxv. 18 of the husband of a wicked wife. Syr-Sin. has "He was troubled in spirit." Cf. ἀνακρίνω, ἀναλύω, ἀναπαύω. Once more we have evidence of the reality of Christ's human nature; see on iii. 5.

τῷ πνεύματι. The higher part of His being, which was distressed by moral obliquity; see on ii. 8.

Τί ἡ γενεὰ αὕτη; He is not asking for information, but expressing regret. See on Jn ii. 23—25, x. 38, xl. 45. His own generation (*v.* 38, xiii. 30; Mt. xi. 16, xii. 41—45; Lk. xi. 29, xvii. 25, xxi. 32; not in Jn) was as wrong-headed towards Him, as the generation to which Moses belonged was towards him (Deut. i. 35, xxxii. 5, 20). As usual, Mt. omits a question which seems to imply that Christ needed to be informed; see on v. 30.

ἀμὴν λέγω. See on iii. 28.

εἰ δοθήσεται. A Hebraistic mode of making a strong asseveration equivalent to an oath. "May God punish me," or some such thought, is understood; Gen. xiv. 23; Num. xiv. 30; Deut. i. 35; Ps. xcv. 11. From 1 Sam. iii. 17 we see how such a form arose. Elsewhere in N.T. it occurs only in quotations from LXX. (Heb. iii. 11, iv. 3, 5). Blass, § 78. 2. Mt. and Lk. add to "There shall no sign be given" the words "but the sign of Jonah."

13. The situation of Dalmanutha being unknown, we do not know what εἰς τὸ πέραν indicates.

14—21. The Leaven of the Pharisees and the Leaven of Herod.

Mt. xvi. 5 b—12. Cf. Lk. xii. 1.

14. ἐπελάθοντο. *They forgot* (R.V.). This is not quite parallel to v. 8, where "He *had* said" best represents the meaning of the imperf. But Burton (§ 48) supports A.V. in rendering "they *had* forgotten" here.

ἐν τῷ πλοίῳ. According to Mt., what follows took place after they had landed on the other side. The "one loaf" is an unimportant detail which is well remembered. Syr-Sin. has "*not* one loaf."

15. διεστέλλετο. In v. 43, vii. 36, ix. 9 we have the aor., as elsewhere in N.T. The imperf. may mean that the charge was given more than once; or, like εἶχον, it refers to the time in the boat,— they were short of bread and He was saying this; or it may be the conve_sational imperf. Mt. has εἶπεν, again changing imperf. to aor.

βλέπετε ἀπό. Not "look away from," but "look and turn away from," "consider and avoid." Cf. φυλάσσεσθε ἀπό (Lk. xii. 15), προσέχετε ἀπό (Mt. vii. 15), φοβηθῆτε ἀπό (Mt. x. 28), and see on αἰσχυνθῶμεν ἀπό (1 Jn ii. 28). This pregnant constr. is not Hebraistic. In a letter of A.D. 41, βλέπε ἀπό occurs in a warning against dealings with Jews (G. Milligan, *N.T. Documents*, p. 50).

τῆς ζύμης. Leaven works imperceptibly and may represent good (Mt. xiii. 33) or bad (1 Cor. v. 6; Gal. v. 9) influence; Ignatius (*Magnes.* x.) has it of both. But it is generally used of bad influence, fermentation being regarded as corruption; fermentation disturbs, inflates, sours. Hence the careful banishment of it during the Passover. Mt. interprets the leaven of the Pharisees (and Sadducees) as their "doctrine," Lk. (xii. 1) as "hypocrisy," and this might apply to Herod also. Bede gives as part of Herod's leaven *simulatio religionis*. The repetition of τῆς ζύμης shows that the leaven of the Pharisees is different from the leaven of Herod, and perhaps irreligion and moral weakness is meant by the latter. Possibly, in thus hurriedly crossing the Lake, they were avoiding being molested by Herod's emissaries. Cf. Lk. xiii. 31. The two leavens were alike in working against Christ. Mk gives no interpretation, and the different interpretations in Mt. and Lk. point to early conjectures.

16. διελογίζοντο πρὸς ἀλλ. ὅτι. Cf. xi. 31. The ὅτι is recitative not causal. See crit. note.

17. Τί διαλογίζεσθε. D and other witnesses add ἐν ταῖς καρδίαις ὑμῶν (ii. 8), which does not harmonize with πρὸς ἀλλήλους. Their dis-

cussion was audible, and their want of apprehension appears to have
surprised Christ Himself.

οὔπω νοεῖτε. "After all the teaching which you have received
and the experiences you have had, are you still so dull of apprehension?" Cf. iv. 13, 40, vii. 18.

πεπωρωμένην. Mt. again spares the Twelve by omitting this
censure; see on iii. 5, iv. 13, vi. 52. Syr-Sin. has "Even until now
is your heart blinded?" *Ex corde induratio manat in visum auditum
et memoriam* (Beng.).

18. ὀφθαλμοὺς ἔχοντες. From Jer. v. 21; Ezek. xii. 2. This
also is omitted in Mt. Cf. Oxyrh. Logia 3, ὅτι τυφλοί εἰσιν τῇ καρδίᾳ
αὐτῶν καὶ οὐ βλέπουσιν, πτωχοὶ καὶ οὐκ οἴδασιν τὴν πτωχίαν.

καὶ οὐ μνημονεύετε. This may be an independent sentence;
either *And do ye not remember?* (A.V., R.V.), or "And ye do not
remember." More probably it is the principal clause of the sentence
which follows, taken interrogatively; *Do ye not remember when I
brake...how many...ye took up?*

19. ἔκλασα εἰς τ. πεντακισχιλίους. The compound, κατέκλασεν
(vi. 41), is not repeated. The use of εἰς instead of the *dat. comm.*
is freq. in late Greek. Cf. εἰς τοὺς ἁγίους (1 Cor. xvi. 1; 2 Cor. viii. 4,
ix. 1), εἰς τοὺς πτωχούς (Rom. xv. 26), etc. It is found in LXX. and in
papyri. Deissmann, *Bib. St.* pp. 117 f.

κοφίνους. See on *v.* 8 and vi. 43.

λέγουσιν αὐτῷ, Δώδεκα. They remember the facts, but they have
failed to see their significance. They were not likely to forget the
abundant store which they themselves had collected after all had been
satisfied.

21. Οὔπω συνίετε; A repetition of the reproach in *v.* 17. Mt.
lessens the reproach by amplifying the question and suggesting the
answer. In Mk Christ continues His education of the Twelve by
letting them find the answer. Their error was twofold; they did not
see that "leaven" in this connexion must be a metaphor; still
worse, they did not see that One who had fed thousands with a few
loaves and fishes was not likely to be disturbed because, in a brief
cruise, they were ill supplied with bread. They were not only ἀσύνετοι
(vii. 18), but ὀλιγόπιστοι (Mt. xvi. 8). Evidently, the manner of
feeding the multitudes had not greatly impressed the disciples. The
second time they are almost as anxious as the first; and in this third
and trifling difficulty they are anxious again.

22—26. A BLIND MAN HEALED AT BETHSAIDA.

22. Βηθσαϊδάν. Bethsaida Julias, perhaps the only Bethsaida on the Lake; see on vi. 45. D and several Old Latin texts read "Bethany," which is probably an error; but there may have been a Bethany on the Lake.

τυφλόν. The Ephphatha miracle (vii. 32 f.) and this are peculiar to Mk, and they have similarities of detail, some of which may have led Mt. to omit both, because they seem to suggest that Christ had difficulty in effecting the cure. In each case He first isolated the sufferer, and He did not heal merely with a word or a touch; and Mt. may not have liked the use of spittle. Moreover, in this case Christ asks for information, and His success in restoring sight is at first only partial. The parallel extends beyond the two miracles: viii. 1—26 is parallel to vi. 30—vii. 37. We have in each case a voyage, a feeding of a multitude, and a miracle of healing by means of spittle and touch.

φέρουσιν αὐτῷ...παρακαλοῦσιν ἵνα. This wording is in both narratives. Of course φέρουσιν does not mean that they carried him; see on xv. 22.

23. ἐπιλαβόμενος τῆς χειρός. *Ipse ducebat; magna humilitas* (Beng.). Partitive genitive; elsewhere Mk uses κρατήσας (i. 31, v. 41, ix. 27); ἐπιλαμβάνω is a favourite verb with Lk. Cf. vii. 33.

πτύσας εἰς τὰ ὄμματα. Spittle was believed to be good for diseased eyes (see on Jn ix. 6), and the use of it would aid the man's faith. In class. Grk ὄμμα is rare in prose, but it occurs several times in LXX.

ἐπηρώτα. The conversational imperf. See on iv. 10 and v. 9. Christ perceived that the weakness of the man's faith was an obstacle, and He endeavoured to strengthen it. He questioned him ὡς μὴ ὁλόκληρον ἔχοντα τὴν πίστιν (Theoph.).

Εἴ τι βλέπεις; See crit. note. Εἰ in direct questions is rare, except in Lk. (xiii. 23, xxii. 49; Acts i. 6, xix. 2, xxi. 37, xxii. 25). There is no need to supply γινώσκειν θέλω or the like.

24. ἀναβλέψας. The man looked up in order to answer the question; the attempt to stretch forth the withered hand is similar (iii. 5). The context nearly always shows whether ἀναβλέπω means "look up" (vi. 41, vii. 34, xvi. 4) or "recover sight" (x. 51, 52). Here and Jn ix. 11 either meaning is possible. Cf. ἀνάγειν, ἀνακαλεῖν.

ἔλεγεν. Conversational.

Βλέπω τοὺς ἀνθρώπους ὅτι. See crit. note. *I see the men, for I perceive people as trees walking.* His sight is imperfect; he knows that what he sees are men, because they walk, but to him they look like trees. The change from βλέπω to ὁρῶ should be marked as in iv. 12.

25. διέβλεψεν κ.τ.λ. The aorists and the imperf. are accurate, and the three verbs form a climax; " he saw (what he then looked at) perfectly (Mt. vii. 5; Lk. vi. 42), there was complete restoration of sight (iii. 5, ix. 12), and he continued to discern (x. 21, 27, xiv. 67) all things, even at a distance, clearly." The adv. is rare and late. It is possible that the gradual restoration of the man's sight was meant as a lesson to the Twelve, symbolizing the gradual removal of their mental blindness.

26. εἰς οἶκον αὐτοῦ. Cf. ii. 19, v. 11, vii. 30. There is no command to keep silence; see crit. note. But quiet meditation, free from intercourse with curious neighbours, is best for him; and over-exercise of his newly recovered power of sight is guarded against.

Μηδὲ εἰς τ. κώμην εἰσέλθῃς. *Do not even enter into the village* (R.V.). No doubt he could reach his home without doing so. Christ had lamented over the people of Bethsaida for their callousness respecting His mighty works (Mt. xi. 21), and their influence on the newly healed would not be for good. The prohibition is only temporary (aor.). Contrast μηδὲ ὀνομαζέσθω (Eph. v. 3) and μηδὲ ἐσθιέτω (2 Thess. iii. 10), where perpetual abstention is enjoined. In both these passages Vulg. has *nec* instead of *ne quidem* for μηδέ: here it follows a corrupt reading. The reading adopted " is simple and vigorous, and it is unique in N.T. The peculiar initial Μηδέ has the terse force of many sayings as given by St Mark, but the softening into Μή by אּ* shows that it might trouble scribes" (W.H.). Even if there were a second μηδέ, " neither...nor " (A.V.) would be wrong; it should be *not even...nor yet.*

27—30. The Confession of Peter.

Mt. xvi. 13—20. Lk. ix. 18—21.

27. ἐξῆλθεν. He left Bethsaida, which had been rebuilt by Philip the tetrarch and named Julias in honour of the daughter of Augustus, and came to the neighbourhood of Paneas, which had been rebuilt by Philip and named Caesarea in honour of Augustus himself (Joseph. *Ant.* xviii. ii. 1). It was called Καισάρεια ἡ Φιλίππου in order to distinguish it from Κ. Στρατῶνος on the coast. Our Lord is once more going northwards, in order to find quiet for the training of the Twelve and for His own preparation for suffering and death. He may also have been avoiding the dangerous dominions of Antipas, because His

hour was not yet come.　But this time, instead of following the
coast to Tyre and Sidon, He goes inland, up the valley of the Jordan
to one of its sources, near the ancient Laish or Dan.　The name
Paneas (preserved in the modern *Banias*, which is near the old city)
points to a heathen population.　It had its Πανεῖον, a grotto sacred
to Pan, and inscriptions containing Pan's name have been found
in the rocks.　Evidently Christ did not seek this region in order to
preach to the inhabitants.　Since the attempt to make Him a king,
His public preaching, even among Jews, seems to have been less.

ἐπηρώτα.　Conversational; see on iv. 10, v. 9.　Mt. has λέγει.

Τίνα με λέγουσιν οἱ ἄνθρωποι εἶναι; This crucial question shows
that the education of the Twelve is now reaching a high level.　It was
mainly for their sake that He asked it; yet He may have asked for information as to remarks which they had heard when He was not with
them; see on v. 30.　But in any case the question was educational;
it would teach the disciples how little effect their mission had had on
the large majority of the Jews.

28.　εἶπαν αὐτῷ λέγοντες.　Mk alone has the superfluous λέγοντες.
See crit. note and cf. vi. 25, vii. 20.　All these conjectures have
been mentioned before (see on vi. 14, 15); Mt. adds Jeremiah.　It is
remarkable that the opinion that Jesus is the Messiah is not mentioned.　Cf. Jn vi. 14, 15.

29.　Ὑμεῖς δέ.　Here again Christ may be asking for information.
But ye, who know so much of My teaching and work, *who do ye say
that I am?* Their knowing the views of other people showed that the
question had been raised in their minds; cf. iv. 41.　He does not tell
them who He is; He draws the truth from their reflexion, and He
expects better things from them than from other men.

ὁ Πέτρος λέγει.　Πάλιν ὁ Πέτρος, ὁ πανταχοῦ θερμός, προπηδᾷ καὶ
προλαμβάνει (Euthym.).　All three assign the reply to Peter, and it
is in harmony with his character and position that he should answer
for the Twelve—the first time in Mk that he does so.　Cf. Jn vi. 69.
But there is divergence as to the wording of his reply; "Thou art
the Christ" (Mk), "*The Christ* of God" (Lk.), "Thou art *the
Christ*, the Son of the living God" (Mt.).　Mt.'s expansion of the
reply corresponds to his expansion of Christ's question.　In each
case he *interprets* the words used; cf. x. 18, 19, 28—30, 40, xiii. 24.
There may be something of expansion and interpretation in the famous
passage, Mt. xvi. 17—19, which he alone records, but that the whole
is invention is not probable.　Mk's omission of it is intelligible; ἵνα
μὴ δόξῃ χαριζόμενος τῷ Πέτρῳ (Theoph.).　It was not one of the things
which Peter reproduced in his teaching.　Salmon, *The Human*

Element, p. 351. This cannot be regarded as a special revelation to Peter; Peter states the conviction of all, and Christ in the hearing of all accepts it as true. Again, we need not suppose that, until Peter made this confession, the Apostles had no idea that Jesus was the Messiah, but we are sure that from this point they know. The strange combination of the aor. ἀποκριθείς with the pres. λέγει is freq. in Mk (iii. 33, ix. 5, 19, x. 24, xi. 22, 33, xv. 2). Mt. xxv. 40 and Lk. xiii. 25 have the still stranger ἀποκριθεὶς ἐρεῖ. Both occur in LXX. Here, as in iii. 33, Syr-Sin. omits ἀποκριθείς.

30. ἐπιτίμησεν. Cf. i. 25, iii. 12. The beginning and end of this narrative afford evidence of its historical character. A writer of fiction would hardly have taken Christ into heathen territory, and that without representing Him as preaching to the heathen; nor would he have said of Him that He extracted a confession of His Messiahship from His disciples and at once forbade them to publish the fact. The Gospel narrative as a whole shows the reason for both facts.

31—33. THE PASSION FORETOLD ; PETER REBUKED.

Mt. xvi. 21—23. Lk. ix. 22.

31. ἤρξατο διδάσκειν. It was indeed a new beginning. Slowly, fitfully, and still very defectively, the Twelve had been brought by Him to see that He was the promised Messiah; and now He began to teach them that the King and Conqueror whom they had been expecting must suffer shame and death. All three connect this prediction with the confession of Peter, and here was another reason for silence. Peter's ὁ Χριστός was true, but what he and the others understood by ὁ Χριστός was not true. In proclaiming Jesus as the Messiah they would have taught much that was erroneous.

Δεῖ. *Must*, because of the Divine decree. This δεῖ comes to the surface all through the life of Christ from His childhood onwards (Lk. ii. 49), and is especially evident during the later stages (Lk. iv. 43, ix. 22, xiii. 33, xvii. 25, xix. 5, xxii. 37, xxiv. 7, 26, 44). The word is thus used of Christ all through the N.T., but this is the only instance in Mk. The necessity is not of man's making, but of God's; the cause is not man's hostility to Christ, but God's love to man. Man's hostility is God's instrument.

τὸν υἱὸν τοῦ ἀνθρώπου. See on ii. 10, 28. In Mk the title is used eight times in passages which predict the Passion or the Resurrection. It is not so used in "Q."

πολλὰ παθεῖν, *multa pati*. The expression is frequent (v. 26;

Mt. xxvii. 19), esp. of the Passion (ix. 12; Mt. xvi. 21; Lk. ix. 22,
xvii. 25). Not in Jn, who neither in Gospel nor Epistles uses πάσχω.
What follows forms a climax; Passion, Rejection, Death—the second
causing the third. If the hierarchy had not absolutely rejected Him,
Pilate would have let Him go.

ἀποδοκιμασθῆναι. *Be rejected* after investigation. Δοκιμασία was
the scrutiny which an official elected at Athens had to undergo to see
whether he was qualified to take office. The Sanhedrin held a δοκιμασία with regard to Jesus, and decided that He was not qualified
to be the Messiah (xii. 10; 1 Pet. ii. 4, 7). The expression is probably
taken from Ps. cxviii. 22. But the idea of rejection *after investigation*
is not in the Hebrew word used there and eleven times in Jeremiah,
where it is generally, but not always, rendered by ἀποδοκιμάζω. Other
renderings are ἀπωθέομαι and ἐξουδενόω, and its meaning is not so
much rejecting after scrutiny as rejecting with contempt. Hort on
1 Pet. ii. 4.

ὑπὸ τῶν πρεσβυτέρων κ.τ.λ. The Sanhedrin is mentioned in all
its fulness, each of its three constituent parts having the article,
which should be repeated in English; cf. xi. 27, xiv. 43, 53. It is as
if each of the three classes had given a separate vote for rejection. In
Mt. xvi. 21 and Lk. ix. 22 the three are under one article, as forming
one body. The ἀρχιερεῖς are usually placed first, as including the
high-priest and (at this time) the ex-high-priests; but cf. Lk. ix. 22,
xx. 19; Mt. xvi. 21. Very rarely are the ἀρχιερεῖς omitted (Mt. xxvi. 57;
Acts vi. 12).

μετὰ τρεῖς ἡμέρας. So also ix. 31 and x. 34. The expression
may be colloquial, a current phrase for a short time, like our "after
two or three days." Mt. and Lk. change it to the more accurate
τῇ τρίτῃ ἡμέρᾳ, which Syr-Sin. and some other authorities read here.
In Hosea vi. 2, "after *two* days" = "on the third day."

32. παρρησίᾳ, *palam.* Here only in Mk, nowhere in Mt. or
Lk., nine times in Jn, and four in 1 Jn. Mk makes it clear that the
disciples' misapprehension of the prediction, esp. as regards the
Resurrection, was their own fault. Jesus Himself spoke quite clearly
and without reserve. Originally παρρησία was used of unreserved or
fearless *speech*; but this distinction is not always observed (Jn vii. 4,
xi. 54). "With openness" or "clearness" is the meaning here.
On this occasion He used no metaphor or parable, such as He employed ii. 20. See on 1 Jn ii. 28, v. 14, where Vulg. has *fiducia.*

ἐλάλει. He dwelt on this subject for some time. Neither Mk
nor Mt. implies that directly Christ mentioned His sufferings and
death Peter interposed; he had time to consider the matter, and he

acted after some deliberation. There may have been impulsiveness, but not such as blurts out an objection on the spur of the moment. Hence Christ's severe condemnation of him. There seems to have been a reading λαλεῖν or ἐκλαλεῖν, for k has *resurgere et cum fiducia sermonem loqui*. See A. S. Lewis, *Light on the Four Gospels from the Sinai Palimpsest*, p. 67.

προσλαβόμενος. Peter can bear it no longer. From his purely human point of view (*v.* 33), a rejected and murdered Messiah seems to him a monstrous contradiction. He thinks that the Master is making a grave mistake; and so he takes Him aside to remonstrate with Him privately. As in the petition of the Syrophoenician woman, Mt. gives the words of the remonstrance, and Syr-Sin. inserts them here. "Then Simon Cepha, *as though he pitied Him*, said to Him, Be it far from Thee," where in the Syriac there is assonance between "he pitied" and "be it far." There is affection in it, but the affection is altogether misdirected and exhibited in a wrong way. Peter's rather patronizing presumption is at first sight surprising, because he had just led the way in confessing that Jesus was the Messiah; but it is "exquisitely natural" (Lagrange).

33. ἐπιστραφείς. Midd. sense, as in v. 30. This graphic touch, freq. in Lk., is in Mt. also. If Peter's rebuke to Him was given privately, His rebuke to Peter must, for the sake of all, be given openly. It was as He turned that He saw the disciples, from whose company Peter had withdrawn Him. Without ἐπί (Acts ix. 35, xi. 21) or πρός (Lk. xvii. 4; Acts ix. 40) after it, ἐπιστρέφ. means "turn round," not necessarily "turn towards." The other Evangelists use στραφείς of Christ's turning to people. Vulg. spoils the effect of ἐπιτιμᾶν...ἐπετίμησεν by translating *increpare...comminatus est*. The latter is the usual translation.

Ὕπαγε ὀπίσω μου, Σατανά. At the end of the Temptation Christ dismissed the evil one with Ὕπαγε, Σατανᾶ (Mt. iv. 10). He recognizes Satan's influence once more in Peter's suggestion that the Messiah can accomplish His work without suffering and death, which is a repetition of the suggestions made in the wilderness. Mt. says expressly that Ὕπαγε...Σατανᾶ was addressed to Peter, and ὅτι οὐ φρονεῖς must be addressed to him. For the moment Peter has identified himself with Satan, and he is banished with similar decision and severity.

Bede tries to mitigate Peter's error, which he thinks sprang *de pietatis affectu* and could not be attributed to the prompting of the evil one. He admires Peter's taking the Master aside, *ne praesentibus ceteris condiscipulis magistrum videatur arguere*. He would give to

"Satan" its original meaning of "adversary"; in this matter Peter's wishes are opposed to Christ's. Origen and Theophylact go still further from the true meaning when they interpret Ὕπαγε ὀπίσω μου as signifying "Follow Me; conform to My will."

The severity of the rebuke is explained by the severity of the temptation. Christ's prayers during the Agony show what it cost Him to resist the suggestion that the triumphant Τετέλεσται could be reached without suffering, and that the Crown might be won without enduring the Cross. The Divine Δεῖ must be accomplished, but Christ's human soul shrank from the accomplishment, and the thought of escaping it had a dire attractiveness. *D.C.G.* art. "The Character of Christ."

οὐ φρονεῖς τὰ τοῦ θεοῦ. It was God's will that His Son should suffer and die, and Peter was setting his love for his Master in opposition to God's love for His Son and His sons. The Apostle who should have been a support had become an occasion of falling. It is a low type of human affection that forbids those who are loved to suffer in a righteous cause. Conformity to the mind of God is the only safe rule. Cf. Phil. iii. 19. Excepting this Saying and Acts xxviii. 22, φρονεῖν in N.T. is confined to the Pauline Epistles; Rom. viii. 5; Col. iii. 2. But the expression φρονεῖν τά is not specially Pauline; cf. 1 Macc. x. 20, and in Dem. *Phil.* 3 we have οἱ τὰ Φιλίππου φρονοῦντες.

34—ix. 1. THE DUTY OF SELF-SACRIFICE.

Mt. xvi. 24—28.   Lk ix. 23—27.

34. τὸν ὄχλον. Cf. vii. 14. Neither Mt. nor Lk. mentions this multitude which comes thus suddenly upon the scene, but Lk.'s characteristic ἔλεγεν πρὸς πάντας indicates that others besides the Twelve are now present. What follows could be appreciated by many outside the Twelve, and self-denial is for all, not for ministers only. Mt. inserts his favourite τότε, thus making this address follow immediately on the prediction of the Passion. In the East a crowd is easily collected.

Εἴ τις θέλει. See crit. note. *If anyone desires to come after Me;* οὐδένα γὰρ ἄκοντα καταναγκάζει (Euthym.). There is no δεῖ, and εἰ θέλει is put first with emphasis. This "catholic doctrine" (Beng.) is almost *verbatim* the same in all three, and we may believe that it was regarded as one of the chief treasures among Christ's remembered Sayings. It seems to have been in "Q"; Mt. x. 38, 39; Lk. xiv. 26, 27, xvii. 33.

ὀπίσω μου ἐλθεῖν. Quite different from ὑπάγειν ὀπίσω μου (v. 33). Among the crowd, partly heathen, were some who came out of mere curiosity, and others who followed without counting the cost. Who ever desires to be a genuine follower must accept the conditions. The idea of ἀκολουθεῖν now takes the place of μετάνοια (i. 4, 15, vi. 12), and the appeal seems to be made to a select few.

ἀπαρνησάσθω ἑαυτόν. He must give up self-worship and self-will. Self is a home-made idol to be put away (Is. xxxi. 7). He must love God with all his powers and his neighbour as himself. The expression is not found elsewhere in N.T.

ἀράτω τὸν σταυρὸν αὐτοῦ. The same verb is used of Simon of Cyrene (xv. 21). This is the first mention of the cross in Mk and Lk., but Mt. x. 38 is earlier. Jn nowhere uses it in a metaphorical sense. The metaphor would be intelligible and amazing to those who heard it. Varus about B.C. 4 had crucified 2000 rebels (Joseph. *Ant.* XVII. x. 10). Quadratus (*B.J.* II. xii. 6), Gessius Florus (*B.J.* II. xiv. 9) and others (*B.J.* v. xi. 1) crucified many. Lk. adds his characteristic καθ᾽ ἡμέραν to the startling metaphor. If the expansion is his own, it shows much spiritual insight; cf. the change from σήμερον to τὸ καθ᾽ ἡμέραν in the Lord's Prayer. In all five passages it is "*his* cross" or "*his own* cross," which intimates that everyone has a cross that no one else can carry. Here the primary reference is to martyrdom; every disciple must be ready for that. To the Twelve, who had just heard the prediction of the Passion, the parabolic Saying would be much more intelligible than to the rest.

ἀκολουθείτω μοι. "Obey Me without question." It is doubtful whether this is a third condition or a return to ὀπίσω μου ἐλθεῖν, "and in that way he will come after Me." The Saying could hardly have been invented.

35. ὃς γὰρ ἐὰν θέλῃ. *For whosoever would save* (R.V.), or *de oireth to oave.* "Will oave" (A.V.) is too like the simple future, a defect found again in A.V. in Lk. xix. 14; Jn vi. 67, vii. 17, viii. 44. The meaning of ψυχή varies in N.T., and we have no exact equivalent in English. It is (1) the physical life, which animates the flesh and perishes in death, x. 45; (2) the immaterial part of man's nature, which does not perish in death, and which is also called πνεῦμα, Lk. i. 46; (3) where man's nature is regarded as threefold, ψυχή is the lower side of the immaterial part, πνεῦμα being the upper, 1 Thess. v. 23, where see Jowett, Lightfoot, and Milligan. Here the word fluctuates between (1) and (2). "Life" must be kept throughout the three verses, the context showing whether physical life or spiritual life is meant. The sweep of this Saying is immense.

The world thinks that "nothing succeeds like success," and that the chief end of human activity is one's own happiness. Experience confirms Christ in teaching that nothing fails like success, for it is generally disappointing and often depraving to character, and that to seek one's own happiness in all things is a sure way of missing it. Bede gives a good illustration; *Frumentum si servas, perdis; si seminas, renovas.* Cf. Jn xii. 24; 1 Cor. xv. 36.

δς δ' ἄν ἀπολέσει. The fut. indic. may be caused by the preceding ἀπολέσει, but the constr. is found elsewhere both in LXX. (Winer, p. 385) and in N.T. (W.H. *App.* p. 172). Cf. Rev. iv. 9. It is, however, exceptional and anomalous.

ἕνεκεν ἐμοῦ. This important condition is in all three reports of this occasion, but not in Lk. xiv. 26, xvii. 33 or Jn xii. 25. Καὶ τοῦ εὐαγγελίου is peculiar to Mk both here and x. 29; see on i. 15. Syr-Sin. has "and whosoever shall lose his life for My gospel's sake."

36. τί γὰρ ὠφελεῖ. See crit. note and cf. 1 Cor. xiv. 6. It is manifest that self-preservation by means of self-sacrifice is the best policy, *for* of what use is it to win everything if one does not preserve one's life, *i.e.* oneself? For τὴν ψυχὴν αὐτοῦ Lk. has ἑαυτόν. Even in this world, no amount of success can compensate for loss of internal peace or deterioration of character. "For what then have men lost their soul, or for what have those who were on earth exchanged their soul?" (Apocalypse of Baruch, li. 15). The sum total of the visible universe, which is passing away, is poor compensation for the loss of what is invisible and eternal. See Dalman, *Words*, p. 167. A.V. has "profit" for ὠφελ. in Mk and Mt., but "advantage" in Lk.; also "lose" for ζημιωθ. in Mk and Mt., but "cast away" in Lk. The latter verb implies that the supremely successful man pays the *cost* with his life. In itself the verb does not include the idea of punishment; that idea comes from the context.

37. τί γὰρ δοῖ. Cf. παραδοῖ (iv. 29, xiv. 10) and γνοῖ (v. 43). The common interpretation, that nothing can compensate a man for the loss of his higher personal life, may stand. But in that case we ought to have "*take*" rather than "give." Therefore the rendering in Tyndale, Cranmer, and the Genevan deserves consideration, "What shall a man geve to redeme his soule agayne?" So also Coverdale, "What can a man geve, to redeme his soule withall?" When he has forfeited it by sinful folly, what can he pay to get it back? The loss is irrevocable. Ἀντάλλαγμα is "an equivalent in value" (Job xxviii. 15; Ecclus xxvi. 14), esp. a marketable equivalent.

38. ὃς γάρ. This fourth and last step in the reasoning looks
back to the start in *v.* 34, and it takes us beyond the experiences of
this life to the final Judgment. Christ is revealing more and more of
the mysteries of the Kingdom. " The possibilities of irreparable loss
are manifold, *for* whoever is guilty of moral cowardice in reference to
Christ's requirements will have to suffer this loss." *Ce verset est
comme le fond du tableau qui fixe les perspectives* (Lagrange). The
compound ἐπαισχύνομαι is freq. in Paul.

μοιχαλίδι. "Apostate"; the ref. is to spiritual adultery, the
worship of Mammon (Jas iv. 4). The man who dares not make a
stand against this disowning of Christ must be prepared to be dis-
owned at the Judgment. The picture of the Judgment is in accordance
with Jewish ideas, and we cannot safely draw inferences from the details. These verses show—and *v.* 35 is accepted even by Loisy as
authentic—that Christ takes into most solicitous consideration the
future condition of each individual soul.

ὁ υἱὸς τοῦ ἀνθρώπου. See on ii. 10. The contrast with *v.* 31 is
great. There it is the *suffering*, here it is the *glorified* Messiah that is
contemplated. Cf. Lk. xii. 8.

τοῦ πατρὸς αὐτοῦ. Only here and xiv. 36 in Mk does Jesus speak
of God as His Father; cf. xiii. 32. God is the Father of the Son of
Man, and the Son of Man is the Son of God.

μετὰ τῶν ἀγγέλων. Here, as in xii. 25, all three record that our
Lord spoke of Angels as beings that really exist. It is not credible
that all the passages in which His teaching on this subject is recorded
have been corrupted by the introduction of the Evangelists' own
beliefs.

CHAPTER IX.

1. ὧδε τῶν ἑστηκότων (BD*) rather than τῶν ὧδε ἑστ. (ACD²L etc.) from Mt.

3. אBCLΔ omit ὡς χιών (Mt. xxviii. 3) and insert οὕτως before λευκᾶναι (characteristic fulness).

6. ἀποκριθῇ (אBC*LΔ) rather than λαλήσει (ADMN etc.). ἔκφοβοι γὰρ ἐγένοντο (אBDLΔΨ 33) rather than ἦσαν γὰρ ἔκφ. (ΑΝΧΓΠ).

7. אBC etc. omit λέγουσα, from Mt. and Lk.

9. καὶ καταβαινόντων (אBCDLNΔ) rather than καταβ. δέ (ΑΧΓΠ). See on i. 14.

12. אBCLΔ omit ἀποκριθείς. See on v. 9.

14. ἐλθόντες...εἶδον or εἶδαν (אBLΔΨ) rather than ἐλθὼν...εἶδεν (ACDΓΠ).

15. ἐξεθαμβήθησαν (אBCDLΔ) rather than ἐξεθαμβήθη (ΑΓΠ).

16. αὐτούς (אBDLΔΨ) rather than τοὺς γραμματεῖς (ACΓΠ).

17. ἀπεκρίθη αὐτῷ (אBDLΔΨ 33) rather than ἀποκριθεὶς εἶπεν (ACΓΠ).

19. αὐτοῖς (אABDLΔΨ) rather than αὐτῷ (C³Γ): C* omits.

20. συνεσπάραξεν (אBCLΔ 33) rather than ἐσπάραξεν (ΑΓΠΨ).

23. אBC*LΔ omit πιστεῦσαι.

24. אA*BC*LΔ omit μετὰ δακρύων, and אABC*LΨ omit Κύριε.

25. BCDΓ omit ὁ before ὄχλος. Syr-Sin. omits τ. ἀκαθάρτῳ.

28. εἰσελθόντος αὐτοῦ (אBCDLΔ) rather than εἰσελθόντα αὐτόν (ΑΓΠ).

29. אB, k omit καὶ νηστείᾳ. Cf. 1 Cor. vii. 5.

31. μετὰ τρεῖς ἡμέρας (אBC*DLΔΨ) rather than τῇ τρίτῃ ἡμέρᾳ (AC³ΓΠ). Cf. viii. 31.

33. ἦλθον (אBD) rather than ἦλθεν (ACLΓΔΠ). אBCDLΨ omit πρὸς ἑαυτούς.

38. Before αὐτῷ, אBΔΨ read simply ἔφη. אBCLΔΨ omit ὃς οὐκ ἀκολουθεῖ ἡμῖν. ἐκωλύομεν (אBDLΔ) rather than ἐκωλύσαμεν (ACΓΠ), and ἠκολούθει (אBCLΔ) rather than ἀκολουθεῖ.

40. ἡμῶν...ἡμῶν (אBCΔΨ) rather than ὑμῶν...ὑμῶν (ADΓΠ), perhaps from Lk. ix. 50.

9 1]

NOTES

41. ἐν ὀνόματι ὅτι (ABC*LΨ) rather than ἐν τῷ ὀνόματι μου ὅτι (DΔ). There are other variations.

42. אCDΔ omit εἰς ἐμέ after πιστευόντων.

44, 46. אBCLΔ and other authorities omit both verses.

45. אBCLΔΨ omit εἰς τὸ πῦρ τὸ ἄσβεστον.

47. אBDLΔΨ omit τοῦ πυρός.

49. אBLΔ omit καὶ πᾶσα θυσία ἀλὶ ἁλισθήσεται, which comes from Lev. ii. 13.

1. καὶ ἔλεγεν αὐτοῖς. The insertion of this introductory formula indicates a break of some kind. The words that follow can hardly be addressed to the multitude (viii. 34), and they may have been spoken on another occasion. Mt., as often, omits Mk's imperf.

Ἀμὴν λέγω ὑμῖν. See on iii. 28.

εἰσίν τινες ὧδε τ. ἐστ. See crit. note. *There be some here of them that stand by* (R.V.). We have ὁ ἑστηκώς or ὁ ἑστώς of a "by-stander," xi. 5, xv. 35 (?); Jn iii. 29; Acts xxii. 25.

οὐ μὴ γεύσωνται θανάτου. *Shall in no wise taste of death* (R.V.); strong negative, as in v. 41, x. 15, xiii. 2, 19, 30. The metaphor is taken, not from a death-cup, but from the idea of bitterness, a bitterness which to the believer is only a taste; Heb. ii. 9. See on Jn viii. 52. The phrase is not found in O.T. Cf. γεύεσθαι μόχθων (Soph. *Trach.* 1101), γεύεσθαι πένθους (Eur. *Alc.* 1069).

ἕως ἂν ἴδωσιν. Cf. vi. 10, xii. 36; the constr. is freq. in Mt. and Lk.

τὴν βασιλείαν τ. θεοῦ ἐληλυθυῖαν ἐν δυνάμει. Mt. expands this, as he expands viii. 29, and here his expansion is a misinterpretation; he has "till ye see the Son of Man coming in His reign," with obvious ref. to the Second Advent, which viii. 38 suggested to him. Probably, when Mt. wrote, "the reign of God come with power" was understood in that sense. See on i. 15, and Dalman, *Words*, p. 133. That interpretation became untenable when all the Apostles had died before the Second Advent; and then other interpretations became necessary, of which the following are chief. 1. The Transfiguration (so most of the Fathers); 2. The Resurrection and Ascension (Cajetan, Calvin); 3. Pentecost and the Spread of Christianity (Godet, Hahn, Nösgen, Swete); 4. The Destruction of Jerusalem (Wetstein, Alford, Morison, Plumptre); 5. The internal Development of the Gospel (Erasmus). The test of correctness is εἰσίν τινες τ. ἐστ. Among the bystanders are some who will see the reign of God come with power, while others will not. That seems to exclude 2 and 3, unless the absence of Judas is held to justify εἰσίν τινες. The Transfiguration could be meant only in the sense that it was a sort of symbol or earnest of the reign of

God; and "shall in no wise taste of death until" could hardly be
used of an event which was to take place in about a week. No modern
writer seems to adopt it. The destruction of Jerusalem was witnessed by a few of those present, and it swept away Judaism, leaving
Christianity in full possession; Moses and Elijah vanished, and Jesus
only, with His ministers, remained. Possibly no single event is intended, but only the solemn declaration that before long, by the power
of God, the reign of God will be firmly established (Lagrange). In
any case, it is not sound criticism to insist that Mt., who so often
expands Christ's words, alone in this case gives His words correctly,
and that, in saying that some of those present would see the Second
Advent, Christ said what has proved to be untrue. Moreover, we have
to remember that Christ's language, especially on this subject, reflects
the pictorial symbolism of later Judaism. Much of it may be oriental
imagery, setting forth the triumphant success of the Gospel, without
any reference to Christ's return in glory. In particular, ἐν δυνάμει
does not refer to "glory" but to "power," viz. the powerful energy
which was manifested wherever the Gospel was preached.

The perf. ἐλήλυθα occurs nowhere else in Mk and nowhere at all in
Mt. It is fairly freq. in Lk. and Jn, but Lk. omits it here, and his
report of the words is the least eschatological of the three.

2—8. THE TRANSFIGURATION.

Mt. xvii. 1—8. Lk. ix. 28—36.

2. μετὰ ἡμέρας ἕξ. If μετὰ ἡμ. τρεῖς means "on the third day"
(viii. 31), μετὰ ἡμ. ἕξ should mean "on the sixth day." Lk. says
"about eight days," which would be no serious discrepancy, even
"if on the sixth day" were certainly the right meaning. There is
no special point in either "six" or "about eight," and the statement
that there was a week's interval is a mark of historic truth, like
"Legion" in v. 9. Other marks of truth are the good connexions
with what precedes and what follows, the fitness of the position in the
Ministry as a whole, and the injunction to silence, a detail not likely
to be invented. Moreover, there is no parallel in O.T., for the illumination of Moses' face has little similarity. The additional details
given by Lk., coupled with his independent wording, suggest that he
had information besides that which he derived from Mk; and the
mention of the Transfiguration in 2 Pet. i. 16—18 shows what
Christians of that age, whatever the date of 2 Pet. may be, believed
respecting it. Its absence from Jn is no difficulty, for that Gospel
omits so much that had been already sufficiently recorded.

The *manner* of the wonder, as in the feeding of the thousands, eludes us, and it is vain to ask in what way Moses and Elijah were visible and audible to the apostles; but the *significance* of it can in some measure be understood. It encouraged the three witnesses, who had been perplexed and depressed by the announcement that the Messiah must suffer and die; and this encouragement would spread to the other disciples, although for a few months they were not to know the reason for it. It intimated that His Kingdom was not of this world; it was no earthly reign. It is also possible that this foretaste of His glory imparted encouragement to the Messiah Himself, analogous to the strengthening which He received from an Angel, when His sufferings had already begun. Hastings' *D.B.* and *D.C.G.* art. "Transfiguration" and the literature there quoted.

παραλαμβάνει. Cf. iv. 36, v. 40, x. 32.

τὸν Ἰάκωβον καὶ Ἰωάννην. One art. for the pair of brothers. Lk. reverses the order and has no art. See on v. 37.

ἀναφέρει. Not a common use of the verb in class. Grk. In Bibl. Grk its general use is offering to God.

εἰς ὄρος ὑψηλόν. The mountain is nowhere named. The Mount of Olives is an extraordinary conjecture. It is not high, and both before and after the Transfiguration Christ is in or near Galilee. Tabor is the traditional scene, perhaps suggested by Ps. lxxxix. 12. In the Eastern Church the Feast of the Transfiguration (6 August) is sometimes called τὸ Θαβώριον. But there was a fortified village on Tabor (Joseph. B.J. iv. i. 8, ii. xx. 6). Hermon, which is over 9000 ft, is now generally adopted. It could easily be reached from Caesarea Philippi in a day or two. Lk. says that Christ went up the mountain to pray (cf. Mk vi. 46), and that it was during His prayer that the Transfiguration took place.

κατ' ἰδίαν μόνους. Characteristic fulness; Mk alone has the rather superfluous μόνους. He is fond of κατ' ἰδίαν (iv. 34, vi. 31, 32, vii. 33, ix. 2, 28, xiii. 3), which Mt. has here, but not Lk. Syr-Sin. omits κατ' ἰδίαν.

μετεμορφώθη. *Transfiguratus est* (Vulg.). See on 2 Cor. iii. 18, where Vulg. has *transformamur* and neither A.V. nor R.V. has "transfigured." See Lightfoot, *Philippians*, p. 131. The word, avoided by Lk., gives us no sure clue as to the nature of the change.

ἔμπροσθεν. Freq. in Mt. and not rare in Lk. and Jn, but here only in Mk.

3. στίλβοντα. Here only in N.T.; in LXX. of the gleaming of polished metal (Nah. iii. 6; 1 Macc. vi. 39; etc.).

λίαν οἷα γναφεύς κ.τ.λ.　See crit. note.　Again we have a fulness
of description which is in Mk alone, but he omits the brightness of
Christ's face.　Γναφεύς occurs nowhere else in N.T.　Cf. ἄγναφος
(ii. 21; Mt. ix. 16), and the paradoxical ἐλεύκαναν αὐτὰς ἐν τῷ αἵματι
τοῦ ἀρνίου (Rev. vii. 14).

ἐπὶ τῆς γῆς.　Not superfluous; it contrasts earthly with heavenly
whiteness.　Syr-Sin. omits λίαν...λευκᾶναι.

4. ὤφθη.　The word used of the appearances of Christ after the
Resurrection (Lk. xxiv. 34; Acts ix. 17, xiii. 31, xxvi. 16; 1 Cor. xv.
5—8).　The three were thoroughly awake (Lk. ix. 32).　The ὅραμα
(Mt. xvii. 9) was no dream.

Ἠλείας σὺν Μωυσεῖ.　Mt. and Lk. have "Moses and Elijah,"
which is the more natural order.　But Elijah was expected to return
(vi. 15, viii. 28), whereas Moses was an unexpected addition; hence
Mk's expression.　The possible reappearance of Moses seems to have
been a later idea of the Jews.　In spite of Deut. xxxiv. 5 and Josh. i.
1, 2, it was believed that he was taken up to heaven alive (Assumption
of Moses).　The power to recognize these representatives of the Law
and the Prophets is analogous to that of St Paul recognizing Ananias
in a vision (Acts ix. 12).　The recognition was necessary for the
purposes of the Transfiguration, and it might confirm them in the
belief that Christ was not overturning the Law and the Prophets, for
the representatives of both were in conference with Him.　"The Law
and the Prophets paid homage to the Gospel" (Loisy).

5. ἀποκριθείς.　See on viii. 29 *sub fin.*　Peter's "answer" was
not to words addressed to him, but to facts which appealed to him.
Cf. x. 24, 51, xi. 14, xii. 35, xiv. 48, xv. 12.　Lk. says that it was uttered
as Moses and Elijah were parting from Christ after talking with Him
about His exodus from this world.　Peter wants them to stay in order
that the existing ecstasy may continue.

Ῥαββεί.　Mk alone preserves the original Aramaic; cf. xi. 21,
xiv. 45, and see on x. 51.　In all these places A.V. obscures a
characteristic feature.　Lk. translates it with his characteristic ἐπιστάτα, Mt. with κύριε.

καλόν ἐστιν.　*It is a good thing that we are here.*　"It is a beautiful
coincidence.　We are very happy, and we can make ourselves useful."
Perhaps he desires that the Master's sufferings, if they cannot be
avoided (viii. 32), may be indefinitely postponed.　*Cette intervention
de Pierre, si elle est malavisée, donne à toute l'épisode le cachet le plus
réel* (Lagrange).

τρεῖς σκηνάς.　He may be thinking of booth-making at the F.
of Tabernacles, which possibly was being celebrated at this time

(Mackinlay); but neither possibility is required to explain Peter's proposal.

καὶ Μωϋσεῖ μίαν καὶ Ἡλείᾳ μίαν. "Not so," says Jerome; "the Law and the Prophets are now in the tabernacle of the Gospel." Here Moses is placed before Elijah.

6. οὐ γὰρ ᾔδει τί ἀποκριθῇ. "Answer" as in *v.* 5. No one spoke to him, and he knew not what to say, yet with his usual impulsiveness he says something. Mt. again spares one of the Twelve and omits this. See on vi. 52.

ἔκφοβοι. Strong compound (Heb. xii. 21); *they became sore afraid* (R.V.), or *they had become*, for the fear preceded and explained the ill-advised utterance. See on v. 8. All three mention this fear, but at different points in the narrative; Mk before the cloud and the voice, Lk. after the cloud and before the voice, Mt. after both cloud and voice.

7. νεφέλη ἐπισκιάζουσα αὐτοῖς. Mt. says that it was "luminous" (φωτινή), which is somewhat out of harmony with "overshadow"; but the etymology of ἐπισκιάζω need not be pressed. Cf. ἐπέφωσκεν of evening coming on (Lk. xxiii. 54). The cloud hung over them and rested above them. Syr-Sin. has "Him" for "them." The luminous cloud represents the Shechinah, symbolizing the Divine Presence, and it is in marked contrast to the petty shelter suggested by Peter. Similarity of sound may have suggested a connexion between Shechinah and ἐπισκιάζω. Cf. the cloud at the Ascension (Acts i. 9), and at the Second Advent (Lk. xxi. 27).

Οὗτός ἐστιν. We have four reports of this Voice, those of the Synoptists and that of 2 Pet., and no two of them agree in wording. These differences are less important than the difference between this Voice and the one at the Baptism, viz. the ἀκούετε αὐτοῦ. At the Baptism (i. 11) the words are addressed to Christ, here to the Apostles. The Law and the Prophets are consummated in Christ, and henceforth the disciples are to listen to Him. Thus the charge of the Heavenly Father agrees with the last recorded words of the earthly Mother, "Whatsoever He saith unto you, do it" (Jn ii. 5). This Voice assured the disciples that, although the Jews might reject Him and the Romans put Him to death (viii. 31), yet He was accepted and beloved by God. The servants who prepared the way have passed; the Son abides (Jn viii. 35). On the proposal to make ὁ ἀγαπητός a separate title of the Messiah, ὁ υἱός μου, ὁ ἀγαπητός, see Hastings' *D.B.* II. 501.

8. ἐξάπινα. To be taken with εἶδον. Here only in N.T., but not rare in LXX. Elsewhere we have ἐξαίφνης (ἐξέφνης, W.H.); xiii. 36;

Lk. ii. 13, ix. 39; Acts ix. 3.   Sudden return to normal conditions.
They expected to see some further marvel.

οὐκέτι οὐδένα.   See on i. 44; neither here nor there is there a
double neg. in Mt.

9—13.   THE DESCENT AND THE DISCUSSION ABOUT ELIJAH.

Mt. xvii. 9—13.

9.   Καὶ καταβαινόντων.   See crit. note.   The Transfiguration
probably took place at night and the descent from the mount on
the following morning (Lk. ix. 37).

ἐκ τοῦ ὄρους.   The ἐκ suggests that they came out of some
secluded spot on the mountain.   BDΨ 33 support ἐκ against ἀπό.

διεστείλατο.   Mk's favourite word; see on v. 43; for αὐτοῖς after
a gen. abs. see on v. 21, for ἵνα see on iii. 9, for διηγήσωνται see on
v. 16.

εἰ μὴ ὅταν.   *Save when* (R.V.) rather than "till" (A.V.).   The
ὅταν, "whenever," leaves the time of the rising again quite indefinite.
This agrees with the prohibition to proclaim Him as Messiah (viii. 30);
to tell of the recent glory would intensify erroneous ideas about Him.
This principle of concealing His Messiahship runs through the whole
of Mk (iii. 12, viii. 30, ix. 9, x. 18).   The Resurrection showed where
His true glory lay.   For ἐκ νεκρῶν see on vi. 14.

10.   τὸν λόγον ἐκράτησαν.   *They kept the saying*; they not only
remembered it but obeyed it; cf. vii. 3, 4, 8.

πρὸς ἑαυτούς.   Amphibolous, but better taken with συνζητοῦντες
(R.V.) than with ἐκράτησαν.   Syr-Sin. has "reasoning with themselves."   They would be familiar with the idea of rising from the
dead, but the special resurrection of the Son of Man perplexed them.
Syr-Sin. has "What is this word that He said, When He is risen from
the dead?"   D and Lat.-Vet. have ὅταν ἐκ νεκρῶν ἀναστῇ for τὸ ἐκ ν.
ἀναστῆναι.   The ἐστί reproduces their wording; "what His rising
again from the dead *is.*"   This questioning is omitted by Mt., who
again refrains from recording the Apostles' want of intelligence; cf. vi.
52, ix. 6, x. 24.

11.   ἐπηρώτων.   Conversational imperf. which Mt., as often,
changes to aor.   Some would place *vv.* 11—13 after viii. 38, and
they would fit that position; but there is no other evidence that
they ever had it.

Ὅτι λέγουσιν.   Here and in *v.* 28 R.V. makes ὅτι recitative; but
it is probably interrogative in both places, as perhaps in 1 Chron.
xvii. 6.   In ii. 16 the reading is doubtful.   The question seems to

imply that the appearance of Elijah after the appearance of the
Messiah had perplexed them. It reminded them of Mal. iv. 5, which
the Scribes interpreted to mean that Elijah would appear again before
the Messiah came. Cf. Ecclus xlviii. 10.

12. Ἠλείας μὲν ἐλθών. The μέν is concessive; "It is true,"
"indeed." The corresponding δέ is lost in the interjected question;
ἀλλὰ λέγω takes its place. Cf. 1 Cor. v. 3; 1 Thess. ii. 18; Rom. vii.
12, x. 1. The correlation μὲν...δὲ... is much less freq. in N.T. than
in class. Grk.

ἀποκαθιστάνει. MSS. differ as to the form used, whether from
ἀποκατιστάνω, which W.H. "with hesitation" prefer (*App.* p. 168),
or ἀποκαθίστημι, or ἀποκαθιστάνω.

καὶ πῶς γέγραπται; This is a direct (R.V.) and not an indirect
(A.V.) question. Christ answers their question with another, which
points to the answer to theirs. "How is it that it stands written that
the Messiah is to suffer? If the Messiah is about to suffer, Elijah must
already have come." This repetition of the prediction that He must
suffer is remarkable, so soon after the glory on the mount.

13. ἀλλὰ λέγω ὑμῖν. *But, so far from this being a difficulty,
I say to you that Elijah moreover is come.* There is no ἐγώ with
λέγω (contrast Mt. v. 22, 28, 32, etc.), because there is no opposition
between what Christ says and what the Scribes say. Christ confirms
the belief that an Elijah must come. His statement goes beyond that
of the Scribes. Not only must he come, but "moreover he is come
and they did to him, etc."

ἐποίησαν αὐτῷ. *They did to him whatsoever they listed.* They
imprisoned him and put him to death. There was no need to say
who had treated "Elijah" in this manner. The phrase is in O.T.
style (1 Kings ix. 1, x. 13; Ps. cxiii. 11; Dan. viii. 4; 1 Macc. vii. 16),
and indicates absolute power. Both Mk and Mt. have ἐποίησαν, which
A.V. renders "have done." R.V. has "did" in Mt., but leaves
"have done" in Mk.

καθὼς γέγραπται ἐπ' αὐτόν. *Even as it stands written about him.*
Antipas and Herodias were foreshadowed in Ahab and Jezebel.

14—29.   CURE OF A DEMONIAC BOY.

Mt. xvii. 14—20.   Lk. ix. 37—43.

14. ἐλθόντες...εἶδον. See crit. note. Written from the point of view
of one of those (Peter) who had been on the mount. Zahn, *Introd. to
N.T.* II. pp. 494 f. Mt. and Lk. are different. The contrast between
the peace and glory on the mount and the conflict below will never be

forgotten so long as Raffaelle's great picture, the last which he completed, survives. Compare Moses on the mount communing with Jehovah, and Aaron compromising with idolatry below.

πρὸς τ. μαθητάς. The Apostles who had not witnessed the Transfiguration.

γραμματεῖς. They had been successfully attacking the nine in the absence of the Master. Their presence in the North is evidence of their watchfulness. Some, however, would omit γραμματεῖς as a gloss—against all evidence—and make the disciples dispute with one another about their failure. We hear no more of these Scribes.

15. ἐξεθάμβησαν. The strong compound is peculiar to Mk in N.T. (xiv. 33, xvi. 5, 6). The crowd were awe-struck at the opportuneness of His unexpected arrival. They leave the disputants and run to welcome the great Healer and Teacher. It is improbable that "traces of the celestial glory" of the Transfiguration struck them with awe. Christ had enjoined silence about that, and such traces would have made silence almost impossible. Vulg. translates both readings, ἐξεθαμβήθη and ἐξεθάμβησαν, *omnis populus videns eum stupefactus est et expaverunt et accurrentes salutabant eum.* Jerome cannot have meant both to stand. Syr-Sin. omits πᾶς ὁ ὄχλος.

16. ἐπηρώτησεν. Only here, *v.* 21, and xii. 28 does Mk use the aor. of this verb; elsewhere the imperf. (v. 9, vii. 5, 17, etc.). Mt. of course omits the question as implying that Christ was ignorant. Cf. v. 9, 30, vi. 38, viii. 12, 23, etc. The question is addressed to the crowd (see crit. note), who had joined in attacking the nine for their failure to heal. Their sympathy would be with the father of the boy. These Apostles had healed people during their mission (vi. 13); why would they not heal the only son (Lk.) of this poor man?

17. εἷς ἐκ τοῦ ὄχλου. The question was addressed to the multitude; the man who was specially interested at once replies. He was eager to secure help before more time was lost.

Διδάσκαλε. Mt., as at *v.* 5, has the more reverent Κύριε. The Aramaic would be Rabbi in both places. The father tells much more than Christ had asked, and his statement is very natural, though not quite accurate. He had set out intending to bring his boy to Christ, but had arrived during His absence, and so had brought him to the disciples (Mt.). The spirit is called "dumb" either because of its effect on the boy, or because it refused to answer when addressed. Lagrange quotes Plut. *De defectu orac.* p. 438 B of a Pythia who gave no response ἀλάλου καὶ κακοῦ πνεύματος οὖσα πλήρης. Cf. Lk. xi. 14; Mt. xii. 22.

18. ῥήσσει αὐτόν. *Convulses him;* Lk. σπαράσσει. But ῥήσσει may mean *dashes him down* (R.V.); cf. Wisd. iv. 19, ῥήξει αὐτοὺς ἀφώνους πρηνεῖς.

ἀφρίζει καὶ τρίζει. Neither verb is found elsewhere in N.T. Each Evangelist describes the symptoms differently, and Hobart (pp. 17— 20) regards three expressions used by Lk. as medical. The father is anxious that Christ should know how grievous his son's case is. Cf. Soph. *Electr.* 709.

ξηραίνεται. *Withereth away*; or perhaps "becomes like a dry stick, bloodless and motionless." Trench, *Miracles*, p. 372.

οὐκ ἴσχυσαν. *They were powerless.* We must distinguish the οὐκ ἴσχυσαν of Mk and Mt. from Lk.'s οὐκ ἠδυνήθησαν, and εἰ δύνῃ (*vv.* 22, 23), and οὐκ ἠδυνήθημεν (*v.* 28); but here "had not strength" (Lk. xvi. 3) would not be suitable.

19. Ὦ γενεὰ ἄπιστος, ἕως πότε ἔσομαι. In all three, who agree much more closely in the wording of Christ's reply than in that of the father's appeal. Throughout the Synoptics, the chief agreements are in Christ's Sayings, which tradition preserved more carefully than narrative or the sayings of others. The whole company, esp. the powerless disciples, are included in the "unbelieving generation." The repeated ἕως πότε is "the Lord's *quousque tandem*" (Swete). There is weariness and disappointment in the reproach. Bede compares it to that of a physician whose directions have not been followed. Cf. Jn xiv. 9; Rev. vi. 10; and with πρὸς ὑμᾶς the πρὸς ἡμᾶς, vi. 3, and πρὸς ὑμᾶς, xiv. 49.

20. καὶ ἰδὼν κ.τ.λ. There is the common confusion of personality between the demoniac and the demon; cf. iii. 11. In any case we have a confusion of construction, as often in Mk. Either ἰδών refers to τὸ πνεῦμα, the masc. being used because Mk thinks of the demon as a person; or ἰδών refers to the boy, and the sentence means "when the boy saw Jesus, straightway he was convulsed by the demon."

συνεσπάραξεν. Also in Lk. Stronger than σπάραξαν (i. 26), where, as here, Syr-Sin. has "threw him down." Cf. συμπληρόω, συντέμνω.

ἐκυλίετο. Here only in N.T., but freq. in LXX. Cf. κυλισμός (2 Pet. ii. 22). The change from aor. to imperf. is accurate.

21. ἐπηρώτησεν. Our Lord is asking for information, as in *v.* 16, vi. 38, viii. 23. Both Mt. and Lk. omit the question. Cf. Soph. *O.T.* 558. *How long time is it since this hath come to him?* Here only in Mk is ὡς used in a temporal sense. In Lk., Jn, and Acts it is very freq.

Ἐκ παιδιόθεν. Pleonastic, like ἀπὸ μακρόθεν (v. 6), and our "from whence," "from henceforth"; παιδιόθεν (ΑΓΠ) or ἐκ παιδίου would suffice. The A text of Gen. xlvii. 3 has ἐκ παιδιόθεν.

22. ὕδατα. The plur. may mean pools and streams. We are not to think of suicidal mania; a convulsion near fire or water often nearly proved fatal. To understand this of feverish alternations of heat and shivering is unnatural.

εἴ τι δύνῃ. When he left home, the father was confident that Jesus could heal his son; but the disciples' failure has weakened his trust in the Master's power. Syr-Sin. has "as much as thou canst do."

23. Τὸ εἰ δύνῃ. See crit. note. Christ quotes with surprise the father's expression of doubt, and τό is a mark of quotation. It depends on the father rather than on Christ whether the son can be healed or not. Christ can heal, if the father has faith (ii. 5, v. 34, 36, vi. 5). The leper (i. 40) doubted whether Christ had the will to cleanse so unworthy a person as himself; this father doubts whether Christ has the power to heal his son. The proposal to retain the common reading and make the inserted verb imperat. (πίστευσαι instead of πιστεῦσαι) does not make the reading more probable. Both δύνῃ (Lk. xvi. 2) and δύνασαι (i. 40; Mt. v. 36) occur in N.T.

πάντα δυνατὰ τῷ πιστεύοντι. As often, Christ states a comprehensive principle and leaves us to find out the necessary limitations. See on x. 27, xiv. 36. Faith enables us to take hold of the power of God to be used in accordance with His will. Syr-Sin. has "all things can happen unto thee, if thou believest."

24. εὐθὺς κράξας. See crit. note. The father does not lose an instant in expressing his desire to raise his trust in Christ to the utmost, though he cannot feel that he completely fulfils the condition implied in τῷ πιστεύοντι. He prays Christ to strengthen his faith, and his prayer has been echoed by thousands since Mk put it on record. "Help me, although unbelieving" is not the meaning, but "Help my faith where it is ready to fail" (Swete). The whole of this impressive conversation (ἵνα ἀπολέσῃ αὐτόν...ἀπιστίᾳ) is peculiar to Mk. The Freer MS. has "the spirit of the child" instead of "the father of the child." This looks like a slip of the careless copyist. See Appendix.

25. ἐπισυντρέχει ὄχλος. *A multitude came running together* (R.V.). Not "*the* people" (A.V.); there is no art. in the true text, and therefore no ref. to the crowd already mentioned. Apparently Christ and the father had drawn away from it (vii. 33, viii. 23) while the boy was being fetched, and now a fresh crowd runs towards the group. The double compound occurs nowhere else in N.T., and both prepositions have point, one knot of people on the top of another. Cf. ἐπισυνηγμένη, i. 33.

Τὸ ἄλαλον. Nom. with art. for voc. See on v. 8. All three have ἐπετίμησεν, but the words of the rebuke and the two verses which follow are peculiar to Mk.

ἐγὼ ἐπιτάσσω. Emphatic pronoun; "It is no longer disciples who speak, but ἐγώ, ὃν οἶδας" (Euthym.).

26. πολλὰ σπαράξας. The masc. here is in favour of ἰδών in *v*. 20 referring to the demon rather than the boy. As if desiring to do as much mischief as possible before leaving. Vulg. has *discerpens* here and i. 26, but *conturbavit* in *v*. 20, thus making the simple verb stronger than the compound; πολλὰ is *multum*, as in v. 10, 23, 38; it might have been *vehementer*, as in v. 43.

τοὺς πολλούς. *The more part* (R.V.), "most of them"; cf. vi. 2, xii. 37. But Mk seems to make little difference between οἱ πολλοί and πολλοί.

'Ἀπέθανεν. As in v. 35, the aor. is used of a death which has just taken place.

27. κρατήσας τῆς χειρός. See on i. 31. Bede points out that healing by means of touch is further proof of the reality of Christ's humanity. Syr-Sin. has "and delivered him to his father."

28. εἰσελθόντος αὐτοῦ. This gen. abs., instead of the participle agreeing with the noun or pronoun following, is in Mk's style; v. 18, 21, x. 17, xi. 27, xiii. 1, 3. See crit. note.

εἰς οἶκον. *Indoors*, as iii. 19. This subsequent questioning is freq., esp. in the privacy of a house (iv. 10, vii. 17, x. 10).

Ὅτι ἡμεῖς; Interrogative, as in *v*. 11, and ἡμεῖς is emphatic. They have been empowered to cast out demons (iii. 15, vi. 7); how is it that they have failed in this case?

29. Τοῦτο τὸ γένος κ.τ.λ. The reply is obscure in two particulars. 1. What γένος? Evil spirits of any kind? or those which render their victims deaf and dumb? 2. Who is to pray? The exorcist? or the victim's friends? or the possessed person himself? Mt. gives a much simpler answer, which may be regarded as interpreting Mk, Διὰ τὴν ὀλιγοπιστίαν. To be effectual, prayer must be accompanied by faith, and the disciples who had proved powerless either had not prayed, or had prayed without faith. They may have thought that the power to heal was inherent in themselves, and that there was no need to pray; or they had had little trust that God would hear their prayer. Mt. sometimes gives his interpretation of Christ's words as having been actually spoken; see on *v*. 1, viii. 29.

ἐν προσευχῇ. See crit. note. The widely diffused addition καὶ νηστείᾳ may be safely rejected as an early interpolation in the interests of asceticism. In Acts x. 30, νηστεύων καὶ is condemned on still stronger evidence (אABC and Versions), while the evidence against τῇ νηστείᾳ καὶ in 1 Cor. vii. 5 is overwhelming. Mt. xvii. 21 is an interpolation from Mk ix. 29 after καὶ νηστείᾳ had been added. Here the internal evidence is as strong as the external. When a demoniac was brought to the disciples to be healed, were they to say, "We must first fast for so many hours"?

30—32. ANOTHER PREDICTION OF THE PASSION.

Mt. xvii. 22, 23. Lk. ix. 43—45.

30. Κἀκεῖθεν. From the neighbourhood of the "high mountain" (v. 2). The best MSS. usually have κἀκεῖθεν: καὶ ἐκεῖθεν (x. 1) is a very rare exception.

οὐκ ἤθελεν. He is still in quest of seclusion for the training of the Twelve. It is noteworthy that in none of these quests is He represented as working a miracle in order to secure seclusion; repeated failures do not induce Him to use supernatural means where ordinary means may suffice.

31. Ὁ υἱὸς τοῦ ἀνθρώπου. The Twelve have by no means grasped the import of the Passion, still less that of the Resurrection, and Jesus continues to instruct them. They know that He is ὁ Χριστός, yet He does not speak of Himself by that title, which might lead them to use it inadvertently in speaking of Him to others, in violation of viii. 30. He continues to use the title which veiled, while to some it suggested, His Messiahship.

παραδίδοται. *Is being delivered up* by the Father *into the hands of men.* This interpretation is as old as Origen (on Mt.) and is powerfully defended by Abbott, *Paradosis*, p. 53 f. If the verb refers to Judas (iii. 19), εἰς χεῖρας ἀνθρώπων is almost superfluous; if God is meant, the addition is almost necessary. Cf. 2 Sam. xxiv. 14; Ecclus ii. 18. There may be a play of words between "Son of Man" and "hands of men." The pres. may mean that the process of delivering is already begun, but more probably is the common usage of pres. for what is sure to take place.

32. οἱ δὲ ἠγνόουν. *But they remained ignorant.* Out of consideration for the Twelve, Mt. omits both their ignorance and their fear. Lk. suggests that, as in the case of the two on the way to Emmaus (Lk. xxiv. 16), they were not allowed to know then, in order that they might remember it afterwards, and see that Christ had suffered with full knowledge and free will. Ῥῆμα is freq. in the other Gospels and not rare in the Epistles, but in Mk is found only here and xiv. 72.

ἐφοβοῦντο. They had heard the severe rebuke to Peter (viii. 33). The question about Elijah was an indirect attempt to obtain an explanation (*v.* 11), and the answer had not made things clear to them. They could not understand the Messiah's rising again, because they did not see how the Messiah could die, and they were afraid of being rebuked for doubting it, or possibly of being told something still more distressing than this general prediction of His sufferings.

33—37. THE QUESTION OF PRECEDENCE.

Mt. xviii. 1—5. Lk. ix. 46—48.

33. ἐν τῇ οἰκίᾳ γενόμενος. *When He had got indoors*, in contrast to ἐν τῇ ὁδῷ. This time it is Christ who asks for an explanation of "what has been said." See on *v.* 28.

Τί ἐν τῇ ὁδῷ διελογίζεσθε; Here Christ asks in order to educate. They would not quarrel about such a matter in His immediate presence; but He got no answer to His question, and therefore the subject of their dispute was known to Him in some other way (Lk. ix. 47).

34. τίς μείζων. They were ashamed to confess such a dispute and were afraid of condemnation. Bede suggests that the preference shown to the three *seorsum ductos in montem* may have led to the dispute. Mt. represents them as asking Jesus, "Who is the greatest in the Kingdom of Heaven?" The use of the comparative, without the art., as equivalent to the superlative is freq in late Greek. Blass, § 11. 3, 44. 3; Winer, pp. 303, 305. For ἐσιώπων, *they remained silent*, see on x. 48.

35. καθίσας ἐφώνησεν τοὺς δώδεκα. Mk alone has this picturesque detail. He commonly sat to teach (see on xiii. 3), but here He may be resting after the journey.

Εἴ τις θέλει. *If any man desireth to be first.*

ἔσται πάντων ἔσχατος. This does not mean that the *result* of striving to be first is degradation, but that the *way* to be first is self-suppression and service (x. 43, 44) ; *de humilitate ad summa crescimus* (Cypr. *De zelo*, 10). This saying is echoed in Ep. of Polycarp 5; see on xiv. 38.

36. λαβὼν παιδίον. A representative of the humblest and simplest of His followers ; τὸ γὰρ παιδίον οὔτε δόξης ἐφίεται, οὔτε φθονεῖ, οὔτε μνησικακεῖ (Theoph.). Syr-Sin. inserts that "He looked at him" before addressing the disciples. Similarly at x. 16 it inserts that "He called" the children before laying His hands on them.

ἐν μέσῳ αὐτῶν. He was sitting as the centre of the group, and therefore ἐν μέσῳ for the child would be παρ᾽ ἑαυτῷ (Lk.), the place of honour. For other instances of Christ's treatment of children see

x. 15; Lk. x. 21, xvii. 2; Mt. xxi. 16. The tradition that this child was Ignatius of Antioch is not found earlier than the ninth cent. (Anastasius Bibliothecarius, Nicephorus Callistus). It is not mentioned by Eusebius, and Chrysostom says that Ignatius had not seen Christ. The title ὁ Θεοφόρος means that Ignatius carried God in his heart, and ὁ Θεόφορος would mean "borne along by God" rather than "carried in the Divine arms." It is futile to guess whose child it was.

ἐναγκαλισάμενος. See on x. 16. In Prov. vi. 10, xxiv. 33 (48) the verb is used of folding the arms with the hands in lazy inactivity. Syr-Sin. omits.

37. ἐν τῶν τοιούτων παιδίων. Anyone of similar childlike character. Nothing is said about his *coming* in the Name of the Lord: πᾶς δὲ ὁ ἐρχόμενος ἐν ὀνόματι Κυρίου δεχθήτω (*Didache* xii. 1).

δέξηται ἐπὶ τῷ ὀνόματί μου. "Receiveth on the *basis* of My Name," "name" being here used in the common signification of "character." He who does this, not because he is fond of children or of simple persons, but because they represent to him the Christlike character, has the honour of having Christ as his guest. Cf. *v*. 39, xiii. 6. Mk also uses ἐν τῷ ὀνόματι (*v*. 38), ἐν ὀνόματι (*v*. 31, xi. 9), and διὰ τὸ ὄνομα (xiii. 13). See on 3 Jn 7; also Deissmann, *Bibl. St.* pp. 146, 196.

οὐκ ἐμὲ δέχεται. Οὐκ = οὐ μόνον. "Not only receives Me" or "Not so much receives Me"; cf. x. 45. "I will have mercy and not sacrifice" (Hos. vi. 6) does not condemn sacrifice but says that mercy is far better; cf. Lk. x. 20, xiv. 12, xxiii. 28; Jn xii. 44. What is negatived in such expressions, as being defective, is included, with a great deal more, in the affirmative clause. Blass, § 77. 12. This Saying is Johannine in tone and carries us far in Christology; cf. Lk. x. 16. Abbott, *Johannine Grammar*, § 25, 93. Both ἀποστέλλω (Mt. x. 40; Lk. ix. 48; Jn iii. 17, etc.) and πέμπω (Lk. xii. 13; Jn iv. 34, etc.) are used of the mission of the Son. See on Jn i. 33.

38—40. MISTAKEN ZEAL FOR THE NAME.

Lk. ix. 49, 50.

38. Ἔφη αὐτῷ. See crit. note. This kind of asyndeton is rare in Mk (x. 28, xii. 24), as in Lk. and Jn, but is freq. in Mt. Nowhere else in the Synoptists is John mentioned as intervening singly. He speaks again with others x. 35 and xiii. 3.

Διδάσκαλε. Lk. has his favourite Ἐπιστάτα (cf. *v*. 5). It is possible that the words ἐπὶ τῷ ὀνόματί μου remind him of the incident

which he mentions. He may mean, " Were we not right in refusing
to receive as an ally one who did not receive Thee as Master ? " Justin
(*Try*. 30) says that in his time the Name of Jesus was used with success
in exorcisms.

ἐκωλύομεν. Conative imperf., as in Mt. iii. 14; cf. xv. 23; Lk. i.
59, v. 6. Or " repeatedly forbade " may be the meaning.

ὅτι οὐκ ἠκολούθει ἡμῖν. *Because he was not following us.* The
exorcist did not profess to be a disciple; and the disciples were indignant, not because he had been rivalling their powers, but because,
without authority, he had been using Christ's Name. Unlike the
juggling exorcists in Acts xix. 13—16, the man was evidently (in
however defective a way) sincere and successful. To suppose that
this exorcist is meant to represent St Paul is a curiosity in criticism.
A representative of St Paul would preach rather than exorcize.

39. Μὴ κωλύετε. *Cease to forbid him*, or anyone like him. Cf. v.
36, vi. 50, x. 14; also the reply of Moses to Joshua's jealous advice
(Num. xi. 29). It is an unworthy interpretation which makes Christ's
words mean, " He gets his living by Me, and therefore is sure not to be
against Me."

40. καθ' ἡμῶν, ὑπὲρ ἡμῶν. See crit. note. It is strange that
Renan (*V. de J.* p. 220) and E. Klostermann (*ad loc.*) should regard
Mt. xii. 30 — Lk. xi. 23 as giving a contradictory rule. Loisy would
have us believe that Mk omitted the other saying at iii. 27 because he
meant to make Christ say something different elsewhere. The two
rules are perfectly harmonious, but this one is to be used in judging
other people, the other rule in judging ourselves. If we are not sure
that others are against Christ, we must treat them as being for Him;
if we are not sure that we are on His side, we have reason to fear that
we are against Him. Both rules show that friendly action and hostility
are incongruous.

**41—50. Results of Helping and of Hindering the Cause
of Christ.**

Mt. xviii. 6—9. Lk. xvii. 1, 2, xiv. 34.

41. ὅς γάρ. The γάρ looks back to *v.* 37, to what was said
before John's interruption. "Receiving" Christ's representative need
not mean anything magnificent; help as humble as a drink of water,
if given for Christ's sake, will assuredly be richly rewarded. Note the
ἀμήν (iii. 28) and the οὐ μή (*v.* 1). It is perhaps fanciful to point out
that the poorest can offer cold water, whereas warm water requires a
fire (Bede).

ὅτι Χριστοῦ ἐστέ. A Pauline expression (Rom. viii. 9; 1 Cor.
i. 12, iii. 23; 2 Cor. x. 7). See crit. note. With the doubtful
exception of Lk. xxiii. 2, Christ is nowhere else in the Synoptic
Gospels called Χριστός, but always ὁ Χριστός. Dalman, *Words*, p. 305,
thinks that the clause is "an unnecessary explanation of ἐν ὀνόματί
[μου]," *i.e.* a gloss by some editor; so also Hawkins (*Hor. Syn.*
p. 152) and Zahn (*Introd. to N.T.* ιι. p. 500). We might more simply
suppose that, as in i. 15, Mk is putting our Lord's meaning into the
language which was usual in his day.

42. σκανδαλίσῃ. See on iv. 17. Just in proportion to the beauty
of the childlike character is the guilt of the man who knowingly
spoils it. Here and in *v.* 43 σκανδαλίσῃ (אBLΔψ) is right; in *v.* 45,
-ίξῃ.

τῶν πιστευόντων. He is speaking of simple Christians in *vv.* 37,
41, 42; it is they who are His best representatives. Will not simple
believers be perplexed and sent astray, when they see Apostles contending for the foremost place?

καλόν ἐστιν αὐτῷ μᾶλλον. *It is good for him, if the choice has to
be made.* Lk. has λυσιτελεῖ αὐτῷ, "it is worth his while." Cf. Mt.
v. 29. Death by drowning is a terrible thing; but in comparison with
causing a simple soul to sin it is an excellent thing. Lk. has ἕνα last
in the sentence, with great emphasis; the context in Lk. is quite
different.

μύλος ὀνικός. A millstone requiring an ass to turn it, therefore
so large that it must sink a man. Lk. has λίθος μυλικός, "a millstone," and ΑΓΠ have the same here; μύλος may be either "a mill"
or "a millstone." The term ὀνικός has been found in papyri dated
respectively 8 Feb. A.D. 33 and 5 Feb. A.D. 70, and in an inscription
c. A.D. 136, having previously been unknown outside Bibl. Grk.
Deissmann, *Light from Ancient East*, p. 76. Cf. Ovid, *Fasti*, vi. 318,
Et quae puniceas versat asella molas.

βέβληται. The most terrible moment is chosen for comparison.
The heavy stone is hanging on to the man's neck (pres.), and he has
been hurled to what must be his death (perf.), and it is the death of
a dog. Cf. Sueton. *Aug.* 67, *Oneratis gravi pondere cervicibus prae-
cipitavit in flumen.*

43. καὶ ἐὰν σκανδαλίσῃ σε ἡ χείρ σου. Seducing simple souls is
disastrously easy work; but still more easy is seducing oneself, by
letting the body lead the spirit astray. The language in the three
instances is parabolic, but the meaning is clear. We sacrifice hand,
foot, or eye, to avoid fatal or incurable maladies. We may have to
sacrifice things still more precious, to avoid the death of the soul.

κυλλός. *Crippled*, originally of "bowed legs," the opposite of βλαισός, "knock-kneed," but also used of the hand; ἔμβαλε κυλλῇ (Aristoph. *Eq.* 1083) "toss into a hand crooked to catch something."

εἰς τὴν ζωήν. In N.T., ζωή occurs more than 100 times, but in Mk only four, twice without (*vv.* 43, 45), and twice with (x. 17, 30). αἰώνιος. In class. Grk, βίος, the life of a human being, is higher than ζωή, the life which men share with brutes and vegetables. In N.T., βίος has its classical meaning of "human life" or "means of life" (xii. 44), but ζωή is greatly promoted, meaning the life which men share with Christ and with God. See on Jn xii. 25; 1 Jn i. 2, ii. 16. Trench, *Syn.* § xxvii; Cremer, *Lex.* p. 272.

ἀπελθεῖν. *Sc.* ἀπὸ τῆς ζωῆς. D has βληθῆναι.

τὴν γέενναν. Excepting Lk. xii. 5 and Jas iii. 6, γέεννα occurs only in Mk and Mt. Not in LXX. The word is a loose transliteration of *Ge-Hinnom*, "Valley of Hinnom," where under Ahaz and Manasseh children were thrown into the red-hot arms of Molech (2 Chron. xxviii. 3, xxxiii. 6; Jer. vii. 31). Josiah (2 Kings xxiii. 10—14) abolished these horrors and desecrated the place by making it a refuse-heap for offal and rubbish, including the carcases of animals, which were consumed, acc. to late writers, by a fire which never went out. This heap was a mass of corruption, devoured by worms and fire, and hence was regarded as symbolizing punishment in the other world. Is. lxvi. 24 shows the beginning of the idea. It is much plainer in Enoch; "This accursed valley is for those who are accursed for ever; here will all those be gathered together who utter unseemly words against God, and here is the place of their punishment" (xxvii. 2). "A like abyss was opened in the midst of the earth, full of fire, and they were all judged and found guilty and cast into that fiery abyss, and they burned" (xc. 26; cf. xlviii. 9). Cf. 2 Esdras vii. 36, *Clibanus Gehennae ostendetur et contra eum jucunditatis paradisus*; Ps. of Solomon xii. 5, xv. 6; Apocalypse of Baruch lxxxv. 13. The site of the Valley of Hinnom is much disputed; Hastings' *D.B.*, *D.C.G.* artt. "Gehenna," "Hinnom, Valley of." The loss of the *m* in "Hinnom" in transliteration to "Gehenna" is repeated in the change from "Mariam" to "Maria."

The confusion caused in all English Versions prior to R.V. by using "hell" to translate both ᾅδης and γέεννα is well known; Lightfoot, *On Revision*, p. 87; Trench, *On the A.V.* p. 21. Hardly any correction in R.V. is more valuable than that of reserving "hell" for γέεννα and simply transliterating ᾅδης.

ἄσβεστον. The fire cannot be extinguished so long as there is fuel to feed it: it "burns as long as sin remains to be consumed" (Swete).

The constr. καλὸν...ἤ, instead of κάλλιον...ἤ, is perhaps Hebraic (Gen. xlix. 12; Hos. ii. 7) but it is found in Hdt. ix. 26 *sub fin.*, ἡμέας δίκαιον ἔχειν τὸ ἕτερον κέρας ἤπερ Ἀθηναίους.

44. See crit. note.

45. ὁ πούς σου. It is lawful, but not necessary, to find different meanings for "hand," "foot," and "eye." The general sense is that even what is most useful and most dear may have to be sacrificed. *Si quid est quo teneris, aut expedi, aut incide* (Seneca, *Ep.* xvii. 1). The picturesque repetition of the same idea with a change of form is an impressive Orientalism. But all three cases are stated hypothetically; "*if* they cause thee to offend." Precious things may be thankfully retained, if they have no evil effects. It is possible that the alliteration between καλόν and κυλλόν, and between καλόν and χωλόν (*vv.* 43, 45), is intentional.

46. See crit. note.

47. μονόφθαλμον. Hdt. iii. 16, iv. 29. In Attic Greek, ἑτερόφθαλμος was preferred to denote one who had lost an eye, μονόφθαλμος being reserved for the Cyclops who never had more than one. Popular language *de minimis non curat* and is not troubled about fine distinctions. An "alternative" is a possibility of one out of *two* things; but "three alternatives" is too convenient an expression to be driven out of use.

τὴν βασιλείαν τοῦ θεοῦ. The same as τὴν ζωήν in *vv.* 43, 45.

βληθῆναι. D and Syr-Sin. have ἀπελθεῖν.

48. ὅπου ὁ σκώληξ κ.τ.λ. This highly metaphorical expression is here part of the true text. It comes from Is. lxvi. 24; cf. Judith xvi. 17; Ecclus vii. 17; Apocalypse of Peter 10. The "worm" and the "fire" are opposed to "life," and seem to denote "destruction"; they can hardly mean life in endless torture. They have no end so long as they have anything to devour. Victor and Theophylact interpret them of the gnawing reproaches of conscience and the memory of shameful things done in this life. Perhaps they point rather to permanent loss, irreparable deterioration of the man's real self. Jews had strange ideas about the unseen world, as that one of the joys of the righteous was to see the torments of the wicked. Christ did not contradict these ideas, but He has left teaching which enables us to correct them.

49. πᾶς γὰρ πυρὶ ἁλισθήσεται. A very difficult statement. Each of the two metaphors is capable of different interpretations, and the two seem to be opposed, for fire destroys and salt preserves. Moreover the connexion with what precedes is not clear. These sentences may be isolated Sayings which Mk has put together here, because the common idea of "salt" seems to unite them, while that of "fire" connects the first sentence with what precedes, although in reality the sentences have no connexion with one another or with the preceding words. If there is connexion with what precedes (γάρ), we must find it with vv. 43—49 as a whole, and not simply with τὸ πῦρ in v. 49. "I have been speaking of fire, *for* with fire of some kind every man shall be salted." The way to escape the penal fire hereafter is to seek the purifying and preservative fire here, the fire of the Divine Presence (Heb. xii. 29; Deut. iv. 24, ix. 3; Mal. iii. 2, iv. 1). A sense of God's Presence burns up all that is base, and preserves all that is akin to Him. *Ignis purgat, et urit, et illuminat, et calefacit. Spiritus sanctus purgat sordes vitiorum, et urit cor ab humore libidinum, illuminat mentem notitia veritatis, et calefacit incendio caritatis* (Herveius Burgidolensis). The Christian, salted and illumined by communing with God, becomes himself salt and light to others. Another possible meaning is that the aim of penal suffering is to purify. See crit. note.

50. καλὸν τὸ ἅλας. *A fine thing is· the salt.* Here τὸ ἅλας is passing in meaning from the Divine to the human; in the next clause it is wholly human. *Nihil utilius sale et sole* (Plin. *H.N.* xxxi. ix 45 102). In LXX. and N.T., τὸ ἅλας is the common form, with τὸ ἅλα (cf. γάλα) as *v.l.* in good MSS. In class. Grk ὁ ἅλς prevails.

ἄναλον. Here only in N.T. and LXX. Apostles without the spirit of devotion and self-sacrifice, selfish Apostles who wrangle for the first place, are as worthless as savourless salt. We have a similar saying in the Testaments (*Levi* xiv. 4); "What will all the nations do, if ye are darkened in ungodliness?"

ἀρτύσετε. The verb means "prepare," and especially "prepare and flavour food" (Col. iv. 6).

ἐν ἑαυτοῖς. See on xiii. 9.

εἰρηνεύετε. See on 2 Cor. xiii. 11. In LXX. it is freq. Elsewhere only in Paul. The fruits of the Spirit are ἀγάπη, χαρά, εἰρήνη (Gal. v. 22). Cf. 1 Cor. iii. 3.

CHAPTER X.

1. καὶ πέραν (אBC*LΨ) rather than διὰ τοῦ πέραν (ANXΓΠ).

2. Φαρισαῖοι (ABLΔΠ) rather than οἱ Φαρ. (אCNVX). ἐπηρώτων (אBCDLMΔ) rather than ἐπηρώτησαν (ANXΓΠ).

5. אBCLΔ omit ἀποκριθείς. Cf. vv. 20, 29, v. 9, vii. 6, xi. 29, 33, xii. 17.

6. αὐτούς (אBCLΔ) rather than αὐτοὺς ὁ θεός (ANXΓΠ) or ὁ θεός (D).

7. אBΨ, Syr-Sin. omit καὶ προσκολληθήσεται...αὐτοῦ.

10. εἰς τὴν οἰκίαν (אBDLΔΨ) rather than ἐν τῇ οἰκίᾳ (ACNXΓΠ). περὶ τούτου (ABCLΓΔ) rather than περὶ τοῦ αὐτοῦ (EFGH etc.). ἐπηρώτων (אBCLΔΨ) rather than ἐπηρώτησαν (ADNXΓΠ).

12. αὐτὴ ἀπολύσασα τ. ἄνδρα αὐτῆς (אBCLΔ) rather than γυνὴ ἀπολύσῃ τ. ἄν. αὐτῆς καί (ANXΓΠ).

13. ἐπετίμησαν αὐτοῖς (אBCLΔΨ) rather than ἐπετίμων τοῖς προσφέρουσιν (ADNXΓΠ).

14. BMNXΓΔΙΙΨ omit καί before μὴ κωλύετε.

16. κατευλόγει τιθεὶς τ. χ. ἐπ᾽ αὐτά (אBCLΔ) rather than τιθεὶς τ. χ. ἐπ᾽ αὐτὰ εὐλόγει (ANXΓΠ).

20. אBΔΨ omit ἀποκριθείς. Cf. v. 5.

21. אBCDΔΨ omit ἄρας τὸν σταυρόν, from viii. 34.

24. אBΔ, k omit πεποιθότας ἐπὶ τοῖς χρήμασιν.

25. διελθεῖν (BCKΠ) rather than εἰσελθεῖν (אANXΓΔΨ), which is an assimilation to what follows.

26. πρὸς αὐτόν (אBCDΨ) rather than πρὸς ἑαυτούς (ADNXΓΠ).

27. אBCΔ omit δέ after ἐμβλέψας.

29. אBΔ, as in vv. 5, 20, omit ἀποκριθείς. BCΔ have ἢ μητέρα ἢ πατέρα. אBDΔ omit ἢ γυναῖκα, from Lk.

32. οἱ δὲ ἀκολουθοῦντες (אBC*LΔ) rather than καὶ ἀκ. (ANXΓΠ). Cf. vii. 24. Wrede (*Messiasgeheimnis*, pp. 96, 275) would omit καὶ ἐθαμβοῦντο. Some Old Latin texts seem to have omitted either ἐθαμβοῦντο or ἐφοβοῦντο.

34. ἐμπτύσουσιν...μαστιγώσουσιν (אBCLΔ) rather than μαστ.... ἐμπτ. (ANXΓΠ). μετὰ τρεῖς ἡμέρας (אBCDLΔ) rather than τῇ τρίτῃ ἡμέρᾳ (ANXΓΠ). Cf. viii. 31, ix. 31.

35. אBCDLΔ have αὐτῷ after λέγοντες.

36. με ποιήσω (א^aBΨ) or ποιήσω (CD) rather than ποιῆσαί με (AXΓΠ).

37. ἀριστερῶν (BLΔΨ) rather than εὐωνύμων (אACDNXΓΠ).

38. ἢ τὸ βάπτισμα (אBC*DLΔ) rather than καὶ τὸ βάπτ. (AC³XΓΠ).

42. καὶ προσκαλεσάμενος αὐτ. ὁ Ἰησοῦς (אBCDLΔ) rather than ὁ δὲ Ἰ. πρ. αὐτ. (ANXΓ). See on i. 14.

43. ἔστιν ἐν ὑμῖν (אBC*DLΔΨ), rather than ἔσται ἐν ὑμ. (AC³NXΓΠ).

46. τυφλὸς προσαίτης ἐκάθητο παρὰ τὴν ὁδόν (אBLΔΨ) rather than ὁ τυφλὸς ἐκάθ. π. τ. ὁδ. προσαιτῶν (AC²XΓΠ).

47. Ναζαρηνός (BLΔΨ) rather than Ναζωραῖος (אACXII).

49. Φωνήσατε αὐτόν (אBCLΔ) rather than αὐτὸν φωνηθῆναι (ADXΓΠ).

50. ἀναπηδήσας (אBDLΔΨ) rather than ἀναστάς (ACXII).

52. ἠκολούθει αὐτῷ (אABCDLΔ) rather than ἠκ. τῷ Ἰησοῦ. See on v. 13, xii. 41.

1—12. THE QUESTION OF DIVORCE.

Mt. xix. 1—12, v. 31, 32. Lk. xvi. 18.

1. Καὶ ἐκεῖθεν ἀναστὰς κ.τ.λ. We have almost the same wording vii. 24, where, as here, a move of a considerable distance is begun. We have perhaps reached the long section in Lk. (ix. 5—xix. 28) which is called "The Journeyings towards Jerusalem." Ἀναστάς does not look back to καθίσας (ix. 35); it is Hebraistic amplification (i. 35, ii. 14, vii. 24, xiv. 57, 60); freq. in Lk. and Acts, twice in Mt., once in Jn. Καὶ ἐκεῖθεν (אBCDΔ) is perhaps unique in N.T. Elsewhere the best MSS. have κἀκεῖθεν, as in ix. 30.

τὰ ὅρια τῆς Ἰουδαίας. A comprehensive expression for Judaea and the adjoining country; cf. v. 17, vii. 24, 31. The εἰς need not be limited to mean simply "up to"; it probably means "into" (A.V., R.V.).

καὶ πέραν. See crit. note.

ὄχλοι. Nowhere else does Mk use the plur., and here D and Lat-Vet. (with Syr-Sin.) have the sing. and they couple ὡς εἰώθει with the action of the multitude. This has much less point than the statement that Christ takes up once more His practice of public teaching. Here again Mt. (xix. 2) substitutes healing for teaching; see on vi. 34. Syr-Sin. has "healed and taught."

2. Φαρισαῖοι. No art.; see crit. note. It is not implied that

they are the same Pharisees as those who assailed Him previously
(ii. 16, vii. 1, viii. 11). But all do what is customary; multitudes
throng Him, He teaches them, Pharisees attack Him. D and Syr-
Sin. omit the approach of the Pharisees, leaving the ὄχλοι as nom. to
ἐπηρώτων.

πειράζοντες αὐτόν. They perhaps had heard that He condemned
divorce (Mt. v. 31, 32), which was recognized by the Law, and they
hoped to get Him committed to a clear contradiction of the Law.
And possibly they wished to embroil Him with Antipas, who had
divorced his wife in order to marry Herodias; but this is less
probable.

3. ἀποκριθείς. He answers their thoughts as well as their words,
and Himself makes the appeal to Moses. Mt., with less probability,
represents Him as allowing them to make the first appeal to what
Moses commanded (ἐνετείλατο). See on xii. 26.

4. Ἐπέτρεψεν. First with emphasis; "suffered," "permitted."
The right of divorce was established by custom, and "Moses" takes
it for granted (Lev. xxi. 7, 14, xxii. 13; Num. xxx. 9); but in certain
cases the right might be forfeited (Deut. xxii. 19, 29). In Deut.
xxiv. 1 f., to which passage reference is here made, the right of
divorce is assumed; and the husband is told that in divorcing he
must observe certain formalities, the chief of which is the writing
(Mk) and giving (Mt.) a βιβλίον ἀποστασίου (βιβ. ἀποκοπῆς Aq., βιβ.
διακοπῆς Sym.), and that in no circumstances may the divorced
woman become his wife again. J. Lightfoot on Mt. gives a specimen of a βιβ. ἀποστασίου, and it expressly mentions the right of the
divorced wife to marry again. The reason for divorce is not stated,
but it could not be adultery; the penalty for adultery was not divorce,
but death (Lev. xx. 10; [Jn] viii. 5). "Moses" neither commanded
nor forbade divorce, but commanded that, if it took place, it must be
done in a certain way and be irrevocable. Driver on Deut. xxiv. 1 f.
Malachi (ii. 14, 15) contends against divorce, but nowhere in N.T. is
there any reference to the passage. Here D and Syr-Sin., with some
Old Latin texts, have both the writing and the giving (*dare scriptum*)
of the βιβλίον.

5. εἶπεν αὐτοῖς. See crit. note.

Πρὸς τ. σκληροκαρδίαν ὑμῶν. First with emphasis; *For your
hardness of heart* (R.V.), "with a view to it," or "in reference to
it." See Gould on the importance of this concession, and Christ
does not condemn Moses for having made it. To be σκληροκάρδιοι
(Deut. x. 16; Jer. iv. 4; Ezek. iii. 7; Ecclus xvi. 10) and σκληροτρά-
χηλοι (Exod. xxxiii. 3; Deut. ix. 6, 13; Baruch ii. 30) had ever been

a reproach against Israel (Acts vii. 51). In Deut. x. 16 and Jer. iv. 4, Aq. has the more literal ἀκροβυστία καρδίας.

τὴν ἐντολὴν ταύτην. Not the command to divorce; there was no such command; but to effect divorce in a certain way.

6. ἀπὸ δὲ ἀρχῆς κτίσεως. Christ directs them to a far earlier authority than that of the written Law. "Moses" has also told us of the original ideal of marriage. Primeval marriage made no provision for divorce. The Creator made pairs, without surplus females. Like "creation," κτίσις may mean either "the creative act" (Rom. i. 20) or "the aggregate of creatures" (Col. i. 23). In 2 Pet. iii. 4 we have the same phrase as here, and in both places the second meaning is preferable. The words ἄρσεν...αὐτούς are from Gen. i. 27, where ὁ θεός occurs in the preceding clause, as the Pharisees would know. It was inevitable that it should be inserted here; see crit. note. Mt. has ὁ κτίσας. But Christ is not opposing the authority of God to that of Moses, as Victor and others think. He is showing that in the Pentateuch we have evidence that the concession made by the Law to debased human nature was not included in the original plan made by the Creator.

7. ἕνεκεν τούτου. In Gen. ii. 24 these words refer to the making of woman out of the rib of man, which *explains* the almost universal fact that a man leaves his parents and clings to a wife. Here, as in 1 Cor. vi. 16 and Eph. v. 31, this momentous fact is made an argument for monogamy. See crit. note.

8. ἔσονται...εἰς. Cf. Heb. i. 5, viii. 10, and see on 2 Cor. vi. 18.

ὥστε οὐκέτι εἰσίν. For the constr. cf. ii. 28; Jn iii. 16; etc. The indic. after ὥστε states an actual result.

9. ὃ οὖν ὁ θεὸς συνέζευξεν. God did not do this by uttering the words quoted in *v.* 7; they are Adam's words, although Mt. assigns them to God. But God has made possible and has sanctioned a relationship between man and woman which is more binding than even that which exists between parent and child. 1 Cor. vii. 10 may refer to this saying.

10. εἰς τὴν οἰκίαν. See crit. note. Again we have a subsequent questioning in the privacy of a house; cf. ix. 28. In ix. 33 it was He who questioned them. Perhaps the εἰς implies the motion to the house; but in late Greek the distinction between εἰς and ἐν is becoming blurred. Blass § 39. 3. Πάλιν refers to the previous questioning by the Pharisees.

11. μοιχᾶται ἐπ' αὐτήν. *Committeth adultery against her.* In answering the Pharisees it sufficed to point out that, from a higher point of view than that of the Mosaic Law, divorce was a falling away from the ideal of marriage set before mankind at the Creation, an ideal which ought to be restored. In answering His disciples He goes further and declares that marrying another after divorce is adultery, which implies that divorce is no real dissolution of the marriage tie. Gould holds that the exception in Mt. xix. 9 is implied here, " because adultery is the real dissolution of the marriage tie. Formal divorce does not break the marriage tie, adultery does break it." Μοιχάομαι in N.T. occurs only in the passages in Mk (*vv.* 11, 12) and Mt. (v. 32, xix. 9) which treat of divorce; the usual verb is μοιχεύω (*v.* 19), act. of the husband, pass. of the wife.

12. This is probably added in order to make it quite clear that in this matter the sexes are equal; neither partner can dissolve the marriage. Jewish law made no provision for a wife to divorce her husband (Joseph. *Ant.* xv. vii. 10); so Mt. omits this verse and substitutes, if the words are genuine (אDL etc. omit), "And he that marrieth her that is put away committeth adultery." Probably to avoid this difficulty D and some other authorities have here " If a woman depart from her husband and marry another." It is rash to see here an accommodation to Roman marriage-law, and therefore evidence of the Roman origin of this Gospel. We need not doubt that Christ uttered the words; but if He did not, love of parallelism would sufficiently account for their being attributed to Him. There may be allusion to Herodias who had deserted her first husband just as Antipas had deserted his first wife.

Neither Mk nor Lk. (xvi. 18) represents Christ as having made any exception to this prohibition of divorce. Mt. twice inserts an exception, παρεκτὸς λόγου πορνείας (v. 32) and εἰ μὴ ἐπὶ πορνείᾳ (xix. 9); an unfaithful wife has ruptured the marriage tie and may, or must, be divorced. It is doubtful whether Christ did make this exception. Mt. may have had independent authority for it; but it is at least as probable that he inserted it, because he felt sure that Christ would not prohibit what the Law allowed, and what perhaps the Church of Jerusalem allowed. These are possibilities. What is certain is that this exception is attributed to Christ in the Gospel which more than any other has influenced Christian thought and practice in this and other matters; and Christians who divorce an unfaithful wife and marry again can claim Scriptural authority for so doing. That Christ made the exception in accordance with Jewish practice, and that Mk and Lk., writing for Gentiles, omitted the exception as being Jewish, is an intelligible theory, but it is not probable. It is safer to point out that in no Gospel does Christ censure Moses for regulating divorce (and thereby sanctioning it) in a defective state of society. The in-

ference is that in similar conditions of society a similar concession
may be made. See Hastings' *D.B.* and *D.C.G.* artt. "Divorce" and
"Marriage"; also Allen on Mt. v. 32, xix. 9.

13—16. CHRIST BLESSES LITTLE CHILDREN.

Mt. xix. 13—15. Lk. xviii. 15—17.

13. προσέφερον αὐτῷ παιδία. Mk and Mt. place this incident
immediately after the discourse on divorce in a house at Capernaum,
and Salmon (*Human Element*, p. 395) makes the attractive suggestion
that the children of the house "were brought to Him to say good-
night, and receive His blessing before being sent to bed." Lk.
intimates that several parents brought their babes (τὰ βρέφη); and
the disciples would hardly have interfered, if only the children of the
house had been brought. Both Mk and Lk. say that the object was
that the great Healer should *touch* the children, which Mt. enlarges
into what He actually did; "that He should lay His hands on them
and pray." Cf. Gen. xlviii. 14. Syr Sin. here has "lay His hands
on them." For the subj. after a past tense see Winer, p. 360; the
opt. is going out of use, and no example of the opt. after ἵνα is found
in N.T. Both Mk (ii. 4) and Mt. (often) use προσφέρειν of bringing
the sick to Christ, and ailments in children are common; even those
who had no ailment would be honoured by His touch. A girl of
twelve is called παιδίον (v. 39, 42), so that we need not think of all
these children as babies; the point is that their being too young to
comprehend His teaching is no reason for keeping them from Him.
In the First Prayer Book of Edward VI. this passage was substituted
in the Office for Baptism for Mt. xix. 13—15, as clearer evidence of
Christ's love for children.

οἱ δὲ μαθηταὶ ἐπετίμησαν αὐτοῖς. See crit. note. To the disciples
it seemed intolerable that the Master, whose strength was sorely tried
by the number of adults whom He taught and healed, should be
expected to attend to little children who had no need of any special
attention.

14. ἠγανάκτησεν. *Was much displeased* (A.V.); cf. *v.* 41, xiv. 4;
Lk. xiii. 14; Mt. xxvi. 8. Another instance of human emotion in
Christ; see on iii. 5. He was indignant that His disciples should put
such a limit on His love and His work as to exclude children. In a
smaller degree it was a repetition of the error of Peter (viii. 32). Peter
wished to keep Him from future suffering and death; the disciples
now wish to keep Him from present trouble and fatigue. Like the
records of their terror at the storm, their misunderstanding about the

leaven, their powerlessness in dealing with the demoniac boy, and their disputing about the first place, this narrative illustrates the candour of the Evangelists in telling what is not to the credit of the Apostles.

Ἄφετε, μὴ κωλύετε. See crit. note. Mt. and Lk. weaken the sharp decisive commands by inserting a connecting καί between them. "Allow them; cease to forbid them" (cf. ix. 39) is doubtless nearer to the original utterance. We have similarly expressive instances of short, unconnected sentences, i. 27, ii. 7, vi. 38, and of short, unconnected rebukes, iv. 39, 40, viii. 17, 18, ix. 19.

τῶν γὰρ τοιούτων. *His, qui similem haberent innocentiam et simplicitatem, praemium promittit* (Bede, from Jerome). This, like ἄφετε and μὴ κωλύετε, is in all three. The gen. is possessive; *For to such belongs the Kingdom of God.* The disciples were trying to keep from the Son of God some of those who were the most fit to be admitted to His presence. The end and aim of His work was to bring people into the Kingdom, and His ministers were turning most promising candidates away. Various writers point out that Jesus says τοιούτων, not τούτων, to show that it is simple character that counts and not tender years.

15. ἀμὴν λέγω ὑμῖν. This solemn warning, "the final lesson of His ministry in Galilee" (Swete), is omitted by Mt., who has recorded similar words xviii. 3, but without the important δέξηται, which implies that the Kingdom is *offered.* "Receiving the Kingdom" means accepting the rule and sovereignty of God. "Entering the Kingdom" means becoming a member of the society in which His rule prevails. The leave to enter is always open to those who qualify themselves for entering.

ὡς παιδίον. With perfect trust, joy, and hope; "even as a weaned child" (Ps. cxxxi. 2).

οὐ μὴ εἰσέλθῃ. *Shall in no wise enter;* cf. ix. 1, 41, xiii. 2, 19, 30.

16. ἐναγκαλισάμενος. The same gesture as in ix. 36; and in both places Syr-Sin. has something different; here "He called them," there "He looked at them." On this occasion the embrace must have been repeated several times, and each repetition would emphasize the rebuke just uttered. "To save Me from possible fatigue, you would have deprived Me, and have deprived these little ones, of the joy of mutual affection." Both here and ix. 36 Mt. omits this beautiful action. He may have thought that it did not harmonize with the majesty of the Messiah.

κατευλόγει. See crit. note. "He blessed them fervently again and again." The strong compound occurs nowhere else in N.T., but it is used of Tobias blessing Sara's parents and of Tobit blessing Sara (Tobit xi. 1, 17). Cf. καταγελάω (v. 40), κατακλάω (vi. 41), καταφιλέω (xiv. 45), etc.

τιθεὶς τὰς χεῖρας. This was all that had been asked, but *plus fecit quam rogatus erat* (Beng.).

17—31. THE RICH MAN'S QUESTION; CHRIST'S ANSWER AND COMMENTS.

Mt. xix. 16—30. Lk. xviii. 18—30.

17. ἐκπορευομένου αὐτοῦ. *As He was going out* of the house in which He had welcomed the children. Mk alone has this detail, and that the rich man ran and prostrated himself. The action indicates youthful impulsiveness; he is quite in earnest (cf. i. 40, v. 22); he has perhaps just heard of Christ's graciousness to the children, and it has kindled his enthusiasm. All three place the coming of the rich man immediately after the blessing of the children, to which it forms an instructive contrast. The children were nearer to the Kingdom than they knew; it did them no harm to be exalted, and they were greatly exalted. The rich man was farther from the Kingdom than he knew; it might do him good to be somewhat abased, and he was abased. Εἰς ὁδόν, as in vi. 8, means *for a journey*, to travel, rather than "into the way" (A.V., R.V.), which would be εἰς τὴν ὁδόν. It is doubtful whether εἰς (Mk, Mt.) simply = τις (a rare use without a substantive), or means that he was by himself. There is reason for conjecturing that εἷς τις νεανίσκος (xiv. 51) is the Evangelist; but that this εἷς is the same as that εἷς τις νεανίσκος is pure conjecture. Lk. calls him ἄρχων, which may mean no more than that he was a leading man. In the wording Lk. often agrees with Mk against Mt., but only once (ἀκούσας, v. 23) with Mt against Mk. See on v. 21 for the pronouns after the gen. abs., and on 1. 15, 40 for the combination of participles.

ἐπηρώτα. Conversational imperf. See on v. 9.

Διδάσκαλε ἀγαθέ. The admiration is genuine, but it is defective; he means no more than that he is seeking instruction from a teacher of great reputation for wisdom and kindness. It is perhaps chiefly the kindness (Mt. xx. 15), as manifested to the children in spite of the disciples' opposition, that is meant; cf. iii. 4; Lk. vi. 45, xxiii. 50. Mt., in order to avoid what seems to be implied in the question which Christ asks in return, transfers ἀγαθός from Διδάσκαλε to τί; "Master, what good thing shall I do?" This makes ἀγαθόν pointless; action

that is to win eternal life must be good. Lk. both here and x. 45 has
τί ποιήσας, as if the speaker thought that one heroic act might win
eternal life. The Philippian gaoler (Acts xvi. 30) asked τί με δεῖ
ποιεῖν; cf. Lk. iii. 10—14, and see Wetstein on Mt. xix. 16.

ζωὴν αἰώνιον. Mk uses this remarkable expression only here and
v. 30; Mt. and Lk. each have it thrice, Jn 17 times, 1 Jn six times.
The expression never varies, but A.V. has "eternal life," "life
eternal," "everlasting life," "life everlasting"; R.V. always
"eternal life." The idea becomes prominent in Jewish thought
in connexion with belief in the resurrection (Dan. xii. 2; cf. Ps. of
Solomon iii. 16; 2 Macc. vii. 9). See on iii. 29, ix. 43; also on
Jn iii. 15 with App. E. In class. Grk κληρονομέω is "receive a share
of an inheritance," "inherit," and is followed by the gen. In Polyb.
and LXX., as in N.T., it has the acc. In LXX. and N.T. the idea of
"inheritance" seems to be almost lost, and that of "sanctioned and
settled possession" to remain. Hort on 1 Pet. i. 4. Mk has it nowhere else.

18. Τί με λέγεις ἀγαθόν; There can be no emphasis on the
enclitic με, which is in all three, but Mt. has τί με ἐρωτᾷς περὶ τοῦ
ἀγαθοῦ; This does not fit the original question, for the rich man
had not asked about "the good." Nor does it fit what follows, for
εἷς ἐστὶν ὁ ἀγαθός ought logically to be ἓν ἐστὶν τὸ ἀγαθόν. Mt. has
evidently changed language which he thought would mislead into
what seemed to him more likely to have been said. His unwilling-
ness to record what might give a low view of the Messiah is apparent
all through his Gospel, and he shrank from saying that Christ
objected to being called good. "Good Master" was a very unusual
form of address; no example has been found in the Talmud, and the
rich man seems to have used it glibly. If it was not a mere compli-
ment to win favour, it was said without consideration. There was
some defect in his use of the epithet. The defect was not that he
failed to see that Jesus was God, as if Christ's reply meant, "God
alone is really good, and you do not believe that I am God. Unless
you do that, I cannot accept the title 'good' from you." This is
the explanation of Cyril, Basil, Epiphanius, Ambrose, Jerome, Bede,
Maldonatus, and Wordsworth. It cannot be right, for the man could
not have understood it, and Christ's words must have had a meaning
for him. What he might have seen and failed to see was that the
good desires of which he was conscious in himself, and the good
words and works which he recognized in Christ, all came from God.
The man was too self-confident, too certain that of his own will and
power he could do what would win eternal life. Christ, by attributing

His own goodness entirely to God (Jn v. 19—30) checks this self-confidence. *Magistrum absque Deo nullum bonum esse testatur.*
οὐδεὶς ἀγαθὸς εἰ μὴ εἷς ὁ θεός. So also in Lk., but there אB omit
ὁ. The saying is quoted in a variety of forms, some closer to Mk and
Lk., some closer to Mt.; *e.g.* Justin *Apol.* i. 16, *Try.* 101; Hippol.
Philosoph. v. 1; and four times in *Clem. Hom.* See W.H. *App.* pp.
14, 15.

19. τὰς ἐντολὰς οἶδας. It is not difficult to know God's will,
He has shown all men the way to eternal life. Mt. gives this interpretation of Christ's words as having been actually spoken; "If thou
wouldest enter into life, keep the commandments." See on viii. 29,
where Mt. expands Christ's question and Peter's reply.

Μὴ φονεύσῃς. So also Lk. and Jas. ii. 11. Mt. and Rom. xiii. 9
have the form used in Exod. xx. and Deut. v., Οὐ φονεύσεις.

μὴ ἀποστερήσῃς. *Ne fraudem feceris* (Vulg.). Mt. and Lk. omit
this prohibition, perhaps as not being one of the Ten Words, and
Syr-Sin. omits it in Mk. It may represent the tenth commandment,
or it may be added by Christ as a special warning to the rich man.
Cf. Exod. xxi. 10; Mal. iii. 5; and Ecclus iv. 1, τὴν ζωὴν τοῦ πτωχοῦ
μὴ ἀποστερήσῃς.

τίμα τὸν πατέρα σου. All three place the fifth commandment
last and omit the first four. Mt. adds the golden rule from Lev. xix.
18, which Mk has at xii. 31. If it had been uttered on this occasion
the rich man could hardly have answered as he did.

20. Διδάσκαλε. See crit. note. This time ἀγαθέ is omitted.

ταῦτα πάντα ἐφυλαξάμην. The man's self-satisfaction and his
ignorance of what the commandments imply are manifest; but he is
not so much praising himself as showing his disappointment at
Christ's answer. He had expected to be advised to undertake something exceptional and difficult, and he is told of the humdrum duties
which every decent person tries to perform. Mt. and Lk. have
ἐφύλαξα. So also in Acts xvi. 4, xxi. 24, as in class. Grk. In LXX.
we have both act. (Gen. xxvi. 5; Exod. xii. 17, xx. 6) and midd.
(Lev. xviii. 4, xx. 8, 22, xxii. 3), without difference of meaning.
Syr-Sin. omits πάντα.

ἐκ νεότητός μου. Mt. omits this and at this point calls him
νεανίσκος, which does not contradict 'from my youth,' for a man of
thirty might be called νεανίσκος.

21. ἐμβλέψας. A concentrated, penetrating look (v. 27, xiv. 67;
Lk. xxii. 61). Christ saw in him the making of a beautiful character
and a valuable disciple, and He loved him for what he was and for
what he might become. This is the only place in the Synoptics in

which love is attributed to our Lord, whereas compassion is often attributed to Him. In Jn compassion is never attributed to Him, love often, and (excepting xix. 31) always love to man. Ἀγαπάω is the verb used of Christ's affection for the family at Bethany (Jn xi. 5) and the beloved disciple (Jn xiii. 23, xix. 26, xxi. 20). See on Jn xi. 5 and xxi. 15. Both Mt. and Lk. omit this mark of Christ's perfect humanity; it indicates that behind Mk is someone who was present, who was intimate with Christ, and who knew from experience how penetrating a look from Christ could be (Lk. xxii. 61). Nothing is gained by taking ἐμβλέψας ἠγάπησεν as hendiadys, *amanter aspexit* (Beng.); moreover, hendiadys requires two substantives, not two verbs.

"Εν σε ὑστερεῖ. Cf. Ps. xxiii. 1. Christ leaves the man's estimate of himself unchallenged. Granting that it is not untrue, there is still something wanting, viz. freedom from the ἀπάτη τοῦ πλούτου (iv. 19). Mt. gives these words to the rich man; "What lack I yet?" He then inserts "If thou wouldst be perfect" as a preface to "Go, sell, etc." Cf. Clem. Alex. *Strom.* iii. 6, p. 537 ed. Potter.

ὅσα ἔχεις πώλησον καὶ δός. Lk. has διαδός. In no other way could the rich man's future be made secure from moral disaster. It was a strong measure, urged as the only prudent course, in his case. Simon and Andrew were not told to part with all that they had, because their hearts were not tied to their possessions; and to give up everything cannot be a duty of general obligation. But every follower of Christ must be ready to adopt it, if the call to do so should come. Cf. Lk. xii. 33. Seneca gives similar advice; *Projice omnia ista, si sapis, immo ut sapias; et ad bonam mentem magno cursu ac totis viribus tende* (*Ep.* xvii. 1). For πτωχός, "abjectly poor" (πτώσσω, "I crouch") see Trench, *Syn.* § xxxvi.

ἕξεις θησαυρὸν ἐν οὐρανῷ. Christ does not promise him eternal life in return for the sacrifice of his possessions; He promises a secure treasure in return for an insecure one; Mt. vi. 19, 20. It is obedience to the second command that will prove decisive.

ἀκολούθει μοι. Pres. imperat. To be continually a follower of Christ is the sure road to eternal life; cf. viii. 34. That a man may give all his goods to feed the poor without being a follower of Christ is quite possible (1 Cor. xiii. 3). *Facilius enim sacculus contemnitur quam voluntas. Multi divitias relinquentes Dominum non sequuntur* (Bede). See crit. note.

22. στυγνάσας...λυπούμενος. Cf. Gen. iv. 5. All three record the grief, but Mk alone has στυγνάσας, for which Mt. and Lk. have ἀκούσας. He was gloomy and sullen with a double disappointment;

no perilous exploit was required of him, but he was asked to part with what he valued most. With a lowering look (Mt. xvi. 3), instead of coming to follow Christ (i. 18, 20, ii. 14), he turned away, deeply pained (note the participles). This is the sorrow of the world which leads to death, τῆς φιλαργυρίας ἡ ἄκανθα τὴν λιπαρὰν ἄρουραν τῆς ψυχῆς αὐτοῦ διελυμήνατο (Euthym.). Στυγνός is freq. in tragedians, but rare in prose; στυγνάζω is rare everywhere. On the Τίς ὁ σωζόμενος πλούσιος of Clem. Alex., which is apparently a popular address on this incident, see *D. of Chr. Biog.* I. p. 565; Swete, *Patristic Study*, p. 49.

23. περιβλεψάμενος. This again points to an eye-witness; see on iii. 5. It is not a concentrated look directed to one person (v. 21), but a glance round the faces of His followers, to judge how this conversation had affected them, and to intimate that He has something to say.

δυσκόλως. Εἰ δὲ πλούσιος δυσκόλως, πλεονέκτης οὐδ' ὅλως (Euthym.). The adv. is in all three, but is found nowhere else in Bibl. Grk. Facts of this kind show that either Mt. and Lk. used Mk or all three used a tradition which was already in Greek. Clem. Alex. (*Strom.* v. 5, p. 662 ed. Potter) has ὁ λόγος τοὺς τελώνας λέγει δυσκόλως σωθήσεσθαι. Cf. Eccles. v. 10, 13.

τὰ χρήματα. "Wealth," esp. money (Acts viii. 18, 20, xxiv. 26), whereas κτήματα, "possessions" (v. 22), seems to refer specially to lands and houses (Acts II. 45, v. 1); but both words are comprehensive. Syr-Sin. has "for them who trust in their riches," and so again in v. 24.

24. ἐθαμβοῦντο. This verse has no parallel in Mt. or Lk., who habitually spare the Twelve. Mk alone uses this verb, and always cf the effect of Christ's words (i. 27) or action (v. 32). Lk. uses θάμβος in a similar way (iv. 36, v. 9). For ἀποκριθεὶς λέγει see on viii. 29 *sub fin.*

πῶς δύσκολον. The adj. has three stages of meaning; "difficult to please about food," dainty; "difficult to please," fretful; "difficult" in any sense, as here. See crit. note. The words omitted by אBΔ and k, one of the most important of the representatives of the Old Latin texts, cannot be original. They do not fit the context and they are less than the truth. The context requires "How hard it is for rich people not to trust in riches, and those who trust in riches *cannot* enter the Kingdom" (Mt. vi. 24). The true text says that it is hard for anyone to enter the Kingdom (Lk. xiii. 24), and therefore very hard for the wealthy (Lk. vi. 24, xvi. 19; Jas. v. 1). This was a solemn warning to Judas. Celsus said that Christ took this from

Plato (*Laws* v. p. 742), but that passage merely says that a man cannot be both very good and very rich.

25. εὐκοπώτερον. In all three: lit. "more capable of being done with easy labour" (εὖ, κόπος); in N.T. always in the comparative (ii. 9; Lk. v. 23, xvi. 17), but εὔκοπος occurs in LXX. and in Polybius. Some commentators would follow D and some Old Latin texts in transposing verses 24 and 25. The transposition looks like a correction, or it may be accidental owing to homoeoteleuton.

κάμηλον διὰ τρυμαλιᾶς ῥαφίδος. There is no need to conjecture that κάμηλος means a cable (Cyril, Theoph.); Euthym. mentions this view without adopting it. Nor need we read κάμιλον, which is said to mean a cable, although the existence of such a word is doubtful. Still less need we make the needle's eye mean a small side-gate for foot-passengers (Shakespeare, *Richard II*, v. v. 17), an explanation which no ancient commentator adopts. Christ's Sayings, like those of other Oriental teachers, are often hyperbolical; "strain out the gnat, and swallow the camel" (Mt. **xxiii.** 24), "whoso shall say to this mountain etc." (xi. 23), "a grain of mustard seed, less than all seeds, becometh a tree" (Mt. xiii. 32), etc. In the Talmud an elephant going through a needle's eye is used to express an impossibility. The saying in the Koran about "not entering into paradise until a camel pass through the eye of a needle" (vii. 38) may come from the Gospels. While τρῆμα (Mt. and Lk.) is classical and fairly common, τρυμαλιά is late and rare; both τρυμαλιά and ῥαφίς ("stitcher") were probably colloquial.

26. περισσῶς ἐξεπλήσσοντο. Cf. i. 22, vi. 2, vii. 37. The O.T. teaches that God rewards good men with wealth, and most men either have it or labour to get it. How amazing, therefore, to be told that wealth is a dire obstacle to salvation!

λέγοντες πρὸς αὐτόν. See crit. note. In Mk, as in Mt., λέγειν πρός is very rare; iv. 41; cf. viii. 16, xi. 31.

Καὶ τίς δύναται σωθῆναι; *Then who in the world can be saved?* Not merely, What *rich* man? There is no hope that anybody will escape the enormous peril; cf. xiii. 20. The καί accepts what is said and carries it on with emphasis; Lk. x. 29; Jn ix. 36; 2 Cor. ii. 2, 16.

27. ἐμβλέψας. As in *v.* 21. Christ neither explains nor softens the strong Saying in *v.* 25, but He shows where the solution of the difficulty is to be found. God has many counter-charms with which to conquer the baleful charm of riches. The disciples had seen this conquest once (ii. 14), and they would soon see it done again (Lk. xix. 1—10). But those who would be freed from the spell must work with Him, otherwise the ἀδύνατον stands (xiv. 10, 11).

πάντα γὰρ δυνατά. The πάντα is not absolute. God's own character places some limits, and there are others which seem to us to exist; but all things that are necessary for the salvation of mankind —and this is the point here—are possible with God. See xiv. 36 and cf. ix. 23; Lk. i. 37; Gen. xviii. 14; Zech. viii. 6. It is an attractive conjecture that the rich man was still within hearing, and that these words were meant to reach him. They touch what seems to have been his chief fault; see on *v.* 18.

28. ἤρξατο ὁ Πέτρος. The asyndeton harmonizes with the Apostle's outburst; cf. Ἔφη αὐτῷ ὁ Ἰωάνης (ix. 38). ℵABC have neither καί (D) nor δέ (KΝΠ). "Then" (A.V.) has no authority.

Ἰδοὺ ἡμεῖς. The pronoun is emphatic; "*we* did not prefer our possessions to Thee." Christ's ἀκολούθει μοι (*v.* 21) would remind him of his own call, and he could hardly help contrasting his own response to it with the behaviour of the rich man. But he could have helped calling attention to the contrast, and the impulsive remark is characteristic. It suggests some such question as that which Mt. supplies, "What then shall be *our* reward?" This, however, is probably Mt.'s interpretation of what was said. See on *v.* 19. The exact question in Peter's mind might be, "Shall *we*, then, inherit eternal life?"

ἀφήκαμεν...ἠκολουθήκαμεν. The change of tense is accurate; "we left once for all...we have followed and continue to follow." Mt. and Lk. have two aorists.

29. ἔφη ὁ Ἰησοῦς. Cf. ix. 38. Jesus treats Peter as the spokesman of the Twelve, and, as often, gives what is not a direct answer to the question, but what either includes the answer or is much more important. Mt. supplies a direct answer by inserting words which were probably uttered on a different occasion (Lk. xxii. 30). Christ treats in a similar way the remark made by Peter about the withered fig tree (xi. 21 f.).

οὐδείς ἐστιν. There will be no exceptions. Everyone who, for the highest motives, has given up what is most dear to him will be abundantly rewarded here and hereafter. See crit. note. Philo (*De Vita Contempl.* p. 474) has a similar list; καταλιπόντες ἀδελφούς, τέκνα, γυναῖκας, γονεῖς.

ἕνεκεν ἐμοῦ καὶ ἕνεκεν τ. εὐαγγελίου. See on viii. 35. There Mt. and Lk. have only the first half. Here each takes a different half and amplifies it. Perhaps all that Christ said was ἕνεκεν ἐμοῦ. See on i. 15 and cf. i. 32.

30. ἐὰν μὴ λάβῃ. "Without receiving," or *but he shall receive* (A.V., R.V.). The construction is imperfect.

νῦν ἐν τῷ καιρῷ τούτῳ. Mk's characteristic fullness again, as in i. 32, 35, 42, ii. 23, 25, etc. Lk. omits νῦν, Mt. omits the whole. Here καιρός is preferred to αἰών as indicating that the period is brief. Mk alone repeats οἰκ. καὶ ἀδελ. κ.τ.λ. in speaking of the recompenses, another instance of superfluous fullness. Mt. puts all the compensations and rewards "in the regeneration," and therefore omits μετὰ διωγμῶν, for there can be no persecutions in the future life. Clem. Alex. quotes as if Christ had asked, "What is the use of the χρήματα in this life?" It is the eternal compensation that is worth having. "A hundredfold" of course means what will compensate a hundredfold; the silly jibe of the Emperor Julian about a hundred wives has no foothold here. Yet even with regard to the happiness of human relationships the great Christian family supplies compensation in kind. The text of D is here very eccentric.

ἐν τῷ αἰῶνι τῷ ἐρχομένῳ. "In the age which is in process of being realized," which is of unlimited duration, whereas a καιρός is necessarily limited.

31. πολλοὶ δὲ ἔσονται. Lk. gives this Saying at an earlier point (xiii. 30); it was probably uttered more than once, and it is capable of more than one application. Many who think that they have earned much will be disappointed, and many who think that they have earned little will be surprised, as the labourers in the vineyard. The fortunate and unfortunate will often change places, as Dives and Lazarus. "The greyhaired saint may fail at last," as Judas, and the greyhaired sinner may be saved, as the penitent robber.

32—34. THE LAST PREDICTION OF THE PASSION.

Mt. xx. 17—19. Lk. xviii. 31—34.

32. Ἦσαν δέ. Note the unusual δέ and see on vii. 24. Translate "Now," not "And" (A.V., R.V.).

ἀναβαίνοντες. As in English, a journey to the capital is "going up." This is literally true of Jerusalem, which is "a city set on a hill" (Mt. v. 14), and the hill stands high above the sea; cf. Jn ii. 13, v. 1, xi. 55; Acts xi. 2, xxv. 1; Gal. ii. 1. The verb is exceedingly freq. in LXX., where it translates about twenty different Hebrew words.

Ἱεροσόλυμα. *Quae urbs illud occidendi Prophetas quasi usu ceperat* (Grotius on Lk. xiii. 33). Mk and Jn always have this Greek form of the name; so also Mt., except xxiii. 37, and Josephus. The Hebrew Ἱερουσαλήμ prevails in LXX., and in N.T. where the name has religious significance, as distinct from mere topographical meaning (Mt. xxiii. 37; Gal. iv. 25; Heb. xii. 22; Rev. iii. 12, xxi. 2, 10). But Lk. uses Ἰερουσαλήμ without religious significance. Both forms have a smooth breathing; the aspirate comes from a mistaken connexion with ἱερός.

ἦν προάγων. As an Oriental shepherd "goeth before" his sheep, who follow with complete docility (Jn x. 4). This graphic detail of His leading for a while in silence and their following in fear is in Mk only; it may be something that Peter remembered well. There are two companies; *the Twelve*, who were awe-struck at Christ's demeanour and fixity of purpose (Lk. ix. 51; cf. Ezek. iii. 8, 9; Is. l. 7), for He had said that He would suffer much at the hands of tl e hierarchy, and He was going to their headquarters; and *the casual followers*, who had an indefinite presentiment that something untoward was impending. But there is no indication of "excitement" in His manner. See crit. note.

παραλαβὼν πάλιν τ. δώδεκα. In all three; it implies the presence of other followers. The verb means "taking *to oneself*" (Jn i. 11, xiv. 3), and therefore *aside* from others (iv. 36, v. 40, ix. 2, xiv. 33). In class. Grk it is freq. of taking a wife or adopting a son. The πάλιν means that He rejoined the Twelve.

ἤρξατο. He renews the unwelcome topic. This is the fourth (not third) recorded prediction (viii. 31, ix. 12, 31). *Apostolis saepius dixit, et indies expressius, ut in posterum testes essent praescientiae ipsius* (Grotius). This is more accurate than Loisy, who says that this prediction is made *en termes identiques*; it is more definite and detailed than the previous predictions, and this has probability on its side. The voluntary character of His death is made clear to the Apostles; He knew the inevitable consequence of going to Jerusalem now.

τὰ μέλλοντα αὐτῷ συμβαίνειν. *The things which were sure to happen to Him* (Mt. xvii. 12, 22, xx. 22; Lk. ix. 31, etc.). On κατακρινοῦσιν α. dat. see Blass § 37. 2.

33. παραδοθήσεται. In all three; see on ix. 31. Mk here has more detail than either Mt. or Lk., but nothing which is not in either Mt. or Lk. That the Sanhedrin will "hand Him over to the heathen" almost reveals that He will be crucified (Jn xviii. 31, 32), for "the heathen" could only mean the Romans. Mt. again gives an interpretation of Christ's words as having been spoken; he records that Christ *said* "crucify." See on *v.* 28.

34. ἐμπαίξουσιν. The verb is peculiar to the Synoptists in N.T. This and what follows are the work of "the heathen." Lk. says that the Twelve "understood none of these things," because "the thing was hidden from them."

μετὰ τρεῖς ἡμέρας. See crit. note. Mt. again substitutes the more accurate "on the third day." The mention of "the third day" in three of the four predictions is important in connexion with the evidence for the Resurrection, and the careful correction of the intelligible, but not quite exact, "after three days" is also important. Lk. corrects it twice and once omits the expression. At the time when the Gospels were written, and indeed considerably earlier (1 Cor. xv. 4), there was a clear and uniform conviction that the life of Him who died on the cross was renewed *after an interval*. Something quite different from His spirit surviving, after leaving the body, took place. With the theory of mere survival after death, "on the third day" becomes as unintelligible as the empty tomb. And the repeated records of the inability of the Twelve to understand these predictions are against the theory that they believed that He had risen because they were so confident that He would rise.

35—45. THE REQUEST OF THE SONS OF ZEBEDEE.

Mt. xx. 20—28. Cf. Lk. xxii. 25.

35. This request is evidence of the Apostles' want of apprehension as to the nature of the Kingdom. Even if there was an interval, which Mt. excludes with his characteristic τότε, it was strange, but hardly "comic" (Bruce), that soon after this detailed prediction of His approaching sufferings and death, two of His most favoured Apostles should trouble Him with an ambitious petition. Perhaps Mt. felt this, for he puts the petition into the mouth of their mother. Tradition probably said that in some way she was responsible for the petition being made, and it looks like a mother's ambition. But they were parties to it, and even in Mt. Christ addresses them and not her. They and Peter had received a special revelation on the mount; and soon afterwards first Peter exhibits a selfish ambition on behalf of all the Twelve (*v.* 23), and then James and John do so on their own behalf. Christ's promise about the twelve thrones (Mt. xix. 28) was remembered; the present journey to Jerusalem was to produce a crisis of some kind (*v.* 33); and the sons of Thunder wished to make sure of a good position in the Kingdom. Evidently the question of "who is the greatest" (ix. 34) has not yet been put to rest. Their asking to have their request granted before they had stated it is almost childish in its simplicity; and the D text represents Christ as promising to do what they wish.

οἱ [δύο] υἱοὶ Ζεβ. The δύο (BC, Memph.) may come from Mt. xxvi. 37; cf. Jn xxi. 2. Their mother's name was Salome, and she seems to have been the sister of Christ's Mother (xv. 40; Mt. xxvii. 56; Jn xix. 25). These brothers, therefore, would be our Lord's first cousins, and hence their hope of preferment. "This was the first ecclesiastical intrigue for high places in the Church" (Sadler). θέλομεν ἵνα. Cf. vi. 25, ix. 30; cf. x. 51. Blass § 69. 4, 5, 6.

37. ἐκ δεξιῶν. Both here and Mt. xx. 21, Vulg. has *ad dexteram tuam*, although *ab dextera* would have been good Latin and closer to the Greek. In English we must say either "on" or "to." See crit. note. Cf. Joseph. *Ant.* vi. xi. 9 on the value of the right hand and the left hand places.

ἐν τῇ δόξῃ σου. The brothers may be thinking of Moses and Elijah at the Transfiguration (ix. 4), or of what was said before it (viii. 38).

38. Οὐκ οἴδατε. They little thought of the two crucified robbers. In spite of His declaration (viii. 34, 35), they did not know that the entrance to the Kingdom is through suffering, and that those who would reign with Him must be ready to endure with Him (Acts xiv. 22; Rom. viii. 17; 2 Tim. ii. 12). On the change from αἰτήσωμεν (*v.* 35) to αἰτεῖσθε, "ask for yourselves," see J. H. Moulton, p. 160.

ὃ ἐγὼ πίνω. He does not reprove them for their carnal ideas about the Kingdom, but He proceeds to correct them. They do not understand the nature of His mission. "Can ye drink?" implies that the cup is no pleasant one, and it is one which He is already drinking. The process is a long one, and the bitterness increases. Mt. interprets it of the Agony, and has μέλλω πίνειν instead of πίνω. "Cup" in the sense of "the contents of the cup" is freq. in literature (Lk. xxii. 20; 1 Cor. x. 16, 21, xi. 25—27). Cf. the "cup" in Gethsemane (xiv. 36), the "cup of God's fury" (Is. li. 17, 22).

τὸ βάπτισμα. Regarding troubles as a flood in which one is plunged is also common in literature (Ps. xviii. 16, lxix. 1, 2; etc.). But here more may be meant. Baptism is immersion with security against sinking; rising again follows. It was therefore a very fit metaphor for the Passion, and Christ had used it before (Lk. xii. 49, 50); but Mk alone reproduces it here. Baptism into water inaugurated the earthly work of the Messiah; baptism into death is to inaugurate His return to glory. For the cogn. acc. see Rev. xvi. 9.

39. Δυνάμεθα. The bold answer is the same in both Gospels; but A.V. suggests a difference, "We are able" (Mt.), "We can" (Mk); and so also in the preceding question.

πίεσθε...βαπτισθήσεσθε. As in the case of the rich man (*vv.* 20, 21), Christ does not question the estimate which James and John have formed of their own characters, nor does He say that all will be of equal rank in the Kingdom. He tells them that they will share His sufferings, and that it is the Father who will assign places in the Kingdom. But the statement with regard to the sufferings is indefinite, and it is forcing the meaning to call it a prediction that the brothers will be put to death for their belief in Jesus Christ. There is no such prediction, and therefore no difficulty as to its non-fulfilment in the case of John. Both suffered, and James was killed by Herod Agrippa I. (Acts xii. 2). John was imprisoned and beaten (Acts iv. 3, v. 18, 40), was banished to Patmos (Rev. i. 9), and continued to confess Christ through a long life. The stories of his having been thrown into a caldron of boiling oil (Tert. *De Praescr.* 36; Jer. *C. Jovin.* i. 26), and of his having drunk poison in the presence of Domitian (*Acta Johannis*), probably arose from a desire to find a literal fulfilment of the baptism and the cup. The statement that Papias said that both John and James were slain by the Jews rests on poor authority; if he did say it, he was probably drawing an inference from Christ's declaration that both brothers should drink His cup. J. A. Robinson, *Hist. Character of St John's Gospel*, p. 79. The belief that Jesus had declared that John would not die could not have become current if John had been slain with James. Nor in that case would the Gospel according to the Hebrews have said that James alone was to drink Christ's cup. Syr-Sin. here has "Ye *may be able* to drink...*ye may be able* to be baptized," and Syr-Cur. has the same, Mt. xx. 23. This change was doubtless made to meet the difficulty that John was not put to death.

40. ἐξ εὐωνύμων. Omens from the left hand were *sinister*, but they were euphemistically called "of good name" to avert ill fortune; εὐωνύμων = ἀριστερῶν (*v.* 37). The former is more freq. in N.T., but the latter is far more freq. in LXX.

οὐκ ἔστιν ἐμὸν δοῦναι. Cf. οὐκ ἐμὲ δέχεται (ix. 37). The rewards will be His to give (Rev. xxii. 12; 2 Tim. iv. 8), but only in accordance with the will of the Father, who "hath given all judgment unto the Son" (Jn v. 22 f. ; Acts x. 42), and He will exercise it when the time and season come (Acts i. 7). Their asking the Son of Man to give the reward, before they had earned it, and before He was glorified, was altogether out of place; it was asking Him to be capricious and unfair. Cf. xiii. 32. This was a favourite Arian text, and as such is often discussed by the Fathers. Hence the addition in some Latin texts of *vobis*, which is retained in the Clementine Vulgate without Greek authority; also in Aeth.

ἀλλ' οἷς ἡτοίμασται. *But* it shall be given to them *for whom it* *hath been prepared* by the Father. This interpretation "by the Father" is certainly right, and it is given by Mt. as having been uttered; cf. *vv.* 19, 28, 33, 38. And δοθήσεται is to be understood. In A.V. "it shall be given" is in italics in Mt., but not in Mk. There is no δοθήσεται in either text. On the reading ἄλλοις for ἀλλ' οἷς see Nestle, p. 37. Syr-Sin. reads ἀλλῷ. Euthym. understands, not δοθήσεται, but ἐκείνων ἐστίν, "it belongs to those for whom it hath been prepared," which comes to much the same. The point is that fitness, and not personal influence, decides these matters; but we may also make ἀλλά equivalent to εἰ μή, "Not Mine to give, *except* to those." This is sometimes denied, but without good reason. ἔπαισε δ' αὐτόχειρ νιν οὔτις ἀλλ' ἐγὼ τλάμων (Soph. *O.T.* 1331): ἡδέα δ' οὐκ ἔστιν ἀλλὰ τούτοις καὶ οὕτω διακειμένοις (Arist. *Eth. Nic.* x. v. 10). In the sense of Divine preparation, ἑτοιμάζω is almost a technical expression (Mt. xxv. 34; Jn xiv. 2; 1 Cor. ii. 9; Heb. xi. 16; Rev. xii. 6, xxi. 2; 2 Esdr. viii. 52). Hatch, *Essays*, p. 51 f.

41. ἀγανακτεῖν. Cf. *v.* 14. Christ had already rebuked the spirit of ambition and jealousy in the Twelve (ix. 35), but it was not extinguished; and the other ten are indignant with the two brothers for trying to get special promotion for themselves. We do not, however, read of the nine being indignant when Christ *gave* special honour to Peter, James, and John. It was the brothers' *asking* for special favour which gave offence.

42. Οἴδατε. Christ's rebuke to the ten is as gentle as that to the two. We have three rebukes of this character, all beginning with an appeal to the *knowledge* possessed or not possessed by the persons addressed; *vv.* 19, 38, 42. Cf. iv. 13.

οἱ δοκοῦντες ἄρχειν. *They which are accounted to rule, qui censentur imperare* (Beza), who are recognized as rulers. This does not mean that they only seem to be rulers, or think themselves such without being so; cf. Gal. ii. 2, 6, 9. It points to the fact that the power of kings depends upon their being recognized as kings. Wetstein gives illustrations of the phrase in different senses. Cf. Susann. 5. The expression is thoroughly Greek (Plato, *Gorgias*, 472 A). Mt. has simply οἱ ἄρχοντες, Lk. οἱ βασιλεῖς, but he places the Saying in the discourses at the Last Supper.

κατακυριεύουσιν. Stronger than κυριεύουσιν (Lk.); cf. κατέκλασεν (vi. 41). R.V. has "lord it" here and 1 Pet. v. 3, and "have lordship" in Lk. Vulg. has *dominantur eis* here, and *dominantur eorum* in Mt. and Lk., the latter being a rare constr., but found in Tertullian and Lactantius.

οἱ μεγάλοι αὐτῶν. "The great officials of the heathen"; the αὐτῶν might refer to οἱ δοκοῦντες ἄρχειν, but more probably it refers to τῶν ἐθνῶν. Syr-Sin. omits the sentence.

κατεξουσιάζουσιν αὐτῶν. The verb is a very rare one; Mt. has it, and two writers could hardly adopt it independently. Again we are in doubt as to αὐτῶν, and again it is better to refer it to τῶν ἐθνῶν. The despotism of heathen monarchs is heavy, and that of the great officials, who act with the monarchs' authority, is as bad or worse. The last αὐτῶν might refer back to οἱ δοκ. ἄρχειν. The officials who govern in the king's name really control the king, whose delegated authority they so use as to govern the king himself; *e.g.* of Pallas and Narcissus, *His uxoribusque addictus, non principem se sed ministrum egit* (Sueton. *Claud.* 25). But this irony would have no point here.

43. οὐχ οὕτως δέ ἐστιν. See crit. note. *But not so is it among you*; οὐχ οὕτως is emphatic by position. "Quite different are the conditions which determine your relations to one another." The disciples had not grasped these conditions, but they existed; it is the submissive childlike spirit that wins promotion (ix. 36, x. 15). Among the heathen it is held that all must serve Caesar; the ideal ruler knows that he must serve all; he is *servus servorum*.

μέγας γενέσθαι. *To become great.* The superlative, in the strictly superlative sense, is very rare in N.T. (Acts xxvi. 5; 2 Pet. i. 4). Either comparative (ix. 34) or positive (as some think here) may take its place. But here it is better to retain "great," as the next verse shows.

44. πρῶτος...δοῦλος. An advance on the previous paradox; supremacy is more than greatness, and slavery is more than service. The higher the rights, the greater the duties. Cf. 1 Cor. ix. 19, and see on 2 Cor. iv. 5. We infer that there are differences of rank in the Kingdom; Mt. v. 19, xi. 11.

45. καὶ γάρ. "And what is more"; giving an additional reason for what has just been stated. Here the contrast between the two systems is at a maximum. In inaugurating the Messianic Kingdom the Messiah Himself renders service rather than receives it, and gives His labour and His life for His subjects. He often received service, both from Angels (i. 13) and from men and women (i. 31, xiv. 13, xv. 41), but that was not the purpose of the Incarnation. And here He does not say that He was sent (ix. 37), but that He *came*—of His own free will—to minister, and to *give*—of His own free will—His life. This is the most definite declaration of the object of His coming into the world that has thus far been recorded; and it is given, not as instruction in doctrine, but incidentally, to enforce a practical lesson. This does not look like invention.

οὐκ...ἀλλά.   See on ix. 37.

διακονῆσαι.   "He emptied Himself by taking the characteristic attributes of a servant." Cf. Jn xiii. 13—15, and see Lightfoot on Phil. ii. 7.

δοῦναι τὴν ψυχήν.   This is the climax; "Greater love hath no man than this " (Jn xv. 13), and this greatest service the Messiah came to render.

λύτρον.   In some way that is beyond our comprehension, the Death and Resurrection of Christ made it easier for mankind to win forgiveness and entrance into the Kingdom in which eternal life is enjoyed.   The supreme change of conditions is spoken of in Scripture under a variety of metaphors, from which we must be very cautious in drawing inferences.   They sometimes overlap, and therefore the same texts would illustrate more than one of them.   Christ's work for us in this respect is spoken of as "ransoming" (x. 45; Mt. xx. 28; 1 Tim. ii. 6; Tit. ii. 14), "redeeming" (Rom. iii. 24; Eph. i. 7; Col. i. 14; Heb. ix. 12, 15), "buying with a price" (1 Cor. vi. 20; 2 Pet. ii. 1; Rev. v. 9), "shedding blood for a new covenant " (xiv. 24; Heb. xiii. 20), "loosing from sins with blood " (Rev. i. 5), "salvation" or "rescue" (Tit. ii. 11; Heb. ii. 10, v. 9; etc., etc.), " propitiation " (Rom. iii. 25; 1 Jn ii. 2, iv. 10), "reconciliation" or "atonement" (Rom. v. 11; 2 Cor. v. 18, 19; Col. i. 20), "justification " (Rom. v. 9). No metaphor can give us more than a fragment of the truth, and this is often mixed with what (for the purpose in hand) is not true.   Interpretation of figurative language is therefore precarious, and drawing inferences from our interpretations may be perilous.   It is perhaps wisest to accept the fact of these blessed results of Christ's Death and Resurrection, without trying to explain the manner of their working. In the present case we do not know whether Christ used a word which was equivalent to λύτρον.   The metaphor may be the translator's, for λύτρον occurs in N.T. nowhere excepting this utterance.   Nevertheless cognate words are common, esp. in the Pauline Epp. and in writings akin to Pauline thought; e.g. ἀντίλυτρον, λυτρόομαι, λύτρωσις, ἀπολύτρωσις, of which the last is far the most common.   But this metaphor of ransom or redemption is not found in the Johannine writings.   See Westcott, *Hebrews*, pp. 295 f., *Epp. of St John*, pp. 83 f.; Deissmann, *Light from Anc. East*, pp. 330, 331.   The different shades of meaning for λύτρον and λύτρα in literature and papyri do not help us much in explaining this passage, which is the basis of Pauline doctrine.   The Apostle would know the oral tradition about it.

ἀντὶ πολλῶν.   The ἀντί does not belong to δοῦναι, " to give instead of many giving," but to λύτρον, " a ransom to buy off many " (Mt. xvii.

27; Heb. xii. 16). And πολλῶν does not mean for His friends, and not
for His enemies. See on Jn xv. 13; 2 Cor. v. 18; 1 Jn ii. 2; 1 Tim.
ii. 6. That we have πολλῶν instead of πάντων is possibly due to Is. liii.
11, 12 (LXX.). The "many" are contrasted, not with "all," but
with " one "; the surrender of one life rescued millions; ὑπὲρ πάντων
γὰρ ἔδωκε τὴν ψυχὴν αὐτοῦ καὶ πάντας ἐλυτρώσατο, εἰ καὶ πολλοὶ θέλοντες
ἐνέμειναν ἐν δουλείᾳ (Euthym.). The preposition commonly used of
Christ's dying on our behalf is ὑπέρ.

46—52. Blind Bartimaeus restored to Sight.

Mt. xx. 29—34. Lk. xviii. 35—43.

46. We once more have three records, and no two agree. Mk and
Lk. give one blind man, Mt. gives two. Mk and Mt. say that Christ
healed as He was going out of Jericho, Lk., when He was approaching
it. Mk and Lk. say that He healed with a word, but they do not quite
agree as to the word, Mt. that He healed with a touch. These discrepancies are of no moment, except as part of the overwhelming
evidence that not every statement in the Bible can be accepted as
historically accurate. See on iv. 41. There is general agreement
that near Jericho, as Jesus was near the last stage in His last journey
to Jerusalem, a blind man called to Him for help, that the crowd tried
to silence him, but that Jesus interfered on his behalf and restored his
sight; and then the man followed Him. As in the case of the storm
on the Lake, Mk gives graphic details, such as an eye-witness might
remember, which Mt. and Lk. omit as unessential.

The Jericho of our Lord's time was a fine city, much augmented
and adorned by Herod the Great, who died there, and by Archelaus,
but it was a mile or more from the old site. So far as we know, this
was Christ's only visit to it. The modern Jericho is a squalid
village.

ὄχλου ἱκανοῦ. This use of ἱκανός = "plentiful" is freq. in Lk.,
Acts, and LXX., but occurs nowhere else in Mk. It is probably
colloquial.

ὁ υἱὸς Τιμαίου Βαρτιμαῖος. Mk alone gives these names, which
indicate that the man was still remembered when the Gospel was
written. With the order of the names comp. υἱὲ Δαυεὶδ Ἰησοῦ (v. 47).
The derivation of Bartimaeus is doubtful. Keim, *Jesus of Nazara*, v.
p. 61; *Enc. Bibl.* art. "Bartimaeus." Mt. viii. 28 has two demoniacs,
where Mk and Lk have only one.

τυφλὸς προσαίτης. See crit. note; also Jn ix. 8. In the Gospel
of Nicodemus i. 6, this man is said to have been born blind. Perhaps

the two miracles are confused. Blind men were proverbially beggars; *Quid aliud caecitas discit quam rogare, blandiri ?* (Quintil. *Declam.* 1). The roads being full of pilgrims on their way to the Passover, beggars would frequent them.

ἐκάθητο παρὰ τὴν ὁδόν. The acc. after a verb of rest is freq. in both N.T. and LXX. (iv. 1=Mt. xiii. 1; Lk. xviii. 35=Mt. xx. 30; Acts x. 6, 32; Gen. xxii. 17, xli. 3; etc.); see also Xen. *Anab.* iii. v. 1, vii. ii. 11. He was by the side of the road and commanding it, so that he could hear all that passed.

47. ὁ Ναζαρηνός. See crit. note and on i. 24.

ἤρξατο κράζειν. Here, as in *vv.* 28, 32, 41, Mk's favourite ἤρξ. is omitted, not only by Mt., but by Lk., who often has it.

Υἱὲ Δαυείδ. This form of address is here in all three twice. It implies that "Jesus of Nazareth" is believed to be the Messiah; and the Messiah would give sight to the blind (Is. lxi. 1). It is remarkable that a blind beggar should, in this Gospel, be the first to give Jesus this title. But the thought was in the air; the beggar shouted what many people were debating in themselves or with one another (Lagrange). The expression occurs again xii. 35=Mt. xxii. 42=Lk. xx. 41, and nowhere else in Mk or Lk. Mt. has it several times, Jn never. Dalman, *Words*, pp. 319 f.

48. ἐπετίμων. It was the crowd in front of Jesus who did this (Lk.); they wanted to silence him before Jesus came up. Like the disciples with the Syrophoenician woman (Mt. xv. 23), they resented the ceaseless importunity; and like the disciples with those who brought their children (*v.* 13), they resented the trouble likely to be given to Christ. They were not objecting, nor does Jesus do so, to his addressing Him as the Messiah. Wrede, *Messiasgeheimnis*, p. 278. Note the imperfects.

ἵνα σιωπήσῃ. This is Mk's usual word (iii. 4, iv. 39, ix. 34, xiv. 61). Lk. has his usual σιγάω, which neither Mk nor Mt. ever uses. Jn uses neither.

49. στάς. So also Mt. As often in Gospel and Acts, Lk. has σταθείς, which is peculiar to him; it may imply taking a conspicuous place.

Φωνήσατε αὐτόν. He makes those who would have silenced the man tell him that his cries have taken effect. Lk. says that He told them to lead the man to Him.

Θάρσει, ἔγειρε, φωνεῖ σε. Mk alone records these words, the rhythm of which has been stereotyped by Longfellow. The people's complete change of attitude, directly they perceive Christ's interest in the beggar, is characteristic of *mobile vulgus*, but it is also evidence of their respect for Him. For θάρσει see on vi. 50.

50. ἀποβαλὼν τὸ ἱμάτιον. It was the most valuable thing that he had, and it might never be recovered; but that is nothing, if only he can reach the Son of David. Syr-Sin. makes him *take up* his garment, as if ἐπιβαλών were the word; and Mrs Lewis adopts this as original.

ἀναπηδήσας. In spite of his blindness; not a moment is to be lost. The graphic word is found nowhere else in N.T., and the whole of this graphic verse is peculiar to Mk. Swete quotes a remarkable parallel from Lucian, *Catapl.* 15. Note the combination of participles.

51. ἀποκριθείς. Answering the man's action. See on ix. 5.

Τί σοι θέλεις ποιήσω; Not here, any more than in *v.* 36, is Christ giving *carte blanche* (Godet) to have anything that may be desired. The man's persistency has shown that he has faith enough, and Jesus now lets the bystanders who would have suppressed him know that this is no common tramp begging for money, but a sufferer who believes in the Messiah's benevolence and power. For the constr. cf. *v.* 36; Lk. ix. 54, xxii. 9. In class. Grk this constr. is more freq. with βούλομαι, which in N.T. is far less common than θέλω.

'Ραββουνεί. See on Jn xx. 16. As in ix. 5, Mk alone preserves the original Aramaic. Mt. and Lk. have Κύριε. See Dalman, *Words*, pp. 324, 327, 340.

ἵνα ἀναβλέψω. We may understand either θέλω or θέλω ποιήσῃς. Here ἀναβλέψω must mean " recover sight " and not " look up." See on viii. 24. *Non terrena dona, non fugitivos honores, a Domino, sed lucem quaeramus* (Bede).

52. Ὕπαγε. Cf. i. 44, vii. 29. Lk. substitutes 'Ανάβλεψον. Mt. reports no word and substitutes a touch. The man's faith being so great, Christ heals with a word instead of the means used viii. 22—26.

ἡ πίστις σου σέσωκέν σε. This again has a rhythm of its own, and it also is omitted by Mt. At v. 34 all three record these words. They do not occur in Jn, who uses σώζω seldom and πίστις never. All three record that the cure was instantaneous, Mk with his favourite εὐθύς and Lk. with his favourite παραχρῆμα. Cf. ii. 12, v. 29.

σέσωκεν...ἀνέβλεψεν...ἠκολούθει. In each case the tense is accurate, and ἐν τῇ ὁδῷ is against the suggestion that ἠκολούθει implies " became a disciple." Bartimaeus went on with Him to Jerusalem. Lk. adds that he praised God and that the people followed his example. Some of them may have been among those who cried " Hosanna to the Son of David " (Mt. xxi. 9, 15) soon after this. As at i. 26, ii. 11, and v. 34, there is no command to keep silence, which would have been useless in the case of a miracle witnessed by a crowd. Moreover, He was soon to be publicly proclaimed as the Messiah.

CHAPTER XI.

1. D, Latt. omit εἰς Βηθφαγή, but the words should probably be retained. τὸ ᾿Ελαιών (B, kr) should probably be preferred to τῶν ᾿Ελαιῶν.

2. οὐδεὶς οὔπω ἀνθρώπων (BLΔΨ) rather than οὐδεὶς ἀνθρώπων (DXΓ); ℵC have οὐδ. ἀνθρ. οὔπω, KΠ have οὔπω οὐδ. ἀνθρ.

3. ἀποστέλλει (ℵABCDLΔ) rather than ἀποστελεῖ (ΠΨ). πάλιν ὧδε (ℵBC*DLΔ) rather than ὧδε (AC²XΓΠΨ).

4. καὶ ἀπῆλθον (ℵBLΔ) rather than ἀπῆλθον δέ. See on i. 14.

7. φέρουσιν (ℵᶜBLΔΨ) rather than ἄγουσιν (ℵ*C) or ἤγαγον (ADXΓΠ). ἐπιβάλλουσιν (ℵBCDLΔ) rather than ἐπέβαλον (AXΓΠ).

8. καὶ πολλοί (ℵBCLΔ) rather than πολλοὶ δέ (ADN). See on i. 14. κόψαντες ἐκ τῶν ἀγρῶν (ℵBLΔΨ) rather than ἔκοπτον ἐκ τῶν δένδρων καὶ ἐστρώννυον εἰς τὴν ὁδόν or ἐν τῇ ὁδῷ (ADNXΓΙΙ).

9. ℵBCLΔ omit λέγοντες.

10. ℵBCLΔΨ omit ἐν ὀνόματι Κυρίου (from v. 9).

11. Here and vv. 14, 15, ὁ ᾿Ιησοῦς is omitted in most MSS., including the best.

19. ὅταν (ℵBCKLΔΨ) rather than ὅτε (ADNXΓ). ἐξεπορεύοντο (ABKΔΠΨ) is probably to be preferred to ἐξεπορεύετο (ℵCDNXΓ), but it may be a correction to harmonize with παραπορευόμενοι (v. 20).

23. ℵBDΨ omit γάρ, ℵBLΔ omit ὃ ἐὰν εἴπῃ.

24. ἐλάβετε (ℵBCLΔΨ) rather than λαμβάνετε (ANXΓΠ).

26. ℵBLSΔΨ omit the verse (from Mt. vi. 15).

29. ℵBCLΔΨ omit ἀποκριθείς. See on v. 9, x. 5. BCLΔ omit κἀγώ.

32. ὄχλον (ℵBCN 33) rather than λαόν (ADLXΓΔΨ), which Mk never uses in his narrative.

33. ℵBCLNΓΔ omit ἀποκριθείς.

1—11. The Messiah's Entry into Jerusalem.

Mt. xxi. 1—11.   Lk. xix. 29—44.   Jn xii. 12—19.

1. Βηθφαγή. The locality is uncertain, and it is doubtful whether it was a village near Bethany or a district which contained it. It is not mentioned in O.T., and nowhere in N.T., excepting these narratives. When Mt. wrote, it was apparently better known than Bethany, which he omits. Wellhausen suspects that Bethany is an intrusion here, inserted because among Christians Bethany was so well known. In that case, Mk ought to omit and Mt. to insert it. Renan (*Vie*, p. 374, ed. 1863) says that passages in the Talmud show that Bethphage was a sort of *pomoerium*, which reached up to the eastern substructions of the Temple.

πρὸς τὸ ὄρος. *Towards the mount* rather than "at the mount" (A.V., R.V.); cf. i. 33, ii. 2, iv. 1.

τὸ Ἐλαιών. See crit. note. Luke xix. 29 and xxi. 37 there is doubt between Ἐλαιών and Ἐλαιῶν. Ἐλαιών, *Olivetum*, is an "olive grove" or "Olivet." Acts i. 12 we have Ἐλαιῶνος, as in Joseph. *Ant.* vii. ix. 2. W.H. *App.* p. 158; Deissmann, *Bib. St.* pp. 208—212; and for description, Stanley, *Sin. and Pal.* pp. 185, 422. There was a tradition that the Messiah would appear there. The Egyptian pretender did appear there.

This arrival took place 8th Nisan (Jn xii. 1); but as the year of the Crucifixion is unknown, it is impossible to say what date that would represent in our Calendar. Either A.D. 29 or 30 or 33 would fit the evidence in the Gospels, and 29 or 30 is generally preferred to 33. The Evangelists do not regard chronology as important, and the small amount which they give us is not always harmonious. Lewin, *Fasti Sacri*, gives the evidence clearly.

ἀποστέλλει δύο. Even as regards trifling missions, our Lord seems to have adhered to His plan of sending the Apostles out in pairs (xiv. 13); see on iii. 14 and vi. 7. Two who had already worked together would perhaps be sent, and Mk's details point to Peter as one of the two.

2. Ὑπάγετε. So also Lk., while Mt. has his favourite πορεύεσθε.

τὴν κατέναντι. We have no means of knowing whether this was Bethany or Bethphage or another village. The two messengers could see it and there was no need to name it. The compound prep. is not classical, but it is freq. in Bibl. Grk.

πῶλον. The young of horse, ass, elephant, dog, and even of man; in the last case it is usually fem., "a filly." The word is in all three and nowhere else in N.T. In LXX. it is usually a young ass; Gen. xxxii. 15, xlix. 11; Judg. x. 4, xii. 14; Zech. ix. 9. Cf. *pullus*, which is also elastic in meaning, but is commonly used of birds. Vulg. has *pullum* here. Mk evidently regards as supernatural Christ's knowledge of what would happen; cf. xiv. 13; Jn i. 48, iv. 50, xi. 11, 14. We may adopt other possibilities, but they receive no support from the Evangelists.

οὐδεὶς οὔπω. See crit. note and on i. 14. The animal is required for a solemn and sacred purpose. The Virgin Birth and the new tomb harmonize with this idea, which is natural and widespread; Num. xix. 2; Deut. xv. 19, xxi. 3; Judg. xvi. 11; 1 Sam. vi. 7: 2 Sam. vi. 3; Ovid, *Metam.* iii. 11; Virg. *Geor.* iv. 540. See Wetstein *ad loc.* and Orelli on Hor. *Epod.* ix. 22.

λύσατε καὶ φέρετε. The change from aor. to pres. is accurate; cf. Acts xii. 8, and contrast Jn xi. 44 (both aor. imper.) and Jas. ii. 12 (both pres. imper.).

3. Tί ποιεῖτε τοῦτο; Either *Why do ye this?* (A.V., R.V.), or "What are you doing?" Vulg. *Quid facitis?*

Ὁ κύριος χρείαν ἔχει. In all three; cf. ii. 17, xiv. 63. There is probably little difference between ὁ κύριος here and ὁ διδάσκαλος xiv. 13; both represent *Rabbi.* See on ix. 5. The Lord's humiliation and poverty continue to the end; even for His triumphal entry into Jerusalem He has to borrow an animal to ride upon. But it was no part of His humiliation that the animal was an ass; Judg. i. 14, v. 10, x. 4; 1 Sam. xxv. 20; 2 Sam. xvii. 23, xix. 26. The ass was quite consistent with a royal personage coming *peaceably.* Moore, *Judges,* p. 274.

καὶ εὐθὺς αὐτὸν ἀποστέλλει πάλιν ὧδε. See crit. note. *And straightway He sendeth him back hither* (R.V. marg.) The Lord will not keep the colt longer than is necessary; He is going to send it back directly. This strongly attested reading is not prosaic and commonplace; it is pleasing and natural. Christ anticipates the owner's anxiety. Mt. turns the promise into a prediction that the owner will at once send the ass and the foal. It is apparently through a misunderstanding of Zech. ix. 9 that he mentions two animals; the "ass" and the "foal of an ass" are the same animal.

4. πρὸς [τὴν] θύραν. *Towards the door,* "close to it"; cf. i. 33, 11. 2, iv. 1. Neither πῶλον nor θύραν has the art. in the true text.

ἔξω ἐπὶ τοῦ ἀμφόδου. Superfluous fulness; there is no need to say both "out of doors" and "in the open street." See on vi. 25. The exact meaning of ἄμφοδον is uncertain; it originally meant a road round some building, and then it seems to have been used for any public road or street. Syr-Sin. has "a court in the street," Vulg. *bivium,* which is too definite. In LXX. (Jer. xvii. 27, xlix. 27) it represents buildings, "palaces"; but Aquila (Jer. vii. 17, xi. 6, xiv. 16) uses it of "streets." In the D text of Acts xix. 28, d has *in campo* for εἰς τὸ ἄμφοδον. Evidently the meaning was elastic.

5. τῶν ἐκεῖ ἑστηκότων. See on ix. 1. Lk. says that they were the owners, which is probable; but in a village everyone knows everyone, and bystanders would see that the disciples were not the owners,

and would ask their business. That the owners were Lazarus and his sisters is not a probable conjecture, even if the village is Bethany. Lk. at any rate would mention this; and none of the family would have questioned disciples of Christ in this way.

Τί ποιεῖτε λύοντες τ. πῶλον; *What do ye, loosing the colt?* (R.V.). " What do you mean by it? " Cf. Acts xxi. 13, τί ποιεῖτε κλαίοντες; " What mean ye by weeping? "

6. καθώς. *Even as.* They delivered Christ's message exactly. Lk. transfers καθώς to their experiences; everything happened exactly as He had foretold.

ἀφῆκαν αὐτούς. The owners let the two disciples go with the colt. They knew ὁ κύριος by reputation and were sure that He would be as good as His word about sending the colt back. They might even " be proud that it should be used by the Prophet " (Swete).

7. φέρουσιν. Cf. i. 32, vii. 32, viii. 22, and see on xv. 22.

ἐπιβάλλουσιν. See crit. note. As the colt had never been ridden, it would have no ἐπίσαγμα.

τὰ ἱμάτια αὐτῶν. B has ἑαυτῶν, " their own upper garments." The officers of Joram took off their garments to make a throne for Jehu, when they proclaimed him king (2 Kings ix. 13).

ἐκάθισεν ἐπ' αὐτόν. The acc. is freq. (*v.* 2, ii. 14, iv. 38; Mt. xix. 28; Jn xii. 14; etc.). In such cases the previous motion may be understood; see on Jn i. 32.

8. πολλοὶ τὰ ἱμάτια κ.τ.λ. The enthusiasm spreads to the multitude. The disciples had taken off their chief garments to form a seat; the multitude take off theirs to form a carpet. There are many examples of this impulse; *e.g.* the story of Raleigh and Queen Elizabeth at Greenwich in Dec. 1581. A close parallel is found in the solemn entry of Buddha Dîpankara (*Buddhavamsa* ii.); " The people swept the pathway, the gods strewed flowers on the pathway and branches of the coral-tree, the men bore branches of all manner of trees, and the Bodhisatta Sumedha spread his garments in the mire, men and gods shouted, All hail! " The similarity, as Clemen remarks, is due to " identity of Oriental customs."

στιβάδας. So the best MSS. It means greenery of any kind, esp. when used as litter (στείβω); " branches " is too definite. R.V. marg. has " layers of leaves."

ἐκ τῶν ἀγρῶν. " Fields " with us suggests " meadows," whereas Mk uses the word of farms or cultivated land, and near to towns most of it would be cultivated (v. 14, vi. 36). See crit. note. Mk alone has this detail, and Syr-Sin. omits it here. All three are silent about the crowd coming with palm branches *from* Jerusalem (Jn xii. 13, 18).

9. οἱ προάγοντες. This might include the Jerusalem contingent, which on meeting Christ turned round and headed the procession.

ἔκραζον. This cry continued; the "earliest hymn of Christian devotion" (Stanley, *Sin. and Pal.* pp. 190 f.; his description of the scene is famed).

'Ωσαννά. "Save, we pray"; but the word seems to have become an expression of praise rather than of prayer. Lk. in choosing an equivalent that would be intelligible to Gentile readers takes δόξα and not σῶσον δή. Contrast *Acta Pilati* i. It is remarkable that Mk gives no translation of *Hosanna*; contrast v. 41, vii. 34, xv. 22, 34. This may be either because, like *Rabbi* (ix. 5), the word was so familiar, or because he himself was in doubt about the meaning. Ps. cxviii., which perhaps celebrates the Dedication of the Second Temple, and is certainly processional, was sung at the F. of Tabernacles, and the palm branches, waved by the crowd from Jerusalem, would easily suggest the ceremonies of that Feast. In the post-communion prayer in the *Didache* (x. 6) "Hosanna to the *God* of David" occurs, and some texts have "Hosanna to the *Son* of David," from Mt. xxi. 9.

εὐλογημένος ὁ ἐρχ. κ.τ.λ. In these words all four agree. Originally they were a welcome to the pilgrim who comes to the Feast; but here they imply that "He who cometh" has a mission from God.

10. εὐλογημένη ἡ ἐρχ. βασ. Here Mk is alone. The cry shows that some in the crowd remembered Christ's teaching about the Kingdom and had some vague idea that this was the inauguration of it. "The coming kingdom of our father David" points back to 2 Sam. vii. 11—16 (cf. Zech. xii. 10), and they think that the glories of David and Solomon may be restored. Their ideas about Jesus of Nazareth were no doubt diverse and indefinite. To most He was a great Prophet; to some He was the Prophet who was to be the Forerunner of the Messiah; to others He was the Messiah Himself, about whom again their ideas were diverse and indefinite. Even without counting the possibility of provoking the Procurator, this public recognition of Jesus as the Messiah or His Forerunner was an audacious thing, evidently not premeditated. He was under the ban of the hierarchy. The Sanhedrin had tried to arrest Him. They had excommunicated the man born blind for saying that He had Divine power. They had made Him an outlaw by calling on all Jews to help in arresting Him (Jn xi. 57). And yet, not only pilgrims from Galilee and countryfolk from the neighbourhood of Jericho, but numbers who came from Jerusalem joined in proclaiming Him as the Messiah (*vv.* 9, 10; Mt. xxi. 9; Lk. xix. 38; Jn xii. 13).

ὡσαννά ἐν τοῖς ὑψίστοις. *Glory in the heaven of heavens*; or, if
the idea of "save" be retained, "May our prayer for salvation be
heard in heaven." Syr-Sin. has "Peace in the highest." Cf. Job
xvi. 19, 20. Mk omits the protest of the Pharisees and the Lamentation over Jerusalem (Lk. xix. 39—44).

11. εἰς τὸ ἱερόν. This defines εἰς Ἱεροσόλυμα more exactly, just
as the approach towards Jerusalem is defined more exactly by εἰς
Βηθφαγή (*v.* 1). The ἱερόν is the whole of the Temple-enclosure or
τέμενος, including the courts open to the air as well as the ναός which
was roofed. See on Jn ii. 14, 20; also Sanday, *Sacred Sites of the
Gospels*, pp. 106 f., with illustration and plan.

περιβλεψάμενος πάντα. This and the remainder of the verse are
peculiar to Mk. For the last time this embracing look is remembered
and recorded (iii. 5, 34, v. 32, x. 23). This time it is all-embracing,
and all the more full of meaning if we think of the Lamentation over
Jerusalem as having been uttered a few hours before. To regard this
as the wondering look of a provincial, who was seeing Jerusalem for
the first time, is entirely to misinterpret its meaning.

ὀψίας ἤδη οὔσης τ. ὥρας. There were still a few days in which
some souls might be reached and in which teaching might be given
which would hold good for all time; but it was too late for anything
to be done that evening. So He went back to Bethany and passed the
night on the quiet slopes of the M. of Olives (Lk. xxi. 37). In the
city He would have been less quiet and less safe; τὰ γὰρ Ἱεροσόλυμα
πάσης κακίας ἐργαστήριον ἦσαν (Theoph.). He takes all precautions
to prevent being arrested before His hour is come.

12—14.　THE BRAGGART FIG-TREE.

Mt. xxi. 18, 19.

12. τῇ ἐπαύριον. This is commonly understood to be Monday
11th Nisan.

ἐπείνασεν. The reality of Christ's manhood is again conspicuous,
and that in three ways. He suffered hunger; until He went up to
the fig-tree, He did not know that it had nothing but leaves; then He
felt disappointment. This hunger is some evidence that at Bethany
He was not under the roof of friends; they would have provided Him
with food in the morning.

13. ἰδὼν συκῆν ἀπὸ μακρόθεν. It was a single tree by the road-
side (Mt.), and its having leaves before the season would make it
conspicuous. See on *v.* 6 for the pleonastic ἀπό.

εἰ ἄρα τι εὑρήσει. *Si quid forte inveniret* (Vulg.). Mt. characteristically omits an expression which implies ignorance in Christ, and he merely states that Christ found only leaves. In the fig-tree the fruit precedes the leaves, and therefore abundance of foliage was a profession that fruit was there, although it was not the time for either. The ἄρα means "in these circumstances"; as there were leaves, there was good prospect of fruit. Ἄρα is rare in Mk (iv. 41), but is fairly freq. in Mt., Lk., and Acts; nowhere in Jn. Cf. Acts viii. 22. Οὖν is also rare.

ὁ γὰρ καιρὸς οὐκ ἦν σύκων. So in אBC*LΔ. *For the season was not that of figs.* It is not easy to see how this is an intimation from the Evangelist that the whole of Christ's action was symbolical; that He was not desiring figs and did not expect to find any on the tree.

14. ἀποκριθείς. He "answered" the deceptive profession of the fig-tree. Cf. ix. 5, x. 51, xiv. 49.

Μηκέτι...μηδείς. The opt. of wishing (φάγοι) occurs 35 times in N.T. But only here and Acts viii. 20 is the wish for something evil. Burton § 176. Neither here nor at i. 44 (see note) is there a double neg. in Mt., whose wording here is different. It is possible that neither Evangelist gives the exact words. Christ may simply have predicted that such a tree would never bear fruit for anyone, a prediction which Peter regarded as a curse. Even if Mk gives the words correctly, they hardly amount to a curse; there is no ἐπικατάρατος or κατηραμένος (Gal. iii. 10; Mt. xxv. 41). Cf. μὴ γένοιτο (Lk. xx. 16). If we are right in regarding the words as a judgment on the tree for its deceitful professions, it is to be noted that it is the only miracle of judgment wrought by Christ, and it is wrought on an insensate object; εἰς τὸ ἀναίσθητον δένδρον ἐπιδείκνυται τὴν δύναμιν (Theoph.). The solemn lesson is given without causing pain. But the symbolical judgment is not pointed out by Christ, still less its application to Jerusalem, which had just exhibited such enthusiasm for Him as the Messiah, and was about to show how deceptive that enthusiasm was by putting Him to death for not being the kind of Messiah that they desired. Time would show this application, when the braggart and barren city, *quae verba sine operibus sonabat* (Bede), was destroyed. The lesson which Christ pointed out was less obvious and of more pressing need (*vv.* 22—25).

It is sometimes suggested that this narrative is only the parable of Lk. xiii. 6—9 in another form. Not only the story, but the moral in each case is different. The parable is a warning against spiritual unproductiveness, and we are not told that the unproductiveness continued, and that the threatened destruction took place. Here there is no warning, and the tree is destroyed, not for producing nothing, but for making a deceptive show of exceptional producing power. Still less satisfactory is the suggestion that this is a case of folklore; there was a withered fig-tree near Jerusalem, and this story was invented to account for it. Withered fig-trees must have been common enough. It is extraordinary objects that excite folklore.

ἤκουον. *The disciples were listening;* they were near enough to hear these unusual words, which were spoken for the sake of the lesson to which they led (*vv.* 21—25). Christ sees in His own disappointment an opportunity for giving instruction that was much needed. The incident could be made a parable, not told, but acted before the disciples' eyes; and *segnius irritant animos* etc. (Hor. *A. P.* 180). The ἤκουον intimates that there is something more to be told.

15—19.   The Cleansing of the Temple.

Mt. xxi. 12—17.   Lk. xix. 45—49.   Cf. Jn ii. 14—22.

15. ἤρξατο ἐκβάλλειν. The work would take some time and He began it at once. He refused to begin to teach in the presence of such a scandal, and in order to be thorough He treated buyers as being as offensive as sellers. In the true text (אABCL) ἀγοράζοντας has the art. The buyers as a class are driven out with the sellers. This market was in the Court of the Gentiles. It was not a common market, but one for the sale of all that was required for the sacrifices and the ritual of the Temple. The Temple-tax (Mt. xvii. 24) might not be paid with heathen coins, and the same rule would apply to offerings to the treasury (xii. 41). Hence the opening for money-changers. The market was sanctioned by the hierarchy, who had a share of the profits, and near the time of the Passover business would be brisk. To a pilgrim, coming to Jerusalem full of awe in anticipation of the unique sanctity of the Temple, the shock of finding himself in the hubbub and contentious bargaining of a bazaar must have been distressing. It is said that at Mecca pilgrims are fleeced in a similar way.

τῶν κολλυβιστῶν. "The rate of exchange," κόλλυβος (Cic. *Verr.* ii. 3, *Att.* xii. 6), was sometimes as high as 10 or 12 per cent. Jn uses κερματισταί also, "dealers in small change," κέρματα.

τὰς καθέδρας. The change from "tables" to "seats" is not accidental. Overturning the tables of money-changers caused spilling of the coins. Overturning the tables of dove-sellers would have caused suffering to the birds; so here He overturned the seats and told the sellers to remove the cages. Syr-Sin. has "tables" in both places. See on Jn ii. 16.

τὰς περιστεράς. "*The* doves" (R.V.); those which were required for the purification of women (Lk. ii. 22 f.) and other offerings (Lev. xii. 8, xiv. 22, xv. 14, 29).

16. οὐκ ἤφιεν ἵνα. Cf. vi. 25, ix. 30, xv. 36. This detail, peculiar to Mk, may be one of Peter's recollections. Making the Temple a thoroughfare seems not to have been formally permitted, but the hierarchy could easily have stopped it, and did not do so.

17. ἐδίδασκεν. Mt. once more (see on vi. 34, x. 1) mentions healing where Mk and Lk. mention teaching; but Mt. records more of Christ's latest teaching than they do. Cf. Acts iii. 2. Although Jesus had allowed Himself to be proclaimed as the Messiah, yet He goes back to His old work of teaching (and healing). He shows that His mission is still, not to reign, but to serve (x. 45); *He went on teaching and saying to them.*

Οὐ γέγραπται; He again appeals to what "stands written," for which they professed such reverence, while they habitually ignored it (ii. 25, vii. 6, 7, x. 6, 7, xii. 10; Mt. xxi. 16). The quotation follows the LXX. of Is. lvi. 7.

πᾶσιν τοῖς ἔθνεσιν. *For all the nations.* Not only Mt., but Lk. also, omit these words, which looks as if Lk. had not Mk before him at this point. The words have special significance, for it was the Court of the *Gentiles* that Christ was restoring to its proper purpose as a "house of prayer." Cf. 1 Kings viii. 41, 42; Jn xii. 20. See on xiii. 10, xiv. 9.

ὑμεῖς δέ. All are held responsible, all who took part in, or countenanced, the traffic. Renan, *Vie*, pp. 215, 344.

πεποιήκατε. More accurate, as covering both past and present, than ἐποιήσατε (Lk.) or ποιεῖτε (Mt.).

σπήλαιον λῃστῶν. *A robbers' den.* A.V. often obscures the not unimportant difference between the mean, purloining κλέπτης and the violent λῃστής, who is more of a "brigand" or "bandit" than a "thief." See on Jn. x. 1 and xviii. 40. These words come from Jer. vii. 11, where the Prophet is exhorting the Jews to avert judgments by repentance, as Christ does here. The reference may be to the extortionate charges; διὰ τὸ ὁμοίως τοῖς λῃσταῖς φιλοκερδεῖν (Euthym.); or λῃστής may be used of any kind of flagrant offender. In any case, as Origen says, these traffickers were doing in the house of prayer τὰ ἐναντία τῇ εὐχῇ.

18. οἱ ἀρχιερεῖς καὶ οἱ γραμματεῖς. So in ℵABCDLΔΠ. The order in A.V. has little authority. For the first time in Mk, Mt. and

Lk., the chief priests appear in active hostility to Christ. Their gains were being touched. It was as when Luther attacked Pope and clergy and denounced the sale of indulgences. If the Temple-market was stopped, "the hope of their gain was gone." Note the change of tense.

πᾶς γὰρ ὁ ὄχλος. So in אBCΔ. Lk. characteristically has ὁ λαὸς γὰρ ἅπας, which calls attention to the fact that the multitude was a Jewish one and representative of the whole nation, for Jews from all parts of the world were now collecting for the Passover. This second γάρ is remarkable; it explains why the hierarchy feared Christ. Not because of His miracles; no one had ever heard of His harming anyone by word or touch; but because this representative multitude was "amazed at His teaching," so different from that of the Scribes, and "hung on His lips, listening."

19. καὶ ὅταν ὀψὲ ἐγένετο. See crit. note. Not ὅτε, but ὅταν: *And every evening they went forth out of the city;* lit. "whenever it became late." Cf. iii. 11, vi. 56. Blass § 63. 7; J. H. Moulton, p. 168. See on *v.* 11. Lk. says the same in very different words.

It is impossible to be certain whether Christ cleansed the Temple twice or only once. There is no improbability in His having done so both at the beginning and at the end of His Ministry (Salmon, *Human Element*, p. 433). If He cleansed it at the beginning, the evil would revive, for the authorities would delight in showing public contempt for His teaching and in resuming their profits. In that case He would deal with it more severely the second time; and His condemnation of it in the Synoptics is more severe than in Jn. See on Jn ii. 17. Mk contains facts which imply an earlier Ministry in Jerusalem. When did Joseph of Arimathaea become a disciple? When did the household at Bethany become friendly, or the owners of the colt, or the owner of the upper room? But at the present time the hypothesis that He cleansed the Temple only once finds more favour. Then which is the true date? Here there is much difference of opinion, for the probabilities are rather equally divided. But in one respect all four Gospels agree about the date; they make it "the first public act in the Ministry in Jerusalem" (J. A. Robinson, *Hist. Char. of St John's Gospel*, p. 21,—an admirable little book). The Synoptists omit the early work in Jerusalem, but they place this significant action at the opening of what they do record of Christ's work there; and in each case His protest against the licensed desecration of "the Mountain of the House" provokes a question as to His own authority (*v.* 28; Jn ii. 18).

20—25. The Lesson of the Withered Fig-Tree.
Mt. xxi. 19—22.

20. πρωΐ. This was the *following* morning (Tuesday), the day in that week about which we have most information, excepting Friday. But the interval between the first and second seeing of the tree may have been shortened in tradition. Mt., as often, enhances the miracle. He banishes the interval altogether; "the fig-tree *immediately* withered away," and the Apostles (not Peter only) express their astonishment at the suddenness of the result. No doubt Mk is nearer the truth in both particulars. There was a considerable interval, and it was Mk's instructor who called attention to the fulfilment of Christ's prediction. The tree may have contributed to its own death by exhausting itself with its premature abundance of foliage.

21. ἀναμνησθείς. Perhaps none of them thought much about it, until the tree was seen in its changed condition. Then Peter remembered the unusual words to which they had listened (*v.* 14).

'Ραββεί. See on ix. 5, x. 51.

ἣν κατηράσω. That is Peter's view; the words as recorded are a prayer rather than a curse, and in them nothing is said about withering, but only perpetual fruitlessness. Hence Peter's surprise. The acc. after καταράομαι is late; we usually find the dat.

ἐξήρανται. Like πεποιήκατε (*v.* 17), the perf. is more accurate than the aor. (Mt., Lk.). In both cases we have the present result of past action.

22. ἀποκριθείς. For the curious combination of aor. part. with pres. indic. see on viii. 29 *sub fin.* No direct answer is given to Peter's remark, which was meant to raise the question of a judgment on the tree. Christ does not gratify his natural curiosity, but gives to all of the Apostles a lesson less easy to see, but of greater importance. See on x. 29.

῎Εχετε πίστιν θεοῦ. Not the "faith which God bestows," but the "faith which relies on Him." *Have faith in God*, faith in the efficacy of prayer. It was this faith which most of them had lacked in trying to heal the demoniac boy (ix. 29); it was through His possession of this faith that His prayer about the tree had been so clearly answered. Note the pres., "continually have."

23. ἀμὴν λέγω ὑμῖν. See crit. note, and on iii. 28.

ὃς ἂν εἴπῃ τῷ ὄρει τούτῳ. "Removing mountains" was a Jewish figure of speech for a very great difficulty, and it would be familiar to the disciples. Like many Oriental teachers, Christ was accustomed

to use strong and picturesque language which to Western ears sounds
extravagant (ix. 45—47, x. 25). Sanday, *The Life of Christ in Recent
Research*, pp. 26 f. Lk. omits the withered tree, but has a similar
Saying in a different connexion, with a sycamine tree instead of
a mountain (xvii. 6). In each case the miraculous passage from
land to sea is effected by faith. The most difficult results are
attainable when faith and prayer are directed towards objects which
are in accordance with the Divine Will (ix. 23). St Paul may have
known that our Lord had used this figure (1 Cor. xiii. 2), but he may
equally well have employed it independently. Origen interprets "this
mountain" as "this hostile object presented by the devil." Armed
with faith and prayer we may say to Satan himself, "Depart," and
he will go. E. A. Abbott, *The Son of Man*, p. 387.

Ἄρθητι καὶ βλήθητι. Aor. of what takes place once for all; cf.
λύσατε (*v.* 2; Jn ii. 19), βοήθησον (ix. 22).

μὴ διακριθῇ. Hort says that Jas i. 6 is "taken from our Lord's
words in Mk xi. 23. Not the mere petition avails, but the mind of
the asker, the trust in God as one who delights to give. *Wavering* is
no doubt the right translation of διακρινόμενος in this verse (Acts x. 20;
Rom. iv. 20, xiv. 23), though singularly enough this sense occurs in
no Greek writing, except where the influence of the N.T. might have
led to its use. It is supported by the versions, the Greek commentators from Chrysostom and Hesychius, as well as by the context
of all the passages. Cf. διαλογίζομαι, 'dispute with oneself' in the
Gospels." N.T. usage makes διακρίνομαι the negation of πιστεύω, for
each, so far as it is true, excludes the other. See crit. note.

24. προσεύχεσθε καὶ αἰτεῖσθε. So אBCDLΔ. See on Jn xi. 22;
προσεύχομαι (nowhere in Jn) is reserved for prayer to God (i. 35, vi.
46); αἰτέομαι may be used of requests to man (vi. 24, xv. 8). Syr-Sin.
omits καὶ αἰτεῖσθε.

πιστεύετε ὅτι ἐλάβετε. *Always believe that ye received them*—"at
the moment when ye asked for them."

25. ὅταν στήκετε προσευχόμενοι. *Whenever ye stand in prayer.*
Christ says "stand" because that was the usual posture among the
Jews (1 Sam. i. 26; 1 Kings viii. 14, 22; Neh. ix. 4; Mt. vi. 5;
Lk. xviii. 11, 13). Yet kneeling was not unusual in cases of special
earnestness (1 Kings viii. 54; Ezra ix. 5; Dan. vi. 10). Christ knelt
(Lk. xxii. 41), and kneeling has become usual among Christians
(Acts vii. 60, ix. 40, xx. 36, xxi. 5; Eph. iii. 14). But the Eastern
Church still prays standing. Stanley, *East. Ch.* p. 159, ed. 1883;
Hefele, *Chr. Councils*, I. p. 435. For the very rare use of ὅταν with
pres. indic. see Winer, p. 388; Burton § 309; Blass § 65. 9.

ἀφίετε εἴ τι ἔχετε κατά τινος. A necessary caution against the supposition, which Peter's remark might encourage, that our curses on other men will be executed by God. "The tree which Thou cursedst is withered away; therefore we may curse with like effect."

ὁ πατὴρ ὑμῶν ὁ ἐν τοῖς οὐρανοῖς. A remarkable expression in this Gospel, and an echo of the Lord's Prayer.

παραπτώματα. "Slips aside," "false steps," and so *transgressions*.
A.V. uses five words for παράπτωμα, "fault," "offence," "fall," "trespass," "sin," of which R.V. uses the last three.

The similar saying, Mt. vi. 14, 15, may have been taken from this passage and inserted, as other Sayings seem to have been inserted, in the Sermon. We infer that the Lord's Prayer had already been taught to the disciples. Christ does not say that our forgiving others suffices to secure forgiveness for ourselves; but refusing to forgive others is a bar to our being forgiven. Cf. Ecclus xxviii. 2; also the Testaments; "Do ye also, my children, have compassion on every man in mercy, that the Lord also may have compassion and mercy on you" (*Zebulon* viii. 1). Nowhere else in Mk does ὁ πατὴρ ὑμῶν occur.

26. See crit. note.

27—33. The Sanhedrin's Question about the Authority of Jesus.

Mt. xxi. 23—27. Lk. xx. 1—8.

27. ἔρχονται πάλιν. Apparently the same day (Tuesday), but later than πρωΐ in *v.* 20; it is called "The Day of Questions." We may think of the scene as the Court of the Gentiles (*vv.* 15—17) in which He was walking, and teaching as He had opportunity. For the constr. see on ix. 28.

οἱ ἀρχιερεῖς κ.τ.λ. See on viii. 31, where, as here, all three elements of the Sanhedrin are mentioned, each with a separate article. The deputation is a formal one, and representatives of each of the three bodies are present. The intrinsic probability of the question which they raise and of the questions which follow is admitted by Strauss. Hausrath (*N.T. Times*, p. 250) gives a vivid description of this "picture with genuine Oriental local colouring."

28. Ἐν ποίᾳ ἐξουσίᾳ; "In the right of what *kind* of authority art Thou acting thus?" Cf. Acts iv. 7. They refer specially to His interference with the hierarchy respecting the Temple-market, but indirectly they challenge His whole career. It was a reasonable question, and they were the right people to raise it. Did He hold that He was clothed with Divine or with human authority? and by whom was it conferred? It was not merely in order to protect the public from an impostor that they pressed this question. They sought to entangle Him fatally. If He claimed Divine authority, He might be convicted of blasphemy. If He claimed human authority as the Son of David, He might be handed over to the Procurator. If He disclaimed all authority, He might be denounced to the people as a convicted impostor. The second question is not a repetition of the first; it at once arises as soon as a claim to any kind of authority is made. Authority must be received from a power that is competent to confer it. Who conferred it on Jesus? Mk alone, with characteristic fulness, adds ἵνα ταῦτα ποιῇς, and Syr-Sin. omits it here. Burton § 215, 216. For ποῖος see on xii. 28.

29. Ἐπερωτήσω. See crit. note. He answers their questions with another question; but the ἐπ- refers to *directing* the interrogation, not to making it *on the top* of previous interrogations. Wünsche says that it was a Rabbinical custom to ask another question by way of a rejoinder; but the custom is general.

ἕνα λόγον. Not "one question" (A.V., R.V.), nor "one thing" (A.V. marg.), but *one statement*. "You have asked me to state My authority. *I will ask you for one statement.*" The "one" is not in opposition to their two questions; it means that a single statement from them may settle the matter. At once they, and not He, are placed in a dilemma. But His reply is not an evasion; if they answered His question, the way to the answer to their question would be clear. As the constituted religious guides of the people, sitting on Moses' seat, it was their place to speak first. The people had declared John to be a Prophet, and John had declared Jesus to be the Messiah. The Sanhedrin knew this, and they had allowed the popular estimate of John to pass unchallenged. That ought to mean that they admitted that John was a Prophet with a commission from Heaven to preach repentance-baptism. Did they admit this? If so, the authority of Jesus was established, for an inspired Prophet had declared Him to be the Messiah. Cf. Acts v. 38, 39, where Gamaliel offers a similar dilemma.

30. τὸ βάπτισμα. The most conspicuous characteristic of John's preaching is taken as indicating his whole teaching as a reformer, just as justification by faith is taken to indicate the teaching of Luther. See on i. 4.

ἐξ οὐρανοῦ. A reverent desire to avoid using the Divine Name caused the Jews to employ various expressions as equivalent, of which "Heaven," as with ourselves, was one (Lk. xv. 18, 21; Jn iii. 27; Dan. iv. 26; 1 Macc. iii. 18, iv. 10, 24, 55; 2 Macc. ix. 20). It is freq. in the Mishna. Dalman, *Words*, pp. 217 f. Cf. ἄνωθεν (Jn iii. 3, 31, xix. 11; Jas i. 17, iii. 15). On the omission of the art. in such phrases see Blass § 46. 5. The second "Answer Me" is omitted by Mt. and Lk. as superfluous.

31. διελογίζοντο πρὸς ἑαυτούς. Does this mean the same as πρὸς ἀλλήλους (iv. 41, viii. 16), and that they discussed with one another what reply they had better give? Mt. thinks this improbable and substitutes ἐν ἑαυτοῖς : the debate took place in the mind of each with the same general result. Lk. takes the other view with συνελογίσαντο. We have similarly doubtful cases, xiv. 4, xvi. 3. Syr-Sin. omits πρὸς ἑ.

32. ἀλλὰ εἴπωμεν. This is probably the interrogative deliberative subjunctive; *But shall we say, From men?* (R.V. marg.). Cf. δῶμεν ἢ μὴ δῶμεν; (xii. 14).

ἐφοβοῦντο τὸν ὄχλον. This abrupt return to his own narrative is in Mk's style, and it is effective. The abruptness is avoided by Mt. and Lk., who include the fear of stoning in the deliberations of the deputation. They both omit ὄντως, which Mk has nowhere else. It qualifies εἶχον (R.V.), not προφήτης (A.V.) ; the people were thoroughly convinced that John was a Prophet. Their joy in recognizing him as such had been intense; and their resentment would have been intense if the hierarchy had attempted to rob them of this satisfaction. Note the strong form ἅπαντες, which is rare in Mk (i. 27, viii. 25), but very freq. in Lk. and Acts; "every one of them had this feeling about John." This use of ἔχω may be a Latinism. Blass § 70. 2.

33. Οὐκ οἴδαμεν. This profession of ignorance is more than equalled in baseness by the profession of loyalty to the heathen Emperor a day or two later (Jn xix. 15). As Bede says, they feared stoning, but they feared the truth still more. These teachers of Israel (Jn iii. 10), who pronounced the multitude to be accursed for its ignorance (Jn vii. 49), declared that they themselves were ignorant whether one whom the multitude had accepted as God's messenger had any commission from Heaven. Again we have aor. part. combined with pres. indic., as in *v.* 22. Syr-Sin. again omits the aor. part.

Οὐδὲ ἐγὼ λέγω. Where would have been the use? If they did not accept John's testimony to His Messiahship, His own testimony to it would have been of no avail. Their confession of ignorance was an abdication of their official position as teachers of the nation, and they had no right now to question His authority. Hence His silence before the Sanhedrin (xiv. 61). He does not say Οὐδὲ ἐγὼ οἶδα, which would have been the exact rejoinder to their reply; and His οὐδὲ ἐγὼ λέγω suggests that they do know but refuse to tell.

CHAPTER XII.

2. τῶν καρπῶν (אBCLNΔ) rather than τοῦ καρποῦ (ADX̄).

3. καὶ λαβόντες (אBDLΔ 33) rather than οἱ δὲ λαβόντες (ACXII).
See on i. 14.

4. ἐκεφαλίωσαν (אBLΨ) rather than ἐκεφαλαίωσαν (ACDN etc.),
which could hardly mean "treated him summarily." אBDLΔ 33
omit λιθοβολήσαντες (from Mt.). ἠτίμασαν or ἠτίμησαν (אBDLΨ 33)
rather than ἀπέστειλαν ἠτιμωμένον (ACNXΓΠ). Syr-Sin. omits καὶ
ἠτίμασαν.

5. אBCDLΔΨ 33 omit πάλιν.

6. The text is confused; read ἔτι ἕνα εἶχεν υἱόν, ἀγαπητόν·
ἀπέστειλεν αὐτὸν ἔσχατον πρὸς αὐτούς (אBLΔ); other witnesses support portions of this reading. In vv. 6, 9, 20, 23, 27, 37, the οὖν is
almost certainly an interpolation. Perhaps x. 9, xiii. 35, xv. 12 are
the only places in Mk in which οὖν is original; xi. 31 is doubtful.
Scribes often inserted particles for the sake of smoothness, as γάρ in
v. 36.

14. καὶ ἐλθόντες (אBCDLΔ) rather than οἱ δὲ ἐλθόντες (ANXΓΠ).
See on i. 14.

17. אBCLΔ omit ἀποκριθείς. See on vii. 6, x. 5. ἐξεθαύμαζον
(אBΨ) rather than ἐθαύμαζον (D²LΔ) or ἐθαύμασαν (ACNXΓΠ).

20. אABC* omit οὖν. See on v. 6.

21. μὴ καταλιπών σπέρμα (אBCLΔ 33) rather than καὶ οὐδὲ αὐτὸς
ἀφῆκε σπέρμα (ADΓΠ).

22. Read καὶ οἱ ἑπτὰ οὐκ ἀφῆκαν σπέρμα (אBCLΔ).

23. אBC*LXΔΨ omit οὖν (see on v. 6) and ὅταν ἀναστῶσιν.

24. אBCLΔ omit καὶ ἀποκριθείς. See on v. 17.

27. אABCDLΔ omit θεός. אBCLΔ omit ὑμεῖς οὖν.

28. εἰδώς (אᶜABXΓΔΨ) rather than ἰδών (א*CDL).

29. אBLΛ omit πασῶν τῶν ἐντολῶν.

30. אBELΔ omit αὕτη πρώτη ἐντολή.

31. δευτέρα αὕτη (אBLΔ) rather than καὶ δευτέρα ὁμοία αὕτη (AXΠ).

32. εἷς ἐστιν (אABLΔ) rather than εἷς ἐστιν θεός (D).

33. אBLΔΨ omit καὶ ἐξ ὅλης τῆς ψυχῆς (from v. 30).

36. אBLΔΨ omit γάρ. See on *v.* 6. ὑποκάτω (BDΨ) rather than ὑποπόδιον (from LXX. of Ps. cx. 1).

37. אBDLΔΨ omit οὖν. See on *v.* 6.

41. אBLΔΨ omit ὁ Ἰησοῦς after καθίσας. See on v. 13.

43. ἔβαλεν (א°ABDLΔ 33) rather than βέβληκεν (ΧΓΠ). βαλλόντων (אABDLΔ) rather than βαλόντων (FHS).

1—12. THE WICKED HUSBANDMEN.

Mt. xxi. 33—46. Lk. xx. 9—19.

1. ἐν παραβολαῖς. Cf. iii. 23, iv. 2. Mk gives only one parable, but Mt. gives three. This and the Sower and the Mustard Seed are the three parables which are in all three Synoptics, and Mt. places this parable between the Two Sons, which treats of work in the vineyard, and the Marriage of the King's Son. During the special training of the Twelve there had been few, if any, parables. In these last days of public teaching Christ *began* to use them again. But, although there probably were several, ἐν παραβολαῖς does not necessarily mean more than one. It is an O.T. phrase, and may be used of a single parable or dark saying, like our "You are speaking in parables." The αὐτοῖς evidently means the deputation from the Sanhedrin; so also Mt. But Lk. says that He began πρὸς τὸν λαὸν λέγειν. If He spoke to the people, He spoke *at* the hierarchy, who were still present. The parable contains an indirect answer to the question which they raised. His authority is that of the Father who sent Him, as He sent the Prophets through many generations; and he warns them of the judgment which awaits them, when they have slain Him as they slew the previous messengers. This story, therefore, might be called an allegory rather than a parable, for it sets forth in a figure past, present, and future events, rather than truths for the permanent guidance of believers. As *v.* 9 shows, the tenants of the vineyard are not the hierarchy but the nation whom they mislead, and the vineyard is not the nation, but the nation's spiritual privileges. It is not intimated that the Jews will be handed over to other leaders, but that their privileges will be handed over to the Gentiles. The whole nation followed the lead of the hierarchy in putting the Messiah to death and shared in the guilt of that act; and it was the whole nation that was dispossessed. Christ is recalling the well-known parable in Is. v. 1—7, and there also the whole nation is condemned. Cf. Jer. ii. 21 ; Ezek. xv. 1—6, xix. 10—14; Hos. x. 1 ; Deut. xxxii. 32. The audience would understand the imagery of the parable. It is somewhat captious

criticism when Loisy says that a man who plants his own vineyard is
not likely to be a lord who takes a long journey, and that an owner
who lives a long way off would not want to be paid in kind with fruit.
It is not said that he planted the vineyard himself, or that he went a
long way off, or that the messengers could not sell the fruit and bring
money for it. Moreover, reasonable hearers do not expect everything
in a parable to be prosaically probable: it suffices that there are no
glaring impossibilities. Lk. makes the story more symmetrical; a
single slave is sent thrice, and the treatment of the messengers becomes steadily worse, until it culminates in the death of the son.
From Lk. comes the reading λέγειν in this verse; אBGLΔ, Latt. Syrr.
have λαλεῖν.

’Αμπελῶνα ἄνθρ. ἐφύτευσεν. Cf. Gen. ix. 20; Deut. xx. 6, xxviii.
30, 39, etc. The termination -ων is similar to -etum in Latin. Cf.
ἐλαιών (xi. 1), δενδρών (Aq. Gen. xxi. 33; 1 Sam. xxxi. 13), ῥοδών, etc.

φραγμόν. In Palestine, fences are commonly of stone, which is
abundant (Num. xxii. 24; Prov. xxiv. 31; Is. v. 5). Stanley, *Sin
and Pal.* p. 421.

ὑπολήνιον. The ληνός (Mt.) was the trough, cut in the solid rock
or lined with masonry, in which the grapes were trodden, and out of
which the juice flowed into the ὑπολήνιον. These details have no
separate meaning. They show that the tenants were well treated by
the owner. The vineyard was protected from wild animals (Num.
xxii. 24; Ps. lxxx. 13; Cant. ii. 15), and there was a complete outfit
for wine-making. Tristram, *Eastern Customs in Bible Lands*, p. 138.

πύργον. A residence for the wine-dressers and a watch-tower
against robbers (Is. i. 8, v. 2).

γεωργοῖς. A generic term including ἀμπελουργοί (Lk. xiii. 7). In
Jer. lii. 16 the two are distinguished. As in the parable of the
Unrighteous Steward, these tenants had a long lease and paid in kind.
All three Gospels have ἐξέδετο (WH. *App.* p. 168; Blass § 23. 3),
which occurs nowhere else in N.T. The verb is used in the same
sense in Plato (*Laws*, vii. 806 D), but in LXX. of giving a daughter in
marriage (Exod. ii. 21; Ecclus vii. 25; 1 Macc. x. 58).

ἀπεδήμησεν. *Went into another country* (R.V.); "far country" is
more than the word means, and the parable implies that the owner
was not far off. Lk. adds χρόνους ἱκανούς. Origen interprets the
absence as meaning the withdrawal of the Shechinah. The cessation
of the theocracy is more probable. In any case, the tenants are not
forgotten. Jehovah frequently reminds them of their duty to Him.
It is like the act of a father who gives his children the opportunity of
right action without constant supervision.

2. **δοῦλον.** *Bondservant* or *slave.* This designation, so degrading among men, becomes a title of nobility when the servant is in voluntary bondage to the Lord. Moses, Aaron, David, and the Prophets are all in a special sense δοῦλοι Κυρίου or Θεοῦ. St Paul was proud of being δοῦλος Ἰησοῦ Χριστοῦ (Rom. i. 1; cf. the greetings in Phil., Tit., Jas, 2 Pet., Jude).

ἀπὸ τῶν καρπῶν. The proportion, or the fixed amount, which they had covenanted to pay is not stated. They refused to pay any rent. Cf. Lev. xix. 23—25.

3. **λαβόντες...ἀπέστειλαν.** He was *sent* to *take* the fruits, and the men *took* him and *sent* him off without any. This is probably a mere accident in expression; Mk is not given to playing on words. The more literary Lk. is more subtle in language; in v. 25 he perhaps does mean to suggest that the man now carried what had hitherto carried him. St Paul is fond of playing on words; see on 2 Cor. i. 13 and App. D. In LXX. δέρω, if the readings are right, means "flay" (Lev. i. 6; 2 Chron. xxix. 34, xxxv. 11); in N.T. it means always "beat." Cf. our colloquial "hide," "give a hiding." For "send empty away" see Lk. i. 53; Gen. xxxi. 42; Deut. xv. 13; 1 Sam. vi. 3; Job xxii. 9.

4. **ἐκεφαλίωσαν.** The verb occurs nowhere else in Greek literature, but there is not much doubt about the meaning; *in capite vulnaverunt* (Vulg.). Mt. substitutes ἐλιθοβόλησαν, Lk. τραυματίσαντες. "Beheaded" would be ἀπεκεφάλισαν (vi. 16), but k has *decollaverunt*. The unnecessary conjecture ἐκολάφισαν has no authority. Syr-Sin. omits the verse.

5. **κἀκεῖνον.** If ἐκεφαλίωσαν be rendered "beheaded," this is "him also"; otherwise "and him." Here, as in most places, κἀκεῖνον, and not καὶ ἐκεῖνον, is found in the best MSS. See on x. 1. Syr-Sin. omits this murder.

πολλοὺς ἄλλους. Loose conversational constr. The statement is true to history, in which both rulers and people are found in constant opposition to the Prophets; *e.g.* 1 Kings xviii. 13, xxii. 27; 2 Chron. xxiv. 20, xxxvi. 15; Neh. ix. 26; Jer. xxv. 3—7, xxxv. 15. Their number makes a telling contrast to ἕνα υἱόν. This is lost in Lk. For μὲν...δὲ... cf. xiv. 21, 38. It is rare in Mk.

6. **ἀγαπητόν.** It is possible to take the term as a Messianic title in i. 11 and ix. 7, but not here. Put a comma between υἱόν and ἀγαπητόν, "one son, a beloved one," *i.e.* an only son (Judg. xi. 34). Cf. Gal. iv. 4; Heb. i. 2. In N.T. ἀγαπητός is used only of Christ or of Christians.

Ἐντραπήσονται. In all three. The meaning seems to be that of

"turning towards" a person to pay respect to him (Lk. xviii. 2;
2 Thess. iii. 14; Heb. xii. 9). But the act. (1 Cor. iv. 14) means
"I put to shame," which may come from "I turn in," *i.e.* "make a
man hang his head," either in reverence or in confusion; cf. ἐντροπή
(1 Cor. vi. 5, xv. 34). This meaning is found in LXX. and in late
colloquial Greek, as shown in papyri. The question of "turning
towards" or "turning in" is unimportant.

This is parable or allegory, not history, and the owner of the vineyard is a man (*v.* 1), who might be mistaken about the effect of sending
his son. He acts, not as God acts, but as He appears to act. God
sometimes seems to repent of His own actions (Jer. xviii. 8, 10, xxvi.
13; Joel ii. 13; Amos vii. 3; Jonah iii. 9); but this is only man's
point of view (Num. xxiii. 13). Cf. Is. v. 4.

7. ἐκεῖνοι δέ. The pronoun places the men at a distance from the
writer in abhorrence; *But those wicked men, the husbandmen*; cf. xiv.
21; Jn viii. 44, x. 1; see on Jn xiii. 30. The scene recalls that of
Joseph's brethren plotting against him; δεῦτε ἀποκτείνωμεν αὐτόν are
their words also (Gen. xxxvii. 20). The killing of the previous
messengers was defiance; the killing of the son might be permanent
gain. Here the parable leaves history and becomes prophecy,
and (as often in prophecy) what is predicted as certain is spoken
of as having taken place. Christ knew that the Jews meant to
kill Him and that He would submit to being killed. The final
messenger to the husbandmen had told them that he was the
son. Christ did the same, at first by signs, and finally in plain words
(xiv. 62).

8. καὶ ἐξέβαλον αὐτόν. They flung out his corpse to the birds
and beasts; a last act of defiance and insult. Mt. and Lk. make
the casting out precede the slaying, possibly because Christ was
crucified outside Jerusalem. Naboth was taken outside the city to be
stoned (1 Kings xxi. 13); also Stephen (Acts vii. 58).

9. ἐλεύσεται καὶ ἀπολέσει. Mt. says that the members of the
Sanhedrin made this reply, and it may represent the presentiments of
some of them; but doubtless it was our Lord who uttered it. It predicts the destruction of Jerusalem, of the Jews as a nation, and of
Judaism as represented by the Temple-worship.

δώσει τὸν ἀμπελῶνα ἄλλοις. The spiritual privileges of the Jews
are to pass to the new Israel, which will consist mainly of Gentiles,
and they "will render Him the fruits of their seasons" (Mt.), otherwise "they also will be cut off" (Rom. xi. 22). Lk. says that Christ's
prediction was received by those whom He addressed with μὴ γένοιτο,
which, though more probable than Mt.'s statement that they them-

selves uttered the prediction, is perhaps Lk.'s idea of what they must
have felt.

10. **οὐδὲ τὴν γραφὴν ταύτην ἀν.** *Have ye not read even this
scripture?* (R.V.). "Did ye never read" occurs ii. 25; Mt. xxi. 16;
cf. Mt. xix. 4, xxii. 31. Ἡ γραφή in N.T. commonly means a particular
passage; the O.T. as a whole is αἱ γραφαί (*v.* 24). See on Jn ii. 22.
Λίθον ὃν ἀπεδοκίμασαν. Attraction to the relative. From the
vineyard in Is. v. we pass to the equally familiar builders in Ps. cxviii.,
part of which had been sung by the multitude at the triumphal entry;
and the quotation is as exact from the LXX. as the LXX. from the
Hebrew. Just as the vine-dressers reject the messengers, so the builders
reject the stone, and with equally fatal result (Mt. and Lk.). Perhaps
we ought to translate "*A* stone" rather than "*The* stone." The
builders rejected many stones, and one of the rejected stones became
"head of the corner." But "The stone" may be right, if Λίθος was
a name for the Messiah (Justin, *Try.* 34, 36). For ἀποδοκιμάζω see
on viii. 31. Γίνομαι εἰς occurs in Lk. and Acts, and is freq. in quotations from LXX. The change of picture from the vineyard to the
builders makes allusion to the Resurrection possible; the slain son
could not be revived in the story, but the rejected stone can be
promoted.

κεφαλὴν γωνίας. A corner-stone uniting two walls; but whether
at the base or at the top is not certain. Some think that it means the
highest stone in the building; cf. Zech. iv. 7. The expression occurs
nowhere but in Ps. cxviii. and the quotations from it here, Acts iv.
11, and 1 Pet. ii. 7, where see Hort. The Psalm is probably connected with the dedication of the second Temple, in the building of
which some such incident may have occurred. Perowne on Ps. cxviii.

11. **παρὰ κυρίου ἐγένετο αὕτη.** Either *From Jehovah this corner-
stone came*, or *From Jehovah this came to pass* = *This was from the
Lord* (R.V.). In the latter case αὕτη is a Hebraism, αὕτη="this
thing." Cf. οὐκ ἐγένετο ὡς αὕτη (Judg. xix. 30); οὐ γέγονεν τοιαύτη
(1 Sam. iv. 7); αὕτη με παρεκάλεσεν (Ps. cxix. 50), where τὸν λόγον
σου precedes. But there is no other instance of this Hebraistic fem.
in N.T. For the constr. cf. *v.* 2, xiv. 43; Jn. i. 6.

12. **αὐτὸν κρατῆσαι.** Cf. iii. 21, xiv. 44, 46, 49, 51.
καὶ ἐφοβήθησαν. We might expect ἀλλ' ἐφοβήθησαν. Cf. vi. 19.
The two statements, however, are put side by side, not in opposition,
but in contrast. The hierarchy were continually trying to arrest
Him, and, just when He had shown that He knew of their murderous
plots, their fear of the people hindered them from arresting Him.
Winer, p. 544 n. A similar fear had kept Antipas from putting the

Baptist to death. In xi. 32 we have their habitual feeling of fear (imperf.); here we have its operation in a particular instance.

ἔγνωσαν γάρ. *Because* they recognized the reference (Lk. xii. 41, xviii. 1; Rom. x. 21; Heb. i. 7, 8) to themselves, they desired all the more to arrest Him.

πρὸς αὐτούς. With emphasis; *that it was in reference to them*, or *against them* (Acts xxiii. 30), *that He spake.*

ἀφέντες αὐτόν. Just the opposite of their desires and endeavours. They dared not take public action against this popular Prophet, all the less so as pilgrims from Galilee were daily increasing in Jerusalem.

13—17. THE PHARISEES' QUESTION ABOUT TRIBUTE.

Mt. xxii. 15—22. Lk. xx. 20—26.

13. ἀποστέλλουσιν. Mk in his conversational style supplies no nominative, and apparently it is the baffled Sanhedrists who send another relay of insidious questioners. Mt. says that the Pharisees are the senders.

καὶ τῶν Ἡρῳδιανῶν. We had this remarkable alliance iii. 6. The Herodians were obnoxious to the Pharisees on political grounds, as the Sadducees were on religious grounds; but the Pharisees were willing to work with either for the destruction of Jesus. The Passover brought all parties to Jerusalem.

ἀγρεύσωσιν. A hunting metaphor, of catching wild animals. The λόγῳ includes both their question and His answer. This verb and παγιδεύω (Mt.) occur nowhere else in N.T., but both are found in LXX. in a figurative sense, as here (Prov. v. 22; Eccles. ix. 12). In different ways all three Gospels call attention to the *hypocrisy* of these questioners. They skilfully act the part of innocent and earnest enquirers, and profess to rely upon His courage and sincerity for an answer unbiased by fear or favour.

14. ἀληθὴς εἶ. They did not believe this, but they knew that Jesus professed it (Jn viii. 14, 16, 18, 40); and we have here indirect confirmation of the Fourth Gospel, in which ἀληθής and the cognate words are freq., whereas ἀληθής occurs nowhere in the Synoptic Gospels, except in this saying.

οὐ μέλει σοι. Cf. iv. 38; Lk. x. 40; Jn x. 13.

βλέπεις εἰς πρόσωπον. In LXX. we have ὁρᾶν εἰς πρ. (1 Sam. xvi. 7), but more often θαυμάζειν πρ. (Lev. xix. 15; Prov. xviii. 5; Job xiii. 10; cf. Jude 16) or λαμβάνειν πρ. (Mal. i. 8, 9, ii. 9; Ecclus iv. 21, 27; cf. Lk. xx. 21; Gal. ii. 6).

ἐπ' ἀληθείας. *On a basis of truth*, or *according to truth* (Lk. iv.

25, xxii. 59; Acts x. 34).   Cf. ἐπ' ἀδείας, ἐπὶ σχολῆς, ἐπ' ἴσης, sc. μοίρας.

τὴν ὁδὸν τοῦ θεοῦ.   Cf. Acts xviii. 26.   The opposite of "evil ways," "ways of sinners," "false ways" (Ps. cxix. 101, 104, 128).
ἔξεστιν δοῦναι.   "Does the Law allow it?"   Cf. εἰ ἔξεστιν (x. 2), οὐκ ἔξεστιν (ii. 24, 26, vi. 18).   Since the deposition of Archelaus, Judaea had paid a poll-tax to Rome, and this question about the lawfulness of paying tribute had been raised by Judas of Galilee (Acts v. 37), whose rebellion, about A.D. 7, is often mentioned by Josephus (*Ant.* xviii. i. 1, etc.).   Like the question about authority, this was in itself a fair one to put to a public teacher; it was one about which the Pharisees (Mt.) and the partisans of Herod might feel perplexed. How could the payment of a poll-tax, which went to the *fiscus* of a heathen Emperor who had robbed the Jews of their freedom, be reconciled with the Law?

κῆνσον.   *Census* from meaning the valuation of a person's estate came to mean the tax which depended on the valuation, and then any kind of impost, which is the meaning here.   The impost being a poll-tax, D and some other authorities have ἐπικεφάλαιον, k *capitularium*.

ἢ οὔ;   The alternative is not otiose; they wish to tie Him down to a plain Yes or No, either of which would land Him in difficulty.

ἢ μὴ δῶμεν;   Deliberative subj. (iv. 30, vi. 24, 37), and hence the change from οὐ to μή.   This second question is omitted by Mt. and Lk., also by Syr-Sin. in Mk., as superfluous fulness, as in i. 32, 42, vi. 25, etc.

15.   **εἰδὼς αὐτῶν τὴν ὑπόκρισιν.**   All three point out that Christ saw their insidious acting, but each uses a different verb and substantive.   Mt. γνοὺς πονηρίαν, while Lk. has his favourite κατανοήσας with πανουργίαν.   One might have expected Mt. to prefer εἰδώς (intuitive knowledge) to γνούς (knowledge gained by experience).

Τί με πειράζετε;   Christ knew why, but His question shows them that He is aware that their question is a trap.

φέρετέ μοι δηνάριον.   *Bring Me a denarius*; φέρετε has far more point than δείξατε (Lk.) or ἐπιδείξατε (Mt.).   Christ knew that no one would have heathen money about him; and, as He had banished the money-changers from the Temple, it would have to be fetched from outside.   This involved a pause, during which the by-standers would speculate as to why Christ had sent for τὸ νόμισμα τοῦ κήνσου (Mt.), the coin in which the poll-tax was paid.   See on vi. 37.

ἵνα ἴδω.   Mk only, but implied in δείξατε.   This is part of the acted lesson.   It is unlikely that Christ had never seen a *denarius*. He knows that it will be stamped as Caesar's.   The copper coins of

the Procurators had no "image" or other figure likely to offend the
Jews. אACD have ἵνα εἰδῶ (ii. 10); "that I may know the answer to
your question."

16. ἐπιγραφή. Existing coins of Tiberius have round the head
TI · CAESAR · DIVI · AVG · F · AVG ·, and on the reverse PONTIF ·
MAXIM. Cf. Τίνα ἔχει χαρακτῆρα τοῦτο τὸ τετρασσάριον; Τραιανοῦ
(Epict. *Dis.* iv. 5). The question there is asked for a didactic purpose,
but a different one.

17. Τὰ Καίσαρος ἀπόδοτε Καίσαρι. The change from δοῦναι to
ἀπόδοτε gives the whole principle. It was not a question of *giving*
what might lawfully be refused, but of *paying* what was lawfully
claimed. The tribute was not a gift but a debt. Caesar gave them
the inestimable benefit of stable government; were they to take it
and decline to pay anything towards its maintenance? The discharge
of this duty in no way interfered with their duty to God. The paying
of the coin, with Caesar's image upon it, to Caesar in no way hindered
a man's giving himself, made in God's image, to God. Οὐδὲν
ἐμποδίζει πρὸς θεοσέβειαν τὸ τελεῖν τῷ καίσαρι (Theoph.): indeed the
one duty was included in the other. Ranke has pointed to this
Saying as having had immense influence on the course of history.
This is true, but largely through misunderstanding; Christ does not
say anything here as to the relations between Church and State.
Lightfoot, *Sermons in St Paul's*, pp. 46 ff.

ἐξεθαύμαζον. All three mention the admiration of the audience.
The answer was complete, and yet, as Lk. points out, there was
nothing to take hold of; the Saying was ἄληπτον. The compound
verb is rare; Ecclus xxvii. 23, xliii. 18; 4 Macc. xvii. 17. Cf. ἐκθαμβέομαι (Mk only in N.T.).

Here some critics place the *pericope* about the Woman taken in
Adultery.

18—27. THE SADDUCEES' QUESTION ABOUT RESURRECTION.

Mt. xxii. 23—33. Lk. xx. 27—28.

18. Σαδδουκαῖοι. Mk mentions them nowhere else; nor does
Lk., except in Acts. Jn nowhere mentions them. In Mt. they are
six times coupled with the Pharisees. We may regard them as the
priestly aristocracy. They were much less numerous than the
Pharisees and much less popular. Josephus (*Ant.* xviii. i. 4) says
that Sadducees who became magistrates professed the views of
the Pharisees, otherwise the people would not have tolerated them,
for a belief in a resurrection had become popular (2 Macc. vi. 26,

vii. 9, 14, xii. 43, xiv. 46). Their denial of a resurrection grew
out of their attitude towards the oral tradition, which the Pharisees
held to be binding, while the Sadducees said that it was not. Both
agreed that the doctrine could not be proved from Scripture, for
against what is said on one side (Job xix. 26; Ps. xvi. 9—11,
xvii. 15; Is. xxvi. 19) must be set what is said on the other (Ps. vi.
5, lxxxviii. 11, cxv. 17; Eccles. ix. 4—10; Is. xxxviii. 18, 19).
To the Sadducees this meant that resurrection was an open question,
and they refused to believe it (Acts xxiii. 8; Joseph. *Ant.* xviii. i. 4,
B.J. ii. viii. 4). Excepting Lk. ii. 34, ἀνάστασις in N.T. is always
resurrection from the dead, a meaning which is very rare and late in
LXX. (2 Macc. vii. 14). It is doubtful whether οἵτινες, "who are of
such a class as to," refers to the Sadducees as a whole, or to those
who came to question our Lord. All Sadducees said that resurrection
was not an article of faith, but some may have believed that it was
true. Lk. confines the denial to those who came; τινες τῶν Σαδ. οἱ
λέγοντες, not τῶν λεγόντων. In all three the denial is given as a
matter of opinion, μὴ εἶναι, as in Acts xxiii. 8. The Corinthian
sceptics declared as a fact that there is no such thing as a resurrection
of dead people, ὅτι ἀνάστασις νεκρῶν οὐκ ἔστιν (1 Cor. xv. 12). These
Sadducees knew that Christ had discomfited their opponents the
Pharisees, and they hoped to succeed where their adversaries had failed.

ἐπηρώτων. Conversational imperf. (v. 9, vii. 17, viii. 23, 27, 29,
etc.). Mt. and Lk. have the aor.

19. Ἐάν τινος ἀδελφός. The allusion is to Deut. xxv. 5, but the
exact words are not quoted; nor do the Synoptists agree in their
wording.

μὴ ἀφῇ τέκνον. Deut. xxv. 5 says "have no *son*," but in LXX.
σπέρμα is used, and the Talmud says that the deceased brother must
have no *child*. Here all three say *child*less. Lev. xviii. 16, xx. 21
forbids marriage with a brother's wife, and this is sometimes interpreted to mean that such marriage is forbidden during the brother's
life. But would it be necessary to forbid such a union? More
probably Lev. gives the rule, and Deut. states an exception to it.
Driver on Deut. xxv. 5—10. The Levirate law is still widely
prevalent in certain tribes in Asia, America and Polynesia. Among
the Jews it does not seem to have been liked, and Deut. allows the
surviving brother to refuse to take the widow. It would be of more
importance to Sadducees than to others. Those who deny individual
immortality find a kind of substitute for it in the continuation of the
family; but to them the dying out of the family means absolute
extinction. See *D.C.G.* art. "Levirate Law."

20. ἑπτὰ ἀδελφοὶ ἦσαν. The example is framed so as to make resurrection appear ridiculous; πλάττουσι τὴν διήγησιν ταύτην. Mt. inserts παρ᾽ ἡμῖν, and D has παρ᾽ ἡμῖν in Mk; but it is not likely that such a case had occurred. The Sadducees perhaps insinuated that the Levirate law showed that Moses did not believe in a resurrection. Christ produces evidence that Moses must have believed in it.

ἀποθνήσκων. "In dying," "at his death." Here again, and throughout in all three, nothing is said about a *son*; it is "leaving no seed," or "being childless."

21. μὴ καταλιπών. See crit. note. *Without leaving seed behind him.* As usual the participle has μή, not οὐ. See on ii. 4, v. 26, vi. 34, viii. 1.

ὡσαύτως. The adv. is amphibolous, but it is best taken with what precedes (A.V., R.V., WH.). In 1 Cor. xi. 25 and 1 Tim. v. 25, ὡσαύτως must be taken with the καί that follows. D omits the third brother and continues καὶ ὡσαύτως.

22. ἔσχατον πάντων. Cf. 1 Cor. xv. 8; Mt. has his favourite ὕστερον, which Mk nowhere uses. See crit. note.

23. τίνος αὐτῶν ἔσται γυνή; See crit. note and WH. *App.* p. 26. They put an extreme case; but less extreme cases were common without the action of the Levirate law. A woman often married twice, and to those who regarded the future life as similar to the present one, the question naturally arose, "Whose wife will she be?" The accepted answer seems to have been, "The wife of her first husband." Christ might have adopted this answer, and it would have sufficed to rebut the Sadducean objection; but such an answer would have confirmed the current debasing views respecting the life to come.

ἔσχον αὐτὴν γυναῖκα. *Got her as wife,* a usual meaning of ἔσχον (Jn iv. 18, 52; Gal. iv. 22; 1 Thess. i. 9; Philem. 7). J. H. Moulton, p. 145. Syr-Sin. omits γυναῖκα.

24. ἔφη αὐτοῖς. See crit. note, and for the rare kind of asyndeton cf. ix. 38, x. 29. Syr-Sin. has "*Our Lord* answered and said."

Οὐ διὰ τοῦτο. *Is it not because of this that ye go astray, that ye know not,* etc.? See on *v.* 10 for similar questions asked by Christ. They thought that they had Scripture on their side, and what was still worse (μηδέ as in vi. 11), they did not realize the power of God (cf. 1 Cor. xv. 34). The latter kind of ignorance is corrected first. But Christ expresses no opinion of the Levirate law; He neither condemns nor confirms it. See on xiii. 5 for πλανάω.

25. οὔτε γαμοῦσιν οὔτε γαμίζονται. The former, as in class. Grk, of the man, the latter of the woman, who is given in marriage by her father (1 Cor. vii. 38).　The questioners did not see that God could not only grant life in another world, but also make it very different from life in this world.　The Sadducees assumed that, unless the conditions of life hereafter are the same as in this life, there can be no future life at all.　Marriage is necessary here to preserve the race, but where all are immortal there is no need of marriage.　In Enoch (xv. 6, 7) the Lord says to the Angels, "You were spiritual, in the enjoyment of eternal immortal life, for all generations of the world.　Therefore I have not appointed wives for you; for the spiritual have their dwelling in heaven."

ὡς ἄγγελοι.　Angels do not marry, because they are immortal, and those who rise from the dead are like them.　This comparison is in all three, and it had special point in dealing with Sadducees, correcting another of their errors (Acts xxiii. 8).　It tells us nothing respecting the manner of the resurrection, but it tells us that those who rise will not die again, and it assures us that such beings as Angels, who live under very different conditions from those under which we live here, exist.　Cf. viii. 38; also xiii. 27 = Mt. xxiv. 31; xiii. 32 = Mt. xxiv. 36; Mt. xiii. 39, 41, 49, xviii. 10, xxv. 31, xxvi. 53; Lk. xii. 8, 9, xv. 10, xvi. 22; Jn i. 52.　It is unreasonable to suggest that in all these passages the Evangelists attribute their own beliefs to Christ, and that He never sanctioned the doctrine by the words which they report.　See Latham, *A Service of Angels,* pp. 52—60.

ἐν τοῖς οὐρανοῖς.　It is remarkable that Mk has this expression, while Mt. has ἐν τῷ οὐρανῷ.　We might have expected exactly the converse.　See on εἰδώς (v. 15) and cf. xiii. 32 = Mt. xxiv. 36.

26.　οὐκ ἀνέγνωτε;　The first-mentioned cause of error, ignorance of Scripture, is now corrected.　We have had a similar question ii. 25 (see note and xii. 10).

ἐν τῇ βίβλῳ Μωυσέως.　This tells us nothing as to the authorship of the Pentateuch or of the passage quoted.　Our Lord uses "Moses" and "David" in the way in which all Jews used them at that time (i. 44, vii. 10, x. 3, xii. 36).　It is incredible that in so doing He was deciding critical questions authoritatively.

ἐπὶ τοῦ βάτου.　"*At* the portion of Scripture known as *The Bush.*" The section which contains the incident of the burning bush was so called.　Similarly, ἐν Ἠλίᾳ (Rom. xi. 2) means in the section which contains the story of Elijah.　Cf. 2 Sam. i. 18.　But ἐπί (not ἐν) makes this explanation somewhat doubtful; ἐπί may be simply local, "at the bush."　This local meaning would be certain if the words ran πῶς ἐπὶ τοῦ βάτου, as A.V. takes them; but ἐπὶ τ. β. πῶς throws the probability the other way. In LXX., as here, βάτος is masc. In Lk. xx. 37 and Acts vii. 35 it is fem.

Christ does not appeal to Dan. xii. 2. He goes to what for every Jew was the highest authority of all, the Pentateuch. That the Sadducees accepted no other books, though asserted by some Fathers, seems to be an error. In the Books of Moses, again and again the doctrine of a future life is to be found by those who have spiritual insight. In Gen. xxvi. 24 and xxviii. 13, after the death of Abraham, God calls Himself "the God of Abraham." In Exod. iii. 6, 15, 16 and iv. 5, after the death of all three, God calls Himself "the God of Abraham, Isaac and Jacob." If God is still their God, they are still alive; for "He is not a God of dead men, but of living." Lifeless things can have a Creator, but not a God. "O ye ice and snow, bless ye the Lord" is poetical personification rather than intelligible worship. Gamaliel is said to have used a somewhat similar argument. God made promises to the patriarchs which were not fulfilled during their life on earth, and of course God's promises to them must be fulfilled ; therefore the patriarchs are still alive or will be revived. Christ's argument is found 4 Macc. vii. 19, xvi. 25, but the date of that book may be later than Mk.

It will be observed that Christ's argument, like St Paul's, does not prove the resuscitation of the material body; it proves the survival of the soul or spirit, which will have a spiritual body suited to it (1 Cor. xv. 35—45). *Christ* says that the living God cannot be a God of dead persons; the continued relation of each one of them to Him as God (note the repetition of Θεός with each name) shows that the personal life of each one of them still survives. *St Paul* says that the continued relation of each believer to the Christ, who has been raised in a glorified Body of which believers are members, secures for each the continuance of bodily life. Death may lessen or destroy their relation to the world of sense, but it intensifies their relation to Christ and to God. Neither Christ nor St Paul tells us the connexion between the spiritual body which is immortal and the material body which is dissolved by death. Science shows us that the material particles of living organisms, in the course of ages, are used over and over again; and to ask Whose shall they be at the Resurrection? is repeating the error of the Sadducees.

27. πολὺ πλανᾶσθε. See crit. note. Mk alone has this. The terse abruptness is characteristic of his preservation of the original manner of utterance; *ye go greatly astray.* Cf. i. 27, iv. 40, ix. 23, x. 14, 18. Religion, the bond between God and man, is indeed a

poor thing, if man's existence ends with death. *Ceux qui ont vécu pour Dieu ne peuvent jamais être morts pour lui* (Loisy).

28—34. THE SCRIBE'S QUESTION ABOUT THE GREAT COMMANDMENT.

Mt. xxii. 34—40. Cf. Lk. x. 25—28, xx. 39.

28. προσελθὼν εἶς τῶν γραμματέων. When the discomfited Sadducees retired, a Scribe came forward and asked a question which was often discussed. Mk takes a favourable view of his intentions and says that his comment on Christ's reply won from Him high commendation. Mt. does far otherwise. He says that the man was a Pharisee (therefore an enemy, according to Mt.), who, so far from being grateful to Christ for refuting the Sadducees about resurrection, put a testing question to Him, apparently to draw a vulnerable reply. The man makes no comment on Christ's reply and receives no commendation. Lk. says that some of the Scribes praised Christ's refutation of the Sadducees, but he does not give this conversation with one of them, perhaps because he has recorded a similar conversation earlier (x. 25 f.). Note the accumulation of participles. Syr-Sin. omits the first and smooths the awkward constr. "And when one of the Scribes heard that He had answered well to those who were questioning Him." See on i. 15.

Ποία ἐστὶν ἐντολὴ πρώτη πάντων; R.V. elsewhere gives the right meaning to ποῖος (Lk. ix. 55; Jn xii. 33, xviii. 82, xxi. 19; Rom. iii. 27; 1 Cor. xv. 35), but neither here nor xi. 28. Sometimes the distinctive meaning is faint or extinct, but here it has point. The Scribe wants to know what *kind* of a commandment is to be put in the highest place. The Rabbis divided the 613 precepts of the Law (248 commands and 365 prohibitions) into "weighty" and "light," but the sorting of them caused much debate. This Scribe wants a principle of classification. The neut. πάντων looks as if πρωτ. πάντων was a colloquial expression used independently of the gender of whatever was "first." Alford suggests that πρῶτος πάντων was treated as one word, "first-of-all"; or perhaps as meaning "first of all things" (Winer, p. 222; Blass § 36. 12). Examples from papyri are wanted; there seem to be none in Greek literature, where πρώτη πασῶν would be correct.

29. ἀπεκρίθη. Our Lord again shows that the answer is to be found in what is very familiar. The questioner had to recite twice daily a text which gave him the principle which he desired. That principle is the love of God, which is indicated in the Second Com-

mandment, "showing mercy unto thousands in them that love Me,"
and is set forth again and again in Deut. as that which ought to be
the leading principle in human conduct (x. 12, xi. 1, 13, 22, xiii. 3,
xix. 9, xxx. 6, 16, 20). It there appears as the first commandment
of all. See Driver on Deut. vi. 5. *Praeceptum non modo maximum
amplitudine, sed etiam primum natura* (Beng.).

κύριος ὁ θεὸς κ.τ.λ. Of the three renderings (A.V., R.V., R.V.
marg.) the first is the more approved rendering of the Hebrew;
"Jehovah our God is one Jehovah"="The Lord our God is one
Lord" (R.V. in Deut. vi. 5 and A.V. here).

30. ἐξ ὅλης τῆς καρδίας σου. This use of ἐκ is classical; ἀλλ'
εἴπερ ἐκ τῆς καρδίας μ' ὄντως φιλεῖς (Aristoph. *Nub.* 86). Mk follows
LXX. in having ἐξ throughout, Mt. follows the Heb. with ἐν throughout, while Lk. (x. 27) begins with ἐξ and changes to ἐν. The powers
with which God is to be loved are thus given by each:

LXX.　διάνοια, ψυχή, δύναμις,
Mt.　καρδία, ψυχή, διάνοια,
Mk　καρδία, ψυχή, διάνοια, ἰσχύς,
Lk.　καρδία, ψυχή, ἰσχύς, διάνοια.

Mt., as usual, prefers a triplet, but he might have made a better one,
for there is as little difference between καρδία and διάνοια as between
δύναμις and ἰσχύς. Except in quotations, no Evangelist uses διάνοια.
Whether we have three or four terms, the meaning is that God is to
be loved with all the powers which man can bring into play, whether
of emotion, intellect or will. No psychological system lies at the
back of the groups or is to be constructed out of them. Cf. the
Testaments, ὑμεῖς δὲ φοβεῖσθε Κύριον τὸν Θεὸν ἡμῶν ἐν πάσῃ ἰσχύι ὑμῶν
(*Zebulon* x. 5): also Apoc. of Baruch, lxi. 1, *ex toto corde suo et ex
tota anima sua*.

31. Ἀγαπήσεις τὸν πλησίον σου. In both cases it is ἀγάπη, as
described 1 Cor. xiii., that is enjoined; φιλήσεις would have been less
suitable, and in the case of love to God very unusual. Both in Exod.
and Deut., the commandments are given in fut. indic. (οὐ ποιήσεις,
κ.τ.λ.), as here. See on x. 19. The Scribe had asked about the
πρώτη πάντων. Christ answers and goes on to show him what the
"first of all" involves; see on 1 Jn iv. 20, 21. The second, which
is involved in the first, is given in the exact words of LXX. (Lev. xix.
18). So also Rom. xiii. 9; Gal. v. 14; Jas. ii. 8, where it is called
βασιλικὸς νόμος. But in none of these passages is the love of God
coupled with the love of one's neighbour; contrast *Didache* i. 2. The
wording of Lev. xix. 18 encouraged Jews to put a very restricted
meaning on τὸν πλησίον: no Gentile was a "neighbour." Contrast

Jn xv. 12; Lk. x. 36. The duty of loving one's neighbour is more evident than that of loving God, yet the latter is prior in dignity and importance; for He is closer to us than our neighbours are, "nearer than hands and feet," and the duty to love Him as our Father is the foundation of the duty to love them as brethren. These two commandments are found side by side in the Testaments, "Love the Lord in all your life, and one another in a true heart" (*Dan* v. 3). Philo (*De Septenario*, p. 282 Mang.) mentions as the two ἀνωτάτω κεφάλαια, εὐσέβεια and ὁσιότης towards God, φιλανθρωπία and δικαιοσύνη towards men. See Sanday and Headlam, *Romans*, p. 376.

32. Καλῶς. The reply of the Scribe is given by Mk alone. Καλῶς is not an interjection. It may be taken either with the preceding εἶπεν, in which case it anticipates νουνεχῶς in *v.* 34, or with the following εἶπας. In favour of the former is the fact that elsewhere Mk begins addresses with Διδάσκαλε (iv. 38, ix. 17, 38, x. 17, 20, 35, xii. 14, 19, xiii. 1). But the full expression in καλῶς ἐπ' ἀληθείας is in Mk's style, where ἐπ' ἀλ. adds strength to καλῶς, but is otherwise pleonastic; "Verely thou hast sayde right" (Coverdale).

ὅτι Εἷς ἐστιν. *That He is one* (R.V.), not "*for* there is one *God*" (A.V.). The Scribe avoids using the Divine Name, and the insertion of θεός in some texts is a corruption.

33. τῆς συνέσεως. This takes the place of τῆς διανοίας without difference of meaning, and τῆς ψυχῆς is omitted.

περισσότερον. *Much more* (R.V.) rather than "more" (A.V.), which would be πλεῖον (Mt. vi. 25): in *v.* 40, A.V. and R.V. are alike defective.

ὁλοκαυτωμάτων. These are a higher species of θυσίαι, viz. those which ascend eucharistically to heaven. We have the same combination and much the same sense in 1 Sam. xv. 22, which may have been in the Scribe's mind. Cf. Ps. xlix. 8—10, l. 18, 19; Jer. vii. 22, 23; Hos. vi. 6.

34. νουνεχῶς. Here only in Bibl. Grk, and nowhere else in our Bible does *discreetly* appear. Polybius has νουνεχῶς several times, combining it with πρακτικῶς and φρονίμως. The Scribe showed νοῦς (1 Cor. xiv. 14, 15; Rev. xvii. 9) or intelligence in seeing that moral duties are far more important than ceremonial observances.

Οὐ μακρὰν εἶ. There may be an allusion to Is. lvii. 19. Cf. Acts ii. 39; Eph. ii. 13, 17. As in the case of the rich man (x. 22), we are left in ignorance as to the ultimate issue. Did the rich man in the end follow Him to whom he had run for instruction? Did this Scribe enter the Kingdom to which he had come so near? Cf. 2 Pet. ii. 21.

οὐδεὶς οὐκέτι. See on i. 44. The Evangelists put this remark in different places. Lk. has it after Christ had silenced the Sadducees. Mt. has it after Christ's question about the Son of David, when all had been doubly silenced, for He had successfully answered their questions and they had failed to reply to His.

35—37. The Lord's Question about the Son of David.

Mt. xxii. 41—45. Lk. xx. 41—44.

35. ἀποκριθείς. Syr-Sin. omits. As in ix. 5, xi. 14, xv. 12, we have ἀποκριθείς of responding to circumstances which elicit utterance. No words are recorded as calling for a reply ; but His critics have been testing Him with questions, and now He closes the debate with a question of His own. Here the question is addressed to the people in His public teaching; Mt. says that the Pharisees gathered together and that He put the question to them. Lk. is indefinite.

Πῶς λέγουσιν. "In what *sense* can they make the statement?" Or "How can they *maintain* the statement?" This, however, may be making too much of πῶς. Perhaps "How can they say?" is all that is meant. The statement has obvious difficulty. As in the case of the Levirate law, Christ does not declare whether the statement is right or wrong; but He intimates that those who make it ought to be able to explain the difficulty. He is not asking a question for the mere purpose of baffling them (see on xi. 29); the answer to it would help them to understand who He was. The people had illustrated the teaching of the Scribes by hailing Him as the Messianic Son of David, and He had accepted that homage, so that His own position was clear. But how did those who resented that homage explain the Psalm?

36. ἐν τῷ πνεύματι τῷ ἁγίῳ. *In the power of the Spirit, the Holy Spirit.* See on i. 23. The fact that the Psalmist was inspired is stated with solemn fulness; and for that fact we may claim the authority of Christ. Among all the sons of men, if there be one who could give an authoritative decision as to whether a writer was inspired or not, He is that one, προφήτης ὑπάρχων (Acts ii. 30). And we may perhaps claim His authority also for the belief that the Psalmist was writing of the Messiah. When we come to the question of the authorship of the Psalm, we are on different ground. We have no right to claim His authority in a matter which is not among things that are spiritually discerned, but is among those which can be decided by study and intelligence. We do not know what Christ believed about the authorship of Ps. cx. If (in the limitation of knowledge to which

He submitted in becoming man) He shared the belief of those who
sat on Moses' seat, we may be sure that He had no intention of
giving an authoritative decision on a question which had not been
raised. "Man, who made Me a judge of such things?" So far as
we can see, supernatural knowledge of the authorship of the parts of
the O.T. would have hindered rather than helped His work, and it
is rash to assume that He possessed it.

But it is not necessary to decide whether our Lord accepted the
Davidic authorship of Ps. cx. His argument is founded on David
being the speaker, and this argument "is justified if the author of
the Psalm lets David appear as the spokesman" (Briggs, *Psalms*, II.
p. 376). See Kirkpatrick on Ps. cx. in this series; Perowne, *Psalms*,
p. 302; Sanday, *Bampton Lectures*, p. 419; Gore, *Bamp. Lectt.* p. 196;
Dalman, *Words*, p. 285; Meyer or Weiss or Plummer on Mt. xxii. 43.

κάθου. This form occurs in the five quotations of this Psalm in
N.T. and is freq. in LXX. See Thackeray, *Gr. of the O.T. in Greek*,
p. 258; also Mayor on Jas. ii. 3, and cf. κάθη in Acts xxiii. 3.

ὑποκάτω. So also in Mt., but Lk. agrees with LXX. and Heb. in
having ὑποπόδιον. The change to ὑποκάτω avoids the tautology of
ὑποπόδιον τῶν ποδῶν. See crit. note.

37. λέγει αὐτὸν κύριον. Cf. A. 10.

καὶ πόθεν; Mt. has καὶ πῶς; We have both in Plato, *Phaedr.*
269 D, πῶς καὶ πόθεν ἄν τις δύναιτο πορίσασθαι;

ὁ πολὺς ὄχλος. The great multitude, "the mass of the people," is
perhaps better than "the common people" (A.V., R.V.). Field
prefers the latter and gives quotations, which, however, can hardly
decide in such a case, for both renderings, as here, make good sense.
At the end, as at the beginning, of His Ministry, His teaching attracted
masses. But with many of them ἤκουεν ἡδέως was like the same fact
in Antipas with regard to the Baptist (vi. 20). They liked the fresh-
ness of His method and the skill with which He answered questions;
they perhaps enjoyed hearing the professional teachers routed; and
some may have appreciated the spiritual strength of His instruction.
But, like Antipas, nearly all of them, when pressed, were ready to
consent to their Teacher's death.

38—40. Christ's Condemnation of the Scribes.

Mt. xxiii. 1—7. Lk. xx. 45—47.

38. ἐν τῇ διδαχῇ αὐτοῦ ἔλεγεν. As often, Mk has imperf. where
Mt. and Lk. have aor. Only a brief denunciation is here common to
all three; somewhat more is common to Mk and Lk.; but the greater

part is in Mt. alone, who, however, has evidently strung together in one discourse denunciations which were uttered on other occasions. Lk. gives some of them in other and more probable settings. With the exception of Lk. xx. 45—47, none of the denunciations which are common to Mt. and Lk. are placed by Lk. as uttered on this occasion. Mt. xxiii. is a mosaic like the Sermon on the Mount. On the other hand, it is likely that more was said on this occasion than is placed here by Mk and Lk.; "in His teaching" almost implies that more was said than is recorded.

Βλέπετε ἀπό. See on viii. 15. Salmon quotes A.V. of this and Lk. xx. 46 as illustrating the differences which arise through independent translation of the same words. Here "*love* to *go* in long *clothing*, and love *salutations* in the *market-places* and the *chief* seats in the synagogues, and the *uppermost* rooms at feasts, which for a *pretence* make long prayers." In Lk. the same Greek words are translated respectively, "desire, walk, robes, greetings, markets, highest, chief, show." Vulg. also varies considerably. Mk's conversational style is illustrated by the coupling of περιπατεῖν and ἀσπασμούς after θελόντων. This use of θέλω = "I like " is found here only (Mk, Lk.) in N.T.

στολαῖς. *Robes* (R.V.) rather than "clothing" (A.V.); cf. xvi. 5. The word implies dignity, as in liturgical vestments or royal robes or festal array (Exod. xxviii. 2; 1 Chron. xv. 27; Lk. xv. 22; Rev. vii. 9, 13, 14). Here and in Lk. xx. 46 Syr-Syn. has "in colonnades" (στοαῖς for στολαῖς).

39. πρωτοκαθεδρίας. These seem to have been at one end of the synagogue, in the centre, facing the congregation. Cf. Lk. xi. 43. Edersheim, *Sketches of Jewish Social Life*, p. 263.

πρωτοκλισίας. *Chief places* (R.V.), not "uppermost rooms" (A.V.). We cannot be sure which these were in our Lord's time, when Jewish customs had been modified by Greek, Roman, and Persian influences. The Talmud says that, in a couch which held three, the middle place is for the worthiest. Greeks commonly had two on a couch, but both Greeks and Romans sometimes had four. *Dict. of Ant.* artt. " Cena," " Symposium," " Triclinium." Becker, *Charicles*, Sc. vi., *Gallus*, Sc. ix.

40. κατεσθίοντες τὰς οἰκίας. Here again we have an easy conversational style; τῶν θελόντων is forgotten. These Scribes abused the hospitality and benevolence of devout women. Widows are mentioned as being those who ought least of all to have been thus treated (Exod. xxii. 22—24; Deut. x. 18, etc.). Josephus (*Ant.* xvii. ii. 4) says of the Pharisees, οἷς ὑπῆκτο ἡ γυναικωνῖτις. The primitive Church seems to have suffered much from the greed of officials (1 Thess. ii. 5; 1 Tim. iii. 3, 8; 1 Pet. v. 2).   See on 2 Cor. ii. 17, viii. 20, xi. 20.

προφάσει. *Sub obtentu prolixae orationis* (Vulg.), but in Lk. *simulantes longam orationem*. They pretended to pray for a long time in order to gain influence over religious people. There was a Rabbinical saying that long prayers make a long life.

οὗτοι. "Such people as these," *isti*, who turn prayer into an instrument of wickedness, "shall receive a sentence of much greater severity." Cf. Jas. iii. 1. They act a part in order to rob the poor and the bereaved, and they employ the most sacred actions in religion in order to do this with success. Others may rob the fatherless and the widow, but they do not make a show of piety in doing so.

41—44. The Widow's Two Mites.

Lk. xxi. 1—4.

41. καθίσας κατέναντι τοῦ γαζοφυλακίου. Some cursives and Syriac Versions say that He stood. The detail is peculiar to Mk. The incident is probably rightly recorded as taking place just after the questions; but it is possible that the Saying about "devouring widows' houses" led to its being recorded. Mk and Lk. have both the Saying and the incident; Mt. (in the true text) has neither. In any case the narrative makes a bright contrast to the despicable avarice of the Scribes. It is not certain that there was any building called the Treasury. In the Court of the Women were thirteen chests with trumpet-shaped openings (*Shoparoth*) on which was inscribed the purpose for which the money put into the opening would be used. These chests, or the place where they stood, had the name of "The Treasury." The strong-room to which the money was afterwards taken cannot be meant here. See on Jn viii. 20. The changes of tenses are accurate and graphic, καθίσας, ἐθεώρει, βάλλει, ἔβαλλον, ἐλθοῦσα ἔβαλεν.

χαλκόν. This would be literally true of the large majority; very few would give silver. The number of givers would be greatly increased by pilgrims coming up for the Passover. Cf. vi. 8.

42. μία χήρα πτωχή. The use of εἷς for τις, common enough in modern Greek, had begun before this period, and this may be an instance; Lk. has τινα. On the other hand, μία may point to her loneliness; it certainly contrasts her with the many wealthy givers. That she had been beggared by the Pharisees, or had been worked upon to give her last farthing, is not suggested by the narrative.

λεπτὰ δύο. The λεπτόν was a Greek coin, the smallest copper coin in use, and Mk tells those who were familiar with the Roman coinage that it was half a *quadrans*, and therefore the eighth of an *as*. Plutarch (*Cic.* 29) says that a quadrans is the smallest copper coin, τὸ λεπτότατον τοῦ χαλκοῦ νομίσματος. Christ knew supernaturally that what she gave was all that she possessed, and we need not ask how the amount which she gave was known. It is said that it was not lawful to give less than two *perutahs* or λεπτά in paying this Jewish anticipation of "Peter's Pence." Cf. Lk. xii. 59 and Mt. v. 26.

ὅ ἐστιν. The neut. is colloquial. Blass § 31. 2 gives no exact parallel; cf. iii. 17, xv. 22.

43. προσκαλεσάμενος. The disciples were not sitting with Him but had to be called. Cf. iii. 13.

'Αμὴν λέγω ὑμῖν. "Ye would not have supposed it, but *verily I say to you.*" See on iii. 28. Lk. has ἀληθῶς.

πλεῖον πάντων. In proportion, and also in the spirit in which she gave; it was in the latter that she was richer than all of them. This principle had been recognized by philosophers; κατὰ τὴν οὐσίαν δ' ἡ ἐλευθεριότης λέγεται· οὐ γὰρ ἐν τῷ πλήθει τῶν διδομένων τὸ ἐλευθέριον, ἀλλ' ἐν τῇ τοῦ διδόντος ἕξει· οὐδὲν δὲ κωλύει ἐλευθεριώτερον εἶναι τὸν τὰ ἐλάττω διδόντα, ἐὰν ἀπὸ ἐλαττόνων διδῷ (Arist. *Eth. Nic.* IV. i. 19). Cf. Xen. *Mem.* I. iii. 3. The means of the giver and the motive are the measure of true generosity.

44. ἐκ τοῦ περισσεύοντος. See on 2 Cor. viii. 12, 14. *Non perpendit Deus quantum in sacrificio, sed ex quanto proferatur* (Bede). Vulg. here has *ex eo quod abundabat illis*; in Lk. *ex abundanti*.

ἐκ τῆς ὑστερήσεως. They had a great deal more than they needed, while she had a great deal less; it was the difference between a surplus and a *deficit*. There is similar irony in 1 Jn iii. 17; "Whoso *hath* the world's goods and beholdeth his brother *having* need." The one possesses wealth and the other possesses the want of it. This irony is marred in R. V. by the substitution of "in need." Vulg. here has *de penuria sua*; in Lk. *ex eo quod deest illi*. Cf. τὸ ὑστέρημα (2 Cor. viii. 14); in N.T. the difference between -σις and -μα has become blurred, *e.g.* βρῶσις = βρῶμα, πόσις = πόμα. Syr-Sin. omits.

ὅλον τὸν βίον. Bíos occurs here only in Mk and nowhere in Mt. or Jn. It means either "the physical life of human beings" (Lk. viii. 14; 1 Tim. ii. 2; etc.) or "means of life" (here, Lk. viii. 43, xv. 12, 30, xxi. 4). The words are another instance of Mk's fulness of expression. See on *v.* 14, where, as here, Syr-Sin. omits what is superfluous. There is a remarkable parallel to this incident in the literature of Chinese Buddhism. A widow enters a religious assembly and says, "Others give costly gifts; I in my poverty can give nothing." Then she remembers that she has still two copper coins and she offers these to the priests. The chief priest pays no attention to the rich gifts of the others, but only to the devout spirit of the poor widow, and he sings a song in her praise. Clemen, *Primitive Christianity and Non-Jewish Sources*, p. 331.

CHAPTER XIII.

2. אBLΨ omit ἀποκριθείς. Cf. vii. 6, x. 5, xii. 17. ἀφεθῇ ὧδε (אBDLΔΨ) rather than ἀφεθῇ (AXΓΠ).

5. אBLΨ omit ἀποκριθείς.

6. אBLΨ omit γάρ here and in v. 7. See on iii. 35.

8. אBLΨ omit καί before ἔσονται. אBDLΔΨ omit καὶ ταραχαί. ἀρχή (אBDLΔΨ) rather than ἀρχαί (AXΓ).

9. BL omit γάρ after παραδώσουσιν. It is probably an insertion.

11. καὶ ὅταν (אBDLΨ) rather than ὅταν δέ (AXΓΔΠ). See on i. 14. אBDΓΨ omit μηδὲ μελετᾶτε.

12. καὶ παραδώσει (אBDLΨ) rather than παρ. δέ (AXΓΔΠ).

14. אBDLΨ omit τὸ ῥηθὲν ὑπὸ Δ. τ. πρ. ἑστηκότα (אBL) rather than ἑστηκός (DΨ) or ἑστός (AΔΠ), from Mt.

15. אBLΨ omit εἰς τὴν οἰκίαν.

18. אBL omit ἡ φυγὴ ὑμῶν.

22. אBDΨ omit καί before τοὺς ἐκλεκτούς, from Mt. Ψ omits τούς.

25. ἔσονται ἐκ τ. οὐρανοῦ (אABC) rather than τοῦ οὐρανοῦ ἔσονται (LΓΔ).

27. DLΨ omit αὐτοῦ after ἀγγέλους. It may come from Mt.

28. γινώσκετε (אB*CXΓΠ) rather than γινώσκεται (AB³DLΔ).

31. παρελεύσονται (אBDXΓΠ) rather than παρελεύσεται (ACLXΔ). BD* omit μή after οὐ, but it may be retained with אACLΓΔΠ. After οὐ μή read παρελεύσονται (אBL) rather than παρέλθωσιν (ACDXΓΔΠ). After οὐ μή copyists often correct fut. indic. to aor. subj. Mt. xv. 5; Lk. xxi. 33; etc.

33. BD, ack omit καὶ προσεύχεσθε, which may come from xiv. 38. Syr-Sin. omits βλέπετε.

1, 2. THE DESTRUCTION OF THE TEMPLE FORETOLD.

Mt. xxiv. 1—3. Lk. xxi. 5, 6.

1. ἐκπορευομένου αὐτοῦ...αὐτῷ. For the constr. see on v. 21 and ix. 28; it is repeated below in v. 3. He was leaving the Temple once more to spend the night at Bethany.

εἰς τῶν μαθητῶν. We do not know which; Mt. says "His disciples," Lk. "some people."

ἴδε ποταποὶ λίθοι. Like ἰδού, ἄγε, φέρε, we have in ἴδε an exclamation, as the nom. shows. Cf. iii. 34, xi. 21. Galileans were not familiar with any such edifice, and this alone may have caused the admiring outburst, as the Temple was being viewed in the evening light. But it is likely that the remark "Your house is left unto you desolate" elicted the ποταποί. It was so grievous to think that desolation was in store for such a building. The late Greek ποταπός (here only in Mk) has lost its local signification and is rendered *qualis*, not *cujas*. It commonly indicates admiration or surprise. "It is almost impossible to realize the effect produced by a building longer and higher than York Cathedral, standing on a solid mass of masonry almost equal in height to the tallest of church spires" (Wilson, *Recovery of Jerusalem*, p. 9). The (perhaps exaggerated) description by Josephus (*B.J.* v. v.) should be read. See also Sanday, *Sacred Sites of the Gospel*, with conjectural restoration; Edersheim, *Temple*, pp. 20 f.

2. Βλέπεις. The sentence is possibly interrogative; "Art thou looking at?" But "Thou art looking at" is more forcible.

οὐ μή οὐ μή. J. H. Moulton states that there are 60 cases of οὐ μή in the Gospels, 54 of which are in actual words of Christ, the remaining 6 being in words addressed to Him (p. 191). Here Mk alone has the double οὐ μή, but Mt. produces the same effect by inserting ἀμὴν λέγω ὑμῖν: "there is not the slightest doubt about the absolute destruction." Cf. vv. 19, 30; Joseph. *B.J.* VII. 1. 1. Robinson, Stanley and others tell us how complete the destruction has been. Whole strata of ruins lie beneath the modern Jerusalem. The disciples would think of this magnificent edifice as the centre of the Messianic Kingdom. To hear the Messiah predict its total overthrow must have been a perplexing experience. The ὧδε (see crit. note) is in all three narratives. D, Lat-Vet. and Cypr. add, "and in three days another shall rise up without hands," from xiv. 58 and Jn ii. 19. WH. *App.* p. 26. Cf. Dan. ii. 34. On Julian's attempt to rebuild see Socr. *H.E.* iii. 20.

3—13. THE DISCIPLES' QUESTIONS AND THE LORD'S ANSWER.

Mt. xxiv. 3—14. Lk. xxi. 7—19.

3. καθημένου αὐτοῦ κ.τ.λ. These details seem to come from one who remembered, and from whom they passed into the primitive tradition. Christ was sitting, as often when He gave instruction

(iv. 1, ix. 35; Lk. iv. 20; Mt. v. 1), on the Mount of Olives, looking across to the Temple. The last detail is in Mk only, and he alone mentions which disciples were with Him.

ἐπηρώτα. Mk's conversational style appears again. When he used the sing. he was thinking of Peter only, and then he goes on to mention the others who were present and who joined in the desire to know what was asked. See on iv. 41. That ἐπηρώτα (אBL 33) is the original reading, and that ἐπηρώτων is a correction, need not be doubted.

κατ' ἰδίαν. What He had to reveal was too solemn and critical to be revealed to all the Twelve (Jn xvi. 12). The four whom He takes with Him are the two pairs of brothers who were called at the beginning of the Gospel.

4. Εἰπὸν ἡμῖν. All three record these two questions, When? and What sign? The disciples want to know how soon the Temple will be destroyed, and what will give warning that the destruction is very near. The sing., τὸ σημεῖον, is in all three; one manifest signal is expected. They accept, without question, that the destruction will take place, just as they accept the equally appalling statement that one of them is a traitor (xiv. 19). They probably assumed that the end of the world would immediately follow the destruction, an assumption which Christ does not directly correct. Experience would do that, as soon as correction was necessary. Εἰπόν is from the 1st aor. εἶπα.

συντελεῖσθαι. Nowhere else in Mk. It is used of days being completed, Lk. iv. 2; Acts xxi. 27; Job i. 5; Tobit x. 7. The πάντα comes last with emphasis, ταῦτα συντ. πάντα being the right order; but the meaning of ταῦτα πάντα is not clear. Christ's reply is about the Parusia. Mt. here makes use of two expressions which no other Evangelist employs, παρουσία and συντέλεια τοῦ αἰῶνος.

5. ἤρξατο. The verb is not pleonastic; He is beginning a new course of instruction. Cf. viii. 31, xii. 1. This is the longest of Christ's utterances in Mk. The only other connected discourses of Christ which Mk gives us are parables, and of those he has only four, against twenty-three in Lk. We need not reject this discourse because it is unique in this Gospel, any more than we need reject the one parable which is peculiar to Mk.

Βλέπετε μή. He takes the second question first, and, as often, gives no direct reply. Instead of telling them of some manifest signal, He bids them be on their guard against false signals. A great deal must take place before the end comes and there will be much deception. All three have βλέπετε μή, and this charge, to "be on their guard," is the main lesson of the chapter; it recurs *vv.* 9, 23, 33 : ἄλλο τοίνυν ἠρώτησαν, ἄλλο ἀποκρίνεται (Victor).

ὑμᾶς πλανήσῃ. *Lead you astray* (R.V.). Cf. xii. 24, 27. The verb is freq. in the Johannine and Pauline writings, and it is used of serious departure from the truth. See on 1 Jn i. 8.

6. ἐπὶ τῷ ὀνόματί μου λέγοντες ὅτι ᾿Εγώ εἰμι. It is obvious that ἐπὶ τῷ ὀν. μου cannot here mean "for My sake" or "with My authority" (ix. 37, 38, 39); it means "usurping My title." Impostors will claim to be the Messiah, as Mt. turns it. And here at once we have some indication that Christ's predictions about the future have become somewhat confused in tradition, words respecting the end of the world becoming mixed with words respecting the destruction of the Temple. None of the seducing leaders who arose between A.D. 30 and 70, *e.g.* Theudas and the Egyptian (Acts v. 36, xxi. 38), seem to have professed to be the Messiah. Simon Magus (Acts viii. 9) may be regarded as an ἀντίχριστος (1 Jn ii. 18) but not as a ψευδόχριστος (*v.* 22). Thus far Mk has told us nothing of Christ's prediction of His return; yet here He speaks of it as an event with which the disciples were familiar. The idea that the end of the world will be preceded by a great intensification of evil occurs in various places of the N.T.; 2 Thess. ii. 3; 2 Tim. iii. 1; 1 Jn ii. 18; 2 Pet. iii. 3; Jude 18.

7 πολέμους καὶ ἀκοὰς πολ. Josephus and Tacitus tell us of plenty; see esp. Tac. *Hist.* i. 2. For ἀκοάς see on i. 28.

δεῖ γένεσθαι. In all three; from Dan. ii. 29; cf. Rev. i. 1. God has so decreed. Cf. *v.* 10 and viii. 31 and mark the characteristic asyndeton; γάρ in *vv.* 5, 7 is an interpolation. "The epigrammatic brevity of Mk is specially striking in this context" (Swete).

οὔπω τὸ τέλος. *Not yet is the end;* Looking back to the disciples' question about συντελεῖσθαι.

8. ἐγερθήσεται κ.τ.λ. Almost verbatim the same in all three. Only here is ἐγειρ. ἐπί τινα found in N.T. Cf. ἐπεγερθήσονται Αἰγύπτιοι ἐπ᾽ Αἰγυπτίους...πόλις ἐπὶ πόλιν καὶ νομὸς ἐπὶ νομόν (Is. xix. 2). Thus far (6, 7, 8 a) we have had religious and social corruptions and conflicts; the disciples are now told that certain natural portents will precede the end, earthquakes and famines, to which some texts add a third. See crit. note.

ὠδίνων. *Of travail* (R.V.) is better than "of sorrows" (A.V.). But it is not certain that the idea of "*birth*-pangs" is to be understood, the pangs which accompany the birth of a new dispensation. That idea belongs more to the persecutions which are mentioned next (9—13).

9. βλέπετε δὲ ὑμεῖς ἑαυτούς. Mk only. The pronouns are in emphatic juxtaposition. "Let other people attend to these disturbances in society and in nature; but do *ye* look to *yourselves*." This use of βλέπω is very rare, but it has been found in a papyrus-letter of A.D. 41; βλέπε σεαυτόν. The reflexive ἑαυτούς with the second person is freq. in N.T. (ix. 50), esp. in Paul; ὑμῶν αὐτῶν, κ.τ.λ. is rare (1 Cor. v. 13). Syr-Sin. omits the words.

παραδώσουσιν. "Your fellow-countrymen will hand you over to councils," *i.e.* to the elders of the local synagogues, who as religious magistrates had considerable authority. See on Lk. xii. 11, xxi. 12. Saul of Tarsus was among the first who fulfilled this prediction as a persecuting Jew, and later as a persecuted Christian. See on 2 Cor. xi. 24. In Mt. x. 17—20 and Lk. xii. 11, 12 we have passages similar to this. They may be doublets; but it is not impossible that these cautions were given more than once.

καὶ εἰς συναγωγάς. These words are amphibolous and are commonly taken with what follows as a pregnant constr.; "and ye shall be taken into synagogues and beaten"; see on *vv.* 3 and 16. "Ye shall be beaten into the synagogues," *i.e.* driven into them with whips, is certainly wrong. It is better to take the words with what precedes; *They will deliver you up to councils and to synagogues; ye will be beaten.* This harmonizes well with the abruptness of the preceding verses. Syr-Sin. has "They shall deliver you up to the *people* and to councils; and ye shall stand before kings and ye shall be *beaten before governors* for My sake, for a testimony to them, *and to all nations.*"

ἕνεκεν ἐμοῦ. Cf. viii. 35, x. 29.

εἰς μαρτύριον αὐτοῖς. *Testimony* to the rulers and kings, who, but for the persecution of Christians, might never have known about Christ. This applies to both Jewish and heathen potentates: St James and St Peter persecuted by Herod Agrippa I. illustrate the former; St Paul before Festus and Herod Agrippa II. illustrates both. A sagacious person might have seen that what is predicted here was probable. Even those who do not admit that Jesus had supernatural foresight need not suppose that this is a pseudoprophecy, constructed to fit the persecutions of Apostles, and attributed to Christ.

10. εἰς πάντα τὰ ἔθνη. First, with emphasis. Gentile readers would appreciate the significance of this, which is clearly brought out in Mk. Cf. xi. 17, xiv. 9. The Gospel is for all mankind.

δεῖ κηρυχθῆναι τὸ εὐαγγ. A glorious compensation for the δεῖ γενέσθαι in *v.* 7. It is a Divine decree that *to all the nations, before the end comes, the good tidings must be proclaimed.* Note the order of

the words. See on i. 14, 15, and cf. Mt. xxviii. 19; Lk. xxiv. 47.
It is probable that in all three Gospels this eschatological discourse is
augmented by the insertion of Sayings, the setting of which had been
lost. Hence the difficulty of interpreting it as a whole.

11. προμεριμνᾶτε. *Be anxious beforehand.* Lk. has the more
classical προμελετᾶν. Cf. Aristoph. *Eccl.* 117; Plato *Soph.* 218 D.
This charge shows the meaning of "take heed to yourselves"; not
that they are to endeavour to escape, but that they are to acquit
themselves worthily. They will have Divine help to bear testimony.

ὃ ἐὰν δοθῇ...λαλεῖτε. This has O.T. parallels; ἐγὼ ἀνοίξω τὸ
στόμα σου, καὶ συμβιβάσω σε ὃ μέλλεις λαλῆσαι (Exod. iv. 12); τὸ ῥῆμα
ὃ ἐὰν εἴπω πρός σε, τοῦτο φυλάξῃ λαλῆσαι (Num. xxii. 35); δέδωκα τοὺς
λόγους μου εἰς τὸ στόμα σου (Jer. i. 9). There is here no encouragement
to ministers to preach without preparation. It is those who are
suddenly called upon to defend the faith before a persecuting tribunal
that may trust to the inspiration of the moment.

τὸ πνεῦμα τὸ ἅγιον. Double article as in xii. 36. In Lk. xxi. 15
Jesus promises that He Himself will supply wisdom. In Lk. xii. 12
it is the Holy Spirit, as here.

12. παραδώσει ἀδελφός. In *v.* 9, παραδώσουσιν is impersonal.
Here we are told who they are that will do this thing—"they of
a man's own household" (Mt. x. 36); *nec ullus est inter eos fidus
affectus, quorum diversa fides est* (Bede). This deadly division in
families is predicted Mic. vii. 1 6; cf. Ezek. xxii. 7, xxxviii 21. It
was regarded as a special feature in the Woes of the Messiah;
2 Esdras vi. 24, xiii. 30—32. Cf. Enoch c. 1; "Brothers will fall in
death one with another, until it streams with their blood like a
river."

ἐπαναστήσονται. The verb implies rebellion against authority
(Judg. ix. 18; 2 Sam. xxii. 40; etc.). Note the plur. verbs, marking
the numerous separate instances of such conduct.

θανατώσουσιν. All three have this verb, which in class. Grk is
used of executions. In Enoch c. 2 it is the fathers who put the sons
to death.

13. καὶ ἔσεσθε μισούμενοι. *Verbatim* the same in all three.
The analytical fut. marks the hatred as a process continually going
on; cf. *v.* 25. It will have its compensations, τὸ γὰρ ἕνεκεν αὐτοῦ
μισεῖσθαι, ἱκανόν ἐστι πάσας ἐπικουφίσαι τὰς συμφοράς (Theoph.). On
the causes of this universal hatred of Christians see Plummer, *Church
of the Early Fathers*, pp. 150 f.

ὁ δὲ ὑπομείνας εἰς τέλος, οὗτος σωθήσεται. Mt. has the same, but
Lk. interprets, "In your endurance ye shall win your souls." Not

εἰς τὸ τέλος, the end spoken of in *v.* 7, but εἰς τέλος, "finally" or "to the uttermost," which is better here, as in 1 Thess. ii. 16. See on Jn xiii. 1 and Ryle and James on Ps. Sol. i. 1. In the Epp. and in Rev. ὑπομονή is freq. as a special virtue of Christians, and it cannot be won without affliction (Rom. v. 3). It means courageous endurance without despondency. See Lightfoot on Col. i. 11; Trench, *Syn.* § 53. With this use of οὗτος comp. that in *v.* 11, vi. 16, xii. 10; that of ἐκεῖνος in vii. 20 is similar. For σωθήσεται in the spiritual sense see viii. 35, x. 36.

14—23. EVENTS CONNECTED WITH THE DESTRUCTION OF JERUSALEM.

Mt. xxiv. 15—25. Lk. xxi. 20—24.

14. "Ὅταν δὲ ἴδητε. Christ is still dealing with the disciples' second question, What warning signal will there be? Thus far He has said no more than that a great deal will happen before the end comes. Now He tells them that the intrusion of "the abomination of desolation" into "a holy place" (Mt.), will be a warning to believers to leave Judaea. According to O.T. usage, βδέλυγμα means any idolatrous object, whether person or thing, such as must excite disgust and abhorrence in every Jew (1 Kings xxi. 26; 2 Kings xvi. 3; etc.). "The abomination of desolation" means that which causes desolation by bringing disaster and ruin. As Mt. points out, the phrase comes from Daniel (xi. 31; cf. ix. 17, 27, xii. 11; and see on 1 Macc. i. 54, 59). Heathen Rome is here indicated.

ἑστηκότα. See crit. note. The temptation to correct the faulty grammar would be great, esp. to ἑστός, which Mt. has here. But ἑστηκότα is no slip of the pen. The masc. shows that the βδέλυγμα is regarded as a person, either in fact or by personification. Cf. καὶ τότε φανήσεται ὁ κοσμοπλάνος (*Didache* xvi. 4). We may understand the Roman general or the Roman army. Loisy suggests "Satan, or his instrument," Antichrist, which is not probable. Syr-Sin. has "*the sign of* the abomination of desolation standing where it ought not," which is right as interpretation.

ὅπου οὐ δεῖ. Mt. makes this more definite by writing ἐν τόπῳ ἁγίῳ, "in a holy place," which may mean the Holy Land (2 Macc. ii. 18).

ὁ ἀναγινώσκων νοείτω. *Let him that readeth understand.* Readeth what? The parenthesis is in Mt. also, but not in Lk. In Mt. the meaning might be "he that readeth the passage in Daniel," for Daniel has just been mentioned as the source of the quotation. But that meaning is much less possible here, for neither Daniel nor any other writing has been mentioned, and Mk could hardly expect Gentile readers to know that the allusion was to Daniel. It is much more probable that in the parenthesis we have, not Christ's words calling attention to those of Daniel, but the Evangelist's words calling attention to those of Christ. At the time when he was writing, the signal which Christ had indicated seemed to be in preparation; the Romans had not yet laid siege to Jerusalem, but it was probable that they would do so, and the abomination might soon be in a holy place. Therefore Christians in Judaea, when they read this Gospel, ought to be preparing for flight. If this is correct, the date of the Gospel can hardly be later than A.D. 67. Lk. omits the parenthetical remark; when he wrote, the destruction of Jerusalem had taken place and the warning would be meaningless. Cf. Rev. i. 3, where ὁ ἀναγινώσκων must refer to the reader of that writing.

τότε οἱ ἐν τῇ Ἰουδαίᾳ...τὰ ὄρη. These important words are the same in all three. The tradition as to the counsel given by the Lord was constant. "Judaea" sometimes, esp. in Lk., means "the Land of the Jews," Palestine; but here it probably means "the province of Judaea," as everywhere else in Mk (i. 5, iii. 7, x. 1), and "the mountains" are the mountains of Judaea. In 1 Macc. ii. 28, Mattathias and his sons ἔφυγον εἰς τὰ ὄρη, forsaking all that they had in the city. The mountains of Judaea were full of caves and recesses, whence Mattathias carried on a guerrilla warfare against the forces of Epiphanes. These retreats had often been hiding places for Israel. Eusebius (*H.E.* iii. 5) tells us that the Christians in Jerusalem received a revelation before the war, in consequence of which they fled to Pella in Peraea, the modern *Tabakât Fahil*. Pella is not in the mountains, but in the valley of the Jordan, so that this warning cannot have been invented afterwards to fit the facts. The Christians may have felt that they were not safe in the mountains, and may have fled on across the Jordan to Pella. Moreover, the story in Eusebius refers to the Christians in Jerusalem; Christ's warning is given to all those in Judaea. Lawlor (*Eusebiana*, Lect. i.) has shown that both Eusebius and Epiphanius probably got what they have to tell us about the flight to Pella from Hegesippus, who may have known some of the fugitives.

15. ὁ ἐπὶ τοῦ δώματος. Lk. gives these words in a very different context and with a spiritual meaning, to teach that indifference to worldly interests is the attitude in which to be ready for the Second Advent (xvii. 31). The meaning here and in Mt. is literal, and intimates that, when once the danger-signal has arisen, no thought of saving property must be allowed to delay flight. The flat roof of houses was used for many purposes, and there were generally outside steps up to it (ii. 4), and by these steps escape would be most quickly made. But the manner of descent is immaterial; it is going down *with a view to save property* that is condemned as folly.

16. ὁ εἰς τὸν ἀγρόν. Perhaps, "The man who *has gone to his* field." But, in late Greek, εἰς answers both Whither? and Where? cf. i. 39, x. 10; in both places inferior texts substitute ἐν for εἰς. In Cornwall "up to" = "at." Here Mt. has ἐν. Blass § 39. 3. See on *v.* 27.

εἰς τὰ ὀπίσω. Freq. in the Gospels (Lk. ix. 62, xvii. 31; Jn vi. 66, xviii. 6, xx. 14; cf. Phil. iii. 13), and in LXX. "The passage recalls Lot's escape from Sodom, Gen. xix. 17" (Swete).

τὸ ἱμάτιον αὐτοῦ. Almost indispensable for a journey (Acts xii. 8): nevertheless the risk in going back to fetch it would be too great. The man would leave it behind in going to work and would wear only a χιτών (vi. 9) = "shirt," or a σινδών (xiv. 51) = "loin-cloth." Cf. Virg. *Geor.* i. 299. See on x. 50.

17. οὐαί. This "woe" is the same in all three; but "woe" is not the best translation. In passages like Mt. xxiii. and Lk. vi. 24— 26 the word suggests an imprecation; "Alas for" is better both here and xiv. 21, as elsewhere in N.T. The word is freq. in Rev., Is., Jer. Cf. Epict. *Dis.* iii. 19 *sub init.* where the ἰδιώτης says οὐαί μοι διὰ τὸ παιδάριον,

θηλαζούσαις. Used both of the mothers (here) and of the children (Mt. xxi. 16); so also in LXX. D here has θηλαζομέναις. "Alas for those women who are unable quickly to fly from home!"

18. χειμῶνος. Gen. of time (Mt. ii. 14; Jn iii. 2; Acts ix. 24). Either "in stormy weather" or "in winter" makes good sense, but the former is better (Mt. xvi. 3; Acts xxvii. 20). Here prayer for temporal advantages is clearly sanctioned. Mt. shows Jewish feeling in adding μηδὲ σαββάτῳ. But Mk may have omitted this as having no interest for Gentile readers. Lk. is altogether different.

19. θλίψις. See on iv. 17. The word is appropriate here as indicating the *pressure* of the siege; but there is no need to expand the meaning into "one prolonged tribulation." As often in Mk, the sentence is quite intelligible, but is rather awkwardly expressed; *tribulation such as there has not been such.* Blass 50. 2, 4. Josephus (Preface to *B. J.* 4) says that in his estimate the calamities of the Jews exceeded those of all mankind from the beginning of the world. Cf. Exod. ix. 18; Deut. iv. 32.

οὐ μὴ γένηται. *And assuredly never shall be;* see on *v.* 2. The Lord looks forward into the limitless future. Cf. Dan. xii. 1; Jer.

xxx. 7; 1 Macc. ix. 27: Assumption of Moses viii. 1. These current phrases look to the past, but Christ includes the ages to come.

20. ἐκολόβωσεν. Lit. "amputated," and so "curtailed"; in 2 Sam. iv. 12 of cutting off hands and feet. God has decided to shorten the days, and they are regarded as shortened.

κύριος. Elsewhere in Mk this use of Κύριος without the art. is found only in quotations; i. 3, xi. 9, xii. 11, 29, 30, 36. It is freq. in Lk. i. and ii. The duration of "those days" is not indicated.

οὐκ ἄν ἐσώθη πᾶσα σάρξ. Hebraistic. The negative belongs to the verb and πᾶσα σάρξ is one term; "*the whole* of mankind would have been *not saved*" = "no flesh would have been saved." In other words, οὐ πᾶς = "no one," not (as in class. Grk) "not every one." Cf. Lk. i. 37; Rom. iii. 20; 1 Cor. i. 29; Gal. ii. 16. "All flesh" is a common Hebraism for the human race; Lk. iii. 6; Jn xvii. 2; Acts ii. 17; etc. The siege lasted only from April or May to September, but the loss of life was immense; and it would have been greater, but for "the elect," whose presence and prayers secured a shortening of the time of destruction. "The elect" probably means the believers who were true to their high calling. See the Apocalypse of Baruch xxi. 2, lxxxiii. 1–6; Enoch i. 1. The superfluous οὓς ἐξελέξατο is in Mk's style; see on i. 32, vi. 25. It is not in Mt.

21. καὶ τότε. "It will be a time of great excitement and much fanaticism, and those who are looking for signs will be easily misled; therefore be on your guard against impostors." In the Sermon Christ points out that at all times, if we want to find the right way, we must beware of seducing guides (Mt. vii. 15—20).

Ἴδε ὧδε κ.τ.λ. Mt's expansion of this is characteristic, as also is Mk's simplicity.

μὴ πιστεύετε. Not "cease to believe," as μὴ φοβεῖσθε (vi. 50) and μὴ κωλύετε (x. 14), but "continually abstain from believing," as μὴ προμεριμνᾶτε (v. 11). Mt. here has aorists.

22. ψευδόχριστοι. We know of none at this time who claimed to be the Messiah, but the word seems to have been loosely used as meaning much the same as ἀντίχριστοι (1 Jn ii. 22, iv. 3; 2 Jn 7).

ψευδοπροφῆται. Cf. Acts xiii. 6; Rev. xix. 20; *Didache* xi. It was, of course, much easier to pretend to be a prophet (Deut. xiii. 1) than to pretend to be the Messiah; and fanatics would have this delusion more easily than the other. See on 1 Jn iv. 1. Syr-Sin. has "prophets of lies."

σημεῖα. Things, whether frequent or rare, which have a meaning beyond their own qualities.

τέρατα. Things which excite amazement or terror, but without necessarily having any meaning. Supernatural acts are often in N.T. called σημεῖα καὶ τέρατα, and often σημεῖα, esp. in Jn, but never τέρατα alone. See on 2 Cor. xii. 12.

πρὸς τὸ ἀποπλανᾶν. "With a view to leading away from the right path." In 2 Chron. xxi. 11 the verb is coupled with ἐκπορνεύω of leading into idolatry, and is used in Prov. vii. 21 of seduction by an adulteress. Cf. 1 Tim. vi. 10.

εἰ δυνατόν. Cf. xiv. 35; Rom. xii. 18. *Si potest fieri* (Vulg.).

τοὺς ἐκλεκτούς. See crit. note. "*Even* the elect" (A.V.) is right in Mt., but not here.

23. ὑμεῖς δέ. *But do ye* (whatever others may do) *take heed* (*vv.* 5, 9, 33, iv. 24; with ἀπό, viii. 15, xii. 38).

προείρηκα ὑμῖν πάντα. The πάντα is qualified by the context, "all that is necessary for your guidance"; cf. vi. 30, ix. 23, xi. 24. He had not foretold the exact date for which they had asked. The verb occurs nowhere else in the Gospels.

24—27. The Close of the Age foretold.

Mt. xxiv. 29—31. Lk. xxi. 25—28.

24. ἐν ἐκείναις ταῖς ἡμέραις. Very indefinite; see on i. 9. We may believe that this is nearer to the expression actually used than the εὐθέως of Mt. Mt. wrote at a time when it was believed that the Second Advent would quickly follow the fall of Jerusalem, and, as often, he gives his interpretations as having been actually spoken; see on viii. 29, ix. 29, x. 19, 28, 33, 38, 40. Christ showed that His Coming would not save Jerusalem from destruction but would follow that destruction. That it would follow quickly (Rev. xxii. 20) was a wrong inference which experience corrected: ἀρχὴ ὠδίνων (*v.* 8) and πρῶτον δεῖ (*v.* 10) imply that the interval would not be short. The language here used is highly symbolical, such as is found in the Prophets and in the apocalyptic literature of the Jews. Cf. Is. xiii. 10, xxxiv. 4; Ezek. xxxii. 7—8; Amos viii. 9; Joel ii. 30, 31, iii. 5. It intimates that mighty results follow when God shows His hand in the government of the world. "It is needless to minimize these words into eclipses or meteoric showers, or to magnify them into actual destruction of sun and moon and stars. They are not events, but only imaginative portrayal of what it means for God to interfere in the history of the nations" (Gould). All three Gospels here speak of catastrophic changes of nature which probably represent catastrophic changes in the social and spiritual world. Guesses as to their exact meaning are not very profitable.

μετὰ τ. θλίψιν ἐκείνην. After the overthrow of Jerusalem.
σκοτισθήσεται. Cf. Lk. xxiii. 45; Rev. vi. 12, viii. 12: also the
Testaments, *Levi* iv. 1; Enoch lxxx. 2—7; Assumption of Moses x. 5,
where we read that the sun will not give light, the horns of the moon
will be broken and turned to darkness, and the circle of the stars will
be shaken.

25. ἔσονται...πίπτοντες. Analytical future, as in *v.* 13; "the
stars will be continually falling." Cf. Lk. v. 10, xvii. 35, xxi.
24.

αἱ δυνάμεις...σαλευθήσονται. In all three. Isaiah (xxxiv. 4) has
these phenomena in reverse order; τακήσονται πᾶσαι αἱ δυνάμεις τῶν
οὐρανῶν...καὶ πάντα τὰ ἄστρα πεσεῖται. Cf. Is. xl. 26. Neither here
nor in 1 Cor. xv. 40 are the heavenly bodies regarded as animated;
the δυνάμεις in Eph. i. 21 and 1 Pet. iii. 22 are different, being akin
to angelic powers.

26. καὶ τότε. "Then, and not till then." Mt. has "*on* the
clouds" (ἐπί); with that exception, all three have the same wording.
ὄψονται. Not, "*ye* shall see." This is another intimation that
those whom He is addressing will not live to see the Second Advent.
Cf. 1 Thess. iv. 16; 2 Thess. i. 7, ii. 8; Rev. i. 8, xix. 11—16;
Zech. xii. 10. Mt. has "Then shall *appear* the *sign* of the Son of
Man."

τὸν υἱὸν τοῦ ἀνθρώπου. The ref. to Dan. vii. 13 is clear, as also in
xiv. 62; see Driver, *ad loc.* pp. 102—109; Westcott on Jn i. 14,
pp. 71—74. Early in the Ministry Christ seems to have begun to use
the title "Son of Man" of Himself (see on ii. 10), and to have made
the application to Himself gradually more clear (see on viii. 31).
But here for the first time He is said to have definitely connected it
with the famous prophecy in Daniel.

ἐν νεφέλαις. Mt. has "*on* the clouds of heaven" (*bis*), Lk. "*in* a
cloud," Dan. "*with* the clouds of heaven," Rev. "*with* the clouds."
We must not insist on a literal interpretation of these words; the
clouds may be part of the symbolism. It is God who moves the
clouds (Is. xix. 1; Ps. civ. 3); and they accompany "the destined
Possessor of universal dominion" (Dalman, *Words*, pp. 242—9).

27. ἀποστελεῖ τ. ἀγγέλους. See crit. note. Although αὐτοῦ is
probably not genuine, we may translate "*His* Angels"; cf. iv. 26, 36,
vi. 32, vii. 2. It is of more moment to make clear that the elect are
His than that the Angels are (Jn vi. 37, 39, x. 14, 16, 27—29, xvii. 2,
6, 9, 24).

ἐκ τεσσάρων ἀνέμων. A colloquial expression found in both O.T.
and N.T. It occurs in a papyrus of the second cent. A.D. (Deissmann,

Bib. St. p. 248). The sentence is an echo of Deut. xxx. 4 and Zech. ii. 6. The meaning is obvious. Cf. Jer. xxix. 14, xxxii. 37.

ἀπ' ἄκρου γῆς κ.τ.λ. The meaning of this is less obvious. "From the ends of heavens to their ends" (Mt.) means "throughout the whole extent of the heavens." But here the antithesis between earth and heaven, while it gives a great impression of vastness, is less easy to understand. It seems to mean "throughout space in all directions." However remote a corner of the universe may be, if any of the elect are there, they will be remembered and gathered in. Cf. 2 Macc. i. 27, ii. 7. For Christ's mention of Angels see on viii. 38 and xii. 25.

28, 29. THE LESSON OF THE FIG-TREE.

Mt. xxiv. 22, 23. Lk. xxi. 29—31.

28. Ἀπὸ δὲ τῆς συκῆς. *Now from the fig-tree*; generic, any fig-tree. Often in parables the art. is thus used; ὁ σπείρων (iv. 3), ὁ ποιμὴν ὁ καλός (Jn x. 11), ὁ ἀγαθὸς ἄνθρωπος (Mt. xii. 35). Fig-trees and olive-trees are specially common in Palestine, but the latter, as being evergreen, would not have served for this lesson. Lk., writing for those to whom the fig-tree might not be familiar, adds καὶ πάντα τὰ δένδρα.

τὴν παραβολήν. As with τοὺς ἀγγέλους (v. 27), we may regard the art. as possessive, "*her* parable" (R.V.). Here and in Mt., A.V. ignores the art., "*a* parable." See on iv. 3.

ὅταν ἤδη. "Whenever this has already taken place."

καὶ ἐκφύῃ τὰ φύλλα. *And putteth forth its leaves* (R.V.). This avoids change of nominative. Lk. has προβάλλω without accusative. Both φύω and ἐκφύω are used transitively in LXX. But some MSS. and versions favour ἐκφυῇ, "and the leaves spring forth," *et nata fuerint folia* (Vulg.).

γινώσκετε. See crit. note. *Cognoscitis* (Vulg.); "ye recognize," "your experience tells you." The remark is true of everyone, and there is no emphatic ὑμεῖς.

τὸ θέρος. Only in this passage in N.T. It certainly means "the summer" and not "the harvest," which would be ὁ θερισμός (iv. 29). Cf. Cant. ii. 11—13.

29. οὕτως καὶ ὑμεῖς. In vii. 18, where no comparison is drawn, καί belongs to ὑμεῖς, "ye also." Here it strengthens οὕτως, *even so ye*, as often (Jn v. 21; Rom. v. 18, 21; 1 Cor. xv. 22; etc.). "Also" may have much the same effect as "even," but we do not need both as in R.V. The ὑμεῖς is emphatic; "anyone can recognize the signs of the fig-tree, but you disciples must recognize the signs of the times "; ταῦτα is not the end, but the signs of the end.

γινώσκετε. This may be indic., as in *v.* 28, but it is probably like μάθετε in *v.* 28, imperat. *Scitote* (Vulg.). There are many passages in which a similar doubt arises, esp. in Jn (v. 39, xii. 19, xiv. 1, xv. 18, 27) and in 1 Jn (ii. 27, 29, iv. 2).

ὅτι ἐγγύς ἐστιν. The nom. is left indefinite, and it is probably impersonal, "the End" (*v.* 7), or "the Kingdom" (Lk.), or "the time" (Rev. i. 3, xxii. 10); but R.V. makes it personal, "He" (Jas. v. 9; Phil. iv. 5). The difference is not great. Lk. omits ἐπὶ θύραις, which illustrates Mk's love of fulness. It is a popular expression for nearness; ἐπὶ τῇ θύρᾳ (Acts v. 9). For the sense cf. 1 Cor. xvi. 22.

30—32. CERTAINTY OF THE EVENT; UNCERTAINTY OF THE TIME.

Mt. xxiv. 34—36.　Lk. xxi. 32—33.

30. ἀμὴν λέγω ὑμῖν. This important Saying (30, 31), with its solemn introduction, has nearly the same wording in all three.

οὐ μὴ παρέλθῃ. *Shall assuredly not pass away;* cf. *vv.* 2, 19, ix. 1, 41, x. 15.

ἡ γενεὰ αὕτη. Here, as elsewhere in the Gospels (see on viii. 12) this expression can hardly mean anything else than Christ's own contemporaries; see esp. Mt. xxiii. 36. To make it mean the Jewish race, or the race of believers, or the whole race of mankind, is not satisfactory. But, if any of these be adopted, the sentence is only an expansive way of saying that *some* persons in some period will see the fulfilment of the predictions. If Christ's own generation is meant, then we may suppose that either (1) tradition has confused what was said of the destruction of Jerusalem with what was said of the End; or (2) the destruction, as removing Judaism, the great obstacle of the Gospel, was the beginning of the End; or (3) the destruction of Jerusalem is a symbol of the End and is treated as identical with it.

31. ὁ οὐρανὸς καὶ ἡ γῆ. The saying is proverbial for what stands for ever. The material universe will one day come to an end, but Christ's words will always hold good. Cf. 2 Pet. iii. 10; Heb. i. 11, 12; Rev. xx. 11, xxi. 1; Ps. cii. 25—27, civ. 29—31; Is. li. 6.

οἱ δὲ λόγοι μου. Not merely this prediction, but the whole of His teaching. Cf. οἱ ἐμοὶ λόγοι (viii. 38) and ὁ ἐμὸς λόγος (Jn viii. 31). The great revelation of the Father's love to His children holds good for ever.

32. περὶ δὲ τῆς ἡμέρας ἐκείνης. This can hardly mean anything else than the great day which will bring to an end αἱ ἡμέραι ἐκεῖναι (*vv.* 17, 19, 24), the day of the Advent (xiv. 25; Lk. xxi. 34; 2 Thess. i. 10; 2 Tim. i. 12, 18, iv. 8). If for a moment the downfall of Jerusalem has been treated as representing the End, this verse (to which there is no parallel in Lk.) definitely distinguishes the two. Christ has given signs by which those who are on the alert may recognize the nearness of the downfall. He now, in very clear and emphatic language, tells His disciples that He can give no hint as to the time of His Advent. He Himself does not know. This is a saying which no Christian would have invented and attributed to Christ. Interpolation (Ambrose) is not credible.

οὐδὲ οἱ ἄγγελοι. *Not even the Angels;* cf. v. 3, vi. 31, viii. 17, xii. 10. Here again Christ solemnly teaches that Angels exist (see on viii. 38, xii. 25) and He has just stated (*v.* 27) that Angels will take part in the stupendous events of that Day. Cf. Mt. xiii. 41, 49, xxv. 31, xxvi. 53.

οὐδὲ ὁ υἱός. *Nor yet the Son.* The other Evangelists represent Christ as speaking of "the Son" in the same absolute manner; Mt. xi. 27; Lk. x. 22; Jn v. 19, vi. 40, xvii. 1. We have οὐ...οὐδὲ...οὐδὲ... Mt. vi. 26, xii. 19 and Rev. v. 3; cf. Rev. ix. 4. It was not for any man, not even the Son of Man Himself, " to know times and seasons, which the Father hath set within His own authority" (Acts i. 7). After the Resurrection Christ does not say that He is ignorant; but at this crisis He was not yet glorified, and in this, as in many other things, He condescended to share the ignorance of His disciples; see on vi. 5, 38, viii. 5, 22, ix. 21, xi. 13; Jn xi. 34. The meaning would seem to be, " The Father has not revealed this, not even to Me, the Son." This, of course refers to the Son *as He then was*, incarnate and not yet glorified. See Gore, *Dissertations*, pp. 77—88.

εἰ μὴ ὁ πατήρ. This goes back to οὐδεὶς οἶδεν: "no one, except the Father," to which Mt. adds "alone" (μόνος), which covers οὐδὲ ὁ υἱός, words which in Mt. are omitted in important witnesses, but are probably to be retained. That the Father knows this season and day is stated in O.T. (Zech. xiv. 7) and in Ps. Sol. xvii. 23, "Behold, O Lord, and raise up unto them their King, the Son of David, in the time which Thou, O God, knowest" (εἰς τὸν καιρὸν ὃν οἶδας σύ, ὁ Θεός). Dalman, *Words*, p. 287.

33—37. THE NECESSITY FOR WATCHFULNESS.

Mt. xxv. 13—15. Lk. xxi. 36.

33. βλέπετε. See crit. note and cf. *vv.* 5, 9, 23. It is a thread which runs through the whole discourse.

ἀγρυπνεῖτε. *Be vigilant*, "Do not allow yourselves to slumber" (ἄγρυπνος = ἄϋπνος). Neither A.V. nor R.V. distinguishes between this and γρηγορεῖτε (v. 37). The verbs differ little in meaning and in LXX. translate the same Hebrew; moreover St Paul uses them indifferently (Eph. vi. 18; Col. iv. 2); but a change in the Greek should be marked by a change in the English. See on 1 Thess. v. 6. Here Mt. has γρηγορεῖτε. Note the characteristic asyndeton and see on x. 14.

ὁ καιρός. "The Divinely appointed"; see on i. 15. Mt. has "the day, nor yet the hour."

34. ὡς ἄνθρωπος. Again a characteristic asyndeton (Mt. inserts γάρ), and a characteristically unskilful constr. There is no apodosis to ὡς (Blass § 78. 1), and forgetting that he has used no finite verb Mk inserts καί before τῷ θυρ. ἐνετείλατο. It is possible that we here have a Hebraism; "It is as when a man"; but to make ὡς look back to ἀγρυπνεῖτε is a forced constr., unlike Mk.

ἀπόδημος. "Gone abroad"; nowhere else in Bibl. Grk. Cf. ἀποδημέω (xii. 1; Mt. xxi. 33, xxv. 14; etc.).

ἀφεὶς τὴν οἰκίαν αὐτοῦ. Superfluous after ἀπόδημος and omitted by Mt. See on i. 32, vi. 25. For the combination of participles see on i. 15.

τοῖς δούλοις...τὴν ἐξουσίαν. To the whole body of his slaves he gave the necessary authority to act during his absence.

ἑκάστῳ τὸ ἔργον. To each individual slave he assigned his proper work.

καὶ τῷ θυρωρῷ. R.V. saves the constr. by rendering καί "also"; but confused constructions are so common in Mk that this refinement is less probable. Cf. iii. 16—18, iv. 15, 26, 31, vi. 8, 9, vii. 2—5, 11, 12, etc. See on Jn x. 3. Neither there nor here is it necessary to give any definite meaning to the door-keeper (Jn xviii. 16). Euthymius makes him to be τὸν ἑκάστου νοῦν, τὸν ἐπιστατοῦντα ταῖς θυρίσι τῆς ψυχῆς. The general lesson of the parable is that all are to watch. Pastors and rulers of the Church may be meant; but the οἰκονόμος (Lk. xii. 42; xvi. 1—8) would seem to represent them (1 Cor. iv. 1; Tit. i. 7). Does θυρωρός look back to ἐπὶ θυραῖς (v. 29)?

γρηγορῇ. A late verb, formed from ἐγρήγορα.

35. πότε ὁ κύριος. The same as πότε ὁ καιρός (v. 23) and ἡ ἡμέρα ἐκείνη (v. 32). See Edersheim, *The Temple and its Services*, p. 120, for striking parallels to this verse.

ἢ ὀψέ. See on vi. 48. These are not technical terms, but popular expressions; ἀλεκτοροφωνία occurs nowhere else in Bibl. Grk, but it is found in Aesop's *Fables*, 79. *Gallicinium* is used in a similar way as a popular term for "before dawn," like our "cock-crow"; *noctis*

gallicinio venit quidam juvenis (Appuleius, *Met.* 8). The mixture of
two adverbs with two substantives, one the acc. of time the other the
gen. of time, is quite in Mk's conversational style; "late, midnight,
at cockcrow, or early."

36. μὴ ἐλθών. Cf. Lk. xii. 37, 38; 1 Thess. v. 6.

ἐξαίφνης. If the suddenness causes disaster, the fault lies with
those who have not watched. They were warned beforehand that
the Coming might be sudden.

37. πᾶσιν λέγω. "No one may think that the warning given to
a few disciples is no concern of his; the warning is given to all
believers." It was probably given more than once and in more
than one form. It has been preserved in more than one form
and in a variety of settings, but this and xiv. 38 are the only places
in Mk, who in this chapter may have included words spoken on
other occasions. Cf. Mt. xxiv. 37—51, xxv. 1—13; Lk. xii. 35—40,
xvii. 26—35, xxi. 34—36. Contrast Ezek. iii. 16—21, xxxiii. 1—9,
where the responsibility is laid on the Prophet.

In his Introduction to Rev. i.—iii. (p. xiii) Hort says: "It has
long been a favourite idea with some Continental writers, an entirely
mistaken one, I believe, that the record of our Lord's own apocalyptic
discourse in the first three Gospels includes a kernel or core transcribed
from a purely Jewish Apocalypse."

The latest theory with regard to Mk xiii. is of a different character:
it is stated with great ability by Mr Streeter, *Studies in the Synoptic
Problem* (edited by Dr Sanday), pp. 180—183, 428—436. It is there
argued that Mk has accepted as a genuine record of a discourse by Christ
what is really a Christian Apocalypse, composed shortly after the fall
of Jerusalem, to encourage the despondent by showing that the delay
of the Coming had been foreseen by the Master, and especially to warn
believers against Anti-Christs and false Christs. It is admitted that
this composition contains a few genuine Sayings of our Lord, *e.g. vv.* 1,
2, 11, 15, 16, and most of 28—32; also that Mt. derived his version
of the discourse from Mk, and not from another recension of this
Christian Apocalypse.

The theory is very far from being proved, and being entirely
destitute of documentary evidence it is incapable of proof. As an
hypothesis it is not required. Even those who deny that Christ had
any supernatural insight into the future cannot point to anything
which must have been written after the event. The one solid fact is
that some Sayings of our Lord as reported by Mt. "conform more
closely to the conventional apocalyptic pattern" than similar Sayings
as reported by Mk, and that there is still less of this conventional

apocalyptic element in the Sayings which are reported by both Mt. and
Lk. But, as Mr Streeter himself admits in a later volume (*Founda-
tions*, p. 112), "the conclusions I was then inclined to draw from it
were, I now think, somewhat too sweeping." There is nothing in
the substance of the discourse which is unworthy of the Master, and
there is nothing in the wording of it that is conspicuously unlike the
style of the Evangelist. In this respect it is very unlike the last
twelve verses of Chap. xvi., which cannot have been written by Mk.
Even in those verses which are supposed to contain no genuine
Sayings of Christ there are things which are characteristic of Mk's
style; *e.g.* the conversational ἐπηρώτα in the sing. (*v.* 3); ἤρξατο (*v.* 5);
freq. asyndeton (*vv.* 7, 8, 9); the superfluous ἣν ἔκτισεν ὁ θεός (*v.* 19),
and οὓς ἐξελέξατο (*v.* 20), and ἐπὶ θύραις (*v.* 29), and ἀφεὶς τὴν οἰκίαν
αὐτοῦ (*v.* 34); asyndeton (*v.* 23); the forcible but illogical combination of earth and heaven (*v.* 27); asyndeton (*vv.* 33, 34); the
combination of participles, ἀφεὶς...καὶ δούς (*v.* 34); loose constructions
(*vv.* 34, 35). It is hardly likely that so many features of Mk's style
would have been found in a discourse, all of which was taken from a
source which *ex hypothesi* was already in writing. Mr Streeter himself points out that Mk "would not have composed the Apocalypse
but, accepting it as authentic, inserted it whole." It is more to the
point to remark with Milligan (*N.T. Documents*, p. 146), that we here
see to how large an extent Christ "availed Himself of current Jewish
imagery in His teaching." We may also remark that throughout the
prediction it is the destruction of the Temple and of Jerusalem that is
prominent; about Christ's own death there is nothing.

CHAPTER XIV.

2. γάρ (אBC*DLΨ) rather than δέ (AC²ΧΓΔΠ).

3. אBLΨ omit καί before συντρίψασα. אBCLΔΨ omit κατά before τῆς κεφαλῆς.

4. אBCLΨ omit καὶ λέγοντες.

5. τοῦτο τὸ μύρον (ABCLΔΠ) rather than τοῦτο (ΜΧΓ) or τὸ μύρον (א). D has τὸ μύρον τοῦτο.

7. αὐτοῖς (אᶜBDLΓΔ) rather than αὐτούς (ΑΧΠ). אᶜBL add πάντοτε, which would be in Mk's style.

9. ἀμὴν δὲ λέγω (אBDΓΔΨ) rather than ἀμὴν λέγω (ACX).

14. τὸ κατάλυμά μου (אBCDLΔΨ) rather than τὸ κατάλυμα (ΑΧΓΠ).

19. ἤρξαντο (אBLΨ) rather than οἱ δὲ ἤρξαντο (ΑDΧΓΔΠ). εἷς κατὰ εἷς (אBLΔ) rather than εἷς καθ' εἷς (ΑDΧΓΠ); cf. [Jn] viii. 9.

22. BD omit ὁ Ἰησοῦς. אABCDLΓΔ omit φάγετε, from Mt.

24. אBCDL omit καινῆς.

25. אCDL omit οὐκέτι, but it may be retained (ΑΒΝΧΓΨ).

27. אBCDLΧΓΔΨ omit ἐν ἐμοὶ...ταύτῃ.

29. Εἰ καί (אBCGLΨ) rather than Καὶ εἰ (ΑΧΓΔΠ).

30. אC*D omit δίς, but it may be retained (ΑΒC²LΧΓΔΠ).

31. אBCDL omit μᾶλλον after ἐλάλει (אBDL).

35. προελθών (אBFMN) rather than προσελθών (ΑCDLΧΓΔ). ἔπιπτεν (אBLΨ) rather than ἔπεσεν (ACD etc.).

43. אBLΨ omit πολύς, from Mt.

45. אBCDLΔΨ omit the second Ῥαββεί.

47. εἷς δέ τις (BCNΧΓΔΠ) rather than εἷς δέ (אALMΨ) or καί τις (D).

50. ἔφυγον πάντες (אBCLΔΨ) rather than πάν. ἔφ. (ΑDΧΓΠ).

51. νεανίσκος τις (אBCL) rather than εἷς τις νεαν. (AEF etc.). D has νεαν. δέ τις. συνηκολούθει (אBCL) rather ἠκολούθει (D) or συνηκολούθησεν (Δ) or ἠκολούθησεν (Α). אBC*DLΔ omit οἱ νεανίσκοι. אBCL omit ἀπ' αὐτῶν.

58. οἰκοδομήσω (אABC etc.) rather than ἀναστήσω (D).

65. ἔλαβον (אABCLNΓΔII) rather than ἐλάμβανον (DG) or ἔβαλον (EMX 33). Nestle (*Text. Crit. of N.T.*, p. 266) argues in favour of ἐλάμβανον.

68. Οὔτε οἶδα οὔτε (אBDL) rather than Οὐκ οἶδα οὐδέ (AMNXΓII) or Οὐκ οἶδα οὔτε (CΔ). אBL (with Syr-Sin. and Memph.) omit καὶ ἀλέκτωρ ἐφώνησεν, and consistently with this אL omit ἐκ δευτέρου in *v.* 72.

70. אBCDΨ omit καὶ ἡ λαλιά σου ὁμοιάζει.

72. εὐθύς before ἐκ δευτέρου should be retained (אBDLM). As in *v.* 30, אC*D omit δίς, but it may be retained (ABC²LNXΓΨ).

1, 2. THE MALICE OF THE SANHEDRIN.

Mt. xxvi. 1—5. Lk. xxii. 1, 2.

1. ᾽Ην δὲ τὸ πάσχα. Mt. puts this remark into the mouth of Christ, and he omits τὰ ἄζυμα, which is either confusing or superfluous. The Passover on Nisan 14 was distinct from the F. of Unleavened Bread, which lasted from the 15th to the 21st (Lev. xxiii. 5, 6; Num. xxviii. 16, 17; 2 Chron. xxx. 15, 21; etc.). But it was usual to treat them as one festival. Josephus does so expressly (*Ant.* II. xv. 1, XIV. ii. 1), though he knows that they are distinct (*Ant.* III. x. 5, IX. xiii. 3). Note the unusual δέ, marking the change of subject, and see on vii. 24, x. 32, xv. 16.

μετὰ δύο ἡμέρας. This is perplexing, and we do not get much help from Hos. vi. 2; "He will revive us after two days or on the third day," where "on the third day" is not the same as "after two days," but adds a day; "after two or three days" is the meaning—a common expression for a period which cannot or need not be exactly defined. If "after three days" (viii. 31, ix. 31, x. 34) means "on the third day," then "after two days" should mean "on the second day," for which αὔριον would have been simpler. But Mk nowhere uses αὔριον. We are probably to understand that what follows took place on the Wednesday, the day before the Synoptic Paschal Supper and two days before the Johannine Passover.

ἐζήτουν. The discussion took some time. Mt., as often, has the aor., συνεβουλεύσαντο, and instead of the Scribes (Mk, Lk.) he has here and in Gethsemane "the elders *of the people.*" Cf. Mt. xxi. 23 = Mk xi. 27.

ἐν δόλῳ. They were agreed about that; the question was what kind of δόλος.

2. Μὴ ἐν τῇ ἑορτῇ. That meant immediate action or postponement for ten days, and the latter might easily involve His escape. When the Galilean pilgrims returned home, He would go with them.

μήποτε ἔσται. *For fear there shall be.* The indic. shows that they regard the result as certain; arrest during the Feast is sure to produce a tumult; μάλιστα γὰρ ἐν ταῖς εὐωχίαις αὐτῶν στάσις ἅπτεται (Joseph. *B. J.* i. iv. 3). Cf. Heb. iii. 12 and Lightfoot on Col. ii. 8.

3—9. THE ANOINTING AT BETHANY.

Mt. xxvi. 6—13. Jn xii. 1—11.

3. ἐν Βηθανίᾳ. That our Lord should be at a supper at Bethany on one of the days before the Passover is what we should expect from xi. 11, 12, and one would gather from Mt. and Mk that the supper took place on the evening of Tuesday or Wednesday. But Jn quite distinctly places it before the Triumphal Entry, perhaps on the Friday of the previous week; see on Jn xii. 1. The precision in Jn is not likely to be erroneous, and we must suppose that Mk, followed by Mt., has recorded this event after others which really preceded it. The wish to bring it into close connexion with the treachery of Judas may have caused the displacement.

ἐν τῇ οἰκίᾳ Σίμωνος. That the owner of the house was called Simon, and that at a meal in his house a woman anointed Christ from an alabaster, are the reasons why, already in Origen's time, this narrative was confused by some persons with that in Lk vii. 36—50. Almost everything else is different, and "the leper" seems to be added here to distinguish this Simon from any other, for Simon was one of the very commonest of names. The difficulty of believing in two anointings is infinitesimal; one such might easily suggest a repetition. Whereas the difficulty of believing that Mary of Bethany had ever been "a sinner" is enormous. There is no evidence of a previous evil life, and what we know of her renders a previous evil life almost incredible.

τοῦ λεπροῦ. We are not told that he was present. If he was presiding as entertainer, he must have been cured of his malady. It is probable that some curable skin diseases were regarded as leprosy; and a cured "leper" might still be known as ὁ λεπρός.

κατακειμένου αὐτοῦ. This second gen. abs. is quite in Mk's conversational style.

γυνή. There is no hint that she was related to Simon; and that she was his wife, daughter, or sister are improbable conjectures. She may have been still alive when Mk and Mt. wrote, but dead when Jn wrote; hence they might prefer not to name her, while he had no reason for abstaining. Or he happened to know her name, whereas they did not. The case of Malchus is parallel (see on *v.* 47).

ἀλάβαστρον. The word is all genders, but in class. Gk the termination is -os, masc. or fem. Boxes or phials for holding unguents were called "alabasters"," even when made of other material; but Pliny says that unguents keep best when kept *in alabastris* (*N. H.* xiii. 2). Cf. Hdt. iii. 20. In N.T., and probably in LXX., μύρον, "ointment," is distinguished from ἔλαιον, "oil." Trench, *Syn.* § xxxviii. Here μύρου is virtually an adj., ἀλ. μύρου = "unguent-box"; and νάρδου πιστικῆς tells what kind of unguent, and of what quality. The kind is that made from a well-known plant found chiefly in India. Tristram, *Nat. Hist. of the Bible*, p. 485. The quality denoted by πιστική is uncertain, but "potable" = "liquid" (πίνω) may be dismissed. "Trustworthy" = "genuine" is possible. Unguents were often adulterated. The only safe course is to transliterate, "pistic," and leave the word unexplained; it evidently implies that the ointment used was specially good. See on Jn xii. 3 and cf. Cant. i. 12.

πολυτελοῦς. Horace offers to give a cask of wine for a very small box of good ointment (*Carm.* iv. xii. 17). Cf. 1 Tim. ii. 9; 1 Pet. iii. 4.

συντρίψασα. Mk alone tells us that she broke the box or phial, possibly in eagerness to pour out the whole contents quickly. Renan's suggestion may be right that she did not wish the alabaster to be used again for a less worthy purpose (*Vie*, p. 373, ed. 1863), just as wine-glasses are sometimes broken to show honour to the person whose health has just been drunk. But this is less probable, for she breaks the alabaster *before* anointing Him, not after. The verb implies violence (v. 4; Rev. ii. 27), but the vessel would be fragile. Note the participles.

κατέχεεν. Mt. retains the imperf. and adds ἐπὶ before κεφαλῆς, which here is probably governed by the κατα-. Verbs compounded with κατά often take a gen.; κατακυριεύω, καταφρονέω, κατεξουσιάζω, κατηγορέω, κ.τ.λ. See crit. note. Jn says that she anointed Christ's feet and wiped them with her hair, as the sinner wiped her tears from His feet before anointing them (Lk. vii. 38). She could anoint either head or feet from behind, as He reclined on a couch.

4. ἦσαν δέ τινες. By his silence as to who these were Mk again spares the Twelve. Mt. says that it was the disciples who were indignant, while Jn states that it was Judas who gave utterance to the resentment, because the loss of the costly ointment meant the loss of money which he could have stolen. In all these cases, Mary,

Judas, Peter and Malchus, earlier Evangelists may have been ignorant of the names or may have suppressed them. Jn knew the names, and when he wrote there was no need for suppression. It is not often that Mk is more considerate of the Twelve than Mt. is.

πρὸς ἑαυτούς. *Among themselves* (R.V.) rather than "within themselves" (A.V.). There would be some exclamations or looks of disapproval. See on xi. 31, where Vulg. has *secum*; but here *intra semet ipsos.*

ἡ ἀπώλεια. A very rare use of ἀπώλεια, which usually has the intrans. meaning of "perdition" (Mt. vii. 13; Jn xvii. 12; etc.). Cf. ὁ οἶνος ἀπόλλυται (ii. 22).

γέγονεν. The destruction has taken place and the loss abides.

5. ἠδύνατο γάρ. Explanation of their strong disapproval. See crit. note.

ἐπάνω δηναρίων τριακοσίων. All one term, and gen. of price; "for over-200-denarii." The ἐπάνω has no effect on the case; cf. ὤφθη ἐπάνω πεντακοσίοις ἀδελφοῖς (1 Cor. xv. 6). See on vi. 37 respecting the amount. Mt., as usual, omits the amount. See on v. 13.

ἐνεβριμῶντο. *They went on murmuring against her.* Mt. has ἠγανάκτησαν.

6. Ἄφετε αὐτήν. This must mean *Let her alone* rather than "Allow her"; *sinite eam* (Vulg.). It was too late to prevent her.

κόπους παρέχετε. Κόπος is a "blow," and hence "worry" or "wear and tear"; Lk. xi. 7; Gal. vi. 17. So also in papyri.

καλόν ἔργον. "It was a beautiful act that she wrought on Me."

7. πάντοτε. First with emphasis; *At all times ye have the poor with you.* It is worth while to distinguish πάντοτε from ἀεί, which is much less freq. in N.T., and is never used by Mk; see on 2 Cor. iv. 10. These words, with *But Me ye have not at all times*, are in all three, and we cannot doubt their authenticity. Considering His teaching about the poor (x. 21; Lk. xiv. 13, 21, xvi. 20; Jn xiii. 29), we may feel certain that no one would have invented such a Saying for Him. The πάντοτε after αὐτοῖς is probably genuine; see crit. note. It emphasizes the permanent possibility of benevolence. There is no contradiction between the promise of His perpetual spiritual Presence (Mt. xviii. 20, xxviii. 20) and this statement that the opportunity of doing honour to His Body would not be perpetual.

8. ὃ ἔσχεν ἐποίησεν. *She did what she could.* This class. use of ἔχω is freq. in Lk. (vii. 42, xii. 4, xiv. 14) and Acts (iv. 14, xxiii. 17, 18, 19, etc.). For the sense see on 2 Cor. viii. 12.

προέλαβεν μυρίσαι. *She hath been beforehand in anointing.* She

anticipated the funeral rite. Jn tells us that myrrh and aloes, but
not unguents, were placed round the Body, and Mk and Lk. say that
women prepared to anoint Him, but that He had risen before they
could do so. So Mary alone has this honour. Μυρίζω is classical,
but occurs here only in Bibl. Grk. Professional embalmers were
called ἐνταφιασταί, and ἐνταφιάζω = "embalm" (Gen. l. 2). So also
in papyri.

9. ὅπου ἐὰν κηρυχθῇ. Cf. Mt. xii. 32. In the first and second
centuries A.D., the substitution of ἐάν for ἄν after ὅπου, ὅς, etc. was
common. Deissmann, *Bib. St.* p. 203; J. H. Moulton, p. 42.

τὸ εὐαγγέλιον. See on i. 1, 14. Mk and Mt. record this promise,
but do not tell the woman's name; Jn tells the name, but does not
record the promise.

εἰς ὅλον τ. κόσμον. Cf. xiii. 10. That salvation is for the whole
of mankind is clearly given in our earliest Gospel. For this use of
εἰς see on i. 39; Winer, p. 517.

μνημόσυνον. Late Grk, freq. in LXX. Syr-Sin. has "when the
gospel shall be preached throughout the whole world, there will be a
memorial of what she has done."

10, 11. THE COMPACT OF JUDAS WITH THE HIERARCHY.

Mt. xxvi. 14—16. Lk. xxii. 3—6.

10. Ἰούδας Ἰσκαριώθ. In mentioning the traitor here each
Evangelist has something characteristic. Mk has Ἰσκαριώθ: he never
has Ἰσκαριώτης. Mt. has ὁ λεγόμενος Ἰσκαριώτης, Lk. has τὸν καλού
μενον Ἰσκαριώτην. All three give without comment the mournful fact
that the traitor was "one of the Twelve." The art. here, ὁ εἷς τ.
δώδεκα, looks as if "one-of-the-Twelve" had become a sort of *sobriquet*
for Judas.

παραδοῖ. See on iv. 29. Although Judas is called προδότης, yet
προδίδωμι is not used of his crime. It is a rare verb in Bibl. Grk, but
here D has προδοῖ and Vulg. has *proderet*. Cf. 2 Kings vi. 11; 4 Macc.
iv. 1. It is not probable that the Sanhedrin had publicly offered
a reward, and that "Judas called in answer to an advertisement."

11. ἐχάρησαν. The offer freed them from a grave difficulty.
Now they could act before the Feast began. They would not have
ventured to make such a proposal to a disciple of Jesus. That one of
His most intimate associates should volunteer to betray Him was an
amazing advantage. Moreover it was evidence that the influence of
Jesus was on the wane, ὅτι καὶ ὑπὸ τῶν μαθητῶν ἤρξατο μισεῖσθαι
(Euthym.).

ἐπηγγείλαντο. So also Lk. (συνέθεντο), while Mt. says that Judas was paid there and then thirty pieces of silver. Such discrepancies are of no moment. In order to identify the coins paid to Judas with the treasure brought by the Magi, the Narrative of Judas of Arimathaea (ii.) makes them pieces of gold. Thirty shekels would be about 120 *denarii*, which would buy what £10 or £12 would buy now. It is not improbable that the priests would be willing to pay in advance so moderate a sum for so great a service, and it is probable that Judas would insist on at least a substantial instalment. Hastings' *D.B.* art. "Money," p. 428.

ἐζήτει. *He began to seek.* Hitherto it had been the hierarchy who were casting about for a good opportunity (xi. 18, xii. 12, xiv. 1). Now it is Judas who has to do so; they have secured a competent agent. What follows shows how he was baffled until after the Supper; the arrangements were carefully kept secret.

It is remarkable how objectively Mk, and indeed all the Evangelists, treat the conduct of Judas. He was an intimate disciple, one of the Twelve, and he betrayed his Friend and Master to His implacable enemies for money and with a kiss. There is no need to say anything more. Probably money was only one of the motives. Judas saw that Jesus had failed, and he hastened to make terms with the victorious side. It is possible that there were selfish elements in his reasons for attaching himself to Jesus, and that these had gone on increasing, to the extinction of nobler motives, as the prospect of personal advancement grew less. That the motives for the betrayal were in any respect good is not credible.

12—16. PREPARATIONS FOR THE PASSOVER.

Mt. xxvi. 17—19. Lk. xxii. 7—13.

12. τῇ πρώτῃ ἡμέρᾳ τ. ἀζύμων. It is possible that here we have the beginning of the divergent chronology respecting the Passover, as given by the Synoptists on the one hand and by Jn on the other. The Synoptists, in a confused and not very consistent way, place the Paschal Supper on Thursday evening. Jn, with great precision and with complete consistency, places the Passover on Friday evening, when it and the Sabbath began simultaneously. The better course is to abide by the Johannine tradition and assume that our Lord, knowing that He could not have the Paschal Supper at the right time, held it a day in advance. It is incredible that the Sanhedrin sat during the Passover night to try Jesus, and that He was executed with the two robbers on the first day of the Feast. **All four**

Evangelists place the Crucifixion on the day before the Sabbath, *i.e.*
on Friday.   The question is, which day was the 14th Nisan?

ἔθυον.   Imperf. of customary action.   The verb, like σφάζω (1 Jn
iii. 12; 1 Sam. xv. 33), although often used of sacrifices, is not
sacrificial in meaning (Lk. xv. 23; Jn x. 10; Acts x. 13).   Here A.V.
has "kill," with "sacrifice" in the margin; in 1 Cor. v. 7 it has
"sacrifice," with "slay" in the margin.   In 1 Cor. x. 20, "sacrifice"
is required by the context.

Ποῦ θέλεις;   The association of the Twelve with Jesus has
become so close that none of them thinks of celebrating the Passover
with his own family.   Relations of some of them would come up to
Jerusalem for the Feast.   They were probably ignorant of our Lord's
intention of having a Paschal Supper before the time.   Christ seems
to have kept both time and place secret till the last.   The treachery
of Judas must not be allowed to act till the appointed hour had come,
and no miracle was needed to effect this; careful precaution sufficed.

13.   ἀποστέλλει δύο.   See on xi. 1.   Lk. tells us that the pair
were Peter and John, probably the oldest and youngest of the Twelve,
certainly two that had been specially selected on previous occasions.
Neither here, nor at the Supper, is there mention of a lamb, and it is
very improbable that there was one.   If the hypothesis that Christ
anticipated the time for celebrating the Passover is correct, the
disciples could not get the priests to kill the lamb before the time.
Moreover, the whole company ought to be present in the Temple at
the killing of the lamb (Exod. xii. 4 6), and two disciples would not
suffice for this.   Above all, there would be no need of a typical lamb,
when the true Paschal lamb was present, ready to be offered, but not
yet slain.

Ὑπάγετε εἰς τ. πόλιν.   This shows that they are outside Jerusalem, perhaps at Bethany.

ἀπαντήσει ὑμῖν ἄνθρωπος.   This remarkable detail is omitted in
Mt.'s very abbreviated narrative.   The man's carrying water shows
that he was a servant, not the owner, who is in the house (*v.* 14).
Slaves or women fetched water for the household (Deut. xxix. 11;
Josh. ix. 21—27; Jn iv. 7).   That this was the master of the house
drawing water on 13th Nisan for making the leaven, is a useless
suggestion; no evidence as to the day can be got from a *servant*
fetching water.   As in the case of the colt (xi. 2, 3), there is room for
doubt whether our Lord had arranged matters beforehand or not.   It
might have been agreed that the man carrying water should be ready
to meet the disciples.   But this is not the impression which the
narratives give us.   Apparently Christ had arranged with the owner

that the Paschal meal should take place at his house; but His telling the disciples that they would meet one of this man's servants, and that by following this servant they would find the house, is evidently regarded as supernatural prescience. If there had been any desire to invent a sign of supernatural prescience, our Lord would have been made to predict something more remarkable than a man carrying a pitcher.

Vulg. is again capricious; here it has *laguenam aquae bajulans*; in Lk. *amphoram aquae portans*, the Greek being the same. So also in what follows; here *Ubi est refectio?* in Lk. *Ubi est diversorium?*

14. Ὁ διδάσκαλος λέγει. In all three; the words show that Jesus was known to the owner, and seem to imply that He had previously asked for a room. Victor would have it that the man did not know Jesus, and that his immediate obedience shows what power Jesus had.

τὸ κατάλυμά μου. Perhaps not the same as the ἀνάγαιον which was granted. Christ may have asked for the common guest-room on the ground floor, but the man gave Him his private room, above the guest-room, the best that he had. On the identification of this ἀνάγαιον with the ὑπερῷον of Acts i. 13, and placing it in "the house of Mary, the mother of Mark" (Acts xii. 12), and the consequent identification of "the goodman of the house" with the father of Mark, see Sanday, *Sacred Sites of the Gospels*, p. 77; Edersheim, *Life and Times*, ii. p. 485; Zahn, *Introd. to N.T.* ii. p. 493. The identifications are very attractive, but the evidence is slight; see further on *v.* 51. That the man with the pitcher was Mark the Evangelist, son of "the goodman," a conjecture as old as Alexander Monachus of Cyprus (*c.* A.D. 550), is almost as improbable as that he was the goodman himself. The μου after κατάλυμα (see crit. note) is important; it proves that Christ had some claim on the owner, and is strong evidence that He had arranged with the man for a room.

15. αὐτὸς ὑμῖν δείξει. A further note of prescience. The man will himself conduct the disciples to the upper room, which will be found in complete order, set out with rugs on the couches. This might mean no more than that the man was certain that the room would be required by some one for the Paschal meal; but it looks as if "the Master" had bespoken a room.

ἀνάγαιον. Anything raised above the ground, "upper floor" (Xen. *Anab.* v. iv. 29), *upper room*. MSS. vary much in spelling; ἀνόγαιον, ἀνώγεων, ἀνώγεως, ἀνώγαιον, ἀνώγεον, but the best MSS. have ἀνάγαιον, which is confirmed by papyri with καταγαίῳ, κατάγειον. The word was originally an adj. and it is so treated in D, ἀνάγαιον οἶκον. The Latin renderings vary also; *cenaculum* (Vulg.), *medianum* (a), *pede plano locum* (b), *in superioribus locum* (c e), *superiorem domum* (d in Lk.).

16. καθώς. *Even as.* Both Mk and Lk. insist on the exact agreement of the disciples' experiences with the details which Christ had foretold, just as Lk. does with regard to the directions about the colt (Lk. xix. 32). Mt. in both places says that the disciples did as they were told. Here he omits the details, and therefore cannot remark on the exact fulfilment of Christ's predictions. Here, iv. 33, and xv. 8, R.V. fails to give the force of καθώς.

ἡτοίμασαν. The apparent contradiction between the room being already ἕτοιμον and the disciples having to "make ready" does not trouble Mk, but it is avoided by Lk. There is no real inconsistency. The room was ready for a meal, but there was no food provided. This the disciples had to see to.

17—25. The Paschal Supper.

Mt. xxvi. 20—29.   Lk. xxii. 14, 19—23.   Jn xiii. 1, 2.

17. ὀψίας γενομένης. The evening of the same day. For a description of the probable surroundings see Edersheim, *Life and Times*, ii. pp. 488 f., *The Temple and its Services*, pp. 194 f.

18. ἀνακειμένων. Cf. ii. 15, vi. 26. The original custom of standing for the Passover had long been abandoned. Instead of commemorating the fear and haste of the flight from Egypt, they enjoyed the security and repose of their abode in the Land of Promise.

Ἀμὴν λέγω ὑμῖν. With all solemnity the amazing disclosure is made. Evidently Judas had escaped suspicion; no one at once thinks of him. Lk. places the disclosure at the end of the section. From this point onwards Lk. treats Mk with very great freedom and evidently has other authority, possibly oral. Sir John Hawkins calculates that Mt. adheres to Mk's language very nearly twice as closely as Lk. does, and there are eleven cases in which Lk. changes the order of Mk, where Mt. retains it (*Studies in the Synoptic Problem*, pp. 76 f.). Cf. Jn xiii. 21.

ὁ ἐσθίων μετ' ἐμοῦ. Mk alone has this. To Orientals it was an additional horror, for hostile action against a man was absolutely precluded by eating bread with him. Cf. Ps. xli. 9. The words come last with tragic effect.

19. ἤρξαντο λυπεῖσθαι. See crit. note. The asyndeton is impressive; the festal meal was at once turned to mourning. But no disciple doubts the truth of the Master's words; sooner than that each suspects himself, πιστεύοντες τῷ τὰς καρδίας εἰδότι πλέον ἢ ἑαυτοῖς (Theoph.). Leonardo's fresco depicts this crisis.

εἶς κατὰ εἶς. This ungrammatical idiom is not found in classical writers, but it and similar expressions are not rare in late Greek; τὸ δὲ καθ᾽ εἶς (Rom. xii. 5); ἀνὰ εἶς ἕκαστος (Rev. xxi. 21); ὁ καθ᾽ εἶς δὲ τῶν φίλων (3 Macc. v. 34); εἶς καθ᾽ ἕκαστος (Lev. xxv. 10, A text, which Deissmann, *Bib. St.* p. 138, is inclined to support). Perhaps the prep. was treated as an adv.

Μήτι ἐγώ; *Surely it cannot be I?* Cf. ii. 19, iv. 21. If Mt. is drawing an inference, it is a safe inference, when he tells us that Judas also asked this question. Not to have asked with the rest would have attracted attention.

20. Εἶς τῶν δώδεκα. This also is peculiar to Mk, as is the probably genuine ἕν (BC*) before τρύβλιον. All three points serve to bring out the enormity of the crime. The traitor is one of the Twelve, eating with Him whom he is about to deliver up to His enemies, and even dipping his morsel in one and the same dish with Him. The τρύβλιον was perhaps the bowl of sauce into which pieces of unleavened bread were dipped. This declaration does not make known who is the guilty one. Later in the meal Christ's giving a dipped morsel to Judas lets John know who is the traitor.

21. ὁ μὲν υἱὸς...παραδίδοται. Here again all three have almost exactly the same words, and they are doubtless original. Obad. 7 or Mic. vii. 6 might have been quoted with effect; but Christ's words have no parallel in O.T. For μὲν...δὲ..., which is rare in Mk, cf. v. 38 and xii. 5.

ὑπάγει. This expresses better than πορεύεται (Lk.) that the going is a going *away* (Jn vi. 67), and such is departure from this life (Jn vii. 33, xiii. 3, xvi. 5, 10, 17). Moreover, the verb implies the voluntariness of His departure; τὸ ἐκούσιον ἡ λέξις ἑρμηνεύει (Victor). Hence καθὼς γέγραπται expresses the exact agreement between His voluntary action and the Father's revealed will.

οὐαὶ δὲ τῷ ἀνθρώπῳ. *But alas for the man;* see on xiii. 17. The οὐαί expresses lamentation over a condition so awful. God's decrees respecting the Son of Man did not require the treachery of Judas. Of his own free will he committed a sin which brought about the fulfilment of the decrees in a particular way, and for that he is condemned. Again and again Christ had tried to win him back; iv. 19, ix. 50, x. 23, xi. 17, xii. 43, xiv. 7 record words which might have influenced Judas, and which in some cases may have been meant for him. This statement of the lamentable condition of ὁ ἄνθρωπος ἐκεῖνος (xii. 7), and this proof that he is still treated with consideration (for he sees that Christ knows of his guilt and yet does not name him), are his Master's last efforts to waken his conscience.

δι' οὗ. In all three; Judas is Satan's instrument (Lk. xxii. 3; Jn xiii. 2, 27) in causing the death of the Messiah.

καλὸν αὐτῷ...ἐκεῖνος. Not in Lk. It is possible to interpret thus; "It were good for the Son of Man if Judas had not been born." But the interpretation is inadmissible. Christ is not speaking of His own fears, but of the fearful condition of Judas. A man may so misuse his life as to make it a curse instead of a blessing. As Jerome (on Mt.) says; *simpliciter dictum est, multo melius est non subsistere quam male subsistere.* Cf. ix. 42 and Enoch xxxviii. 2. The repetition of ὁ ἄνθρωπος ἐκεῖνος closes the utterance with a mournful cadence; "good were it for him if he had not been born—that man." Cf. ii. 20. Syr-Sin. omits the cadence. The departure of Judas may perhaps be placed here. It is impossible to determine whether he partook of the Eucharist or not.

22. ἐσθιόντων αὐτῶν. The Evangelist seems to be anxious to make clear that two memorable events of that evening, the disclosure about the presence of a traitor (*v.* 18), and the Institution of the Eucharist, took place during the meal.

λαβὼν ἄρτον. He took one of the cakes of bread and acted as He did at the feeding of the 5000 (vi. 41) and of the 4000 (viii. 6), breaking, blessing, and distributing to the disciples. But on this occasion there is no distribution by the disciples to others. That came later, when, in accordance with the Lord's command (1 Cor. xi. 24—26), the Eucharist became a permanent Christian rite. Syr-Sin. omits λαβών, "as they did eat bread." We cannot insist that ἄρτος must mean leavened bread, and that therefore the meal cannot have been the Passover. The conclusion is right, but the premise is precarious. It is unlikely that at such a time the disciples would provide leavened bread.

St Paul's account of the Institution is the earliest; but that of Mk and Mt. is independent of it. Their narrative has some features which are not in his; εὐλογήσας of the bread and εὐχαριστήσας of the cup, Λάβετε of the bread, λαβὼν εὐχαριστήσας ἔδωκεν of the cup, their all drinking of it, the Blood being ἐκχυννόμενον ὑπὲρ πολλῶν, and the declaration οὐ μὴ πίω...τοῦ Θεοῦ. On the other hand, St Paul gives two features which are not in Mk or Mt. He places a considerable interval between the bread (during supper) and the cup (after supper), and he records the important charge τοῦτο ποιεῖτε εἰς τὴν ἐμὴν ἀνά-μνησιν. What seems to be the true text of Lk. is silent about both.

Five features are in all four narratives; taking bread, thanksgiving or blessing, breaking, "This is My Body," and the mention of a cup. The first three give us ritual which may be said to be Divinely appointed.

There is probably no difference in meaning between εὐλογήσας (vi. 41 of the 5000) and εὐχαριστήσας (viii. 6 of the 4000). Both are used of the bread, and refer to the utterance in which Christ blessed God and gave thanks. Both verbs contain the εὖ which appears also in εὐδοκία and εὐαγγέλιον. It is remarkable that there is so little agreement as to the exact words spoken; the exact words are not of supreme importance. It is having the mind of Christ and acting in His spirit that must be secured.

τοῦτό ἐστιν τὸ σῶμά μου. Our Lord's human Body was present and His Blood had not yet been shed. Therefore all carnal ideas respecting the meaning of these words are excluded. Few words in Scripture have given rise to more controversy. All that it concerns us to know is certain; that those who rightly receive the Eucharist spiritually receive Christ. How this takes place has not been revealed and cannot be explained. Nor is any explanation necessary for right reception. See Hastings' *D.B.* art. "Lord's Supper" and the literature there quoted; also Robertson and Plummer on 1 Cor. xi. 23 f.

23. λαβών...εὐχαριστήσας. Characteristic combination of participles; see on i. 15.

ἔδωκεν...ἔπιον. Mk adds πάντες with emphasis, and Mt. transfers πάντες to Christ's command. It was not necessary to state this of the bread, which Christ seems to have given to each one; in any case, each has his separate morsel. But the cup was handed to only one of them. Some might have passed it without drinking, or it might not have gone the whole way round. Mk desires to make clear that all drank. In the later ritual of the Passover several cups were passed round at intervals. It is futile to attempt to identify the Eucharistic cup with one of these. The ritual may or may not have been the same.

24. τὸ αἷμά μου. No narrative makes mention of the blood of the Paschal lamb. "My Blood *of the covenant*" is an allusion to Exod. xxiv. 6—8, where see Driver. The attempts to show that the Lord's Supper was celebrated with bread alone have failed as signally as the attempts to derive the breaking of bread from the Eleusinian mysteries.

τὸ ἐκχυννόμενον. *Which is being shed;* what is near and certain is spoken of as present. Cf. ἀποφορτιζόμενον, Acts xxi. 3.

ὑπὲρ πολλῶν. *On behalf of many,* "many" being opposed, not to "all," but to "one" or "few." Christ was one dying for many and for a great many more than His personal disciples. These "many" are one of the parties to the covenant with God which is ratified by the Blood of Christ. See on x. 45.

25. οὐκέτι οὐ μὴ πίω. Characteristic accumulation of negatives; cf. iii. 27, ix. 8, xi. 2, xii. 34, etc. The οὐκέτι (see crit. note) implies that Christ partook of the cup, in accordance with what is known of Paschal ritual, before passing it to the disciples. He partakes of this Paschal supper, but it is His last. In these mysterious words He seems to be bidding farewell to the Jewish dispensation under which He had lived. This saying also could hardly have been invented. The prescribed Jewish blessing, before drinking wine, runs "Blessed art Thou, O Lord our God, King of the Universe, who createst the fruit of the vine" (*Authorized Daily Prayer Book*, p. 287).

τοῦ γενήματος τῆς ἀμπέλου. An O.T. expression for wine (Num. vi. 4; Is. xxxii. 12; Hab. iii. 17). In all three Gospels here, as in 2 Cor. ix. 10, γένημα (γίνομαι), not γέννημα (γεννάω), is right. The latter is right Mt. iii. 7, xii. 34, xxiii. 33; Lk. iii. 7. Deissmann, *Bib. St.* p. 184.

καινόν. Not νέον as in ii. 22; it is not the newness opposed to maturity, but the newness opposed to what is obsolete, the newness of the new heaven, that is meant. Our Lord retains the common picture of the Kingdom as a festal scene in which there is a banquet; the picture suggests "love, joy, and peace," which are chief among spiritual possessions. The picture is found in both O. and N.T. Cf. 2 Esdr. ii. 8; Book of the Secrets of Enoch, viii.

26 — 31. DEPARTURE TO THE MOUNT OF OLIVES. DESERTION AND DENIAL FORETOLD.

Mt. xxvi. 30—35. Lk. xxii. 31—39. Jn xiv. 31, xviii. 1.

26. ὑμνήσαντες. They sang one or two Psalms, probably cxxxvi., or cxv.—cxviii., before leaving the room.

ἐξῆλθον. This perhaps corresponds with Jn xiv. 31 (see notes there), but more probably with Jn xviii. 1. Going out of the city to the Mount of Olives was His usual practice (xi. 1; Lk. xxii. 39), and therefore would not surprise the Eleven. Probably even St John did not know that Judas would accomplish his treachery that night.

27. Πάντες. There will be no exception; not one will stand the shock of the arrest and execution of the Master.

Πατάξω τ. ποιμένα. This quotation differs from both A and B texts of LXX. and also from the Heb. See on Zech. xiii. 7 and also

Swete, *Intr. to O.T. in Greek*, p. 393. The quotation is made by Christ, not by Mk, and the truth of the saying has often been verified in history. The change from the imperat. (πατάξατε or πάταξον in LXX.) to the future (Mk, Mt.) makes the saying more suitable to the context, for it is God who will smite the Shepherd. The saying may have been a proverb before Zechariah used it, and it may have existed in both forms. In Zech. the sheep are the members of the Jewish Church; here they are primarily the Apostles (*v.* 50), but other followers may be included.

28. ἀλλά. Mt. has δέ, which does not mark so clearly the contrast between the sad scattering of the flock through the death of the Shepherd and its happy reunion through His Resurrection; *After I am raised up.*

προάξω. The verb suggests another contrast; between His going before them to Jerusalem to suffer and die (x. 32) and His going before them to a meeting place in the chief scene of their life with Him. This prediction of a meeting in Galilee is required to explain xvi. 7 and Mt. xxviii. 16, and we may be sure that it was uttered. As usual (viii. 31, ix. 31, x. 34), Christ adds to the prediction of His death the comforting promise of rising again; but it seems to have made little impression on the Apostles until after its fulfilment. Even then they derived little comfort from it until He appeared to them. That they believed that He had appeared to them because they were so convinced that He would rise again is against all the evidence that we possess.

29. ὁ δὲ Πέτρος. For the second time Peter impulsively contradicts a prediction of the Master, whose severe rebuke (viii. 33) has for the moment been forgotten. The emphatic repudiation of the possibility of his own faithlessness is thoroughly characteristic of his affection and of his self-confidence. On a former occasion he claimed credit for the whole band (x. 28). Here he claims exemption from weakness for himself. He admits the possibility of the others breaking away.

Εἰ καί. See crit. note. This combination indicates that what is supposed is conceded as being a fact (Lk. xi. 8, xviii. 4; 2 Cor. xii. 11; etc.). The exact difference between εἰ καί and καὶ εἰ is not easy to mark in English, and is not always the same. In most of the instances of καὶ εἰ in N.T. καί is a mere conjunction, "and if"; *e.g.* Mt. xi. 14. Winer, p. 554.

ἀλλ' οὐκ ἐγώ. We often have ἀλλά after εἰ καί. Anything else may be possible, *but* not that Peter will fail. It is strange that Jerome should say of this *non est temeritas.*

30. Ἀμὴν λέγω σοι. The prediction of his almost immediate failure is made with great solemnity : λέγω σοι is in all four Gospels, and Lk. and Jn are quite independent of the other two and of one another. Lk. and Jn place the prediction in the supper-room, Mk and Mt. place it during the walk from the room to the Mount of Olives, and Lk.'s narrative differs considerably from Jn's. Some suppose that there were three predictions, two in the room and one afterwards. It is unlikely that the prediction was repeated. These divergences about details are of little moment, and we have no means of determining which tradition is nearest to the actual facts. See on Jn xiii. 38.

σὺ σήμερον ταύτῃ τῇ νυκτί. The σύ, though omitted by ℵCDΔ and Old Latin texts, is probably genuine ; it answers to Peter's confident ἐγώ. We have here another instance of Mk's fulness, and of Mt. and Lk. each taking different parts of Mk's full expression, Lk. having σήμερον and Mt. ταύτῃ τῇ νυκτί. See on i. 32, 42, xv. 26. According to Jewish reckoning the day had begun at sunset, and σήμερον would mean " before the next sunset." "This night " therefore greatly abbreviates "to-day." The denial will take place within a very few hours.

δίς. This may safely be regarded as original ; see crit. note. It is confirmed by the Fayûm fragment, and the fact that Mt., Lk., and Jn mention only one cock-crowing makes omission more probable than interpolation. Travellers tell us that in the East cocks crow with extraordinary regularity at certain hours, about twelve, two, and five o'clock. Tristram, *Nat. Hist. of the Bible*, p. 221. But our Lord is not predicting the hours at which the denials will take place ; nor is the obvious meaning, that before the cock crows a second time there will have been three denials, the only point. Our Lord foretells that the first cock-crowing will not stop the denials ; in spite of this warning, Peter will still persist that he does not know Christ. The declaration, therefore, is pregnant with meaning, " *Thou*, who art so confident that thou at any rate wilt never be offended, within twenty hours, nay within six, wilt not only be offended, but wilt have denied Me, not once nor twice only, and that in spite of at least one warning signal." Cf. ὅτε τὸ δεύτερον ὦ ἀλεκτρυὼν ἐφθέγγετο (Aristoph. *Eccl.* 390) ; *Quod tamen ad cantum galli facit ille secundi* (Juv. ix. 106). The form ἀλέκτωρ is more common in poetry, ἀλεκτρυών in prose, and the Fayûm fragment has ἀλεκτρυών here ; it has also the more usual κοκκύζω of the crowing.

τρίς. In all four Gospels ; and the Synoptics all have the strong compound ἀπαρνήσῃ, which occurs only in this connexion and in that of denying oneself (viii. 34 = Mt. xvi. 24); ἀρνέομαι is much more common (*vv.* 68, 70; etc.).

31. ἐκπερισσῶς ἐλάλει. Peter is not silenced, but continues (imperf.) to protest vehemently (ἐκπ. here only in N.T.) that not even the fear of death would induce him to deny his Master. In his vehemence he does not see that he is charging Christ with uttering false predictions.

πάντες ἔλεγον. Here again the imperf. is in place; one after another they echoed Peter's protestations. As often, Mt. prefers an aor. Neither Lk. nor Jn mentions this.

32—42. The Agony in Gethsemane.

Mt. xxvi. 36—46. Lk. xxii. 40—46. Cf. Jn xviii. 1.

32. Γεθσημανεί. Only Mk, followed by Mt., gives the name, which may mean "oil-press." They call it a χωρίον, a "piece of ground" or an "estate." Lk. and Jn use the still more indefinite τόπος, Jn adding that there was a garden there. We are in doubt as to whether Gethsemane was the garden or was next to it; also whether the traditional site is the true one. It has been regarded as the site since the Empress Helena visited Jerusalem, A.D. 326; but trustworthy information may have perished long before that. Josephus says that Titus cut down all trees on that side of the city (*B. J.* vi. i. 1). This would obliterate traces, and there were no Christians left to keep a true tradition. Lk. says that Christ went thither "according to His custom," and Jn says that He "often" resorted there. By going elsewhere, Christ might have baffled Judas; but Judas was now allowed to know where to find Him.

Καθίσατε ὧδε. This is spoken to the eight who are left near the entrance. Lk., who omits the separation of the three from the eight, says that He at once told the disciples to pray. His Gospel in a special sense is the Gospel of Prayer.

ἕως προσεύξωμαι. *Until I have prayed.* Cf. Lk. xii. 59, xv. 4, xvii. 8, xxii. 34; Jas. v. 7. There is not much difference in meaning between this and "while I pray" (A.V., R.V.), but similar constructions should be treated alike. Vulg. has *donec orem*; Beza, *usque dum precatus fuero.* The omission of ἄν in such cases is freq. in papyri. J. H. Moulton, p. 168.

33. παραλαμβάνει. Cf. v. 40, ix. 2. At other times we find Jesus seeking solitude for prayer (i. 35, vi. 46), but in this great crisis He desires sympathy, and He selects those who will be least likely to misunderstand His intense distress. His selecting these three once more would surprise neither them nor the rest. The view that the "young man" of *v.* 51 was already in the garden, and was a witness of the Agony, seeing much which the three lost while they were slumbering, cannot be regarded as probable. It was probably the march of the band coming to capture Jesus that woke him and drew him to the spot.

ἤρξατο ἐκθαμβεῖσθαι. The ἤρξατο is not *otiose*; He has a new experience in emotional suffering—mingled amazement and terror. Cf. ix. 15, xvi. 5, 6. Mt., as often, shrinks from attributing purely human feelings to Christ. Under the sanction of his own περίλυπος, he substitutes λυπεῖσθαι.

ἀδημονεῖν. Mt. retains this as covered by περίλυπος. The word is not in LXX., and only once again in N.T., Phil. ii. 26, where see Lightfoot. The derivation is uncertain, but the word seems to imply distress and dismay.

34. Περίλυπός ἐστιν ἡ ψυχή μου. The reality of Christ's humanity is again evident; it shrinks from the Cross. Mention of His ψυχή is rare, and that fact may warn us not to be curious in attempting to pry into "the Self-consciousness" of Christ. We know very little about it. See on Jn xi. 33, xii. 27.

ἕως θανάτου. Cf. 1 Kings xix. 4; Jonah iv. 9.

μείνατε ὧδε καὶ γρηγορεῖτε. The change of tense is intelligible. They were at once to cease from accompanying Him, and were to continue to be watchful. Once more they were selected as witnesses. They had seen Him wresting a victim from death; they had seen Him in the glory of the Transfiguration; and now they were to see Him in the humiliation of His Agony. Syr-Sin. omits the charge. Mt. adds μετ' ἐμοῦ.

35. προελθὼν μικρόν. See crit. note. "About a stone's cast" (Lk.). They could not only see but hear.

ἔπιπτεν...προσηύχετο. Here Mt. does well in changing the first imperf. to aor., and inferior texts have ἔπεσεν in Mk. The prayer continued after the fall.

παρέλθῃ ἀπ' αὐτοῦ ἡ ὥρα. Mk only. The *hora fatalis* (*v.* 41; Jn vii. 30, xii. 27, etc.) is meant.

36. καὶ ἔλεγεν. Here again, as in the Institution of the Eucharist, there is remarkable difference as to the words used; see on *v.* 22. Lk. gives only one prayer. Mk gives two and says that the second was the same as the first. Mt. gives three, the second differing from the first, but the third the same as the second. There is substantial agreement between all three as to the wording of the first prayer.

Ἀββᾶ ὁ πατήρ. As in *v.* 41 and vii. 34, Mk gives the Aramaic. Christ spoke both Aramaic and Greek, and it is not improbable that

in the opening address He used first one language and then the other.
Repetition, whether in one language or two, is the outcome of strong
feeling and is impressive ; Martha, Martha (Lk. x. 41), Simon, Simon
(Lk. xxii. 31), Jerusalem, Jerusalem (Mt. xxiii. 37). This is much
more probable than that ὁ πατήρ is Mk's translation of Ἀββᾶ.
Translation injected into such a prayer would be unnatural. But it
is possible that Mk here attributes to Christ a form of address which
had become usual in public worship. Nom. with art. instead of voc.
is freq. in N.T. ; see on v. 8. Lk. has πάτερ, Mt. πάτερ μου. See on
Gal. iv. 6.

πάντα δυνατά σοι. See on x. 27. Mt. softens this to εἰ δυνατόν
ἐστιν, Lk. to εἰ βούλει.

παρένεγκε. "Carry past, without causing Me to drink, this cup
of suffering and death." In class. Grk the words would mean,
"Place this cup at my side" (Hdt. i. 119, 133 ; Plato, *Rep.* p. 354) ;
but in Plutarch the verb is used in the sense of removing (*Camill.* 41).
In Heb. xiii. 9 and Jude 12 it is used of being swept out of one's
course and carried astray. *Orat transire calicem, ut ostendat vere quod
et homo erat* (Bede). The view that our Lord's Agony was nothing
but His sorrow for the sins of men is not found in the Gospels. The
metaphor of a cup is used in O.T. of both good and bad fortune
(Ps. xvi. 5, xxiii. 5; Jer. xxv. 15; Is. li. 17; etc.). In N.T. it is
specially used of Christ's sufferings (x. 38, 39 ; Jn xviii. 11).

ἀλλ' οὐ τί ἐγὼ θέλω. Lk. has his favourite πλήν and brings the
wording closer to that of the Lord's Prayer ; πλὴν μὴ τὸ θέλημά μου
ἀλλὰ τὸ σὸν γινέσθω. With this condition it is lawful to pray, as for
other temporal blessings, so also for the removal of suffering. Which-
ever wording we adopt, the petition is proof of the existence in Christ
of a human will, distinct from, but always submissive to, the Father's
will. Mackintosh, *The Person of Jesus Christ*, pp. 220—222, 294—
299, 399. Note the οὐ, not μή, the effect of which is "But I am not
asking," or "But the question is not."

37. εὑρίσκει. As in the case of the braggart fig-tree (xi. 13), He
discovers the fact by coming and seeing ; and what He sees evokes an
expression of surprise and disappointment. But the reality of His
human nature is here most conspicuous in His prayers.

οὐκ ἴσχυσας. *Hadst thou not strength?* "Was thy will not
strong enough to comply with My request during a single hour?"
This shows that Christ's prayer had lasted a considerable time ; they
had heard some of it, and then had fallen asleep—"for sorrow," as
Lk. in extenuation states. As on the Mount of Transfiguration,
physical weariness had conquered, and He treads the winepress alone

(Is. lxiii. 3). The reproach is addressed to Peter the boaster, who had promised to die with Him, if need be (vv. 29, 31), and the old name "Simon" is used here, as in Jn xxi. 7, perhaps to suggest that he was not acting in accordance with the new name, or to remind him of the time when he was called.

38. προσεύχεσθε ἵνα μή. Change from sing. to plur. Pres. imperat. of continuous prayer, and ἵνα μή is *that...not* (R.V.) rather than "lest" (A.V.). Here all three agree, and the words which follow again recall the Lord's Prayer. But no Gospel, either here or elsewhere, states that Christ charged the disciples to pray for *Him*. They are to pray for themselves in their πειρασμοί, as He prays for Himself in His. But He prays for them also and for others (Jn xvii. 8, 15, 20). The contrast between Christ's praying in His temptation and the disciples' prayerless self-confidence (v. 31), and subsequent slumber, is great.

πειρασμόν. The word occurs nowhere else in Mk, and nowhere at all in Jn. It is perhaps true that in N.T. πειρασμοί generally means trials sent by God rather than temptations sent by the evil one, but here the latter sense prevails. See Hort on 1 Pet. i. 6.

τὸ μὲν πνεῦμα πρόθυμον. This is quoted in the Ep. of Polycarp 7 as a Saying of Christ, see on ix. 35. Owing to Christ's training of the disciples, their spiritual nature was ready to respond to Divine calls, but the weakness which is inherent in man's lower nature still sometimes prevented the responsiveness from taking effect. *Quantum de ardore mentis confidimus, tantum de carnis fragilitate timeamus* (Bede). Human action requires the co-operation of spirit and flesh, and the flesh is often a clog to good action, or even an opponent to it (1 Pet. ii. 11; cf. Rom. vi. 19, viii. 3, 9). When the flesh is regarded as a successful opponent of the spirit, it may be said to be strong rather than weak. All depends upon the point of view.

39. τὸν αὐτὸν λόγον εἰπών. "Saying the same *words*" (A.V., R.V.) is a little too definite; it means "speaking to the same effect." The statement would be quite true if He made the same petition in different words, as reported by Mt.

40. εὗρεν. As in v. 37. This and οὐκ ἤδεισαν are the two main verbs, ἦσαν γάρ being a parenthesis.

οὐκ ἤδεισαν τί ἀποκριθῶσιν. Again a parallel with the Transfiguration; see on ix. 6. After their boasting (v. 31), they had no excuse to offer for their failing to watch.

41. ἔρχεται τὸ τρίτον. Mk omits the third going away and the third prayer. Cf. 2 Cor. xii. 8; Num. xxiv. 10; 1 Sam. iii. 8.

Καθεύδετε τὸ λοιπόν. The first reproaches (v. 37) were questions;

the form of the second is not recorded. This may be a question. "Are ye going to sleep on and take your rest?" "Is it quite impossible to induce you to watch and pray?" Syr-Sin. omits τὸ λοιπόν, which, however, is no obstacle to making the sentence interrogative. Even if "Sleep on now and take your rest" be understood as mournful irony rather than a conceded permission, it does not fit on well with the words which immediately follow.

ἀπέχει. Mk only. In papyri we find ἀπέχω used by persons who receive money and give a receipt. Deissmann, *Bib. St.* p. 229. Possibly the impersonal ἀπέχει would mean "settled," "the transaction is at an end." The traditional rendering "Enough," *Sufficit*, seems to be right, however that meaning may be reached. The Old Latin renderings differ considerably, but they point to some such signification as "the consummation is here," "the hour is come." The exclamation may have been preceded by an interval of some duration. See Field, p. 39.

παραδίδοται. *Is being delivered up into the hands of sinners.* See on ix. 31, x. 33.

42. ἐγείρεσθε. The disciples are still on the ground.

ἄγωμεν. Cf. i. 38. *Let us be going,* not to escape, but to meet the traitor (Jn xviii. 4). "At the fitting time He did not prevent Himself from falling into the hands of men" (Orig. *Cels.* ii. 10).

ὁ παραδιδούς. So also in Jn. Peter and John knew who he was (Jn xiii. 23—26). The multitude to which Judas was acting as guide was now within hearing and perhaps within sight. Cf. i. 14.

43—50. THE TRAITOR'S KISS AND THE ARREST OF JESUS.

Mt. xxvii. 47—56.　Lk. xxii. 47—53.　Jn xviii. 2—12.

43. εὐθύς...παραγίνεται. These words are peculiar to Mk, and εὐθύς is doubly characteristic; in itself and in being superfluous; cf. vi. 25. Nowhere else does Mk use παραγίνομαι, which is very freq. in Lk. and Acts.

ἔτι αὐτοῦ λαλοῦντος...Ἰούδας εἷς τῶν δώδεκα. These words are in all three. Cf. v. 35; Mt. xii. 46; Lk. viii. 49; also xiv. 10; Mt. xxvi. 14. Jn says εἷς ἐκ τῶν δώδεκα (vi. 71, xx. 24). Judas and Jesus are the only persons named in this section, and Judas is named without any epithet of abhorrence; to call him "one of the Twelve" is enough. The narrative is quite passionless.

παρὰ τῶν ἀρχ. κ.τ.λ. The three sections of the Sanhedrin are again clearly marked by separate articles; see on viii. 31. The ὄχλος would be composed of those who approved of the arrest, and they had taken any weapons that were ready to their hands. The Sanhedrin would take care that the Galilean pilgrims were not informed of their plans. Nothing is told us of the eight disciples who had been left near the entrance. Judas would have to pass them.

44. δεδώκει. No augment, as often (xv. 7, 10, xvi. 9; Lk. vi. 48, etc.). The omission is not rare in class. Grk, partly for convenience, but chiefly for sound. It is most freq. in compounds.

ὁ παραδιδούς. *He who was betraying Him.*

σύσσημον. A sign previously arranged, a concerted signal or *token* (A.V., R.V.); more definite than σημεῖον (xiii. 4), which Mt. has here. The word occurs nowhere else in N.T. and is rare in LXX. The Sanhedrin did not wish to be embarrassed by arresting disciples, who would have little influence without their Master (v. 27), and hence the necessity for a token by which He could be distinguished from them. Jn omits it; see on Jn xviii. 5. The reports of so exciting a scene, with such rapid action and in imperfect light, would be sure to differ considerably. But it is not likely that the kiss is a fiction. Few details in history have made such an impression on men's minds.

φιλήσω. The meaning "kiss" is common in class. Grk and in LXX., but in N.T. it is used only of Judas; φίλημα is used of the "kiss of peace" in Paul and 1 Peter.

αὐτός ἐστιν. *He is the man.* Cf. Lk. xxiv. 21.

κρατήσατε αὐτόν. See on iii. 21, vi. 17.

ἀπάγετε ἀσφαλῶς. Cf. v. 53, xv. 16; Acts xii. 19. Ἀπάγω frequently has the meaning of "arrest," "take before a tribunal," "put in prison" (Hdt. Plat. Dem. and also in papyri). For his own sake Judas would be anxious that there should be no failure; he could never face the Master again. Moreover he knew that Jesus possessed mysterious powers, and that hitherto he had always escaped; iii. 6, xi. 18; Lk. iv. 30; Jn vii. 44, 45, viii. 59, x. 39, xi. 53, 57, xii. 19. That Judas had warned the men whom he led of Christ's supernatural power is not probable; but there was the possibility of rescue. Latin versions differ widely in their rendering of ἀσφαλῶς: *caute* (Vulg.), *firmissime* (f), *diligenter* (d), *cum omni sollicitudine* and *cum monitione* (some MSS. of Vulg.). Nearly all have *ducite*, but more accurately *abducite* (q).

45. ἐλθών...προσελθών. Characteristic combination of participles; cf. i. 31, 41. But, though the expression is clumsy, it is intelligible and graphic. Judas arrives, recognizes Jesus, and at once comes up to Him.

εὐθύς. Mt. adopts this and it is by no means superfluous. Judas allows no delay to give a chance of escape, and he is anxious to get his own share in the matter over. See crit. note.

κατεφίλησεν. The change from φιλήσω (v. 44) to the compound seems to show that καταφιλέω here has its classical force of kissing affectionately. Often in Xen. it has this meaning and always in N.T. (Lk. vii. 38, 45, xv. 20; Acts xx. 37). In LXX. it is perhaps too freq. to be always understood in this sense. See on x. 16. That the kiss of Judas was a very demonstrative one seems to be the meaning of Mk and Mt., and there may have been an embrace to prevent movement. Lk. appears to shrink from recording the actual kiss, but he records Christ's rebuke to Judas for this monstrous form of treachery, and his record of what Christ said differs strangely from that of Mt. Mk records no rebuke, and he does not mention Judas again. The narrative in Jn, without being contradictory, is utterly different, and we cannot put the accounts together in proper order. As remarked before, impressions as to what took place would differ even among those who were present, and tradition would introduce other differences.

46. ἐπέβαλαν τὰς χεῖρας. This is the commonest use of ἐπιβάλλω in N.T. Cf. Lk. xx. 19, xxi. 12; Jn vii. 30, 44, etc. Note the 2nd aor. with 1st aor. termination (אB) and see on εἴδαμεν, ii. 12.

47. εἶς δέ τις. Both Mk and Lk. have τις, but Mt. omits it. It suggests that the writer could name the εἶς, if he thought it wise to do so. Here, as in the cases of Mary anointing Christ, and of Judas murmuring at her, the later records are more definite than the earlier. Mk says that this assault was committed by a certain person, Mt. and Lk. that it was done by one of Christ's followers, Jn that it was the act of Simon Peter. After Peter's death, and long after the event, no harm would be done in giving the name. Jn alone gives the name Malchus; as an acquaintance of the high-priest (Jn xviii. 15) he would know his slave's name. Malchus may have been the first to lay hands on Jesus, and hence Peter's impulsive attack on him. Peter's mingled affection and self-confidence are again conspicuous. He does not think of the risk to himself, nor does he stop to consider what good it would do to wound one man, and him a mere subordinate. His μάχαιρα was probably a large knife rather than a sword; there were two such weapons in the party (Lk. xxii. 38).

ἀφεῖλεν. *Took off.* In no other connexion is ἀφαιρέω used in N.T. of physical sundering; but cf. Gen. xl. 19; Exod. xxix. 27; 1 Sam. xvii. 46, etc. Both Lk. and Jn specify the *right* ear, a very rare instance of agreement between Lk. and Jn in narrative, as distinct from Mk and Mt. Mt. alone records Christ's rebuke to Peter, and Lk. alone records the healing of the ear. In some cases diminutives retain their force in N.T., *e.g.* πλοιάριον (iii. 9), κυνάρια (vii. 27); but here ὠτάριον (Mk, Jn) and ὠτίον (Mt.) = οὖς (Lk.).

48. ἀποκριθείς. He answers their action, their manner of arresting Him, as if He were a dangerous bandit; see on ix. 5 and xi. 14. This remonstrance is the same in all three; Jn omits it.

ἐξήλθατε. See on ἐπέβαλαν, *v.* 46.

συλλαβεῖν. *To arrest*; Lk. xxii. 54; Jn xviii. 12; Acts i. 16, etc.

49. καθ᾽ ἡμέραν...ἐν τῷ ἱερῷ. The words are in all three, and they cause no difficulty, even if none of those who had heard Him teach were present in Gethsemane. Those who had ordered His arrest knew that every day, in a most public place, He was to be found. The allusion is probably to the last few days, not to the earlier teaching in Jerusalem.

ἤμην. This is the usual form of the 1st pers. imperf. in N.T. (Mt. xxv. 35; Jn xi. 15; Acts x. 30, etc.).

πρὸς ὑμᾶς. Lk. has μεθ᾽ ὑμῶν, but πρός *c.* acc. indicates not merely proximity or accompaniment, but intercourse; see on Jn i. 1 and 1 Jn i. 2.

ἀλλ᾽ ἵνα. Something is understood; "but *you did not arrest Me then*, in order that." Mt. supplies *all this has come to pass.* See on Jn ix. 3 and 1 Jn ii. 19.

αἱ γραφαί. See on xii. 10, 24. In Jn it is always ἵνα ἡ γραφὴ πλ. (xiii. 18, xvii. 12, xix. 24, 36).

50. ἔφυγον πάντες. See crit. note. The πάντες comes at the end with emphasis; *and they forsook Him and fled—all of them.* Peter, after striking one useless blow, flees with the rest; cf. *vv.* 27, 29. It was evident that He was not going to use His miraculous power to prove His Messiahship, and they left Him to the fate which He had often foretold.

51. καὶ νεανίσκος τις. See crit. note. This strange incident has so little to do with the narrative, and is so out of harmony with the tone of it, that we wonder why it was inserted. It cannot be part of Peter's reminiscences, for he had fled before it occurred, and he would not regard the matter as instructive. It can hardly be part of the story which he habitually told, and it would not be likely to be part of the primitive tradition. The patristic guess that the young man was St John is excluded by the fact that he had already fled. James, the Lord's brother, is less improbable, but has little to recommend it. Much more probably the young man was the Evangelist himself. This hypothesis gives an adequate reason for the insertion of the incident. The matter was of intense interest to him, and some who read his Gospel would know who was meant. He does not give his name, for he does not wish to pose as the one adherent of Jesus who did not fly until an attempt was made to arrest him. If the Evangelist was the son of "the goodman" in whose house the Paschal meal was celebrated (see on *v.* 14), then his appearance at this crisis is intelligible. The house was near Gethsemane, and the noise and lights of the band led by Judas may have awakened Mark, who—taking the first thing that came to hand as a covering—ran out to see what was happening. As his father knew Jesus (*v.* 14) and was perhaps a disciple, Mark would be greatly interested, even if he were not himself a disciple. All this hangs together very well, but the evidence for it is slender. The suggestion that the incident is given as a specimen of the animosity of Christ's foes against anyone who seemed to sympathize with Him, is not very convincing. As in the case of "the father of Alexander and Rufus" (xv. 21), the Evangelist seems to assume that some of his readers will know who is meant; but it is the interest to himself that causes the adventure of the young man to be recorded. Zahn, *Introd. to N.T.* II. p. 494; Mk "paints a small picture of himself in the corner of his work."

σινδόνα. This may mean either an article of clothing or a coverlet caught up to serve as clothing. Of the perfect housewife (Prov. xxxi. 24) it is said σινδόνας ἐποίησεν καὶ ἀπέδοτο, which Toy explains as "probably a square piece of cloth that could be used as an outer garment or as a night-dress"; and Moore thinks that the 30 linen garments which Samson wagered (Judg. xiv. 12) were "rectangular pieces of fine and therefore costly linen stuff, which might be worn as an outer garment, or as a night-wrapper." The Talmud says that such a piece of linen might be used as a curtain or a shroud. We may conjecture with Bengel that a young man who had a σινδών as a wrapper came from a well-to-do household. Cf. Acts xii. 8.

52. καταλιπών. Often used of leaving behind (xii. 19, 21), or abandoning completely (x. 7; Lk. v. 28). In N.T. this compound is far more freq. than λείπω. All these minute details show that, if Mk is not giving his own experiences, he has got information from one who was there. That Mt. and Lk. should omit this incident is natural. That a later editor has inserted it in Mk is very improbable. What would be the object of such insertion? If the young man was Mark, or some one whom he knew very well, we have a reasonable explanation of its presence in this Gospel.

53—65. The Trial before the High-Priest.

Mt. xxvi. 57—68.   Lk. xxii. 63—71.   Cf. Jn xviii. 12—14, 19—24.

53. πρὸς τὸν ἀρχιερέα. Caiaphas, as Mt. states. Neither Mk
nor Mt. mentions Annas, and Mk never *names* Caiaphas, but presum-
ably in Mk "the high-priest" always means Caiaphas. Jn says that
they took Jesus to Annas first. He had been high-priest A.D. 7—14,
and had been deposed by Valerius Gratus, Pilate's predecessor. But
probably some Jews regarded him as the true high-priest, although
his son-in-law Caiaphas acted as high-priest A.D. 18—36. They seem
to have lived together in the same palace. See on Jn xviii. 13.

συνέρχονται. The Sanhedrin, with its three component sections,
is ready to meet at once; and the three sections are mentioned
separately, as if to show how representative the assembly was, and
how widely spread was the responsibility. Late as the hour is, the
witnesses are ready also. All has been carefully prepared. The
Synoptists distinguish two ecclesiastical trials, an informal one during
the night, when the chief business was transacted, and a formal one
by daylight to confirm the proceedings. Nothing done in the night
was valid.

54. ὁ Πέτρος ἀπὸ μακρόθεν ἠκολούθησεν. When the first panic
was over, Peter's affection re-asserted itself; and perhaps there was
some shame at this pitiful result of his self confident professions; but
his fears keep him at a distance. All three have μακρόθεν, but Mk
alone has the superfluous ἀπό (v. 6, viii. 3, xi. 13), and here it is Mt.
who has the imperf., while Mk has the less accurate aor. After Jesus
had been taken inside the palace, Peter, with the help of a disciple
who was probably St John (see on Jn xviii. 15), obtained admission
to the αὐλή, *atrium*, or open court, from which the room in which
the Sanhedrin was sitting could be seen. There he sat with the
Levitical guard, warming himself. Jerusalem is 2500 feet above the
sea, and the nights in spring are cold. The superfluous εἰς—ἕως ἔσω
εἰς— is in Mk only. That it was Judas who got Peter admitted is
incredible.

πρὸς τὸ φῶς. Both Mk and Lk. notice this. His care for his
comfort was fatal; the firelight caused him to be recognized. Xeno-
phon uses φῶς in the sense of fire (πῦρ). Syr-Sin. omits the words.

55. ἐζήτουν...οὐχ εὕρισκον. Their failure to get evidence on
which He could be condemned to death was as continuous as their
seeking for it. Ecclesiastical tribunals have often been prone to
decide first and then seek for evidence to justify the decision.

56. ἴσαι...οὐκ ἦσαν. *Agreed not together;* cf. Deut. xvii. 6, xix.
15; Num. xxxv. 30. The words might mean "were not just and
impartial," but hardly "were not adequate," which would rather be
ἱκαναί (Plato, *Sym.* 179 B, *Hip. Mi.* 369 c).

57. ἐψευδομαρτύρουν. This repetition is in Mk only. Syr-Sin.
omits.

58. Ἡμεῖς ἠκούσαμεν αὐτοῦ. *We ourselves heard Him.* This
characteristic fulness is again peculiar to Mk. The report of the
words is in Mt. different and shorter; "*I am able* to destroy the
temple *of God,* and *to* build it in three days.*" How far the report of
what the witnesses said has been influenced by the recollection of
what Christ actually said, or by the interpretation of what He said, it
is impossible to determine. It is not incredible that Christ's remarkable utterance made two years before (Jn ii. 19) was remembered,
and was now brought up against Him in a perverted form. Of course
Christ had not said that He would destroy the Temple. On the other
hand it is possible that He had said something similar recently. His
prediction of the destruction of the Temple (xiii. 2) may have become
known, and to a Jew that would seem to be blasphemy, for the
Temple was the token of the Presence of God. Cf. Rev. xi. 1, 2.
They did not see that in killing the Messiah they doomed the Temple
to destruction. Cf. Acts vi. 14, where Stephen's saying on the
subject is quoted against him. For διὰ τριῶν see on ii. 1, and for
ἀχειροποίητον see on 2 Cor. v. 1.

59. οὐδὲ οὕτως. Mk only. Mt. regards the statement that they
were false witnesses as sufficient. Mk states with satisfaction that
even about this definite charge their statements did not tally. According to Jn ii. 19 Jesus had said "Destroy...and I will raise."

60. Οὐκ ἀποκρίνῃ οὐδέν; This is a separate question (A.V., R.V.).
Vulg. runs the two questions into one; *Non respondes quicquam ad
ea quae tibi objiciuntur ab his?* The Greek in Mt. is the same,
with the omission of one negative, but there Vulg. has *Nihil respondes
ad ea quae isti adversum te testificantur?* Both these translations
treat τί as if it were πρὸς ἅ. We might take τί as ὅ τι, "nothing as to
that which"; but the two questions are more terse and more in Mk's
style. The double negative is in Mk's style; see on *v.* 25.

τί οὗτοί σου κ.; "What explanation is there of all this testimony
against Thee?" The high-priest adopts this paternal tone in order
to get evidence from Christ Himself which they had failed to get from
their witnesses. Syr-Sin. make this a separate question, as also does
Victor.

61. ἐσιώπα καὶ οὐκ ἀπεκρίνατο οὐδέν. So אBCL 33. Again
the double negative and superfluous fulness; Mt. has ἐσιώπα only.

Euthymius gives two reasons for the silence; βλέπων μὲν καὶ τὸ δικαστή-
ριον παράνομον, εἰδὼς δὲ καὶ ὅτι μάτην ἀποκρινεῖται παρὰ τοιούτοις.
With regard to the first, the Sanhedrin had no right to make Him
a prisoner, no right to hold a nocturnal sitting, no right to use false
witnesses in support of an iniquitous prejudgment. Moreover, by
declaring their inability to decide whether the Baptist had a Divine
commission, they had abdicated. There was nothing for Him to reply
to, for all evidence against Him had broken down. All three Gospels
have ἀπεκρίνατο (Mt. xxvii. 12; Lk. xxiii. 9). The aor. mid. is rare
both in LXX. and N.T. (Lk. iii. 16; Jn v. 17, 19, but not xii. 23;
Acts iii. 12).

πάλιν...ἐπηρώτα. This does not mean that the high-priest repeated his question, but that he made another appeal. The appeal is
quite a new one. Jesus had accepted the acclamations of those who
hailed Him as "He that cometh" and as "the Son of David." Did
He Himself claim to be the Messiah? the Son of the Blessed? The
latter expression would be used in order to avoid using the Divine
Name. Mt. substitutes "the Son of *God*," having stated that
Caiaphas put this question with a solemn adjuration, Ἐξορκίζω σε
κατὰ τοῦ Θεοῦ τοῦ ζῶντος. After such words there was no point in
avoiding the Divine Name. Jewish thought had by no means always
identified the Messiah with the Son of God. But it was sometimes
done; *e.g.* Enoch cv. 2; 2 Esdr. vii. 28, 29, xiv. 9; and Caiaphas
would know this. For the Sanhedrin's purpose it was much more
important that Jesus should be got to claim the latter title. The
populace had not hailed Him as the Son of God; if He could be led
to say that He was the Son of God, a charge of blasphemy could be
established. Elsewhere in N.T. εὐλογητός is a predicate of ὁ Θεός in
doxologies.

62. Ἐγώ εἰμι. Jesus admits the right of the high-priest to ask
this question and replies at once. For the first time in this Gospel
He publicly declares in full and solemn language Who He is. The
reference to Dan. vii. 13 would be understood by those present. Mt.
gives the less definite reply Σὺ εἶπας, "That was *thy* saying," which
might be assent, or denial, or neutral, according to circumstances.
Cf. xv. 2. Here what follows shows that, if Σὺ εἶπας was the expression used, it was equivalent to Ἐγώ εἰμι.

τὸν υἱὸν...τῆς δυνάμεως. These words are in all three. They tell
the Sanhedrin that a day will come when the positions will be reversed
and He will be passing sentence on them (Rev. i. 7). In τῆς δυνάμεως
we have another substitute for the Divine Name. Dalman, *Words*,
pp. 200, 306—308.

μετὰ τῶν νεφελῶν. See on xiii. 24, 26. The clouds are doubtless symbolical. Such symbolism was part of the mental furniture of a Jew, although some Jews may have understood the symbols literally.

Early in the Ministry Christ had begun to give a partial revelation of His Messianic character by calling Himself "the Son of Man"; He had given clearer intimations in private to the Twelve; He had accepted Peter's confession of His Messiahship; He had refused to rebuke those who had publicly proclaimed Him as the Messianic King at the triumphal entry; and now before the Sanhedrin and before Pilate He acknowledges His full right to the title. To Pilate He explains that He is no earthly king, no rival of the Emperor. No explanation of His Kingship or of His Sonship is given to the hierarchy. They knew the import of His words, as the action of the high-priest shows.

63. διαρήξας τοὺς χιτῶνας. In this he was doing no more than duty required. The high-priest was forbidden to rend his clothes for his own misfortunes (Lev. x. 6, xxi. 10), but, when acting officially, he was bound to do so as a protest against any expression that was regarded as blasphemous, and the Talmud prescribes the exact way in which it was to be done. Originally a spontaneous way of expressing grief, perhaps much older than Judaism, it ended in becoming even more formal than our wearing of black or the duration of court mourning. The LXX. expression is διαρ. τὰ ἱμάτια, but τοὺς χιτῶνας occurs in the captains' lamentations for the death of Holofernes (Judith xiv. 19), and in the Ep. Jer. 31 the idolatrous priests are described as having τοὺς χιτῶνας διερρωγότας. Apparently Caiaphas acted in accordance with rule. It was the under-garments which had to be torn. This punctilious observance of ceremonial detail (cf. Jn xviii. 28), accompanied by gross violation of important regulations and of clear principles of justice, was very characteristic. Christ ought to have been arrested before sunset and by the witnesses, and there seem to have been other violations of established rules (Brodrick, *The Trial and Crucifixion of Jesus Christ*, pp. 30, 65).

Τί ἔτι χρείαν ἔχομεν μαρτύρων; The question reveals that they had been seeking witnesses for the purpose of condemning Him, and the satisfaction of the conspirator is apparent through the distress of the official. What the court must regard as a blasphemous utterance shocked the high-priest, but such an utterance was exactly what he and the other Sanhedrists were desiring to elicit. Cf. Plato *Rep.* 340 A, καὶ τί, ἔφη, δεῖται μάρτυρος; αὐτὸς γὰρ ὁ Θρασύμαχος ὁμολογεῖ.

64. ἠκούσατε τῆς βλασφημίας. The sentence may be interroga-

tive (WH.), but more probably it is categorical (A.V., R.V.), and we may keep the aor. in English; *Ye heard the blasphemy.* The thing heard is rarely in the gen., and here Mt. has the acc. Cf. Lk. xv. 25.

τί ὑμῖν φαίνεται; *What do you think of it?* This might mean, "Do you regard His utterance as blasphemous?" But it probably meant, "What treatment ought to be His?" The blasphemy was assumed.

οἱ δὲ πάντες. The πάντες may be exact. It is not likely that Joseph of Arimathaea (Lk. xxiii. 51) or Nicodemus (Jn vii. 50, xix. 39) was present at this nocturnal meeting; but Mt. omits the doubtful πάντες.

ἔνοχον εἶναι θανάτου. This is certainly accurate. They could decide that He was *worthy* of death; but, the sitting being illegal, the Sanhedrin had no power to pronounce any sentence. That was done later, after daybreak.

65. ἤρξαντό τινες ἐμπτύειν. The τινες, in contrast with the preceding πάντες, must mean some members of the Sanhedrin. That Roman soldiers should be guilty of such brutality (xv. 19) is not wonderful; but that members of the supreme court should exhibit their malignity in this way shows the temper in which they had come to judge their Prisoner. Christ had prophesied the spitting, but as done by the heathen (x. 34). Lk. records the prediction of the spitting (xviii. 32), but not the fulfilment of it. The more classical καταπτύω does not occur in N.T. or LXX. The covering of the face has no connexion with the Roman custom of covering the head of a criminal before crucifixion. Cic. *Pro Rabir.* iv. 13, v. 16. Syr-Sin. omits the covering. Κολαφίζω means "strike with the fist" (1 Cor. iv. 11; 2 Cor. xii. 7, where see note; 1 Pet. ii. 20).

Προφήτευσον. This might have come immediately after the covering of the face; even then the meaning would not have been quite obvious. Mt. gives it clearly. Jesus was challenged to declare by His Messianic power who His unseen assailant was.

οἱ ὑπηρέται. The underlings of the Sanhedrin, the Levitical guard. "Did strike Him with the palms of their hands" (A.V.) is certainly wrong as regards the verb. We must read ἔλαβον (see crit. note); *they caught Him.* The meaning of ῥαπίσμασιν is less certain. It may have its original meaning of blows with a rod, but it is more probable that the later meaning of slaps with the open hand is to be retained here. Cf. Is. l. 6. *They caught Him with blows* is a safe rendering, leaving it open whether the blows were inflicted with the hand or with rods. Κονδύλοις ἔλαβεν has been found in a papyrus of this period, and Wohlenberg illustrates the unusual form of expression from Cic. *Tusc.* ii. 14, *Spartae pueri ad aram verberibus accipiuntur.*

Euthymius remarks with what candour (φιλαληθῶς) and with what
freedom from partiality (ἀπαθῶς) the Evangelists narrate. No con-
cealment of the sins of Apostles, no exaltation of the Master, and no
abuse of His enemies.

66—72. Peter's Three Denials of His Master.

Mt. xxvi. 69—75.   Lk. xxii. 56—62.   Jn xviii. 17, 25—27.

66. μία τῶν παιδισκῶν. We have four accounts of the three
denials. They exhibit, what is frequently found in honest witnesses,
agreement in the main features combined with considerable difference
in the details. The four records may be reduced to three, for Mt. is
dependent on Mk. It is possible that Lk. is sometimes influenced by
Mk, but in this section Mk, Lk., and Jn may be regarded as three
independent witnesses. All four agree that the person who provoked
the first denial was a woman, but they do not agree as to what she
said, and they agree still less as to Peter's reply. This παιδίσκη was
a female slave in the high-priest's household. See notes on Jn xviii.
25—27. The second denial is given very briefly by all four; but the
first and third are reproduced with much fulness in Mk.

67. ἰδοῦσα...ἐμβλέψασα. Mk's common combination of participles; see on i. 15. Neither word is superfluous. She saw some
one with whom she was not familiar; and, after she had looked at
him steadily (viii. 25, x. 21, 27), she saw that he was the person
whom a disciple of Jesus had asked her to admit (Jn). Probably
Peter's manner betrayed disquietude and sympathy with the Prisoner
in the room overlooking the court.

Καὶ σύ. (Mt., Jn.) "Thou as well as the other whom I know."

τοῦ Ναζαρηνοῦ. Mk only (i. 24). The epithet is emphatic by
position and is spoken with contempt; see on Jn i. 47. Mt. has "the
Galilean," Lk. and Jn neither.

68. ἠρνήσατο. All three have this aor. and also the οὐκ οἶδα,
which Mk gives with characteristic fulness, Οὔτε οἶδα οὔτε ἐπίσταμαι
κ.τ.λ. This may be taken in three ways; "I neither know nor
understand what *thou* sayest" (R.V.); "I neither know Him nor
understand what *thou* sayest"; "I neither know nor understand.
What art *thou* saying?" (WH.). The second way has the advantage
of bringing out the difference between οἶδα and ἐπίσταμαι and thus
justifying the use of οὔτε...οὔτε: moreover Lk. supplies αὐτόν after
οἶδα. Here again (see on *v.* 30) Mt. takes one half, and Lk. the other
of Mk's full statement; οὐκ οἶδα αὐτόν (Lk.), οὐκ οἶδα τί λέγεις (Mt.).

εἰς τὸ προαύλιον. Here only in Bibl. Grk. *The vestibule* or
forecourt rather than "the porch" (A.V., R.V.). Mt. says "the

porch" (τὸν πυλῶνα), which would be near to the προαύλιον. Experience had shown that it was dangerous to stand in the light of the fire. That καὶ ἀλέκτωρ ἐφώνησεν is an interpolation may be regarded as certain, though R.V. admits the words. See crit. note.

69. ἡ παιδίσκη. Near the porch the portress would be likely to notice him again, and she began to point him out to the bystanders. Mt. assigns this act to a different woman, ἄλλη, while Lk. says that it was a man, ἕτερος, and that he addressed, not the bystanders, but Peter himself. Jn says that this second attack was addressed direct to Peter, εἶπον αὐτῷ, but he does not say by whom, and he states that it took place while Peter was warming himself by the fire. These divergences are of no importance; οὐ γὰρ ἐξηκρίβωται τοῦτο τῇ μνήμῃ τῶν γραψάντων (Victor). The main facts, that Peter was again assailed, and that he again denied, are given clearly by all. No doubt several people attacked him, while he shifted from one part of the courtyard to another.

70. πάλιν ἠρνεῖτο. Mk alone changes from aor. to imperf.; "he kept on denying." This almost implies that several persons had assailed him.

μετὰ μικρόν. Lk. says about an hour later.

οἱ παρεστῶτες ἔλεγον. The imperf. is accurate. Lk. assigns the third attack to ἄλλος τις, and Jn says that he was a kinsman of Malchus, and had seen Peter in the garden. All three Synoptists state that Peter was now recognized as a Galilean; little, however, is known about the Galilean dialect or pronunciation which betrayed him. Dalman, *Words*, p. 80; Schürer, *Jewish People*, II. i. p. 10.

καὶ γάρ. *And what is more*, introducing an additional reason for suspecting him. His dress may also have suggested Galilee.

71. ἀναθεματίζειν. Lk. and Jn omit the cursing and swearing. The cursing would mean that he declared himself to be anathema, if what he said was not true; cf. Acts xxiii. 12; Gal. i. 8, 9; 1 Cor. xvi. 22. Both the manner and the substance of his denial have increased. First he denied once that he was a follower of Jesus. Then he denied this several times. Now in very strong language he denies that he knows "this man of whom ye speak"; he cannot even now name the Master.

72. εὐθύς. So also Mt. and Jn, while Lk. has his favourite παραχρῆμα. See crit. note. All four notice how quickly the cock-crowing followed on the third denial. Mk alone has ἐκ δευτέρου, which אL omit, as אCD omit δίς in *v.* 30. Lk. alone records Christ's turning and looking at Peter; but all the Synoptists record that he remembered Christ's prediction of the three denials and that this made him weep.

ἀλέκτωρ ἐφώνησεν. *A cock crew.* None of the Gospels has the
definite art., which A.V. and R.V. everywhere insert.

τὸ ῥῆμα. As in ix. 32, this refers to a particular utterance. Jn
uses only the plur., but always of separate sayings; see on Jn iii. 34.

δὶς φωνῆσαι. See crit. note. It is remarkable that in the omission of δίς here and v. 30, and of ἐκ δευτέρου in v. 72, authorities vary:
א omits in all three places, C* omits δίς in both places, but not ἐκ
δευτέρου, L omits ἐκ δευτέρου, but not δίς in either place.

καὶ ἐπιβαλὼν ἔκλαιεν. We must be content to share the ignorance
of all the ages as to what Mk means by ἐπιβαλών. At an early period
(D, Latt. Syrr.) καὶ ἤρξατο κλαίειν was substituted for καὶ ἐπιβαλὼν
ἔκλαιεν. Euthymius regards ἐπιβαλών as meaning ἀρξάμενος, and
J. H. Moulton (p. 131) quotes a Ptolemaic papyrus as confirming this
—ἐπιβαλὼν συνέχωσεν τὰ ἐν τῇ ἑαυτοῦ γῇ μέρη, which he translates,
"he set to and dammed up." Lagrange points out that here the
meaning may rather be, "he threw on earth and made a dam."
Other unusual meanings for ἐπιβαλών are "in response to this," and
"with vehemence" (πικρῶς, Lk.). Neither is satisfactory. In iv. 37
we have τὰ κύματα ἐπέβαλλεν εἰς τὸ πλοῖον, but that hardly justifies
"flung himself into space" as the meaning of ἐπιβαλών. Nor is
"stopped suddenly," as if striking against an obstacle, more probable.
If we refuse to give any exceptional meaning to ἐπιβαλών, something
must be understood. Theophylact supplies τὸ ἱμάτιον. He explains
it by ἐπικαλυψάμενος τὴν κεφαλήν. Covering the head is sometimes an
expression of grief (2 Sam. xv. 30, xix. 4), and Field follows Salmasius
and C. F. A. Fritzsche in adopting this meaning. It is perhaps a little
less violent to supply τὴν διάνοιαν, "when he thought thereon, he
wept" (A.V., R.V.). But in all these cases closer parallels than those
which are put forward in justification are needed. The superiority of
ἔκλαιεν (Mk) to ἔκλαυσεν (Mt., Lk.) is evident. Jn, who greatly
abbreviates his friend's denials (οὐκ εἰμί, οὐκ εἰμί, πάλιν ἠρνήσατο),
omits the weeping; when he wrote, Peter's repentance and heroic
death were known in all the Churches.

It is possible to exaggerate Peter's baseness for the sake of pointing
a moral. His coming to the high-priest's palace, and being ready to
enter the court where the Levitical guard was in attendance, was
courageous. His remaining there after he had been repeatedly
charged with being an adherent of the Accused was still more
courageous. He must have known that he ran the risk of being
arrested for his violence in the garden, and for this he was prepared.
But he was not prepared for the awkward remark made by a woman.
The lie once told was persisted in, and he quickly went from bad to
worse.

CHAPTER XV.

1. ποιήσαντες (ABNXΓΔΠΨ) rather than ἑτοιμάσαντες (אCL).

3. אABCDLΓΠ omit αὐτὸς δὲ οὐδὲν ἀπεκρίνατο.

4. κατηγοροῦσιν (אBCDΨ) rather than καταμαρτυροῦσιν (AMNX ΓΔ).

6. ὃν παρῃτοῦντο (א*AB*Δ) rather than ὅνπερ ᾐτοῦντο (אᶜB³CNX ΓΠ). ῞Οσπερ occurs nowhere in N.T.

7. στασιαστῶν (אBCDKNΨ) rather than συνστασιαστῶν (AΔ).

8. ἀναβάς (אBD) rather than ἀναβοήσας (ACXΓΠ). אBΔ omit ἀεί.

12. אBCΔΨ omit θέλετε.

14. περισσῶς (אABCD) rather than περισσοτέρως (XΓ), which occurs nowhere in the Gospels.

20. τὰ ἱμάτια αὐτοῦ (BCΔΨ) rather than τ. ἱμ. τὰ ἴδια (ΛPXΓΠ). σταυρώσωσιν (אBXΓΠ) rather than σταυρώσουσιν (ACDLNΔ).

28. אABC*³DXΨ omit the verse, also k Syr-Sin. The.

33. καὶ γενομένης (אBDLΔΨ) rather than γεν. δέ (ACXΓΠ). See on i. 14.

34. For ἐγκατέλιπες, D has the surprising reading ὠνίδισας: d, however, has *dereliquisti*. But c has *exprobrasti*, i has *in opprobrium dedisti*, k* *maledixisti*. See Burkitt in *J.T.S.* i. p. 278; Nestle, p. 266.

39. אBLΨ omit κράξας after οὕτως.

40. אBL omit ἦν after ἐν αἷς.

41. אBΨ omit καί after αἵ, while ACLΔ retain καί and omit αἵ.

44. ἤδη ἀπέθανεν (BD) rather than πάλαι ἀπέθ. (אACL etc.). Change to avoid repetition.

45. πτῶμα (אBDL) rather than σῶμα (ACXΓΔΠΨ).

46. ἔθηκεν (אBC²DL) rather than κατέθηκεν (AC*MXΓΠ), the more usual verb.

47. τέθειται (אᶜABCDΔΠΨ 33) rather than τίθεται (MΓ).

1—15. THE TRIAL BEFORE THE PROCURATOR.

Mt. xxvii. 1—26. Lk. xxiii. 1—3, 18—25.
Jn xviii. 28—40, xix. 4—16.

1. εὐθὺς πρωΐ. *Directly it was morning*, *i.e.* as soon as it was lawful to transact business. They must get everything settled with Pilate before the Paschal Lambs were killed that afternoon. The real business was done at the nocturnal meeting, of which Mk and Mt. give a detailed account, and therefore describe the formal confirmation in the morning very briefly. Lk. records the later meeting only, and transfers to it features of the midnight sitting. Some items would have to be gone through twice. There is no exact parallel to εὐθὺς πρωΐ, but εὐθὺς τοῖς σάββασιν, "on the very first sabbath" (i. 21) is near it.

συμβούλιον ποιήσαντες. "Held a consultation" (A.V., R.V.) is very likely right, but συμβούλιον may mean the result of consultation, "a plan of action." Mt., as usual, has συμβ. ἔλαβον. See on iii. 6.

οἱ ἀρχιερεῖς. The three elements of the Sanhedrin are given, but differently from xiv. 53. With characteristic fulness (xiv. 58, 61, 68) Mk adds καὶ ὅλον τὸ συνέδριον, which Mt. omits as superfluous. Lk. has simply his characteristic words ἄπαν τὸ πλῆθος αὐτῶν.

δήσαντες. He had been bound in the garden (Jn xviii. 12, 24), and probably unbound in the high-priest's palace. It was important to show to Pilate that they regarded Him as dangerous, and it is said that binding intimated that He had been declared to be worthy of death.

παρέδωκαν Πειλάτῳ. Mk assumes that his readers know who Pilate was; he never calls him ὁ ἡγεμών. The Procurator had come from Caesarea, the Roman capital, to keep order during the Passover. He probably occupied Herod's palace, as Florus had previously done (Joseph. *B. J.* ii. xiv. 8, xv. 5). The hierarchy hand Jesus over to him to get their sentence of death confirmed; see on Jn xviii. 31. Pilate of course would not listen to a charge of blasphemy, so they accuse Him of being seditious, forbidding tribute to Tiberius, and assuming the title of "king." Pilate would not understand "Messiah," but "king of the Jews" would be intelligible enough. Pilate does not take their word for it; he begins to investigate the case himself; and here we may have much of the exact language used, for Pilate would converse with our Lord in Greek.

2. **Σὺ εἶ ὁ βασιλεὺς τῶν Ἰουδαίων;** The question is identical in all four. The Jews themselves say "King of Israel" (*v.* 32), but to Pilate they would say "King of the Jews." The σύ is emphatic and expressive of surprise; He certainly did not look like one who would claim kingly power. For ἀποκριθεὶς λέγει see on iii. 33 and viii. 29.

Σὺ λέγεις. Christ recognizes Pilate's authority and his right to ask, and His Σύ also is emphatic; "That is *thy* statement." Christ neither affirms nor denies it; He gives what Theophylact calls ἀμφίβολος ἀπόκρισις. He could not say that He was not King of the Jews; on the other hand He was not a king in Pilate's sense. But the reply is probably nearer to assent than to denial; see on xiv. 62. Σὺ λέγε s is in all three; not in Jn.

3. **κατηγόρουν...πολλά.** "Accused Him *of many things*" (R.V.), *in multis* (Vulg.), or *much*, the usual meaning in Mk. See on i. 45.

4. **ἐπηρώτα.** Probably the conversational imperf. See on v. 9. But Pilate may have asked the question several times.

Οὐκ ἀποκρίνῃ οὐδέν; See on xiv. 16.

πόσα. "What *grave* charges" may be meant as well as "how many."

5. **οὐκέτι οὐδέν.** Again a double negative; Lk. omits οὐκέτι. The accusations were false, like those before the Sanhedrin, and Christ did not reply to them in either case. The proceedings are more intelligible when we learn from Jn that in private Christ explained to Pilate that His Kingdom was not of this world. Pilate's questions He answers, but He makes no reply to the false statements of the Sanhedrin. Yet, without Jn, we should not understand why Pilate did not condemn Jesus when He did not clearly renounce all claim to be King of the Jews.

6. **κατὰ δὲ ἑορτήν.** Neither "at *that* Feast" (A.V.) nor "at *the* Feast" (R.V.) is quite accurate; it means *at festival-time*. *Singulis diebus festis* (k) is better than *per diem festum* (Vulg.).

ἀπέλυεν...παρῃτοῦντο. See crit. note. *He used to release*, and his releasing corresponded to their requesting; both were customary. Nothing is known of this custom beyond what is told us in the Gospels, but it is in accordance with Roman policy. At the *lectisternium* prisoners were sometimes released (Livy v. 13); but here only one prisoner, specially chosen by the people, can be set free. A papyrus of about A.D. 87, quoted by Lagrange (*ad loc.*) and by Milligan (*N.T. Documents*, p. 79), gives a nearer parallel. Phibion, guilty of violence, is brought before C. Septimius Vegetus, governor of Egypt, who says to him ἄξιος μὲν ἦς μαστιγωθῆναι...χαρίζομαι δέ σε τοῖς ὄχλοις. The mob did not wish Phibion to be scourged, and the governor "makes them a present of him."

7. ἦν δὲ ὁ λεγόμενος Βαραββᾶς. *Now there was the man called Barabbas*, a somewhat unusual expression; cf. Mt. xxvi. 14; Jn ix. 11. The name is probably a patronymic, Bar-Abba, "son of Abba," or "son of a father"; but it is not certain that Abba was used as a proper name so early as this. The interpretation "son of a Rabbi," διδασκάλου υἱός or *filius magistri*, is ancient, but it is not correct. Bar-Rabban would become Βαρραββάνας. It was inevitable that the choice between "a son of a father" and "the Son of the Father" should be pointed out. The remarkable reading which inserts "Jesus" before "Barabbas" in Mt. xxvii. 16, 17 is almost certainly a corruption. WH. *App.* p. 19.

τῶν στασιαστῶν. See crit. note. "The members of a faction, the revolutionaries." They are spoken of as notorious. The word occurs here only in Bibl. Grk. The classical form is στασιώτης.

οἵτινες. "Who were of such a character as to" (iv. 20, xii. 18). They were desperadoes.

πεποιήκεισαν. No augment, as usual; cf. *v.* 10, xiv. 44. In Deut. xxii. 8, φόνον ποιεῖν is used of causing death by omitting to put a parapet round one's roof. Excepting this verse, στάσις = "popular disturbance" is peculiar to Lk. and Acts; in Heb. ix. 8 it = "standing posture"; in LXX. it represents eight Hebrew words. Here Syr-Sin. has "had done wrong and committed murder."

8. ἀναβάς. It might be natural to speak of going *up* to the Praetorium; but in fact the Praetorium stood high. Mk is silent as to the temper of the people when they started; they soon became hostile to Jesus.

ὁ ὄχλος ἤρξατο αἰτεῖσθαι. In Jn, Pilate takes the initiative and offers to "release the King of the Jews" in honour of the Passover, this being one of his devices to free an innocent prisoner without exasperating the populace. In Mt., Pilate offers the alternative of Jesus or Barabbas. Will they have one who was falsely accused of stirring up sedition, or one who was guilty of both sedition and murder? It is much more likely that, as Mk and Jn state, Pilate simply offered to release Jesus. He was most anxious to set Him free; he cared nothing, and possibly knew nothing, about Barabbas. To suggest him to the people would lessen the chance of their accepting Jesus.

9. Θέλετε ἀπολύσω. We have the same constr. x. 36, 51, xiv. 12.

10. ἐγίνωσκεν. *He was becoming aware.* Pilate was shrewd enough to see that there was violent *animus* against Jesus and that

the charges against Him were untrue. Jewish leaders were not likely to resent a Rabbi's being hostile to Rome: they were quite capable of resenting the success of a rival Teacher. His real crime was that He had been too popular, and it was this which led Pilate to hope that the proposal to release Him in honour of the Feast would be welcomed by the people. But he made a mistake in calling Him "the King of the Jews." Such a title in the mouth of a Roman official must seem to be contemptuous; he would have done better, had he called Him "the Prophet of Galilee."

11. οἱ δὲ ἀρχιερεῖς. It was the hierarchy, and neither Pilate nor the people, who first suggested Barabbas. We are not told what means they used to change the attitude of the people towards Jesus. But the citizens far outnumbered the Galilean pilgrims, and with the city mob Barabbas may have been a sort of hero, like Dick Turpin, or, if he was a revolutionist rather than a highwayman, he may have been like Wat Tyler. The fickleness of the multitude in this case seems extraordinary, even beyond that which is often found in *mobile vulgus*. But it was a fatal shock to sentiment to see the supposed Messiah standing bound and helpless before the heathen Procurator. No true Messiah would endure such an indignity. The change of feeling was catastrophic and complete. They had been deceived and made fools of, and they were quickly made ready by the priests to propose the cruelest of punishments for the impostor. Judas had betrayed Him, the Eleven had deserted Him, and we need not be astonished at the fickleness of the populace. Loisy's incredulity is quite out of place. Lagrange compares the sudden collapse of Boulanger's popularity in April 1889. For ἀνασείω cf. Lk. xxiii. 5.

12. Τί οὖν ποιήσω ὃν λέγετε. See crit. note. *What then am I to do with Him whom ye call.* Delib. subj. rather than fut. indic. (R.V.). The more usual constr. is ποιεῖν τινί τι, but that does not mean quite the same as ποιεῖν τινά τι. The latter is "to do something *with* a person," the former is "to do something *to* a person." Here ὅν may = τούτῳ ὅν, but the other constr. is simpler. Pilate was within his duty in offering to release Jesus for the Feast and in letting the people choose Barabbas in preference. But he had no right to let them decide what was to be done with Jesus. He wanted to avoid the responsibility of condemning Jesus, and above all to avoid a tumult at the Passover. If the Jews were bent on having the life of an innocent Galilean, the responsibility was theirs. At all costs he must prevent an insurrection which would have to be put down by his troops. That would mean much bloodshed and the raising of awkward questions at Rome. Mt. interprets Pilate's thoughts by putting into his mouth the words, "I am innocent of this blood" (BD, Syr-Sin.).

13. οἱ δὲ πάλιν ἔκραξαν. This does not mean that they had previously asked him to crucify Jesus. They had previously asked him to free Barabbas (*v.* 11), and now they make *another* request. Or πάλιν may merely mean in *reply* to Pilate, in which case πάλιν = "thereupon." Their reply was made with the uttermost promptitude, and was probably suggested by the priests when they urged the people to ask for Barabbas.

14. Τί γὰρ ἐποίησεν κακόν; In all three Synoptists. "I can hardly do that, *for* what evil hath He done?" This is well expressed by "Why" (A.V., R.V.). Pilate falls lower and lower. While acting as Roman judge, he allows clamorous Jews to dictate his decision, and even argues with them, and that in a way which declares that he regards their decision as iniquitous. He says, "You are sentencing an innocent man to crucifixion," and their only answer is to shout the iniquitous decision again with vehemence. See crit. note and cf. x. 26 and Acts xxvi. 11.

15. τὸ ἱκανὸν ποιῆσαι. *Satisfacere*, a Latinism found in Polybius and other late writers, but nowhere else in N.T., and perhaps nowhere in LXX. Pilate is cowed and becomes the henchman of the hierarchy.

ἀπέλυσεν αὐτοῖς τ. Βαραββᾶν, καὶ παρέδωκεν τ. Ἰησοῦν. This contrast is in all three Synoptists and was evidently part of the primitive tradition; and all four Evangelists have παρέδωκεν of this last step in the great παράδοσις. Judas delivers Him up to the guards, the guards to Annas, Annas to Caiaphas and the Sanhedrin, the Sanhedrin to Pilate, Pilate to Herod, Herod to Pilate, Pilate to the executioners. And all these details are part of God's delivering up His Son for the redemption of mankind.

φραγελλώσας. Another Latinism (φλαγελλώσας, D): in x. 34 and Jn xix. 1 we have the usual μαστιγόω. In Mk and Mt. the scourging is closely connected with the crucifixion, and capital punishment often included both; Livy xxii. 13, xxxiii. 36; Cic. *In Verr.* v. 62; Joseph. *B. J.* II. xiv. 9, v. xi. 1. In Jn the scourging is one more attempt made by Pilate to save at least the life of Jesus; he hopes that the Jews will be satisfied with this; see on Jn xix. 1.

Mk and Mt. have no dat. after παρέδωκεν, but ἵνα σταυρωθῇ implies "to the soldiers." Jn says αὐτοῖς, viz. to the priests. Lk. says τῷ θελήματι αὐτῶν, which means to the will of the people. Pilate delivered Jesus up to both priests and people when he handed Him over to the soldiers to be crucified. In the Gospel of Peter Herod gives the sentence, and the guilt of the execution is attributed to him and the Jews. In the *Acta Pilati* (B. x.) the Jews execute the sentence as soon as Pilate has pronounced it.

16—20 a. THE MOCKERY BY PILATE'S SOLDIERS.

Mt. xxvii. 27—31.   Jn xix. 2, 3.

16. Οἱ δὲ στρατιῶται. Some of the troops under the command of the Procurator, brought to Jerusalem to maintain order during the Feast. Again we have δέ to mark a change of subject; see on vii. 24, x. 32, xiv. 1, xv. 16.

ἔσω τῆς αὐλῆς. This implies that the scourging had been inflicted elsewhere; but whether inside the building, or outside, is not clear.

ὅ ἐστιν πραιτώριον. This loose conversational statement is quite in Mk's style, and Blass' proposal to substitute τοῦ πραιτωρίου is not needed. Whether the αὐλή was partly or wholly roofed, or not roofed at all, it is strange that it should be identified with the whole building. Probably the αὐλή was the only part that was open to the public, and therefore, when people spoke of the Praetorium, they meant its αὐλή. Or Mk in his conversational manner may be stating "I mean the *praetorium*-court "; but, even if we were sure of this, we should not be justified in altering his wording. It is perhaps possible that the soldiers' quarters in the Procurator's palace is meant. In A.V., πραιτώριον is translated in five different ways. In the Gospels it seems always to mean the residence of the Procurator. See on Jn xviii. 28.

ὅλην τὴν σπεῖραν. Again a loose conversational expression; it obviously means all the members of the cohort who were within hearing at the moment. The men on duty in connexion with the trial and the execution summon all who are near at hand to come and make sport of "the King of the Jews." Possibly σπεῖρα does not mean a full cohort of 500 or 600 men.

17. ἐνδιδύσκουσιν αὐτὸν πορφύραν. Double acc. both here and *v.* 19. Cf. Lk. xvi. 19 of Dives. Mt. for πορφύραν has χλαμύδα κοκκίνην, Jn has ἱμάτιον πορφυροῦν. All three mean some bright coloured garment to represent a royal robe; see on Jn xix. 2, 3 and cf. the Gospel of Peter iii. 7. There are parallels in the Testaments (*Zebulon* iv. 10; *Benjamin* ii. 3); and the behaviour of pirates to their captives, as described by Plutarch (*Pomp.* 24), is a striking illustration. Several others are quoted by Lagrange.

ἀκάνθινον στέφανον. It is impossible to determine what plant was used for this purpose, and conjectures are very various. But the use of στέφανος instead of διάδημα does not prove that the soldiers mock Him as conqueror rather than as king. The whole context indicates mock homage to royalty.

18. Χαῖρε βασιλεῦ τῶν 'Ιουδαίων. The soldiers are playing at *Ave Caesar* and mingling brutal outrage with it. In the Gospel of Peter the formula is "Judge righteously, O king of *Israel*," and the title on the cross is "This is the king of Israel"; see on *v.* 32. Lk., having given the mockery by Herod and his guards (xxiii. 11), omits the mockery by Pilate's troops, and the one incident may have led to the other, for some of Pilate's soldiers probably accompanied Him and witnessed Herod's brutality. But Pilate did not join in the mockery, as Herod did. Herod was exasperated with Jesus for not gratifying his curiosity. Pilate was exasperated, not with Jesus, but with the priests, for preventing him from setting Jesus free. On the voc. βασιλεῦ (not ὁ βασιλεύς) see J. H. Moulton, p. 70.

19. τιθέντες τὰ γόνατα. Possibly a Latinism; *ponentes genua.* Cf. Lk. xxii. 41; Acts vii. 60. Note the imperfects.

20. ἐξέδυσαν αὐτὸν τὴν πορφύραν. The double acc. is classical. The change from the imperfects in *v.* 19 to the aorists in *v.* 20 has point. Nothing is said about the crown of thorns, but it was probably taken off when other signs of mock royalty were removed. The centurion would not have allowed the mockery to continue when the march to the place of execution began. Pictures are misleading in this respect, as in various details of the crucifixion. In the most ancient representations of the crucifixion the Saviour does not wear a crown of thorns. The verse should have ended at τὰ ἱμάτια αὐτοῦ.

20 b—22. The Road to Calvary.

Mt. xxvii. 31 b—33. Lk. xxiii. 26—33 a. Jn xix. 16, 17.

καὶ ἐξάγουσιν. The change of tense and of behaviour point to a change of nominative. The soldiers off duty are left behind, while the centurion and his assistants take charge of the Prisoner and add neither insult nor brutality to what they are bound to do in their treatment of Him. At first, according to custom, Jesus bore the cross, or at any rate the cross-beam, Himself (Jn xix. 17). The soldiers seeing that it was more than He could carry transferred the burden to Simon. Place a colon after σταυρώσωσιν αὐτόν.

21. ἀγγαρεύουσιν. Originally a Persian expression of impressing people into serving the couriers of the Great King (Hdt. viii. 98), similar to the *cursus publicus* in the Roman Empire. Cf. *operae* *publicae* and the French *corvée*. But papyri and other evidence show that as early as B.C. 250 the word was used in a more general sense and at last was applied to compulsory service of any kind. Deissmann, *Bibl. St.* pp. 86, 87; Hatch, *Essays*, p. 37. Cf. Mt. v. 41. אַ*B* read ἐγγαρεύουσιν, which probably represents local pronunciation and is thought by some to point to an Egyptian origin for those two MSS.

παράγοντά τινα. Elsewhere in the Gospels the verb is used only of Jesus "passing by" (i. 16, ii. 14; Mt. ix. 9, 27; Jn ix. 1); and outside the Gospels only in the sense of things "passing away" (1 Cor. vii. 31; 1 Jn ii. 8, 17). Syr-Sin. omits the word.

Σίμωνα Κυρηναῖον. In all three Synoptists; his name and origin were well remembered. There was a strong colony of Jews in Cyrene, planted there by Ptolemy I. They had equal rights with the citizens and often gave trouble (Joseph. *Apion.* ii. 4, *Ant.* XIV. vii. 2, XVI. vi. 1, 5, *B.J.* VII. xi. 1, *Vita* 76; Eus. *H.E.* iv. 2; cf. 1 Macc. xv. 23; 2 Macc. ii. 23). Simon may have been a member of the Cyrenean synagogue (Acts vi. 9). It is unlikely that he is the same as "Symeon that was called Niger" who is mentioned with "Lucius of Cyrene" (Acts xiii. 1).

ἐρχόμενον ἀπ' ἀγροῦ. *Coming from the country.* This need not mean that he was coming from *work* in the country, and it certainly was not a case of coming home from work in the evening. If he was an inhabitant of the district, he may have come to buy or sell, or in connexion with the Passover; but he may have been a pilgrim come up for the Feast. We cannot use this statement as evidence for determining the day.

τὸν πατέρα Ἀλεξάνδρου καὶ Ῥούφου. Mk only. When he wrote, Alexander and Rufus were known to many for whom he wrote, and Simon was not. Mk wishes to interest his readers in the narrative. For the purposes of the narrative it is of no moment whether Simon had sons or what their names were. Cf. xiv. 51, 52. There may here be confirmation of the tradition that Mk wrote in Rome. Alexander is not to be identified with any other Alexander in N.T. The name was very common in the East, and no Alexander otherwise known to us is likely to be the same man. Rufus, on the other hand, is a rare name in the East, though not rare in Rome, and he may be the Rufus of Rom. xvi. 13, in which case his mother was well known to St Paul. He may also be the Rufus of the Ep. of Polycarp (ix.). But this conjecture is of as little value as that of Origen, who thinks that Simon of Cyrene may have been converted by St Mark.

ἄρῃ τὸν σταυρόν. In viii. 34 the same expression is rendered

"*take up* his cross" (A.V., R.V.), but here "*bear* his cross." Why
not "take up" in both places? Vulg. has *tollo* in both, and Mk may
have intentionally used the same verb in both passages. We need not
be afraid of apparent discrepancy from Lk., who says that the soldiers
laid the cross *on* Simon, ἐπέθηκαν αὐτῷ. What Christ had hitherto
carried was transferred to Simon. Pictures sometimes represent
Simon as merely helping Christ to carry the cross.

22. φέρουσιν αὐτόν. This may mean that He was so exhausted
that the soldiers had to carry Him for the remainder of the way
(i. 32, ii. 3); but it probably means "bring, conduct" (vii. 32,
viii. 22, ix. 17, 19, xi. 2, 7). Latin versions have *perducunt, ad-
ducunt, duxerunt*; k has *ferunt illam*, "bring the cross."

Κρανίου τόπος. Mk, Mt., and Jn give this as the meaning of
Golgotha, while Lk. has simply Κρανίον, which favours the view that
it was so called from the shape of the rock. That Jews allowed the
skulls of criminals to lie there unburied is incredible, though Jerome
seems to accept it: in that case it would have been called the "place
of *skulls*." The legend that Adam's skull lay there, thus bringing
the fatal death of the first Adam into connexion with the lifegiving
death of the second Adam, appears to be believed by Ambrose. But
Chrysostom gives it as a mere report, and Jerome rejects it as an
attractive interpretation of the name and *mulcens aurem populi, nec
tamen vera*. The Ethiopic Melchisedek legend makes *Golgotha* itself
to be Adam's skull. *Golgotha* is not a pure transliteration, but is a
Greek modification, for the sake of euphony, of *Goulgoltha, Gougaltha*,
and *Gogoltha*. The familiar "Calvary" comes from Vulg. *Calvariae
locus*, Lk. *Calvariae*. We have not sufficient evidence to decide either
the site or the origin of the name. The literature is large. Sanday,
Sacred Sites, pp. 54, 68—77; *D.C.G.* art. "Golgotha." Nor is the
route through the city to it known. What is called the *Via Dolorosa*
is a mediaeval conjecture.

23—32. THE CRUCIFIXION AND THE FIRST THREE HOURS.

Mt. xxiii. 34—44.   Lk. xxiii. 33 b—43.   Jn xix. 18—26.

23. ἐδίδουν αὐτῷ. *They offered Him* (R.V.). "They tried to
give Him"; the conative imperf. Cf. ἐκωλύομεν αὐτόν (ix. 38). Mt.,
as often, has the aor. where Mk has the imperf., and in this case is
less accurate.

ἐσμυρνισμένον οἶνον. Wine medicated with myrrh and perhaps
other drugs, to act as an anaesthetic. Syr-Sin. has "sweetened with
spice." Mt. has χολή, "gall," instead of myrrh; both were bitter,

and Mt. may have wished to recall Ps. lxix. 22. Euthymius
erroneously suggests that a nauseous drink was offered to Him in
mockery to increase His sufferings. It is said that there was a
women's guild in Jerusalem which supplied condemned criminals
with potions for deadening pain before execution. "Give strong
drink unto him that is ready to perish, and wine unto the bitter in
soul; Let him drink and forget his poverty, and remember his misery
no more" (Prov. xxxi. 6, 7) may have suggested this custom. Christ
refused to be stupefied and have His mental faculties obscured; His
mind must be free to surrender His life by an act of will. Had He
drunk the potion, Christendom might have lost the Words from the
Cross. When Dr Johnson was told that without a miracle he could
not recover, he said that he would take no more opiates, "for I have
prayed that I may render up my soul to God unclouded."

24. σταυροῦσιν αὐτόν. All the Evangelists pass over the horrors
of the process of crucifixion in reverent silence. There is no attempt
to excite emotion by detailing them. We have no means of determining whether our Lord's feet were nailed or tied, for Lk. xxiv. 39
is not decisive. In the Gospel of Peter, before the burial, nails are
taken from the hands only, which indicates that "Peter" knew the
Fourth Gospel. The Synoptists say nothing about the nailing, and
Jn speaks only of the hands (Jn xx. 25, 27). Writers and painters,
perhaps influenced by Ps. xxii. 17, have commonly assumed the nailing of the feet, and this is probably correct (see Meyer on Mt.). In
that case each foot would almost certainly be nailed separately.

διαμερίζονται τὰ ἱμάτια. This was not an exceptional brutality;
the clothing of an executed criminal was a perquisite of the executioners. All four call attention to the parting of the garments in
wording which is influenced by Ps. xxii. 18, which Jn (xix. 24) quotes
verbatim from LXX. The Hebrew distinguishes the upper and under
garments, as does Jn in his narrative; LXX. and the Synoptists
do not.

βάλλοντες κλῆρον ἐπ᾿ αὐτά. Here again the Evangelist who was
present is more definite than the Synoptists. He records how lots
were cast for the under-garment only, while the upper was divided
into four.

τίς τί ἄρῃ. Lit. "Who should take what," *quis quid tolleret*
(Vulg.). The double question occurs nowhere else in N.T., though
some authorities have it Lk. xix. 15, ἵνα γνῷ τίς τί διεπραγματεύσατο.
Syr-Syn. omits it here. It is not rare in class. Grk. ἡ τίσι τί ἀπο-
διδοῦσα τέχνη δικαιοσύνη ἂν καλοῖτο (Plato *Rep.* 332 D). Similarly πῶς
τί; Field, pp. 43, 44, quotes other instances.

25. Ἦν δὲ ὥρα τρίτη. Mk alone gives this note of the hour, which creates a difficulty with Jn xix. 14, where the *Ecce Homo* is placed at the sixth hour. Suggestions of a false reading in either place may be rejected, and forced interpretations of plain language are unsatisfactory. The least unsatisfactory solution is the not quite baseless conjecture that Jn reckoned time as we do, and that his sixth hour is our 6.0 a.m., but it can hardly be called probable. See notes *ad loc.* On a day of exceptional excitement, with prolonged darkness at midday, traditions as to the time of day might be very confused and divergent; but a difference of two or more hours can hardly be explained in this manner.

καὶ ἐσταύρωσαν αὐτόν. The καί couples the fact of crucifixion already mentioned with the time of day, so that καί = ὅτε, which some cursives substitute. We sometimes use " and " in the sense of "when"; " it was noon and he arrived."

26. ἦν ἡ ἐπιγραφὴ τῆς αἰτίας αὐτοῦ ἐπιγεγραμμένη. A *titulus*, stating the crime for which he was to suffer, was commonly fastened to the criminal's neck before he was taken to execution, but we lack evidence as to its being fastened to the cross. The space above the head would be likely to be used in this way.

Just as no two authorities agree as to the words used at the Institution of the Eucharist, or as to the prayers in Gethsemane, or as to Peter's denials, so no two Gospels agree as to the wording of the title on the Cross. All four, however, have Ὁ Βασιλεὺς τῶν Ἰουδαίων. St John had gazed at it and read it repeatedly, and he is doubtless accurate in stating that these words were preceded by Ἰησοῦς ὁ Ναζωραῖος, and that the inscription was in the two languages of the country, Aramaic and Greek, as well as in the official Latin. The Gospel of Peter gives the improbable wording, " This is the King of *Israel*." Pilate would know no such expression; cf. *v.* 32.

27. δύο λῃστάς. *Two robbers* (R.V.); see on xi. 17, xiv. 48. They may have taken part in the insurrection in which Barabbas had shed blood; but no hint is given of any such connexion. More probably they were bandits, and may have been some of those who caused the road from Jerusalem to Jericho to be notorious for danger (Lk. x. 30). They had probably been condemned at the same time as Jesus, for they know how His case differs from theirs (Lk. xxiii. 40, 41, 42). The names of the two robbers are given with extraordinary variety in the Apocryphal Gospels and other legendary sources; but, on the whole, Dismas or a similar name is given to the penitent robber, and Gestas or a similar name to the impenitent. Titus and Dumachus

(Θεομάχος), Joathas and Maggatras, Zoatham and Chammatha, Matha and Joca, are other variants.

ἕνα ἐκ δεξιῶν. Such are the right and left hand places for which James and John had asked (x. 37).

28. See crit. note. The interpolation is based on Lk. xxii. 37 and Is. liii. 12. It is not Mk's habit to point out the fulfilment of Scripture. See WH. *App.* p. 27.

29. οἱ παραπορευόμενοι. Syr-Sin. omits. Cicero (*In Verr.* v. 66) says that public places along the highways were chosen for crucifixions; that the sufferers might serve as scares to criminals and warnings to passers by. The executed were treated as vermin, nailed to a tree or door. To this public place outside Jerusalem "passers by" would be brought by animosity, curiosity, business, or accident. The expression at once recalls Lam. i. 12, ii. 15; but Ps. xxii. 8 may also bo in the minds of the Synoptists. In O.T. "shaking the head" is often given as a sign of mock pity or derision; 2 Kings xix. 21; Ps. xxii. 7, cix. 25; Job xvi. 4; Is. xxxvii. 22.

ἐβλασφήμουν. Cf. Acts xiii. 45, xviii. 6; Rom. iii. 8.

Οὐά. Here only in Bibl. Grk. It oxpresses respect or amazement, genuine or sarcastic, while οὐαί, which is frequent in LXX. and N.T., expresses pity. There is much the same difference between *vah* and *vae*.

ὁ καταλύων. Nom. with art. for voc., as often; cf. v. 8, 41, ix. 25; and especially Rev. xviii. 10.

30. σῶσον σεαυτόν. These words are in all three. Lk. attributes them to the soldiers, who may have caught them from the passers by. They are the gibe of men who discredited Christ's wonderful works. If it was really true that He could raise the dead, of course He could come down from the cross.

31. οἱ ἀρχιερεῖς...μετὰ τῶν γραμματέων. On such a day, the eve of the Passover and of the Sabbath, these priests and scribes must have come on purpose to mock. Judges capable of striking and spitting at their Prisoner (xiv. 65) would be equally capable of making derisive remarks in His hearing. They talk *at* the dying Sufferer, not like the passers by, *to* Him. Their scornful remarks to one another are meant to be heard by Him and by others. See on x. 34. But the Evangelists let the malignity of the hierarchy speak for itself; they record it without denouncing it. Loisy remarks that it is improbable that the majority of the Sanhedrin would be present at the crucifixion. Perhaps so, but Mk does not say that they were. Enough were there to justify the statement that the priests and the scribes flung about insulting words.

"Άλλους ἔσωσεν. These words also are in all three. *He healed others; Himself He cannot heal.* This is a freq. meaning of the verb in the Gospels (iii. 4, v. 23, 28, 34, vi. 56, x. 52; etc.). The prince of the demons, they said, helped Him to heal others (iii. 22), but He can get no such help for Himself. In the Gospel of Nicodemus the saying is expanded thus: " Others He saved, others He cured, and He healed the sick, the paralytic, the lepers, the demoniacs, the blind, the lame, the dead; and Himself He cannot cure." His enemies had never been able to deny the fact of His miraculous healings.

32. ὁ Χριστός. Alluding to His declaration before the Sanhedrin (xiv. 62).

ὁ βασιλεὺς 'Ισραήλ. Alluding to the title on the cross. It is probably from this expression (Mk, Mt.) that the Gospel of Peter gets the idea that the wording of the title was "This is the King of *Israel.*" Jews would say "of Israel," but Pilate would write "of the Jews."

ἵνα...πιστεύσωμεν. Mt. has καὶ πιστεύσομεν, turning the saying into a promise to believe. They failed to understand Moses and the Prophets, and they did not believe Him of whom they wrote, even when He raised the dead. But when He Himself rose, many of the priests became obedient to the faith (Acts vi. 7).

ὠνείδιζον. As in *vv.* 29 and 31, the imperf. expresses continued action. Mt. retains the imperf. in all three places. We may suppose that Mk and Mt. were ignorant of the subsequent conduct of the penitent robber. The frequent reviling of the other robber was much better known and was commonly spoken of as done by " the robbers." So Cyril of Jerusalem, Ambrose, and Augustine. Origen, Chrysostom, and Jerome suppose that both robbers at first reviled, and that afterwards one of them changed and rebuked the other. This is less probable. Much less satisfactory is the suggestion that ὠνείδιζον (Mk, Mt.) means much less than ἐβλασφήμει (Lk.); both *reproached* Jesus, but only one *railed on* Him. There is little difference in meaning between the two verbs (Lk. vi. 22; Rom. xv. 3; Heb. xi. 26; 1 Pet. iv. 14), and they are sometimes coupled (2 Kings xix. 22). Vulg. here has *conviciabantur*, in Mt. *improperabant.*

33—41. THE LAST THREE HOURS AND THE DEATH.

Mt. xxvii. 45—56.　Lk. xxiii. 44—49.　Jn xix. 29, 30.

33. The divergence in the records here and at *v.* 36 need not surprise us. Eyewitnesses in a time of excitement seldom agree exactly as to what they saw and heard, and exact agreement is a reason for suspecting collusion. Reports of what was said and done at the execution of John of Leyden at Münster in Jan. 1536, written by eyewitnesses immediately afterwards, differ widely as to what took place.

ὥρας ἕκτης. All three Synoptists say that the darkness began at the sixth hour and lasted till the ninth; and "over the whole *land*" (A.V., R.V.) is doubtless the meaning of ἐφ' ὅλην τὴν γῆν. As in the case of Egypt (see Driver on Exod. x. 23), the darkness was local, and it may be ascribed to natural causes. At the Paschal full moon an eclipse would be impossible, and we need not suppose that Lk. xxiii. 45 means this. An eclipse is given as the cause in the *Acta Pilati*, but Origen points out the impossibility. Extraordinary darkness at noonday, extending for miles, is not a very rare phenomenon, and there is no sound reason for doubting the fact on this occasion, although some critics suggest that Amos viii. 9, quoted by Irenaeus (IV. xxxiii. 12) as a prediction of it, caused the midday darkness to be imagined. The Gospel of Peter enlarges upon the completeness of the darkness. Granting the fact, it was inevitable that Christians should believe that in this case Nature was expressing sympathy with the sufferings of the Redeemer, or pronouncing the infliction of them to be a work of darkness, or predicting the fate of those who had tried to extinguish the Light of the World (Origen), or refusing to look upon a crucified Lord and aid by its light those who blasphemed Him (Jerome). We have no right to condemn such beliefs as certainly untrue. "If He thunder by law, the thunder is yet His voice." See on Amos viii. 9 and Godet on Lk. xxiii. 44, 45. Syr-Sin. omits ἐφ' ὅλην τ. γῆν.

34. ἐβόησεν. Like the cry with which He expired, this utterance was a φωνὴ μεγάλη (v. 37). It is the only Word from the Cross recorded by Mk and Mt., and in both Gospels it is given in the original Aramaic, but texts vary somewhat as to the transliteration. Whether Jesus uttered the first word in the Aramaic or the Hebraistic form is, as Dalman remarks, of little moment. "The latter appears to have the greater probability in its favour, as being the less natural in the Aramaic context. It is conceivable that, to secure greater uniformity, one copyist corrected ἠλεί to ἐλωεί, so that the whole should be Aramaic, while another changed λεμὰ σεβαχθανεί into λαμὰ [ἀ]ζαφθανεί, so as to have the whole in Hebrew" (*Words*, p. 54). Here D has ἠλεί, and it would be easier for ἠλεί than ἐλωεί to be twisted into 'Ηλείας. Allen thinks "it is difficult not to believe that Christ quoted the Psalm in Hebrew, *Eli Eli lama azabhtani*" (*Studies in the Syn. Prob.* p. 305). In that case the Aramaic form in Mk is given for the sake of those to whom Aramaic was more familiar than Hebrew. But

even if ἐλωεί be original, there is no difficulty. It was not a case of
accidental mishearing. The man, in derision, purposely misquoted
the word which Christ had uttered. As to the next word we have
λαμᾶ (BD), λεμᾶ (אCLΔ), λιμᾶ (AKMPXΓII), and λειμᾶ (EFGHSV) as
variants, and there are as many of σαβαχθανεί. But the *asabtani* in
German Bibles has no MS. authority, any more than *Bnehargem* for
"Boanerges" (iii. 17).

'Ο θεός μου. LXX. also has the nom. with the art. (see on *v.* 29),
while Mt. has Θεέ μου. In N.T. there is perhaps not much difference
in tone between the two usages; cf. *v.* 18. On the other hand, LXX.
and Mt. have ἵνα τί, while Mk has εἰς τί. In Mk and Mt., though not
in LXX., the μου is repeated; even in this time of apparent desertion,
Christ recognizes God as His God. And both Mk and Mt. omit
πρόσχες μοι, which is in LXX. but not in the Hebrew. The character
of the cry is full guarantee for its historical truth. No Christian
would have attributed such words to the Messiah, had He not uttered
them. It is possibly because of their perplexing mystery that Lk. and
Jn omit them, and that the Gospel of Peter changes them into ἡ δύ-
ναμίς μου ἡ δύναμις, κατέλειψάς με. This is one of the Docetic traits
in that book, which treats the crucifixion as if it were devoid of
suffering. There is a passage in the Testaments (*Joseph* ii. 4—7)
which might serve as a moral drawn from this cry of mental agony.
Οὐ γὰρ ἐγκαταλείπει Κύριος τοὺς φοβουμένους αὐτόν...Ἐν βραχεῖ ἀφί-
σταται εἰς τὸ δοκιμάσαι τῆς ψυχῆς τὸ διαβούλιον...Ὅτι μέγα φάρμακόν ἐστιν
ἡ μακροθυμία, καὶ πολλὰ ἀγαθὰ δίδωσιν ἡ ὑπομονή. On the reading
ὠνίδισας (D) for ἐγκατέλιπες see crit. note. In the Defence of Christianity generally attributed to Macarius Magnes (A.D. 400) "it is
remarkable that the objector knew both ὠνείδισας and ἐγκατέλιπες and
regarded them as distinct utterances" (Swete).

35. Ἠλείαν φωνεῖ. This is ironical and means "The helpless
Messiah wants the Messianic Forerunner to come and help Him," or,
more simply, "wants Elijah to succour Him." It is said that Elijah
was regarded as the helper of the helpless.

36. γεμίσας σπόγγον ὄξους. Lk. omits this, having mentioned
at an earlier stage that the soldiers mocked Him by offering Him ὄξος,
i.e. the *posca* or sour wine provided for them, and possibly for the
sufferers. The sponge and the stalk may have been ready for the
latter purpose, or the sponge may have been a stopper for the jar.
Sponge is mentioned nowhere else in the Bible, but its use is often
mentioned elsewhere, and it would be common in places near the
sea. Jn says that it was Christ's "I thirst" which led to this incident, and again he has the definiteness of an eyewitness. He remem-

bers the jar of wine and that the "reed" was a stalk of "hyssop," which was not our *Hyssopus officinalis*, for that does not grow in Palestine. A stalk of two or three feet long would suffice. Pictures with the feet of the Crucified above the heads of the spectators are misleading. So tall a cross would be troublesome to carry and difficult to fix upright.

The accumulation of participles is characteristic (see on i. 15) and περιθείς is exact, the sponge being round the top of the stalk and crowning it (*v.* 17; cf. xii. 1). Ps. lxix. 22 perhaps suggested ἐπότιζεν, which is the conative imperf., like ἐδίδουν in *v.* 23. Mt. here retains the imperf.

λέγων "Αφετε ἴδωμεν. Here Mt. differs completely. He says that it was the *companions* of the giver of the wine who cried, "Αφες ἴδωμεν, *i.e.* "Let Him alone"; or "Leave off; let us see whether Elijah is coming to save Him." Apparently Mt. had some authority which he preferred to Mk. In each case there is a doubt as to "Αφετε or "Αφες, whether it means "Let be" (A.V., R.V.), or coalesces with ἴδωμεν, as in ἄφες ἐκβάλω (Mt. vii. 4). "Αφετε might mean, "Let me alone," "Don't stop me." But, whatever rendering we adopt, it is evident that Mk and Mt. follow different traditions as to what took place. "Αφες ἴδω occurs Epict. *Dis.* iii. 12 *sub fin.*

37. ἀφεὶς φωνὴν μεγάλην. The recurrence of the verb is purely accidental. The great cry is in all three Synoptists, and it shows that Christ did not die merely of exhaustion.

ἐξέπνευσεν. The change from imperfects to aorists is accurate. No Evangelist says that Christ "died"; He gave up His life by an act of will, *He yielded up His spirit*; κατ' ἐξουσίαν, ὅτε ἠθέλησεν, ἀποθνήσκει (Euthym.). Mk and Lk. say ἐξέπνευσεν, Mt. ἀφῆκεν τὸ πνεῦμα, Jn παρέδωκεν τὸ πνεῦμα. The last expression indicates that this "great cry" is to be identified with the last Word; Πάτερ, εἰς χεῖράς σου παρατίθεμαι τὸ πνεῦμά μου (Lk.). See on Jn xix. 30. The Gospel of St Peter has ἀνελήμφθη, "He was taken up," another expression with a Docetic tinge. A discussion of the physical causes of the death of Christ is unnecessary, and lack of evidence precludes the attainment of any satisfactory result. We may abide by the words of Scripture that He "lay down His life that He might take it again" (Jn x. 17).

38. τὸ καταπέτασμα κ.τ.λ. All three mention the portent of the rending of the Temple-veil, about which we have no further information. Possibly the Evangelist regards it as the Temple rending its clothes in grief for the death of the Messiah, a death which sealed its own doom, *lamentans excidium loco imminens* (*Clem. Recog.* i. 41).

The Gospel of Peter has it, and there is a passage in the Testaments
(*Levi* ix. 3) which predicts that "the veil of the Temple shall be rent,
so as not to cover your shame "; but in the latter passage ἔνδυμα may
be the true reading rather than καταπέτασμα. Jerome says that in
the Gospel according to the Hebrews there was a statement that
superliminare templi infinitae magnitudinis fractum esse atque divisum,
which points to a tradition of some extraordinary occurrence. The
veil in question is that between the Holy Place and the Holy of
Holies, and it is mentioned nowhere else in N.T., for Heb. ix. 3
refers to the Tabernacle. Its rending might signify that by the death
of Christ the exclusiveness of the Jewish religion was done away, and
that even the Holy of Holies was now accessible to all who desired to
enter.

ἀπ' ἄνωθεν. Mt. omits the superfluous ἀπό. See on ἀπὸ μακρόθεν
(v. 6).

39. ὁ κεντυρίων. One of Mk's Latinisms, already used by Polybius. In Mt., Lk., and Acts we have ἑκατοντάρχης or -χος. All three
call him "*the* centurion," the one whose duty it was to see the
sentence of execution carried out, *supplicio praepositus*. Legend gives
the name of Longinus (λόγχη, Jn xix. 34) to him and to the soldier
who pierced the Lord's side, apparently identifying the two. Bede
calls him Legorrius. He was standing close by, opposite the middle
cross, and it was his duty to keep strict watch, which would be all
the more necessary during the darkness, and what he had noted
greatly impressed him. Legend says that he was healed of sore eyes
by Christ's blood, which fell on him during his watch, and that he
became a Christian martyr. The Gospel narrative is very different.

ὅτι οὕτως ἐξέπνευσεν. The manner of Christ's death, especially
the confidence with which He committed His spirit into His Father's
hands, completed the conviction which had been growing in him.
All three Evangelists endeavour to describe this heathen soldier's
attitude towards Christ's death. He was awe-struck. This was no
dangerous or despicable criminal. This Man was not merely innocent
but righteous (Lk.), and he was quite right in claiming God as His
Father (Mk, Mt.). In this way Mk confirms Lk.'s report of Christ's
last Word, which Mk himself does not record. He also, in recording
the centurion's comment, reveals his own feeling about the Gentiles.
The moment after the death of the Messiah the power of that death
is recognized by a heathen who had taken part in inflicting it. This
heathen echoes the exordium of the Gospel. See on i. 1. The
centurion had *perhaps* been told that Jesus had supernatural powers
and claimed to be Divine. But he had himself heard Him, with His

dying breath, address God as His Father, and he knew that dying men do not tell wanton lies. The centurion, no doubt, meant far less than the truth when he called Jesus "a son of God." But at least he meant that he had never seen a better man die a nobler death. Lk. says that in this confession the centurion "glorified God"; *i.e.* he unconsciously did so. Augustine (*De Cons. Ev.* iii. 20) treats the differences between the narratives well. The good character of the centurions in N.T. has often been noticed; cf. Mt. viii. 5—13; Acts x. 22, xxii. 26, xxiii. 17, 23, 24, xxiv. 23, xxvii. 43. Roman organization produced and promoted men of fine character. See Polybius vi. 24.

40. ἦσαν δὲ καὶ γυναῖκες. The centurion was not the only person who regarded the death of Christ with reverence and awe. *There were also women, beholding from afar* (R.V.). Cf. v. 6, viii. 3, xi. 13, xiv. 54. They had no mind to see more of the horrible details of the crucifixions, still less to hear the derisive language of Christ's triumphant enemies. His Mother and her sister, Mary of Clopas, with Mary Magdalen, had been near the Cross for a time, but they had come away, and the beloved disciple had taken the first to his own home; but the two others with Salome had joined a group at a distance and still remained. Lk. gives no names, but says that "all His acquaintance" were there also. Are the disciples included in οἱ γνωστοὶ αὐτῷ? John had probably returned to the cross; but where were the Ten?

M. ἡ Μαγδαληνή. *Mary of Magdala.* Mk has not mentioned her before, but assumes that she is known to his readers. Gratitude for her great deliverance (xvi. 9; Lk. viii. 2) had made her a devoted follower. The common identification of her with the "sinner" of Lk. vii. 37 is a monstrous error, which ought never to be repeated.

M. ἡ Ἰακώβου τ. μικροῦ κ. Ἰωσῆτος μήτηρ. Syr-Sin. has "Mary the *daughter* of James the less, the mother of Joseph"; but *Mary the mother of James the less (little) and of Joses* (A.V., R.V.) is right. She was the wife of Clopas (Jn xix. 25), who is certainly not the same as Cleopas (Lk. xxiv. 18) and cannot with any certainty be identified with Alphaeus. See on iii. 18. James and Joses are mentioned, not as being famous, but in order to distinguish their mother from other Marys. They are not the James and Joses of vi. 3. James was called ὁ μικρός probably because of his *stature*, but Deissmann (*Bib. St.* p. 144) suggests *age*. "The younger" would probably have been ὁ μικρότερος (Gen. xlii. 32), or ὁ νεώτερος (Gen. xlii. 34; Lk. xv. 12), or ὁ ἐλάσσων (Gen. xxv. 23).

Σαλώμη. Mk treats her also as known to his readers. Mt. gives no name but substitutes "the mother of the sons of Zebedee," who has been previously mentioned by him (xx. 20). She was probably the sister of Christ's Mother. See on Jn xix. 25.

41. ἐν τῇ Γαλιλαίᾳ. This limitation is in all three. These numerous women were pilgrims who had come from Galilee for the Passover; they were not "daughters of Jerusalem."

42—47. The Burial.

Mt. xxvii. 57—61.   Lk. xxiii. 50—56.   Jn xix. 38—42.

42. ὀψίας. A vague word, here used of the time between 3.0 p.m. and sunset.

ἐπεὶ ἦν παρασκευή. This is pointed out by Lk. also. The Sabbath began at sunset, and there must be no delay. If Joseph had not been prompt, Christ's enemies would have had His Body put, with those of the two robbers, into the grave where criminals were interred (Jn xix. 31). Even if the Sabbath had not begun that evening, it would have been contrary to Jewish law to allow the bodies to remain unburied after nightfall. See Driver on Deut. xxi. 22, 23; Joseph. *B. J.* iv. v. 2. Παρασκευή is the regular name for Friday in the Greek Church. Mk explains the term for Gentile readers; nowhere else does he use ἐπεί. Προσάββατον occurs Judith viii. 6 and in the title of Ps. xcii. (xciii.).

43. ὁ ἀπὸ Ἀριμαθαίας. The site of Arimathaea is unknown. It has been identified by some with Ramah, the birthplace and burial-place of Samuel. Its full name was Ramathaim-zophim, "Double Height of the Watchers" (Stanley, *Sin. and Pal.* p. 224). The ἀπό suggests that Joseph had ceased to reside at Arimathaea, and his having a tomb at Jerusalem and being a member of the Sanhedrin shows that he had settled in the city. Mt. says that he was πλούσιος, Lk. that he was ἀγαθὸς καὶ δίκαιος, which may all be summed up in Mk's εὐσχήμων. Only a person of good position and bearing would have had much hope of at once being admitted to an audience with Pilate.

ἦν προσδεχόμενος. Cf. Lk. ii. 25, 38.

τολμήσας. *Took courage*; see Field, p. 44. It required courage to go to the Procurator on such an errand. He was no relation of the Crucified, and therefore had no claim to this favour, and his being a member of the Sanhedrin might be fatal. The Sanhedrin had that day driven Pilate to condemn an innocent person to death,—a humiliating and exasperating thought for a Roman judge, and Pilate would know nothing of Joseph's having taken no part in this crime. Above all, there was danger as to what the Sanhedrin would do, when they heard of Joseph's visit to the Procurator. But reverence and affection for the Master gave him the necessary courage.

44. ἐθαύμασεν. Pilate's astonishment and questioning of the centurion are in Mk alone. Pilate would suspect an attempt to get possession of the Body before death had occurred. Death in a few hours was rare, and Eusebius (*H.E.* viii. 8) says that martyrs, even when nailed to the cross, sometimes were guarded till they died of hunger (see Heinichen's notes). Josephus (*Vita* 75) tells us that among a number of crucified captives he found three of his acquaintances still alive, and got Titus to have them taken down. Two died under medical treatment, but one recovered. In the *Digests* (xlviii. 24, Ulpian) it is ordered that the bodies of the executed are not to be buried without permission, that permission may be refused, and should be refused in cases of high treason (*majestatis*). See Lagrange.

45. ἐδωρήσατο τὸ πτῶμα. *He granted the corpse* (R.V.). The verb occurs again 2 Pet. 1. 3, 4, of Divine favours, and nowhere else in N.T. In LXX. it is used of Divine (Gen. xxx. 20) and royal (Esth. viii. 1) favours. Nowhere else is Christ's Body called a πτῶμα, *cadaver*, a word which has a contemptuous sound, like "carcase"; cf. vi. 29; Mt. xxiv. 28; Rev. xi. 8, 9. Hence Mt., Lk., and Jn use σῶμα, which many texts have here. But to Pilate Christ's Body was a πτῶμα or *cadaver*; and after his pitiable conduct in surrendering Jesus to the priests he may have been glad to make some amends by granting Joseph's request without a fee, as ἐδωρήσατο rather implies. On the other hand, ἀποδοθῆναι (Mt.) might imply that it was given in return for something paid. See on xii. 17.

46. ἀγοράσας σινδόνα. Joseph may have done this and made arrangements with Nicodemus before going to the Procurator. Both were members of the Sanhedrin and had agreed to act together. This σινδών might make the strips (ὀθόνια) which were wound round the Body along with the spices which Nicodemus brought. *Ex simplici sepultura Domini ambitio divitum condemnatur, qui ne in tumulis quidem possunt carere divitiis* (Bede). For ἐνείλησεν cf. 1 Sam. xxi. 9.

λελατομημένον. Rock-hewn tombs are common round about Jerusalem, and would commonly be used for well-to-do persons. Like the colt and the gravecloths, the tomb had not been used before, for Joseph had had it made for himself. See on Jn xix. 41. One wall would be cut with a stone shelf, on which the Body was laid, and a large stone, circular like a millstone, would be lying flat against the outside rock, ready for closing the opening. Two men might roll it into its place, but to roll it back would be a difficult task for women (xvi. 4). A globular stone would be much heavier, and it would not so completely close the opening as to exclude wild animals.

μνημείον. This is the word most frequently used of the sepulchre by all four. It perhaps has no shade of difference in meaning from μνῆμα. In the Byzantine sepulchral inscriptions at Jerusalem the usual word is θήκη, from the use of τίθημι, as here, of burial. See crit. note.

47. M. ἡ ᾿Ιωσῆτος. This probably means "the *mother* of Joses" (*v.* 40); if she had not been mentioned before, "the daughter of Joses" would be the probable rendering. D, ff n q and Syr-Sin. have "the daughter of James." These two women had watched the pious work of Joseph and Nicodemus, who *may* have had assistants, but might wish to do without them. They desired to see the last of the Master, and to know exactly how to arrange for their own pious work. Apparently, after the men had departed, the two women still sat on and gazed.

Some critics suggest that all these details have been invented in order to make a foundation for the theory of the Resurrection. Such criticism renders history impossible. The strongest evidence can be shown to be possibly untrue by such methods. Mk's simple narrative is thoroughly coherent. The women witness the hasty burial before sunset on Friday. When the Sabbath is over at sunset on Saturday, they buy spices. Very early on Sunday they set out to use the spices, evidently without any hope of a Resurrection. Their experiences at the tomb lead them to believe that Jesus is risen.

CHAPTER XVI.

2. τῇ μιᾷ τῶν σαββάτων (אBLΔ 33) rather than τῆς μιᾶς σαββάτων (ACLΠ). B omits τῇ. D has μιᾶς σαββάτου.

4. ἀνακεκύλισται (אBL) rather than ἀποκεκύλισται (ACXΓΔΠ).

8. אABCD omit ταχύ.

9. παρ' ἧς (CDL) rather than ἀφ' ἧς (AXΓΔΠ), an obvious correction.

17. C*LΔΨ omit καιναῖς.

18. AD omit καὶ ἐν ταῖς χερσίν.

The question of the genuineness of the last twelve verses is discussed in the Introduction (pp. xliii ff.). The time has come when discussion ought not to be necessary. Writers and preachers might be allowed to assume that these verses are no part of the Gospel according to St Mark with as much freedom as they assume that the words about the Three Heavenly Witnesses are no part of the First Epistle of St John. There are cases in which the evidence on one side is so strong that no amount of evidence on the other side, however voluminous and imposing, can shake it; and this is one of them. The interesting facts pointed out by Professor A. C. Clark (*The Primitive Text of the Gospels and Acts*, pp. 73 f.) do not make the genuineness of these verses more probable.

1—8. The Visit of the Women to the Tomb.

Mt. xxviii. 1—8. Lk. xxiv. 1—10. Cf. Jn xx. 1—18.

1. διαγενομένου τοῦ σαββάτου. *When the Sabbath was past* (A.V., R.V.). The verb is used of passing intervals of time in Acts xxv. 13 and xxvii. 9; cf. 2 Macc. xi. 26. After sunset on Saturday they bought ἀρώματα, a comprehensive term for sweet-smelling substances, whether solid or liquid. They proposed to pour these over the Body as it lay wrapped in gravecloths. Christ's words to Judas (xiv. 8) might suggest this. When they had finished their preparations it was too dark to do anything at the tomb; they must wait till dawn on Sunday.

2. ἀνατείλαντος τοῦ ἡλίου. *When the sun was risen.* Mk's fondness for fulness of expression (xiv. 58, 61, 68) here leads him into inconsistency. If the sun had already risen, it would not be λίαν πρωί. Mt. becomes still more confused about the time of day. Elsewhere (i. 32, ii. 20, vi. 35, xiv. 30), when Mk gives two notes of time, Mt. omits one (viii. 16, ix. 15, xiv. 15, xxvi. 34). Here he gives two which are even less harmonious than Mk's two. Mk confuses the time of the women's leaving home with the time when they reached the tomb. Mt. confuses the time when they bought the unguents with the time of their setting out to use them. At the latter hour it was still dark (Jn), which agrees with λίαν πρωί here. Even if λίαν πρωί means only "as early as they possibly could," it does not harmonize with "at sunrise."

τῇ μιᾷ τῶν σαββάτων. So also Lk. and Jn. Lit. "On day one of the week," not (as Coverdale in Lk.) "upon one of the Sabbathes." Here and in Jn, Vulg. has *una sabbatorum*, in Lk. and Acts xx. 7 *una sabbati*. This is a more important point than the hour of starting or of reaching the sepulchre. All the Evangelists agree that the tomb was found empty on the morning of Sunday.

3. ἔλεγον πρὸς ἑαυτάς. Cf. xi. 31, xiv. 4. Two of them had seen Joseph and Nicodemus, possibly with assistance and a lever, roll the stone to close the tomb, and they began to discuss among themselves whom they could get to open it. Here k has a strange interpolation about a sudden darkness at the third hour and Angels coming down from heaven and going up again with the risen Christ.

4. ἀνακεκύλισται. *Is rolled back* (R.V.), has been rolled back and remains so. Rolled back ἐκ τῆς θύρας, as Mk accurately says, rather than ἀπὸ τοῦ μνημείου (Lk.). It was probably rolled sideways and was leaning against the rock. The ἀνα- implies that it had gone back to the place whence Joseph and Nicodemus had moved it. See crit. note. Mk may have believed that the risen Christ had moved the stone, but he gives no hint of this belief. He states what those who were there reported; ἀνακεκύλισται is their exclamation.

ἦν γὰρ μέγας σφόδρα. It was so large that they could see at a distance that it had been rolled back. But the words may be a belated remark to explain why they were anxious about the matter; and D with other authorities have the remark at the end of *v.* 3. All four Evangelists state that the stone had been removed. Mt., as

at the Crucifixion, mentions an earthquake about which the other
three say nothing; also that an Angel rolled away the stone and sat
on it. This looks like conjectural explanation of a well-known fact.
In Mk the Angel is found inside the tomb. Lk. and Jn mention two
Angels. What is said about Angels is in harmony with Jewish modes
of thought, but it may also be substantially in harmony with fact.
We cannot safely attribute all the details of the narrative to Jewish
ideas of what would be likely to happen rather than to experience
of what did happen. We know so little about the nature of Angels
that it is rash to be peremptory as to what is credible or not. On
the whole subject see Swete, *The Appearances of our Lord after the
Passion*; also the introductory note to Jn xx. Jn mentions only one
of the women mentioned here, and his narrative about her is quite
different.

5. νεανίσκον. Mk leaves us to infer that this was an Angel.
The sobriety of all four narratives is in marked contrast to the
grotesque story in the Gospel of Peter, and it leaves us with the
impression that there is a basis of solid fact. Cf. 2 Macc. iii. 26, 33,
x. 29, xi. 8. We must allow (1) for the intense excitement of the
women at finding the sepulchre open and empty, (2) for the diversity
of the impressions which each of them received, and (3) for the
difficulty which each of them would have in describing her own
experiences. We must also allow (4) for the unintentional inaccuracy
with which those to whom they told their experiences would repeat
what they had been told. It is more reasonable to believe that facts
have been misunderstood and misreported, than to believe that there
are no facts, but that all the narratives are the outcome of delusion
or deliberate fiction. The substantial facts, common to all the
narratives, are that early on Sunday morning women went to the
tomb to see the Body which had been placed there, and that what
they sought was not found; the tomb was empty. The explanation,
slowly grasped at the time and confirmed afterwards, was that He
had risen. All this is more like sober history than myth.

στολὴν λευκήν. See on xii. 38.

ἐξεθαμβήθησαν. See on ix. 15. *They were amazed* (R.V.), but no
doubt something of fright (A.V.) was mingled with their astonishment.

6. ὁ δὲ λέγει αὐταῖς. As on the Lake (vi. 49, 50), the figure
which they see shows by addressing them that he is no mere phantasm;
and he addresses them in much the same way.

Μὴ ἐκθαμβεῖσθε, *Cease to be amazed*, = θαρσεῖτε, "Be of good
cheer." What follows may be taken interrogatively, "Is it Jesus
that ye are seeking? That is useless labour."

τὸν Ναζαρηνόν. Mk alone has this touch; it would appeal to Christ's friends from Galilee. See on i. 24.

τὸν ἐσταυρωμένον. Cf. 1 Cor. i. 23, ii. 2; Gal. iii. 1; He is now permanently "the Crucified."

ἠγέρθη. "You are too late; He is already risen." Hence the aor. rather than the perf. That He remains raised is not here the main point. One might have expected οὐκ ἔστιν ὧδε to have come first, as in Mt. and Lk., but Mk puts the supreme fact first and then gives the evidence for its truth. "He is risen. Do you doubt that? The tomb is empty; look at the place where the Body was laid." As we know from Jn, the graveclothes were lying there, but the Body had gone from within them. The Angel speaks with marvellous simplicity and directness. The short sentences, without connecting particles, are very impressive, and his calmness is in marked contrast to the women's excitement.

7. ἀλλὰ ὑπάγετε. Mk only. "Do not linger here wondering, *but* go to those who greatly need the knowledge of this fact." We may say that the Apostles needed the glad tidings even more than the women; but it was those who sought that were the first to find. The energy of the women had its reward.

καὶ τῷ Πέτρῳ. "And in particular to Peter." Here again we seem to have Peter behind the Evangelist. This special encouragement, sent to the chief Apostle, who was still lamenting his threefold denial, would be treasured and repeated by him. *Vocatur ex nomine ne desperaret ex negatione.* No other Evangelist reports this mention of Peter, but it is in harmony with St Paul's statement that there was a special manifestation "to Kephas" (1 Cor. xv. 5), and with the report quoted by Lk. (xxiv. 34), that Christ had appeared "to Simon." The three statements mutually confirm one another.

Προάγει ὑμᾶς εἰς τ. Γαλιλαίαν. This seems to look back to xiv. 28. The predictions that He would rise again had made too little impression on the Apostles; and it was therefore all the more necessary to remind them that He had appointed a meeting-place in Galilee. They might be sure that all would be done *even as* (καθώς, as in i. 2, ix. 13, xi. 6, xiv. 21) He said to them. In iv. 33, xiv. 16, and here, R.V. has simply "as" for καθώς. The appendix (*vv.* 9—20) contains no note of this appearance in Galilee.

8. ἐξελθοῦσαι ἔφυγον...εἶχεν. The change from aor. to imperf. is impressive. Their flight from the tomb was instantaneous; the trembling and astonishment were lasting. Terror at the supernatural utterance had held them fast for a few moments. As soon as the utterance ceased, their first impulse was to get away from the scene

of such awful experiences and from the cause of such unwelcome
emotions. It is clear from what follows that it was not eagerness to
deliver the Angel's message which made them fly in such haste.

εἶχεν γὰρ αὐτὰς τρόμος καὶ ἔκστασις. This use of ἔχω of the grip
of fear and pain is common; ἔχουσιν δέ μου τὰς σάρκας ὀδύναι (Job xxi.
6), ὠδῖνες αὐτοὺς ἕξουσιν (Is. xiii. 8). Cf. Job xxxi. 23; also Hom. *Il.*
iv. 79. Elsewhere in N.T. τρόμος is always connected with φόβος
(1 Cor. ii. 3; 2 Cor. vii. 15; Eph. vi. 5; Phil. ii. 12). Mk seems to
wish to show that fear was not the only emotion. See on v. 42.

οὐδενὶ οὐδὲν εἶπον. The double negative again; cf. xiv. 60, 61,
xv. 4, 5, etc. At first their tremor was so great that they were unable
to think of the gracious and joyous contents of the Angel's utterance,
and they quite forgot to communicate the glad tidings to others.
They were too frightened to think of anything but escape; all which
is true to nature. Mt. records the later stage, when "great joy"
was mingled with their fear, and then they ran to tell the disciples.
Lk., with his fondness for πᾶς, says that they told "*all* these things
to the Eleven and to *all* the rest." We may reasonably suppose that,
if we had the conclusion of this Gospel, we should have some account
of the transition from a terrified silence to a joyous eagerness to
communicate the good news, and also perhaps some report of the
delivery of the special message to Peter.

ἐφοβοῦντο γάρ. It is difficult to believe that Mk intended to end
his Gospel at this point and in this exceedingly abrupt way. It is
possible that ἐφοβοῦντο γάρ is not even a finished sentence, but that
the words introduce a statement as to what it was that they feared
when for a time they told no one what they had seen and heard.
Still, as ix. 6 shows, this need not be so; but ix. 6 does not support
the theory that ἐφοβοῦντο γάρ is meant to close even the section about
the visit to the tomb. The words give us the impression of a ragged
edge to an imperfect document.

9—11. The Appearance to Mary Magdalen.

Jn xx. 11—18.

9. Ἀναστὰς δὲ πρωὶ πρώτῃ σαββάτου ἐφάνη. These words
again give the impression of a ragged edge. The preceding passage
has no proper conclusion. This passage has no proper beginning, for
there is no nom. to ἐφάνη. Evidently something has preceded in
which Jesus has been mentioned. The two edges do not fit one
another. Whatever these twelve verses may be, they were not written
as a conclusion to Mk's account of the first hours of the first Easter

Day. Instead of giving the sequel of the first visit to the tomb, they
begin with another account of the first visit to the tomb, agreeing
with that of Jn, but not agreeing with that of Mk. Mary Magdalen,
one of the three women mentioned by Mk, is here quite alone, and
she is introduced, not as a person who has just been mentioned, but
as a person who needs to be described. In xv. 40, 47 and xvi. 1 she is
named as one about whom the reader is sure to know; here she is
introduced as a stranger. We should probably take πρωί with
ἀναστάς rather than with ἐφάνη.

πρώτῃ σαββάτου. The expression is found nowhere in Mk, who
never uses either σάββατον or σάββατα in the sense of "week."
Contrast v. 2 and parallels. Excepting Lk. xviii. 12, "the week"
in N.T. is generally plural, τῶν σαββάτων. The nearest parallel to
πρώτῃ σαββάτου is κατὰ μίαν σαββάτου (1 Cor. xvi. 2).

ἐφάνη. Another expression not found elsewhere in N.T. In
Lk. ix. 8, ἐφάνη is used of the reappearance of Elijah, but nowhere is
this verb used of an Appearance of the risen Lord. Contrast Lk. xxiv.
34; Acts xiii. 31, xxvi. 16; 1 Cor. xv. 5—8.

παρ' ἧς ἐκβεβλήκει. A third expression not found elsewhere.
The usual constr. is ἐκβάλλω ἐκ. Where ἐκ is not suitable we have
ἀπό, as in Acts xiii. 50; Exod. x. 11, xxiii. 31; Lev. xxi. 7, etc.;
παρά is not suitable.

ἑπτὰ δαιμόνια. Lk. states this in his first mention of Mary
Magdalen (viii. 2); it indicates an obsession of special malignity. It
is out of place to suggest a parallel with the "seven other spirits
more evil than himself" (Mt. xii. 45), or a contrast with "the seven
Spirits which are before His throne" (Rev. i. 4, iii. 1). We have no
ground for thinking that Mary of Magdala had been exceptionally
wicked, or that demoniacs generally were persons of very vicious lives.
See on xv. 40. Seven is a typical number, as made up of two other
typical numbers, three and four. These ideas about numbers are
widely spread, and there is no need to suppose any borrowing from
astrology, or Mazdeism, or other foreign sources. Plurality on an
impressive scale is meant. The demons could not be counted.

10. ἐκείνη πορευθεῖσα. This use of ἐκεῖνος, merely to recall the
main subject, is very freq. in Jn (i. 8, 18, 33, v. 11, 37, 39, 43, etc.),
but is not in Mk's style; yet we have it three times in this appendix
(10, 11, 20). And πορεύομαι, so very freq. in Mt., Lk., Jn, and
Acts, occurs only once in Mk (ix. 30), and then with the definite
meaning of travelling; yet we have it three times in six verses (10—
15).

τοῖς μετ' αὐτοῦ γενομένοις. This periphrasis for the disciples is found in no Gospel; it is as comprehensive as Lk.'s "to the Eleven and to all the rest."

πενθοῦσιν καὶ κλαίουσιν. This was an early fulfilment of what had been foretold (Jn xvi. 20). The disciples were mourning and weeping while the world was rejoicing in keeping the Feast; but the sorrow was soon to be turned into joy. The two verbs are often combined (Lk. vi. 25; Jas iv. 9; Rev. xviii. 11, 15, 19). The Gospel of Peter has ἐκλαίομεν καὶ ἐλυπούμεθα, but there is reason for believing that the Mk known to that writer ended at *v.* 8.

11. κἀκεῖνοι. Here and *v.* 13 the crasized form is found in the best MSS.; καὶ ἐκεῖνοι (iv. 20) is a very rare exception.

ἐθεάθη. Like ἐκεῖνοι as here used, this is a Johannine word (1 Jn i. 1, iv. 12, 14; Jn i. 14, etc.), and it occurs nowhere in Mk. It was the persistent testimony of those who had had this experience, that they had *seen* the risen Lord with their own eyes; and few believed that He was alive again until they had seen Him. That the confident expectation of seeing Him again led the disciples to believe that they had seen Him is quite contrary to clear evidence.

ἠπίστησαν. Unbelief was the general result when the testimony of others was received; Thomas was only one of many sceptics (*v.* 16; Lk. xxiv. 11, 41; Jn xx. 24). Ἀπιστέω (here and *v.* 16) is not found in Mk.

Whether or no we regard the narrative about the visit of the three women to the tomb (*vv.* 1—8) as referring to the same event as that which is recorded here and Jn xx. 11—18, it is remarkable that Christ's Appearance to Mary Magdalen, with or without other women, is not mentioned by St Paul, when he enumerates those who, from personal experience, could be cited as witnesses for the reality of Christ's Resurrection. Jn also, when He calls the Appearance at the Sea of Tiberias "the third time" of Christ's manifesting Himself (xxi. 14), does not count the Appearance to Mary which he himself records. Women were not official witnesses; and perhaps from the first it was noticed that, owing to emotion and excitement, the story which they told was not coherent. St Paul begins with the "first" of the Apostles and ends with the "least" of them, giving six Appearances in all. St John gives three Appearances, at all of which he himself was present. But, if in examining the witnesses for the Resurrection "the believer is confronted with details that do not harmonize, the unbeliever has to explain away the triumphant progress of the new sect" (Burkitt). Can the success and vitality of the Christian religion be explained, if Jesus of Nazareth died on the cross and never rose again?

12, 13.   Appearance to Two Disciples.

Lk. xxiv. 13—22.

12. Μετὰ δὲ ταῦτα. Μετὰ ταῦτα or τοῦτο is a Lukan and Johannine expression, but it is not found in Mk.   The two are the two who
were walking to Emmaus on the evening of Easter Day.

ἐφανερώθη.   Jn has the same verb in the same sense (Jn xxi. 1, 14).

ἐν ἑτέρᾳ μορφῇ.   The meaning is not clear.   It cannot mean that
He was glorified as at the Transfiguration.   It might mean that He
was in a form different from that in which He appeared to Mary; she
took Him to be a gardener, the two regarded Him as an ordinary
wayfarer.   It probably means that His form was different from that
in which He had previously been known to them; but it has little
point unless one knows that the two disciples failed to recognize
Him.

εἰς ἀγρόν.   The position of Emmaus is unknown.   *El Kubeibeh*
about seven miles N.W. of Jerusalem is perhaps the most probable
conjecture; but either *Kulonieh* or Beit Mizzeh nearer to Jerusalem
on the W. may be right.   *Amwâs*, about twenty miles N.W. of
Jerusalem, is impossible, although Christian writers from Eusebius
to the Crusades take the similarity of name as decisive.

13. κἀκεῖνοι.   See on *vv.* 10 and 11.

οὐδὲ ἐκείνοις ἐπίστευσαν.   This does not agree with Lk. xxiv. 34,
where the two, on their return from Emmaus, are greeted with the
news that the Lord is risen and has appeared to Simon.   But Thomas
did not believe this, and there may have been others who were
convinced neither by these two nor by the Ten.   The compiler of
these notes is evidently not copying from Lk., and what follows seems
to show that he had been told that the Apostles had refused to believe
the evidence from Emmaus.   The Apostles may have been allowed to
hear of the Resurrection before seeing the risen Christ in order that
they might know from personal experience what it was to have to
depend upon the testimony of others, as would be the case with their
converts (Jn xx. 29, 31).   See Hort on 1 Pet. i. 8.

14—18.   The Appearances to the Eleven.

Lk. xxiv. 36—43.   Jn xx. 19—23.   Cf. 1 Cor. xv. 5 f.

14. Ὕστερον.   These verses seem to be a summary of what the
writer had heard or read respecting manifestations of the risen Lord
to the Apostles on and after Easter Day.   What may have been said

on different occasions is strung together and assigned to a single occasion, the scene of which seems to be Jerusalem. But the narrative does not seem to be dependent on the Canonical Gospels, although the language is less unlike the language of those Gospels than *vv.* 9—13 are. "Ὕστερον, seven times in Mt. and once each in Lk. and Jn, is found nowhere in Mk, who prefers ἔσχατον.

αὐτοῖς τοῖς ἕνδεκα. *To the Eleven themselves* (R.V.), *ipsis undecim* (Beza), *i.e.* to the official body as distinct from Mary Magdalen and the two unnamed disciples. "The Eleven" proves nothing as to the presence of Thomas; both "the Eleven" and "the Twelve" are used to designate the Apostolic College, independently of the exact number (Jn xx. 24; 1 Cor. xv. 5). The terms *Decemviri* and *Centumviri* were used in a similar manner. Cf. the English "hundred."

ὠνείδισεν. Nowhere else is this verb used of Christ's rebuking His disciples, not even when Peter ventured to rebuke Him (viii. 32, 33). R.V. renders "upbraid" here and Mt. xi. 20, but "reproach" xv. 32; Mt. v. 11, xxvii. 44; Lk. vi. 22. Vulg. commonly has *exprobro*, but also *convicior* (xv. 32), *inpropero* (Mt. xxvii. 44), and *dico omne malum adversus* (Mt. v. 11).

ἀπιστίαν καὶ σκληροκαρδίαν. Nowhere else is either of these grave faults laid to the charge of the Apostles. They had shown ὀλιγοπιστία (Mt. xvii. 20), had had πεπωρωμένην τὴν καρδίαν (viii. 17); but they were neither unbelieving nor impenitent. We conclude that the words are not Christ's but the narrator's, who seems to have been much impressed by the fact that many of Christ's disciples treated the report of His Resurrection as something too good to be true. He emphasizes this (*vv.* 11, 13, 14; cf. 16, 17).

It was probably because the change from this severe rebuke to the commission in *v.* 15 appeared to be intolerably abrupt that an insertion was made of a reply on the part of the disciples. Respecting this interesting interpolation, of which we have now recovered the whole in the original Greek, see Appendix. But there is point in the abrupt change which this interpolation seeks to mitigate. The disciples are told, not merely to believe, but to *preach to all the world*, what they themselves had doubted. In a similar way Christ shows to Saul of Tarsus, not merely that he must cease to persecute Him, but how great things he must suffer for His sake (Acts ix. 16).

15. καὶ εἶπεν αὐτοῖς. This introductory formula intimates that there is some break between *v.* 14 and *v.* 15. What follows was probably said on a different occasion, perhaps a week later. Between Lk. xxiv. 43 and 44 there is a similar break.

Πορευθέντες. See on *v.* 10. This is their primary duty, to go

into. all the world and proclaim the good tidings. Note the strong
form ἄπαντα, and cf. Rom. x. 18 and Rev. xiv. 6.

πάσῃ τῇ κτίσει. *To the whole creation* (R.V.). Contrast the
limitation when the Apostles were first sent out, Mt. x. 5, 6. Except
in the phrase ἀπ' ἀρχῆς κτίσεως (x. 6, xiii. 9), in which it means the
creative act rather than the sum of that which is created, κτίσις is not
found elsewhere in the Gospels. It is fairly freq. in Paul, esp. in
Romans.

16. ὁ πιστεύσας. It is no longer faith in the Resurrection that
is specially emphasized, as in *vv.* 11, 13, 14, but faith in the Gospel
message, in Christ, the Son of God, who had died and risen again, as
the Saviour of the world.

βαπτισθείς. Baptism involves profession of the necessary faith;
but *quisquis credidit, baptismum suscepit* (Beng.), just as in the
Eucharist, *crede et manducasti* (Aug.) holds good. Baptism is required where it may be had, and it is regarded as part of the means of
salvation (Tit. iii. 5; cf. Gal. iii. 27). See esp. 1 Pet. iii. 21, ὑμᾶς σώζει
βάπτισμα, δι' ἀναστάσεως Ἰησοῦ Χριστοῦ, we are saved through baptism
by virtue of the Resurrection. The disciples were already accustomed
to baptize (Jn iv. 2), but their main duty was to preach, as here
stated, for it is by the word of God (1 Pet. i. 23) that men are saved.

σωθήσεται. In the spiritual sense. Just as faith is necessary for
the healing of the body (ii. 5, v. 34, ix. 23, x. 52), so also it is
necessary for the healing of the soul. This higher meaning of σώζω
is found viii. 35, x. 26; also in xiii. 13, which guards against the
supposition that if one has but believed and been baptized one is safe;
there must be "endurance to the end." The meaning in xiii. 20 is
different.

ὁ δὲ ἀπιστήσας κατακριθήσεται. *But he that disbelieveth shall be
condemned* (R.V.), *condemnabitur* (Vulg.). The rendering "shall be
damned" is seriously misleading. Whatever may be the authority of
this appendix to Mk, it gives no sanction to the damnatory clauses of
the *Quicunque vult*. The error begins with Wiclif, and although it is
corrected in the Rhemish Version, it is retained in A.V. Cf. ὁ μὴ
πιστεύων ἤδη κέκριται (Jn iii. 18), where the ἤδη and the use of κέκριται
rather than κατακέκριται (a verb found in no Johannine writing) are
safeguards against misinterpretation. In the case of ὁ ἀπιστήσας there
was no need to say anything about baptism; that of course was
rejected.

17. τοῖς πιστεύσασιν. The writer does not say τῷ πιστεύσαντι,
nor does he add πᾶσιν. His own experience must have taught him
that not each individual believer, but only some of those who believed,

had these χαρίσματα ἰαμάτων (1 Cor. xii. 30); πολλὰ τοιαῦτα πολλοῖς παρηκολούθησαν ἁγίοις (Euthym.), and even that may be too strong. In any case, the promise was to the Church collectively. The writer would not have put into the mouth of Christ a prediction which everyone knew had not been fulfilled. On the other hand, both in 1 Cor. xii. 10 and Gal. iii. 5, St Paul treats the possession of extraordinary powers by some of his converts as a well-known fact. Cf. Jn xiv. 12.

ἐν τῷ ὀνόματί μου. These words are placed first with great emphasis. The power is not their own to be used for their own aggrandisement. Cf. ix. 38; Acts iii. 6, xvi. 18, xix. 13. The disciples had already exercised this power (iii. 15; Mt. x. 1; Lk. ix. 1, x. 17). Justin repeatedly testifies that in his day the power of thus exorcizing demons was possessed by Christians, who were more successful with the Name of Jesus Christ than Jews were with the Name of the God of Abraham (*Try.* 30, 85, *Apol.* ii. 8). Tertullian bears similar testimony (*Apol.* 23, *Ad Scap.* 2, 4). Origen says, "We ourselves, by the use or prayers and other means which we learn from Scripture, drive demons out of the souls of men" (*Cels.* vii. 67). Soon there arose the idea that the mere uttering of the Name of Jesus had a magical effect, which cannot have been Christ's meaning. The exact meaning of "in My Name" depends upon the context; *e.g.* "by My authority and power," "in My character," "as My representative." Cf. Jn xiv. 13, xv. 16, xvi. 24, 26.

γλώσσαις λαλήσουσιν. Cf. Acts ii. 4, x. 46, xix. 6; 1 Cor. xii. 10, 28, xiv. 5 f. Irenaeus states that this continued in his day (v. vi. 1), as well as the driving out of demons (ii. xxxii. 4). Thus far all that is mentioned in this summary of what Christ promised to the disciples is confirmed by statements in N.T. as well as by other evidence. In the next verse elements which seem to be akin to legend are mingled with well-attested facts.

18. ὄφεις ἀροῦσιν. Christ's words to the Seventy (Lk. x. 19), which mean that they will triumph over fraud and treachery (cf. Ps. xci. 13), would easily be understood literally, and what is said here may be an inference from that, or from what happened to St Paul at Malta (Acts xxviii. 3—6). There is no need to think of Moses' rod or the brazen serpent. Even if ἐν ταῖς χερσίν be omitted (see crit. note), "take up in their hands" must be the meaning. "Remove" or "drive away" (Luther, *vertreiben*), as in 1 Cor. v. 2, or "kill" (Euthym., Theoph., ἀφανίζειν), as in Lk. xxiii. 18; Jn xix. 15; Acts xxi. 36, is certainly not the meaning. The extermination of snakes is not regarded as a special work of believers. The writer thinks of them as miraculously preserved from the bite of venomous creatures.

θανάσιμόν τι πίωσιν. The famous legend about St John drinking hemlock without being harmed (Hastings' *D.B.* II. p. 682 *a*) may have grown out of this verse or x. 39. Eusebius (*H.E.* iii. 39) quotes from Papias a similar story about Justus Barsabbas, and there are many such. Nowhere else in Bibl. Grk is θανάσιμος found; in class. Grk it means "near death" of persons and "deadly" of things. The narrator understands the words literally in each case. He is not thinking of spiritual serpents or spiritual poisons. The cessation of the power of serpents and poisons and wild beasts is often given as a feature of the Golden Age (Is. xi. 8, 9, xxxv. 9, lxv. 25; Ezek. xxxiv. 25; Job v. 22, 23; Hos. ii. 18). Virgil has the same idea (*Ecl.* iv. 24, viii. 71, *Geor.* ii. 152).

χεῖρας ἐπιθήσουσιν. The hands which can take up serpents with impunity can heal the diseases of their fellows. Christ Himself used this method of healing, and the Apostles did so also (vi. 5; Acts ix. 12, 17, xxviii. 8). It is remarkable that anointing with oil (vi. 13; Jas. v. 14) is not mentioned. It is perhaps accidental, but the order in which the signs are placed runs thus; casting out demons (time of Christ); speaking with tongues (Apostolic Age); taking up snakes and drinking poison (Growth of Legend); healing by laying on of hands (all ages). Contrast Mt. xxviii. 20.

καλῶς ἕξουσιν. The expression is classical, but is not found elsewhere in N.T., but κακῶς ἔχοντες is not rare (i. 32, 34, ii. 17, vi. 55).

19, 20. THE ASCENSION OF THE LORD AND HIS COOPERATION WITH HIS DISCIPLES.

Lk. xxiv. 50—53. Acts i. 9 f.

19. Ὁ μὲν οὖν κύριος. The οὖν (rare in Mk) refers to what precedes, the μέν (also rare in Mk) anticipates the δέ in *v.* 20. The Lord did one thing, those whom He had addressed did another.

ὁ κύριος Ἰησοῦς. In Lk. xxiv. 3 this combination is possibly a very early interpolation; it is freq. in Acts and Epistles, but is found nowhere else in the Gospels. Even if we omit Ἰησοῦς we have an expression which is not found in Mk or Mt., but is coming into use in Lk. and Jn. The use in xi. 3 is different.

μετὰ τὸ λαλῆσαι αὐτοῖς. This need not be confined to the condensed summary of Christ's farewell addresses given in *vv.* 15—17. It may mean "After all His communications with them."

ἀνελήμφθη. Cf. Acts i. 2, 11, 22 and 1 Tim. iii. 16, where the same verb is used; also Acts i. 9, where ἐπαρθῆναι also regards the Ascension from the side of the Divine power rather than that of Christ's own will and act. But the latter is also recognized; ἀναβαίνω, Jn vi. 62, xx. 17 (*bis*), Eph. iv. 8; πορεύομαι, 1 Pet. iii. 22; διέρχομαι, Heb. iv. 14. As we might suppose it is the former view that is taken of Elijah; he "was taken up" (2 Kings ii. 11; Ecclus xlviii. 9; 1 Macc. ii. 58). In the Greek Church the regular name is ἡ 'Ανάληψις, *i.e.* the Assumption rather than the Ascension.

ἐκάθισεν ἐκ δεξιῶν τοῦ θεοῦ. A highly metaphorical phrase to indicate the transcendent glory of the Ascended Lord. In this glory He was revealed to the dying Stephen, not, however, sitting to rule and judge, but standing to succour and save (Acts vii. 55, 56). The sitting is mentioned Eph. i. 20; Col. iii. 1; Heb. i. 3, 13, viii. 1, x. 12. xii. 2. This session at God's right hand signifies permanence, rest, and dominion,—in glory, majesty, and felicity (Ps. cx. 1)—after the toils, humiliations, and sufferings of life upon earth. Τὸ μὲν καθίσαι δηλοῖ ἀνάπαυσιν καὶ ἀπόλαυσιν τῆς θείας βασιλείας· τὸ δὲ ἐκ δεξιῶν τοῦ Θεοῦ οἰκείωσιν καὶ ὁμοτιμίαν πρὸς τὸν Πατέρα (Euthym.). Excepting *v.* 5, the regular phrase in Gospels and Acts is ἐκ δεξιῶν (x. 37, 40, xii. 36, etc.), but in the Epistles ἐν δεξιᾷ, which CΔ have here, prevails. Pearson, *On the Creed*, Art. vi. 275 f., gives many quotations to illustrate the metaphor.

20. ἐκεῖνοι δέ. The Apostles and their colleagues in the ministry of the word; cf. *vv.* 10, 11, 13.

ἐξελθόντες. This shows how condensed this summary of Apostolic labour is. Much took place before there was a Church at Jerusalem which could send out missionaries to preach everywhere.

συνεργοῦντος. The verb is found nowhere in the Gospels, and it is used nowhere in the N.T. of Christ cooperating. In Rom. viii. 28 it is used of the cooperation of God, if ὁ Θεός is the right reading. In the Testaments we have ὁ Θεὸς συνεργεῖ τῇ ἁπλότητί μου (*Issach.* iii. 7; *Gad* iv. 7).

βεβαιοῦντος. *Confirming.* The verb is not found elsewhere in any of the Gospels, but it is often used of confirming a bargain. Deissmann, *Bib. St*, p. 109.

ἐπακολουθούντων. This verb also is not found in the Gospels. The ἐπί indicates the direction of the attesting signs; see on 1 Tim. v. 10 and cf. 1 Pet. ii. 21. In papyri, ἐπηκολούθηκα is found in accounts in the sense of "verified." That may be the meaning here; "signs which authenticated the word" (G. Milligan, *N. T. Documents*, p. 78). Perhaps the best comment on the verse is Heb. ii. 4, a passage which "is of deep interest as shewing the unquestioned reality of miraculous gifts in the early Church; and the way in which they were regarded as coordinate with other exhibitions of divine power" (Westcott).

APPENDIX

ADDITIONAL NOTE ON Mk xvi. 14.

The now well-known interpolation in this verse was known to Jerome, who says that it existed in "some copies and especially Greek MSS." (*Dial. c. Pelag.* ii. 15), and he quotes a portion of the reply put into the mouths of the Apostles. His quotation runs thus: *Et illi satisfaciebant dicentes; Saeculum istud iniquitatis et incredulitatis sub Satana est, qui non sinit per immundos spiritus veram Dei apprehendi virtutem. Idcirco jam nunc revela justitiam tuam.* Instead of *sub Satana est qui* some MSS. have *substantia est quae*, which yields very poor sense and is now known to be certainly wrong. For in 1907 Mr C. L. Freer bought in Cairo a very interesting MS. of the Four Gospels in Greek, and the text of Mk contains the whole of the interpolation of which Jerome has given part in a Latin translation. This Greek MS. is believed to be of the fifth or sixth century; indeed some critics have thought that it may be of the fourth. The order of the Gospels is that of DX and the old Latin MSS., viz. Mt., Jn, Lk., Mk, and the MS. (or that from which it was copied) seems to have been made from different texts. The text of Jn is superior to that of Mt. In Jn it generally agrees with B, in Mt. generally with the later official or Byzantine text. In Lk. down to viii. 12 it agrees mainly with B, and for the rest of the Gospel mainly with the later text. These features, however, do not greatly concern us. In Mk the text varies, but it has one or two unique readings. In i. 27 it has "What is this new, this authoritative teaching, and that He commandeth even the unclean spirits and they obey Him?" In ix. 24 it has "the spirit of the child" instead of "the father of the child." But for us the most interesting feature is that it contains the appendix to Mk (xvi. 9—20) and after *v.* 14 has the interpolation in question. The text of it runs thus:—

κἀκεῖνοι ἀπελογοῦντ(ο) λέγοντες ὅτι ὁ
αἰὼν οὗτος τῆς ἀνομίας καὶ τῆς ἀπιστίας
ὑπὸ τὸν Σατανᾶν ἐστιν ὁ μὴ ἐῶν τὰ ὑπὸ
τῶν πνε(υμ)άτων ἀκάθαρτα τὴν ἀλήθειαν

τοῦ θ(εο)ῦ καταλαβέσθαι (καὶ) δύναμιν. διὰ
τοῦτο ἀποκάλυψον σοῦ τὴν δικαιοσύ-
νην ἤδη, ἐκεῖνοι ἔλεγον τῷ Χ(ριστ)ῷ καὶ ὁ
Χ(ριστὸ)s ἐκείνοις προσέλεγεν ὅτι πεπλήρωται ὁ ὅρος τῶν ἐτῶν τῆς ἐξουσίας τοῦ
Σατανᾶ, ἀλλὰ ἐγγίζει ἄλλα δ(ε)ινά· καὶ ὑ-
πὲρ (τ)ῶν [ἐγὼ] ἁμαρτησάντων (ἐγὼ) παρεδόθην
εἰς θάνατον ἵνα ὑποστρέψωσιν εἰς τὴν
ἀλήθειαν καὶ μηκέτι ἁμαρτήσωσιν,
ἵνα τὴν ἐν τῷ οὐρανῷ πν(ευματ)ικὴν καὶ ἄ-
φθαρτον τῆς δικαιοσύνης δόξαν
κληρονομήσωσιν. ἀλλὰ πορευθέντες . . .

This is evidently the work of a careless and unintelligent scribe, and the text here and there is evidently corrupt, but the disciples' reply to Christ's rebuke is clear enough, and what He said to them in resuming His address is also fairly clear. We may render the whole thus :—" And they excused themselves (Rom. ii. 15; 2 Cor. xii. 19), saying that this age of lawlessness and unbelief is under Satan, who, through the agency of unclean spirits, suffereth not the truth and power of God to be apprehended (Eph. iii. 18). For this cause reveal Thy righteousness now, they said to Christ. And Christ addressed them, The limit of the years of the authority of Satan has been fulfilled, but other terrors draw nigh. And for the sake of those who have sinned I was delivered over unto death, that they may return unto the truth and sin no more, that they may inherit the spiritual and incorruptible glory of righteousness which is in heaven. But go ye into all the world, etc."

When we had only the short extract in Jerome, Zahn was inclined to believe that it was not a gloss, but a bit of conversation handed down by tradition (*Introd. to N.T.* ii. p. 472). The words attributed to Christ have not much resemblance to those which are preserved in the Gospels; they most probably represent what some Egyptian Christians of the second or third century thought that He might have said.

INDICES

I. GENERAL

II. GREEK

An asterisk denotes that the word is not found elsewhere in N.T., and such words are included in the index, even if there is no note on them in the commentary. A dagger denotes that the word is not found in LXX.

CAMBRIDGE: PRINTED BY JOHN CLAY, M.A. AT THE UNIVERSITY PRESS